A Clearing in the Forest

A CLEARING
in the Forest

Law, Life, and Mind

Steven L. Winter

The University of Chicago Press
Chicago and London

Stephen L. Winter has taught at Brooklyn Law School, University of Miami School of Law, The American University, Washington College of Law, and Yale Law School. He is former chair of the American Association of Law Schools section on Law and Humanities and former assistant counsel for the NAACP Legal Defense Fund.

The University of Chicago Press, Chicago 60637
The University of Chicago Press, Ltd., London
© 2001 by The University of Chicago
All rights reserved.   Published 2001
Printed in the United States of America
10 09 08 07 06 05 04 03 02 01   5 4 3 2 1

ISBN (cloth): 0-226-90221-8

Library of Congress Cataloging-in-Publication Data

Winter, Steven L.
    A clearing in the forest : law, life, and mind / Steven L. Winter
        p.   cm.
    Includes index.
    ISBN 0-226-90221-8 (cloth: alk. paper)
    1. Law—Philosophy.   2. Law—Methodology.   I. Title.
    K235 .W576   2001
    340'.1—dc21
                                                    2001000748

⊗ The paper used in this publication meets the minimum requirements of the American National Standard for Information Sciences—Permanence of Paper for Printed Library Materials, ANSI Z39.48-1992.

For Lynn, with love

CONTENTS

Thomas Cole, *Home in the Woods* (1847). Reynolda House, Museum of American Art, Winston-Salem, North Carolina. (Photo by Alan Perlman)

SOME YEARS ago, while journeying in the mountains of North Carolina, I passed by a large number of 'coves,' as they call them there, or heads of small valleys between the hills, which had been newly cleared and planted. The impression on my mind was one of unmitigated squalor. The settler had in every case cut down the more manageable trees, and left their charred stumps standing. The larger trees he had girdled and killed, in order that their foliage should not cast a shade. He had then built a log cabin, plastered its chinks with clay, and had set up a tall zigzag rail fence around the scene of his havoc, to keep the pigs and cattle out. Finally, he had irregularly planted the intervals between the stumps and trees with Indian corn, which grew among the chips; and there he dwelt with his wife and babes—an axe, a gun, a few utensils, and some pigs and chickens feeding in the woods, being the sum total of his possessions.

The forest had been destroyed; and what had 'improved' it out of existence was hideous, a sort of ulcer, without a single element of artificial grace to make up for the loss of Nature's beauty. Ugly, indeed, seemed the life of the squatter, scudding, as the sailors say, under bare poles, beginning again away back where our first ancestors started, and by hardly a single item better off for all the achievements of the intervening generations. . . .

Then I said to the mountaineer who was driving me, "What sort of people are they who have to make these new clearings?" "All of us," he replied. "Why, we ain't happy here, unless we are getting one of these coves under cultivation." I instantly felt that I had been losing the whole inward significance of the situation. Because to me the clearing spoke of naught but denudation, I thought that to those whose sturdy arms and obedient axes had made them they could tell no other story. But, when they looked on the hideous stumps, what they thought of was personal victory. The chips, the girdled trees, and the vile split rails spoke of honest sweat, persistent toil and final reward. The cabin was a warrant of safety for self and wife and babes. In short, the clearing, which to me was a mere ugly picture on the retina, was to them a symbol redolent with moral memories and sang a very paean of duty, struggle, and success.

—William James, *On a Certain Blindness in Human Beings* [1]

THERE IS a virtual revolution going on within the cognitive sciences. Basic-level categorization, radial categories, image-schemas, conceptual metaphor—these and other findings are transforming our fundamental understanding of the mind. Indeed, what we are learning about reason and categorization bears little resemblance either to the conventional wisdom or to regnant philosophical theories. In this book, I bring these advances in cognitive theory to bear upon Law and the underlying issue of freedom and constraint in human affairs. The picture that will emerge is profoundly different and substantially more complex than the one that animates both our conscious, day-to-day thinking and the most sophisticated scholarly debates.

By far the most important conclusions to emerge from this recent work on cognition are two: first, that imagination is central to the cognitive process; and, second, that imagination is embodied. The workings of the mind simply cannot be understood without appreciating the pivotal role of embodied imagination in all aspects of cognition, language, and thought. The implications are momentous. On one hand, we are discovering that human thought is irreducibly imaginative. On the other, we are learning that—contrary to the conventional wisdom—human imagination operates in an orderly and systematic fashion. This insight alters the contours of entire debates in disciplines such as law, philosophy, and literary theory. In this book, we will explore how what we are learning about the human mind changes our understanding of law and, ultimately, of ourselves.

The project rests on the straightforward premise that a better theory of the mind should facilitate a better understanding of the products of the mind. Law is one of those products and, so, should be amenable to an analysis informed by the tools of cognitive theory. This would not be true, of course, if the mind were just a neutral processor of objective, external information or merely a manipulator of symbols. So, too, there would be no point in such a study if the mind were just a construct of culture and discourse or if there were no constraints on the subjective processes of human creativity. But, ongoing work in quiet corners of the cognitive sciences indicates that the mind itself is an embodied process formed in interaction with the physical and social world. Meaning arises in the imaginative interactions of the human organism with its world, and these embodied experiences provide both the grounding and structure for human thought and rationality. In short, recent developments in the cognitive sciences suggest that a competent model of human knowledge can be developed outside the traditional limitations of the representational/correspondence view, on one hand, and the skeptical or coherence views, on the other.

To those familiar with contemporary philosophical debates, this may seem a pointless or pyrrhic exercise. Richard Rorty, for example, maintains that "no roads lead from the discovery of the organism's various interfaces with the world to criticisms of the organism's views about the world, or, more generally, from psychology to epistemology." [1] Rorty's claim is that an understanding of human cognitive processes will not provide a foundational ground from which to identify those views that are objectively "right" and authoritatively reject those that are "wrong." Just so. It does not follow, however, that an understanding of how our cognitive processes work cannot be useful in criticizing and reconstructing what we think we "know."

It is common ground among many students of the philosophy of language, including Rorty, that there is no objective description of reality separate from our conceptual schemes. This is so because, as Hilary Putnam explains, there cannot be "any inputs which are not in themselves to some extent shaped by our concepts, by the vocabulary we use to report and describe them, or any inputs which admit of only one description, independent of all conceptual choices." [2] Sophisticated legal thinkers have been aware of this fact for some time now because they must constantly grapple with the enigmas that arise as a consequence. Justice Frankfurter, for example, pointed out the inherent difficulty in ascertaining the "voluntariness" of a confession, which is neither a brute fact nor a purely legal conclusion but, in his words, "an amphibian." "This is so," he explained, "because the concepts by which language expresses an otherwise unrepresentable . . . reality are themselves generalizations importing preconceptions about the reality to be expressed."[3]

This insight implies, however, that there *is* something quite important to be gained in understanding how our conceptual system is structured. To the extent that the conceptual system has substantive effects on what we think and what we know, it is imperative that we understand those effects. It has been a mainstay of feminist, critical race, and critical legal theory that knowledge is partial and that legal decisionmaking is, therefore, inevitably lacking in "objective" justification. But there still remain the questions of what partialities produce particular decisions and how they do so.

For anyone who has practiced law, the significance of these questions should be readily apparent. As a lawyer for the NAACP Legal Defense Fund, I spent eight exceptionally rewarding years litigating prison conditions, police practices, and other civil rights cases. More than anything else, I learned to appreciate the ways in which good legal strategies are a function of social and cultural dynamics that owe little indeed to the force of legal logic. I learned how the cultural, the social, and the political create possibilities for reform through litigation quite beyond those sanctioned or even hinted at by the governing legal standards.[4]

What enables effective action is not transcendental truth but pragmatic knowledge—that is, the smaller human truths that best explain how we think and act within the complex social webs that we inhabit (and that inhabit us). What legal actors need, therefore, is something like a cognitive map of the cultural models and other social constructs that animate thinking and decisionmaking among lawyers, judges, and laypersons alike. This task requires a set of tools quite different from the analytic skills and normative theories that dominate the study of law today. The promise of cognitive theory lies precisely in its ability to make explicit the unconscious criteria and cognitive operations that structure and constitute our judgment. It is by laying bare these cognitive structures and their impact on our reasoning that we can best aid legal actors—whether advocates or decisionmakers—who wish to understand the law better so that they can act more effectively.

But the benefits of cognitive theory to law are not merely technical and strategic. First, to expose the infrastructures of legal reasoning is also to facilitate a more penetrating critique, one that cuts to the very root of suffocating conventional wisdom. Second, to pose the ostensibly descriptive question of how law works is, necessarily, to inquire into the substance and ontology of Law. This inquiry will lead inexorably to the most profound issues of meaning and autonomy in human affairs. Once we have explored the cognitive and social underpinnings that make law possible, our entire conception of the law will be turned on its head: Though we conceptualize it as an authority that rules over us, we will find that law is but one consequence of more pervasive cultural processes of meaning-making. And this insight will bring us face-to-face with the conclusion that what actually stands behind the majestic curtain of Law's rationality and impartiality is nothing other than ourselves and our own, often unruly social practices.

A central theme of my argument concerns the difficulties inherent in the traditional understandings of both mind and reason. The traditional view takes for granted that reason is linear, hierarchical, propositional, and definitional. I refer to this standard view as "the rationalist model" or, more simply, "rationalism" to emphasize that it is, after all, only one possible model of reason and, thus, that it operates as a kind of "ism." There is a better alternative that is grounded or "bottom-up" (rather than deracinated or "top-down") and that is flexible and adaptive (rather than definitional and static). These distinctions make all the difference: As we will see with respect to a range of issues in philosophy of language and law, rationalist accounts systematically (and paradoxically) distort what they seek to clarify and render more precise. The frequent result is an appearance of error or indeterminacy where a more complex order in fact prevails. We shall repeatedly watch as phenomena that appear so disorderly in rationalism's harsh light resolve into sensible, predictable patterns once they are considered in light of recent developments in cognitive theory.

This book, in other words, is *anything but* an argument against reason. What I take issue with is only a particularly cramped, though nonetheless canonical view of what reason must be. The central question of this book is not *whether* we are rational but *how* we are rational. And that question in turn provides the basic plan of the book: To understand how we do law, one must first understand how we are rational. Chapter 1, which serves as a general introduction, outlines the problem and introduces some of the concepts such as metaphor and image-schemas that suggest a more productive alternative. The next three chapters elaborate the basic concepts: the grounding and embodiment of thought; the structure of metaphorical thought; and categorization understood as an active, adaptive, socially motivated process. These chapters develop some of the empirical evidence from which these concepts arise, though for reasons of economy the treatment is expository and suggestive rather than exhaustive or definitive.

Chapter 5, on narratives, serves as a bridge to the law-focused arguments of the book. This chapter develops the implications of radial categorization as a flexible and productive process. This discussion serves as a vehicle for exploring the questions of regularity and constraint in law that I take up in the balance of the book. Chapters 6 and 7 examine the process of decision according to precedent, providing in-depth analyses of two areas of law. Here, the contrast with rationalism will be particularly stark: The decisions that appear so indeterminate when viewed on rationalist assumptions will become systematic and orderly once understood as products of a radial category. These two chapters also begin the inquiry, central to the argument of the book, concerning the nature and grounding of legal concepts.

Chapter 8 analyzes rules and rule-following. We will find not only that rules do not and cannot work in a rule-like fashion, but also that rules necessarily depend on the very cultural practices they are supposed to regulate. The next two chapters extend the investigation into the nature of constraint in law. Chapter 9 examines the form of legal analysis commonly referred to as "reasoning by analogy." Chapter 10 examines three significant cases of change in modern American law and shows that even such dramatic innovations take place only *by means of* the structures of cognitive and cultural constraint. The two final chapters conclude the inquiry into the nature of law: Chapter 11 summarizes the argument of the book by contrasting the distortions of the rationalist approach to law with the regularities that emerge when one considers legal decisionmaking as a dynamic process shaped by cognition, categorization, and persuasion. Chapter 12 presses the argument to its radical conclusion. Though we identify "Law" with its positivist manifestations in statutes and court decisions, law is—both in concept and reality—neither more nor less than an artifact of our collective contributions to legal meaning. Once we understand that law is not an external "thing" that exists above or apart from us, the way will be open to a different, more productive notion of freedom.

A word about methodology. I will be drawing (both directly and indirectly) on extensive empirical work in psychology, anthropology, neuroscience, and linguistics that has taken place over the last thirty years. But a great deal of the evidence that I will be discussing comes directly from ordinary language use. Many will find this strange; people still tend to think, like Lewis Carroll's Humpty Dumpty, that words mean what *they* want them to mean. But language is an empirical phenomenon no less than any other form of human behavior. Economists study market transactions (and all sorts of other conduct); sociologists study social behavior; and linguists study language—all in an effort to discern regularities and induce rules. Philosophers of language—and here we may include literary theorists—

take language as an a priori capable of being theorized without regard to the actual patterns of current (synchronic) usage or historical (diachronic) development. But the evidence, as we shall see, is remarkably inconsistent with their theories. Indeed, as I hope to persuade you, the data support a radically new and different view.

This talk of data and empirical evidence will be comforting to some, distressing to others. Those in the latter group will point out that all evidence is theory dependent; the postmodernists among them will emphasize that everything is a matter of interpretation, and that it is interpretation all the way down. Is cognitive theory anything more than just another empiricism with all its well-known problems?

The short answer is "no," and for reasons already alluded to. It is worth pausing on this point because it sets the stage for much of the argument to follow.

The contingency of knowledge may be an ineluctable human truth (paradoxical as that may sound). But it does not follow that we can have no useful knowledge or that every view is as good as every other. The lack of objective foundations for our knowledge does not translate into radical skepticism unless, as Martha Nussbaum puts it, "metaphysical realism is the only form of truth worth having." [5] To put the point another way, the claim of radical indeterminacy is itself theory dependent; it is, moreover, dependent upon theoretical assumptions that are themselves quite foundationalist. For, implicit in this claim is the assumption that there are only two categorical possibilities: *Either* correspondence is possible *or* it is not; *either* everything is objective, in which case we can talk meaningfully of evidence and data, *or* everything is up for grabs, in which case all "facts" are merely a matter of interpretation.

The first thing to notice about this line of reasoning is that both poles of the opposition between foundationalism and indeterminacy assume the very same foundationalist premises concerning what counts as constraint. In this way, many putative postmoderns who confidently believe they have transcended foundationalism remain captives of the ironic paradox that, in chapter 1, I refer to as "antinomial capture." The second thing to notice is the totalizing, all-or-nothing quality of the reasoning. Constraint is assumed to mean total constraint—i.e., determinacy—and, by the law of the excluded middle, the only alternative is no constraint at all.

Once these assumptions are spelled out, however, they lose much of their plausibility. Radical indeterminacy would be true if and only if objective foundations were the sole form of constraint imaginable. Of course, the fact that another form (or degree) of constraint is imaginable does not yet prove that it is true. That is the burden of my argument. But, at least, we have cleared the ground for the possibility.

If it is simultaneously true that all evidence is theory dependent and that every view is not as good as every other, then how are we to evaluate claims to knowledge? We can do so, of course, only within the finitude of our own situation.[6] As I have argued previously (and pursue again here), persuasion is constrained by the beliefs and understandings that one already holds.[7] Thus, any appeal to evidence can be an appeal only to the conventional criteria of comprehensiveness, elegance or parsimony, and pragmatic usefulness: Does the proposed account explain all the data? Does it do so with the fewest assumptions or postulates possible? Does it provide a hypothesis that works for purposes of explanation, prediction, and action? What I hope to show is that by these customary standards, cognitive theory better accounts for the evidence than either objectivism or any of the various forms of skepticism. This is not a claim to transcendental truth but to the only kind of provisional, human truth we can have.

Ultimately, I hope to persuade you that this view is "correct" because it makes the most sense in terms of what—upon reflection—you already know to be true of your own experience. If cognitive theory is correct that human understanding is contingent on the kinds of bodies that we have and the ways in which those bodies interact with our environment, then it is grounded in a reality that to a very large degree is shared by all human beings. If cognitive theory is correct, then there are constraints on reason and knowledge—although not of the foundationalist sort. This understanding will yield a view of reason as grounded, but not determinate; as imaginative, but not free; as regular, but not entirely predictable. In short, it will yield a view of reason and knowledge as the profoundly human phenomena we know them to be. And *that,* as Wallace Stevens says, is the most profound truth one could reasonably care to convey:

> To say more than human things with human voice,
> That cannot be; to say human things with more
> Than human voice, that, also, cannot be;
> To speak humanly from the height or from the depth
> Of human things, that is acutest speech.[8]

ACKNOWLEDGMENTS

THIS BOOK pulls together (hopefully, in a more-or-less coherent narrative) ideas worked out in a series of articles written over the ten-year period beginning in 1986. During that time, I benefited from the comments, suggestions, and insights of many, many people. I am grateful to George Lakoff, Jan Deutsch, Mark Turner, Michael Fischl, Frank Michelman, Jon Simon, Stanley Fish, Tom Grey, Jennifer Jaff, Bob Post, Milner Ball, Owen Fiss, Paul Kahn, Pat Gudridge, Terry Anderson, Bruce Ackerman, Mark Tushnet, Pierre Schlag, and Tony Amsterdam. Sheldon Leader, Larry Joseph, and Dick Markovits read the manuscript and provided remarkably thoughtful comments, for which I am very much in their debt. I also want to express my sincere thanks to the participants in the Brooklyn Law School brown bag series and to the many students in my Jurisprudence Seminar over the years, who sat through numerous chapters and shared with me their reactions and insights. I owe a special debt to my colleagues Gary Minda, Larry Solan, and Bailey Kuklin for the untold hours of discussion that have helped me clarify my thoughts: Their contributions are deeply embedded in the pages that follow. And special thanks to Marvin Frankel, who not only did a *mitzvah* in taking care of Aaron but also made it possible for me to finish this book.

The work of many wonderful research assistants over the years has been invaluable; I am grateful to Louis Moritz, Terry Tracht, Mark Richardson, Rachel Courtney, Emilio Boehringer, Suzanna Chiu, and Judy Falk. Judy and Suzanna deserve to be singled out for recognition; they have my heartfelt thanks. I also want to thank Geoff Huck, John Tryneski, and all of the people at University of Chicago Press for their enthusiasm and support at every stage of this project. Work on this book was greatly facilitated by the financial support of the University of Miami School of Law and Brooklyn Law School.

While a majority of the book is new, portions of several chapters have appeared in various guises and are reprinted here by permission: Chapter 1 first appeared in *Metaphor & Symbolic Activity*. Chapter 3 appeared in substantial part in the *Harvard Law Review*. Portions of chapters 8, 9, and 10 first appeared in the *Texas Law Review*; portions of chapters 4 and 8 appeared in the *Connecticut Law Review*.

Jeremy Paul and Mark Johnson read and commented on every chapter; I am indebted to them for their incalculable support and devoted friendship. My wife Lynn provided love, nurturance, sustenance, and substantive insight; without her there would, of course, be no book.

Dick Posner merits his own paragraph. It was enough that he reached across gulfs of both politics and method to offer his friendship and encouragement. But, Dick also read the entire manuscript twice: first, chapter by chapter as it came out of my computer and then, again, when the book was complete. Each time, he responded with his trademark, hand-typed, pages-long letter of line-by-line suggestions. (Well, the last was an e-mail.) No one knows how he does it. (I asked; he won't say.) But I, like many others, am glad that he does. Thanks so very much.

As I finished this book, I wondered if I would be able to express how profoundly I have been moved, influenced, and inspired by John Coltrane and Ornette Coleman. So, it was a happy surprise when I came across the perfect line in Rafi Zabor's wonderful novel, *The Bear Comes Home* (1998). Let me say that I simply cannot imagine living except "while Coltrane burned his way to God on a minor blues or Ornette raised his saxophone and centuries of cognitive imprisonment fell to the dust" (77). One need only hear what Coltrane does with *Greensleeves* or Ornette with a Bach prelude to understand how *very* much the human mind can do.

Port Washington, N.Y.
December, 2000

CHAPTER I

A Clearing in the Forest

EARLY IN Robert Bolt's *A Man for All Seasons,* Sir Thomas More and his future son-in-law, Roper, clash over the value of fidelity to law in the face of evil. At this point in the play, Sir Thomas is Lord Chancellor. His aide, Richard Rich, has just left the room. Though Rich comports himself as the devoted assistant, it is already apparent that he will betray Sir Thomas. Both Roper and Alice More urge Sir Thomas to have Rich arrested. Alice protests that Rich has been allowed to go unharmed.

Sir Thomas demurs. "And go he should if he was the Devil himself until he broke the law." Roper objects to the notion that the Devil should be given the benefit of the law. Sir Thomas challenges him: "What would you do? Cut a great road through the law to get after the Devil?" Exactly so, Roper declares, "I'd cut down every law in England to do that." Sir Thomas retorts:

> Oh? And when the last law was down, and the Devil turned round on you—where would you hide, Roper, the laws all being flat? This country's planted thick with laws from coast to coast—man's laws, not God's— and if you cut them down—and you're just the man to do it—do you really think you could stand upright in the winds that would blow then?[1]

These lines resonated so powerfully with Felix Frankfurter that, as his theater companions report, he could not contain himself. "'That's the point,' he kept whispering to us in the dark, 'that's it, that's it.'"[2]

Not everyone shares Justice Frankfurter's ardent reaction. What we do share, however, are the underlying cultural metaphors that structure the logic of this passage. Even those who reject the naïveté of Frankfurter's (and Sir Thomas's) faith in the law nevertheless deploy this imagery to understand and describe the experience of law from the inside. In his *Critical Phenomenology of Judging*,[3] Duncan Kennedy reflects on the judge's experience of precedent. He conceptualizes the cases as arrayed in fields, identifying six typical field configurations. Two of these field configurations—the impacted field and the case of first impression—"represent constraint and freedom as they are conceived by the legal tradition itself." In the impacted field, "boundaries are long straight lines" that are "reinforced at regular intervals with precedents whose holdings exactly track the line." The case of first impression, in contrast, "is a kind of clearing of freedom in the endless forest of constraint." When the judge acts, he "fills in a part of the clearing" and, thus, precludes his or her freedom for the future (538–39).

Because these expressions employ highly conventional metaphors, they seem comfortable and familiar. To many, they are nothing more than clichés. For most lawyers and legal scholars, metaphor is merely a matter of expression—useful for rhetorical purposes, but perilous to reason. This is the import of Cardozo's overworked dictum: "Metaphors in law are to be narrowly watched, for though starting as devices to liberate thought, they end often by enslaving it."[4] Eminent philosophers such as Donald Davidson and Richard Rorty understand metaphor as entirely devoid of semantic content. They view metaphors as, at most, powerful devices that can affect the senses and sometimes give birth to new meanings.[5] Underlying this view, is the assumption that linguistic meaning is socially contingent and essentially arbitrary.

Developments in cognitive theory overturn all these views. Even the trite metaphorical expression "forest of constraint" is surprisingly rich in conceptual content, nonarbitrary in meaning, complex in structure, and systematic in operation. This "simple" expression involves no fewer than five conceptual metaphors that are a significant, entrenched part of our conceptual system. Conceptual metaphors of this sort make possible comprehension, define patterns of inference, and enable semantic productivity. They are, so to speak, part of the unconscious rules of our language-game. Without them, we could not even think.

Why does any of this matter? Since cognitive theory purports to describe the way the mind works, it follows that—to the extent it is correct—it can describe only what we are already doing all the time. So what is to be gained by uncovering the underlying patterns of thought?

A lot. Much of what we know is at the level of tacit knowledge. We can ride bicycles, compose new sentences, and make complex judgments about all sorts of everyday things without conscious effort or thought. Cognitive theory offers the tools to make this tacit knowledge explicit. It thus makes it possible to open up and examine a great many important things that otherwise must remain opaque—things such as "judgment" and "conscience." Moreover, once these conceptual tools are brought to bear, many things we thought we understood look very different. In fact, much of what we take for granted with respect to knowledge, reasoning, and categorization must now be reconceived in light of what we are learning about the mind.

This revolution has far-reaching ramifications for law, both how we do it and how we think about it. Riding a bicycle can be reduced to laws of physics, but no one thinks that we learn to ride a bicycle by mastering those formal expressions. So, too, much of what we do in law—applying rules, characterizing precedents, making or predicting decisions in litigated cases—can be described in the analytic terms of legal doctrine. But it is widely recognized that the surface logic of the discipline does not govern the decisionmaking process. John Dewey made this point three-quarters of a century ago,[6] and it has since been acknowledged all across the jurisprudential spectrum.[7] Rather, if we can perform the operations of "legal reasoning" (and many of us can), it is because we have assimilated the tacit knowledge that makes the rules comprehensible, defines the patterns of legal inference, and enables the productivity of crucial legal categories. Cognitive theory opens a window on these operations; it makes it possible to specify them, describe them, and better understand their strengths *and* limitations. In subsequent chapters, we will explore how rule-application and decision according to precedent work in terms of basic-level categorization, idealized cognitive models, prototype effects, and radial categories.

Thus, at the first level, cognitive theory is important to law because it explains how we do what we do. This is no mean feat, as those familiar with the scholarly debates know. We have endured literally generations of controversy over the fundamental question of whether law works at all. Many maintain that lawyers and judges properly trained in their craft are in fact able to resolve problems reliably using the traditional tools. The critics, however, argue that legal doctrines do not and cannot control outcomes because they do not generate determinate solutions to legal questions. Cognitive theory explains why neither side of this tense debate has it quite right. Legal decisionmaking does reproduce in predictable patterns that are no more or less regular, no more or less susceptible to study and categorization than any other human phenomenon. On the other hand, there is nothing about this process that is "objective" or "determinate" in the way promised by the analytic logic that dominates the surface of the discipline.

At the second level, then, cognitive theory is important to law because it responds to—or, rather, radically transforms—many of these traditional jurisprudential debates. The conventional understanding of law confronts an insuperable paradox. It is the essence of our concept of law that it operates as an external constraint, much like the impenetrable vegetation of the forest. Yet this very conception already places law in the domain of metaphor and imagination, which is to say in the *internal* realm of the human mind. We cannot even talk about law without metaphorically treating it as an OBJECT: Courts "make" law; criminals "break" the law; vigilantes "take the law into their own hands." The contradiction is devastating. Because the desired constraint is internal to the mind, the conventional view is defenseless against the various subjectivist critiques that have been leveled against it.

Within the assumptions of the subject-object dualism that frame much of the current legal debate, there are only two alternatives: Either the object constrains the subject, or the subject must command the object; if the law does not carry with it objective constraints, then it follows (or so the argument goes) that all outcomes are subjective and politically motivated. This is one (necessarily caricatured) version of the indeterminacy critique first developed by the legal realists and later extended by the critical legal studies movement. It assumes that there are no meaningful constraints on purposive decisionmaking except, perhaps, those that are arbitrary and entirely contingent. Thus, Kennedy has argued that since constraint is not an objective property of the legal materials themselves—like the physical obstruction of the trees that impede my movement—it can only be the delusory product of a "properly" socialized subjectivity.* Indeed, in his most recent work, Kennedy argues that adjudication is marked by a denial of the inevitably ideological work of the judge; on Kennedy's view, those who claim to be constrained by the law are acting in something like Sartrean "bad faith."[8] But these conclusions do not follow because, as I hope to demonstrate, there is another alternative that is both theoretically more robust and better supported by the empirical evidence.

At the third and most profound level, cognitive theory is important to law because it alters the traditional understanding of freedom and constraint upon which the conventional picture of law rests. Ultimately, I aim to exploit the insight to be gained from cognitive theory to induce a gestalt

---

* Kennedy wrote: "I am perfectly aware that the rule is not a physical object and that deciding how to apply it involves a social, hence in some sense subjective process" (561).

switch that—much like the reversal that William James experienced during his travels in Appalachia—inverts the conventional metaphor of forest and clearing. I will be using advances in the study of the mind to present a picture in which the law is the clearing that emerges as a consequence of the relentless cultivation of human imagination. Perhaps most important of all, I will be arguing that what we are learning about the mind radically transforms the traditional understanding of constraint and, with it, our very concept of freedom.

The linchpin of this argument is a *theory of imagination*. This will seem an oxymoron to many because, on the conventional understanding, imagination is not the kind of thing one can have a theory about. Imagination is commonly understood as a kind of cognitive wild card. On the standard view, imagination is that quintessentially subjective—and, therefore, inexplicable—faculty of absolute, unfettered creativity. But not everyone sees it this way. Paul Ricoeur, for example, maintains that: "Innovation remains a form of behavior governed by rules. The labor of imagination is not born from nothing. It is bound in one way or another to the tradition's paradigms." [9]

Recent studies in the cognitive sciences support this latter view. Of course, any survey of the area will reveal that cognitive science is a contentious field still dominated by traditional rationalist assumptions about mind and reason. But the outlines of an alternative, more productive view are already in place. An important, early treatment is Hubert Dreyfus's critique of artificial intelligence as inadequate to the situated and embodied nature of actual human intelligence. [10] These insights have been taken up in different ways in the pioneering work of George Lakoff and Mark Johnson and of the Nobel laureate Gerald Edelman. [11] The emerging picture is of a human rationality more subtle and complex than anything even conceivable under the standard view. The outlines of this emergent view can be plotted along three principal axes.

1. *Human thought is irreducibly imaginative.* Because cognition must be dynamic and adaptive—that is, enabling successful application and adjustment to contingent and changing situations—it cannot consist solely or even primarily of passive operations that depend upon content and correspondence. It follows that cognition is not principally representational, propositional, or computational, but rather involves processes that are imaginative, associative, and analogical. A growing body of empirical and theoretical work demonstrates that human brain processes are *imagistic* and *cross-modal*. They are imagistic in that they involve highly schematic images that are not dependent on any particular sensory modality such as the

visual, the kinesthetic, or the spatiotemporal.[12] They are cross-modal in that the different sensory modalities do not operate as discrete systems. Rather, they combine to form global mappings—"dynamic structure[s]" that, as Edelman explains, are "altered as the sampling by different sensory sheets and its input-output correlations are changed by motion and behavior" (54–56).

2. *Imagination is embodied, interactive, and grounded.* Imagination is embodied in the sense that it emerges from the neural structure of the brain. "There is," Edelman points out, "no such thing as software involved in the operation of brains, and the evidence overwhelmingly indicates that the morphology of the brain matters overwhelmingly" (30). Rationality, in other words, is a function of our particular human "wetware." Concretely, this means that our embodied interactions with the physical and social world form the substrata of imagination—the "raw material," so to speak, of which the cognitive processes are made. There is nothing magical or mystical about this; it is, rather, a consequence of the cross-modal character of neural processes. Imagination, therefore, is dependent on the kinds of bodies that we have and on the ways in which those bodies interact with our environment. It is grounded in the sense that it is contingent on these experiences.

3. *Imagination operates in a regular, orderly, and systematic fashion.* Indeed, it is now possible to describe the structures of imagination. These mechanisms, which we will explore in some depth, include mental operations such as basic-level categorization, conceptual metaphor, metonymy, image-schemas, idealized cognitive models, and radial categories.

As suggested by even this initial summary, these are large and difficult claims. They are not separate points but are related to one another in complex ways. Together, they transform our understanding of reasoning and categorization.

WHAT'S WRONG WITH REASON

At the start, I want to be clear about exactly what is at stake in this argument: One of the principal claims of this book is that one cannot have an account of meaning, rationality, intellectual change, law, or any other human phenomenon without an understanding of imagination and its central, constitutive role in the interaction between the human organism and the environment.[13] Quite simply, no field remains untouched by what we are finding out about the mind.

In revolutionizing our understanding of human categorization,[14] for example, cognitive theory transforms everything that depends on categories—including phenomena as prosaic as rules and as obscure as "judgment." So, too, many of the basic assumptions concerning reason that go unquestioned by philosophers and legal theorists must be revised or abandoned in light of what we are learning about the human mind. The recognition that human rationality is grounded in experience requires rejection of both the determinacy aspired to by analytic logic *and* the arbitrariness assumed by most social coherence theories.* The import of transfigurative processes such as metaphor is that there can be no linear, algorithmic function that links experiential input to imaginative output. But neither is rationality purely arbitrary, subjective, or radically indeterminate; it is framed and constrained by the systematic nature of these conceptual processes. In the terminology of cognitive theory, human rationality is *motivated.*† To put the point somewhat paradoxically: An imaginative rationality is indeterminate in more-or-less predictable ways.

Consider, again, the stakes for law. As highlighted by the exchange between Roper and Sir Thomas, the entire enterprise rises or falls on the existence of constraint. For several decades now, law and legal theory have been haunted by this question. Many fear that if there are no constraints, judges and other legal actors will be free to impose their personal values or political preferences.[15] As a consequence, the debate within the jurisprudential mainstream has focused on the proper source of constraint: Is it the text of the rule, the intent of the drafters, the policy or values behind the provision, or some other touchstone in political or moral theory?

What is striking, however, is how much this debate takes for granted. Each of the mainstream positions simply assumes that reason is available to control and direct the movement from authoritative source to the logical decision of a concrete case. On the standard view, legal reasoning consists in abstracting from a judicial opinion or other authoritative legal text the principles that express the necessary and sufficient conditions, properties,

---

* The social coherence view of meaning is related to a view of indeterminacy of reference of language terms. On this view, words do not "fit" the world at all: One can speak meaningfully only of language systems as a whole; the only constraint is internal consistency; and the meaning of any single term is determined solely by its relations to other units in the language network. On this view, social conventions determine how, of a variety of possible ways, each such holistic system "carves up" the world.

† The concept of motivation, which we will explore in chapter 4, has nothing to do with subjective intent, but rather refers to what *makes sense of*—that is, what structures, constitutes, and enables—a particular thought or expression.

or criteria that characterize it. Then, one decides the next case by determining whether it corresponds with this abstracted form of which the original is only a manifestation (as in a judicial decision) or expression (as in a rule).[16]

This approach is workable, however, only if two conditions are met: (1) the principles, properties, or criteria must accurately fit the social world; and (2) there must be a single, logical trajectory from principle to concrete application. Otherwise, objectivity is impossible; there would be no guarantee that the "right" principles had been extracted nor that they had been properly implemented in the case at hand. Rather, there would be every risk that the "controlling" principles were themselves colored by value assumptions and their application skewed by individual purposes. Indeed, without the constraint of a precise and reliable reason, many different outcomes could be "justified" by reference to any given principle.

That is exactly the charge of the indeterminacy critique, which denies both possibilities (1) and (2).[17] Although this critique takes several different forms, it generally subscribes to a perspectivalist position: It rejects the assumption that there is a single, privileged view of reality and, instead, sees every person or group as having an equally valid but different perspective on the world. In the relativist version of the indeterminacy critique, reasoning and categorization are not natural or given but are relative to particular languages, cultures, histories, or conceptual schemes.[18] On this view, legal doctrines are often masks for power because they purport to derive from the neutral application of objective reason by a disinterested judiciary when, all the while, they are merely expressions of the needs or values of the culture's elites.[19] In the more extreme subjectivist version of this critique, reason and categories are seen as a function of an actor's purposes, desires, or beliefs. On this view, legal doctrines and rules are virtually infinitely manipulable in light of one's instrumental and political purposes. On either view, reasoning from principle has only the appearance of objectivity. It, thus, has the vice of false legitimation without the saving grace of real constraint.

Both sides of this controversy, however, assume the same ideal of reason as top-down, linear, definitional, and characterized by closure (as in the law of the excluded middle). One side affirms this rationalist model of reason; the other denies its efficacy. On this model, reason is propositional (i.e., transparent and truth-conditional), hierarchical (i.e., particulars are subsumed under general rules or principles), analytic and reductive (i.e., things are analyzed and explained in terms of their basic components or elements), and essentialist (i.e., distinguishing between necessary and contingent properties and assuming that, by definition, the former are constitutive). Procedurally, reason issues in hierarchies, definitions, distinctions, values, criteria of evidence, and measures of adequacy. On this account, imagination is the antithesis of reason and, for all practical purposes, a synonym for indeterminacy.

Much of this may seem self-evident because it characterizes so much of what, within the Western tradition, we assume rationality is about.[20] In academic circles, the rationalist model has something of the status of an ideology. As such, it is largely impervious to refutation on empirical grounds. There is irony in this, but no surprise. As Thomas Kuhn observes, even science is largely resistant to data that does not conform to its reigning paradigms.[21] Nevertheless, as we shall see in the next few chapters, the empirical evidence suggests that surprisingly little of human rationality actually fits the rationalist model. Instead, the data present a picture of a human rationality that is bottom-up rather than top-down, imaginative rather than linear, flexible rather than definitional, and characterized by openness rather than closure (as in radial categories). Indeed, as we shall see in chapter 3, the rationalist model is itself just a special case of metaphorical thought.

The hegemony of the rationalist model is such that it retains its hold notwithstanding the widespread rejection of its underlying premises, for the rationalist model is systematically related to an objectivist worldview. By "objectivist," I refer to a general position that understands the world as made up of determinate, mind-independent objects with inherent characteristics or "essences."[22] It follows from this view that reason is a matter of propositions that are capable of representing or "mirroring" those objects, their properties and relations, in a linear, undistorted fashion. Categories are organized in terms of the common properties that are the necessary and sufficient criteria of membership.* Distinctions are the logical means by which we discriminate between apparently similar things that "in fact" are in different categories. Principles are high-order generalizations that serve as fundamental laws that accurately characterize essences or relationships.

But undermine the foundational assumption—i.e., that it is the "true" objects of the world about which we reason—and the entire rationalist apparatus falls with it. As Stanley Fish puts it: "Remove the connection between observable features and the specification of meaning, and you also

---

* Even social coherence views, which recognize categorization as humanly constructed, treat categories as about objects with ascertainable properties or criteria that establish their commonality. This is no less true of ontological relativism, which maintains that objects are only individuated relative to a conceptual scheme.

remove everything else that is supposedly independent of context; entailment [and] contradiction . . . become as variable and contingent as presupposition."[23] Thus, if the anti-foundationalist insight is correct—that is, if reason is not grounded in the observable, objective facts of the world—then there is no reason to assume that rationality issues in propositions, that things have determinable essences, that distinctions of kind are a basic unit of logic, or anything else. If reason is solely the product of historical and cultural forces, then it should be "variable and contingent" in form as well as substance. It may be, in Nietzsche's famous phrase, nothing more than a "mobile army of metaphors, metonymies, anthropomorphisms."[24]

It is remarkable, therefore, that many who reject objectivism nevertheless continue to adhere to the rationalist model. Leading anti-foundationalists such as Stanley Fish and Richard Rorty persist in the view that reason within an "interpretive community" or "normal discourse" consists in the same old rationalist repertoire of propositions, definitions, distinctions, and the like.[25] Thus, although they firmly reject its foundational framework, both Fish and Rorty nevertheless maintain the entire superstructure of the objectivist model of rationality.

The hegemony of the rationalist model is even more strikingly revealed among those who deny its efficacy in law. In a widely noted article, Joseph Singer argues that legal doctrine cannot be determinate because it is not internally consistent. One such inconsistency, he notes, takes "the form of rules with exceptions or of principles with limiting counterprinciples." This would not be a problem, of course, if one could fix and justify the exceptions. But, Singer argues: "Because the line between the rule and the exception or the principle and the counterprinciple may be moved, we require a *metatheory* at a higher level of generality to tell us where to draw the line."[26] So, too, Duncan Kennedy contends that legal argument consists of matched pairs of policy positions that cancel each other out. Although he acknowledges that we are frequently "able to distinguish particular fact situations in which one side is more plausible than the other," he maintains nevertheless that the law is indeterminate.* "The difficulty," he explains, "is that there are no available *metaprinciples* to explain just what it is about these particular situations that make them ripe for resolutions."[27]

What Singer and Kennedy both fail to explain is why only a metaprinciple will do. This requirement would make sense on the rationalist

---

* In his most recent work, Kennedy has refined his position to argue only that localized demonstrations of indeterminacy are nearly always possible. I consider this version of the argument in chapter 11.

model with its top-down structure, in which particulars are subsumed under general rules and high-order principles govern all lower-order functions. But these, after all, are the *critics;* they purport to deny the efficacy of rationalism.[28]

There are two ways to interpret this otherwise peculiar insistence on the rationalist model. The first, more charitable explanation is that Singer and Kennedy are making an internal critique, attacking law on its own (rationalist) assumptions. The problem with this interpretation, however, is that it means that they have nothing to say to those who explain (or defend) existing legal practices along more modest—typically Wittgensteinian—lines as a form of life rather than a formal or logical system.[29] This suggests a second, more revealing explanation: that Singer and Kennedy are insisting upon the rationalist model because it is only against the backdrop of such strongly rationalist assumptions that the law appears so indeterminate and vulnerable to manipulation. In this ironic way, the most ardent critics of rationalism in law turn out to be unwitting victims of the droll paradox I call "antinomial capture"—that is, more often than not, the price of opposition is that one is defined precisely by what one most vehemently rejects.* The ironic bottom line is that both the mainstream and the opposition not only agree but insist upon the very same premises concerning what counts as constraint.[30]

Developments in cognitive theory make it possible to talk about innovation and constraint free from the distorting grip of these objectivist assumptions. True, legal materials do not produce patterns that conform to the rationalist expectations of precision, hierarchy, and determinacy. But it does not follow that law is indeterminate; we may just be looking for the wrong patterns. Propositional legal rules promise determinate answers, but the largely imaginative structure of thought yields, instead, a different pattern of decisionmaking. As I argue in chapter 6, much of the perceived indeterminacy of law results from the superimposition of a rationalist model for law upon a much more complex process of human reasoning.

Thus, the second principal claim of this book is that we must shift our focus away from *meta*structures (or the lack thereof) to the cognitive and cultural *infra*structures, if we are going to make any sense of the phenomenon of law. There is regularity in law, but it derives neither from logic nor from rules. We *are* able to distinguish particular fact situations in which one

---

* It is rather like the analysand who, reacting to the therapist's insight that her mother was a powerful influence on her life, exclaimed: "That's not true. It's not true at all. I am nothing like my mother. In fact, I am exactly the opposite in every respect."

argument is more plausible than another, and there is nothing mysterious in this. The insight that rationality is imaginative and grounded means, quite simply, that we use physical and social experience and general cultural knowledge to categorize and understand. Using the tools of cognitive theory, we can now make much of this tacit knowledge explicit. Once we have applied these tools to understand law, we will find that legal decisionmaking produces predictable patterns that both include and account for innovation. I refer to the resulting view—which I introduce in chapter 6 and develop in succeeding chapters—under the counterintuitive rubric of "law as persuasion." It is conventional to think of persuasion as an unruly factor that distorts the law in its appeal to extrarational considerations. But just the opposite is true: Regularity in law is a function not of logic or objectivity, but of the cognitive and social constraints that attend the process of persuasion. Indeed, in chapter 11, I derive this conclusion from the law's own claim to neutrality.

GIANT STEPS

With the stakes thus firmly in view, we can return to the opening passages from Bolt's *A Man for All Seasons* and Kennedy's *Critical Phenomenology* for a first canvass of the claim that human rationality is both imaginative and simultaneously embodied, grounded, and systematic in operation. To do so, however, it is necessary to introduce the concepts of *metaphor* and *image-schema*.

I start with these concepts for three reasons. First, metaphor provides a particularly accessible way in which to demonstrate these complex claims concerning embodiment, grounding, and systematicity. The examples— like the opening passage from *A Man for All Seasons*—are familiar and, therefore, easy to follow. Second, because metaphors are frequently structured by underlying image-schemas, this initial examination of the concept of metaphor also helps elucidate the claim that cognition is imagistic. Third, because metaphor involves knowledge transfer across domains (from the Greek *meta pherein,* "to carry over"), it provides a useful illustration of what is at issue in the claim that cognition is cross-modal. I want to be clear, however, that this focus on metaphor is didactic rather than definitive. It is not my claim that "everything is metaphor," nor that metaphor is more basic or pervasive than other cognitive mechanisms. Phenomena such as basic-level categorization, idealized cognitive models, prototype effects, and radial categories are important aspects of cognition that hold equal if not greater significance for our understanding of law. But that is getting ahead of the story.

As understood in cognitive theory, metaphor is a matter of thought and not mere language. It refers to a tightly structured set of conceptual mappings in which a target domain is understood in terms of a source domain of more readily comprehended embodied or social experience.* This conceptual mapping is conventionally represented by means of a mnemonic of the form TARGET-DOMAIN-IS-SOURCE-DOMAIN. But this is only a representation; the metaphor is the set of conceptual mappings and not the mnemonic. Similarly, it is important not to confuse the metaphor, which is the conceptual mapping, with the many metaphorical expressions that are its linguistic manifestations.[31] We comprehend and reason by means of the conceptual mappings, not—as assumed by philosophers like Davidson—by means of language and propositions.

Both the conceptual nature of metaphor and its independence of particular linguistic expressions are nicely illustrated by the passages with which I started the chapter. Thus, it was immediately recognizable that the excerpts from both Duncan Kennedy and *A Man for All Seasons* employ the same conceptual metaphor even though the latter never actually uses the expression "forest of constraint." Similarly, Kennedy's impacted field— in which "boundaries are long straight lines" that are "reinforced at regular intervals with precedents whose holdings exactly track the line"—is readily comprehended as using the same imagery of motion and constraint, even though it communicates the idea without the particular metaphorical instantiation of "forest."

These metaphorical mappings, moreover, define semantic content. Consider the exchange between Roper and Sir Thomas. Roper's desire to set aside the law in the face of evil is characterized by Sir Thomas as a desire to "cut a great road through the law." In contrast, Sir Thomas insists that the Devil himself should be free "until he broke the law." Both these representations—both "cutting" and "breaking"—connote abrogation of the law's constraint. Yet, one senses that there is a difference between them. In condemning Roper's understandable zeal, Sir Thomas does not equate it with the corruption of someone like Rich. Instead, he makes a pragmatic appeal to Roper's long-term self-interest in maintaining the law's integrity. At the same time, however, Sir Thomas's rebuke intimates that there is some-

---

* "Experience" is used as a shorthand for the human organism's interaction with its physical and social world. But it is not intended to suggest that there is some unmediated experiential foundation for our knowledge. As we shall see in the next chapter, this in not even true of perception. And the fact that many of our cognitive constructs are grounded in *social* experience means that our very ability to construct a world is, in an important sense that we shall explore below, highly constrained.

thing much worse—something more destructive—about Roper's proposed course of action. None of this is contained in the propositional content of the exchange. How do we know this?

Although the expressions "to break the law" and "to cut a great road through the law" both connote abrogation of the law's constraint, they are premised on different metaphorical mappings that indicate different *kinds* of abrogation. The "breaking" in the phrase "to break the law" is not the destruction or elimination of the law, but a breach or transgression (from the Latin *trans gredi,* "to step across" or "to step beyond") of its limits. We can verify this by examining the range of related conventional expressions. If what were mapped was the act of destruction, then we would expect to find other expressions that correlated with that conceptual image. But, absent some very special contexts of usurpation (of which Watergate might be an example), it would be peculiar to say that an ordinary criminal had "wrecked," "ravaged," "destroyed," "demolished," or "obliterated" the law. So, too, when someone breaks the law, we do not "fix," "remake," "rebuild," "reconstruct," or "reassemble" it. Rather, when the law has been broken the appropriate corrective is to "reestablish law and *order*" and "*bring* the malefactor *to* justice." Thus, the "breaking" in the phrase "to break the law" is a *breaking out* of the boundaries or constraints set by the law. Correspondingly, law-abiding people stay "*within the bounds* of the law" unless they can find a "technical *loophole.*" Devious people may try to "*get around* the law," but those who defy the law outright become *outlaws* because they are "*outside the boundaries* of the law." [32] To the same effect is the phrase from the Lord's Prayer, "Forgive us our *trespasses.*"

"To cut a great road through the law," in contrast, connotes destruction. When Roper says that he would "cut down every law in England" to get the Devil, we know that this is not merely a matter of temporary suspension of the law for noble purposes. In this metaphor, the constraint of the forest maps onto the restrictions of the law and the act of cutting down the forest maps onto the wholesale elimination of those restrictions. Thus, Sir Thomas's rebuke is precisely that, in leveling the forest to get at the Devil, Roper is risking the complete obliteration of the law. And that is more worrisome than a mere violation of its limits, for it would eliminate the constraints that protect us from the excesses of others.

This passage from Bolt's play also illustrates the way in which metaphorical mappings define patterns of inference. Roper would have Sir Thomas invoke the authority of his office to stop Rich. In other words, he is not exhorting Sir Thomas to break the law, but rather to use his legal power to remove existing legal constraints. This removal of constraint is the basis for Sir Thomas's characterization of Roper's suggested course of action as "cut[ting] a great road through the law." And this characterization in turn structures Sir Thomas's subsequent argument. When Roper responds that he would "cut down every law in England" to get the Devil, Sir Thomas asks him to reflect on the consequences of that action: "When the last law was down and the Devil turned round on you—where would you hide, Roper, the laws all being flat? . . . Do you really think you could stand upright in the winds that would blow then?"

This exegesis of the metaphorical structure of the passage might be of little more than literary interest except for two facts. First, each and every one of these expressions and the accompanying patterns of inference are the product of a more general, conceptual metaphor. Second, these conceptual metaphors are neither arbitrary nor mere products of chance and history, but are grounded in our most basic embodied experience.

As embodied organisms, we achieve upright posture and balance in the world. We experience our bodies as structured wholes with identifiable parts. We individuate objects outside ourselves. We propel ourselves through space to obtain desired objects. Sometimes, our way is blocked by an obstacle and we must exert additional force to overcome or avoid it. Some objects (like our bodies) are so configured as to contain other objects (our *in-*sides). Each of these quite basic interactions with the world is generalizable, and each is in fact generalized across a series of other domains. Each of these generalizations is a "recurring structure" or "repeatable pattern" by which we are able to understand the world as a "unified place that we can make sense of." [33]

The very capacity of the brain to recognize patterns and form concepts depends on these structures of bodily experience. These basic structures or *image-schemas*—such as BALANCE, PART-WHOLE, OBJECT, SOURCE-PATH-GOAL, FORCE-BARRIER, and CONTAINER—provide structure to human thought and a measure of apparent unity and determinacy in our interaction with the world.* Image-schemas are neither representations nor literal "pictures" but, as we shall see in the next chapter, schematics that emerge from cross-modal linkages in neural processes that transcend any specific sensory modality. [34]

Our most basic logical operations are structured by these image-

* I say "apparent" because although these basic constructs arise from embodied experiences of the human organism in the world, they say nothing about the nature of the world itself. This point is critical because the cognitive claim with respect to embodiment is sometimes misread as a reintroduction of objectivism or empiricism.

schemas. For example, building on the work of Eve Sweetser,[35] Mark Johnson has demonstrated how the SOURCE-PATH-GOAL, FORCE-BARRIER, and CONTAINER schemas structure modal verbs such as "must," "may," "shall," "can," and so on.[36] So, too, these image-schemas are the basis for conceptual metaphors that are indispensable to legal and moral reasoning. Whether we are *weighing* the evidence, engaging in interest *balancing*, applying a multipart *balancing* test, or trying to achieve a Rawlsian "reflective equilibrium," [37] we are engaged in mental operations dependent on the BALANCE schema. Conceptual metaphors of this sort are not only reflected in our language, but also in our cultural iconography: hence, the scales of justice.

Image-schemas also provide the predicate for conceptual metaphors that organize diverse areas of human interaction, including some of our most fundamental concepts. Consider, again, the passage from *A Man for All Seasons*. When Sir Thomas asks Roper whether he would "cut a great road through the law *to get after* the Devil," he is employing the general conceptual metaphor ACTIONS ARE MOTIONS. In this metaphor, the experience of physical motion is mapped onto abstract social or intellectual actions. The mapping is systematic, which means that each of the entailments from the domain of physical mobility—the experience of blockage, containment, and movement through space toward desired objects—is also carried over to the target domain of abstract social action. This mapping thus yields a series of correlative metaphors, in which:

- ◆ CONSTRAINTS ON ACTION ARE CONSTRAINTS ON MOTION
- ◆ PURPOSES ARE DESTINATIONS
- ◆ IMPEDIMENTS TO PURPOSES ARE OBSTACLES TO MOTION

In a corollary of these metaphors, life is conceptualized as a purposive journey. This yields expressions like "it's time to *get on* with your life" and "I *overcame* my problem with alcohol." [38]

These conceptual metaphors and their attendant metaphorical mappings make sense of a tremendous range of common expressions. For example, the ACTIONS ARE MOTIONS metaphor explains why a person active in his or her community is a *mover and shaker* or why someone who pulls rank is said to be *throwing one's weight around*. Correspondingly, since CONSTRAINTS ON ACTION ARE CONSTRAINTS ON MOTION, a person too busy to *get free* is said to be *all tied up* with work. So, too, the LIFE IS A JOURNEY metaphor explains why an individualist is colloquially described as *marching to the beat of a different drummer*, and the PURPOSES ARE DESTINATIONS metaphor accounts for the ubiquitous *light at the end of the tunnel*.

The concept of a judicial trial provides an interesting example because these metaphors structure a host of routine legal expressions that might otherwise be thought quite arbitrary. Thus, the general metaphors PURPOSES ARE DESTINATIONS and ACTIONS ARE MOTIONS yield as a special case a metaphorical conception in which ADJUDICATION IS MOVEMENT ALONG A PATH. This is what makes sense of the conventional idioms in which litigation is a judicial *proceeding;* the parties cite supporting *grounds* for their *motions;* the plaintiff must *carry the burden* of proof; a presumption may shift the burden of *going forward;* and parties may decide to *forgo* (from the Old English *forgan* or *foregan,* "to pass by") their procedural rights.

But such conceptual metaphors do more than explain a few idiomatic expressions. Rather, conceptual metaphors like these characterize patterns of semantic productivity and everyday reasoning. Take the conceptual metaphor PURPOSES ARE DESTINATIONS. When we have completed 50 percent of a task—any task, whether physical or intellectual—we know that we are at the *midpoint* in our efforts or *halfway there.* As we *near the end* of our undertaking, we know that we will *meet our goal.* And, when we have finished, we have completed what *we set out to do.* So, too, a project has a *point;* it can be *far along* or *at an impasse;* it can hit a *snag* or grow *by leaps and bounds.*

Many of the basic concepts and routine expressions used in moral and legal reasoning are organized by these same conceptual metaphors. For example, we understand our moral and legal obligations in terms of the CONSTRAINTS ON ACTION ARE CONSTRAINTS ON MOTION metaphor. Thus, we are *bound* by our promises and contracts, although we sometimes try *to get out of* such commitments by asking the other party to *release* us. And, as illustrated by the discussion of the "forest of constraint" expression, our fundamental conception of law is premised on the metaphors ACTIONS ARE MOTIONS and CONSTRAINTS ON ACTION ARE CONSTRAINTS ON MOTION.

This conceptual mapping is reflected quite clearly in the modern debate over the proper parameters of judicial review. In an early due process opinion, Justice Frankfurter observed that judicial interpretation "must *move within the limits* of accepted notions of justice." [39] Justice Black, who was more skeptical of what he referred to as the "*ambulatory* power to declare laws unconstitutional," [40] believed that judicial review could be restrained by adherence to the language of the constitutional text: "The early settlers undertook to *curb* their governments by *confining their powers within written boundaries,* which eventually became written constitutions." [41] More recently, the dispute among the several opinions of the justices in the Supreme Court's 1992 decision reaffirming *Roe v. Wade* and the right to choice relied

on these same conceptual metaphors. Thus, the joint opinion of Justices
O'Connor, Kennedy, and Souter rejected Justice Scalia's faith in the constitutional text "as a means of *curbing* the discretion of federal judges." [42]
Chief Justice Rehnquist in turn complained that the joint opinion's "undue
burden" standard "will do nothing to prevent 'judges from *roaming at large*
in the constitutional field' *guided only by* their personal views." [43] And Justice Scalia condemned the standard as a "rootless" attempt "to preserve
some judicial *foothold* in this *ill-gotten territory.*" [44] In each of these cases,
judicial action is conceptualized as self-propelled motion in need of some
external legal constraint; the presumed alternative is conceptualized as
movement according to desire or personal preference.*

This examination of the ostensibly hackneyed expression "forest of
constraint" has so far revealed four rather significant points. First, where
one might have assumed that such a cliché is arbitrary in meaning, it turns
out to be grounded in basic embodied experience. Second, where one might
have assumed that an idiom of this sort is merely a matter of colorful expression, it turns out to be rich in conceptual and semantic content. Third,
where one might have assumed that such a colloquialism is just an isolated
trope, it turns out to be a product of underlying conceptual metaphors that
constitute a quite significant part of our conceptual system. Fourth, where
one might have assumed that a figurative expression of this sort is subjective and quixotic, it turns out to be highly conventional and quite regular
and orderly in its use. In short, we have seen that imaginative rationality is
embodied, grounded, and systematic in operation.

About the only thing we have not yet accounted for is the specific metaphorical instantiation of "forest." This, too, is premised on a standard conceptual metaphor; in fact, we have already encountered a variant in which
law is treated as a metaphorical OBJECT. The underlying metaphor—part
of a larger metaphorical system to which we will return in chapter 3—
conceptualizes ideas as objects. This metaphor is what motivates conventional legal conceptions such as "findings of fact" and the "holding of a
case," or Holmes's famous metaphor the "marketplace of ideas." [45] In this
last example, ideas are metaphorical commodities that are bought, sold,
and traded. As this example suggests, the IDEAS ARE OBJECTS metaphor can
be further elaborated by introducing particular kinds of objects—such as
commodities, products, or food—that emphasize different features or di-

---

* Hence the derivation of the word "bias," which originally referred to a line diago-
nal to the grain of the fabric.

mensions of the concept "idea." For example, the IDEAS ARE COMMODITIES metaphor focuses on the transactional nature of ideational exchange. In this metaphor, persuasion maps onto selling, acceptance maps onto buying, monetary valuation maps onto the assessment of significance, and the competition of the market maps onto the struggle for acceptance in the domain of public opinion.*

When we reason about the genesis or demise of ideas, we commonly use the metaphor IDEAS ARE PLANTS. In this metaphor, the life cycle of a plant maps onto the duration of an idea. Thus, an idea can *blossom, flower, bear fruit,* or *die on the vine.*[46] We can observe both aspects of this mapping at work in the passage from *A Man for All Seasons.* When Sir Thomas reminds Roper that law is humanly constructed and, therefore, perishable, he exclaims: "This country's planted thick with laws from coast to coast." Correspondingly, the destructible nature of plant life maps onto the fragility of law. Accordingly, Roper can "cut down every law in England" to get after the Devil.

These metaphorical expressions illustrate how the systematicity of metaphorical thought makes possible both semantic productivity and conceptual creativity. The systematic mapping of entailments from source domain to target domain enables us automatically to extend a conceptual metaphor by modeling other aspects in the source domain. We saw an example of this in the case of the ACTIONS ARE MOTIONS metaphor, in which each of the entailments from the domain of physical mobility is carried over to the domain of abstract action to yield a network of related metaphors such as CONSTRAINTS ON ACTION ARE CONSTRAINTS ON MOTION. Similarly, we can produce an indeterminate number of conventional metaphorical expressions by instantiating the entity (or action) in the source domain with a specific example—e.g., "*tied up* with work" for CONSTRAINTS. Finally, we can generate supplementary metaphors by replacing the source domain entity (or action) with a related kind of entity (or action) that provides a different set of entailments—e.g., PLANTS for OBJECTS.†

This systematicity also enables the creation of new metaphorical expressions. Indeed, we have already encountered several example of this phe-

---

* This is what yields such conventional expressions as "that idea isn't *worth* much" or "with the right *packaging* that idea just might *sell.*"

† This list is not exhaustive: The systematicity of metaphorical thought also includes the way in which "inconsistent" metaphors can be combined to work together. Lakoff and Johnson refer to this as "metaphorical coherence," which is possible when different metaphors share entailments.

CHAPTER 2

Embodiment

BY ONE, our son Charles was running at full tilt and beginning to talk (though "ball" and "Dada" were his only words at this point). He padded into our bedroom as I was shining my shoes one day. He was intrigued by this new activity and determined to participate. "Daddy is polishing his shoes," I said, in a vain attempt to deflect him. I let him take the shoe brush and watched patiently as he swiped at my shoes in an awkward imitation of my movements. I gently repossessed the brush and resumed. Charles padded out of the room, only to return moments later holding my hair brush and swiping at his hair with the same awkward movements he had used moments earlier.

Though the term "brush" had not been used, Charles nevertheless understood that these two things—the shoe brush and the hair brush—were part of the same category. He recognized this despite their different uses (which he also seemed to appreciate), "fitting" these things together on the basis of the common motor movements that he acted out.

This simple story illustrates several of the more profound conclusions to have emerged from the cognitive sciences in the past thirty years. Suffice it to say that these findings overturn many of our most taken-for-granted assumptions about human rationality. For example, it is widely assumed that categories and concepts are a matter of common features or identifying criteria. Yet, as this story suggests, it is our patterns of interaction with the world, rather than perceptions of common features such as bristles or wooden handles, that largely govern the way in which we as humans categorize it. So, too, it is axiomatic among philosophers of language (and most law professors) that thought is necessarily a matter of language and propositions. Yet, as this story suggests, there is thought without language; this is possible because thought originates in our sense of spatial and kinesthetic orientation in the world. In both these ways—and many others—human cognition is a fundamentally *embodied* activity.

This chapter explores the embodiment claim along two different dimensions. The first section examines how our embodied interactions with the physical world govern the way in which we as humans categorize it.* We will see how these categorizations are reflected in language, and we will take a preliminary look at how this process is related to neural architecture. The second section reviews some fundamentals of how neurons in the brain are organized in functioning networks; it then considers some of the profound implications that this arrangement holds for cognition. The third section builds on this discussion of neural processes and takes a look at the role of imagistic thought in higher-order aspects of cognition.

BACK TO BASICS

"When you dissect a human brain," Henrietta Leiner told the *New York Times,* "you can see with the naked eye an enormous cable of 40 million nerve fibers descending from the cortex to the cerebellum. I knew how much information it could send. I was just floored. I thought this is some terrific computer down here." [1] (The optic tract, in contrast, consists of only about a million neural fibers.) But there was one catch: The cerebellum (which lies just above the brain stem) was known to regulate bodily functions such as motor control and balance. So what could all those connections be for?

There are still skeptics who insist that the massive connections between the cerebellum and the higher brain serve only motor functions. But the evidence to the contrary is mounting. Connections from the cerebellum's neodentate nucleus run to the frontal and prefrontal areas of the brain and extend at least as far as Broca's area, which is known to participate in language functions. [2] Positron Emission Tomography (PET scan) shows areas of the cerebellum active in word-selection tasks, such as generating verbs, even

---

* This discussion also lays the groundwork for chapter 4, where I explore the ways in which knowledge is organized in experientially meaningful gestalts (e.g., some brushes are for shoes, others for hair) rather than as simple features-bundles or acontextual lists of data. That more complete picture will enable us to see the ineluctably *social* dimension of knowledge and categorization.

when speech is not involved.[3] Frank Middleton and Peter Strick used herpes simplex virus to trace neural pathways in monkey brains and confirmed the existence of *output* connections from the basal ganglia and the cerebellum's dentate nucleus to nonmotor areas of the prefrontal cortex. These cortical areas, moreover, are reciprocally connected to these two "lower" brain structures in a loop that is separate from but parallel to those serving motor areas.[4] Perhaps most significantly of all, dramatic enlargement of the frontal cortical lobes in human evolution was concomitant with development and enlargement of the neodentate. In monkeys, in contrast, the neodentate is not yet differentiated; in apes, it is not fully enlarged.[5]

Though these findings challenge the conventional wisdom in neuroscience, they are not really surprising: Gerald Edelman, for one, insists that "there is an intimate relation between animal functions (especially movement) and the development of the brain."[6] The evidence from cognitive psychology and linguistics is both strong and long-standing. In his classic text *Social Psychology,* Roger Brown observed that "cognitive categories of the first level may be redundantly transmitted by names and by conventional actions."[7] As he explained:

> When Lewis' son first looked upon the yellow jonquils in a bowl and heard them named *flowers* he was also enjoined to smell them and we may guess that his mother leaned over and did just that. When a ball is named *ball* it is also likely to be bounced. When a cat is named *kitty* it is also likely to be petted. Smelling and bouncing and petting are actions distinctively linked to certain categories. We can be sure they are distinctive because they are able to function as symbols of these categories. In a game of charades one might symbolize *cat* by stroking the air at a suitable height in a certain fashion, or symbolize *flower* by inclining forward and sniffing. (318)

Brown observed that this "first level" of categorization "is neither consistently very abstract nor consistently very concrete. It is rather consistently functional." He noted, moreover, that this first level of categorization is "followed by an endless process of further categorization which moves in both the abstract and the concrete direction" (321).

These insights have been confirmed both in field work by the anthropologist Brent Berlin and in experimental work by the cognitive psychologist Eleanor Rosch.[8] They found that there is a level of categorization that is psychologically basic in the sense that: (1) categories at this level are learned earliest and named first; (2) category names at this level are the shortest and most frequently used in the language (e.g., "dog," "cat," "ball," "chair," "car," "dime"); (3) things at this level are remembered more readily and identified more quickly; (4) items at this level are perceived holistically, as a single gestalt, rather than identified by specific, distinctive features; and (5) there tend to be distinctive motor programs for interacting with objects at this level. (As Brown noted, flowers "are marked by sniffing actions but there are no actions that distinguish one species of flower from another" [318].)

Rosch (who mostly studied artifacts and implements) characterized this level of categorization as the *basic level* in contradistinction to higher-order, *superordinate* categories and more specific, *subordinate* categories.* For example, "chair" is a basic-level category, "furniture" a superordinate category, and "rocker" a subordinate category. Superordinate categories are, by definition, the most inclusive; subordinate categories are the most specific. One might think that superordinate categories would, as a general matter, be the most useful because they incorporate the most information. Rosch found, however, that most of our knowledge is organized at the basic level: When subjects were asked to list attributes of various categories, they listed very few attributes at the superordinate level (e.g., animals), most of what they knew at the basic level (e.g., dogs), and little additional information at the subordinate level (e.g., golden retrievers). For the same reason, basic-level categories are the most useful for practical purposes: If you wanted to know whether you would be able to sit when you observe my class, you would not ask whether there is any furniture in the room because you may arrive to find nothing but tables and desks. (Nor would you be likely to inquire about anything as specific as a rocker, since almost any other kind of chair would do.) So, too, the person who delivers our mail will be more interested in knowing that we do not have a dog than in finding out either that we have an animal (a gerbil) or that we do not have a cocker spaniel.

But basic-level categorization is more than a matter of practicality. To get a sense of the embodied basis for basic-level categorization (and of the difference between basic-level and superordinate categories), try the following thought experiment: Close your eyes and picture a chair. Now, close your eyes and try to picture a furniture. You cannot—at least not one that isn't a basic-level object such as a lamp, table, or chair. The reasons are,

---

* Berlin, who studied the way in which Tzeltal speakers in Chiapas categorized plants and animals, called it the "folk-generic level" because it corresponded with scientific categorization at the level of the genus—that is, the level at which oaks are distinguished from redwoods and elephants from giraffes, raccoons, foxes, etc.

first, that one can perceive lamps, tables, or chairs in terms of a single over-all shape, but there is no overall shape for pieces of furniture in general (i.e., that would encompass lamps, tables, chairs, beds, etc.). Second (and, as we shall see in the next section, relatedly), we have special motor programs for interacting with basic-level objects such as lamps, tables, and chairs but no motor program for pieces of furniture in general. Consequently, one can form a mental image of a generic chair but not of a generic piece of furniture.

"What determines basic level structure," Lakoff observes, "is a matter of correlations."[9] The basic level represents the point at which gestalt perception, motor interaction, mental image formation, and general knowledge correlate. The next section examines some of the neural architecture underlying this correlation. In the meantime, note three things:

First, it is easy to see how basic-level categorization might arise as an evolutionary adaptation. To survive, every organism must be able to negotiate its physical environment successfully. Basic-level categorization is organized not in terms of the objective qualities of the physical world itself, but rather in terms of the ways in which we as humans interact with the objects in our environment: the way we perceive them, image them, and physically engage with them by touching, grasping, stroking, sitting, walking, and otherwise moving in relation to them. Categorization, moreover, is itself an adaptive mechanism. As Rosch observes, categorization at the basic level shows the greatest degree of commonality within categories (e.g., "dog") and of discontinuity between related categories (e.g., "dog" and "cat"). Basic-level categorization thus serves "to maximize the information-rich cluster of attributes in the environment" (37).

Second, basic-level categorization creates the impression of an objective reality that "corresponds" with our mental representations of it. But this impression is deceptive. Of course, categories at the basic level "fit" the physical world fairly well; if they did not, we would hardly have survived as a species. In other words, it is simply a truism that human sensorimotor capacities evolved to foster successful adaptation: As Edelman remarks, "evolution teaches us that the selection of animals formed to carry out functions that increase their fitness is at the very heart of the matter" (31). It remains true, however, that the "attributes" that define the basic level are not inherent properties of things-in-the-world but *interactional properties* relative to the embodied ways in which we as humans comport ourselves.

Third, the empirical findings with respect to basic-level categorization hold implications for our understanding of brain structure and function. This is the import of Edelman's just-quoted remark: that evolution necessarily expresses itself through the natural selection of biological form. The brains that evolved to categorize the world at the basic level are brains formed to think imagistically, to conceptualize in terms of embodied interactions, and to integrate those varied interactions adaptively in experientially meaningful gestalts.

SURFING THE NET

Taking a break from my work on this chapter, I logged onto the Internet and fired-up my browser. The browser is set to CNN as the start-up page; on that particular day, CNN had a photo-story on Hemingway's Key West house. The house is open to the public as a kind of museum; its only current residents are the numerous descendants of Papa's six-toed cats. We had visited the house on a weekend excursion to Key West in the late 1980s. Out of curiosity and nostalgia, I clicked on the thumbnail to enlarge the picture and begin the virtual tour. As the photo opened in my browser, I experienced the overpoweringly foul odor of too many cats (all the more startling given that years of chronic sinusitis have severely eroded my sense of smell). A few weeks later, I was talking to my friend Jeremy who told me of a similar incident that occurred when he was eighteen. He had gone to visit his grandfather, who was convalescing from a stroke that left him completely paralyzed on one side. Alert and able to talk, Jeremy's grandfather began to reminisce about his childhood in Russia. He spoke vividly and with increasing verve as he described how he loved to climb the trees at his boyhood home. Jeremy's grandfather suddenly stopped as they both looked on in amazement: In the excitement of his reminiscence, he was making climbing motions with *both* hands.

Such stories are really quite commonplace. They nicely illustrate the point made in the opening chapter: The brain is neither a passive recorder of external stimuli nor a mere processor of symbols, but a dynamic associative mechanism whose active correlations shape what we perceive and how we think. (Recall Edelman's previously quoted observation that "there is no such thing as software involved in the operation of brains, and the evidence overwhelmingly indicates that the morphology of the brain matters overwhelmingly.")

It is still relatively early in the study of the brain. Many fundamental issues, such as how much of the brain is specialized and how much plastic to experience, have yet to be determined; many things we think we know are likely soon to seem dated. What follows, therefore, is on the order of a sketch or emerging picture. Still, what we can comfortably say at this point is in many respects quite revolutionary in its implications.

"Information" in the brain is not stored in discrete locations like pigeonholes nor coded on individual brain cells as on the chips of a computer. To the extent there is anything like a "record" of a memory or event it lies in the multitudinous connections or synapses between very large numbers of neurons. Each neuron has an axon that makes contact across a synapse with the body (soma) or dendrite of another. Electrical activity down the axon causes the release of a chemical neurotransmitter that in turn induces or inhibits the electrical activity of the next neuron. Each time the firing of one neuron stimulates (or inhibits) the firing of the next, the chemical connections between those neurons (that is, the ability to reproduce the same chemical activity)* is strengthened.[10]

These neurons are organized in networks ("neural nets") consisting of groups or "populations" of hundreds or thousands of neurons linked together by these synaptic connections.[11] These synaptic connections can have varying strengths or "weights" that stimulate (or inhibit) to varying degrees the firing of other neurons in the group. Once these synaptic connections have been sufficiently forged, either during development or in response to repeated experience, the network can reproduce the previous pattern of neural activation. Memory, in other words, is a dynamic property of populations of neurons; the basic mechanism is synaptic change, but memory occurs as a *system* property.

These neural networks are, in turn, connected to many other networks. Antonio and Hanna Damasio give the simple example of a person as she picks up a cup of coffee:

> Her visual cortices will respond to the colors of the cup and of its con
> tents as well as to its shape and position. The somatosensory cortices will
> register the shape the hand assumes as it holds the cup, the movement of
> the hand and the arm as they bring the cup to the lips, the warmth of the
> coffee, and the body change some people call pleasure when they drink
> the stuff.

The brain, they emphasize, does not merely register events in the world but "also records how the body explores the world and reacts to it." Even

---

* As Edelman explains, these changes can occur both "presynaptically by changes in the amount and the delivery of transmitter, and postsynaptically by alteration of the chemical state of receptors and ion channels, the units on the postsynaptic side that bind transmitters and let ions carrying electrical charge (such as calcium ions) through to the inside of the cell" (19).

though these neural processes may occur in different portions of the brain, the person nevertheless experiences them in a unified, coherent way and can recall them as such. The Damasios hypothesize that "the records that bind together all these fragmented activities . . . are embodied in ensembles of neurons" they call convergence zones, where

> the axons of feedforward projecting neurons from one part of the brain converge and join with reciprocally diverging feedback projections from other regions. When reactivation within the convergence zones stimulates the feedback projections, many anatomically separate and widely distributed neuron ensembles fire simultaneously and reconstruct previous patterns of mental activity.[12]

Edelman's reentrant cortical integration (RCI) model provides a parallel, though in many ways more elegant, account. On this account, the primary functional units are neuronal groups organized into "mappings" and special kinds of feedback loops that (for reasons we shall see in a moment) he refers to as "reentrant pathways."

Mappings were discovered in the nineteenth century by Gustav Fritsch and Julius Hitzig. A mapping consists of a sheet of neurons in the brain linked to a receptor sheet (e.g., the retina or the touch cells of the skin) in such a way that when the receptor sheet is stimulated (as by light or touch) the corresponding neurons in the mapped group also respond. Many such maps (though by no means all) are topographic, which means that neighboring locations in the receptor sheet are also neighboring locations in the corresponding map.

These neural maps also connect with each other; indeed, Edelman notes that the fibers composing these connections are among the most numerous in the brain.* These "reentrant" connections allow maps to interact with one another. For example, one map may receive stimulation from receptor sheets that respond to visually detected angles; a second receives signals from a receptor sheet that responds to an object's overall movement. Or one map may respond to sight, another to touch. (Let us refer to these simply as map_1 and map_2.) The reentrant signals between these maps correlate their responses: "This means that, as groups of neurons are selected in a map, other groups in reentrantly connected but different maps are also

---

* For example, the corpus callosum—the structure that connects the right and left hemispheres of the brain—contains approximately 200 million such fibers.

selected" (85). In other words, certain active combinations of neurons in map$_1$ signal (i.e., stimulate) an otherwise independent set of neurons in map$_2$. If this happens repeatedly, the synaptic connections that join these combinations—that is, the synaptic connections between map$_1$ and map$_2$—will be strengthened.

Note that, as Edelman points out, topographic connections enable maps to correlate neural responses without any higher-order supervisor. (In philosophical terms, there is no need to postulate an homunculus or "little man" inside the brain who directs the action.) Note, too, that the reentrant connections between two otherwise independent topographic maps (e.g., between the angle mapping and the movement mapping or the visual mapping and the touch mapping) "serve to 'map the maps' to each other" (90, fig. 9-4)—that is, the signals from map$_1$ (let us say, the angle mapping) are *reentered* into map$_2$ along with that map's independent input (if any) from the receptor sheet responding to movement. Finally, note that these kinds of connections are not "limited to a pair of maps or to any one moment in time" (87). Not only can *multiple* maps be coordinated in this way, but their interactions can be coordinated *dynamically* as they vary in real time in response to body movements and changes in the environment.* In this way, the maps can combine to form *global mappings* "containing multiple reentrant local maps (both motor and sensory) that are able to interact with nonmapped parts of the brain" (89).

Though many more steps are necessary to explain higher functions such as consciousness, note that even this truncated sketch provides a working account of the neurological basis for image-schemas and metaphor. As we interact with a physical object such as a box, for example, we perceive it in several dimensions concurrently—vision, touch, body attitude, motor movements. Each of these sensory inputs is mapped from its receptor sheet to its corresponding map in the brain. Reentrant connections among these topographic mappings "map the maps" to each other; they do so, moreover, across several sensory dimensions simultaneously—i.e., the visual, the kinesthetic, and the spatiotemporal (including position, orientation, shape, movement, and velocity).[13] The resulting pattern is not represented in a discrete place in the brain, but rather consists in the overall global mapping. The result, in other words, is not a "picture" of a box, but rather, as Edelman explains, a composite constituted by the "*correlation* between different

---

* To put the matter in perspective, the visual system of the monkey must integrate over thirty different maps for color, orientation, movement, etc. (85–86).

kinds of categorizations" (119). The "images" that we experience in consciousness are an emergent quality of these global mappings—like the schematic mental image of a "chair" that you called up in response to the thought
experiment in the previous section—not actual, concrete pictures of specific
things as they exist in the world.[14]

Since it is also possible to have mappings of global mappings, one would
expect categorizations of perceptual categorizations: "box-like" things, for
example. But this higher-order mapping is not itself a sense perception; it
is, rather, an abstraction or mental construct that synthesizes a "recurring
structure" or "repeatable pattern"—in this case a CONTAINER schema.[15]

Metaphor extends these processes one step further. Remember that
metaphor is a conceptual mapping from a source domain to a target domain that preserves inferential structure, as in the ACTIONS ARE MOTIONS
mapping discussed in the previous chapter. This means that metaphor is an
expected consequence of topographic mappings. As in all topographic
mappings, the structure of the source domain is preserved in the target domain because the neurons of the former map to (i.e., stimulate) the latter
through reentrant signaling (or its equivalent). How do these connections
form? Consider the simple but pervasive conceptual metaphor MORE IS UP
(and its correlative, LESS IS DOWN). In this mapping, the abstract domain of
quantity or value correlates with relative changes along the vertical axis in
the spatial domain, as in the following expressions:

- my stocks *plummeted*
- her fame *skyrocketed*
- nationwide, crime is *down*
- productivity is way *up*

It is easy to see how this correlation occurs. The neural networks characterizing each of these domains "are coactivated in everyday experience, as when
we pile more books on the desk and their height goes up" or add water to
a container.[16] If the mappings are connected by reentrant pathways, co-
activation will strengthen the connections. Once those connections have
formed, the *relations* in the source domain of verticality will be preserved
by the mapping and, therefore, can form the basis of inferences in the target domain of quantity. If something shoots up, it is propelled quickly upward and in a very short time is much higher than before: Hence, the phrase
"her fame *skyrocketed*" indicates a sudden and substantial increase in
celebrity (in contrast, say, to a steadily building career). Metaphor, then, is

a neural mechanism that enables networks used in sensorimotor activity also to serve as the substrates that make abstract reason possible. This, in a nutshell, is Edelman's view:

> Because concepts are considered to require the mapping (and therefore the classification) of global mappings, the use of image schemata related to bodily states in the organization of thought and language is an expected characteristic in conscious organisms. Image schemata involve concepts connected to positions or states of the body as it relates to objects or events—for example, "obstacle," "resistance," "object," "motion," "containment," and "blockage." . . . Such schemata, frequently reflected as *metaphors* in the language of *Homo sapiens,* may already function in animals with conceptual capabilities and primary consciousness.[17]

Consider the implications of this sketch of neural processes. In the first place, it explains why cognition is experientially grounded—specifically, why cognition is contingent on our embodied interactions with the physical and cultural artifacts in the environment. The synaptic changes necessary to connect groups of neurons into working networks could never arise in the first place without the neurological input generated by motor activities, perception, and internal physical processes. This process of synaptic strengthening through use is the reason that memory and the mastery of new skills require repetition and practice. The converse is also true: Once a set of synaptic connections has been forged, little or no conscious effort is necessary to repeat the performance; this is why an oft repeated habit or skill sometimes seems to happen "on its own" either without our awareness or, even, when we consciously intend otherwise.

Second, and more controversially, this account suggests that the brain is to some significant degree a self-organizing system (given the evolutionary development of appropriate structures in the brain such as those that allow reentrant connections). Indeed, the processes we have examined thus far are basically enough to account for perceptual categorization: Computer simulations constructed on this model are capable of categorization, undirected learning, and appropriate adaptive behavior; all that is needed in addition is some input for value-driven behavior—e.g., the knowledge that "long, thin, wiggly things with a rattle on one end can kill you" or "ingesting objects of this sort makes the discomfort in one's stomach go away."[18] Exactly how much of the brain is self-organizing and how much is "hard-wired" is, as indicated earlier, still a matter of some disagreement. But it is nevertheless clear that some postgenetic organization is taking place. In the 1970s, researchers removed half of the visual area in the gold-fish brain and found, nevertheless, "that the ingrowing fibers from the whole retina cram themselves into the remaining neural space and all make con-nections."[19] Language areas of the brain are normally in the left hemi-sphere, but young children who have had their entire left hemispheres re-moved because of epilepsy nevertheless develop language areas in the right hemisphere.[20] Edelman reports (25–28) experiments with other species that show differences in the neural mappings and connections of even geneti-cally identical twins.* And there is evidence from computer simulations that suggests the possibility that the process of self-organization in response to organism experience could begin in utero.[21]

Third, a necessary corollary of this integration via mappings and reen-trant connections is that brain processes, by their very nature, are synthetic and constitutive rather than propositional and analytic. To be clear, the in-tegration of mappings via the strengthened synaptic connections of reen-trant pathways means that the brain *constructs* rather than *mirrors* the re-ality with which it interacts.† This is conspicuously so in cases like those at the beginning of this section: When I *saw* the picture of Hemingway's Key West house, I *smelled* the cats even though they obviously were not in my office (and even though I can barely smell). The same process of construc-tion is what occurs in our everyday perception of the world; indeed, it is how we *have* a world.

Most of the time, of course, we experience these perceptions as simply "corresponding" to an objective reality; it is only when something goes awry that the constitutive nature of cognition becomes apparent. Kuhn gives a marvelous example of an experiment by Jerome Bruner and Leo Post-man in which subjects were shown playing cards from an anomalous deck

---

* To be clear, there is no particular mystery in this; nor is there any contradiction be-tween the self-organization claim and the claim that brain functions depend on the evolu-tionary development of various structures and connections. Michael Gazzaniga puts it deftly: "This does not mean that brain development is not driven by genetic factors. What it does mean is that the developing brain has evolved in the context of a particular envi-ronment. The genetically driven sequence of events occurs with the expectation that cer-tain signals are forthcoming from the environment" (38). William Wimsatt's concept of generative entrenchment nicely characterizes this more complex and contingent under-standing of the role played by the genes. (*See* sources cited in note 19.)

† As with basic-level categorization, the success of our day-to-day interactions with the world creates the misimpression that our mental representations "correspond" to ob-jective reality. But it does not follow that our evolutionary success arose because of a ca-pacity to mirror reality. As long as there are other adaptive strategies that might have served equally well, evolution may well have followed a different course. I discuss some alternatives below.

containing a red six of spades and a black four of hearts.[22] Subjects repeatedly misidentified the irregular cards; it took many exposures before subjects even detected that something was askew and an average of forty exposures before correct identifications were made. Even then, the error rate
was more than 10 percent. As Kuhn observes:

> Novelty emerges with difficulty, manifested by resistance, against a back-
> drop provided by expectation. Initially, only the anticipated and usual
> are experienced even under circumstances where anomaly is later to be
> discovered. . . . Further acquaintance, however, does result in aware-
> ness of something wrong . . . [which] opens a period in which percep-
> tual categories are adjusted until the initially anomalous has become the
> anticipated. (64)

He concludes: "What a man sees depends both upon what he looks at and
also upon what his previous visual-conceptual experience has taught him
to see" (113).

The constitutive quality of mental processes is also evident in the common experience of gestalt illusions. In the Kanizsa triangle (fig. 2.1), we *see*
a bright, almost iridescent triangle in the center of the figure even though
there is actually nothing there; the contour, brightness, and depth effects
are illusory. The integration of different cues from perceptual maps for angle,
shape, and occlusion creates the *experience* of definite contours even though
there are none. That these perceptions arise from ordinary processes of integration is backed up by computer simulations constructed on Edelman's

FIGURE 2.1   The Kanizsa Triangle

The illusory features of the inner triangle are constructed by the cerebral cortex from
contextual cues through integration of perceptual submodalities relating to contour and
occlusion. Cover the black dots and the illusory triangle will recede and disappear.

RCI model, which produce these as well as other well-known gestalt effects such as that of structure from motion.[23]

Though some may see these gestalt illusions as "cognitive errors," it should be apparent, rather, that the underlying neural mechanism arose as a successful evolutionary adaptation. As Edelman observes: "Any gestalt patterning that allowed more adaptive action would have led rapidly to natural selection for particular reentrant circuits and functional segregation" (89). This selection might have occurred in one of two ways. One consequence of the integration process as I have described it is that once an association is forged in experience, it can be reactivated when one of its connected mappings is activated. This means that effective recall or recognition is possible on less-than-perfect information (just as the picture of Hemingway's house induced retrieval of the olfactory dimension of that experience). The efficiency gains are obvious, especially in a world where less-than-perfect information is a commonplace. A second consequence of integration is that actions can be tightly bound to perception (recall the climbing motions made by Jeremy's partially paralyzed grandfather) without the need for conscious mediation. The ability to link categorical responses to categorical perceptions in an automatic and immediate fashion provides substantial adaptive advantages.* Just think of all the times that, as a driver, you hit the brakes without thinking in response to the unexpected actions of other drivers or, as a pedestrian, automatically glanced from side-to-side before entering the street.

It is conventional, both within lay culture and in much of the cognitive sciences, to think of the brain on the model of a computer. But, while there is much to be learned from computer simulations, this view is limited by the simple and, ultimately, decisive fact that brains are analog not digital. More precisely, brains are biological systems whose operations reflect their particular physiology. As Lakoff and Johnson note: "The brain uses neurons, not languagelike symbols. Neural computation works by real-time spreading activation, which is neither akin to prooflike deductions in a mathematical logic, nor like disembodied algorithms in classical artificial intelligence, nor like derivations in a transformational grammar."[24] Human rationality, in short, is the function of an embodied brain that takes shape (i.e., forges its

---

* Of course, it must be true that the resulting judgments and actions tend overall to contribute to rather than imperil survival. This would be true either if they were more accurate than not *or* if they were biased more toward false positives (perceiving and reacting to danger where there was none) than false negatives (perceiving no danger in situations of actual peril).

connections) in the context of real-world interactions and experience. The brain is, as a consequence, primarily associative and adaptive rather than propositional and truth-conditional. And it is highly synthetic, contributing to perception and experience as much as responding to it. To paraphrase Merleau-Ponty (perhaps the first philosopher of embodiment), we might say that the brain thinks in terms of its situation, forms its categories in contact with its experience, and modifies that situation and that experience by the meaning it thus constitutes.[25]

THOUGHT WITHOUT LANGUAGE

"A picture's worth a thousand words" may sound like a cliché. But some of our greatest minds have attested to the central role of images in reason. Einstein attributed his genius not to his facility in mathematics, but to his ability to visualize: He claimed to reason by combining images of a "visual and muscular type," converting them "laboriously" into words and equations only afterward. His first insights into the theory of relativity, for example, occurred when he imagined himself riding on a beam of light looking back at a frozen clock tower or imagined himself chasing after and, then, matching the speed of a beam of light.[26] Famously (though ambiguously), Holmes exhorted us to "think things not words."[27] Finding "a form of words" was for Holmes, too, something that came after and required additional work.[28]

What is the evidence for the role of images in thought? It will help if we begin by separating these different (though related) uses of the term "image." Images of the sort invoked by Einstein are better understood as examples of metaphor. More specifically, they are image-based metaphors in which the visualized scene serves as the source domain whose inferential structure can be mapped to the abstract (in this case) scientific domain.* Perhaps the best description of this process comes from Donald Schön's well-known paper on generative metaphor.[29] Schön tells of a group of researchers struggling with their latest invention: a paintbrush made of synthetic bristles that did not work very well. Finally, one of the researchers exclaimed, "You know, a paintbrush is a kind of pump!" This insight, Schön explains, led the researchers "to notice new features of the brush and of the painting process":

* So, too, there are metonymical mappings in which a concrete image can represent the abstract concept to which it is related—the "Statue of Liberty" for "freedom," for example. (*See* note 21.)

As the researchers explore the paintbrush in light of the possibility of its being a kind of pump, they focus on new features of the brush (the spaces between the bristles, for example); they regroup and reorder features in relation to one another (perceiving the paint as a liquid that flows through the spaces between bristles); and they rename the new grouping of elements (bristles become the "walls" of "channels"). (260)

It is significant that the participants are involved in a particular concrete situation; at the same time that they are reflecting on the problem, they are experiencing the phenomenon of the problem. . . . It is as though the effort to map onto one another descriptions which initially resist mapping cause the participants to immerse themselves, in reality or imagination, in concrete situations which are information-rich. (277)

Here, as in the Einstein example, the researchers are drawing on a concrete, information-rich source domain and mapping its relational structure to a less-well-known target domain (the paintbrush). Only subsequently are these insights formalized in a "theory" of "pumpoids" that accounts for the range of hydraulic phenomenon characteristic of pumps, paintbrushes, washcloths, and mops (257–60).

In contrast, the "things" referred to by Holmes are neither image-based metaphors of this sort nor the mental images described by Edelman, but basic-level categories of objects and actions. This is apparent in another, parallel passage from Holmes: "We need to think of things instead of words—to drop ownership, money, etc., and to think of the stream of products; of wheat and cloth and railway travel." [30] Indeed, we can see Holmes engaged in just this kind of reasoning process in *McBoyle v. United States*.[31] *McBoyle* concerned the question whether a federal statute prohibiting interstate transportation of a stolen "vehicle" applied to airplanes. Holmes concluded that it did not, remarking that "'vehicle' calls up the picture of a thing moving on land." I return to *McBoyle* in chapter 8, where I examine it more critically. For present purposes, however, note how Holmes's thought experiment illustrates a truism about basic-level categorization: One cannot generate a mental image of a superordinate category such as "vehicle" that isn't an image of a basic-level category such as "car" or, presumedly for a nineteenth-century gentleman like Holmes, a horse-drawn carriage.

Both Schön's paintbrush and Holmes's vehicle are examples of image-based thought, though—the subjective reports notwithstanding—these cases could be redescribed in propositional terms. Both cases are different than (though ultimately related to) the kind of mental images discussed in the previous section. In the first case, an image of one thing makes it possible to reason about another by a mapping of its inferential structure (with or without language) to the target domain. In the second, we see a decisionmaker invoking the limits on mental imagery as a reason for confining the reach of a legal category—that is, to effectuate the policy of providing fair notice of criminal prohibitions. Thus, although Holmes's reasoning is not itself imagistic, it rests crucially on the assumption that ordinary linguistic competence depends upon imagistic capacities rather than propositional truth as might be expressed in a set of necessary and sufficient conditions of the term "vehicle."

Still, one might say that all this is, so to speak, postlinguistic. What is the evidence for image-schemas of the sort described by Johnson and Edelman? What proof is there that image-schemas figure in anything we might call "reasoning"?

One kind of proof is evidence from language use discussed in chapter 1: As we shall see throughout the book, this sort of evidence is overwhelming and extends from basic linguistic competence through the most abstract, conceptual examples of legal reasoning.* But there is also experimental evidence showing both that cross-modal images exist and that they figure in human reasoning long before the development of language.

Recall that the basic claim is that to map vision, touch, and kinesthetic sensation into a single, overall sense experience is to map a kind of "image" or "schema" that is independent of any particular sensory modality. The most dramatic evidence for such cross-modal processes comes from experiments conducted with people who have been blind from birth and with infants between the ages of two and a half and four months.

Roger Sheperd, Stephen Kosslyn, and Lynn Cooper performed important experiments regarding the mind's capacity to rotate, scan, and perform various other operations on mental images. These experiments were later repeated by other researchers using congenitally blind subjects. Despite the fact that these subjects had never *seen* a cube or sphere, they were largely able to replicate the results obtained with sighted subjects.[32] (The principal difference was that sighted individuals perform the tasks faster.) Since these

---

* The next chapter examines the metaphorical system that underlies our basic concept of communication. Chapter 5 shows how the general category of "narrative" and the subcategory of "argument" are both structured in terms of a few basic image-schemas. Chapter 8 explores the imagistic reasoning behind legal conceptions of state action. And chapter 10 examines the metaphorical dimensions of First Amendment jurisprudence and the image-schematic structure of Chief Justice Hughes's reasoning in the landmark case of NLRB v. Jones & Laughlin Steel Corp., 301 U.S. 1 (1937).

blind subjects could have perceived these shapes only via touch and movement, their ability to perform these tasks successfully confirms the crossmodal nature of these mental "images." *

Additional evidence comes from a series of brilliant experiments by Elizabeth Spelke and her colleagues. In these experiments, Spelke successfully challenged the prevailing view—identified most closely with Jean Piaget[33]—that children's capacity to represent or reason about object constancy, persistence, and identity does not develop until about eighteen months when their sensorimotor activities are successfully coordinated and internalized. Because no direct communication with or verbal self-report by infants is possible, the key was to establish a way to measure infant cognition. The method they used, referred to as "habituation," measures spontaneous looking time: When infants are shown a familiar display, spontaneous looking time declines; when they are shown a new or unfamiliar display, spontaneous looking time demonstrably increases. Using this method, Spelke and her associates tested infants of various ages to see whether they were capable of representing hidden objects and reasoning about their movements.[34]

The infants were presented with a series of paired events involving object occlusion, blockage, and movement. Portions of the events were screened from view in each case; the infants would then be shown one of two outcomes. Half of the cases presented normal outcomes given the physical configuration of the array; the other half presented outcomes that were physically impossible. For example, four-month-old infants were shown a

---

* Kosslyn (458–59 n.55) identifies an interesting aspect of the original studies that he describes as "the most striking finding about image transformations." The time it takes to rotate, enlarge, or alter a mental image increases with the size and the complexity of the task. He finds this odd "because mental images are not real objects and hence are not constrained by the laws of physics." He apparently thinks that the mind should be able to transform mental images instantaneously, as in successive snapshots. He suggests that "spatial relations encoding subsystems (categorical and coordinate)" may be used to monitor the progress of object manipulation, but he concludes that this "cannot be the entire solution to the puzzle" because "it does not explain the apparently constant rate of rotation." Accordingly, he argues, plausibly, that there is "noise" in the system that is reflected in the need to adjust the image as it is manipulated.

Consider an alternative explanation: The mental image, which is as much kinesthetic as visual, is being "rotated" by or in coordination with programs for motor movement. This *would* account for the constant rate of rotation, since we do not ordinarily move objects in a jerky, spasmodic, or intermittent manner. (Indeed, when we do it seems funny; think of John Belushi in *Animal House*.) In this connection, consider Edelman's claim that the cerebellum "plays a very specific role in the timing and smoothing of successions of movements" and that such smooth movements are essential to categorization (105). This would accord with Kosslyn's first suggestion that a spatial relations subsystem is involved.

stage with a table and a ball. A screen was then set up to block the infant's view of the table. The infant watched while the ball was dropped behind the screen; the screen was then removed. In one condition, the ball rested on the table; in the other, it rested on the floor of the stage underneath the table. In another experiment, five-month-olds were shown a stationary block and a rotating screen. At the outset, the screen lay flat on the table in front of the block. In the first condition, the screen was rotated upwards until it reached the block; in the second, is was rotated a full 180° through the place where the block had been. In yet another experiment, four-month-olds were shown a block that partially occluded a moving rod. The infants were then shown two items: an intact rod and a broken rod corresponding to the visible areas of the object in the original occluded display.

In one of the most interesting experiments, four-month-olds held two attached rings, one in each hand, screened by a cloth that blocked their view both of the rings and of their own bodies. In one condition, the rings were attached by a string so that they could be moved independently; in the other, they were attached by a solid bar and could be moved only as a unit. The infants were then shown alternating displays of connected and separated rings (in each case, completely stationery).

In all these cases, habituation was measured to determine whether the infants recognized or were surprised by the result of the display. On the basis of these responses, Spelke and her associates showed that infants between two and a half and four months can represent and reason about objects they no longer perceive, correctly inferring that a "hidden object would move on a connected, unobstructed path" (Spelke 1992:621). The experiment with the rings, moreover, showed that "objects are perceived under the same conditions whether they are seen or felt. Objects do not appear to be apprehended by separate visual and haptic mechanisms but by a single mechanism" (Spelke 1988:175). Spelke and her colleagues concluded, therefore, that "objects are apprehended by a relatively central mechanism . . . that organizes events in ways that extend beyond the immediately perceivable world in space and time. This mechanism organizes the layout into bodies with at least four properties: *cohesion, boundaries, substance,* and *spatio-temporal continuity*" (Spelke 1988:180). Additional experiments established that infants begin to show an understanding of gravity by six months (Spelke 1992:626) and of *containment* by eight months.[35]

These experiments show conclusively that the capacity both to individuate objects and reason about them is prior to and independent of language. This capacity is plainly cross-modal—i.e., it is not dependent on a particular sensory modality. Moreover, it is *constitutive* in the sense that it organizes cognizance of objects not directly perceived (such as the occluded rod) and events (the movement of the ball behind the screen) into meaningful units consistent with the normal properties of objects (i.e., cohesion and substance) and movement (i.e., direction and inertia). It is, to be precise, conceptual rather than perceptual.[36]

A Programmatic Note

Virtually all of twentieth century legal thought has been shaped by the legal realist confrontation with the formalism conventionally associated with Christopher Columbus Langdell, dean of the Harvard Law School in the late nineteenth century.[37] The legal realists of the 1920s and 1930s— along with such predecessors as Holmes, the early Roscoe Pound, Wesley Newcomb Hohfeld, Arthur Corbin, and Walter Wheeler Cook—relentlessly attacked the formalist belief that general concepts and rules could provide a logical, reliable means for deciding cases. Robert Gordon suggests that much of the legal realist program could be described with two of Holmes's famous slogans: "Think things not words," and "General propositions do not decide concrete cases."[38] To which we might add yet another of Holmes's maxims, "The life of the law has not been logic: it has been experience."[39]

Legal realism had many strands, most of which are evident in law and legal education today. The residue of the realist preference for legislative discretion and administrative decisionmaking can be still be glimpsed in constitutional law. The realist emphasis on "social policy" analysis, the open balancing of competing interests, and purposive reasoning is now a familiar, highly conventional part of mainstream judicial decisionmaking—"albeit in a form that bears precious little resemblance to the far subtler version that the realists seemed to have had in mind."[40] The realist concern for inquiry into empirical and social facts as a basis for reforming law is reflected, on the left, in the law and society movement and, on the right, in the writings of Judge Posner and many associated with the law and economics movement. The rule and fact skepticism of the most famous realists—Karl Llewellyn and Jerome Frank—and the concomitant sense that the deductions of formalist jurisprudence were just masks for decisions reached on other grounds can be seen in the critical legal studies movement's reassertion and reinvigoration of the claims that law is political and indeterminate. Finally, the related instrumentalism and consequentialism of the realists can be seen in sometimes extreme form in the political polarization of the academy—where there is a fairly distinct right and left that mostly talk past each other—and in the various movements of identity-politics theory.

What is largely missing today is careful attention to what we might call the "epistemic" dimension of legal realism. Of course, each of the realists' current heirs have epistemological positions and commitments. But, as reflected in all three of Holmes's aperçus, the antiformalism and anticonceptualism of the legal realists represented a particular claim about the role of abstraction in human reasoning and about the way in which humans think, categorize, and learn. Neither Holmes nor Llewellyn was an epistemological nominalist. As Tom Grey points out, "much of Holmes' actual work was devoted to the abstract and conceptual ordering of doctrine into a structured and coherent system" that smacks uncomfortably of the "doctrinal legal 'logic' . . . that Holmes so famously contrasted with 'experience.'" [41] In a similar vein, my colleague Clark Remington has nicely documented how Llewellyn struggled with the problem of generalization when he wrote the Uniform Commercial Code.[42] As William Twining notes, for Llewellyn it was chiefly a question of finding the *right* level of generalization.[43]

Not just in his later discussion of situation-sense, but also in his earlier work, Llewellyn was particularly alert to the importance of categorization to law.[44] At the same time, however, Llewellyn like Holmes had assimilated the lessons of the American pragmatists and understood that our categories and generalizations have no meaning outside our practices and activities— that is, outside of experience. Thus, Llewellyn summarized the legal realist movement with this observation:

> We have discovered that rules *alone,* mere forms of words, are worthless.
> We have learned that the concrete instance, the heaping up of concrete
> instances, the present, vital memory of a multitude of concrete instances,
> is necessary in order to make any general proposition, be it rule of law or
> any other, *mean* anything at all.[45]

Experience, categorization, meaning—these are among the central issues of contemporary cognitive science. It is not difficult to imagine that if Llewellyn and the other legal realists were alive today, they would be the first to turn to the study of the mind better to understand life and law.

That, in any event, is the spirit in which this book now proceeds.

CHAPTER 3

What Is Metaphor?

CONVENTIONAL VIEWS of reason—and, particularly, of legal reasoning—emphasize the objective, the literal, and the linear. Such views see metaphor either as a distortion of thought or as an evocative but dangerously imprecise rhetoric. But these conventional views are distorting: the expression of a narrow, rationalist conception of reason that is both inconsistent with the evidence of actual language use and inadequate to the rigors of effective legal reasoning. Metaphor is a central modality of human thought without which we cannot even begin to understand the complex regularities of the products of the human mind.

This chapter takes up the question of metaphor in language. Fundamentally, an understanding of metaphor as *cognitive* and *conceptual* transforms the basic assumptions about reason upon which standard accounts of categorization and law both depend. This chapter thus prepares the way for the succeeding examinations of how categorization works and how law is possible. In particular, a cognitive understanding of metaphor provides a more genuinely pragmatic alternative to the insistence on dichotomous thinking that so dominates and distorts contemporary legal thought.

The Master's House

In *The Wallace Stevens Case,* Tom Grey promotes Stevens's poetry as a useful antidote to the absolutist tendencies of conventional legal thought. Lawyers and legal theorists, he notes, are prone to "the habitual and institutional rigidities of binary thought." [1] Judgment must be for either the plaintiff or the defendant. A legal rule either applies to the case at hand or does not. Legal doctrine aspires to consistency and integrity: A legal principle is expected to explain all the cases, or it is considered unreliable and indeterminate. Each of these practices exemplifies legal thought's adherence to the rationalist model in which concepts and categories are defined oppositionally—that is, in terms of the properties that are present or absent (P or not-P). Consequently, as Grey pointedly observes, "Legal theory is too often characterized by absolutists and disappointed absolutists shouting past each other" (6).

Grey suggests that Stevens's poetry offers a "pragmatic middle way" that transcends the traditional oppositions between reality and imagination, the literal and the metaphorical, prose and poetry, law and literature—even law and equity. For Grey, Stevens's poetry teaches us always to hear both sides of these polar oppositions because each pole represents an incomplete, yet useful perspective. At the same time, this poetry counsels that "even when these perspectives are recognized as limited, they will nevertheless survive the transcending moment of recognition" (73).

In this last statement, however, Grey manages to affirm the very binarism that he aspires to transcend. As a pragmatist, Grey is committed to the view that every discourse is a function of conventions and understandings specific to that practice.[2] But the concepts, procedures, and methods of argumentation that constitute his practices as a lawyer are deeply implicated in the rationalist model.[3] This leaves Grey with no way to escape the very tradition that he seeks to inform with his pragmatist insights. He cannot deliver the promised pragmatist "middle way" because he is mired in the old categories, wedded to the old conceptual tools. Grey continues to adhere to the conventional notion in which concepts and categories are defined oppositionally. As a consequence, his own analysis remains afflicted by residual commitments to the objective, the literal, and the rational.

Consider Grey's initial question. To ask whether Stevens's poetry is relevant to law is already to presuppose a categorical distinction that, in point of fact, not everyone recognizes.[4] The distinction between law and literature is natural enough for those steeped in the Enlightenment tradition that privileges the objective over the subjective, the literal over the metaphorical, and the rational over the imaginative. But Grey maintains that Stevens's poetry offers pragmatic therapy for just this tendency toward dichotomization. Yet, when all is said and done, Grey still declares that "law is law, poetry is poetry." "Jurisprudence," he tells us reassuringly, "is not the same as poetics; . . . *Law is poetry* is indeed only a metaphor" (3, 110–11).

With the use of "indeed" and "only," Grey unwittingly signals his residual rationalist and objectivist commitments: It is as if, by virtue of its metaphorical quality, the similarity between law and poetry were somehow less than real. This conclusion would come as no surprise from a dyed-in-the-wool objectivist. After all, it was Locke who insisted upon literal prose "if we would speak of things as they are" and condemned metaphor and other figurative speech as "perfect cheat."[5] But Grey is a pragmatist. Pragmatists dispense with the picture of words as fitting the world and, instead, conceive of them as tools of interaction with it. For the pragmatist, therefore, a metaphor such as "law is poetry" may be useful or not; it may be harmful or not; it may enable some insights or preclude others. But, for the pragmatist, a metaphor can never be unreal or false in any but this relative sense. Certainly, it cannot be unreal solely because of its metaphorical character. *That* conclusion would follow only upon objectivist assumptions that posit some other access to a world—here, the world of law—as it *literally* is.

But even if he were a more consistent pragmatist, Grey's project would fare no better. Pragmatists suppose that, simply by rejecting the correspondence view of meaning, they have successfully transcended the objectivist paradigm. Not so. Although pragmatists conceive of words as tools of interaction with the world rather than as representations of it, they nevertheless continue to understand those tools in much the same way as their objectivist predecessors. In practice, this understanding conduces to an atavistic account of metaphor that—like Grey's meditation on the affinities of law and poetry—actually reinscribes the very paradigm that it claims to have superseded. It is, as the feminist Audre Lorde has remarked, difficult to dismantle the master's house with the master's own tools.[6]

We can do better, but only if we bring to bear the new conceptual developments in cognitive theory. These developments—particularly with respect to cognitive metaphor—pose a forceful challenge to the rationalist model in all its variants, including its most pragmatic one.

PASSING THEORIES

Contemporary pragmatists such as Richard Rorty follow Nietzsche's view that the literal is nothing more than "worn out metaphors which have become powerless to affect the senses."[7] "Old metaphors," Rorty maintains, "are constantly dying off into literalness, and then serving as a platform and foil for new metaphors."[8] On this view, "truth" is the product of the "strong poet" who creates the metaphors that succeed by dying: "A sense of human history as the history of successive metaphors would let us see the poet, in the generic sense of the maker of new words, the shaper of new languages, as the vanguard of the species" (20).

One might hear in Rorty's view an echo of Shelley's characterization of poets as "the unacknowledged legislators of the world."[9] Rorty, however, distinguishes his Nietzschean view of metaphor from that of the Romantics. As he presents it, the Nietzschean view does not merely invert the binary schema of the Enlightenment to exalt the poet over the scientist or legislator. Rather, Rorty explains that the objectivist, the Romantic, and the Nietzschean value different things. The objectivist values the literal and its ability to represent an external reality. The Romantic esteems metaphor and its capacity to express inner truth. But the Nietzschean rejects both forms of "discovery" in favor of the genius of self-creation. Rorty puts it plainly: "To change how we talk is to change what, for our purposes, we are" (19–20).

We can draw the distinction between the Romantic and Nietzschean views of metaphor yet more sharply. The Romantic believes that metaphors express a deeper meaning; Rorty believes that metaphors do not express anything at all. Rorty subscribes to Donald Davidson's view that metaphors have no cognitive content: "Metaphor can, like a picture or a bump on the head, make us appreciate some fact—but not by standing for, or expressing the fact."[10] As Rorty wryly observes, "Tossing a metaphor into a conversation is like suddenly . . . slapping your interlocutor's face, or kissing him" (18).

On Davidson's account, metaphor "uses no semantic resources beyond the resources on which the ordinary depends" (245). He means two things by this claim. First, an expression is not metaphorical because of any special or coded meaning; a metaphor means only "what the words, in their most literal interpretation, mean, and nothing more" (ibid.). Consequently, an expression is metaphorical solely by virtue of its *use:* It causes one to notice a similarity one would not otherwise have noticed. Second, metaphor is just another occasion for radical interpretation—which, on Davidson's account of meaning, is all that ordinary communication is about anyway.*
As Rorty explains it, the distinction between the literal and the metaphorical is a distinction only between familiar and unfamiliar noises: The familiar noises—the literal—are those we already know how to handle because they already have a place in our language-game; the unfamiliar noises—the

---

* Thus Davidson notes that "all communication by speech assumes the interplay of inventive construction and inventive construal" (245).

metaphorical—set us off looking for new ways in which to manage, cope, or understand (17–18).[11]

Davidson's view that metaphors are noncognitive rests on two philosophical presuppositions. The first is that thought is a matter of language and propositions. On this view, the only meaning a metaphor *can* have is its ordinary propositional sense because, to put it simply, that is the only kind of meaning that a philosopher like Davidson recognizes.* A metaphor, Rorty says, is not a "truth-value candidate" (18). The second presupposition is that language is socially contingent and entirely arbitrary. As Rorty explains Davidson's view, you and I can communicate because your

> guesses about what I am going to do next, including what noises I am
> going to make next, and my own expectations about what I will do or
> say under certain circumstances, [have] come more or less to coincide. . . .
> To say that we come to speak the same language is to say, as Davidson
> puts it, that "we tend to converge on passing theories." (14)[12]

Given this understanding of communication, it makes perfect sense to think—as Rorty does—that metaphors are rather like slaps, kisses, gestures, grimaces and other equally whimsical behaviors; it makes perfect sense to say—as Davidson does—that "there is no test for metaphor that does not call for taste" (245). If communication is only a matter of forming "passing theories" of one another's propositional intentions, then it should not matter what kinds of terms are employed.

Developments in cognitive theory undermine both of these philosophical presuppositions: Thought is not primarily linguistic and propositional, but embodied and imaginative; language is neither entirely arbitrary nor merely socially contingent, but grounded in our embodiment and motivated by our interactions with the physical and social world. With the collapse of these presuppositions, Davidson's entire view of metaphor falls. This is perhaps most clear if we consider his well-known claim with respect to what he calls "dead metaphors."

According to Davidson, an expression ceases to be metaphorical—it "dies"—once it becomes familiar and conventional. At that point, it is just another literal statement that conveys a (new) propositional meaning. Davidson gives the following example. Suppose that at one time only humans

---

* Hence, for Davidson, a metaphor's propositional meaning may be either false, as in "he's a lion," or trivially true, as in "business is business."

and other animals had literal mouths. Now, however, bottles and rivers are said to have mouths too.

> When "mouth" applied only metaphorically to bottles, the application
> made the hearer *notice* a likeness between animal and bottle openings.
> (Consider Homer's reference to wounds as mouths.) Once one has the
> present use of the word, with literal application to bottles, there is noth-
> ing left to notice. There is no similarity to seek because it consists simply
> in being referred to by the same word. (252)

The claim that there is nothing left to notice is, as Rorty says, essential to Davidson's account.* For Davidson, the meaning of a word is only its use in a language-game; a metaphor is just the performative effect of using an expression unconventionally to prompt one to notice something new or to notice something in a new way.

In contrast, Paul Ricoeur maintains that no theory of metaphor can work "without including imagining and feeling, that is, without assigning a *semantic* function to what seem to be mere *psychological* features."[13] Missing entirely from Davidson's account is any role for conceptual mappings of the sort discussed in chapter 1 or for the imagistic-kinesthetic modalities of thought described in chapter 2. But, once one recognizes such nonpropositional meanings, Davidson's entire account of metaphor—including the distinction between so-called "live" and "dead" metaphors— begins to unravel quickly. His account of live metaphor fails because a metaphor can and does have a nonpropositional, cognitive content that is not a mere matter of use. His account of dead metaphor fails because, once we understand how live metaphors work, it turns out that most putatively dead metaphors work in just the same way. We can develop this argument by examining three extended examples.

Consider, first, Davidson's own example. For him, "mouth" is a conventional dead metaphor with respect to bottles and rivers but a live metaphor with respect to wounds. Accordingly, there should be nothing more to notice about the first three cases (animal mouths, bottles, and rivers) other than the contingent fact that they now share a single linguistic designation. Similarly, there should be nothing to notice about the provenance or cogni-

---

* "It is essential to Davidson's view that dead metaphors are not metaphors, just as it is essential to the opposing 'metaphysical' view, common to Black and Searle (and to the view of Hesse, Mark Johnson and George Lakoff that language is 'shot through' with metaphor) that dead metaphors still count as metaphors" (169 n.24).

tive content of Homer's poetic achievement. As Rorty says: "To ask 'how metaphors work' is to ask how genius works. If we knew that, genius would be superfluous" (172).

The problem, of course, is that in each case there *is* something to notice. Each of these propositionally different cases—animal mouths, bottles, rivers, *and* wounds—shares the same imagistic quality: an opening through which liquids spill out. As Ricoeur explains, this capacity to generate schematic images is precisely how we establish resemblance. "Imaging or imagining, thus, is the concrete milieu in which and through which we see similarities." [14] It is *because* they are imagistically homologous that the propositionally different cases of animal mouths, bottles, and rivers are comprehensible as a single, conventional linguistic category—that is, "mouth." (As we will see in chapter 4, these propositionally different cases form a simple radial category motivated by a single imagistic model.)

This imagistic homology also enables Homer's arresting image of wounds as mouths. Mouths not only emit liquids but also are the openings through which our thoughts emerge as speech. Thus, a person "cries *out* in pain" or, in divulging a secret, is said to have "spilled the beans." Each of these expressions makes use of the IDEAS ARE OBJECTS metaphor that we first encountered in chapter 1; as we will see in a moment, this conventional conceptual metaphor is part of a larger metaphorical system that in fact defines our most basic notions of communication. Homer's poetic metaphor exploits this metaphorical conception by mapping the image of a mouth crying out for assistance onto that of a wound oozing blood.

There is, of course, a difference between Homer's striking trope and a conventional expression like "the mouth of the river." Indeed, the intuitive appeal of Davidson's distinction between "live" and "dead" metaphors is that it seems to capture just this difference. This intuition is nevertheless mistaken. Davidson's distinction is not about the difference between novel and familiar metaphorical expressions. If it were, it would be a trivial view with which no one would bother to disagree. But Davidson's claim is hardly trivial. His claim is that metaphor has no cognitive content; his claim is that metaphor does no work other than its performative effect of prompting one to notice something (i.e., a propositional truth) in a striking way. Thus, Rorty maintains that "nothing in existence prior to the metaphor's occurrence is sufficient to understand the metaphorical use. That is just why we call it 'metaphorical'" (167). Yet, as we have seen, even so poetic a creation as Homer's trope is enabled and made comprehensible by an image-mapping in which the image of a mouth as an opening through which objects emerge is mapped onto that of a bleeding wound.[15]

When Rorty says that nothing before its first occurrence adequately explains such a metaphorical use, he is correct in the limited sense that there is nothing in any existing language-game that sanctions such an unusual analogy. Thus 3,000 years later, Homer's figure of speech retains the power to startle and disturb. His metaphorical description of wounds as mouths endures as a striking metaphor because, despite its imagistic coherence, it remains aggressively unconventional. Homer's juxtaposition of the typically inviting image of a human mouth—a site of communicative or sensuous contact—with the normally frightening image of a wound seeping blood violates our conceptions of identity and order. In this, at least, Davidson is right: "Novelty is not the issue. What we call the element of novelty or surprise in a metaphor is a built-in aesthetic feature we can experience again and again" (252–53). Note, however, that there is nothing mysterious or subjective about this aesthetic feature; it is not, as Davidson says, merely a matter of taste. Rather, the aesthetic quality of the trope is susceptible to analysis precisely because the metaphor has cognitive content.

We can develop this point with a second example. Consider a cliché such as "the proof of the pudding is in the eating." This maxim has a conventional, propositional meaning that the fully acculturated person recognizes immediately. On Davidson's account, there should be nothing left to notice once one has acquired this conventional meaning. But, once again, there is something to notice: the precise relation of the metaphor to the semantic meaning of the cliché. Someone unfamiliar with the cliché can reason to its propositional meaning metaphorically. That a pudding appears to have gelled does not mean that it is any good; it can look good and still be a failure because it has not congealed on the inside or because it tastes bad. If you know these concrete facts about puddings, then you can infer the cliché's more general suggestion that one adopt the pragmatist's test for truth and value: Does it work? It is suitable for the purpose?

These examples show that thought is not purely linguistic and language is not purely arbitrary, as Davidson and Rorty suppose. Rather, metaphors are imagistically motivated (as in "the mouth of the river") or experientially grounded (as in "the proof of the pudding") such that someone who has never heard the expressions before can nonetheless reason to their propositional meaning by metaphorically mapping their concrete or literal meaning onto a different, more abstract domain.[16] Metaphors, in other words, do have cognitive and semantic content. The fact that a fully acculturated person can go straight to the conventional meaning—i.e., automatically, without the need consciously to retrace the inferential steps—does not indicate that a metaphor is "dead," only that it need not be conscious.

These processes of metaphorical inference are performed unconsciously all the time; indeed, they are indispensable to meaning. Their indispensability is painfully apparent in cases of decompensating mental illnesses such as psychosis. It is a standard psychiatric procedure to use clichés like "the proof of the pudding is in the eating" to test cognitive functioning. People suffering from decompensation are unable to go beyond the concrete explanation of the phrase (e.g., you don't know whether its really pudding until you've eaten it).* On Davidson's account, this inability would show only that the person had somehow "forgotten" a bit of propositional knowledge. In fact, however, people suffering from mental illness experience deterioration in their cognitive functioning such that they are no longer able to move from the cliché's concrete, literal meaning to its more abstract, metaphorical meaning.

Once one recognizes such unconscious processes of metaphorical reasoning, the questions change radically. The issue of a metaphor's vitality can no longer be judged by whether the expression has become conventional, whether it can still readily be recognized as metaphorical, or whether it is used propositionally to refer to a new, previously "mistaken" referent (such as "mouth" for the terminus of a river). Rather, to determine whether a metaphorical expression is still live, one must engage in an entirely different analysis. First, one must examine the underlying conceptual mapping that structures its semantic content. Then, one must see whether the mapping is systematic—that is, does it account for a range of expressions, including related or complementary conceptions. Finally, one must look to see if the mapping is still productive—that is, does it enable ordinary speakers to reason in terms of the metaphor such that they can extend it automatically.

This kind of analysis is not even permissible on Davidson's view. But this bit of philosophical dogmatism leaves a whole lot of data unaccounted for. We can take the argument the final step by turning to our third example: a range of conventional expressions that, though they would appear to be obviously "dead" metaphors, turn out to be cases of systematic conceptual metaphors that are very much alive in contemporary English.

Consider the word "perception." The Latin *capere* means "to take," as in the common-law writ of capias that authorized seizure of the defendant. *Percipere*, a compound derivation, means "to lay hold of." This is the source of the verb "perceive," which encompasses both sensory processes such as seeing and intellectual processes such as understanding. Most speakers of

---

* According to my wife, the cliché that works best for this purpose is "people in glass houses shouldn't throw stones."

ordinary English are unlikely to be aware of this etymology. For them, "perceive" has a literal meaning that corresponds with "understand." Today, "perceptive" is more likely to connote keen insight and understanding than good vision or an acute tactile sense. Thus, the word "perceive" would appear to be a dead metaphor.

It turns out, however, that there are many words premised on the same conceptual mapping in which the physical process of holding is mapped onto the cognitive operation of knowing. A lawyer may scrutinize a document or examine a witness, but the Latin sources *scrutari* and *ex agmen* mean "to pick through garbage" and "to pull out from a row," respectively.[17] Similarly, "comprehend" comes from the Latin *com* + *prehendere* "to grasp together," and "apprehend" comes from *ab* + *prehendere* "to seize."

The fact that the etymologies of apparently unrelated words like "perceive," "scrutinize," "examine," and "comprehend" are products of a single conceptual metaphor troubles the dead metaphor view in several respects. As with our analysis of "mouth," it suggests that meaning is not merely a matter of a word's arbitrary use in a language-game, but rather corresponds to the cognitive content of a supposedly dead metaphor. But unlike "mouth," which is an isolated imagistic metaphor with only a limited number of uses, these cases indicate a phenomenon of greater depth and scope. The fact that the same metaphorical mapping is at work in otherwise unrelated lexical items provides additional evidence of thought at a level other than the purely linguistic—that is, of prelinguistic conceptual capacities that are imagistic and nonpropositional. This is how a single metaphorical mapping can be the basis for what would otherwise appear to be independent linguistic expressions.

Moreover, these cases—"perceive," "comprehend," and so on—represent only the tip of the proverbial iceberg. They are premised on an underlying conceptual metaphor that is part of a much larger metaphorical system first identified by Michael Reddy as the CONDUIT metaphor.[18] It consists of a systematic set of mappings from the source domain of physical objects to the target domain of mental operations, as follows:

Source Domain		Target Domain
PHYSICAL		MENTAL
object	⟶	ideas
seeing	⟶	knowing
container (vehicle)	⟶	words
content	⟶	ideational content

sending	⟶	communicating
grasping (receiving)	⟶	understanding
container (receptacle)	⟶	mind

In this conceptual mapping, a concept or idea is understood as an object subject to inspection, physical manipulation, and transportation; words are vehicles for conveying this ideational "content"; and the resulting cognitive operation is understood as an acquisition or "taking in" of that object. These conceptions can be represented by the mnemonics IDEAS ARE OBJECTS; KNOWING IS SEEING; WORDS ARE CONTAINERS; COMMUNICATION IS SENDING; UNDERSTANDING IS GRASPING; and THE MIND IS A CONTAINER.

Eve Sweetser has found that throughout the history of the Indo-European languages, this mapping and its attendant conceptual metaphors have served as "semantic pathways" for etymological development. Two things about this pattern of language change are particularly significant. First, the direction of change is invariably from the concrete to the more abstract. Thus, words for grasping and seeing have consistently become words for knowing *but not the other way around*—that is, words for knowing never become words for grasping. Second, this phenomenon cannot be discounted as a mere cultural contingency. These semantic changes have occurred "independently in different branches across an area of thousands of miles and a time depth of thousands of years" (9). Moreover, as Sweetser notes, there is "evidence that this metaphorical structure is not restricted to Indo-European" (22). In Hebrew, an Afro-Asiatic language, the word *davar* (דבר) means both "word" and "thing"; conjugated as a verb, the same word yields *l'dabear* (לדבר), "to speak." Closely analogous are the English words "propound" (from the Latin *proponere*, "to set forth") and "proposition" (from the Latin *propositio*, "a setting forth").

Another particularly noteworthy example is the word "metaphor." As we saw in chapter 1, the word derives from the Greek *meta pherein*, "to carry over." What makes "metaphor" interesting is the fact that the word's contemporary meaning is so obviously a live incident of the conceptual metaphors WORDS ARE CONTAINERS and COMMUNICATION IS SENDING. As Grey notes, "Metaphor is the figure of movement, of carrying across, of transport (you can ride a literal *metaphora*, the public bus, in Athens today)" (61). Thus, a metaphor "carries over" a meaning from one context to another. Even more importantly, as Grey's parenthetical reveals, the literal meaning that connotes physical motion and transportation remains very much alive in contemporary Greek.

These examples raise a fundamental point that represents something of a coup de grâce to the dead metaphor view. One might try to avoid the thrust of the etymological evidence and save the Davidsonian view by arguing that entire metaphorical systems can die, too. But contemporary usage demonstrates that the CONDUIT metaphor-system is very much alive. Consider the following perfectly ordinary passage:

> The professor *delivered* a superb lecture, but only the exceptional students were able to *take it all in*. The less gifted students had to *struggle* before they *grasped* the point. It *takes* more to master a concept than to *assimilate* a *piece* of information.

These expressions cannot be accounted for as additional products of a supposedly dead metaphorical system because each of these words—"deliver," "take," "struggle," "grasp," and so on—retains its meaning in the domain of physical activity. To save the dead metaphor view, one would have to explain these as cases of polysemy, in which the same word had developed different meanings and uses. But, as was true with "mouth," this explanation must ignore the systematic connections between these meanings. Each of these cases of synchronic polysemy is motivated by the CONDUIT metaphor—the same metaphorical system that explains the diachronic semantic development of words like "perceive."

The dead metaphor view cannot survive the evidence of ordinary language use. The CONDUIT metaphor-system enables the average English speaker automatically to extend the conceptual mapping by modeling other actions in the physical domain. Thus, *any* word that signifies physical acquisition can be used to signify intellectual understanding: I can *get* your point, *catch* your drift, *field* questions, *discard* faulty assumptions, *dig up* a case on point, *save up* good arguments for later use, *wrench* a point out of context, *wrestle* with a difficult concept until either I *make it my own* or admit that it *continues to elude me,* or note that a previously *settled* issue is now *up for grabs*. Each of these cases of polysemy—in which words that signify physical possession (or its lack) also connote knowing (or its lack)—is motivated by the conceptual metaphors IDEAS ARE OBJECTS and UNDERSTANDING IS GRASPING.

These conceptual metaphors not only enable ordinary linguistic competence but can be seen at work regardless of whether the expression is literal, colloquial, or poetic. Such familiar idioms as "cramming" (for an exam) and "airhead" are contemporary products of the metaphors IDEAS

ARE OBJECTS and THE MIND IS A CONTAINER. In both cases, the mind is conceived of as a container that is either "stuffed" with or "empty" of ideas. If we add the conceptual metaphor UNDERSTANDING IS GRASPING, we get such common expressions as "she has a mind like a steel trap" or "his mind's a sieve." By the same token, Stevens can employ the IDEAS ARE OBJECTS metaphor in exquisite poetic formulations. Thus, he declares that "everything we say . . . [is] a cast / Of the imagination, made in sound"[19] and, "The poem is the cry of its occasion, / Part of the res itself and not about it."[20]

Where Davidson sees only a "dead" metaphor, we have found a systematic set of conceptual mappings that account for a broad range of language data. These findings have several remarkable implications. The ability of this metaphorical system to account for semantic change, polysemy, and the synchronic production of new usages (such as "airhead") indicates that these metaphors are a live part of our conceptual system. The invariability in these trajectories of semantic change over the course of linguistic history presents a picture of metaphor as a systematic and orderly part of the cognitive process. The persistence of this metaphorical system through time and across cultures suggests that it represents a significant, entrenched part of the human conceptual system. And the consistency of this metaphorical system across categories traditionally understood as separate (such as ordinary language and poetry) indicates that there is a common human rationality at work. Rather than the creation of particular genius, metaphor emerges as part of the common, imaginative core of human rationality.

On Davidson's account, the cross-cultural nature of these conceptual metaphors and their consistency across time, space, and genre could only be a remarkable coincidence. Rorty, in fact, takes just such a view.* Although coincidence is always a possible—and technically irrefutable—explanation, it remains a highly implausible account of phenomena of this magnitude and consistency. Besides, it fails completely to explain the synchronic vitality and continuing productivity of these same conceptual metaphors.

The cognitive thesis, in contrast, has a cogent explanation for the regularity and endurance of these conceptual metaphors: Concepts like KNOWING IS SEEING and UNDERSTANDING IS GRASPING are embodied; they emerge from the species-wide experience of learning about one's world through sight and touch.[21] The persistence of these metaphors is further strength-

---

* "Our language and our culture are just as much a contingency, as much a result of thousands of small mutations finding niches (and millions of others finding no niches), as are the orchids and the anthropoids" (16).

ened by the fact that they are deeply embedded in our conceptual system. As Sweetser explains, these conceptual metaphors are aspects of a yet more general metaphor in which the mind is conceived as a body moving through space and cognitive operations are understood in terms of vision and movement (46). This MIND-AS-BODY metaphor, which we will revisit below, provides the semantic pathway that enables words for "path" to come to mean "however." Thus, we have *any way* in English (as in: "Any way you construct the argument, it always comes out . . .") and *tuttavia* in Italian (literally, "all roads") (28, 46).

As a conceptual matter, pragmatist accounts of language and meaning rely heavily on notions of random change and the contingencies of continued use to explain linguistic behavior. As we shall see in the next section, this theoretical bias is a product of pragmatism's antinomial capture. In contrast, cognitive theory's claim that human rationality is an embodied process that is experientially grounded and imaginatively elaborated provides a single, elegant hypothesis that explains a wide range of linguistic and semantic phenomena, including diachronic development, synchronic usage, and continuing productivity. By the standard criteria of comprehensiveness, parsimony, and falsifiability, cognitive theory thus affords the best available account of the actual data of language use.

THINKING IS THE BEST WAY TO TRAVEL

The dead metaphor view is but one consequence of pragmatism's continued adherence to the assumptions of the rationalist model it has supposedly transcended. Consider Rorty's celebrated denunciation of philosophy's obsession with the problem of representation:

> It is pictures rather than propositions, metaphors rather than statements,
> which determine most of our philosophical convictions. The picture
> which holds traditional philosophy captive is that of the mind as a great
> mirror, containing various representations.[22]

In framing the issue as pictures versus propositions and metaphors versus statements, Rorty replicates just those institutional rigidities of binary thought that have dominated philosophy's obsession with accuracy of representation. So, too, the assumptions that underlie Davidson's view of metaphor mirror the standard rationalist dualisms. On one hand, meaning is presumed to be propositional and truth-conditional. On the other hand, metaphors and other language terms are assumed to be merely a matter of taste. As with Grey's "indeed only a metaphor," these presuppositions atavistically reproduce the key rationalist dichotomies between the objective and the subjective, reality and imagination.

We can observe the same ironic predicament in Judge Posner's pragmatist manifesto. Posner argues that "practical reason"—including greater reliance on empirical work in other disciplines—is superior to the logic, rules, and other analytic devices that currently dominate legal practice. He first exposes the limited usefulness of syllogistic reasoning. Posner introduces this argument with a discussion of the famous syllogism "All men are mortal; Socrates is a man; therefore Socrates is mortal":

> That premise says, in effect, here is a box, labelled "men," with a bunch of things in it, every one of which is "mortal." The second premise tells us that the things in the box have name tags and that one of the tags says "Socrates." When we pluck Socrates out of the box we know he is mortal because the only things in it are mortals.
>
> We thus find the syllogism's validity compelling by virtue of a metaphor, the metaphor of the box. (It may seem odd that one's confidence in the validity of logic should be bolstered by a metaphor—yet this is clue to the limitations of logic and the cognitive importance of metaphor.)[23]

There is an oddity here, but it is not the one identified by Posner. No Nietzschean would find anything odd in the discovery that logic is underwritten by metaphor; it was Nietzsche, recall, who said that truth is nothing more than worn out metaphors that have lost their power to affect the senses. If Posner finds it odd that logic should be validated by metaphor, it is only because he subscribes to Davidson's view that metaphors have no cognitive content. Thus, following Davidson, Posner refers to metaphors and similes as "powerful though alogical modes of persuasion" (456). "Metaphor, narrative, simile, and analogy . . . bring [no] new facts to light" but serve only "to jar people out of their accustomed ways of thinking" (150–51). Like Grey (and, no doubt, for similar reasons), Posner holds fast to the rationalist distinctions between logic and metaphor, fact and narrative, law and literature.[24] Posner sets out to criticize logic's continued hold on the legal profession. But, like Grey, his pragmatist mission is compromised by his residual rationalist commitments.

Still, Posner's observation of the connection between logic and metaphor is correct in several crucial respects. He is certainly right that this fact provides a clue to the cognitive importance of metaphor. And Posner is onto something quite important when—notwithstanding his adherence to Davidson's theory of metaphor—he recognizes that the metaphor of the box plays a *cognitive role* in shaping the "truth" of logic. What Posner does not get quite right, however, is the precise nature of that relation.

Because Posner adheres to the rationalist model, he understands logic and metaphor as standing in opposition to one another. Just as he contrasts fact-based argument with the merely persuasive function of metaphor and narrative, he sees metaphor as demarcating the limits of logic. But, to appreciate the cognitive importance of metaphor fully would be to see that the relation of metaphor to logic is one of entailment, not antithesis. The discovery that human rationality is embodied means that basic body states like BALANCE and other image-schemas provide the primary structure of human reason. Logic, in other words, is *constituted* and *enabled* by metaphor. Logic is not a truth about the world whose validity is coincidentally supported by metaphor; the "truth" of logic is, rather, a function of human cognitive processes. As a product of human minds, logic is structured in just the same way that other human concepts are structured—that is, imagistically and metaphorically. In other words, the metaphor does not verify our reasoning as true or correct. Rather, it explains why we reason as we do.

Indeed, on close examination, much of the rationalist model's core conception of reason turns out to be structured metaphorically. Consider, first, Grey's unexceptional description of the pleasures of reason: "Both deduction and clear vision are naturally *felt* as cold, linear, satisfying in their impersonality" (92). This statement strikes all the chords of the Enlightenment conception of reason as a disembodied faculty that is rigorous, precise, and objective. Yet, on a second look, this statement proclaims—and is an instantiation of—the metaphorical quality of reason: Reason is *cold*; it is *rigorous*; it is *linear*; it is *clear*; it is *felt*. Despite its ambition to see itself as disembodied and impersonal, the rationalist model's fundamental depiction of reason depends on metaphorical extensions of embodied experiences like temperature and rigor (from the Latin *rigere*, "to be stiff").

These conventional characterizations of reason as cold, clear, rigorous, and linear are neither accidental nor incidental. Each derives from systematic conceptual metaphors that are entrenched aspects of our language and thought. And each corresponds with a substantive position that is integral to the rationalist model.

Consider the conventional conception of "cool reason." It derives from related metaphors in which emotions such as anger or lust are conceptualized as heat. These conceptual metaphors are part of a larger, more complex metaphorical system that has been extensively documented and analyzed by George Lakoff and Zoltán Kövecses.[25] Although much of the analysis would take us beyond the scope of this discussion, three points bear mentioning. First, these conceptual metaphors (technically, a metonymy and a metaphor) are not arbitrary but embodied. The primary conceptual metaphor for anger—ANGER IS THE HEAT OF A FLUID IN A CONTAINER—is grounded in the physiological responses of increased skin temperature and pulse rate that frequently accompany that emotion.* Second, this metaphorical system defines inferential relationships between various expressions for anger. Thus, the ANGER IS THE HEAT OF A FLUID IN A CONTAINER metaphor explains why a person in a "towering rage" has not "kept his cool," why someone who is "still stewing" has not yet "blown her top," and why, when a person is angry, "adding fuel to the fire" can be dangerous. Third, the conceptual metaphors for anger substantially overlap those for lust. A principal example of this overlap is the conceptual metaphor LUST IS HEAT. This is why a relationship can be *steamy* and a person can be *all steamed up;* it is why one can have *smoldering sexuality* as well as *smoldering anger.*

It should be easy enough to see why reason is "cold." For the rationalist model, the distinction between reason and the emotions is a fundamental binary opposition. This is true in two senses. First, the rationalist model treats reason and emotion as completely dichotomous: Reason is thought to involve no feelings; the emotions are believed to have no cognitive content. Second, the rationalist model understands reason and emotion as antithetical qualities: Where reason rules, the emotions are held in check; conversely, when one is overcome by emotion, reason is impossible. This antithesis is the basis for the stock notion that one should not let one's judgment be *colored* or *clouded* by passion. (These expressions are obviously premised on the KNOWING IS SEEING metaphor, to which we will return below.) Reason is "cold" because its presence is thought to depend on the absence of the "hot" emotions like anger or lust (P or not-P). Reason is, in a word, *dispassionate.*

These notions are so deeply ingrained in our tradition, our culture, our

---

* This conceptual metaphor is what motivates such expressions as "he's a *hothead*," "she lost her *cool*," and "that makes my *blood boil*." In fact, almost any synonym for "boil" also has a conventional connotation of anger—e.g., to simmer, steam, stew, burn (as in "she's doing a slow burn"), fume, seethe, smolder, or churn (as in "he's churning inside").

language, and our thought that the sharp distinction between reason and the emotions seems almost self-evident. But this substantive position is a product of our conceptual system, not a fact about the world. The work of Lakoff and Kövecses demonstrates that our concepts of anger and lust are quite rich in cognitive content and structure. In related work, Lakoff and Johnson have shown how these metaphorical concepts enter into reasoning about sexuality and structure the perception in which attractive women are seen by some as "provocative."[26] So, too, the rationalist view of reason and emotion as antithetical is not consonant with the range of human experience. People can feel passionate about their work (although, for a variety of reasons, this is often frowned upon). To much the same effect, Grey reads Stevens "to show that truth-seeking and pleasure-seeking are so blended in both science and poetry as to be in practical terms inseparable" (90). And, though there are times when we are so angry that we "see red," there are other times when our anger stimulates rather than interferes with our ability to calculate and plan.

Why is reason "rigorous" and "linear"? Both metaphorical expressions are products of the MIND-AS-BODY metaphor. This general metaphor is, as noted above, the basis for more particular metaphors such as KNOWING IS SEEING and UNDERSTANDING IS GRASPING. In this general metaphor, the mind is conceptualized as a body moving through space and various entailments of travel are mapped onto intellectual operations. Sweetser explains:

> Logical structures and conversational structures are . . . understood in
> terms of physical traveling and motion. An argument or a conversation
> follows or covers some particular path through the mental areas it tra-
> verses. Thus we say "That was off the track of the argument," "The pro-
> fessor guided his students through the maze of tax law," "They didn't let
> him get very far into the subject," or "Where were we?" (46)

This specific metaphor can be represented by the mnemonic AN ARGUMENT IS A JOURNEY. It consists of a systematic set of mappings from the source domain of journeys to the target domain of rational argument.* The mappings are as follows:

---

* Journeys function as an entailment-rich source domain for several other important conceptual domains. As alluded to in chapter 1, journeys provide the source domain for an extensive and vital conceptual metaphor for life; in chapter 5, we will see that this metaphor plays a central role in organizing our concept of narratives. So, too, in chapter 8, we will find that the metaphorically related notion of a path structures our concept of a rule. We will find, moreover, that this shared source domain is not the only aspect of conceptual structure that narratives, rational arguments, and rules have in common.

Source Domain		Target Domain
JOURNEY	⟶	ARGUMENT
traveler	⟶	thinker
point of departure	⟶	premises
terrain	⟶	subject matter
vehicle	⟶	theory
route	⟶	logical structure
exploration	⟶	investigation
distance covered	⟶	amount of argument completed
obstacles	⟶	objections
destination	⟶	conclusion

A journey can be arduous or harsh; consequently, one entailment of this metaphor is that just as a traveler must be hardy if she is to make it to her destination, a good argument requires *strong* or *rigorous* reasoning if it is to succeed. Conversely, bad reasoning leads to a *weak* or *lame* argument. In much the same vein, reason is *linear* because a good argument, like a good route, marks the shortest path between two points. Conversely, a bad or confused argument is *convoluted, oblique,* or simply *wanders off point.*

The traditional assumptions that reason must be rigorous and linear are metaphorical inferences rather than objective truths. William James delighted in turning the trope *reason is rigorous* on its head, mocking the "tender-mindedness" of the rationalist insistence on formal and theoretical elegance and extolling the superiority of the pragmatist's "tough-minded" tolerance of plurality and ambiguity.[27] The dogma that reason must be linear is open to a similar critique. No one who has studied the Talmud could possibly question its analytical rigor. Yet, its style of reasoning and organization—which, tracking oral exchanges in the talmudic academies of Palestine and Babylonia, sometimes borders on stream of consciousness—stands as a sixty-volume tribute to the intricate, often convoluted rhythms of the human mind. The rationalist model's insistence on linearity mistakes the difficulties of exposition for the limits of reason. "The problem," as Herbert Wechsler once observed to my law school class, "is that we think things 'in the round,' but we can speak them only one at a time."

As with the other expressions, the conventional understanding of reason as "clear" is an entailment of a basic conceptual metaphor. Rationalism aspires to what Grey aptly identifies as the Platonic, Lockean, and Cartesian "ideal of discursive transparency" (101) because we understand cognitive functions by means of the metaphors KNOWING IS SEEING and WORDS ARE CONTAINERS. A well-reasoned argument is "clear" because it is *open* or *ac-*

cessible and, thus, available to perception. Conversely, a poorly reasoned argument is *murky* or *opaque*. It is the CONDUIT metaphor-system, and not some transcendental truth about pure reason, that makes sense of so many of our conventional expressions about reason and communication.* There is nothing wrong or mistaken in the rationalist model's striving for lucidity (from the Latin *lucere*, "to shine"), but this aspiration simply makes no sense apart from our metaphorical conception of reason.

Indeed, some of the most basic notions of the rationalist model are metaphorical entailments of the CONDUIT metaphor-system. Or perhaps it would be more accurate to say that some of the most basic notions of the rationalist model are a consequence of taking these metaphors too literally. Conceptual metaphors such as UNDERSTANDING IS GRASPING and IDEAS ARE OBJECTS are cognitively entrenched and operate without reflection. Consequently, one can too easily come to see the world as composed of discrete, mind-independent bits of reality. Indeed, rationalists are forever insisting that we face up to the cold, *hard* facts or that, properly understood, there really is something called *hard* law after all. So, too, the assumption that thought is a matter of propositional intentions that are set forth in a linear fashion is a more sophisticated version of the basic conceptual mapping in which ideas are objects and communication is sending. (Recall that "proposition" derives from the Latin *propositio*, "a setting forth.") By the same token, philosophy's obsession with the problem of representation is a correlate of the KNOWING IS SEEING metaphor. As Rorty famously puts it: "The picture which holds traditional philosophy captive is that of the mind as a great mirror, containing various representations."

Consider, in this regard, Posner's exposition of the syllogism "All men are mortal; Socrates is a man; therefore Socrates is mortal." The logic of this syllogism depends upon the rationalist model of a category. On this model, a category (or concept) is defined in terms of the properties that are present or absent (P or not-P). All things that share property P—in this case, mortal humans—are in the category; things that do not share that property (not-P) are not. Posner, in other words, is absolutely right about the metaphor of the box: As figure 3.1 illustrates, rationalist categorization according to common properties conceives of categories as metaphorical containers.

The use of the CONTAINER schema to structure the concept "category"

---

* Consider such examples as: "Which *view* do you espouse?" "This theory really *sheds some light* on our problem." "That was a *brilliant* remark." "I *see* what you're saying." "That's an *insightful* idea." "The students here are very *bright*."

FIGURE 3.1   Categorization and "P or not-P" as CONTAINER metaphor

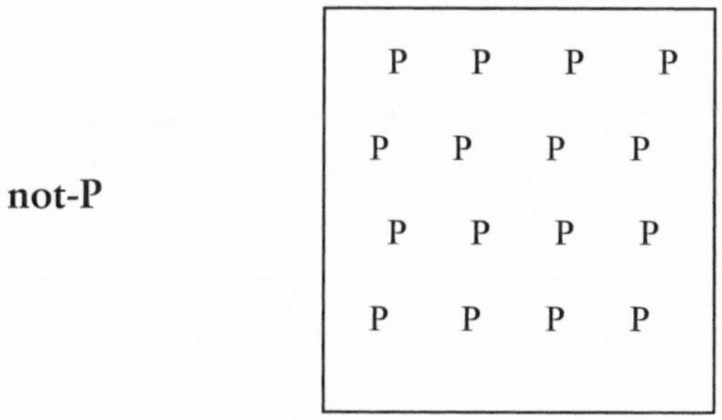

not-P

P	P	P	P
P	P	P	P
P	P	P	P
P	P	P	P

(and "concept") leads to the inference that categories (and concepts) have well-defined boundaries. This inference in turn yields several fundamental rationalist assumptions about reasoning and categorization. It structures the notion of a distinction as a dichotomous choice. It yields the conventional tautology of formal logic: P or not-P. This principle may also be taken as true for propositions, in which case P or not-P yields the law of the excluded middle. The inference that categories have well-defined boundaries also yields the notion that category membership is, as Posner notes, a matter of shared characteristics and, therefore, can be specified in necessary and suffi-cient criteria.

Once again, however, these quite fundamental rationalist assumptions turn out to be just that. Take the assumption that concepts and categories have well-defined boundaries. The world does not come that way; think of the category "tall people." Or consider the dichotomous categories "day" and "night," which, as everyone recognizes, fail to represent adequately the intermediate states of dusk and dawn.* In a similar vein, the logic of cate-gorization on the rationalist model is that every category member should be the same in the relevant respect. Yet, as we will see in the next chapter, there is the well-documented phenomenon of prototype effects in which some category members are perceived as better examples of the category and serve as cognitive reference points that enter into reasoning about the cate-

---

* Such graded phenomena can be dealt with by means of fuzzy logic without doing much violence to the rationalist model. But, though fuzzy logic is a powerful tool that rep-resents an improvement on the basic rationalist model, it is not an adequate account of the full range of human categorization. Fuzzy logic works best for simple graded categories like "day" and "night"; it does not always adapt well to more complex forms of catego-rization such as cluster models.

gory. Indeed, the empirical evidence indicates that humans actually categorize in ways that, for the most part, bear little resemblance to the rationalist model.

Pragmatists like Rorty believe they have superseded the crude subject-object picture with the behaviorist maneuver in which language is viewed not as a medium "in which we form pictures of reality, but as part of the behavior of human beings." [28] The problem is not with this insight—which is invaluable. Rather, the problem is that pragmatists have no idea how the linguistic behavior of human beings actually works. Worse yet, they insist that there is nothing there to understand; for them, language behavior is just the product of random and inexplicable practices. But this pragmatist credo is yet another product of antinomial capture; it is an artifact of the rationalist's assumption of the logical truth of P or not-P, in which concepts are differentiated by the presence or absence of defining properties: *Either* representation is possible, *or* it is not; *either* language accurately corresponds to the world, *or* it is entirely arbitrary and contingent. In short, pragmatists conclude that there is no theory of language to be had because they accede to the rationalist conception of what a theory of language must be.

Despite their best efforts to transcend the subject-object dichotomy, pragmatists remain trapped by the totalizing, all-or-nothing quality of their reasoning. (And little wonder, given that these dichotomies are themselves rooted in the CONTAINER schema, with its entailments of rigidity and closure.) In the next chapter, we will see how the notion of radial categories transforms our fundamental understanding both of what a category is and of how it functions. Indeed, this new understanding of categorization vaporizes the notion of rigid boundaries that defines not only the rationalist understanding of categories and concepts, but also the entire set of traditional dualisms—between the body and the mind, reality and imagination, the objective and the subjective—that provide the formative matrix for rationalist thought.

One can go further only by attending to the implications of recent developments in cognitive theory. The discovery that human rationality is embodied dissolves the mind/body dichotomy. The insight that human rationality is imaginative and adaptive displaces the pragmatists' reductive behaviorism with a more detailed, nuanced account of how we interact with and construct our world. An understanding of the cognitive importance of metaphor promises to collapse the very distinction between reality and imagination: "The question," as Paul Ricoeur puts it, "is whether the functioning of metaphorical sense does not put to the test and even hold at bay this very dichotomy." [29]

JUST THE STATUS OF OUR CONCEPTIONS

In *Connoisseur of Chaos,* Wallace Stevens derides both the disposition to binary thought and the desire to seek resolution in dialectical synthesis. "We cannot go back to that," Stevens tells us. "The squirming facts exceed the squamous mind, / If one may say so." [30] Here, Stevens suggests that the mind that understands everything in dichotomous terms is a reptilian mind: too covered with squamae (epidermal scales), too far down the evolutionary scale to succeed in its task of understanding a squirming world of contingency and flux. "And yet," Stevens instructs us, "relation appears. / A small relation expanding like the shade / Of a cloud on sand, a shape on the side of a hill."

What is this relation? Why is it expanding? Ricoeur suggests an answer when he observes that "to imagine is not to have a mental picture of something but to display relations in a depicting mode." [31] For Ricoeur, imagination consists not in the capacity to create or invent new symbolic representations but in the ability to generate and correlate mental images. Metaphor is just that cognitive operation—that is, the process by which the mind projects a conceptual mapping from one knowledge domain to another.

To put it differently, metaphor is the imaginative capacity by which we relate one thing to another and, in so doing, "have" a world. Thus, a conceptual mapping like the CONDUIT metaphor-system enables us to use all of the entailments of experience in the object domain to structure operations in the intellectual domain. Metaphor is, therefore, a *projection,* in the sense that the entailments and internal relations of the source domain, such as the experience of manipulating physical objects, are carried forward to a target domain, such as that of intellectual operations. And metaphor is an *expansion* in the sense that it is a nonreductive function: To conceive of understanding as grasping, for example, is to gain a sense of "grasp" as a cognitive operation without losing or supplanting its physical meaning.

It follows that conceptual metaphors like UNDERSTANDING IS GRASPING are not literal or truth-conditional statements about the world but imaginative tools that are "true" to the extent that they successfully enable our day-to-day interactions. Once we understand that metaphors are our way of having a reality, the questions that preoccupy pragmatists like Davidson or Posner will no longer be pertinent. We will not ask what a metaphor *means,* but how it does the *work* that it does. We will not ask whether metaphor validates a rule of logic, but instead will attend to the logic that it enables. Indeed, once we understand that metaphors are our way of having a reality, the important question about any metaphor is the genuinely

pragmatic one: What (partial) reality does it enable? As Lakoff and Johnson note, "What is at issue is not the truth or falsity of a metaphor but the
perceptions and inferences that follow from it and the actions that are sanctioned by it." [32]

Precisely because they are not reductive functions that make literal
truth-claims, conceptual metaphors can be combined in ways that—to a rationalist sensibility—can seem only analytically inconsistent. In this way,
they provide a versatile and highly adaptable repertoire for managing an often difficult and diverse environment. Consider, for example, the metaphors
IDEAS ARE OBJECTS and UNDERSTANDING IS GRASPING. These conceptions
imply that knowledge is inert and that, once acquired, it remains a static
and unchanging asset. But, as we have seen, we also employ the more general MIND-AS-BODY metaphor that conceptualizes cognitive operations in
terms of movement and exploration. This metaphorical conception captures both the dynamic quality of intellectual processes and the necessarily
perspectival nature of human knowledge, which, after all, is always knowledge from "a point of view." By using both sets of mappings, we are able to
re-present mental processes without the reductivism that might follow from
reliance on a single metaphor. This twofold flexibility of metaphorical
thought—that is, its capacity for imaginative relation and for metaphorical
coherence—enables us to function better in and adapt more successfully to
a "squirming" and highly complex world. It enables the kind of adaptations
that would not be possible if we tried to pin down a multidimensional world
with speech that is literal and truth-conditional.

In this light, consider Stevens's aphorism from the *Adagia,* "Reality is
a cliché from which we escape by metaphor." [33] We could take this to mean
that reality and metaphor are separate things: The former is just the state of
stasis that precedes the movement of the latter. But this interpretation ignores the full import of "cliché," which connotes the conventional quality of
reality as well as its triteness. Thus, a more plausible interpretation would
equate Stevens's aphorism with the Nietzschean view that reality (like truth
and literality) is a cliché or dead metaphor. Indeed, elsewhere in the *Adagia,* Stevens seems to endorse just this view, saying: "Metaphor creates a
new reality from which the original appears to be unreal" (195). But then
Stevens appears to reject this view, counseling: "There is no such thing as a
metaphor of a metaphor. One does not progress through metaphors. Thus
reality is the indispensable element of each metaphor" (204). Similarly,
Stevens observes elsewhere: "The material of the imagination is reality and
reality can be nothing else except the usable past" (309).

In these adages we see Stevens struggling with the question later posed by Ricoeur: What does metaphorical sense do to the traditional dichotomy of reality and imagination? Taken together, these adages exploit all the possible combinations of the reality-imagination complex: Metaphor is contingent on reality. But reality is only a cliché—what Stevens elsewhere calls a "stiff and stubborn, man-locked set" of conceptions.[34] From this vantage point, metaphor appears as the imaginative means of escape to a "new" reality. Once we are ensconced in that new perspective, however, the former reality will no longer seem merely a cliché; it will seem unreal and *false*. But that can be possible only if the new "reality" is already taken for granted *as* reality—that is, if it has already become a cliché. We have come full circle. There is no difference between "cliché" and "metaphor." Both are conventional ways of having a reality.

Stevens's aphorisms thus presage Thomas Kuhn's famous insight that reality is paradigm-dependent. This is particularly clear when one compares the second aphorism—"Metaphor creates a new reality from which the original appears to be unreal"—with Kuhn's description of the perceptual changes that accompany a paradigm shift:

> Looking at the moon, the convert to Copernicanism does not say, "I used to see a planet, but now I see a satellite." That locution would imply a sense in which the Ptolemaic system had once been correct. Instead, a convert to the new astronomy says, "I once took the moon to be (or saw the moon as) a planet, but I was mistaken."[35]

Paradoxically, the notion of a paradigm shift helps us see that it is useless to think of cliché as "false," for it can be no less true (and no more false) than metaphor. To think of cliché or metaphor as "false"—or, as Grey suggests, as something "that hides from the mind the world as it really is" (71)—is already to commit the objectivist fallacy, positing some other access to a world as it *really* is. By the same token, it would be a mistake to conclude that metaphor is epistemically superior to cliché. Metaphor, too, is a contingent relation, because "reality is the indispensable element of each metaphor."

On this reading, Stevens's aphorisms suggest that there is no opposition between reality and imagination.[36] Imagination is our way of worldmaking, our mode of engagement. The difference between cliché and metaphor is not the difference between true and false, new and old, better or worse, conventional or creative, but only a difference in our understanding of the *status* of our conceptions. Both cliché and metaphor are the world as it is enabled through our conceptions of and interactions with it.

This more pragmatic understanding, in which "cliché" and "metaphor" both denote our imaginative way of having a reality, is particularly congruent with our earlier exploration of everyday language. The "literal" consists largely of metaphors that are not recognized as such—not because they are "dead," but because they are so conventional and, hence, clichéd. Conversely, as we have seen, what we take to be original poetic metaphor is often just a novel instantiation of a conventional conceptual metaphor or an unconventional use of an otherwise ordinary image.

In this light, we can return to Grey's initial question about the relevance of poetry to law. If metaphor is an essential aspect of human rationality, there can be no difference in kind between the "rigors" of reason and the demands of poetry. As Stevens himself observed, "One is not a lawyer one minute and a poet the next. . . . I don't have a separate mind for legal work and another for writing poetry. I do each with my whole mind." [37] The metaphors that animate both standard English and poetic formulations also motivate our legal conceptions. Chapter 10, for example, examines how Holmes used conventional metaphors derived from the CONDUIT metaphor-system in elaborating his famous "marketplace of ideas" metaphor that has been so crucial to the development of modern First Amendment doctrine. And chapters 8 and 12 explore how such basic legal concepts as rules, rights, and "Law" itself are structured metaphorically.

Conventional legal reasoning is relentlessly reductive, imposing propositional rules and other necessary and sufficient criteria for decisionmaking upon a more complex human reality. But the squirming world of contingency and flux is not so easily domesticated. We think that by drawing distinctions we are clarifying the law and making it more precise. Yet, the fact of the matter is frequently otherwise. Chapters 6, 7, and 11 explore examples of the ways in which the procrustean rationalism of standard legal reasoning distorts and obscures the flexibility and creativity indispensable to a functioning legal system. Indeed, as we shall see throughout this book, the imaginative quality of everyday human rationality enables us to accommodate complexity in ways that the conventional notion of dichotomous categories and rule structures simply cannot.

CHAPTER 4

Radial Categories

WE HAVE seen that, although they are imaginative, the processes of basic-level categorization, image-schemas, and conceptual metaphor nevertheless operate in a regular, orderly, and systematic fashion. This chapter completes our initial examination of the conceptual structures of imagination. Here, I introduce such empirically documented phenomena as radial categories, conceptual metonymy, "chaining" within a category, prototype effects, and idealized cognitive models. Together, these developments transform our notion of categorization almost beyond recognition and, with it, everything that depends on categories.

The picture that emerges bears surprisingly little resemblance to conventional wisdom. On the standard view, categorization is nothing more than classification according to common properties.[1] Yet, many of our most elementary and familiar categories defy that logic. The conventional view treats the notion of a category as an a priori conceptual structure that, consistent with the logic of P or not-P, is homogenous in content (at least in the relevant respect). But, it turns out, categories are both varied in kind and complex in structure. On the standard view, categories are descriptive, definitional, and rigidly bounded. The empirical evidence, in contrast, presents a picture of categorization as an imaginative and dynamic process that is flexible in application and elastic in scope. The conventional view understands categories as distinct from purpose or, at least, conceptually indifferent to it. But the data demonstrate otherwise. Even for apparently descriptive categories, function or purpose serves as an integral element of or frame for categorization. Along much the same lines, many descriptive categories are normatively infused rather than value-neutral.

In short, categories are not the passive objects or terms of thought that the rationalists and their subjectivist opposition suppose them to be.* To the contrary: *Categorization is the very process of reasoning itself.* And that, as they say, is the whole ball game.

UNCOMMON COMMONALITIES

George Lakoff entitled his brilliant work on human categorization and cognition *Women, Fire, and Dangerous Things.* When I first talked about the book with friends and colleagues, many of them would naturally inter-polate the word "other" after the word "and." This parapraxis reflects the underlying assumption of rationalist categorization, which is also a staple of legal reasoning: Items (e.g., fact patterns) are subsumed under the same gen-eral category (e.g., covered by the same legal rule) because they share some common property. All things that share property P are in the category; all things that do not have that property—that is, not-P—are not members of the category. On this logic, a category should always be susceptible to defi-nition in terms of the necessary and sufficient conditions (that is, the rele-vant Ps) for category membership.

In choosing the book's title, Lakoff was having a good laugh at the ex-pense of the rationalist in us. The title refers to a real language that actually has a syntactic gender category that includes both women and fire—but not, of course, because they are both considered dangerous. The category is *ba-lan* in Dyirbal, an aboriginal language of Australia. In addition to women, fire, and dangerous things, it includes also water, nondangerous birds, ex-ceptional animals like the duckbilled platypus, and the sun.

The explanation for this seemingly odd grouping is complex: The pri-mary categories are *balan* and *bayi,* and the central category members are women and men, respectively. In Dyirbal mythology, the moon and the sun are husband and wife. Thus, the sun, which is female, is *balan.* Fire is like the sun; water is used to put out fire; rivers are bodies of water; all of these are thus categorized together. Animals are classified with human males as *bayi.* Unusual or dangerous animals, however, are marked in the language by placing them in the opposing category, *balan.* Dyirbal myth also has it

---

* In other words, categories are not rigid and fixed, but neither are they merely the plastic medium of intentional manipulation and control. Purpose, as we shall see, is a shared dimension of category-structure that makes possible some of its built-in flexibility.

that birds are the spirits of dead women; they are *balan*. Dangerous birds like the hawk, however, are marked as *bayi*.[2]

We cannot dismiss this sort of categorization as an irrational artifact of some primitive culture. Much of our own categorization equally defies the rationalist logic that defines categories and concepts in terms of necessary and sufficient conditions. This is the point of Wittgenstein's famous example:

> Consider for example the proceedings we call "games." I mean board-games, card-games, ball-games, Olympic games, and so on. What is common to them all?—Don't say: "There *must* be something common, or they would not be called 'games'"—but *look and see* whether there is anything common to all.—For if you look at them you will not see something that is common to *all*, but similarities, relationships, and a whole series of them at that.

Wittgenstein characterized these similarities and relationships as "family resemblances" in which "we see a complicated network of similarities, overlapping and criss-crossing: sometimes overall similarities, sometimes similarities of detail."[3]

Many treat Wittgenstein's demystifying critique of rationalist categorization as the final word on the subject. But what appears arbitrary or erratic from one theoretical perspective may nevertheless turn out to be orderly and systematic when considered from another. On the basis of extensive empirical evidence in linguistics, anthropology, and cognitive psychology, Lakoff has shown that the similarities and relationships captured by Wittgenstein's notion of family resemblance can be further specified. Much of our categorization takes the form of *radial categories*. A radial category consists of a central model or case with various extensions that, though related to the central case in some fashion, nevertheless cannot be generated by rule. Because they may derive from the central case in different ways, the extensions may have little or nothing in common with each other beyond their shared connection to the central case (79–114).

Consider an example from Benjamin Lee Whorf that, at first blush, seems to confirm the view that linguistic meaning is arbitrary and contingent solely on context and use:

> Take the word "hand." In 'his hand' it refers to a location on the human body, in 'hour hand' to a strikingly dissimilar object, in 'all hands on deck' to another reference, in 'a good hand (at cards)' to another, whereas in 'he got the upper hand' it refers to nothing but is dissolved into a pattern of orientation.[4]

To Whorf's list, we might add "lend a hand" (i.e., give assistance), "give her a hand" (i.e., applause), and "would you hand that to me." These diverse uses of the word "hand" simply cannot be accounted for by any set of necessary and sufficient conditions.

Whorf's example of "hand"—like Wittgenstein's "game" and Davidson's "mouth"—makes categorization seem as arbitrary and unpredictable as a fictive category from a story by Borges or as the child's diversion in which one lists "twenty-seven things to bring on a picnic."[5] But this misimpression is merely an artifact of the rationalist insistence on the logic of P or not-P.[6] If one assumes that categorization can be only a matter of necessary and sufficient criteria, then there are only two possibilities: (1) Save the rationalist model by redefining the uses of words like "hand" as cases of homonymy—that is, "different" words that sound the same but have disparate meanings—or (2) conclude that categorization is arbitrary, entirely contingent on context and convention.* In either case, the rationalist model's all-or-nothing logic obscures the systematic connections that link these different uses in a single categorical structure.

In chapter 3, we saw how the propositionally different uses of the word "mouth" nevertheless constitute a coherent linguistic category that is metaphorically structured by a single image-mapping. Thus, the polysemous uses of "mouth" form a radial category that takes the human (or animal) mouth as its central case. Extensions are generated by means of an image-mapping to other apertures through which things flow. The standard extensions—the mouth of the river, the mouth of a bottle, or the mouth of a tunnel—are fixed by convention. Unusual extensions such as Homer's description of mouths as wounds—or a phrase like "the yawning gates of hell"—are related metaphorical expressions that have nevertheless remained unconventionalized.

Whorf's example is also best described as a radial category. The different senses of the word "hand" are polysemous cases of the same word related to each other by a common model or central case. Each use of the word "hand" is related to the basic-level sense referring to the human limb. The "hour hand" is a metaphoric projection of human body structure; we also

---

* Both conclusions are consistent with the notion that meaning is contingent on context and use: the second directly, the first by treating each context and use as a separate "word." And each conclusion, in its own way, retains the rationalist notion of categorization. The first does so by reducing the data to fit the theory—that is, by fragmenting the uses of "hand" into narrower categories that can be reduced to necessary and sufficient criteria. The second does so paradoxically—that is, by maintaining the integrity of the rationalist notion of a category but denying its validity. (*See* note 8.)

FIGURE 4.1   "Hand" as a Radial Category

METAPHORICAL EXTENSIONS   METONYMICAL EXTENSIONS

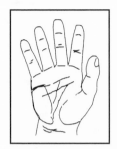

all hands on deck

hour hand   a hand of cards

                                           lend a hand

the upper hand   give a hand

                                           hand that to me

refer to the clock as having a "face." (In much the same way, a bottle of the
right shape can have a "neck" as well as a "mouth.") "The upper hand" is
an instantiation of the more general conceptual metaphor CONTROL IS UP,*
in which human body orientation and its entailments are mapped onto more
abstract experiences of control.[7] For humans, the experience of being upright in the world is inextricably related both to control over our bodies (ever
try to stand drunk?) and to the ability to exercise control over many aspects
of our environment (ever try to cook on your hands and knees?). In an experientially motivated case like CONTROL IS UP, that which is pragmatically
good and useful in our interactions with the world is UP in a basic, nonarbitrary sense. Rather than merely dissolving into a pattern of orientation, as
Whorf suggests, the expression "the upper hand" has a strong experiential
grounding.

    "All hands on deck," "a good hand at cards," "lend a hand," "give her
a hand," and "hand that to me" are all cases of metonymy. A metonymy is
a conceptual mapping that uses knowledge of PART-WHOLE relations to des-
ignate an entity either by means of one of its conceptually significant parts
or by means of some other entity to which it is conceptually related.[8] Examples include such conventional phrases as "my wheels" to refer to one's
car and "the White House" to refer to the president or his administration.

---

* This is what motivates such familiar expressions as "I have control *over* her"; "I am
on top of the situation"; "He's in a *superior* position"; "She's at the *height* of her power";
"He is *under* my control"; and "I'm *low* man on the totem pole."

Like metaphors, metonymies are experientially grounded. Sailors do their jobs with their hands; we lend assistance or give applause with our hands; we hold our playing cards in our hands; and we use our hands to transport objects. Each of these metonymies is an experientially motivated extension of the central meaning of "hand."

Thus, the linguistic category "hand" is a radial category, as represented in figure 4.1. It has a central case and certain conventionalized extensions. These extensions are not rule-governed, and they cannot be reduced to necessary and sufficient criteria. But neither are they arbitrary. Although the various extensions have little in common with one another besides their relation to the central case, each extension is related to that central case by means of an experientially grounded metaphor or metonymy.

"Mouth" and "hand" are simple radial categories. Each consists of an uncomplicated (in these cases, embodied) central model with a single ring or tier of extensions generated by only one or two conceptual processes. *Balan* provides a more interesting example because it involves complexity in three different dimensions: (1) It has several tiers or layers of extensions; (2) these extensions are governed by a variety of different conventions; and (3) many of these extensions bear no relation to the central case but are related only to previous extensions.

Balan takes human females as its central case (the contrasting category, *bayi*, takes human males as its central case). Some category extensions, like the sun and birds, are governed by mythological connections. Others are experientially motivated. Fire, for example, is included on the basis of its phenomenological similarity to the sun, a first-order category member. Water, too, is linked only to a previous extension and not the central case. In this instance, the linkage is premised on the experiential knowledge that water is used to put out fire. Rivers and other bodies of water are included by extension. Finally, category extensions such as dangerous animals are governed solely by convention. Most animals, most fish (those used for food), and weapons used for hunting are classified as *bayi*—that is, together with those who hunt. Dangerous animals, however, are classified as *balan* in order to mark them in the language. Although this marking is purely conventional, it is nevertheless experientially motivated in the sense that it serves the highly practical function of linguistically coding knowledge necessary for survival. In this pragmatic way, even apparently arbitrary conventions can turn out to be framed and constrained by a culture's basic, embodied interactions with its world.

Balan, thus, provides an example of chaining within a category: Some extensions are incorporated on the basis of their relation to an existing category member rather than to the central case. Chaining within a category is neither unusual nor unique to exotic languages or cultures. Lakoff and Brugman have shown that the English preposition "over" is an elaborate radial category that, in addition to other processes, is formed by extensive chaining (416–61 [case study 2]). Lawyers, moreover, are quite familiar with the phenomenon of chaining within a category. Not only is it one basis for "slippery slope" arguments but, as I will explain in chapter 9, it is also a staple of what lawyers refer to as "reasoning by analogy."

At first blush, linguistic categories like "mouth," "hand," and *balan* seem trivial: For the most part, they do not enter into reasoning, evaluation, or judgment; nor do they seem to be of any particular importance to our conceptual systems. Yet, even these relatively simple radial categories hold profound implications for our understanding of reasoning and categorization.

First, they belie the conventional view of categorization as merely a matter of classification according to common properties. Even elementary linguistic categories such as "mouth" and "hand" are organized imaginatively; even our "simplest" categories turn out to be rich in conceptual content and structure. These examples demonstrate, moreover, that basic linguistic competence already involves conceptual reasoning that employs image-mappings, metaphors, and metonymies.

Second, the fact that a category can be formed by means of several imaginative conceptual processes undermines the conventional view of categories as definitional, homogenous, and rigidly bounded. A linguistic category like "mouth" can be specified in necessary and sufficient conditions that are formulated in terms of the underlying image-mapping. But a linguistic category like "hand," which is composed of several different metaphors and conceptual metonymies, cannot be reduced to necessary and sufficient criteria. So, too, the phenomenon of chaining as a mode of category extension means that categories are not necessarily definitional and homogenous; by the same token, they need not have determinate boundaries. And the more extended the process of chaining, the more a category will diverge from the rationalist presumption of P or not-P.

Third, although particular radial categories such as *balan* are contingent cultural artifacts, the *phenomenon* of radial categorization is a product of an imaginative human cognition that transcends culture. Just as the rationalist notion of a category is a metaphorical product of the CONTAINER schema, radial category structure is conceptualized metaphorically in terms of the CENTER-PERIPHERY schema. This use of the CENTER-PERIPHERY schema to structure the way in which we categorize our world has a powerful experiential grounding in our necessarily egocentric perception of the world *around* us. We would expect to find radial categories in many (if not all) languages and cultures, and we do. *Balan* in Dyirbal and *hon* in Japanese were the first two radial categories documented by Lakoff.* Although it is not possible to say whether radial categorization is universal, it is certainly cross-cultural.

Fourth, the Dyirbal categories *balan* and *bayi* illustrate that linguistic categories—no less than metaphors—can have semantic content and enter into cognitive functioning. Not only does *balan* code information about which animals are dangerous, but this knowledge is plainly expected to enter into reasoning and to influence behavior. In effect, Dyirbal treats linguistic categorization as a social resource for preserving and transmitting important cultural knowledge. As we shall see in later sections, this last point is a general one. Many language categories reflect socially governed functions or purposes. Just as Dyirbal groups water together with fire and prey together with hunters, many of our own linguistic categories are organized experientially. Just as Dyirbal linguistic categories contain important information with survival value, many of our own linguistic categories encode important—though, sometimes, highly controversial—normative values.

When Some Category Members Are More Equal Than Others

In a series of landmark experiments, Eleanor Rosch found that people regularly rate some category members as better examples of their respective categories than others. Robins and sparrows, for example, are consistently judged better examples of the category "bird" than ducks, owls, or penguins.[9] Rips found that such goodness-of-example ratings actually enter into reasoning: When told that the robins on an island had a disease, people concluded that the ducks on the island were likely to succumb as well. But, when the sequence was reversed and subjects were told that the ducks were ill, the prediction no longer held.[10] Amos Tversky and Daniel Kahneman found that people thought it more probable that an earthquake in California would cause a flood in which 1,000 people drowned than that there would be a flood anywhere in North America in which 1,000 people

---

* *Hon* is characterized by a central image-schema that is extended by metaphoric projections (104–10).

drowned (even though an earthquake together with a flood is less likely than either alone).[11]

What accounts for such findings? These goodness-of-example judgments and their associated patterns of inference—collectively referred to as *prototype effects*—cannot be explained within the rationalist model. Because the rationalist model defines category membership in terms of common properties, every category member should be the same in the relevant respect. (Recall Posner's description of the category "men" as a box "with a bunch of things in it, every one of which is 'mortal.'")[12] Accordingly, every member should be an equally good example of the category.

From the rationalist perspective, the temptation is strong to see these prototype phenomena as some form of "cognitive error." This, in effect, is the tack taken by the most influential efforts to rescue the rationalist model from the implications of these findings. Those efforts take the form of hybrid "core-plus-identification" theories of categorization. They postulate that categories consist of a definitional core expressed in terms of necessary and sufficient conditions and a supplementary psychological identification procedure based on judgments of typicality or some other such heuristic.[13]

As we shall see shortly, the empirical evidence does not bear out these interpretations. But even if one were to accept the rationalist characterization of prototype effects as (in Tversky and Kahneman's words) a form of cognitive or psychological "fallacy" (304), the underlying questions would nevertheless remain: Why are some category members judged better examples of a category than others? And how is it that these prototypes enter into reasoning?

To answer these questions, we will ultimately need an entirely different account of human categorization. That account is provided in the next section, which reviews the evidence with respect to idealized cognitive models. First, however, we need to consider some additional data with respect to prototype effects. Those data support four conclusions: (1) Prototype effects are pervasive both in scope and in reach; (2) they are cross-cultural; (3) they are not a single, discrete phenomenon but are produced by a complex of different neurological processes; and (4) they are epiphenomenal— that is, they are secondary *effects* and do not characterize the structure of categorization itself.

1. *Pervasiveness.* Prototype phenomena are pervasive in two senses. First, they are not limited to any particular kind of category but are widespread. Second, they are systematically manifest in various cognitive functions. Rosch found prototype effects with respect to a wide variety of object

categories (e.g., chairs, birds, etc.).[14] She found, moreover, that prototypes function as *cognitive reference points* in memory and other mental processes. When asked to list examples of a category, subjects tended to produce lists of prototypical examples of the relevant category. So, too, when subjects were asked to judge the truthfulness of statements (e.g., "a chicken is a bird"), response time was shorter for prototypical cases than for nonprototypical cases.[15]

Similarly, prototype effects are reflected in learning. Children learn category membership of prototypical examples first.[16] This finding has been replicated with adults. The Dani, an aboriginal culture of New Guinea, have only two color categories: *mili,* which incorporates the dark-cool colors— black, green, blue; and *mola,* which incorporates the light-warm colors— white, red, yellow. Rosch found that the Dani were perfectly capable of learning and memorizing names for colors not represented in their language, but that they were more successful learning prototypes or "focal" colors (i.e., the commonly chosen "best" examples of a given color) than "nonfocal" colors.[17] In the same way, adult Americans asked to master artificial categories in the laboratory were able to assimilate the experimentally designed prototypical cases more easily and quickly than other category members.[18]

Subsequent research by Lawrence Barsalou and his colleagues discovered that transitory, ad hoc categories such as "things to do on the weekend" or "what to take from one's home in a fire" also display prototype effects.[19] Even numbers—the very archetype of a rationalist category specifiable in necessary and sufficient conditions—display prototype effects: Some natural numbers (the single-digit ones) are reliably rated better examples of the category "odd numbers" than others.[20] These prototype effects, moreover, are an ordinary part of mathematical reasoning. We regularly employ just such prototypes whenever we "round off" a number to the nearest multiple of five in order to make computation easier and quicker.[21]

2. *Cross-cultural manifestations.* Some prototype effects transcend language and culture. Brent Berlin and Paul Kay found that speakers of languages with different color categories nevertheless identify the same hues or "focal" colors as best examples of the relevant color category. In fact, they found greater agreement on these prototypes across cultures than within cultures.[22] For example, in a culture with a single category for the colors blue and green (Tarahumara, a Uto-Aztecan language of Mexico, has a single word, *siyóname*), people do not choose turquoise (the halfway point on the color spectrum) as the prototype. Rather, they choose either "focal"

green or "focal" blue as the best example—i.e., the same prototypes chosen by English speakers for the categories green and blue.[23]

3. *Multiple neurological bases.* Prototype effects with respect to color appear to be direct products of the relevant neurophysiology. Color perception is organized in terms of three types of paired neurons. Two of these pairs are organized as opponent-response cells, which means that when one cell of a pair fires its counterpart is correspondingly inhibited. These two opponent-response pairs respond to red-green and yellow-blue wave lengths, respectively. The nonopponent-response pair responds to relative brightness across the entire color spectrum. Operating separately, the members of this pair determine white and black; operating together, they determine gray; operating with the color sensitive opponent-response cells, they determine the relative brightness of the particular hue. Not only can these three types of paired cells operate in tandem, but they each operate at about twenty different levels of intensity. In this way, a limited set of elements is able to code as many as 10,000 different hues across the entire color spectrum.[24]

The prototype effects relating to the four primary colors—red, yellow, green, and blue—occur when only one set of opponent-response cells is activated. For example, "focal" blue occurs when the blue-yellow cell ($+B -Y$) fires at its optimal rate, the yellow-blue cell ($+Y -B$) fires at a corresponding level below its basal rate (i.e., its normal rate of firing), and the red-green cells ($+R -G$ and $+G -R$) both remain at their basal rates of firing.[25]

Not all prototype effects are direct products of particular types of neurons, but they can nevertheless be accounted for—at least in general outline—in terms of the properties of the models of neural architecture described in chapter 2: neural networks and reentrant processing.

As discussed previously, a neural net consists of a group of hundreds or thousands of neurons linked together by their synaptic connections. These synaptic connections can have varying strengths or "weights" that, to varying degrees, stimulate or inhibit other neurons in the group. These synaptic connections are developed and enhanced in response to the organism's experience. Once its connections are strengthened in this way, a network is capable of reproducing the same pattern of neural activation.

We can see the implications with the case of color. Perception across the entire color spectrum is expressed through the gradations and combinations of just six paired elements arrayed along three dimensions or axes: red-green, yellow-blue, and relative brightness. In other words, every color that humans can perceive corresponds to a unique combination or triplet of activation levels along these three axes. Perception of the color purple, for example, requires the firing of the +R −G and +B −Y cells (with the corresponding inhibition of the +G −R and +Y −B cells) along with the activation of the nonopponent-response cells that respond to darkness. Variations in the amplitude of this activation pattern yield related colors—such as lavender, violet, or indigo—that cluster around purple: lavender, when the activation of the brightness cells is amplified; violet, when the darkness cells fire more strongly; indigo, when the intensity of the +B −Y cells increases. Thus, the method for coding color in terms of particular patterns of neural firings produces phenomenological similarities and relations that cluster around particular colors: Violet is *like* purple; lavender is, too, but *farther away,* and so on.[26] In other words, the neurological coding system itself produces prototype effects.

Though this account is only suggestive, it is consistent with the known properties of neural networks. Computer simulated neural nets actually do develop prototype effects. R. P. Gorman and T. J. Sejnowski trained a neural net to distinguish sonar echoes and to discriminate between those echoes generated by mines and those by rocks. As a result of its training, the net develops distinct subspaces for coding mine-echo and rock-echo vectors, the central region of which "contains a sort of 'prototypical hot spot,' a spot at which a five-star or prototypical instance of the relevant type gets coded. Less typical, incomplete, or noise-degraded echoes end up coded at various distances from the relevant prototypical hot spot."[27]

Properties of neural nets account for many of the observed characteristics of prototype phenomena. As we saw with color perception, gradations in synaptic weights and consequent differences in the amplitude of activation patterns account for degrees of category membership.[28] Other features of neural networks illuminate how prototypes can function as cognitive reference points. Although different models of neural networks have somewhat different characteristics, one property shared by all of them is that the activation of one part generally stimulates the rest of the network.[29] The existence of connections between related neural groups, moreover, means that the activation of one network can stimulate other related networks. Thus, it is easy to see how a prototype can "stand for" a category: Regardless of whether one is conscious of it, activation of the prototype has the effect of activating the entire category.

On much the same principle, the activation of a prototype can have the downstream effect of stimulating a variety of related categories. As the leading text on parallel distributive processing explains:

People are good at generalizing newly acquired knowledge. If you
learn a new fact about an object, your expectations about other similar
objects tend to change. If, for example, you learn that chimpanzees like
onions you will probably raise your estimate of the probabilities that gorillas like onions. In a network that uses distributive representations, this
kind of generalization is *automatic*. The new knowledge about chimpanzees is incorporated by modifying some of the connection strengths so as
to alter the causal effects of all similar activity patterns. So if the representation of gorillas is a similar activity pattern over the same set of units,
its causal effects will be changed in similar ways.[30]

This account corresponds almost precisely with the kinds of inferences-
from-prototypes found by Lance Rips. More importantly, the shared quality of the connections in neural nets yields a spontaneous capacity to generalize much like our own.

Corroboration also comes from the work of Bradley Seebach and his
colleagues, who tested whether language skills previously thought innate
could be the result of prenatal learning in response to experience in utero.
They took a neural net consisting of five "cells" that had previously been
used to model the kitten's visual cortex. They exposed it to a set of seventy-
four pronunciations of the unvoiced stop consonants [ka], [pa], and [ta] as
articulated by a single speaker. As the researchers explain, this approach is
"conceptually different from learning to recognize consonants as if they
were unrelated, indivisible units." On the rationalist assumption that categories conform to the logic of P or not-P, one would expect to "train the
network on a data base containing all stop consonants in a variety of contextual situations. . . . In this manner the net might be 'taught' to accept all
[k] sounds and reject all non-[k] sounds in many different environments."[31]
But Seebach and his colleagues wanted to test the network's ability to discriminate between *related* sounds. Aside from voicing, the English stop consonants are differentiated by the place of articulation: [ka] is articulated
with the back of the tongue; [pa] with the lips; and [ta] with the tip of the
tongue touching the aveolar ridge just behind the upper front teeth. "To develop a neuron's selectivity for a subphonemic feature that distinguishes the
consonant [k] from the consonants [p] and [t] (place of articulation), . . . the
best training set is one that contains only that feature distinction" (7474).

The training was unsupervised—that is, the network was trained
with random presentations of the stimulus set without the usual "back-
propagation" or feedback. Because of the limited number of cells in the net,

FIGURE 4.2   Cell Configuration, Self-Trained Neural Net

cell	1 [ta]	2 [ka]	3 [ka]	4 [pa]	5 [ta]
	Short high freq.	Long mid-to- low freq.	Long high freq.	Long low freq.	Long high freq.

only "5 features were extracted from the 440-dimensional original space." Cells 2 and 3 responded to [ka], with its long-duration burst across several frequencies; cell 4 responded to [pa], with its long, low-frequency burst; and cells 1 and 5 (though principally 1) responded to the short, high-frequency sound characteristic of [ta]. The results are summarized in figure 4.2. The trained net was able to identify and distinguish the sound successfully at a 98 percent rate of accuracy. It was, moreover, able to generalize that knowledge and classify new stimuli such as unvoiced stop consonants articulated by two additional speakers and voiced stop consonants articulated by all three speakers at a 96 percent rate of accuracy.

As represented in figure 4.2, the unprogrammed network instantiates what might be described fairly as a radial category. Note that the cells' organization is not linear: Recognition of the [ta] syllable is distributed across cells 1 and 5 rather than grouped together (as with the syllable [ka]). At the same time, the organization is not random. The central case (like Gorman and Sejnowski's "hot spots") consists of the characteristic long duration, high-frequency sound of the stop consonant [ka]. The nearer cells encode variations in frequency; the more distant cells are characterized by variations in sound duration.

On this interpretation, the category formed by the stop consonants centers on the convergence of the very different properties of duration and frequency, which implies that prototype effects may be produced by categories involving gestalt conditions—i.e., a confluence of factors whose sum is psychologically more fundamental than the individual parts. For categories with such gestalt structure, it will be the case that only some category members will display all the appropriate conditions; others (the extensions) will lack some or nearly all of the relevant qualities. Accordingly, any model of neural processing able to produce gestalt phenomena should also account for this variety of prototype effects.

As we saw in chapter 2, Edelman's RCI model of integration by means of reentrant signaling between global mappings is just such an account. As Edelman observes:

> The examples of reentry given in the RCI model indicate that it is possible
> through reentrant maps to generate integrated responses that could pro-
> vide bases for certain gestalt properties. . . . The major point, for which
> the model stands as a key example, is that because of its recursive nature
> and its involvement in global mappings, reentry also permits exchanges
> of signals in higher-order brain areas.[32]

In other words, the same capacities that enable the brain to integrate otherwise segregated perceptual submodalities to produce gestalt structures
should serve equally well to integrate the disparate neural activation patterns that constitute different subdimensions of a concept or category.

4. *Epiphenomenal character.* The evidence of the psychological reality
of prototype effects is overwhelming. It might seem natural, therefore, to infer that prototypes literally constitute mental representations and that prototype effects actually characterize category structure. Early on, Rosch assumed just that.[33] On this view, a prototype might compose the central case
of a category, and the goodness-of-example ratings might directly reflect the
structure of a category that is graded by degree of similarity to that central
case. Such categories would, of course, produce prototype effects, and they
can be modeled quite effectively in fuzzy logic.[34] But, as early as 1978, Rosch
warned that "to speak of a single entity that is the prototype is either a gross
misunderstanding of the empirical data or a covert theory of mental representation." The data, she explained, are consistent with many different models of category structure. The only model that does not fit the known facts
about prototype effects is the traditional one that defines categories in terms
of necessary and sufficient conditions.[35]

Nevertheless, there is an experimental literature purporting to assess
"prototype theories" of categorization of the sort that Rosch disclaimed.
These studies usually assume that prototype-based categories are organized
by typical features and that the category prototype consists of "the exemplar with average values on all of the dimensions along which the category's
exemplars vary."[36] Many of these studies announce the superiority of "exemplar models" of categorization, in which categories are "represented
simply as collections of exemplars."[37] But such conclusions are misleading.
One cannot prove the superiority of one's favored theory by testing it only
against a theory that no one really thinks is true. (Early on, Rosch identified exemplar models of categorization as but one of several different approaches—including both propositional and imagistic models—that accorded with the data on prototype effects.) Moreover, as even some of the
proponents of exemplar theory point out, many of the experiments "have

favored exemplar-based processes because they have featured small exemplar pools (about four items) and poorly differentiated categories."[38] Given these and other substantial theoretical limitations,* it is difficult to assess the value of many of these claims. Indeed, even exemplar theorists have noted that so-called prototype models better fit category-learning for some kinds of categories and at earlier stages of learning than do exemplar models.[39]

In any case, here is what we do know: Prototype effects cannot actually characterize category structure because there are many categories that are not graded but that, nevertheless, produce prototype effects. For example, some categories that are formally defined by necessary and sufficient criteria, like the odd numbers, still display prototype effects. So, too, nonclassical categories like "hand" that are not graded nevertheless produce prototype effects. Thus, a poker hand is surely a less prototypical example of the category "hand" than is the human limb. But, just as surely, it would be quite inaccurate to characterize a poker hand as lower on a graded scale of "hands" or as a "lesser" or "second-rate" hand. In the same vein, monopoly and baseball are prototypical games. But Frisbee and ring-around-the-roses are no "less" games, even though they are not prototypical.

In sum, graded categories will produce prototype effects, but not all categories with prototype effects are graded. Other kinds of category structure also produce prototype effects, such as categories formed by metaphoric and metonymic models (such as "hand" or "mouth") and categories characterized by imagistic and other models with gestalt properties. The question thus remains whether there is a unifying model that accounts for the prototype effects of these different kinds of categories.

One such contender is the set of "core-plus-identification" theories. These theories, recall, postulate that categories consist of a definitional core (the necessary and sufficient criteria) and a subsidiary, typicality-based identification procedure responsible for prototype effects. The evidence from neural networks, however, appears to contradict this view. The spreading activation patterns observed in neural nets suggest that prototypes are not

* In addition to the assumption that categories are organized around some form of feature recognition (rather than around imagistic and other interactional properties), these studies also frequently use highly abstract, fabricated categories—collections of nonsense syllables like *buno-kypa* and *mufa-vosy* or sets of stick figure insects with randomly distributed attributes. Recall that the original work of Rosch and Berlin studied real-world categories. (*See* chapter 2.) If the evolutionary assumption is correct—that human cognitive processes evolved as an adaptation to real-world interactions and needs—then the use of artificial stimuli in the laboratory may (or may not) force subjects to use unfamiliar strategies in identification.

just some "additional" identification mechanism but part of the "core" process of categorization. This latter interpretation is in fact borne out by data from independent research.

Barsalou and his colleagues conducted a series of experiments designed to test category stability.[40] They used a variety of category-related tasks to do so. In one experiment, half the subjects were asked to list average characteristics of a category's exemplars and half were asked to provide ideal characteristics. In a second experiment, "prototype subjects" were asked to list characteristics that were typical of a category's exemplars, while "definition subjects" were asked to provide a strict dictionary definition of the category. Barsalou and his colleagues found the greatest category stability (both across subjects and with the same subject across time) for the prototype and definition subjects. Moreover, category stability was virtually the same for prototype and definition subjects (.45 and .44, respectively, for across-subject tests; .67 and .66, respectively, for within-subject tests), and both groups "produced essentially the same properties overall and the same proportion of dictionary properties." Significantly, however, the prototype subjects produced this information *faster* than the definition subjects (7.99 seconds per property versus 9.40 seconds per property). In other words, subjects asked to produce prototypical characteristics accessed the *same* information about the relevant category, but they did so *more efficiently* than those asked to specify definitions.

The mechanisms that produce prototype effects must be integral to cognition and categorization, or they would not be reflected in the speed and efficiency of mental processing. Moreover, the fact that prototype effects encompass both "best examples" and reliable relative goodness-of-example ratings for other category members indicates that these mechanisms are internal aspects of category structure rather than supplementary judgments of frequency, familiarity, or "representativeness." In addition, the category structure that produces prototypes must be constitutive of concepts, or the resulting prototypes would not enter into reasoning—that is, we would find neither the kinds of asymmetric conclusions identified by Rips nor the apparently faulty inference patterns reported by Tversky and Kahneman.

Is the Pope a Bachelor?

The category "bachelor" is generally taken as the paradigm of a P-or-not-P category. Ronald Dworkin uses it as such, proclaiming that "bachelorhood holds of unmarried men."[41] But not every unmarried man is an equally good example of a bachelor. James Bond is surely a more proto-typical bachelor than Tarzan or the pope. Why should this be so?

We can effectively inquire into the conceptual basis of these prototype effects by considering the following sentences, either of which would be deemed correct by an ordinary English speaker:

1. *Technically,* the pope is a bachelor.
2. The pope may not be married, but he isn't *really* a bachelor.

These sentences and the intuitions they represent are problematic on the ra-tionalist model. Given the logic of P or not-P, the pope cannot be both a bachelor and not-a-bachelor. In other words, by the law of the excluded middle, he can be only one or the other. The rationalist, therefore, must ac-cept Dworkin's definition as an analytic truth and conclude that the pope *is* a bachelor. Moreover, the rationalist must reject as erroneous the intuition expressed in sentence 2.

In fact, it is the rationalist's premises and not these intuitions that are erroneous. Indeed, the rationalist's narrow, definitional view excludes every-thing that makes sense of the category "bachelor" and, with it, everything that makes sense of the intuitions expressed in the above sentences. Words, as Charles Fillmore explains, do not stand alone; they "represent catego-rizations of experience, and each of these categories is underlain by a moti-vating situation occurring against a background of knowledge and experi-ence." To understand whether a person is a bachelor, one must first ask "what reason a speech community might have found for creating the cate-gory represented by the word." [42] Fillmore explains:

> The noun *bachelor* can be defined as an unmarried adult man, but the noun clearly exists as a motivated device for categorizing people only in the context of a human society in which certain expectations about mar-riage and marriageable age obtain. Male participants in long-term un-married couplings would not ordinarily be described as bachelors; a boy abandoned in the jungle and grown to maturity away from contact with human society would not be called a bachelor; John Paul II is not prop-erly thought of as a bachelor.[43]

In other words, a "bachelor" is an unmarried man only with respect to an assumed set of background conditions in which there is a human society, a social institution of heterosexual marriage, a typical marriageable age, and a man who is not disqualified from marriage for some other reason. But these assumed conditions do not take into account such social realities as homosexuality, the priesthood, or the fact that people live together without getting married.

The intuitions represented by sentences 1 and 2 reflect just these complexities: The pope fits the formal definition of "bachelor" because he is an unmarried adult man. At the same time, however, he is not "really" a bachelor because the background conditions that "motivate" or *make sense of* the category simply do not hold for the pope. In general, the use of a hedge such as "technically" or the "but . . ." clause in sentence 2 signals a divergence from our ordinary background assumptions on the topic.[44] These departures are particularly revealing of category structure because they mark the absence of some expected dimensions of the standard category. The hedge "technically" indicates that the example conforms with the category's formal, reductive definition as given in some expert domain but that it nevertheless lacks some important feature or features of that category. (It is in just this sense that a formal definition can fairly be said to be "reductive.") The "but . . ." formulation marks a divergence from the prototypical or idealized conditions that form the presupposition of the sentence. In sentence 2, for example, the "but . . ." clause reflects the fact that the pope does not fit the ordinary assumption that single men are interested in women socially and sexually.

The observed prototype effects with respect to the category "bachelor" are a consequence of this kind of categorical structure—variously described as frames, scripts, schemas, scenarios, stock stories, and idealized cognitive models.[45] As Gerry López explains, the world

> is never approached as if it were *sui generis,* but rather is seen through these stock structures. Once the principal features of a given phenomenon suggest a particular stock structure, that structure shapes our expectations and responses. This use of stock structures resolves ambiguity and complements "given" information with much "assumed" information.[46]

Suppose, to use a well-known example, we enter a restaurant, seat ourselves, and are then confronted by a human with pad and pencil. Does this stranger want to hear our life stories? Challenge our right to enter the premises? Take our bet on the afternoon race? Any of these scenarios are possible and, on particular occasions, may in fact be the case. Yet, we "know" immediately that the person is asking for our order because we have automatically and unreflectively assumed a "restaurant scenario" that organizes our understanding of the events around us.[47]

A prototype effect is a consequence of this kind of idealized and conventionalized knowledge structure. Some cases will fit the model better than others. Or, to put it the other way, some models will "fit" the world more-or-less well. "Bachelor" produces prototype effects because, as Lakoff explains (70–71), bachelorhood holds of unmarried men only within the right context. In this case, the model that represents (or *re*-presents) that context characterizes some portions of the social world well and other portions quite poorly. Thus, even though "bachelor" is not a graded category, it nevertheless produces prototype effects.

Lakoff's concept of an *idealized cognitive model* (ICM) provides a more general approach to this idea of category structure. Similar to Fillmore's notion of a frame, an ICM is a "folk" theory or cultural understanding that organizes knowledge of events, people, objects, and their characteristic relationships in a single gestalt structure that is experientially meaningful as a whole. For example, our understanding of the words "buy," "sell," "cost," "goods," "advertise," "credit," and so on are meaningful in terms of an ICM of a commercial transaction that relates them together as a structured activity. The use of any of these words individually evokes an entire picture or model—that is, a holistic standardized account of some area of human endeavor. Among the features that typically constitute an ICM are:

- ontological entities (including actors, objects, places, events, states, actions, etc.)
- properties of those entities
- relations between those entities
- temporal sequences of events and actions
- internal structures of events
- causal relations between events
- other patterns of inferences and relations among entities or events

An ICM is idealized because it does not "fit" actual, lived situations in a one-to-one correspondence. Rather, as we saw with "bachelor" (and as we shall explore in greater depth in the next two sections), an ICM captures our "normal" expectations as they are shaped by cultural practices and conditions. These expectations, therefore, tend to reflect only probabilistic truths about our day-to-day experiences; typically, they also embody a culture's normative values and ideals. An ICM, in other words, represents the set of default assumptions operative within a culture.

The concept of an idealized cognitive model improves on its predecessor conceptions (frames, scripts, schemas, etc.) in two important respects. First, it provides a more general, overarching abstraction capable of accommodating the many different forms of categorical and conceptual structures identified in the literature. Second, it provides a more supple theoretical tool that better explains the complexities of radial categories.

Not all concepts can be captured adequately by the propositional model of a frame or script, though these models do capture "bachelor." Other models are organized by means of metaphors, image-schemas, and image-mappings; accordingly, they require a different set of conceptual tools capable of conveying their operation and structure.[48] The next chapter, for example, explores how a single metaphoric and image-schematic model motivates an extensive and quite diverse radial category that includes both folktales and conventional scholarly argument. Chapter 7 analyzes the metaphorical model that underlies "under color of" law and related areas of state action doctrine. Chapter 10 examines the generative role played by some familiar metaphors—including Holmes's famous "marketplace of ideas"—in the emergence of a modern First Amendment. Still other models are metonymic; this is the case, as Lakoff points out (84–88), with familiar social stereotypes.

Each of these models differs for the others, but despite these differences, they are all ICMs and, thus, share several features: (1) They are grounded in or draw upon direct physical or cultural knowledge; (2) they are highly generalized in order to capture and relate together a broad range of particularized fact situations; (3) they are not objective representations of reality but idealizations that effectively characterize some but not all of the varied situations that humans confront in their day-to-day interactions; and (4) they all produce prototype effects.

We can illustrate this last point by turning to the second advantage of the cognitive models approach: its greater usefulness in describing the complexities that arise from radial categories. Consider the many conventional subcases of the category "mother." There are *working* mothers, *unwed* mothers, *biological* mothers, *birth* mothers, *genetic* mothers, *surrogate* mothers, *single* mothers, *adoptive* mothers, *foster* mothers, and good-old-fashioned *stepmothers*.

Many of these subcases cannot be explained in rationalist, set-theoretic terms: A working mother is not simply one of the subset of mothers who have jobs; neither is an unwed mother one of the subset of mothers who are not married.* Thus, an unwed mother who gives her child up for adoption and then goes out and gets a job is not a "working mother." This is so even though she *is* working and is—at least, technically—still a mother. By the same token, suppose that the child is then adopted by an unmarried woman who is a full-time, tenured professor at an Ivy League law school. *She*, no doubt, is a working mother. But it would be odd—if not, indeed, insulting—to describe the author of *The Alchemy of Race and Rights* as an unwed mother.[49] So, too, a woman whose husband had died and left her with young children would not be referred to as an unwed mother.

"Surrogate mother" raises yet a different problem. The term is conventionally used to refer to the biological mother—who may be both birth mother and genetic mother—and not to the woman who subsequently adopts and cares for the child. Why is it the birth mother and not the adoptive mother who is understood as the substitute?

Fillmore's notion of a frame is only partially helpful in sorting out these complications. The central case of "mother" assumes natural childbirth by a married woman who is the child's primary nurturer and caretaker. The subcases mark divergences from these stereotypical assumptions. In subcases like "adoptive mother" and "single mother," for example, the modifier signals that the subcase varies from the central model in the specified dimension. In subcases like "birth mother" and "genetic mother," in contrast, the modifier signals that the subcase coincides with the central model only in the specified dimension. But this frame-based approach does not explain the expressions "working mother" and "unwed mother" because, as we have seen, a case can diverge from the central model in the specified dimension and still not be so characterized. And this approach says little about which mother is the "real" mother and which the "surrogate."

What does account for these phenomena is the fact that the category "mother" has a much more complex internal structure than can be captured by Fillmore's notion of a frame. The assumptions that characterize the central model for "mother" give rise to a prototype effect in the form of the once prevalent social stereotype of the mother as housewife. In this traditional stereotype, the mother is a married woman who is her child's *full-time* caretaker. A working mother is defined in contrast to this stereotype. A biological mother who is no longer responsible for her child's nurturance

---

* For the same reason, the category "mother" cannot be specified in necessary and sufficient conditions for membership. There is no single set of criteria that encompasses biological mothers, birth mothers, and genetic mothers, on one hand, and surrogate mothers, adoptive mothers, and foster mothers, on the other.

is not a "working" mother even if she has a job because, as Lakoff observes, "only mothers for whom nurturance is an issue can be so categorized" (80–81). As a prototype, the housewife stereotype continues to anchor the "mother" category, notwithstanding its increasing social disintegration. Thus, the decline of the traditional stereotype has not led to a change in the central case but rather to the emergence of the new subcategory of *full-time* mother, which is defined in contrast to the increasing prevalence of working mothers.

The concept "mother" is a cluster model characterized by the convergence of several cognitive models, including a birth model, a nurturance model, and a marital model. These models are independently productive: The nurturance model, for example, is what motivates the verb form "to mother." As Lakoff notes (76, 82), moreover, "Daddy" is defined relative to the nurturance model. (I can happily report that my children frequently call me "Momma.") It is the birth model, in contrast, that motivates the expression "the mother lode." Similarly, the birth model is what motivates the metaphorical use of the term to connote causation, as in the familiar adage "Necessity is the mother of invention" and Wallace Stevens's remarkably poetic line "Death is the mother of beauty." [50]

"Surrogate mother" is defined relative to the marital and nurturance models. "Unwed mother," in contrast, presupposes the birth model, which is why adoptive mothers are not unwed mothers, regardless of their marital status. But even this explanation is incomplete; as Lakoff points out, "we would normally not use the term [*unwed mother*] . . . for a millionaire actress who chose to have a child out of wedlock" (82). Rather, as with the surrogate mother submodel, the unwed mother submodel is further characterized by a negative social stereotype. At the core of this stereotype is the assumption that the unwed mother cannot or does not want to care for her child. This stereotype, too, produces prototype effects: A teenage mother is a prototypical unwed mother; the television character Murphy Brown, who both wants and is prepared to care for her child, is not. This same social logic—in which the nurturance model is *normatively* privileged—accounts for the meaning of "surrogate mother." The surrogate mother, like the unwed mother, is prepared to give up her offspring to someone else. The woman who undertakes to nurture the child is the one who is socially esteemed as the "real" mother. Conversely, the birth mother is denigrated as the "substitute" because she does not care for the child she bore.

To summarize, the concept "mother" is a complex radial category characterized by a cluster of converging models. The cluster model itself produces prototype effects, but so do several of the submodels. The cognitive models approach thus provides a particularly valuable theoretical tool that enables richer and more detailed descriptions of complex categories—descriptions, moreover, that better explain actual patterns of usage than do competing conceptualizations.

The concept of an idealized cognitive model also elucidates the phenomenon of prototype effects. In general, we can say that prototype effects occur with any graded category, any radial category (including those based on metaphorical models), and any cognitive model that involves gestalt conditions. In all these cases, there will be some category members that will most fully embody all of the characteristic attributes or features of the category and other category members that either lack some of those traits or exhibit them only to a lesser degree. We might say, with an ironic nod to Dworkin, that prototypes hold of nonbinary structures.

Feminist Tellers and Rationalist Faith

The cognitive models approach provides straightforward explanations for the apparently illogical patterns of inference described by Rips and by Tversky and Kahneman. The asymmetric inference patterns found by Rips occur because less central subcategories or category members are understood as variants of the central model. In other words, the patterns of inference would run in both directions—that is, from robins to ducks and vice versa—if the relationship between central case and subsidiary category member were linear or if both were derived in parallel fashion. This would be true, for example, if the category members were deduced from some common principle or derived from some set of necessary and sufficient criteria. Because, however, peripheral category members are constructed as modifications of the central case, they represent nonlinear functions that necessarily produce asymmetric patterns of inference.

The Tversky and Kahneman findings also result from the operation of mental models. Tversky and Kahneman found that people's predictions of events violated the logic of probability theory: For example, the probability that an earthquake in California will cause a flood in which 1,000 people drown is necessarily lower than the probability of a flood causing 1,000 fatalities *anywhere* in North America, because the latter prospect necessarily includes not only the former scenario *but many others as well*. Yet, Tversky and Kahneman found that with respect to examples like this one, subjects consistently rated the conjunction (earthquake + flood) more probable than its constituent parts. They explain this logical fallacy as a consequence of cognitive models. "It is . . . natural and economical for the probability of an event to be evaluated by the degree to which that event is representative of an appropriate mental model" (295). In other words, the apparently erroneous probability judgment is a prototype effect. The prototypical case is deemed more likely than its propositionally broader variant because it better fits our mental model of the relevant domain.

But how does a conjunctive event like "a California earthquake that causes a flood" come to be a prototype in the first place? Certainly not because it is such a common event. Rather, as Tversky and Kahneman explain, the prototypicality of the conjunction is itself a consequence or byproduct of the underlying model. As noted earlier, a cognitive model typically includes among its features representations of relations between entities and events. An ICM of a commercial transaction, for example, relates buyers and sellers together in a structured activity that contains particular roles and relations. Understandably, causal connections will be among the most important relations modeled by an ICM. The conjunction errors found by Tversky and Kahneman occurred when the conjoined events tracked stereotypical causal relations or when the questions otherwise employed elements that fit together in the relevant mental model (304–8).

This last point bears emphasis: *Tversky and Kahneman used conjunctive conditions that were designed to elicit prototype effects.* Not surprisingly, they found precisely those effects. Their conclusions, therefore, must be viewed with a certain amount of caution. Examples such as the California earthquake problem establish that conjunction errors do occur. But there is reason to question their broader suggestion that these results represent a fundamental problem with reasoning by means of cognitive models.

Tversky and Kahneman acknowledge that their problems "were constructed to elicit conjunction errors" and, consequently, concede that "they do not provide an unbiased estimate of the prevalence of these errors." They nevertheless argue that, because "the conjunction error is only a symptom of a more general phenomenon" of reasoning by means of mental models, the "basic phenomenon may be considerably more common than the extreme symptom by which it was illustrated" (311). Tversky and Kahneman want to have it both ways, in fact. On one hand, they acknowledge that although the "focus on bias and illusion is a research strategy that exploits human error, . . . it neither assumes nor entails that people are . . . cognitively inept." On the other hand, they offer just that conclusion: "The evidence does not seem to support a truth plus error model, . . . and we suspect that incoherence is more than skin deep" (313).

We should reject Tversky and Kahneman's "suspicion" because it is an artifact of their rationalist presuppositions. Consider a typical Tversky and

Kahneman question. Subjects were asked to rate the likelihood of the following predictions:

- a complete suspension of diplomatic relations between the USA and the Soviet Union, sometime in 1983
- a Russian invasion of Poland, and a complete suspension of diplomatic relations between the USA and the Soviet Union, sometime in 1983

Subjects ranked the second scenario more probable, even though, as the researchers observe, "*suspension* is necessarily more probable than *invasion and suspension*" (307–8). But this conclusion is true only in the abstract: In other words, this conclusion is true only on a rationalist, set-theoretic understanding in which the set of events represented by "suspension of diplomatic relations" necessarily includes the subset represented by "invasion and suspension."

But people don't think in the abstract; they think in the concrete.[51] In the concrete, most people would judge the prospect of a complete suspension of diplomatic relations between the United States and the former Soviet Union as extremely unlikely—that is, at least without a lot more information that might plausibly justify so drastic an action. More precisely, Tversky and Kahneman presume that subjects understand the first scenario in a *literal*, propositional fashion. A cognitive models approach, in contrast, would expect subjects to understand the two scenarios and evaluate the probability of each only relative to some background ICM that provides a context within which the predictions are rendered meaningful. It would expect subjects to bring to these predictions a set of understandings concerning the nature of international relations, the reasons that nations establish and maintain diplomatic relations, the costs that are incurred when relations are suspended, and the kinds of grounds on which suspension of relations might be deemed appropriate. When asked to rate the probability that superpower adversaries like the United States and the former Soviet Union would completely suspend diplomatic relations, subjects could be expected to understand and evaluate that question relative to the default assumptions embodied in those background understandings. Consequently, we would expect subjects to rank the first prediction as unlikely since they would evaluate it against a background web of understandings in which suspension of diplomatic relations is understood as a dangerous and drastic act. At the same time, the identical assumptions would render the second prediction more plausible precisely because those assumptions provide a context in which such action might make sense.

We can put the point more generally by recalling López's observation that people do not approach statements concerning potential states of affairs as if each were sui generis. Rather, they perceive and discriminate new circumstances in terms of an eliciting model (or models) that "resolves ambiguity and complements 'given' information with much 'assumed' information." [52] In these terms, the subjects would understand the two predictions presented by the researchers as disjunctive alternatives: In effect, they would perceive the first statement as a prediction that the two superpowers would suspend diplomatic relations without adequate reason (which, obviously, is improbable). Thus, the subjects probability rankings are not only perfectly consistent with probability theory, they are eminently reasonable.

We can observe the same pattern with a second of Tversky and Kahneman's questions. Subjects were given a personality sketch of someone named Linda and then asked to rate the likelihood of various statements about her. They were told that Linda had been a philosophy major and that as a student she had been an activist concerned with issues of discrimination and social justice. Subjects were then asked to rate the likelihood that Linda was (among other things): (1) an active feminist; (2) a bank teller; and (3) a bank teller who is an active feminist. Eighty-five percent rated it more likely that Linda was a feminist bank teller than a bank teller. The researchers obtained similar results with more sophisticated subjects (i.e., graduate students with training in statistics and probability theory) and with a series of increasingly transparent attempts to highlight the logical fallacy (299–300). But when the personality sketch was omitted, "almost all respondents obeyed the conjunction rule and ranked the conjunction (bank teller and active feminist) as less probable than its constituents" (305).

As noted earlier, Tversky and Kahneman conclude that conjunction errors occur when there is a causal relation between the model established by the personality sketch and the attributes given in the question (e.g., feminist bank teller). Tversky and Kahneman, although correctly identifying the role of cognitive models in producing such prototype effects, wholly fail to consider the role that such models play in structuring their respondents' understanding and evaluation of the questions. If they had considered this, they might have realized that those subjects' responses do not necessarily violate the conjunction rule.

As Tversky and Kahneman note, "the stereotypes of bank teller and feminist are mildly incompatible" (305). Accordingly, the likelihood that a feminist like Linda would choose to work in a gender-stereotyped job such as a bank teller is relatively low. Not surprisingly, subjects rated that prediction quite low—which is what we would expect given what we know about Linda's values, beliefs, and likely motivations. That Linda is a *feminist* bank teller, on the other hand, is more probable, if only because that prediction preserves some consistency of character and belief over time.* In other words, we could expect subjects to process the contrast between statements 2 and 3 as if they read "Linda is a feminist bank teller" and "Linda is [just] a bank teller." Given what we know about human motivation (in this case, information supplied by a background model and the personality sketch) the latter *is* unlikely. In contrast, subjects correctly evaluated the abstract probabilities—that it is more likely that a random person is a bank teller than that she is a feminist bank teller—when the form of the question did not provide the personality sketch.

As we have seen again and again, one corollary of the principle of antinomial capture is that incoherence is often just an artifact of rationalism's too rigid insistence on the deracinated model of formal logic. Subjects' predictions do not conform to the deductive, mechanical logic presumed by probability theory and tested for by Tversky and Kahneman for the simple reason that human categorization does not follow the propositional, set-theoretic model to which they accord normative status (313). When those predictions are reconsidered on a cognitive models approach, what appeared irrational turns out to be perfectly logical. Tversky and Kahneman's broad suggestion that incoherence is a common consequence of reasoning by means of cognitive models is exposed as little more than the bias of their rationalist faith: Although people's predictions do violate the logic of probability theory some of the time, Tversky and Kahneman's more expansive claims are a product of their rationalist-inspired misinterpretations of the data.

Most of the time, people's predictions of real-world behavior focus quite rationally on concrete, context-dependent assessments of the probabilities. Reasoning by means of cognitive models represents a perfectly rational adaptation to the needs of contextual decisionmaking. Real-world judgments require discriminations that are sensitive to motivational and situational complexities, and that is just what reasoning in terms of cognitive models provides. Moreover, as Barsalou's findings suggest, reasoning in terms of cognitive models and the resulting prototype effects yields significant overall efficiencies in cognitive processing.

Consider the vast amount of everyday knowledge (e.g., where a door

---

* Presumably, subjects would rationalize the nonprototypical career choice by positing a scenario in which economic circumstances or some other external factor compelled Linda to accept the available employment.

leads, what a red light means, how one behaves in a supermarket) that the average human needs in order to function successfully in the physical and social world. The sheer mass of it would overwhelm one's cognitive resources if it were necessary to recall this information consciously before it could be used. Consider the case of the beginning driver whose hesitancy and conspicuous difficulty are a direct consequence of the need to mediate all of her actions and decisions consciously. Learning to drive is a process of internalizing and making tacit both the physical skills of operating a vehicle and the basic rules of the road. Only then will the novice driver be able to focus attention on the road and learn to coordinate with the traffic around her.

Effective adaptation to one's physical and social environment is dependent on the embeddedness or *sedimentation* of innumerable background conceptions. The buildup of meanings and assumptions permits a person to employ previously internalized cultural conceptions without the need to synthesize them anew.[53] In this way, the sedimentation represented by cognitive models enables a person to operate at relatively higher levels of abstraction and complexity, "opening the way for innovations that demand a higher level of attention."[54]

Twenty-Two Words for Snow

Fillmore's genuinely pragmatic conception of motivation changes our whole notion of categorization. Fillmore's insight is that words such as "mother" and "bachelor" represent categorizations of experience that a speech community adopts for a *reason*. To know why a community has a category such as "unwed mother" or "bachelor" is to know something about how that community lives, the things it values, the norms it obeys. It has long been recognized that categorization is socially contingent in the sense that different societies use different categories. But the fact that categorization is motivated means that it is socially contingent in the more important sense that many of a society's categories encode its customary functions, its standard repertoire of purposes, its conventional roles, its approved modes of behavior. Once we recognize that function and purpose serve as elements of or frames for those categories, we cannot escape the conclusion that categorization is a profoundly *normative* process.

There is no mistaking, for example, the patriarchal values and assumptions that characterize the central case of "mother." Nor can one make sense of the "bachelor" category absent the entire set of quite traditional normative expectations about marriage, family life, and gender roles. These normative expectations are clear once one considers that, as Fillmore points out, there is no female equivalent for "bachelor" (which is why the 1960s television show *The Dating Game* had to coin the term "bachelorette").[55] The closest counterpart is "spinster"; but this term represents a different, largely negative stereotype of a woman past marrying age who is, moreover, presumed beyond sexual interest. Categories such as "mother," "bachelor," and "spinster" participate in and reproduce an entire set of contingent cultural understandings that reflect unreconstructed notions of gender roles. They exemplify the way in which language encodes and preserves sedimented social understandings long past their point of obsolescence.[56]

Categorization is socially contingent in the third sense that it is dependent or *contingent on* cultural conditions and practices that are themselves constantly in flux. As more women work outside the home, for example, the "working mother" subcategory has increasingly come to define our expectations. Consequently, the new subcategory *full-time* mother has emerged through a process of chaining as a kind of back-formation defined in contrast to working mother. Developments in reproductive technology have led to the fragmentation of the *biological* mother into *birth* mothers, *genetic* mothers, and *surrogate* mothers. Social changes such as the escalating divorce rate and the widespread entry of women into all sectors of the job market have led to the increased prevalence and acceptance of *single* mothers. So, too, in the last few decades, "bachelor" and "spinster" have lost currency in the face of massive upheavals in social and sexual mores. These anachronistic terms have largely been replaced by the uniform, nongendered "singles." What we see in these cases is a motivated process of categorization operating in a flexible and dynamic fashion and proliferating new subcategories through chaining and transformations of the underlying cognitive models.

The flexibility of language-categories—that is, the capacity to accommodate variations of context and purpose—is not unique to social categories like "mother." Although it may appear that basic-level categories like "snow" and "chair" are statically descriptive, they are no less motivated than any other category employed by a given speech community. It is not just the Inuit (the so-called Eskimos) who have many different words for snow.* English "boasts not just *snow, slush,* and *sleet* and their derivatives but also count nouns like *avalanche* and *blizzard,* technical terms like *hardpack* and *powder,* expressive meteorological descriptive phrases like *flurry*

---

* Lakoff wryly observes: "Possibly the most boring thing a linguistics professor has to suffer . . . is the interminable discussion of the 22 (or however many) words for snow in Eskimo" (308).

and *dusting,* compounds with idiosyncratic meanings like *snow cornice,* and so on." [57] Inuits, skiers, and ordinary automobile drivers all need a finely differentiated language for snow in order to perform their respective activities successfully. Thus, although descriptive categories may be *defined* without reference to purpose or function, they operate nevertheless as motivated tools reflective of cultural purposes and needs. As such, they display the same sensitivity and adaptability to context and purpose as other linguistic categories.

"Snow" exemplifies how localized domains of experience ground different categories or vocabularies.[58] But, at least in one respect, it is not particularly representative of the flexible capacity of linguistic categorization: Snow, even in its many varieties, can still be characterized by way of common properties specifiable as necessary and sufficient conditions. But radial categories, with their more-or-less patterns of membership, better reflect the dynamic quality of much linguistic categorization. This ability to distinguish among category members is a crucial part of the ordinary linguistic competence that makes it possible for humans to function in and adapt successfully to the flux and complexity of the real world.

Consider the following example:

> Suppose you say to me, "We're having a discussion group over tonight, and I need four more chairs. Can you bring them?" I say "Sure," and show up with a hardback chair, a rocking chair, a beanbag chair, and a hassock. Leaving them in your living room, I report to you in the kitchen, "I brought the four chairs you wanted." In this situation, my statement is true, since the four objects I've brought will serve the purpose of chairs for an informal discussion group. Had you instead asked me to bring four chairs for a formal dinner party and I show up with the same four objects and make the same statement, you will not be appropriately grateful and will find the statement somewhat misleading or false, since the hassock, the beanbag chair, and the rocker are not practical as "chairs" at a formal dinner. This shows that our categories (e.g., CHAIR) are not rigidly fixed in terms of inherent properties of the objects themselves. What counts as an instance of a category depends on our purpose in using the category.[59]

A rationalist might say that this example shows only how pragmatics and subjective purpose modify meaning (and introduce ambiguity). We can test this interpretation by refining the hypothetical. Suppose all you know is that a friend called and left the message, "Come at eight; bring a chair."

You are not sure whether a dinner party or discussion group is in the offing. You decide to play it safe and bring a dining room chair because it would be appropriate in either case. This, then, would seem to be the best candidate for the "literal" meaning of the word "chair." But suppose that having received the same message, you arrive home to discover your spouse engaged in an impromptu card game. All the dining room chairs are occupied, so you grab the only available chair and head to your friend's home. The host opens the door and, seeing you with rocking chair in hand, says (with obvious annoyance),"Why did you bring *that!*" "But," you respond defensively, "you said bring a *chair.*"

You would, of course, be right: There is no question that a rocker is *literally* a chair, that it is a full-fledged member of the category "chair," that you had faithfully complied with your host's request to the best of your ability under the circumstances. Nevertheless you failed to bring the right *kind* of chair. Although the dining room chair and the rocker both fall within the literal meaning of "chair," they are not equally "chairs," which is to say that the category "chair" has an internal structure that varies with purpose and use.

In a basic-level case such as "chair," the central model is organized in terms of function relative to human body structure. Competent English speakers naturally and unreflectively evaluate particular instances (like a rocker or hassock) in terms of its relative fit both with their particular culture's idealized model of a chair and with the particular purpose at hand. Given this structure, prototypical chairs will be appropriate in nearly every context. But many category members within the category's "literal" purview will not function in every context that calls for a chair. Moreover, borderline cases like a hassock may be treated as "peripheral" or "related" instances of the category that are included only in certain circumstances. In other words, the prototypical cases constitute only a subset of any category; the broader, "literal" reach of any category is subject to expansion or adjustment relative to purpose because context and purpose are routinely built-in, constitutive dimensions of linguistic categorization.

Thus, our whole notion of categorization *does* change once we have grasped the implications of the concept of motivation. "A concept," Llewellyn wisely noted, "is built for a purpose. It is a thinking tool. It is to make your data more manageable in doing something, in getting somewhere." [60] Once we understand that categories are motivated, we can no longer see them as just static or stable classifications of like objects or states of affairs. Categorization must be dynamic if it is to accommodate the motivational and situational complexities of real life; it is an adaptive process that requires evaluation of context and purpose (even if unconsciously and automatically). In other words, categorization is already a form of decisionmaking, of reasoning, and of judgment. Because context-dependent decisionmaking is the crux of law, ordinary categorization is an indispensable and often decisive element of legal decisionmaking. As Llewellyn put it: "If there is the slightest doubt about the classification of the facts—though they be undisputed—the rule cannot decide the case; it is decided by the classifying." [61]

RATIONAL ANIMALS

We can consolidate this long and difficult chapter by considering the operation of a simple legal rule. The example comes from Fred Schauer, who offers it to illustrate his formalist claim that the "literal" language of a rule can constrain legal decisionmaking in a way that reasoning from the purpose of the rule does not. However, what the example in fact establishes is that one cannot even parse a rule without making use of everything we have learned about prototypicality, function-based categorization, and normatively infused judgment.

Schauer asks us to consider a rule prohibiting "live animals on the bus." [62] Does it bar a live goldfish in a sealed plastic bag? Schauer indicates that because the fish is literally an "animal," the prohibition should apply. A decisionmaker interpreting the rule in light of its purpose, on the other hand, would allow the fish because it does not threaten the kind of mischief (e.g., disturbing the passengers) contemplated by the rule. For Schauer, this split between the rule and its underlying purpose is a consequence of the rule's formulation in language:

> The language in which a rule is written and the purpose behind that rule can diverge precisely because that purpose is plastic in a way that language is not. . . . It is because purpose is not reduced to a concrete set of words that it retains its sensitivity to novel cases, to bizarre applications, and to the complex unfolding of human experience. [63]

To Schauer, what distinguishes a rule *as* a rule is the relative inflexibility of its language—what he elsewhere ascribes to the phenomenon of "entrenched generalizations" that are supposed to impede "the possibility of an infinitely sensitive and adaptable language." [64]

I put aside until chapter 8 the more detailed argument concerning the nature of rules, how they work, and the fatal problems of rule formalism and legal positivism. But at this stage, it is already clear that Schauer's account is utterly implausible. How can the decisionmaker parse the rule without being sensitive to "the complex unfolding of human experience?" Suppose a passenger boards the bus carefully carrying a specimen case containing slides for a microscope. Upon inquiry, the driver ascertains that the slides contain live paramecia. Must the driver bar the paramecia from the bus? If that seems silly, consider that—as organisms that "can move voluntarily, actively acquire food and digest it internally, and [that] have sensory . . . systems that allow them to respond rapidly to stimuli"—paramecia fall within the literal definition of an "animal."[65]

The deep problem is that a literal approach to the rule is literally impossible. If the rule does not apply literally to the paramecia, then why does it apply literally to the goldfish? After all, the dictionary also defines "animal" as "a mammal, as opposed to a fish, bird, etc."[66] Worse yet, if paramecia and goldfish are literal animals, then why do we allow *humans* on the bus? Humans, too, are literally animals: We are mammals with sensory systems who respond to stimuli and move voluntarily.

The entire notion of literal language is, in fact, incoherent—if by literal language we mean any reductive view of meaning as reference that functions after purpose and context have been shorn away. For, as the rule regarding animals on the bus demonstrates, meaning *requires* an understanding of context and purpose. There is nothing "simple" or "literal" about this rule— *nor could there be.* If examples of this sort have a naïve "cat on the mat" quality to them, it is only because they are chosen from basic-level categories in order to illustrate persuasively the "relatively" unproblematic nature of meaning. But, as we saw with the "clearing in the forest" trope discussed in chapter 1, what is psychologically simple because conventional and familiar may nevertheless involve quite complex cognitive processes.

Because the rule employs the superordinate category "animal," its "literal" scope potentially covers the entire domain that runs from paramecia all the way to Homo sapiens. From the specification of that category, we know only that the rule certainly applies to such prototypical category members as dogs, cats, and the like—if it applies to anything. To know (that is, to judge) how much of the "literal" reach of the category to include in the rule, we must interpolate what we know about the category "bus"—what it is for, who uses it, what types of problems or disturbances might concern its passengers, and so on. This implicit consideration of "bus" is how we know automatically that the rule prohibiting live animals on the bus cannot possibly apply to *us;* it is how we know *without having even to consider it* that humans are not animals for purposes of the rule. By the same token, it is this general background knowledge that makes the paramecia and goldfish cases seem silly to all but the most rigid bureaucratic mind-set.

In other words, the "bus" concept frames the category "animal"—just as the concepts "dinner party" and "discussion group" differentially framed the category "chair." It is this framing that enables the identification of those extensions of the category that are relevant to the purposes of the rule and those that are not. In this way, the rule forms its own gestalt structure or ICM consisting of the interaction of these two categories, *and this ICM itself produces prototype effects.*

The "hard" cases are those that match these prototypes relatively closely without actually fitting the representative case—seeing-eye dogs, for example, assuming no formal exception. Only in such cases does the decision-maker *need* consciously to consult the rules underlying purposes and values to determine whether the particular instance fits the model marked out by the rule. Considering what one knows about buses and seeing-eye dogs, the decisionmaker might reason that the dog's leash and special training palliate the need for the rule's application in light of its purpose. But even so, there is no difference in kind between the conscious recourse to the policies behind the rule and the tacit knowledge or unconscious process by which we "know" that the rule does not apply to humans or, indeed, to paramecia.

In short, even the "simplest" rule makes sense only against the backdrop of a massive cultural tableau that provides the tacit background assumptions that render it intelligible. Formalists just do not understand human cognition. Meaning is not a property of words or of the categories they signify, but of human thought. For this reason meaning cannot be reduced either to literal language or to analytic definitions that neglect the motivations behind human categorizations of experience. Word-categories and rule-categories always retain their sensitivity to novel cases, unusual applications, and the complex unfolding of human experience.

CHAPTER 5

Compositional Structure

ONE OF the figures of the Jewish communities of eastern Europe was the *magid,* an itinerant teller of tales who spoke in synagogues on the Sabbath. One of these, the Magid of Dubnow, was famous for his ability to come up with just the right story or parable on any subject for every occasion. An admirer once asked the magid how he did it: How could he learn and remember so many stories and parables? The magid responded with the following story.

A traveler walking in the forest came across an extraordinary sight. On every tree, there was a target with an arrow dead center. Marveling at the marksmanship, the traveler followed the trail of bull's-eyes in search of the archer. Eventually, he came across a small boy with a bow and arrow. The traveler asked the boy where he had learned such skillful archery. "Well," the boy explained, "first I shoot at a tree. Then I draw a target around the arrow."

"It's the same with me," said the magid. "First I find out the subject, then I make up a story to fit." [1]

Robert Cover maintains that "law and narrative are inseparably related." [2] If so, the magid's tale is threatening because it epitomizes the conventional view of storytelling as the height of subjectivity. Many people assume that a storyteller is free to tell any story, expressing any message she desires. This intuitive view seems yet more compelling when the narrator is a powerful official like a judge, backed by the might and authority of the state. If law is fused with narrative, then it seems to face precisely the problem of subjectivity that it strives so hard to avoid.

This fear is symptomatic of what Merleau-Ponty calls "the rationalist's dilemma: either the free act is possible, or it is not—either the event originates in me or is imposed on me from outside." [3] But this fear is mistaken. The judge, no less than others, is enmeshed in and dependent upon the structures of social meaning that make communication possible. That, in a sense, is Cover's larger point.[4] As we have seen, moreover, imagination is systematic and orderly rather than chaotic or anarchic. Thus, it is precisely *because* storytelling is an imaginative and profoundly social process that it is highly structured and quite regular in operation.

This chapter develops the profound implications of radial categorization by idealized cognitive models. It does so by introducing the idea of structure as *compositional*—that is, as a process that constrains and enables rather than determines.[5] I show how a single, elegant model animates both an endless number of stories *and* an array of narrative-types, extending all the way from folktales to the avant-garde.[6] Instead of the reified notion of structure as static and deterministic, we will examine how imaginative structure is simultaneously systematic and dynamic, predictable but not determinate.

This discussion concretizes several of the claims of the previous chapter. Narrative provides a particularly rich and detailed example of a radial category whose imaginative structure makes it highly flexible and productive. Narrative also provides an opportunity to describe further the make-up and workings of ICMs. Most importantly, this discussion of narrative serves as a vehicle for exploring the issue of indeterminacy in law. The same processes of narrative construction and reconstruction are implicated in the construction and interpretation of law. Cognitive models play an indispensable role in recognizing, constructing, and interpreting stories of all types, just as they enable us to make sense of and apply a simple rule prohibiting animals on the bus. Thus, this chapter completes the framework for chapter 8's examination of legal rules and chapter 10's account of innovation. Following a rule, it turns out, is much like following a story. And innovation in law is, with one interesting modification, a lot like composing a story.

Thus, this chapter illustrates what is perhaps the most important lesson of this book. In the same way that our cognitive models enable us to recognize stories *as* stories and to determine (i.e., interpret) their meaning, so, too, do they shape our expectations and perceptions with respect to what we deem credible, what we perceive accurate, what we find persuasive. To illustrate this point, I consider the ongoing debate over the role of narrative

in law. The jurisprudential mainstream has been deeply conflicted about
the relevance of narrative. Where Ronald Dworkin and Owen Fiss have invoked the idea of narrative to bolster the law's claim to rigor and meaning,[7]
other scholars have expressed skepticism about the turn to narrative in legal scholarship.[8] But close examination of these claims reveals the degree to
which they rest on little more than the expectations engendered by our conventional categories or models. Indeed, the apparently self-evident difference between standard legal scholarship and the more voguish narrative approaches is nothing more than an artifact of the most banal conventions.
Fanciful as it may sound, standard legal scholarship is just a special case of
storytelling. Conversely, narrative is just a particularly powerful kind of rational argument.

THE TRAVEL SECTION

The word "narrative" derives from the Latin *narrare* ("to tell") and
gnarus ("having knowledge or experience").[9] There is an intimate relation
between *narrare* as "telling" and *gnarus* as "having experience." There is no
telling that is not based in experience and no experience that is not already
a telling. To put it differently, reason is a faculty that occurs only in embodied social creatures situated in and interacting with a physical and social environment. Meaning is neither "in us" nor "out there" but resides in
the imaginative processes by which we order experience and make it meaningful. As Cover says, narratives "are the trajectories plotted upon material
reality by our imaginations."[10]

Like all human understanding, therefore, there is an important sense in
which narrative understanding is "constructed." But it does not follow that
narrative is subjective, arbitrary, or unconstrained. To the contrary, narrative is comprehensible only against an elaborate cognitive background.
Both the storyteller and her audience depend on that background to establish order and meaning, even when—or, perhaps, *especially* when—they
are unaware of doing so.

How does this process of narrative understanding work? Consider a fa-
vorite story from my childhood: a midrash about the patriarch Abraham as
an eight-year-old child.[11]

Terach, Abraham's father, was a maker of idols. Terach left his shop one
day, leaving his son in charge. When Terach returned, he found all but one
of the idols smashed. The remaining idol was the largest of those in the shop.
It stood with a stick tucked under one of its arms. Terach confronted his son
about the destruction. Abraham explained that a woman had brought a

bowl of flour as an offering to the idols, that the idols quarreled over the offering, and that the largest of the idols took a stick and destroyed the others. Terach reacted with incredulity and anger: "Why do you make sport of me?" Abraham responded: "Should not your ears listen to what your mouth is saying?"

This delightful story of hypocrisy and iconoclasm is comprehensible because the reader automatically invokes her accumulated background knowledge to make sense of the events it recounts. First, the reader automatically combines an idealized cognitive model of commercial activity (in which it is understood that it necessary to have someone to mind the store) with a model of filial relations (in which it would be appropriate for a father to ask a son to do so and appropriate for the father to hold the son accountable). Second, the reader makes sense of the moral of the story by invoking and contrasting two opposing understandings or models of idol worship. In one, it is understood that idols are believed to have powers and that idol worshipers make offerings to them. In the other, it is understood that idols are totemic human constructions without any actual powers. Each of these models is evoked by metonymic terms such as "father," "son," "shop," "idol," and "offering." These individual models or scripts are essential subparts invoked unreflectively to make sense of the story. The reader brings these scripts to the story, ready to engage in a joint process of construction.

The use of these models is necessary but hardly sufficient to the process by which the reader makes meaning out of the midrash. How is it that this artifact of an ancient culture is easily recognizable as a story? How is it that even without knowing that the purpose of the midrash is to teach a religious lesson, one knows to abstract a moral? How is it that the reader knows he or she is expected to side with Abraham and not with Terach as the property owner or with the woman as the victim of the social processes of idolatry? The answer is that we have an idealized cognitive model for the concept "story." This model serves as "a cognitive template against which new inputs can be matched and in terms of which they can be comprehended." [12] The internal structure of the model is what yields these insights: first, that the story has a moral and, second, that the moral intended by the author can be obtained unreflectively only by taking Abraham's point of view.

For an account to be perceived as a coherent narrative, it must be more than a "simple succession" or "enumeration of events in serial order"; it must be "a configuration." [13] This configuration has a PART-WHOLE structure of a particular type: In Aristotle's famous description of the prerequisites of a proper story, "a thing is a whole if it has a beginning, a middle, and an end." [14] But it is not just any beginning, middle, and end; otherwise,

Aristotle's dictum would reduce to the rather ridiculous tautology that a story is a story if it starts, rattles on for a bit, and then concludes. Rather, a story is conceptualized as movement along a path, the sequence of its events configured by means of the SOURCE-PATH-GOAL schema.[15] As Ricoeur remarks:

> To *follow* a story is to *move forward* in the midst of contingencies and peripeteia under the *guidance* of an expectation that finds its fulfillment in the "conclusion" of the story. This conclusion . . . gives the story an *"end point."* . . . To understand the story is to understand how and why the successive episodes *led to* this conclusion. (66–67)[16]

We do not think it much of a story if the account *goes nowhere,* if it has no *point.*[17] (This is why a story can have a *peripeteia*—that is, a sudden turn of events or unexpected reversal.) The role of the SOURCE-PATH-GOAL schema in elaborating the concept of story structure is related to the COMMUNICATION IS SENDING mapping of the CONDUIT metaphor and to the conceptualization PURPOSES ARE DESTINATIONS. The reader understands the narrative to be asking him or her to follow the story to its end; the reader, therefore, expects the story to have a point. Because the act of narration is understood as a communicative act, the reader expects that the narrator intends that point as the moral.[18]

The use of the SOURCE-PATH-GOAL schema has three additional entailments that are central to our understanding of a story as a structured whole. First, the concept of movement along a path toward a goal obviously entails a moving entity, usually a person. This traveler is the protagonist of the story; it is whom the story is about. Second, consistent with the conceptualization LIFE IS A JOURNEY, we expect the protagonist to face certain obstacles that must be overcome, usually by force. This provides an agon—a struggle, contest, or dramatic conflict—as the focus of the narrative.[19] As illustrated in figure 5.1, this initial sketch gives us the most basic story structure: a simple travel scenario.

It is commonplace in literature that actual journeys provide central thematic structure—as in the biblical story of Jacob's struggle with the angel,[20]

FIGURE 5.1   Simple Travel Scenario

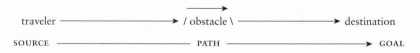

FIGURE 5.2   Extended Travel Scenario/Basic Travel Story

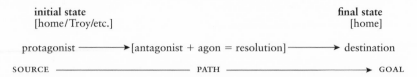

Homer's *Odyssey*,[21] virtually the entire canon of Russian folktales,[22] or a modern work like Jack Kerouac's *On the Road*.[23] In these larger narratives, the PART-WHOLE structure is experientially grounded in our knowledge of journeys. This JOURNEY structure provides a natural starting and ending point in the protagonist's home and a natural beginning and ending for the time dimension of the story. Even *On the Road*, a novel of ultimate rootlessness, begins and ends in New York.

Typically, the OBSTACLE entailment of the travel scenario is filled out in the story domain with an agon that takes the form of an encounter and conflict with an antagonist. Figure 5.2 illustrates this extended travel scenario.

Not all stories fit so neat and ready-made a structure as that provided by a journey. Nevertheless, the SOURCE-PATH-GOAL schema remains central to the ways in which stories are constructed. The third entailment of this schema is that it provides the story's internal conception of time.[24] This conception is consistent with our conventional understanding of "time," which is structured in terms of two SOURCE-PATH-GOAL metaphors.* Thus, the time structure of a narrative is not dependent upon any correspondence to the "real world," nor is it constructed in terms of the narrative itself; rather, it is grounded in our metaphorical conception of time by means of the SOURCE-PATH-GOAL schema.

Often, the elaboration of intelligible beginnings and endings is structured by a BALANCE schema. As illustrated in figure 5.3, a scenario of this type begins with the description of a status quo: an initial state in which life is in harmonious balance. Something disturbs that balance—a need, a lack, a deprivation, or a transformation. The protagonist sets out to restore the balance. There is conflict and resolution. The original state is restored, or

---

* Both of these metaphors conceptualize time in terms of motion. In one, time moves toward us—e.g., "the hours *fly by*" or "the time will *come*." In the other, time is stationary and we move toward and through it—e.g., "the days *ahead*" or "the weeks *past*." Because these conceptualizations are metaphorically coherent, we can use them together, which yields such otherwise contradictory statements as: "I'm *looking forward* to midsemester break, which will be all next week and the week *following*."

FIGURE 5.3   Basic Transformation Scenario

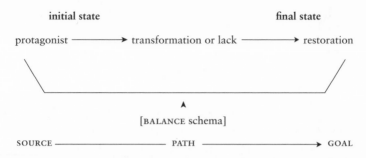

some new balance is attained. In its prototypical form, this schema yields the clichéd fairy-tale ending: "And they lived happily ever after." But the same balance configuration can be observed even in a nonprototypical novel like *On the Road*. The book opens with the line: "I first met Dean not long after my wife and I split up." At the close of the book, the narrator meets quite by accident "the girl with the pure and innocent dear eyes that I had always searched for and for so long." Within two pages, he bids Dean Moriarty good-bye.[25]

The scenarios described so far are only embryonic narratives. We are now ready to assemble these into a model sufficiently rich to account for the concept "narrative." Narrative is understood by means of an ICM structured in terms of four schemas: the PART-WHOLE, the SOURCE-PATH-GOAL, the BALANCE, and the FORCE-BARRIER schemas. These schemas serve as a kind of genetic material or template for a wide variety of stories in which the plot structure follows a protagonist through an agon to a resolution. As illustrated in figure 5.4, the simple traveler becomes the more generalizable protagonist. The antagonist is, typically, the agent that causes the transformation or lack. The protagonist meets the antagonist, and a struggle ensues. This struggle provides an agon as the pivotal point of the narrative; its resolution also restores the initial imbalance and provides a sense of closure. The story structure itself allows the reader clearly to infer the motivation of the protagonist.

More elaborate stories can be constructed by means of recursive structures in which the protagonist may go through a series of agones until a final resolution or new balance is achieved. To use an example from Vladímir Propp's extensive study of Russian folktales, the protagonist is often in need of a magical agent like a sword or a steed with which to defeat the primary antagonist and redress the initial disequilibrium. The magical agent is usually obtained as a result of a fight or verbal encounter (often involving a

FIGURE 5.4   ICM of Basic Story Structure

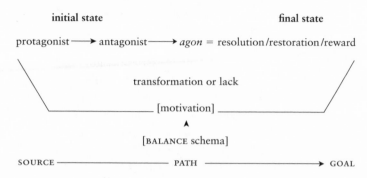

strategic deceit by the protagonist) with a character whom Propp designates a *donor*.[26] This donor scenario is, thus, an agon within the agon that is the larger story.

We can illustrate the functioning of this ICM of basic story structure by completing and analyzing the midrash about Abraham and the idols. Abraham, it will be remembered, took a stick and smashed all but one of his father's idols. He placed the stick in the hand of the remaining idol and blamed the destruction on that survivor. His father reacted angrily, recognizing the impossibility of his son's story. Abraham responded by pointing out the hypocrisy of his father's position.

"Thereupon," the midrash continues, Terach "seized him and delivered him to Nimrod." Both Terach and Abraham's brother, Haran, were present. King Nimrod challenged Abraham's impudence, and the following argument ensued:

> "Let us worship the fire!" he [Nimrod] proposed. "Let us rather worship water, which extinguishes the fire," replied he. "Then let us worship water!" "Let us rather worship the clouds which bear the water." "Then let us worship the clouds!" "Let us rather worship the winds which disperse the clouds." "Then let us worship the wind!" "Let us rather worship human beings, who withstand the wind." "You are just bandying words," he exclaimed; "we will worship nought but the fire. Behold, I will cast you into it, and let your God whom you adore come and save you from it." Now Haran was standing there undecided. If Abram is victorious, [thought he], I will say that I am of Abram's belief, while if Nimrod is victorious, I will say that I am on Nimrod's side. When Abram descended into the fiery furnace and was saved, he [Nimrod] asked him, "Of whose belief are you?" "Of Abram's," he replied. Thereupon he seized him and

cast him into the fire; his inwards were scorched and he died in his father's presence. Hence it is written, AND HARAN DIED IN THE PRESENCE
OF ('AL PENE) HIS FATHER TERAH.[27]

This story is structured as a recursive series of agones in which Abraham bests successively more powerful antagonists until he has achieved his
primary goal. First, Abraham engages in uneven combat with the helpless
idols. Then, he bests his father in argument. This agon is, of course, verbal;
but the practice of verbal argument is itself understood in terms of combat
through the structural metaphor RATIONAL ARGUMENT IS WAR.[28] Abraham
wins this agon with his father, who then delivers him to the king. Abraham
uses his verbal and logical facility to best Nimrod, too. So Nimrod subjects
Abraham to a test of fire, which he survives as well. From his first encounter
with the inert figures, through that with his father, the king, and, finally, the
elements, Abraham remains victorious.

The denouement, however, concerns the death of Abraham's brother. If
one assumes that the rabbis of the midrash intended a lesson of faith, then
the death of Haran can be understood—as it has been traditionally—to underscore the seriousness of the moral of the story: Faith in God is not a simple
question of belief; it is a matter of commitment—of life and death. On this
view, Haran's death and its attendant lesson become the logical stopping
place of the story because that is how the narrators chose to frame it.

But this subjectivist view misses something important: the role of the
BALANCE schema in the construction of this meaning. Moreover, it misses
the way in which the automatic and unreflective understanding that a story
has balance also supports alternative readings. Let me demonstrate the role
of the BALANCE schema in structuring both the traditional and a revisionist
reading of this midrash.

The traditional reading has power because the midrash starts with a picture of the emptiness of idol worship: Abraham assails his father for the vacu-
ousness of his trade in and worship of idols when he lacks any belief in their
power. When Haran proclaims his belief in Abraham's faith, we know that
this, too, is hollow. For his false faith, Haran suffers a specific punishment:
"his inwards [a]re scorched" and he becomes as hollow as his opportunis-
tic protestation of belief. This symmetry between hollow faith and hollow
inwards is reflected in the statement that "Haran died *'al pene*" [literally,
on the face of] his father Terach." *Panim*, the Hebrew word for "face," is a
variant of *penim* (both spelled פנים), which means "insides." On this reading,
Haran dies because of Terach's moral hollowness.

The midrash, however, contains another BALANCE configuration that suggests another meaning. At the start, Abraham exploits the absence of his father to destroy his father's handiwork physically. When confronted about this act, Abraham uses his intellectual prowess to mock the authority of his father. He is then taken before a king whose very name means "rebelled against": The word *nimrod* (נמרד) is formed from the passive of the Hebrew verb *mered* (מרד), which means "to rebel." Confronted with Abraham's facility, Nimrod's authority fares no better than Terach's. By the end of the story, both authority figures have been deposed. At this point, Abraham's moral power—his faith—becomes the agent of his brother's destruction. And so we have come full circle: In the absence of any authority, either father or king, Abraham succeeds in the destruction of his father's offspring and, thus, of a rival for his father's affection. "Hence it is written, and Haran died on the face of his father Terach." On this reading, the reference to Terach's face is to the competition between Abraham and Haran for their father's affection. Here, the "on the face of" is an experientially grounded metonymy in which the face stands for the emotions it displays.* In this revisionist reading, the story is not so much a tale of the triumph of Abraham's monotheistic faith as it is a variant of a systematic biblical theme about the rivalry between brothers that starts with the story of Cain and Abel.[29]

In these alternative readings, we can see how a single schema provides the structure for substantially different readings of the same story. This is the import of the idea of structure as compositional. Humanly constructed meanings are not determinate, but the possibilities are nevertheless framed and constrained by the systematic nature of our cognitive processes. The ICM of narrative is a particularly powerful illustration of this phenomenon of compositional constraint because it shows how a single schema or model can both support multiple meanings and, at the same time, circumscribe what those meanings can be.

CONTINGENCY AND COMPOSITIONAL CONSTRAINT

The ICM of narrative is representative of a more general point: To appreciate that cognition is embodied is to change our very conceptions of contingency and constraint. The questions become more subtle: Contingent on what? Constrained in what ways and to what degree?

Like Claude Lévi-Strauss's *bricoleur*,[30] imagination works with the ma-

---

* This metonymy—in which the face is the source of love, blessing, and salvation—is common in the Bible. *See Numbers* 6:25–26; *Psalms* 80:20. It is still conventional, as in the expression "his face *lit up* when he saw her."

terials at hand. Many of the basic elements, like the BALANCE schema, are embodied. Many more consist of idealized cognitive models grounded in social practices such as those that ground the categories "bachelor" and "mother." Still other elements emerge from routine social interactions with the shared objects of a society. "It is there," Merleau-Ponty observes, "that the deposit of its practical categories is built up, and these categories in turn suggest a way of being and thinking to men." [31]

Constraint, therefore, is both obligatory and indispensable. Our very ability to "have" a world is dependent on the preexisting social practices and conditions that form both the grounds of intelligibility for and the horizons of our world.* Moreover, because these social constructions are reproduced at the level of cognition, there is an important sense in which we unconsciously replicate and maintain our socially constructed contexts. For us, in other words, contingency is *foundational.* To put the point yet more strongly: The grounded nature of cognition means not only that constraint and contingency are inescapable, but also that *constraint and contingency are one and the same.* [32]

This conclusion runs counter to much contemporary discourse, which identifies contingency with arbitrariness and radical indeterminacy. But this conflation rests on the assumption that systems of meaning are nothing more than chance products of history and tradition. And, as we saw in chapter 3, this pure social coherence view is itself a mistaken product of rationalist expectations about what a theory of meaning must be. By the same token, the conflation of contingency with indeterminacy is yet another artifact of antinomial capture, produced by the now-familiar all-or-nothing assumption in which the only alternatives are the polar ones of total constraint or none at all.

The whole question of constraint looks quite different once one lays such rationalist presuppositions aside. [33] Indeed, the notion of contingency as constraint and foundation is a corollary of the embodiment of cognition. For those still ensnared in residual rationalist assumptions, any mention of embodiment is easily mistaken for an old-fashioned foundationalism because

---

* The automobile, which has shaped social attitudes in profound ways, is perhaps the best example. Its pervasiveness and the subsequent development of the interstate highway system have given rise to the particular contemporary configuration of our cities as central business districts ringed by highways that provide access to suburbs and satellite work sites. This configuration entails not only categories like "suburb" and "inner city" but entire sets of values and lifestyle patterns characteristic of those locales. And the impact of the automobile goes deeper. Consider the television advertisement that advises the viewer to buy a particular make because: "It's not just your car; it's your freedom."

it seems to offer the sort of Archimedean point upon which to rest a system of justification. But just the opposite is true: There can be no possibility of transcendence when our very ability to have a world is contingent on the kinds of bodies we have and on the ways in which those bodies interact with our physical and social environment.

As Martha Nussbaum puts it: "The importance of context and particularity for us as we are is inseparable from the fact that we are bodily finite beings of a particular sort, beings who go through time in a particular way." [34] There is no way to get outside of time and existence, no way to escape the field of social interaction that is the self and that the action of the self maintains, no way to transcend—even for a moment—the constitutive action in which the self is already situated and in which the self is always implicated. [35] We are, thus, contingent beings in the sense of the original Latin *contingentem*—"touching on all sides." As Merleau-Ponty observes: "Whatever truth we may have is to be gotten not in spite of but through our historical inherence." [36]

This understanding of embodiment and social contingency as structuring, enabling, and constituting meaning is profoundly inconsistent with any rationalist notion of foundations. Because cognition is irreducibly imaginative, the grounding of meaning in embodiment cannot accomplish precisely what foundations are normally presumed to do—that is, to yield determinate functions that link experiential input to linguistic output in a fixed or linear manner. Rather, grounding experiences provide compositional elements capable of elaboration and, as we saw in the previous chapter, gestalt configurations capable of subtle adaptation to context.

The disparate readings of the midrash—both of which are structured by the same metaphorical conception of a story as a balanced whole—provide one such example of the way that compositional structure constrains but does not determine meaning. Conceptions of morality provide another: It is hard to imagine a human system of moral reasoning that is not motivated by the BALANCE schema. [37] But it does not follow that there is anything determinate about human notions of morality, for the BALANCE schema structures conceptions of moral obligation as disparate as the retributive nostrum "an eye for an eye," its rabbinic interpretation as a requirement of monetary compensation for physical damage, and the conceptually more extended injunction of the New Testament to "turn the other cheek." [38] To put it another way, human conceptualizations of morality are not arbitrary in the sense that they can be just anything. On the other hand, the imaginative, metaphorical nature of these conceptualizations means that they can be many things of a specified, related type.

This pattern of similarity amid difference is an expected consequence of the embodiment of cognition. The claim that human rationality is embodied has an obvious universalist dimension. But because the embodiment of cognition precludes any possibility of transcendence or determinacy, this claim is neither objectivist nor foundationalist in anything like the usual sense. Rather, an embodied rationality is necessarily culturally relativist. This is readily apparent with respect to cognitive models grounded in the variable social experiences of different cultures. Such models differ across cultures and unconsciously shape different expectations and different (though often translatable) ways of perceiving and understanding the world. But cultural relativism is equally if less obviously a product of the more directly embodied bases of cognition. If imaginative, transfigurative processes such as metaphor preclude the possibility of fixed or linear functions linking experiential input to linguistic output, then they are, by definition, capable of being elaborated in more than one way. Accordingly, different cultures can and do employ these embodied experiences in different ways to construct different meanings. There is, therefore, more than one way in which the world can be understood; there is no privileged understanding of rationality in the sense that one way of thinking and talking is a better or "truer" representation of the world.

Given the general nature of the human organism and its environment, there is a stock of relatively stable and well-defined experiences shared by all human beings. For example, human bodies are such that we all experience ourselves as having a front and a back. This is experientially true rather than culturally determined: Simply put, we are more successful in the world if we can see where we are going. The concepts of FRONT and BACK are then metaphorically projected onto various inanimate objects. If I am facing a bush, I categorize the portion facing me as the "front" of the bush. The metaphorical projection to the bush of this particular FRONT-BACK orientation is governed by the language conventions of standard English. In Hausa, a language of West Africa, the same embodied schema and the same metaphorical projection produce the opposite mapping: The "front" of the bush is the far side of the bush—i.e., the side that is facing in the same direction as the speaker.[39] In other words, different cultures elaborate and deploy the same embodied schemas in different, yet related imaginative conceptualizations.*

---

* It should be emphasized that these phenomena, though cultural, are cognitive and not a matter of a particular language. I have been told that linguists doing field research in

This example is, perhaps, too easy. But it typifies the way in which an embodied rationality frames and constrains, rather than determines, meaning. One consequence of this general phenomenon of relative constraint is that instead of the polar alternatives of universality or cultural contingency, we find extensive cross-cultural similarities in the elaboration of basic metaphors. (After all, there is no a priori reason that social contingency should be an all-or-nothing matter.) Given that the narrative ICM is constituted by such basic image-schemas as SOURCE-PATH-GOAL and BALANCE and by the conceptual metaphor LIFE IS A JOURNEY, it is not surprising that the same basic story structure appears in many disparate cultures. We have already seen this model in social and historical artifacts as diverse as the midrash and the Russian folktale. We can observe the same model among yet more distant cultures. In comparing variations of a common mythological story among tribes in British Columbia, for example, Lévi-Strauss reports a basic story line that displays exactly the same structural subparts catalogued by Propp.[40]

Art of the Improvisers

My account of basic story structure raises important questions of scope and application: How could such a simple model explain the proliferation and development of narrative-types extending from the heroic epic through the modern novel to more avant-garde literary forms? The answer is that the ICM of basic story structure operates as the central case that supports a much larger and quite important radial category. As the central case, it describes only the prototypical story. In other words, although it characterizes the conditions sufficient for an account to be recognizable as a story, the ICM does not delimit or define the necessary and sufficient conditions of all stories. Rather, other narrative forms are understood by reference to and as variants of this idealized story structure.

In this way, the elaboration of nonprototypical narratives is simultaneously imaginative and constrained. The central model provides a structure that is sufficiently generalizable to encompass widely varying particulars and, thus, an endless number of instantiations. At the same time, the model is sufficiently schematic to provide a compositional scaffold for an indefinite number of variations and adaptations. As Ricoeur observes: "Rule-governed

---

Harlem in the late 1960s found native English speakers who followed the Hausa conventions rather than those of standard English.

deformation constitutes the axis around which the various changes of paradigm through application are arranged" (70). Extensions are formed by adaptation, modification, and studied distortion of the idealized central model of story structure.

This phenomenon of structural elaboration accounts for the robust productivity of the deceptively simple ICM of basic story structure. The simplest cases of elaboration are those in which the narrator modifies the sequence of the elements of the story by, for example, sending the hero off on a journey before the subject of the quest has been identified.[41] Other familiar examples include the flashback, a device familiar in film narratives but no less common in visual narratives such as painting.[42] In any of these cases, we can have the agon before the lack, or even the denouement before the introduction of the antagonist, and so on. Any of these "disordered" narrative configurations make sense because the reader can be expected to reconstruct and make sense of the story in terms of the ICM of a prototypical narrative.*

More importantly, the schematized nature of the ICM creates the possibility of innumerable instantiations. The protagonist can be hero or antihero. The antagonist slot need not be filled by an actual villain but can be instead the object of the protagonist's affection, as in a romance. Pursuit and courtship are the agon in this case, reflecting the cultural understanding LOVE IS WAR—as in the conventional "battle of the sexes" or the familiar proverb "all is fair in love and war." The antagonist slot can also be filled by a character trait of the protagonist. In that case, the agon can be the protagonist's struggle with his or her own character flaw, as is common in classic tragedy. In this genre, the balance of the narrative is often obtained by the use of the UP-DOWN schema and the symmetry of the protagonist's rise to and fall from power. In other cases, the narrative's agon need not produce a positive resolution but can result instead in a lesson learned by the protagonist. This is frequently the case in moral narratives like *Aesop's Fables*, where the hero loses the confrontation with self or other but gains an insight worth having.

The possibilities of elaboration are almost endless. Yet, the comprehensibility of each instantiation is maintained by the relative economy of struc-

---

* Vladimir Nabokov's *Pale Fire* (1955) is an ingeniously constructed example in which the narrator misreads an entirely unrelated poem as a veiled reference to the story of a deposed eastern European monarch. The story is presented piecemeal in footnotes to the text of the poem. The reader is thus challenged to reconstruct the story line much as a detective—or academic—might piece together the parts of an intellectual puzzle.

ture provided by the basic model. Certain elaborations become conventionalized as recognizable genres: the myth, the folktale, the joke, the romance, the tragedy, the comedy of manners, the novel. In this way, the basic ICM of story structure both permits infinite instantiations and supports an indefinite number of conventionalized extensions.

Avant-garde narrative is a special kind of variant that requires additional attention because it seems in no way to fit the ICM that I have described. To understand the phenomenon of avant-garde narrative, it is necessary to delve a bit deeper into the construction of prototypical narratives. In tracing the basic ICM of narrative and sketching the means of its structural elaborations, I have only begun to describe the possible complexities. Around the bare bones of this typical story structure, the narrator can hang the muscle of the particular plot, the sinew of the connective episodes, the flesh of particular characterizations, the pigment of descriptive or mood-defining passages, and as many layers of conscious and unconscious meaning as the mind inevitably devises.

How is this done? Roland Barthes provides a useful microcosmic division of the functional units of narrative into *nuclei, catalysers, indices,* and *informants.* Nuclei "constitute real hinge points of the narrative (or of a fragment of the narrative)." Catalysers "merely 'fill in' the narrative space separating these hinge functions." Informants identify the time and place of the story. Indices, "a more or less diffuse concept," are atmospheric, characterizational, psychological. For Barthes, the nuclei can be related into a "logical succession" he calls a "sequence." He gives as an example "the homogeneous group 'Having a drink.'" Each of these sequences "constitutes a new unit, ready to function as a simple term in another, more extensive sequence." [43]

Here, Barthes describes in his structuralist vocabulary the role of ordinary ICMs in forming the semantic units, if you will, of narrative structure. Similarly, Ricoeur's account of narrative (55–56) refers to the "conceptual networks" that make up one's understanding of a concept like "action." Narrative understanding, he explains, presupposes "a familiarity with the conceptual networks constitutive of the semantics of the action" and "with the rules of composition that govern the diachronic order of a story" (56). In other words, as described with respect to the midrash about Abraham and the idols at the start of the chapter, narrative understanding requires general cultural knowledge both of the ICMs of various everyday events and of the ICM of narrative by which they are configured into a coherent composition called a "story."

Particular instantiations of narrative have one additional dimension im-

portant to our inquiry. There is virtually no limit to the catalysers that can
be introduced between the sequences of a plot or between the nuclei of a sequence. As Barthes explains:

> This generalized distortion is what gives the language of narrative its spe-
> cial character. A purely logical phenomenon, . . . it ceaselessly substitutes
> meaning for the straightforward copy of the events recounted. On a
> meeting in 'life', it is most unlikely that the invitation to take a seat would
> not immediately be followed by the act of sitting down; in narrative these
> two units, contiguous from a mimetic point of view, may be separated
> by a long series of insertions. . . .
>   Distended, the functional nuclei furnish intercalating spaces which
> can be packed out almost infinitely; the interstices can be filled in with a
> very large number of catalysers. (119–20)

Thus, not only can individual stories instantiate and reorder the elements of
the ICM of narrative in different ways, they can also bend, shape, and fill out
the subparts of the narrative in diverse ways and to varying degrees.

With this more extensive explanation of the structure of narrative, it
should be easy to see how more avant-garde narrative is developed. In Tom
Stoppard's *Rosencrantz and Guildenstern Are Dead*,[44] for example, the narrative structure of the play is parasitic on the story line of *Hamlet*. The latter play provides the more prototypical protagonist, antagonist, and agon;
the narrative of the Stoppard play is an elaborate filling out of the interstices
of the plot from the point of view of Rosencrantz and Guildenstern, two of
Shakespeare's minor characters. Much of this intercalation consists of extended waiting scenarios, with an extra dollop of ennui and angst about the
meaning of it all. Even so, the primary structure of Rosencrantz and Guildenstern's experience is of serial journeys (to Elsinore, to England) for unknown
purposes and to unknown ends. Thus, the basic configuration and meaning
of the play is a composite of the simple travel scenario and the LIFE IS A JOUR-
NEY metaphor.

To be sure, Rosencrantz and Guildenstern experience their own agones
—with the players, the pirates, and, more deviously, with Hamlet himself.
But compared to the more prototypical agones of *Hamlet*, theirs seem random and capricious. That, of course, is also part of the intended theme: Because meaning is something that we as humans construct, it is always easier to see order and structure in the lives of others at a remove than it is to
be certain of meaning and purpose when confronted first hand with the un-
controllable contingencies of one's own life.

Stoppard's play is influenced by Samuel Beckett's landmark *Waiting for Godot*.[45] At first glance, the structure of *Godot* appears to be even less obviously related to the ICM that I have described. Yet, as Barthes points out, *Godot* can be understood as "yet another game—this time extreme—with structure." As Barthes puts it, the scenario has been "extensively catalysed" (120 n.1). Beckett has simply adopted and extended a basic waiting scenario, which he announces quite plainly both in the title and throughout the play (e.g., "Time has stopped." [28]). Even so, Beckett employs quite conventional imagery to make his allegory fully comprehensible: The action (such as it is) takes place at the side of a road; Vladimir and Estragon are identified as fellow travelers.[46] Beckett thus explicitly evokes the travel scenario that is so central to our conventional understanding of narrative. Moreover, Beckett invokes other conventional metaphorical conceptualizations familiar to the literary tradition. He identifies the character of Pozzo with the conventional poetic metaphors LIFE IS A DAY and its derivative LIFE IS LIGHT.* Thus, in act 1, Pozzo counsels Vladimir and Estragon that "if I had an appointment with a . . . Godot . . . , I'd wait until it was black night before I gave up" (27). And, in act 2, Pozzo (now blind) laments: "They give birth astride of a grave, the light gleams an instant, then it's night once more" (77–78).[47]

Even nonstandard narratives like *Godot* are nevertheless comprehensible in terms of the same structural processes and conventional metaphors as more prototypical narratives. Indeed, the strategy of even the most unstructured narrative is to draw upon the reader's natural urge to seek order and meaning; this, Ricoeur observes, is the modus operandi of the fully avant-garde work, "which, as in Joyce's *Ulysses,* challenges the reader's capacity to configure what the author seems to take malign delight in defiguring. In such an extreme case, it is the reader, almost abandoned by the work, who carries the burden of emplotment" (77). Joyce explicitly dares the reader to configure his work as an ordinary travel scenario by giving the book the name of the hero of Homer's *Odyssey.*

To summarize, the category "narrative" forms a radial category consisting of a central case and related conventionalized extensions. The central case is structured in terms of the idealized cognitive model I have sketched; the extensions are variants of this structure, often configured in conven-

---

* Familiar examples are the lines from Shakespeare's *Sonnet* 73 ("In me thou seest the twilight of such day / As after sunset fadeth in the west"); the famous soliloquy in *Macbeth,* act 5, scene 1, spoken by Macbeth just before his death ("Out, out, brief candle!"); and Dylan Thomas's poem, *Do Not Go Gentle into that Good Night.*

tionalized genres. Even the most peripheral cases are nevertheless understood in terms of the model from which they depart. In this way, the concept "narrative" is systematic and structured but not determinate in elaboration.

This flexibility of structure, however, is not the principal source of the indeterminacy or ambiguity of narrative meaning. Rather, the source of indeterminacy is the ineluctable process of cognitive mediation—what Ricoeur calls "the threefold mimesis" (52–77). At no point in the narrative process is there a one-to-one correspondence between the content of the narrative and any real-world referents; at each point, the account is constructed, reconstructed, and reconstructed yet again. The narrator does not tell her story from the raw, unmediated data of life but rather assembles and makes use of the preexisting cultural ICMs with which she apprehends the world. The narrator then configures these nuclei to form a recognizable story-pattern with an apprehensible meaning. By the time the reader confronts the story, the original experiences and ideas have been twice rendered and shaped by cultural and narrative forms. The reader inevitably transfuses the narrative with her own reconstructive effort, decoding the plot and the message in relation to the ICMs that she brings to the process of reading, understanding, and interpreting.[48]

Two things follow from this account: *First,* because understanding narrative is itself a process of imaginative reconstruction—in Nelson Goodman's words, of worldmaking[49]—it necessarily involves the reader's imaginative engagement with and entry into that world. Those within a culture share a stock of cultural ICMs that they use to reconstruct the world invoked by the author. But, in doing so, readers necessarily become coauthors of and participants in that world. As Ricoeur observes: "What is interpreted in a text is the proposing of a world that I might inhabit and into which I might project my ownmost powers" (81). The imaginative reconstruction required for understanding and interpretation implicates the audience as ineluctable partners in a world that the story only evokes.

We can illustrate this phenomenon with an incident retold in Seymour Chatman's essay on film narrative. To crystallize the difference between text and film, Chatman's essay uses an example from Jean Renoir's film adaptation of Guy de Maupassant's *Une Partie de campagne.* In the story, de Maupassant introduces Henriette: "She was a pretty girl of about eighteen; one of those women who suddenly excite your desire." Chatman describes how in the film Renoir conveys this same sentiment by showing the points of view of men of different ages and social situations as they ogle Henriette on a swing. Chatman reports that when he first presented the paper, several conference participants objected to the sexism of his example. "The objection," he notes with some credulity, "seemed to be not about the voyeurism itself but about the willingness of the audience to go along with it." Chatman defends his use of the example, characterizing the identification as "purely aesthetic." A reader "must be able to participate imaginatively in a character's set of mind, even if that character is a nineteenth-century lecher," because this "is simply the way we make sense" of alien viewpoints.[50] Exactly so; but Chatman misses the irony of his own account, which confirms the very charge he intends to refute. For it is precisely this process of *imaginative participation* that is the gist of the criticism: The offensive quality of this vignette is that to follow the story, the audience is being asked to go along with the act of voyeurism—and it does so. The complaint is precisely that the audience becomes an accomplice in the narrator's sexism.

On the other hand, this same process of imaginative participation makes narrative a potentially powerful transformative tool. A story invites the audience into the world of the narrator. In large part, that world will be constructed of culturally shared ICMs. But within this constructed story-world, there will be depicted concrete experiences that are unfamiliar or unknown to the audience. Through the process of projection that makes possible narrative understanding, the audience will imagine itself confronted by these experiences; it will be challenged to make sense of them through its own past experiences; indeed, it must do so in order to understand the story-events as a coherent story-experience of its own. The concrete power of the imagery with which the reader can be confronted—the boy drawing the targets around the arrows, Abraham smashing the idols—can be used directly to engage the audience in the cognitive process by which it regularly makes meaning in its day-to-day world. The act of making sense of the projected experience of the story, in other words, will be mimetic of the process by which humans always make meaning. The audience "lives" the story-experience and, thus, is brought personally to engage in the process of constructing meaning out of the experience of another. In this way, the audience achieves a measure of understanding and empathy. To paraphrase Nelson Goodman: In narrative, experience moonlights as intersubjective meaning.[51]

Second (and conversely), because understanding is a matter of imaginative reconstruction, indeterminacy is a byproduct of the process of communication itself. Communication is possible because humans share the experience of embodied interaction with their physical and social environments. Those interactions give rise to conceptual structures—image-schemas, conceptual metaphors, idealized cognitive models—through which we construct sense and meaning. People within a given culture share a stock of ICMs that, from an epistemological point of view, are no more than useful cultural theories for organizing and making sense of experience. The very usefulness of these cognitive structures inheres in their schematized, generalizable form; this form, in turn, gives rise to a lack of determinacy in elaboration and interpretation. Communication is possible, but there are no guarantees. Readers may be *constrained* to interpret a narrative by means of preexisting ICMs, and to do so in a way that conforms to a cultural ICM of story-types. But there is nothing that *determines* the particular instantiations chosen in the interpretive process. The reader attempts to reconstruct the world invoked by the author and usually succeeds. But the reader remains free to invoke alternative ICMs not intended by or not shared with the author; the reader remains free, therefore, to construct alternative meanings.

We have already seen how the midrash of Abraham and the idols can be read in two different ways, both of which conform to the text of the story, its indices (like the name *Nimrod* and the biblical referent "on the face of"), and the cognitive constraint of the BALANCE schema. Each of these competing interpretations is constructed relative to a different ICM that serves as an alternative template for organizing the meaning of the story. The traditional interpretation is enabled by viewing the midrash relative to a paradigm of faith. The revisionist interpretation is rendered by reading the same story through the lens of a modern, Freudian paradigm. The traditional reading recreates the worldview of the narrator and, thus, enables the reader to approximate the author's intended religious lesson. The revisionist reading assumes a different interpretive stance and, therefore, reconstructs a story of sibling rivalry and Oedipal conflict. From what we know about the rabbinic worldview, we can readily conclude that we have obtained a meaning different from the authors' intent. But, from within the modern, psychoanalytic paradigm, we can and do presume that we have reconstructed an unconscious meaning perhaps unknown to, but nevertheless "intended" by, the rabbis.

Not all alternative interpretations present themselves as potentially coherent, unconscious intentions of the author. A slight divergence of culture between narrator and audience can sometimes make miscommunication inevitable. In *Telling the American Story,* Livia Polanyi recounts just such a failure. Her Dutch colleagues would ask why she chose to leave behind friends, family, and country to accept an academic appointment in Amsterdam. She would explain that she had moved because of the job and the opportunities it offered. Inevitably, her Dutch interlocutors would express puzzlement and disbelief. Despite her sincere efforts at explanation, the conversation invariably ended with a sense of distance, distrust, and betrayal.

Only after several years was Polanyi able to reconstruct the cause of the miscommunication. She had given a truthful explanation that reflected the cultural significance of work and professional ambition to an American. Her Dutch interlocutors, however, interpreted the explanation from a cultural perspective that did not recognize these as proper topics of personal, intimate conversation. Relative to their assumptions about conventional motivations for life choices and proper interpersonal communication, the American explanation that "presented a self which was rational, sensible, business-like, work-oriented, committed and serious" appeared to the Dutch interlocutor as "cold, calculating, uncaring, work-obsessed, ambitious, and slightly inhuman." The Dutch, therefore, would conclude that the speaker "was rejecting their attempts at intimacy by giving them a story which could not possibly be believed." [52]

Because narratives are constructed relative to such pregiven understandings, meaning and communication are vulnerable to cross-cultural distortion. Because narrative meaning is an interactive process that requires reconstruction by the reader, who must reinsert the ICMs of the story's nuclei back into their place in the story line, there is never determinacy in interpretation. On both sides of the narrative interaction, the process of construction is constrained. But on neither side is it determinate or objective in anything but this relative sense.

The ICM of narrative, thus, illustrates the more general phenomenon of relative constraint. A single cognitive model constructed of embodied schemas and basic conceptual metaphors supports the imaginative elaboration of an impressive array of narrative-types. The same model appears in many different cultures and in manifestations that represent quite different social assumptions and practices. At the same time, it is this embodied but culturally elaborated ICM of narrative that allows one immediately to recognize the novel, the midrash, and the work of avant-garde literature as examples of the same "thing," as instantiations of the same process.

PEAS IN A POD

In the late 1980s and early 1990s, storytelling emerged as a conspicuous, new methodology in legal scholarship. This development in turn spawned a secondary literature reflecting on how such work is to be evaluated. Criticizing this methodology as insufficiently analytic, many people seemed to assume that narrative scholarship is merely a matter of *reportage*. Others questioned how storytelling is to be evaluated for truth and representativeness.

Supporters of narrative scholarship argued that storytelling captures modalities of meaning that cannot be expressed in more conventional legal analysis. There is something to this view; but as a categorical claim it is overstated. In an important sense, there is no difference in kind between storytelling and more orthodox argumentation. On one hand, standard scholarship also consists of highly conventionalized forms of analysis arranged in familiar—and, thus, largely invisible—patterns. On the other, storytelling, too, represents intellectual work that configures "the facts" into a recognizable story line with a particular kind of point or moral. In that sense, every story reflects an intellectual or political point of view that can be analyzed critically as would any other type of scholarship.

To illustrate the similarity between storytelling and legal argument, consider the modal law review article. It begins by identifying a problem in some area of the law. Perhaps the cases are in disarray and cannot be reconciled. Perhaps the well-settled policy or principle underpinning some area of legal doctrine does not jibe with important decisions that are nevertheless accepted as intuitively correct. The article proposes to resolve this difficulty through the rigorous application of some new or more powerful theoretical tool. To this end, it turns for insight and illumination to some recondite area—economic theory, rational choice theory, Lacanian psychoanalysis, Rawlsian philosophy, or maybe just a new and more painstaking analysis of the debates surrounding the ratification of the Fourteenth Amendment. Fortified with the learning thus achieved, the article returns to the doctrinal matter at hand. It skillfully wields its newly won insight to work out the initial puzzle and settle any remaining questions. Because real-life conclusions are rarely so neat, the recalcitrant cases are recharacterized, ignored, or disapproved as wrongly decided.

This should resonate, I trust, as a fair description of articles you have read. (I discuss a prominent exemplar below.) But this description should also feel familiar in another, quite different way. For the argument-structure I have sketched follows exactly the outline of the Russian folktale as catalogued by Propp. There is an initial deprivation or lack. The protagonist sets out to right the wrong and restore the initial balance. There is a fight or verbal encounter with a donor through which the protagonist obtains the sword or other magical agent that will be instrumental in the successful completion of his quest. A conflict ensues in which the hero uses the newly won tool to defeat the primary antagonist and redress the initial imbalance. The original state is restored, or some new balance attained.

To a rationalist sensibility, the striking resemblance between the Russian folktale and the modal law review article may seem odd or disturbing. But it is hardly surprising from a cognitive perspective. One would expect there to be an idealized cognitive model for scholarship and for other forms of rational argument, just as there is for any other mental domain. Given what we know about the domains of "narrative" and "argument," one would also anticipate that the models might be related. For one thing, it is quite conventional for the agon slot of the narrative ICM to be filled out by a verbal conflict, as we have seen. More importantly, as discussed in chapter 3, our understanding of rational argument is structured in part by the conceptual metaphor AN ARGUMENT IS A JOURNEY. The parallel conceptual mappings from the source domain of JOURNEYS—that is, of a traveler, a distance covered, obstacles overcome, a destination reached—provide a categorical linkage between the narrative and argument ICMs. Narrative and argument are, in other words, different cases of the same pattern—indeed, of the same pattern of neural firings.

Thus, the "narrative" radial category encompasses rational argument as an extension or specialized subcase. In this subcase, the JOURNEY dimension of the basic-story ICM is satisfied by means of the conceptual metaphor AN ARGUMENT IS A JOURNEY. The protagonist slot is filled out by the central idea or theory of the argument. The antagonist is the mistaken idea, author, or theory under challenge. The dispute between the two contending views serves as the agon of the "narrative" via the conceptual metaphor RATIONAL ARGUMENT IS WAR.

On this view, the insistence that narrative scholarship should be judged by the same standards as more conventional scholarship leads to a pernicious irony. In theory, the structural similarity between the two would seem to support unitary standards. In practice, however, it results in a covert privileging of more "traditional" scholarship whose shortcomings are often masked by the very conventionality of its form. We can better appreciate this point by again recalling López's observation that people never approach the world as if it were sui generis. Rather, we perceive and discriminate new data in terms of our existing models: "Once the principal features of a given phenomenon suggest a particular stock structure, that structure shapes our expectations and responses." [53]

Standard scholarship participates in the rationalist model. Accordingly, it is read in light of the rationalist model's core conception of reason, which, as we saw in chapter 3, is metaphorically understood as rigorous and linear, cold and dispassionate, impersonal and objective. The more closely a scholarly work adheres to the standard format, the more likely it is to be perceived as conforming to rationalist standards of rigor and precision. As a consequence, many of the common weaknesses of conventional scholarship are obscured by the expectations prompted by its familiar form.

Narrative scholarship, in contrast, prompts precisely the opposite set of assumptions. Storytelling is understood as the height of subjectivity. It is seen as literary rather than literal, a matter of emotions and aesthetics rather than cool reason. As a consequence, narrative scholarship is taken to exemplify the personal and the subjective. Accordingly, as we shall see shortly, it elicits disproportionate—one might even say obsessive—attention to accuracy at a level of detail virtually never demanded of conventional scholarship.

This covert privileging of traditional scholarship over narrative scholarship has another aspect. In telling a story, the narrator invites us to enter a constructed world. Because we share basic cultural assumptions about how that narrative world is constructed, we know automatically that we are being asked to view that constructed world from the point of view of the protagonist. Our very success in understanding the story is simultaneously the storyteller's success in persuading us, at least temporarily, to imagine the world in a particular way. We can underscore the power of this process by considering those occasions when the narrator fails and the audience does not accept the characterizations of events "imposed" by the narrator. This response may be especially strong—even violent—if the audience is being asked to see protagonists and villains who do not fit its concepts of identity and order. An audience, for example, that unconsciously harbors stereotypes about Blacks and women may react with disbelief when it cannot recognize what it perceives as unlikely portrayals of characters or events.[54]

When we unconsciously invoke the narrative ICM to re-cognize a story, the internal structure of the model provides patterns of inference and expectations—such as the intended point of view or moral—that enable us to reconstruct its intended meaning. The expectations engendered by unconsciously held models subserve the process, crucial to the dramatic arts, referred to as "the suspension of disbelief." If a suspense drama is done well, for example, the hero's uncanny ability to arrive in the nick of time provokes our relief rather than our skepticism. Because it is part of the fabric of our expectations, we actively engage in the contrivances of plot and character necessary to make the story work.

Although we do not consciously identify scholarship as a subcase of the

narrative genre, standard scholarship nevertheless benefits from the unreflective expectations engendered by the narrative ICM. In this sense, it is no different than other kinds of tacit knowledge (such as the ability to ride bicycles
and compose sentences) that we use effortlessly and—except when we encounter some difficulty—quite unreflectively. (Thus, we could even say that
it is precisely *because* standard scholarship fits so seamlessly with the "narrative" model that it fails to signal its cognitive underpinnings.) But the tacit
working of the narrative ICM means that we are also unaware of the degree
to which we depend on the entailments of that model to carry arguments and
sustain patterns of inference that might otherwise seem unpersuasive.

Consider Dworkin's argument in *Law's Empire.* "Chapter 1," as Dworkin explains, reviews "classical theories or philosophies of law" and shows
that legal positivist "theories are unhelpful because paralyzed by the semantic sting" (68). Dworkin designates as "semantic" those theories that attempt
to delineate the criteria by which propositions of law are judged "true."
The problem with such theories is that they cannot capture the nature of the
actual disagreements amongst judges. Dworkin illustrates the point with
discussions of several famous decisions (13–33).[55] He proposes to solve the
problem by defending a view of law as an interpretive concept. To that end,
he examines the history of an imagined community, its practices of courtesy, and the nature of debates over the best explication of those practices.
This thought experiment enables him to develop a general theoretical account of interpretation that, though it "take[s] us far from law," provides
"the foundation of the rest of the book. The *detour,*" he assures us, "is *essential*" (49–50; emphasis added).

One can scarcely imagine a clearer announcement of what Propp designates the donor scenario. True to the dictates of form, Dworkin develops
an account of interpretation by which he claims to "have drawn the semantic sting" (87). By the book's end, he has also employed this account
of interpretation to reconsider and defend the series of decisions discussed
at the start. This is a prodigious instrument, no doubt. What could it be?
Dworkin explains:

> Constructive interpretation is a matter of imposing purpose on an object
> or practice in order to make it the best possible example of the form or
> genre to which it is taken to belong. It does not follow . . . that an inter-
> preter can make of a practice or work of art anything he would have
> wanted it to be . . . [f]or the history or shape of a practice or object con-
> strains the available interpretations of it. (52)

Famously, Dworkin analogizes law to the writing of a chain novel by successive authors, with the chapters held together by a commitment to the principle of interpretive integrity and the presumed constraints of the story thus far (225–38).

If Dworkin's notions of constructive interpretation and law as integrity have intuitive appeal, they are nevertheless unpersuasive. As Stanley Fish has argued, the authors of the subsequent chapters remain free to reinterpret the plot, the characters, or the genre in ways that drastically change the enterprise.[56] Indeed, even Dworkin acknowledges that the conceptualization of "best" is itself relative to interpretive strategies and commitments (52–53, 234–35). A story should, therefore, always be subject to radical reinterpretation and reconstruction in light of other ways of being in the world—unless it has its own essence, its own fundamental quality. Dworkin explicitly rejects such objectivist assumptions.[57] He asserts instead that as the story proceeds, the very accretion of detail progressively constrains subsequent authors because they must account for the data within their own interpretive conceptions of what a coherent story can be.

But this claim will not wash either. As we have already seen, the accretion of detail does not foreclose alternative interpretations even within a single interpretive conception like the ICM of narrative. Because the ICM is sufficiently generalized to allow many instantiations and many different elaborations, the details of a given story can be reordered in terms of many other points of view. Thus, Stoppard has no difficulty turning the story line of *Hamlet* into an existentialist meditation on the meaninglessness of life, simply by changing the point of view from that of Hamlet to that of Rosencrantz and Guildenstern.* Similarly, it was easy to reinterpret a completed story like the midrash about Abraham and the idols in light of a Freudian paradigm. Both this revisionist interpretation and the traditional one effectively account for the vast majority of the details, including the hidden elements like the indices. Which reading makes the midrash the best that it can be?

Dworkin's conceptions of constructive interpretation and law as integrity seem to work not because they are analytically sound, but because

---

* Alan Ayckbourn uses this device of perspectival shift to almost perfect effect. In his play *The Norman Conquests* (1975), the events among an extended family spending the weekend together in the parent's home are told through three performances over three nights. Each night's performance covers the same time period and the same overall events but takes place in a different room of the house. By the third performance, the meaning of the events viewed on the first night appears entirely different.

they are the beneficiaries of our suspension of disbelief. Analytically, something is "best" only relative to our set of idealized assumptions or model of what we think it should be—a point that, as we have seen, Dworkin concedes. Thus, as Fish points out, Dworkin's notion of integrity is logically indistinguishable from and necessarily collapses back into the cultural values that unconsciously animate the practice or object under consideration.[58] To take two of Dworkin's pivotal examples (53–59), because there is an unconscious, unreflective dimension to thought there can be "unintended" meanings that even the author might subsequently affirm. And, because this unreflective level of thought is structured by means of culturally shared ICMs, there appears to be no discontinuity between the reconstruction of an author's "intent" and the "intent" or "purpose" of social practices such as courtesy or law.

Thus, interpreting a practice to make it "the best it can be" is not a constraint; it is a tautology. Constructive interpretation is what we do every time we speak, read, or write. It is the ordinary cognitive process by which one configures new input in a manner that makes sense—in a manner, that is, that makes of the input a coherent whole or a "best example" of an existing idealized cognitive model or reigning paradigm. Constructive interpretation is, in other words, nothing more than the phenomenon of prototype effects presented in fancy philosophical dress. If Dworkin succeeds in leading us to think that he has said more, it is only because he has exploited the fabric of our expectations and engaged us in the active contrivances of plot and character necessary to make his story work.

We can see the same process in reverse in criticisms of narrative scholarship. Consider Patricia Williams's well-known Benetton story. Williams saw a sweater in the store window that she wanted to purchase for her mother for Christmas.

> I pressed my round brown face to the window and my finger to the buzzer, seeking admittance. A narrow-eyed, white teenager wearing running shoes and feasting on bubble gum glared out, evaluating me for signs that would pit me against the limits of his social understanding. After about five seconds, he mouthed "We're closed," and blew pink rubber at me. It was two Saturdays before Christmas, at one o'clock in the afternoon; there were several white people in the store who appeared to be shopping for things for *their* mothers.
>
> I was enraged. At that moment I literally wanted to break all the windows of the store and *take* lots of sweaters for my mother. . . .

I am still struck by the structure of power that drove me into such a blizzard of rage. There was almost nothing I could do, short of physically intruding upon him, that would humiliate him the way he humiliated me. . . . In the wake of my outrage, I wanted to take back the gift of appreciation that my peeping in the window must have appeared to be. I wanted to take it back in the form of unappreciation, disrespect, defilement. I wanted to work so hard at wishing he could feel what I felt that he would never again mistake my hatred for some sort of plaintive wish to be included.[59]

There is much to admire in the elegance, symmetry, and emotional resonance of Williams's account. (Note the multiple balance configurations in this passage.) But the more common reactions to her story are skepticism and disbelief: Many people seem to doubt that an upper-middle class, professional woman would be excluded from a store on the basis of race. The editors of the *University of Miami Law Review,* which first published this story, initially refused to include the references to Benetton and to Williams's "round brown face," claiming that they feared a libel suit. Students in a Stanford Law School class questioned whether the story wasn't a lie made up "to make all white people feel guilty" (242 n.5). Even Judge Posner, who clearly respects and praises Williams's "powerful gift for narration," questions whether she *really* pressed her face against the window and asks how she *knows* the sales clerk excluded her because she is Black.[60]

Did this event really happen to Pat Williams? *Of course* it did. (To this day, her eyes flash with anger whenever the subject of Benetton comes up.) So, why the skepticism? And why this fixation on the accuracy of every detail? For Anne Coughlin,[61] it is a matter of the cultural expectations that readers bring to autobiography—expectations that impose on the author an implied contract of truthfulness and candor.* Posner sees it as a matter of adherence to the professional norms of lawyers and scholars. But what really gnaws at these critics is the specter of the magid's tale, the anxiety provoked by the rationalist's dilemma: Constraint must come from the outside—from the world of fact—or we are helpless before the mad forces of subjectivity. It derives from a view of subject-object relations that, if not

---

* Coughlin suggests that, consistent with this implied contract, the Miami law review editors may have been innocently seeking confirmation of doubted details. But she fails to explain how this rationalizes their attempted excision of Williams's "round brown face"— a crucial point that Coughlin never in fact addresses.

crude, is nevertheless recrudescent. Thus, Coughlin explicitly maintains that autobiography is a realist discourse "devoted to the distinction between events that are 'in principle observable or perceivable' outside the narrative and those that reside solely inside the world constructed by a storyteller." [62] Posner takes a more sophisticated tack, but he nevertheless poses the question as one of subjectivity versus truth. On one hand, he ponders whether "one-sidedness is an endemic risk of the literary depiction of reality" (380). On the other, he tells us that pragmatists "may be dubious about truth with a capital T, but they respect those lowercase truths that we call facts" (377).

The lesson of cognitive theory—not to mention much contemporary philosophy—is that nothing is observable "in principle" outside our frames of reference. [63] By the same token, there is nothing that can exist "solely" in the world constructed by a story. (If there were, it would be incomprehensible to us.) [64] Rather, everything we observe and every story we construct depends upon the preexisting cultural ICMs with which we apprehend the world. It is a commonplace of contemporary thought that even scientific facts are paradigm-dependent. [65] It follows that subjectivity, too, must be culturally contingent. There can be no purely subjective perceptions free of our value-laden, culturally shared categories and understandings. In this sense, Williams could no more "make up" the fact of her exclusion than she could fail to notice the degree to which race matters in our society.

In a different context, Posner observes that the "pragmatist's real interest is not in truth at all, but in the social grounds of belief" (390). Just so. By implication, pragmatists should be judiciously self-critical about what they take as "fact," for there is always the real danger that one's assessments of fact turn on social orthodoxies that are partial, mistaken, or soon-to-be-obsolete. Pragmatists, in other words, should be particularly self-conscious of Stevens's caution that reality is only a cliché, a stiff and stubborn, man-locked set of contingent cultural conceptions. Not to heed this admonition is to risk that version of the objectivist fallacy in which one mistakes one's socially situated intuitions for "lowercase truths."

We can bring this point into sharper focus by posing a variant of Clark Freshman's question. [66] When so many are skeptical of Williams's account, why is it that no one questions Dworkin's rendering of the debates among the citizens of courtesy? One might respond, of course, that the contrast between an imaginative thought experiment like Dworkin's and a first-person narrative like Williams's is a distinction that makes all the difference. But, from whichever side one views this distinction, it rests on preconceptions that do not withstand analysis.

Consider Dworkin's so-called thought experiment: He does not *imagine* the practices of courtesy of a fictitious community but discusses our own social and historical customs. Initially, peasants doff their hats to the nobility. Eventually, "views about the proper grounds for respect . . . change from rank to age to gender. . . . The rule that men must rise when a woman enters the room . . . might be taken as a paradigm for a certain season" (47–49). Later still, understandings of respect change "from a view that external show constitutes respect" to one in which "respect is a matter of feelings," and from the view that respect should be "directed to groups or to natural properties" to one in which respect is owed "to individuals for individual achievement" (72).[67] Dworkin's "invented" community is just a conventional account of our own cultural history. This correspondence, moreover, is anything but fortuitous: Dworkin's account of the interpretive attitude in the development of a practice must be believable if we are to perceive it as allegory rather than mere fable. And we would not find it believable if it did not provide a plausible account of things with which we are already familiar. For the argument to work, in other words, it must appeal to our experience of and intuitions about our own social and historical practices of courtesy.

So, one might ask, did the practice of rising when a woman entered a room *really* serve as a paradigm for courtesy? And how does Dworkin *know* (to take a particularly crucial and controversial claim) that "a social scientist must participate in a practice [such as courtesy] if he hopes to understand it" (55)?[68] No one asks these questions, of course, because these are taken to be analytical arguments rather than factual assertions. But these claims *could* be taken as empirical. Suppose, for example, Dworkin is all wet about the social evolution of courtesy. Suppose that a careful historical study were to show that courtesy developed as a result of wildly contingent, even random social circumstances. In that event, the self-described "foundation" for Dworkin's view of law as integrity would crumble. In that event, we just might suspect that law, too, is an epiphenomenal manifestation of diverse cultural forces and social circumstances.

Consider the point from the opposite side: What would be different if the Benetton story were just an allegory? Perhaps it would lose the authority and credibility we ordinarily attribute to first-person narratives. But that is just what the critics deny when they question the reliability of Williams's account. So what would be lost? The persuasiveness of the story as an allegory would, like Dworkin's thought experiment, depend upon its congruence with our background assumptions about and experience in the consumer marketplace. If we do not believe that rational store owners turn away willing customers with the wherewithal to pay, then we are likely to distrust this allegory. We might conclude that it misrepresents reality. We might concede that it *could* happen but dismiss it as an unusual or aberrant event. Perhaps it occurs only when, as Posner hypothesizes, the clerk is a disloyal, lazy, or irresponsible employee (373).

The irony is that the Benetton story would be no less true—and perhaps more persuasive—if it were an allegory. Because Williams presents the story as a first-person account, the critics are able to bypass their own background assumptions to focus instead on the credibility and reliability of the storyteller. Had she presented it as an allegory, her critics might have been led to confront the bias of their own intuitions. A frankly fictitious story might have prompted readers to consider the likelihood of such mistreatment more directly. Had they done so, the critics might have encountered the *New York Times*'s 1991, front-page article on the endemic discrimination experienced by even affluent African Americans when they try to participate in the market.

> In interviews, blacks of all ages, regions and economic levels tell similar stories of bad service, public humiliation and legal harassment when confronted by representatives of service industries that, the blacks say, do not acknowledge blacks' growing economic power, private resources and buying patterns.[69]

"The result," the *Times* added, "has been an increasing impatience and rage among middle class blacks."

Indeed, had the critics considered the mistreatment of African Americans more directly, they might have discovered that even Oprah Winfrey—one of America's wealthiest people *and* one of its best known faces—experienced the same mistreatment as Pat Williams. On national television, Oprah described how she stopped at a New York City boutique, pushed the buzzer seeking admission, and was refused entry—her limousine parked in full view at the curb. "We saw the people in the store," said Oprah, "but they wouldn't let us in." [70]

The more general point is the one I have stressed throughout this chapter: Credibility and persuasion are a matter of the same tacit cognitive processes as comprehension. Because each involves categorization and conceptualization, each is contingent on the ICMs by which we cognize our worlds. Whether allegory or first-hand account, the Benetton story seems problematic to many white critics only because it represents a reality largely alien to their experience. By the same token, the story's value has nothing to do with whether it is a painstaking factual account or an artful fiction. Irrespective of genre, the story's value lies in its ability to convey in a powerful, affective way an everyday reality of African American life about which the rest of us need to know. Indeed, if the various skeptics were more familiar with this shameful side of American life, they might never have doubted the Benetton story in the first place.

Daniel Farber and Suzanna Sherry claim that storytelling, as "personal narratives devoid of analysis," fails as scholarship because it is generally "impossible to make counter-arguments." [71] But this position founders on its too simplistic premise. Farber and Sherry treat stories as nothing more than "concrete depictions of events" representing "unadorned account[s] of personal experiences." [72] But there are no "unadorned accounts" because there is no unmediated access to the raw data of a life—not even one's own. A storyteller can experience her life only in terms of the cultural understandings that give form to its events. She must assemble her story from that stock of understandings, configuring them in a recognizable story-form that a reader can unpack. Readers can try to enter into and understand the experiential assumptions that shape those perceptions and characterizations of events, as the author hopes. They can honestly disagree with the storyteller's perceptions and characterizations, as Posner does. Or they can test the empirical basis for the author's assumptions and understandings, as they could with respect to Dworkin's allegory about the citizens of courtesy. But to suggest that narrative scholarship precludes debate because stories entail nothing more than rote description is to betray both a latent objectivism *and* a stunning lack of imagination.

Consider, as a final exhibit, Williams's discussion of the Tawana Brawley incident, in which it was claimed that a Black fifteen-year-old had been brutalized and raped by white police officers. After describing in some detail the abject condition in which Ms. Brawley was found, Williams concludes that the teenager must have

> been the victim of an unspeakable crime. No matter how she got there.
> No matter who did it to her—and even if she did it to herself. Her condition was clearly the expression of some crime against her, some tremendous violence, some great violation that challenges comprehension. And it is this much that I grieve about. The rest of the story is lost, *or irrelevant in the worst of all possible ways.* (170; emphasis added)

Posner brands this "an evasion." "If she did it to herself," he confidently (and reductively) asserts, "it was not a crime, at least not a crime against her" (375).* But Williams's studied finesse of the question of "what really happened" is not an evasion; it is a deliberate attempt to get at a larger social and psychological truth. And that truth is one that a careful reader might already have learned from the Benetton story.

From its first public telling, it has always struck me that the most remarkable—and least remarked upon—aspect of the Benetton story is Williams's description of her reactions: "I was enraged. At that moment I literally wanted to break all the windows of the store and *take* lots of sweaters. . . . I am still struck by the structure of power that drove me into such a blizzard of rage. There was almost nothing I could do, short of physically intruding upon him, that would humiliate him the way he humiliated me. . . . I was quite willing to disenfranchise myself. . . . My rage was admittedly diffuse, even self-destructive" (45–46). I have represented people in prison and on death row, so perhaps I am more alert to these disturbing emotions. But I know of no single statement that so acutely captures the violent, self-destructive rage provoked by the day-to-day oppressions and petty humiliations of race in America. If that self-destructive rage can provoke a teenager like Tawana Brawley to inscribe "Nigger" and "KKK" on her own body, if it nearly provoked a highly educated, well-socialized, and self-controlled person like Pat Williams to smash windows and steal sweaters, then it is no wonder that the Black community suffers from the furious litany of social problems—crime, AIDS, drug addiction, neglect of children, anti-Semitism—that Posner so chillingly recounts (374–75). Those conditions are clearly the expression of some crime—and even if they do it to themselves. Maybe especially then.

As a philosophical matter, questions of "truth" are the wrong ones for pragmatists like Posner to be asking. In chapter 3, I argued that the important and genuinely pragmatic question with respect to any metaphor is not its truth or falsity but the perceptions and inferences that follow from it and the actions that are sanctioned by it. So, too, for stories. Farber and Sherry maintain that scholarship should incite debate. I agree. Pat Williams's narratives present perceptions, provoke insights, and motivate action in direc-

---

* Posner says that Williams "manages to avoid mentioning that the charge . . . was fraudulent" (375). But Williams does report the conclusion of the New York attorney general, along with some quite critical comments of her own about one of Ms. Brawley's prominent advisors (170–72).

tions that this society all too tragically neglects. Why aren't Farber and Sherry debating *that?*

Academic insistence on analytic rigor and truthfulness is hardly surprising. But the value of scholarship is in its ability to add to our knowledge and deepen our understanding. What distinguishes storytelling from more conventional argument is only that it uses the cognitive power of the concrete in a way that the abstracted rhetoric of the law ordinarily does not. Narrative asks the reader to engage directly in the process of meaning-making. At its best, as in Pat Williams's work, narrative scholarship prods our social and intellectual horizons in a way that Dworkin's deracinated discussions of law as integrity could only hope to achieve. From that perspective, the solemn insistence on "traditional" standards seems swathed in irony: It resembles nothing so much as one more rationalist idol, its blunted ax tucked under its arm as it stands guard over the shattered pieces of its predecessors.

CHAPTER 6

The Doctrinal Wheel

IN *Lassiter v. Department of Social Services,* the Supreme Court held that indigent parents faced with state-initiated proceedings to terminate their parental rights were not necessarily entitled to appointed counsel. Justice Stewart's majority opinion proclaimed that "the Court's precedents speak with one voice about what 'fundamental fairness' has meant" in this area. The "pre-eminent generalization" that emerged was a presumption that the right to appointed counsel ordinarily applies only when the litigant stands to lose his or her physical liberty. Measured against that presumption, Ms. Lassiter could not establish a right to counsel in her case.[1]

In dissent, Justice Blackmun read the same cases to show that "incarceration has been found to be neither a necessary nor a sufficient condition for" the appointment of counsel. On his view, the threatened loss of any "sufficiently substantial or fundamental" liberty interest required consideration of the need for counsel in light of the nature of the proceedings. Given the fundamental nature of the liberty interest in matters of family life and the "adversarial, formal, and quintessentially legal" character of the termination proceeding, the dissent concluded that counsel should automatically be appointed in all parental termination cases (40–44).

Cases like *Lassiter* provoke surprisingly little consternation among lawyers, who understand that precedents *never* speak with a single voice. Famously, Karl Llewellyn described the traditional doctrine of precedent as "Janus-faced" and "not one doctrine . . . but two . . . which, applied at the same time to the same precedent, are contradictory of each other."[2] Subsequent scholars have stressed the manipulability of precedent by pressing the point familiar from the preceding chapters: Texts are never self-declaring but must always be interpreted relative to some background set of understandings and purposes. But, while cogent, neither of these positions explain the opinions in *Lassiter*. For this is not a case where one side read the precedents expansively, while the other confined the decisions to their facts. Nor is this a case where each side provided a credible interpretation that, like the traditional and revisionist readings of the midrash, could account for the prior cases in all (or even most of) their details.

Rather, *Lassiter* exemplifies the distorting effects of rationalism in law. Both majority and dissent tried to reduce the relative complexities of a radial category to a single, generalized principle or set of necessary and sufficient conditions. Consequently, neither side could provide a satisfactory account of the precedents; each side either recharacterized the problematic cases or simply ignored them. *Lassiter* thus epitomizes how adherence to the rationalist model makes law seem more unpredictable and incoherent than it is or need be. The inability of either side to distill the cases down to a single principle produces the appearance of indeterminacy and infinite manipulability, when, in fact, a different order prevails.

This chapter and the next each examines an area of legal doctrine that can better be explained as a radial category. In offering this account, I do not claim that cognitive explanations of legal doctrine can yield determinate, "right" answers to legal questions. Rather, I intend to show that legal reasoning already (indeed, on my account, *necessarily*) produces radial categories that are systematically misunderstood and distorted by the attempt to dissect them into standard analytic categories. By observing the process of legal reasoning from the perspective of cognitive theory, we will be able to give better descriptive and predictive—though not necessarily prescriptive—accounts of law and legal doctrine.

The particular doctrinal categories I have chosen—the right to counsel and a series of legal rules respecting action "under color of" law—illuminate a range of issues with respect both to categorization and to legal reasoning. They represent different types of models, different kinds of radial categories, and different sorts of legal categories. The right-to-counsel decisions are structured by a three-factor, scalar model forming a complex graded category. In this instance, the disputes between the justices concern disagreements over extensions of the category. Even so, we shall see how the dissent's arguments for extension manifest the constraints of the central model. The "color of law" cases, in contrast, are organized by a metaphorical model that cuts across a series of ostensibly separate doctrinal areas related by a common underlying conceptual problem. Differences among category members are a function of differences in the policies and purposes underlying the disparate doctrines. Here, the legal disputes are shaped by different understandings of governmental action rather than by disagreement over extensions from the central case.

Finally, these chapters begin an inquiry into the grounding of legal concepts. Although the right-to-counsel decisions represent the relatively straightforward case of a model grounded in specifically legal practices, we will find nevertheless that the application of the model often depends upon general cultural understandings independent of these legal practices or conceptions. In contrast, the "color of law" decisions discussed in the next chapter present a particularly complex and interesting case of a legal concept grounded in more general practices and experiences.

DISTORTING PRECEDENT

The primary issue in the cases leading to *Lassiter* was whether the right to appointed counsel should be administered by an across-the-board rule or determined case by case against a more general standard of fundamental fairness. Initially, the Court applied a rule in federal criminal cases and a standard in criminal cases arising in the state courts.[3] The rule was extended to state felony cases in *Gideon,* to the juvenile justice system in *Gault,* and, in *Argersinger* and *Scott,* to misdemeanor cases involving a sentence of imprisonment.[4] In these beginnings, one can discern some basis for Stewart's "pre-eminent generalization" that the right to appointed counsel normally obtains only in cases involving physical liberty.

But as the Court extended the right to due process hearings into the administrative process, it continued to consider—and sometimes carried over—the right to appointed counsel. In *Vitek v. Jones,* the Court held that even though valid convictions "undoubtedly . . . extinguish a defendant's right to freedom from confinement," a convicted prisoner was nevertheless entitled to a hearing before being involuntarily transferred to a state mental facility for treatment. A four justice plurality would have required that the prisoner be represented by legal counsel; Justice Powell, who provided the necessary fifth vote, differed only in concluding that a qualified nonlawyer such as a mental health professional could function as the prisoner's advocate.[5] In *Gagnon v. Scarpelli,* the Court held that probation could not be revoked without a hearing. Notwithstanding the fact that probation revocation results in a loss of liberty, the Court held that the right to appointed counsel at such hearings should be determined on a case-by-case basis.[6]

And in *Parham v. J.R.*, the Court held that the due process rights of children committed to mental institutions by their parents are satisfied by a "hearing" consisting of the nonadversary review conducted by a qualified medical decisionmaker.[7]

Clearly, Blackmun is correct: Incarceration is neither a necessary condition (as demonstrated by *Vitek*) nor a sufficient condition (as established by *Gagnon* and *Parham*) for the right to counsel. But it is not just the results in these cases that are inconsistent with Stewart's "pre-eminent generalization." Nothing in the discussions in these cases even suggests that the Court gave the physical liberty factor the presumptive weight that Stewart claimed for it. Both opinions in *Vitek* focused primarily on the technical, medical nature of the proceeding, the prisoner's relative incapacities, and the consequent need for an advocate's assistance to make the hearing meaningful.[8] In *Gagnon*, the Court explicitly took the rehabilitative character of the proceeding as its "first point of reference" on the counsel issue; in declining to introduce counsel into every revocation proceeding, the Court stressed that due process does not "require that the significant interests in informality, flexibility, and economy must always be sacrificed." [9]

But, while Stewart's characterization of the precedents is not persuasive, neither is Blackmun's. Where cases like *Vitek* and *Gagnon* seem indifferent to the liberty factor, cases like *Argersinger, Scott,* and *Gault* appear unconcerned with the character of the proceedings. Both in *Argersinger* and *Gault,* the Court adopted an across-the-board rule notwithstanding arguments that counsel was unnecessary or counterproductive given the informal or rehabilitative nature of the respective proceedings.[10] In both cases, moreover, the Court emphasized how much the outcome of a misdemeanor or juvenile proceeding is comparable to that of a felony trial. Thus, in *Argersinger,* the Court rejected as beside the point the argument that the prior cases had all involved felonies: "Their rationale has relevance to any criminal trial, where an accused is deprived of liberty." [11] In *Gault,* the Court observed simply: "A proceeding where the issue is whether the child will be found to be 'delinquent' and subjected to the loss of his liberty for years is comparable in seriousness to a felony prosecution." [12] But the case posing the greatest difficulty for the dissent is *Scott.* There, the Court adopted actual imprisonment, exclusive of other circumstances, as the "defining line" for the right to counsel in misdemeanor cases.[13]

If neither account is fully persuasive, both nevertheless have support in the cases. This seems to confirm the claim that legal reasoning cannot constrain decisionmaking because reasoning from precedent cannot generate determinate solutions to legal questions. On this view, the precedents will always be sufficiently rich in competing arguments and rationales that skill-ful lawyers should be able to extract a version of the case law favorable to their side.[14] And, in a sense, it is hard to quarrel with this view: It credibly describes the self-conscious practices of lawyers and judges engaged in liti-gation. On each side, lawyers massage the precedents to construct an ac-count that makes the law the best it can be—from their strategic point of view, that is. Each side then presents its theory of the law to the court. The judges either adopt the account provided by one side or, replicating the pro-cess, develop yet further accounts.*

But, though this may be a credible description of current practices, it does not follow that it provides a cogent or compelling account of either law or legal reasoning. The claim that reasoning from precedent can always (or, at least, usually) support equally plausible alternative characterizations assumes that if there is no set of necessary and sufficient criteria capable of accounting for all the decisions, then there cannot be any comprehensive "best" version of the precedents. This assumption rests, in turn, on two mistaken premises: (1) that an analytic account specified in terms of neces-sary and sufficient criteria is the only form that a rational explanation can take; and (2) that the process of reasoning—in this case, of legal reason-ing—is solely or even primarily a matter of conscious thought. There is, of course, nothing novel or unusual about these premises; both are tenets of the rationalist model. But this means that the indeterminacy claim is only as good as the rationalist model that sustains it. The indeterminacy critique, in other words, is paradigm-dependent.

Consider the same issue in terms of an alternative paradigm. As we saw in chapter 4, legal rules (whether rules or standards) depend on processes of categorization. Rules not only employ categories (such as "animals" or "bus") but also delineate categories of regulated behavior or of legal action (e.g., "If factors X and Y, then take action of type Z"). But, as chapter 4 demonstrated, very little of human categorization comports with premises 1 and 2 above. Rather, even the "simplest" linguistic categories are rich in con-ceptual content and imaginative structure that cannot be reduced to neces-sary and sufficient conditions. Moreover, we routinely use these complex imaginative processes without the least conscious awareness. So, too, even the "simplest" cases of legal decisionmaking (for example, whether to allow

---

* Both sides will not always be able to produce alternative accounts with the same degree of plausibility exhibited in *Lassiter*. Moreover, sometimes it is not the law that is in dispute but the existence or characterization of the relevant facts. Other times, as was true in *Lassiter,* the dispute turns on competing characterizations of both the law and the facts.

the goldfish or paramecia on the bus) make use of sedimented tacit knowledge in the form of cognitive models (ICMs) that the decisionmaker employs automatically and unreflectively—that is, without the need to recall
them to consciousness.

From a cognitive perspective, therefore, one would not expect necessary and sufficient conditions for the application of a legal rule any more
than one would expect necessary and sufficient criteria for the categories
"mother" or "hand." Rather, one would expect legal categories to be organized by idealized cognitive models grounded in some experientially
meaningful gestalt. These models would produce prototype effects: Some
category members—that is, those that most fully embody the characteristic features of the model—would readily be perceived as paradigmatic examples of the category and could be expected to serve as cognitive reference
points in reasoning about the category. Other category members would either lack some of the model's characteristic features or exhibit them only to
a lesser degree. One would anticipate, therefore, that as the courts applied
the legal rule to the varied factual situations produced by the complex unfolding of human experience the actual pattern of decisions "under" the
rule would manifest a radial category.

On this model of rationality, the right-to-counsel cases provide a nearly
perfect example of the pattern of decisionmaking that Llewellyn described
(with characteristic panache) as the "shaping and joining of complementary
hubs and spokes and rims to form a doctrinal wheel." [15] The right-to-counsel
cases cluster around two foci: Some decisions center on the threatened loss
of physical liberty; others concentrate on the character of the proceeding.
The latter factor is, in turn, analyzed along two distinct dimensions. First,
the decisions consider the purpose of the proceeding: To what degree is it
accusatory and adversarial or rehabilitative and avowedly benevolent? Second, they examine the relative formality or technical difficulty of the proceeding and the impact of the resulting complexity on a layperson's ability
to participate meaningfully in the process without the assistance of an expert
advocate.

From a rationalist perspective, these two lines of precedent seem inconsistent with one another because they appear to employ entirely distinct
criteria. From a cognitive perspective, however, these considerations are but
different components of a single, coherent model.

The first thing to notice in reconstructing that model is that these several considerations are complementary rather than competing: They converge in the felony criminal trial where the gravity of the sanctions is understood to go hand in hand with (if not, in fact, to mandate) formal trial

procedures, rules of evidence, and a rigorous testing of the state's case.* Indeed, it is generally true that the degree of procedural protections afforded the individual increases the more serious are the consequences of adverse state action.[16] Thus, the second thing to notice is that these considerations are not monolithic, all-or-nothing qualities. Liberty, complexity (or formality), and adversariness are all matters of degree. The various considerations in play in the right-to-counsel cases, in other words, are graded concepts.

The case of "mother" illustrates how a category characterized by the convergence of several cognitive models produces a radial category that resists characterization by necessary and sufficient conditions. The right-to-counsel decisions present the analogous case of a single model characterized by the convergence of several graded concepts. The case law resists characterization in necessary and sufficient conditions because, although it is generally true that these factors correlate with one another, such is not always the case. Variations in relations between the factors occur as a result of differences in purpose and subject matter.

Like any form of human categorization, legal categories are motivated. Just as the concepts "dinner party" and "discussion group" differentially frame the category "chair," the liberty and complexity/formality factors are differentially framed by the purpose of the proceeding. When the proceeding is largely accusatorial—that is, when it assesses blame, expresses condemnation, or is otherwise understood as stigmatizing—the liberty factor · is positively correlated with formality and, thus, increased complexity. But when the proceeding is predominantly rehabilitative—that is, when it is benevolently oriented toward treatment—this nominally shared objective overrides the linkage between liberty and formality and typically results in a proceeding that is informal and nonadversarial. Similarly, the subject matter of the proceeding can independently determine its complexity and, thus, the need for assistance.

Consequently, there is no uniform distribution of the liberty, complexity/formality, and adversariness factors across all the relevant cases. In the central case of the felony trial, the severity of the sanctions and the accusatorial nature of the proceedings entail a degree of formality and legal complexity that the Court now understands to require "the guiding hand of counsel at every step in the proceedings."[17] But the cases can vary from the central case along any of the three axes and to any degree. The result is a ra-

---

* Beyond incarceration, the sanctions include the social stigma of conviction and such civil disabilities as loss of the right to vote, disqualification from holding public office, and ineligibility for various professional licenses.

dial category that—analogous to the neurological sketch of color perception discussed in chapter 4—produces prototype effects.

The first-order extensions are those cases that, though they diverge
from the central case in one or more dimensions, strongly manifest the core
components of the felony trial. Thus, the Court extended the right to counsel to juvenile justice proceedings despite the informal nature of the proceedings, their ostensibly rehabilitative aim, and their formal characterization as "civil" rather than "criminal." It did so because it judged the
deprivation of liberty to be as severe as in an adult felony proceeding: Gerald Gault, who was 15, was committed to an "industrial school" for up to
six years; there, the Court noted, "his world is peopled by guards, custodi-
ans, state employees, and 'delinquents' confined with him for anything from
waywardness to rape and homicide." The Court observed, moreover, that
the determination of delinquency "has come to involve only slightly less
stigma than the term 'criminal' applied to adults." It pointed out that, notwithstanding confidentiality rules, juvenile convictions were frequently reported to the FBI, other law enforcement agencies, the military, and potential employers. Given the character of juvenile incarceration and the stigma
of a delinquency determination, the Court concluded that the only real "difference between Gerald's case and a normal criminal case is that safeguards
available to adults were discarded in Gerald's case." [18]

So, too, the Court extended the right to counsel to misdemeanor cases
resulting in incarceration notwithstanding the facts that they are often less
complex (and sometimes more informal) than the typical felony case and
that, by definition, misdemeanor cases involve a lesser deprivation of liberty.* The majority stressed that "the prospect of imprisonment for however short a time will seldom be viewed by the accused as a trivial or 'petty'
matter and may result in quite serious repercussions affecting his career and
his reputation." Accordingly, the Court concluded that—given their shared
accusatorial and punitive character—the rationale of the felony cases was
equally relevant to misdemeanor cases resulting in incarceration. [19]

Vitek represents the converse line of extension. Here, the liberty factor
is only weakly present, since transfer from prison to a mental facility changes
only the relative conditions of confinement. Unquestionably, the technical
complexity of the subject matter is what gives rise to the right to counsel in

---

* A crime is classified as a misdemeanor if it is punishable by a sentence of up to one
year. In *Argersinger,* both the majority and dissent agreed that there is no necessary correlation between the gravity of the offense and the complexity of the legal issues.

such cases. Even so, the contrast with *Parham* makes clear that the complexity factor leads to the appointment of counsel only because the Court viewed the transfer proceeding within a frame more accusatorial and adverse than rehabilitative and benevolent. Thus, the majority explained that an adversarial hearing was required because of "the stigmatizing consequences" of the determination of mental illness and the "qualitatively different" consequences of transfer to a mental institution, where the prisoner is subject to compulsory psychiatric treatment.[20] *Vitek*, in other words, represents a first-order extension that varies from the central case along the liberty dimension. But the transfer proceeding is understood as sufficiently adversarial and complex to be included as an extension of a category that centers on the criminal trial.

The second-order extensions are those cases where the factors fall in the middle range. Thus, in *Gagnon*, the Court stressed the essentially rehabilitative and benevolent role of the probation officer; but it also recognized that the relationship becomes adversarial once the officer decides to recommend revocation.[21] The Court rejected the argument that counsel should never be appointed, pointing to the technical difficulties presented once the proceeding becomes an adversarial contest requiring the cross-examination of witnesses or the analysis of complex documentary evidence.[22] To the argument that *Gideon* and its progeny had rejected the case-by-case approach, the Court deemed it "a sufficient answer" that the revocation of probation represents only a "limited" deprivation of the "conditional" liberty interest of someone who has already been convicted.[23] Thus, in *Lassiter*, Stewart characterized *Gagnon* as establishing that "as a litigant's interest in personal liberty diminishes, so does his right to appointed counsel" (26).

The outliers—where there is no counsel and little process—are those cases in which the Court finds the rehabilitative purpose paramount. In such cases, the ostensible congruity of interests among the participants is presumed to assure that the decision will be controlled by concern for the person's welfare. Thus, in *Parham*, the Court held that when parents voluntarily commit their children to a mental institution, the state need provide only a nonadversarial review consisting of an examination by and the independent medical judgment of a qualified physician. Significantly, the Court emphasized those factors that suggested the rehabilitative and benevolent rather than the accusatorial and adversarial character of the commitment decision. It stressed the state's interest in providing appropriate treatment.[24] It expressed concern that a formal hearing would pit the parents against their child as adversaries, to the detriment of both the parent-child relationship and the child's prospects for successful treatment.[25] The Court also downplayed—but did not deny—the stigmatizing effects of the commitment decision.[26]

To summarize, the right-to-counsel cases form a radial category organized by an idealized cognitive model consisting of these three graded factors. This model is not arbitrary but is grounded in the Anglo-American practices of an adversarial criminal trial.[27] (Or, to put the same point differently, the model is a contingent historical product of those practices.) The three factors are not of equal weight, nor do they operate as independent variables. Rather, they are related to one another in conditional or asymmetric ways. First, and most important, the adversariness factor forms a purposive frame for the other two: If the case falls low on the continuum that runs from the rehabilitative and benevolent to the accusatorial and the adversarial, then little process will be accorded the individual even when physical liberty is at stake and even if the subject matter is complex (as in *Parham*). Second, within that frame, the complexity factor sometimes acts as an independent variable and other times as a dependent variable that correlates with the liberty factor. When the complexity of the proceeding arises from the subject matter (as in *Vitek*), these two factors are independent. But when complexity is a product of the formal nature of the process, this factor acts as a function of the other two. This dependency is clearest in the case of an informal proceeding in which liberty is at stake, as in juvenile cases prior to *Gault*. There, the strength of the liberty and adversarial factors prompts the Court to increase the formality of the process by introducing counsel into the proceedings.

Two Challenges

Consider two potential challenges to this account of the case law—one conventional, the other critical. The first asks how this cognitive approach differs from standard doctrinal analysis: How is this three-factor cognitive model any different than the standard multifactor balancing test that has become an increasingly prevalent part of constitutional adjudication? The second, more skeptical challenge inquires whether cognitive theory really improves on standard legal analysis: Is a cognitive approach any more determinate than conventional forms of legal reasoning?

The first challenge has superficial plausibility. Each of the considerations described as elements of an unconsciously held ICM are discussed in the opinions (though not in every case). Moreover, there is more than a passing resemblance between the three-factor model and the conventional doctrinal forms known as the "totality of the circumstances" and "multi-factor balancing" tests (a point we will return to in chapter 8). Indeed, each of the factors I have described has an ostensible corollary in the three-part balancing test developed in *Mathews v. Eldridge* and applied in *Lassiter*. Under that test, the Court determines what due process requires by weighing the private interest at stake, the risk of error under the existing procedures, and the government's interest in maintaining those procedures.[28] The private interest appears to correlate with the liberty factor, the risk of error with the complexity factor, and the government interest with the adversariness factor.

Still, there are important differences between the three-factor model and the balancing test developed in *Mathews v. Eldridge*. First, the *Eldridge* factors are more general than those I have outlined. Complexity may be the form that the risk of error factor takes in the counsel context, but the other *Eldridge* factors encompass a broader and, therefore, more equivocal assortment of concerns.[29] For example, the government interest factor usually focuses on the state's interest in a just and accurate determination, on one hand, and the cost of additional procedures, on the other. The private interest factor extends beyond the liberty factor to include individual interests with no independent constitutional stature—like treatment or sustenance[30]—that can also be marshaled in support of more streamlined or efficient procedures.

The more important difference is that, compared to the three-part cognitive model, the *Eldridge* test is underspecified in the sense that it is completely silent on the conceptual relations between its factors: One simply "weighs" or "balances" the *Eldridge* factors against one another without any indication either of their relative importance or of the role that any particular factor is supposed to play in the analysis. Yet, as we have seen, the adversariness factor is qualitatively more important, in that it frames the value and meaning of the other two factors.

We can put this point in bas-relief by noting how Stewart's majority opinion treats the strength of the private interest (the liberty factor) as presumptively determinative. As a matter of conventional doctrine, this weighting of the private interest factor is doubly problematic. On one hand, nothing in *Eldridge* or its progeny suggests that the private interest factor should bear this weight; indeed, Stewart first derives the presumption external to the *Eldridge* test and then, in an unprecedented move, places it in the pan against the net weight of the *Eldridge* factors (26–27, 31). On the other hand, the presumption itself is difficult to square with precedents such as *Vitek* and *Parham*. In fact, Stewart does not even try. Of *Vitek*, he says only that "an indigent prisoner is entitled to appointed counsel before being involuntarily transferred for treatment to a state mental hospital (25–26)." *Parham* he simply fails to mention.

In contrast, a cognitive account of the right-to-counsel cases makes better sense both of the actual pattern of decisionmaking and of the arguments offered in those cases. Consider Stewart's presumption in light of the three-part, graded model described above. We have seen that a model consisting of the intersection of several graded concepts will produce prototype effects. In this instance, the three factors converge in the central case of the modern felony trial that, as the prototype, serves as a cognitive reference point for reasoning about the category. Thus, the decisions treat the felony trial as the yardstick against which the right to counsel in other proceedings is measured. This yardstick is explicit in *Gault*'s insistence that a delinquency proceeding "is comparable in seriousness to a felony prosecution" and implicit in *Argersinger*'s conclusion that felony and misdemeanor cases are comparable because "an accused is deprived of liberty." The centrality of the felony trial is evident, as well, in the way that the right-to-counsel cases cluster around the criminal process and its adjuncts: *Vitek* concerns the disposition and treatment of an incarcerated state prisoner, and *Gagnon* involves the administration of probation and parole.

Stewart's "pre-eminent generalization," in other words, is a prototype effect. It expresses a probabilistic truth about the operative conditions of a radial category that nevertheless includes such extensions as *Vitek* and *Gagnon* and such counterexamples as *Parham*. Stewart maintains that "the Court's precedents speak with one voice" in declaring that a person's right to appointed counsel generally exists "*only* when, if he loses, he may be deprived of his physical liberty" (26–27; emphasis added). But this heavy-handed rhetoric disguises a conceptual sleight of hand. The invocation of the voice of authority signals that Stewart is about to invest with presumptive normative force what is, in point of fact, only a defeasible default condition of category membership. What begins as a prototype effect is thus transformed into an argument against the extension of the category to cases lacking one of the attributes of the typical category member. One might think that Stewart is only engaging in the conventional legal practice of drawing distinctions. But, on its own terms, Stewart's "pre-eminent generalization" is only presumptive and not categorical. It is, rather, an example of what I have described elsewhere as a "radical prototype effect,"[31] in which the salience of the prototype colors or distorts the more variegated discriminations characteristic of radial categorization.

Radical prototype effects take two forms. In the "assimilation-to-prototype effect," the prototype so overshadows the rest of the category that one does not distinguish the variants from the prototype of the idealized cognitive model. This is the familiar problem that attends social stereotypes, as when all the members of a group are perceived or assumed to be like the prototypical member.[32] Stewart appears to make this mistake when he summarily treats *Vitek* as if it were a typical loss-of-liberty case. In the "reduction-to-prototype effect," the variants of the central model are not even perceived as instances of the same category. The effect is to reduce the category to its central case—as when someone insists that modern art is not "real" art. Reduction-to-prototype effects are common incidents of legal reasoning because they parallel the rationalist model's strategy of reducing categories to necessary and sufficient criteria. Stewart's presumption seems a clear instance of this phenomenon.

Although a cognitive approach provides a more refined, comprehensive account of the right-to-counsel decisions than does conventional legal doctrine, it might still be vulnerable to the skeptical challenge. Thus, a critic might ask why *Vitek* is characterized as an accusatory proceeding while *Parham* is said to be rehabilitative. Couldn't one "flip" those characterizations, emphasizing the treatment dimension of the transfer in *Vitek* and the stigmatizing effects of the commitment in *Parham?* In *Gault,* the Court noted the older legal understanding that because he "can be made to attorn to his parents, to go to school, etc.," a child "has a right 'not to liberty but to custody.'" What, the critic might ask, makes *Gagnon* a case of conditional liberty and *Gault* not? Couldn't the Court have argued just as plausibly that as a practical matter, revocation of probation works a complete deprivation of liberty, while juvenile incarceration "merely provides the 'custody' to which the child is entitled"?[33]

This second challenge also has surface plausibility, but it misconceives the nature of the argument. Nothing *prevents* a judge from characterizing *Vitek* as rehabilitative and *Parham* as adversarial. Judges can and do characterize the facts, and they often do so in ways that are inconsistent with previous decisions. Consider an example from the right-to-counsel cases. Writing for the majority in *Gagnon,* Justice Powell defended the appropriateness of a case-by-case approach notwithstanding its apparent repudiation in *Gideon* and *Argersinger.* He explained that probation revocation cases are informal proceedings in which the need for assistance arises not from the nature of the process but from the peculiar character of the individual case. In contrast, he argued that criminal trials always require counsel because they are specialized proceedings governed by formal rules of evidence and procedure in which the state is represented by a professional prosecutor.[34] Yet, just the year before, Powell had rested his dissent in *Arger-singer* on the ground that procedures in misdemeanor cases are often informal—presided over by lay judges and presented by arresting officers rather than professional prosecutors.[35]

But, if it is undeniable that judges engage in characterization and interpretation, it hardly follows that legal decisionmaking is indeterminate or that legal doctrine is infinitely manipulable.* Consider what it would mean to accept the skeptic's claim that "in every interesting case, lawyers can generate plausible, conventional legal arguments on both sides of the question." [36] There would still remain the questions of *how* legal actors come to make the characterizations they do and *why* others find those interpretations persuasive.

In other words, it hardly suffices to show that alternative arguments are *plausible* when the name of the game is *persuasion:* Whether one is litigating a case or counseling a client, the challenge of the lawyer's craft is to devise ex ante (i.e., with predictability) a position that will prevail ex post. To do that, the lawyer must construct an argument or draft a document that will convince some subsequent set of legal decisionmakers to take the desired action. Indeed, even on the most cynical view of judicial decisionmaking—in which the judge merely invokes some plausible doctrinal argument to justify a decision made on other (presumedly political) grounds—the lawyer is nevertheless engaged in the endeavor of persuasion. Much the same is true for judges, who must persuade other legal actors, whether they be colleagues on an appellate bench, the judges of a higher court, or the general audience of lawyers, legislators, and citizens. None of this could occur (indeed, the entire enterprise would be futile) unless there were some shared set of understandings that made it possible to gauge the likely course of the decisionmaking process.

It is precisely here that cognitive theory makes its most powerful contribution. From a cognitive perspective, it does not matter that legal decisionmaking is a product of tacit knowledge rather than doctrinal logic.[37] The process is one of persuasion. To ask about the characterizations that people are likely to find convincing is to inquire into what will make the most sense to them under the circumstances. It is to inquire into the nature of their categories and concepts—for it is our categories and concepts that

---

* To the contrary, the transparency of Powell's recharacterization in *Gagnon* cuts against any strong claim of doctrinal indeterminacy. If legal doctrine were, in fact, infinitely manipulable, judges should never have to resort to such conspicuous stratagems in order to harmonize inconsistent results.

define our expectations and, in so doing, powerfully shape what we find believable, what we judge accurate, what we experience as cogent, compelling, and convincing. Persuasion, as we saw in chapter 5, is a function of the cognitive models by which we cognize our world.

The skeptical challenge derives its force from the conventional understanding of law as a matter of prescription. For law to operate *as* law, on this view, there must be some disciplining external constraint on the discretion of the legal decisionmaker. It could be an objective quality of the legal materials—that is, of the facts and holdings of the cases—or a higher-order reason for the differing characterizations (the proverbial "principle" or "metatheory"). But once legal decisionmaking is understood as a process of persuasion, it is quite irrelevant that legal materials are indeterminate because subject to different interpretations. Legal materials do not decide cases, people do. Constraint, therefore, can exist only within the collective decisionmaking processes of some actual community of people.[38] Because judges, too, are dependent on the structures of social meaning that make communication possible, their range of *effective* operation is restricted by the complex social webs they inhabit and that, in turn, inhabit them. Constraint, as the preceding chapter tried to show, is internal and relative.

The fact that legal decisionmaking fails to conform to the categorical patterns promised by the criterial logic of legal doctrine—e.g., that the similarly stigmatizing consequences of commitment are valued differently in *Vitek* and *Parham*—is beside the point. For law to operate as law, it is necessary only that the processes of persuasion operate to constrain decisionmakers in predictable ways. If they do, it does not matter whether the outcomes meet rationalist requirements of analytic rigor. The system can operate as "law" as long as the potential outcomes are predictable—that is, as long as the bases for decisions are widely (if tacitly) shared.

Understanding legal decisionmaking as but an instance of everyday processes of categorization (here, as mediated by persuasion) satisfies this reconceived notion of law because it enables us to identify the regularities that one might reasonably expect to find. As a form of categorization, legal decisionmaking should display all the characteristics of reasoning by means of ICMs. Thus, we would expect that patterns of actual decisionmaking would manifest radial structure; that legal decisionmaking would be motivated by social practices or grounded in general cultural knowledge; that legal decisionmaking would exhibit the same kind of context-sensitive and normatively infused judgment typical of categorization generally; that legal decisionmaking would manifest gestalt properties such as framing and other holistic or ecological relations both within and between categories;

and, consequently, that legal decisionmaking would display various kinds of prototype effects. As we have seen, the right-to-counsel cases display just such cognitive regularities.

By the same token, much of the apparent indeterminacy of characterization disappears once the cases are evaluated in light of these expected regularities. Consider the first of the skeptical questions posed above. Why is the transfer in *Vitek* seen as accusatory and adversarial, while the commitment in *Parham* is understood as rehabilitative? If a factual situation or case has no essential quality, the answer can lie only in the interpretive processes of the decisionmakers. The previous section described the deliberative process in the right-to-counsel cases as characterized by an idealized cognitive model consisting of three graded factors in which the adversariness factor serves as a frame for the other two. But the judge does not *begin* with this model and then reason to the conclusion she likes. Rather, the judge begins with a gestalt perception or overall impression of the situation that is already informed by her general cultural knowledge about such transactions or events, about the roles and relationships of the various actors, and about the conventional purposes or functions that will animate their actions. In other words, the judge does not approach the facts as if they were sui generis. Rather, as Llewellyn explained long ago, the judge sees them in the first instance as examples or representatives of categories already endowed with social meaning.[39]

Thus, even if one assumed that a cognitive model were "applied" in the same sense that one consciously applies a rule, it would still have to be "applied" to the facts as apprehended by the judge, which means that in cases like *Vitek* and *Parham,* the judge's appraisal of the adversariness factor would be relative to (which is to say, constrained by) the background ICMs that provide the contexts within which the facts of the case are rendered meaningful. Here, the concepts "prison" and "parent" provide different categorical frames for the judge's assessment of the adversariness of the commitment decisions in *Vitek* and *Parham.* Simply put, the involuntary transfer in *Vitek*—initiated by prison authorities after the prisoner had set his mattress on fire while in solitary confinement—is more obviously adversarial than the "same" action initiated by one's mother. Thus, not only do the decisions in *Vitek* and *Parham* exhibit precisely the kind of gestalt properties that cognitive theory would predict, but these framing effects are responsible for the context-sensitive discriminations that are usually explained with a vague and conclusory reference to "judgment."

We have seen repeatedly that the familiar and conventional may nevertheless be conceptually complex. The same is true of these framing effects, which subsume prototype effects. In chapter 4, we observed that a legal category forms its own gestalt structure or ICM that produces prototype effects. Above, we have seen how a prototype such as the modern felony trial serves as a cognitive reference point in reasoning about a legal category. A comparable operation is at work here: The framing concept—"prison" or "parent"—will itself be structured by a complex ICM. (Remember the concept "mother.") This ICM will be motivated by cultural experience, will be normatively loaded rather than value-neutral, and will produce prototype effects. These prototype effects (and the normative assumptions they embody) will in turn enter into reasoning and influence the framing. Thus, it is the conception of the typical "parent" or "prison" that frames the Court's assessment of the adversariness factor.

This prototype effect is explicit in *Parham*, where the majority relied on the presumption that parents and social workers act in the best interests of the child.* The Court appreciated that the presumption would not always hold; it recognized, for example, the unfortunate reality of child abuse and neglect. But it considered that fact as a ground for caution rather than as "a reason to discard wholesale those pages of human experience that teach that parents generally do act in their child's best interest." [40] The Court, in other words, understood that—as with any prototype—the presumption reflects idealized assumptions derived from cultural experience and, as such, is only probabilistically true.

The second skeptical question can be answered in much the same fashion as the first. One can plausibly recharacterize *Gault* as a case of conditional liberty and, thus, as on a par with *Gagnon*. But this recharacterization makes sense only within a set of formal, largely antiquated legal conceptions of guardianship and custody. As soon as one broadens the focus to consider what makes sense in *social* terms, the cogency of the analogy fades quickly: The typical relationship between child and parent is not at all like the typical relationship between defendant and parole officer. Similarly, a transfer from the custody of one's parents to that of the state reform school ordinarily works a bigger change in life circumstances than the shift from the supervision of the parole officer to that of the prison guard. In sum, the alternative characterizations that seemed plausible as a matter of legal argument become weak and unpersuasive once the facts are evaluated in terms of their social meanings.

* *Parham* was a class action. One of the class representatives was committed by his mother. The other, J. R., was committed by the Department of Social Services after his (seventh set of) foster parents requested that he be removed from their home.

With respect to both the *Vitek-Parham* and *Gault-Gagnon* sets of comparisons, the apparent indeterminacy of characterization is a product of the
unrealistically thin criterial logic that is the nominal "stuff" of legal reasoning. The cases in each pair share a common element: the stigmatizing
consequences of commitment in *Vitek* and *Parham;* some degree of formal
legal custody in *Gault* and *Gagnon.* If commitment and stigma are viewed
as necessary and sufficient conditions of the right to counsel, then *Vitek* and
Parham are irreconcilable. But once these elements are understood as components of an adversariness factor that is itself defined by a larger social
framework of roles and relationships, the ostensible conflict evaporates.
Similarly, the shared "custody" element in *Gagnon* and *Gault* is the product of a formal legal characterization that fails to distinguish different social
situations.

The indeterminacy identified by the skeptical challenge is merely an artifact of its deracinated model of reason. Merleau-Ponty explains:

> Human acts lose all their meaning when detached from their context and
> broken down into their component parts (like the gestures of the man I
> can see but do not hear through the window of a telephone booth). . . .
> It is easy to strip language and actions of all meaning and to make them
> seem absurd, if only one looks at them from far enough away.[41]

Because the skeptical challenge depends on a highly abstracted conception
of reason, it simply is not germane to an account that understands meaning
as grounded in experience and motivated by complex social practices. The
skeptical challenge merely confirms by negative implication the truism that
all meaning is meaning in a context.

Relative Indeterminacies

Context, as illustrated by chapter 4's discussion of Tversky and Kahneman, is exactly what reasoning by means of cognitive models is all about.
Understanding legal decisionmaking as a matter of reasoning by means of
cognitive models has five significant advantages over its more familiar com-
petitors. First, it enables concrete and detailed accounts of the context-
sensitive discriminations typical of the judicial process. Where more conventional accounts can explain contextual decisionmaking only by reference
to some obscure faculty like "judgment," an account of legal reasoning in
terms of cognitive models makes it possible to specify the parameters that
constitute judgment and govern legal decisionmaking.

Second, a cognitive account illuminates how and why legal decisionmakers adopt the interpretations of the facts that they do. The characterizations actually embraced in the Court's opinions in *Vitek, Parham, Gagnon,* and *Gault* are those that conform to the default assumptions embodied in widely shared cultural ICMs. To be clear: These characterizations and assumptions do not state objective or necessary truths. They are, rather, probabilistic truths or idealizations that characterize our "normal" expectations as they are shaped by cultural practices, conditions, values, and beliefs. Consequently, they represent the understandings—like the notion that parents generally act in their child's best interest—that a court is most likely to find credible and persuasive. They are also the characterizations that a judge could reasonably expect most others to find convincing.

Third, an account of legal reasoning in terms of cognitive models clarifies some of the social constraints on judicial decisionmaking. The judges' characterizations and assumptions will be constrained in the sense that they are contingent on the prevailing social practices that motivate and ground the culture's ICMs: Every characterization is not as good (which is to say, as persuasive) as every other, given a particular set of cultural practices and conditions. Moreover, the fact that cognition is grounded means that even the judges' "own" categories are already constrained by the socially constructed contexts in which they find themselves. In a real and important sense, therefore, judges are *predisposed* to replicate and reflect prevailing cultural practices and conditions.[42] This is especially true when the judges are concerned not to be condemned as "imposing their own values" or dismissed as "out of touch with reality."

Fourth, the judges' characterizations and understandings will also be constrained in the sense that they will be governed by prototype effects: Some category members will play a disproportionate role in reasoning and decisionmaking. Because of the gestalt nature of cognitive processes, the conceptual system will also display ecological properties. In *Vitek* and *Parham,* for example, the prototypes of general cultural categories powerfully influenced the Court's understanding and application of an otherwise unrelated legal category.

Prototype effects will also characterize how judges sort cases into legal categories. Judge Hutcheson, a legal realist judge of the 1920s, famously described his decisionmaking process:

> I, after canvassing all the available material at my command, . . . give my imagination play, and brooding over the cause, wait for the feeling, the hunch—that intuitive flash of understanding which makes the jump-spark connection between question and decision.[43]

Mainstream legal scholars have criticized, even ridiculed, this description as subjective and irrational. But this description merely anticipated (by fifty years) what contemporary cognitive science has documented as prototype effects. We now know that recognition factors are higher and response time shorter for prototypes than for nonprototypical category members. We know, too, that activation of a prototype has the effect of activating the entire category of which it is the exemplar.* Judge Hutcheson had it exactly right: Confronted with the factual and legal characterizations of the parties, the judge must identify an appropriate model (or models) that yields a framework for understanding the situation and deciding the case. In these circumstances, a prototype will powerfully influence the judge's thinking not only because it will catch the judge's attention, but also because it will prompt the relevant categories for consideration.

Fifth, a cognitive account of legal decisionmaking provides the conceptual tools with which to rescue legal theory from the straitjacket of the rationalist model's all-or-nothing assumptions. On that model, constraint is understood to mean determinacy and, by the law of the excluded middle, the only alternative is indeterminacy. When the decisions fail to measure up to the rationalist's expectations of objectivity and determinacy (as they inevitably do), the rationalist (including her analogue, the antinomial captive) can conclude only that "anything goes." Cognitive theory, in contrast, allows more meaningful and precise descriptions of the complex patterns of flexibility and constraint in legal decisionmaking.

Consider, for example, Duncan Kennedy's description of the experience of freedom and constraint in rule application. He describes the dilemma of a hypothetical prolabor judge trying to decide a suit to enjoin a lie-in by striking bus drivers. The judge works through the precedents, their opposition to "how-I-want-to-come-out," and the possible recharacterizations that could turn the workers' actions into the exercise of a First Amendment right. He conceptualizes the precedents as arrayed in "fields" that fix "a boundary between permitted and forbidden acts."

> As we move from fact-situation to fact-situation across the field, the
> speech policy gets weaker, and the property policy stronger, until at the
> boundary they are in equilibrium. . . . At points not on boundaries, one
> or another set of policies predominates. The policies are to be under-

---

* Because a prototype is the paradigmatic example that most fully embodies the characteristic features of a model, the activation of the pattern of neural firings that constitutes the prototype is in a direct sense the activation of the category itself.

stood as gradients; they are strongest in the "core," where a given general rule seems utterly obvious in its application and also utterly "appropriate as a matter of social policy." The argument set supporting the general rules diminishes in force as we move from the core outward toward the periphery, and ultimately to a boundary with another rule.[44]

Kennedy's depiction bears a striking resemblance to the more technical description of a cognitive account. On his account, the legal rule derived from precedent possesses the graded structure of a radial category and produces prototype effects—that is, cases "where a given general rule seems utterly obvious in its application and also utterly 'appropriate.'"

A cognitive account of the same material makes it possible to specify precisely why a rule "seems utterly obvious" and "utterly appropriate" at its "core." One would first reconstruct the cognitive model at work in the First Amendment cases, the normative understandings and assumptions that it encodes, and the social practices that motivate it (a task I take up in chapter 10). One would then be in a position to explain why the rule "diminishes in force as we move from the core outward toward the periphery" and to make predictions about the nature of the arguments for and against extension of the rule.

In the right-to-counsel cases, for example, the graded character of the three-factor model provides a metric that rationalizes the pattern of decisionmaking. Cases like *Gault* that diverge from the central model only slightly (or in one dimension only) make relatively strong candidates for extension. But, as the cases vary from the central model to a greater degree (or along two or more dimensions), the Court is predictably more free to deviate from precedent. Social, political, and ideological values play a role in judicial decisionmaking, but the underlying concepts frame and constrain the instrumentalist choices in the sense that they make certain choices meaningful and render others implausible or unpersuasive. One can say that the model's graded character creates the *forensic space* for disagreement over extension of the right to counsel. Thus, Powell's *Argersinger* dissent relied on the relative informality of the procedures in misdemeanor cases to argue against extension of *Gideon*'s across-the-board rule, while the majority emphasized the strength of the liberty and adversariness factors. But the case-by-case approach prevailed just a year later in *Gagnon,* where Powell's majority opinion stressed the diminished strength of all three factors.

In other words, to describe a line of cases in terms of idealized cognitive models, radial categories, and prototype effects is to give an account of the extent of constraint decisionmakers can be expected to experience in "applying" the law. Elaboration or expansion of a legal category will be governed by regularities in cognitive processing that include motivation, chaining, and metaphorical extension (topics I return to in chapter 10's discussion of innovation). For present purposes, the most prominent of these regularities are those that arise from the compositional structure of idealized cognitive models. The compositional elements of an ICM will provide the conditions of possibility that enable the extension of a legal category and—at the same time and for the same reason—constrain the scope of meaningful (that is, potentially persuasive) argument.

We can see manifestations of compositional constraint in *Lassiter*. In declining to extend the automatic right to counsel to parental termination proceedings, Stewart utilized the model's graded character in two ways. He drew on it most prominently in introducing the presumption that there is a right to appointed counsel only when physical liberty is at stake. But he also justified a case-by-case approach to the appointment of counsel on the ground that parental termination cases, like cases of probation revocation, vary greatly in complexity and, thus, in the need for legal assistance (31). To the majority, in other words, *Lassiter* represented only a second-order extension of a model that centers on the modern felony trial.

Given that model, and given Stewart's presumptive weighting of the liberty factor, one would have expected the dissent to minimize the importance of the criminal trial—that is, one would have expected the dissent to construct an account of the precedents that reformulated the category such that the criminal trial appeared as an incidental rather than prototypical category member. Surprisingly, however, Blackmun, too, invoked the criminal trial as the yardstick against which to measure the right to counsel in other proceedings. In arguing that the formal character of the termination proceeding necessitated the appointment of counsel, he began by asserting: "The method chosen by North Carolina to extinguish parental rights resembles in many respects a criminal prosecution" (42–43). Moreover, he characterized the parental termination proceeding as having "an obvious accusatory and punitive focus" and described "the State's role [as] clearly adversarial and punitive" (48).

From a rationalist perspective that insists on criterial accuracy and rigor, Blackmun's attempt to recharacterize the proceedings as more nearly like a criminal trial must seem both imprecise and unpersuasive. Indeed, the dissent's characterization prompted Chief Justice Burger to write separately to insist that the "purpose of the termination proceeding at issue here was not 'punitive.' On the contrary, its purpose was protective of the child's best interest" (34). And, in a strict sense, Burger was right: The purpose of terminating Ms. Lassiter's parental rights was not to punish her for being a bad mother but to secure the best interests of her son, William, by placing him permanently with adoptive parents who could better care for him.

From a cognitive perspective, however, Blackmun's recharacterization represents an entirely sensible—even predictable—argument for at least three reasons. First, his attempt to assimilate the parental termination proceeding to the category prototype mirrors, and partly offsets, the reduction-to-prototype effect of the majority's presumption. The presumption emphasizes that the right to counsel normally extends only to criminal cases. Blackmun's attempted assimilation-to-prototype acts as a partial corrective; it points out that cases that *resemble* the criminal trial, such as *Vitek,* also entail the right to appointed counsel. Second, and relatedly, Blackmun's characterization of the termination proceeding as "punitive" is a (somewhat crude) attempt to evoke both the prototype and the underlying cognitive model that forms the basis of that resemblance. The termination proceeding is, in Blackmun's exact words, "accusatory and punitive" or "adversarial and punitive." Thus, his point is that the adversariness factor is particularly compelling in a termination case. Given the normative privileging of the nurturance model, the allegation that a parent "has, without cause, failed to establish or maintain concern or responsibility as to the child's welfare" is uniquely stigmatizing (44). (The quotation is from the state's legal papers.) A determination that someone is an unfit parent assesses blame and expresses condemnation in a way that cannot be compared to a determination that someone has a mental illness.* On this view, *Lassiter* represents a first-order extension at least as compelling as *Vitek.*

Third, and most important, Blackmun's argument manifests the compositional constraints of the central model. One could abstract a criterial account that makes the criminal trial appear incidental, but it would not really be persuasive. The fact of the matter is that the right to counsel arose in the context of the felony criminal trial and only later was extended to other cases. It is hard to escape the fact that the criminal trial *is* the category prototype. An argument that seeks to reformulate the legal category in broader terms may very well be effective with those who generally favor the extension of due process protections. But an argument for the extension of

---

* Thus, Blackmun observed that "the procedure devised by the State vastly differs from the informal and rehabilitative probation revocation decision in [*Gagnon*] . . . and the essentially medical decision in *Parham*" (44).

the right to counsel to a new procedural context will be most persuasive to the largest number of people if it can tie the new case directly to the core instance of the existing legal category.

As noted at the outset, a cognitive account of the right-to-counsel decisions does not provide determinate, "right" answers to specific legal questions: The three-factor cognitive model for the right-to-counsel cases does not *tell* you how *Lassiter* should be decided. Rather, it describes the forensic space within which doctrinal debate over the right to counsel takes place. Moreover, the model provides a more cogent framework for analyzing, understanding, and formulating arguments in right-to-counsel cases. Stewart's presumption appears more comprehensible but less defensible when it is understood as a radical prototype effect deployed in an effort to reduce the category to its prototypical cases. The majority's treatment of *Lassiter* as a second-order extension comparable to *Gagnon* is an artifact of its deliberately myopic focus on the only one of the three factors (the liberty factor) on which the case falls low on the scale.*

Conversely, Blackmun's arguments gain both coherence and strength when they are understood as expressions of the three-factor model. When the parental termination proceeding is considered in light of that model, the intensity of the adversariness and complexity factors militate rather strongly in favor of the appointment of counsel. Indeed, if one were to map the radial category structured by that model, *Lassiter* would appear closer to such first-order extensions as *Argersinger, Scott,* and *Vitek*. Under *Argersinger* and *Scott,* a person facing thirty days in jail for disturbing the peace is entitled to counsel. I suspect that most people would consider a misdemeanor conviction for breach of the peace as less serious and less stigmatizing than a solemn, judicial determination that one is unfit to be a parent. So, too, most people would regard thirty days in jail as preferable to the complete, irrevocable severance of all ties with their child.

Even so, the ultimate decision in a case like *Lassiter* will be strongly influenced by one's assumptions and beliefs concerning the competence of state child-welfare agencies and the utility of lawyers in achieving better outcomes. Doctrinally, these considerations might have been taken up in *Lassiter* under the *Eldridge* "risk of error" factor—though they received scant attention in the opinions. Although these considerations do not factor into

---

* Indeed, the reduction of a complex area of law to a single principle, purpose, or policy is a tried and true method for narrowing its scope. Consider, for example, the way in which the current Court has employed an exclusive focus on deterrence to narrow the scope of the Fourth Amendment's exclusionary rule.

the cognitive model directly, they are part of the set of background motivations against which the three-factor model will be viewed. In other words, the compositional constraints of the model will govern to the degree that the decisionmaker is committed to deciding according to precedent or in need of persuading others who are. Within that frame, the further the case lies from the central model, the greater the force these background considerations will have.

A cognitive account denies neither that there is indeterminacy in legal reasoning nor that social, political, and policy considerations play an important role in legal decisionmaking. What a cognitive account does claim is that it is possible to explicate the kinds, degrees, and reasons for the relative indeterminacy that one experiences in working with legal materials. We can categorize these indeterminacies as *indeterminacy of extension, substantive indeterminacy,* and *indeterminacy of paradigm.* By *indeterminacy of extension,* I refer to the lack of fixed, generative rules or principles that determine extensions from the central case of an ICM. By *substantive indeterminacy,* I refer to indeterminacy that arises as a consequence of the contingent nature of our cognitive models. By *indeterminacy of paradigm,* I mean the indeterminacy that results from the law's commitment to the rationalist model of logic and categorization.

Indeterminacy of extension is a consequence of the radial structure of thought. When the facts of a case match the ICM that motivates the precedent or legal principle, most legally trained observers committed to applying the rule will experience the rule as having sufficient structure to constrain decision. As the facts vary from the model, however, greater indeterminacy will result. The degree of "fit" or variance is not an objective given but a function of the existing models; as Putnam admonishes, "there are [no] inputs which are not in themselves to some extent shaped by our concepts."[45] Concepts and categories, in other words, have ontological effects. These ontological effects can also be observed in the compositional constraints that govern the extension of cognitive models. But these constraints are relative rather than absolute; extensions are motivated but not determined.

It follows, however, that much of what is well structured in legal reasoning never comes before us or seems trivial. It tends to remain out of sight because it is automatic, uncontroversial, or easily resolved. Conversely, much of what is problematic in law concerns extensions of—or, as will appear in a moment, conflicts between—existing models. Thus, though law is hard at work much of the time, it cannot do the one thing we most want to depend on it for: to decide the difficult, controversial cases.

Substantive indeterminacy has two dimensions: synchronic and diachronic. Synchronically, substantive indeterminacy arises when there are multiple models for characterizing the same conditions or events. Is burning a draft card properly classified as political speech, as destruction of government property, or as obstruction of a lawful state function? * Multiple models occur because factual situations have no objective qualities or "essences" and because human conceptual systems are not organized hierarchically in terms of higher-order postulates that insure the consistency of lower order concepts and categories. Rather, concepts and categories are grounded in particular contexts or gestalts of meaningful human interaction—e.g., mother, bank teller, journey—and imaginatively extended "outward" to other, related cases and "upward" to more abstract levels. The bottom-up and center-out character of cognition means that concepts and categories often have a local and contextual quality. At the same time, the category prototypes will be relatively stable because of the experiential grounding of these concepts and categories. Synchronically, substantive indeterminacy will arise at the peripheries of the relevant categories: Is the beanbag chair or hassock a "chair" for purposes of the invitation? Is a goldfish or paramecium an "animal" within the meaning of the rule? Is a lie-in a trespass or a lawful demonstration?

Diachronically, substantive indeterminacy arises because the grounding of cognitive models in social practices and experiences necessarily implies social contingency. Because law is grounded in the same cultural ICMs as every other aspect of human rationality, it is no less parasitic on general cultural conflict and change. Wide fluctuations in doctrine can occur as a result of social conflict or change. Old categorizations change in substantive ways—which is good as well as bad. In this sense, law is not a surrogate for politics so much as it is one of the forms in which political discourse takes place.

Indeterminacy of paradigm arises from the disparity between the rationalist model of legal discourse and the cognitive model of human reasoning. The rules proposed by the rationalist legal thinker present themselves as propositional and syllogistic, but human rationality is neither. Propositional legal rules promise determinate answers, but the imaginative structure of thought yields a different pattern of decisionmaking. This lack of fit

---

* Kennedy's lie-in hypothetical is designed to capitalize on this phenomenon by positing a situation that could be characterized either as an interference with the employer's property or as the exercise of a First Amendment right (though, in point of fact, it is weighted against the latter description).

between the professed and the experienced in legal reasoning is perceived as indeterminacy.

Indeterminacy is exacerbated by the rationalist model, which distorts the normal processes of human reasoning in predictable ways. In seeking propositional principles, syllogistic rules, and determinate factual statements as necessary and sufficient criteria, conventional legal reasoning creates greater indeterminacy because it abstracts and simplifies a more complex experience; its very partiality falsifies what it tries to capture. In this way, both the majority and dissenting opinions in *Lassiter* represent typical rationalist dissections of a more complex three-factor model that better captures the actual range of the right-to-counsel decisions. To see the decisions as embodying only one or the other dimension is to miss much of what is actually going on in these cases.

CHAPTER 7

What Is the "Color of Law"?

THE COMIC, Steven Wright, doesn't like Halloween. "I see a person in a cop uniform," he explains, "and I don't know whether it's a cop or just a person in a cop uniform." Then, after a pause: "Of course, that's all a cop is—a person in a cop uniform."

The law has wrestled with this problem for centuries. It arises whenever the acts of governmental officials are subject to legal scrutiny. Because every official is also a private citizen, it is never completely clear when an official has acted *as* an official. The mirror-image problem occurs whenever a question of governmental responsibility arises. As Justice Frankfurter once observed, a government can act only through its agents.[1] But the only people capable of acting for the state may, at any given moment, be acting either as public officials or as ordinary private citizens.

Strikingly, the common law resolved this problem of role ambiguity by relying on a legal metaphor—"under color of office"—to mediate the application of legal restrictions on the exercise of state power. Surprisingly complex in structure, the expression is actually premised on two different metaphorical conceptions—one embodied, the other culturally contingent. The first conception involves a subset of the now familiar CONDUIT metaphor-system; the second consists of a metaphor and a metonymy grounded in quite specific historical practices. Notwithstanding these differences in origin and structure, both metaphorical concepts share the connotation of an action that presents a false or deceptive appearance. More importantly, this meaning-rich metaphor represents a sophisticated response to the conceptual problems raised by cases of official misconduct—a response, moreover, that is not possible on more conventional legal reasoning.

Too Much or Too Little

The problem of who or what is the "state" has proven remarkably recalcitrant to ordinary legal analysis. The difficulty is that there is no "state" apart from the ambiguous social actors that represent it. As an entity, the "state" is an entirely conceptual construct that exists only because we conceptualize it *as such;* in the language made familiar by critical legal studies, the state is a reification.[2] But it is a reification of a very particular kind, because this reification is indispensable to the phenomenological experience of the state. Without the concept "state" there would be only groups of similarly clad thugs impinging on our autonomy or protecting us (at a price, no doubt) from other such groups. In this sense, the state is an imaginative social product over and above its personnel and other material manifestations. The state is a *social institution,* which means that it exists precisely to the extent that people internalize and act on the cultural meaning it represents.[3]

Usually, it requires a period of radical political instability to make us aware of the abstract, socially constructed nature of the state.[4] The Supreme Court faced a version of this problem in 1849, when it was asked to decide which of two sets of competing claimants was the lawful government of Rhode Island. The case, a trespass action, arose when an officer under the charter government broke into the home of an adherent of the competing faction to effect a warrantless arrest. The case turned on which set of actors represented the legitimate state of Rhode Island. The Court concluded that there were no meaningful criteria for choosing between the competing factions and, therefore, that the case presented a political question.[5]

But even in the ordinary case where there is only a single, popularly accepted government, the state's identity remains contingent in two senses. First, it is dependent on the unstable, inherently ambiguous character of its agents. This dependency makes it difficult to determine in any "objective" or "logical" way when the state has caused an injury and when a mere private actor—who only incidentally happens to have a secondary identity as a state agent—is the "real" cause. Second, the state's identity is contingent because the socially constructed nature of the concept "state" means that there is no determinate way in which to decide when it is a governmental entity that has acted: Just as the citizens can withhold their consent from an authority they view as illegitimate, a legal system can withhold its authorization from the acts of its officials. When it does, the resulting doctrinal difficulties are monumental. Is an illegal act by a state official state action?[6] If the answer to that question is "yes" (as it is), is that act shielded by the state's sovereign immunity under the Eleventh Amendment?[7] And if the answer to the latter question is "no" (as, in fact, it is), then how does one resolve the contradiction between these two inconsistent characterizations?

It might seem that the obvious solution to the problem is to identify the state with only those who act pursuant to the specific authorization of its positive law. But this position—which I refer to as *the reductive approach*—obliterates much of what is supposed to be accomplished by the commitment to governmental accountability represented by the ideal of "a government of laws and not of men."[8] In a simplistic sense, the reductive view seems to fit well with the rule-of-law ideal. A governmental officer who fails to comply with the rules specifying her official conduct is no longer viewed as acting for the state and is instead treated as any other wrongdoer.[9] But the reductive approach quickly proves incoherent because there *is* no government apart from the men (and women) who instantiate it. This incoherence becomes manifest under either of two circumstances: (1) when the issue is the enforcement of constitutional constraints on actions that are peculiarly governmental—the Eleventh Amendment problem, for example; or (2) when the system is designed to invoke third-party constraints that are defined in terms of official action.[10]

Worse yet, the search for reliable objectified criteria proves either too much or too little. If state action is identified with state permission, then every actor—public and private, official and unofficial—is always acting as "the state."[11] Conversely, if state action is reduced to direct authorization by positive law, then strictly speaking no putatively illegal act could be attributed to the state until its highest court had upheld it against legal challenge.[12] Here, again, the rationalist tools of standard legal analysis lead to confusion rather than clarity.

Sheriffs, Sureties, and the "Colour of Their Office"

Today, the difficulties caused by the constructive nature of the state arise most frequently in the context of constitutional litigation under section 1983, the Reconstruction Era civil rights act that provides redress for constitutional violations committed "under color of" state law.[13] But the underlying conceptual problem was familiar to the common law, which for centuries used the "color of office" concept to mediate appropriate legal controls over sheriffs and other officers. The phrase "Colour of his Office" first appeared in an English statute of 1275 that prohibited seizures of property without a warrant or other proper authority.[14] As Sir Edward Coke explained in his annotation of the statute:

> *Colore officii* is ever taken in malam partem, as *virtute officii* is taken in bonam: And therefore this implyeth a seisure unduly made against law.
>
> And he may doe it *colore officii* in two manner of wayes: Either when he hath no warrant, or when he hath a warrant, and doth not persue it.[15]

A statute of 1444 prohibited sheriffs and their officers from taking "under color of their office" any "thing . . . to their use, profit, or avail, of any person by them . . . to be arrested or attached, nor of none other for them, for the omitting of any arrest or attachment" or for "mainprise, letting to bail, or eschewing any ease or favour to any such person so arrested." The statute was enacted to curb extortion and other abuses of the bail bond process by local sheriffs, who would release debtors upon the posting of an indemnification bond in an amount exceeding the original debt.[16] The statute delineated the categories of prisoners who were eligible for bail. It expressly excepted from bail those arrested upon execution for debt, specified the form required for bail bonds, and provided that "if any of the said sheriffs . . . take any obligation in other form by colour of their offices, that it shall be void." [17]

The statute was tested in *Dive v. Maningham*. Thomas Maningham had been arrested for debt by the sheriff of the county of Bedford, Lewis Dive. Notwithstanding the statute, Dive accepted a £40 surety bond from Thomas's brother to admit him to bail. When Dive sued the brother on the bond, he defended on the ground that the bond was void under the statute. In response, Dive argued that the bond was not covered by the statute because the clause specifying the form of bail bonds "for any cause aforesaid" referred only to bonds in cases eligible for bail under the statute. Since Thomas Maningham's release was obviously unlawful under the statute, Dive continued, the bond was not covered by the provision rendering void any nonconforming obligation. On this logic, the bond was like any contract enforceable at common law.[18]

The court held that the clauses prescribing the form of bonds and voiding nonconforming bonds applied as well to bonds entered into for nonbailable offenses: "so that if the sheriffs or other officers will let prisoners at large, they must do it at their peril, for by this statute their safe conduct, that is to say, the obligations to save them harmless, is cut off and destroyed." [19] Alternatively, the court reasoned that

> if the obligation is not void for this cause, it seems to me that (if it is taken in other form than the statute limits) these words, viz. *colore officii,* will

make it void for it is to be considered that Thomas Maningham . . . was
in execution under the custody of the plaintiff, not as Lewis Dive, but as
sheriff, for the writ to take Thomas Maningham was directed to him as
sheriff, and so as officer he had the custody of him, then when he took
the obligation, he took it as officer, but he took it unduly, for he was not
bailable, but yet he took it as sheriff, *ergo* he took it *colore officii sui;*
for this word *colore officii sui* is always taken . . . in *malam partem,* and
signifies an act badly done under countenance of an office, and it bears
a dissembling visage of duty, and is properly called *extortion.* As if an
officer will take more for his fees than he ought, this is done *colore officii
sui,* but yet it is not part of his office, and it is called extortion, which is
no other than robbery, but it is more odious than robbery, for robbery is
apparent, and always hath the countenance of vice, but extortion, being
equally as great a vice as robbery, carries the mask of virtue, and is more
difficult to be tried or discerned, and consequently more odious than
robbery. Wherefore here inasmuch as the obligation was made for the
deliverance of Thomas Maningham, who was in the custody of the plaintiff as officer, it cannot be denied but that he took the obligation for his
deliverance *colore officii,* although it was not *virtute officii sui.*[20]

I have quoted this passage at length because the court's difficulty with
the role ambiguity problem is so striking. What the court obviously found
troubling was that, as quoted above, the clause rendering the obligation
void appeared to be addressed to sheriffs acting in their official capacity.*
Yet, on the reductive approach, an unauthorized or illegal act is not a genuine act of the state itself. Indeed, the statute at issue in *Dive* opened with
the king's disavowal of "the great perjury, extortion, and oppression" committed by his sheriffs and their deputies.[21] Nevertheless, the court concluded
that Dive had acted in his official capacity even though his actions were
plainly outside his rightful authority: "When he took the obligation, he
took it as officer, but he took it unduly, for he was not bailable, but yet he
took it as sheriff, *ergo* he took it *colore officii sui.*" In this way, the court
addressed the duplicitous quality of the sheriff's actions "badly done under
countenance of an office, and [bearing] a dissembling visage of duty." As
Maningham's counsel argued: "*Colore officii* implies that the thing is under

---

* This is what makes sense of Dive's claim that the debt was outside the statute: If the
obligation was not taken in his official capacity, then it was just a contract between two
private parties no different than any other obligation at common law.

pretence of office, but not duly, and the office is no more than a cloak to deceit, and the thing is grounded upon vice, and the office is as a shadow thereto."[22]

Nineteenth-century American courts faced the problem of role ambiguity in a variety of contexts. The issue arose with some frequency in suits alleging that in executing a writ of attachment, the sheriff had in fact seized goods belonging to the wrong person. Because sheriffs were likely to be people of limited means, a party injured by the sheriff's unlawful act would seek recovery against the sureties on the officer's bond to perform the duties of his office faithfully. If the sheriff's act were treated as the unlawful act of a private actor, the injured party could not recover against the sureties because, as some courts reasoned, "there being no authority, there is no office, nothing official."[23]

Thus, from the sureties' perspective, a fully reductive analysis would have ensured a "heads I win, tails you lose" situation: "The argument, if sound, would preclude a recovery in any case against the sureties. If an authority could be shown, their defence would be complete; if there was none, the act would be extra official, and not within the scope of their undertaking."[24] Accordingly, even the most reductive courts recognized that the bond would be forfeited and the sureties liable in cases of nonfeasance or misfeasance. They drew the line, however, at cases of malfeasance: "A trespass is certainly not faithful performance of the office, or any performance at all."[25]

But other, less reductive courts recognized that wrongs committed under a claim of authority were *colore officii* and retained their official character. "A seizure of the goods of A, under color of process against B, is *official misconduct*. . . . The reason for this is, that the trespass is not the act of a mere individual, but is perpetrated *colore officii*."[26] As another court explained: "He does this in his character of sheriff, *colore officii*, and not as a naked trespasser without color of authority."[27] Accordingly, the majority rule—later adopted by the Supreme Court for federal officers—gave the injured party recourse against the sureties in cases of malfeasance such as a wrongful attachment.[28]

In the twentieth century, the Supreme Court interpreted section 1983's "under color of law" to include deprivations of constitutional rights caused by state officers acting in violation of state law or otherwise without authority. Following its earlier decision interpreting the parallel criminal provision of the 1866 civil rights act,[29] the Court in *Monroe v. Pape* construed the phrase to refer to the "misuse of power, possessed by virtue of state law and made possible only because the wrongdoer is clothed with the authority of state law." [30]

How does "under color of law" express this meaning? Why is action "under color of office" contrasted to that of a "a *naked* trespasser"? And what does any of this have to do with the problem of role ambiguity?

THE VICE SQUAD

A more conventional analysis might view the "color of office" expression as nothing more than a term of art that arbitrarily acquired its meaning through consistent historical usage by judges and legislators. But, that would miss most of what is interesting and important about the phrase. The expression represents a sophisticated conception motivated by the particular social practices and experiences relating to governmental officers. That conception is not only systematically elaborated in legal reasoning, but also plays a surprisingly important role in legal contexts where the doctrinal term "color of law" is ostensibly irrelevant.

In chapter 5, I observed that there is no a priori reason that social contingency should be an all-or-nothing matter. The "color of office" concept is an interesting case in point because it actually consists of two different metaphorical mappings: In one case—what I call the *false light* notion— the source domain comes from perceptual experience. In the other—which I refer to as the *guise of authority* concept—the source domain is a series of related but historically contingent practices. The two metaphors share various entailments, including the central sense of "color" as false or deceptive appearance. The different legal senses of "color" and the various doctrinal interpretations of the phrase "under color of law" form an extensive radial category organized around that central sense.

We have seen that a metaphor is the set of conceptual mappings and not the many metaphorical expressions that are its linguistic manifestations. For example, a conceptual metaphor like CONTROL IS UP motivates many different metaphorical expressions, such as "he's *under* my thumb" or "she's *on top of* the situation." Conversely, metaphorical expressions that use the same linguistic term can represent entirely different conceptual metaphors. Thus, the expressions "slow *up!*" and "he's cooking *up* a storm" are not instances of a single "up" metaphor, but different metaphorical expressions predicated on different conceptual metaphors—in this case CONTROL IS UP and ACTIVITY IS UP, respectively. [31]

Accordingly, a single linguistic expression can represent more than one conceptual mapping. This is true of "under color of office" (or "under color of law"), which is premised on two different but metaphorically coherent mappings. The first, relatively less important sense of the legal expression is predicated on the CONTROL IS UP metaphor together with a subset of the CONDUIT metaphor-system: KNOWING IS SEEING and its corollary, IDEAS ARE LIGHT-SOURCES.[32]

In its literal sense, color is "the quality or attribute in virtue of which objects present different appearances to the eye, when considered with regard only to the kind of light reflected from their surfaces."[33] The metaphorical expression "under color of law" uses two entailments of our everyday knowledge of color. The first is that color is a quality of surfaces and, therefore, may reveal absolutely nothing about the interior or substance of the object under view. Thus, the "color of law" metaphor expresses much the same sense as the conventional aphorisms "looks can be deceiving" and "don't judge a book by its cover." The second experiential entailment is that color perception is highly dependent upon the quality of light. We know that if we view an object in diminished light or in light other than white light, the color we see will not be true.

Consistent with CONTROL IS UP, the simple phrase "under law" expresses the sense of lawful action—i.e., that the person's (or institution's) actions are governed by the law. Action "under color of law" is action that has only the appearance of being governed by law—i.e., it is not action "under law," but only "under the *color* of law." Thus, a deprivation of rights "under color of" state law connotes an injury by an officer acting with an air of authority that is deceptive or tainted.* Or, as Maningham's counsel argued, the officer presents himself to the victim in a false light so that "the thing is grounded upon vice, and the office is *as a shadow thereto.*"

This sense of "color" as false light is systematic both in ordinary English and in legal discourse. The common notion that metaphor is merely "colorful" language in contradistinction to "clear" prose is, as we saw in chapter 3, a familiar instance of these conceptual metaphors. Shakespeare uses the phrase "under the color of" to connote deception in *Two Gentlemen of Verona.*[34] Another example is the legal concept of a colorable argument, which connotes an argument that has surface plausibility (i.e., "color") but that when examined closely or thought through clearly is nevertheless wrong. As one court explained: "'Colorable' is defined as 'having the appearance, especially the false appearance, of right.'"[35] Thus, "color"

---

* This sense of "color" is not related to the conventional expression "true colors." (As in "he may seem nice, but wait until he shows his *true colors.*") As we will see shortly, "true colors" is related to the second sense of "color of law."

also signifies pretextuality.[36] A related usage appears in eighteenth- and nineteenth-century English law concerning contempt of Parliament "under colour of law," which refers to both illegal actions and false accusations.[37]

In legal doctrine, the term "color" invariably connotes some degree of falsity, ranging from fraud to pretext to mistaken appearance. In *Woolsey v. Dodge,* the federal circuit court rejected the defendant's contention that "the mode of giving jurisdiction in this case is merely colorable; or in other words that it is a fraud upon the law."[38] The term had a different but related connotation in the rather charming medieval doctrine of "colour." A "colour" was a common-law pleading device that was used to avoid pleading the general issue and, thus, take the case away from the jury. It allowed the defendant to convert the issue to a question of law "by giving the plaintiff a 'show' or 'colour,' i.e. by imagining a fictitious title for the plaintiff, specious, but inferior to his own, and asking the judgment of the Court upon it."[39] A similar usage appears in various nineteenth-century American property law doctrines. Under state statutes of limitation for cases of adverse possession, a defendant with "color of title" who had been in possession for the requisite period could defeat a plaintiff with superior title: "Color of title, even under a void and worthless deed, has always been received as evidence that the person in possession claims for himself . . . adversely to all the world."[40]

There is a related usage of "color of law" as "pretense or appearance of law" that was widespread in English political culture during the second half of the seventeenth century. Howard Nenner describes the concept of colour of law as a potent political and rhetorical tool used by both sides in the political struggle between king and Parliament that culminated in the revolution of 1688. "The argument could be completely wrong and at the same time totally convincing. All that was really required was the application of legal principle to the political problems at hand. Of little consequence was the relevance of the legal procedures employed. The 'colour of law' was usually quite enough."[41] Used in this sense, the phrase "legal color" or "by colour of law" was a positive assertion invoked to maintain the appearance of continuity and legitimacy in the face of substantial legal change.

Notwithstanding the prevalence of these metaphorical expressions premised on the false light mapping, it is the second metaphorical sense of "color of law" as guise of authority that animates the reasoning in the most important American cases dealing with official misconduct. Moreover, it is this other sense that best captures the doubled ambiguity caused by the constructive quality of the state and the ambiguous character of its agents.

One less familiar connotation of "color" comes from heraldry, where it refers concretely to the tints employed in heraldic crests. An early use of the term referred to the insignia of a knight.[42] A contemporary usage that bears much the same sense is that of "colors" as referring to the flag (and, hence, the flag's bearers as the "color" guard). In these expressions, "color" is a metonymy where the color—which is often more striking or more quickly and easily perceived than the design—stands for the entire emblem.[*]

The original expression "by Colour of his Office" dates from the thirteenth century statute of Edward I, a time when many of the king's officers and agents would actually have worn the king's coat of arms. As it is used in this early statute, the metonymic expression "color of office" signified conduct that had all the trappings and indicia of an official act even though it was without sufficient warrant in law. Thus, the phrase "color of office" is a compound metonymic expression: "Color" stands for the king's coat of arms, and the coat of arms stands for the office (and/or the king himself). The phrase is also a metaphorical expression once the metonymy is extended to represent the general *concept* of official misconduct (that is, without regard to the actual dress of the governmental agent). "Color of office," then, is a metaphor that is based on a metonymy; it signifies the appearance or guise of authority.

The experiential grounding for this metaphor continues in contemporary practices like the uniforms and insignia of the military and police. Thus, in *Monroe,* Justice Douglas explained "that Congress has power to enforce the Fourteenth Amendment against those who carry *a badge of authority of a state,* . . . whether they act in accordance with their authority or misuse it."[43] The underlying idea remains the same: The officer's attire or vestments signify the office, both in the practical sense that they indicate the wearer's position and in the symbolic sense that they represent the honor and authority of the office. Thus, to *invest* in office (from the Latin *vestīre,* "to dress") is "to clothe *with* or *in* the insignia of an office; hence, *with* the dignity itself."[44] It was conventional in the nineteenth century to say that one was "vested in office," and the installment of new officers is still referred to as an "investiture."

Significantly, the modern cases dealing with the meaning of state action rely on metaphorical understandings derived from this sense of "color of office." In *Ex parte Virginia,* where the federal statute at issue did not con-

---

[*] This is the sense employed in "to show one's true colors" and "acting under false colors." Note that this usage is invariably plural; when used metaphorically, it is usually modified by "true" or "false." Accordingly, this does not appear to be the basis for the metaphor at work in § 1983. If it were, the statute might have said something like: "Every person who, under the true [or false] colors of state law deprives . . ."

tain the words "under color of law," the Court first invoked the guise of authority conception to resolve the state action question:

> Whoever, by virtue of public position under a state government, deprives another of property, life, or liberty, without due process of law, or denies or takes away the equal protection of the law violates the constitutional inhibition; and as he acts in the name and for the state, and *is clothed with the state's power,* his act is that of the state. This must be so, or the constitutional prohibition has no meaning. Then the state *has clothed one of its agents* with power to annul or to evade it.[45]

Dissenting in *Monroe,* Frankfurter conceded that the conduct of the police was state action "because they are *clothed with an appearance of official authority* which is itself a factor of significance in dealings between individuals. . . . The *aura* of power *which a show of authority carries* with it has been created by state government."[46]

In both these quotations (as in the earlier quotes from *Monroe*), the metaphorical sense of "color of office" as guise of authority is the basis for an inference pattern in which the outward appearance of official power—a "show of authority" under state law—explains why official misconduct falls within the reach of the Fourteenth Amendment. Significantly, none of these quotations concerns the interpretation of the statutory phrase "under color of law"; in each case, the pivotal inference that action constituting an abuse of state authority is nevertheless state action prohibited by the Fourteenth Amendment is supplied by the "color of office" metaphor.

We can observe the complementary metaphorical inference pattern at work in Eleventh Amendment cases. In *Ex parte Young,* the Court applied the ultra vires doctrine to avoid the state sovereign immunity problem, explaining that "the officer proceeding under such [unconstitutional] enactment comes into conflict with the superior authority of that Constitution, and he is in that case *stripped of his official or representative character* and is subjected *in his person* to the consequences of his individual conduct."[47] Commentators have criticized these "classic" doctrines of state action and ultra vires as logically inconsistent; justices have treated *Young* as an embarrassing but necessary fiction.[48] But the inconsistency arises only on a reductive analysis that reifies the state and treats it as a stable "thing" separate from the actual persons who act in its name, for it is only on that reductive view that the governmental agent who acts illegally can be said to act not qua agent, but qua private person amenable to a common-law action for redress.

But a social construction like "the state" has no "real" or "physical" identity separate from the persons who embody it; the state is real because the cultural meaning that it represents has been internalized and actualized by the society in question. Thus, as the Court pointed out in *Ex parte Virginia,* the Fourteenth Amendment "must act upon persons, not upon the abstract thing denominated a state."[49] Each of these persons is wrapped in the social meaning that is the state; the officer is the provisional embodiment of the state, whether he is following its dictates or flaunting them. An official who abuses his office exploits this social meaning, in effect transforming the state into a government of men and not of laws. Consequently, there is no inconsistency. When the officer acts, he acts *as* the state because he is clothed with its authority. But when called to account for his actions in violation of that trust, he is liable as an individual now "stripped of his official or representative character and . . . subjected in his person to the consequences of his individual conduct."

It is precisely these connotations that are captured by the "color of office" metaphor. It expresses the way in which the trappings of office provide a veneer of authority, proclaiming that the officer acts with the full power and prestige of the state. At the same time, however, the metaphor connotes the constructive character of that representation—the fact that beneath the uniform and insignia of authority is a person who, in any given case, may not conform his behavior to the legal requirements of his office.

The real problem with *Young* is that it conflates the *colore officii* concept with the doctrine of ultra vires. Where the common law distinguished official misconduct from the act of a "naked trespasser," *Young* treats the two as if they were the same. If *Young* has a fictive quality, it is because it fails to recognize the metaphorical quality of its own reasoning—as if the officer actually were "stripped of his official character" and reduced to a "naked trespasser." This conflation leads to the rather bizarre bit of transcendental nonsense in which the Court says: "State officials sued for damages in their official capacity are not 'persons' for purposes of the suit because they assume the identity of the government that employs them. . . . By contrast, officers sued in their personal capacity come to court as individuals."[50] The fiction common to both of these doctrines is that the officer is not sued as an individual tortfeasor at common law but as a state official who has violated constitutional norms. These are not mistakes that arise under the nonreductive, metaphorical understanding expressed by the *colore officii* concept.

The "color of office" metaphor is both subtle and sophisticated. At the first level, it connotes the sense in which the office may serve to camouflage or mask misbehavior. As Maningham's counsel maintained, "*colore officii* implies that the thing is under pretence of office, but not duly, and the office is no more than a cloak to deceit." Accordingly, the "color of office" metaphor shares with the false light concept the metaphorical entailment of deceptive appearance. As noted in *Dive,* the metaphor conveys that the more serious evil of official misconduct is that the injury is compounded by deception: "As if an officer will take more for his fees than he ought, this is . . . robbery, but it is more odious than robbery, for robbery is apparent, and always hath the countenance of vice, but extortion, being equally as great a vice as robbery, carries the mask of virtue."

At the second level, the "color of office" metaphor expresses the sense that official misconduct does not have the same social meaning as a private wrong like robbery because, as Frankfurter acknowledged, the wrongdoers "are clothed with an appearance of official authority which is itself a factor of significance in dealings between individuals." The metaphor signifies the dual character of the officer who is both a person and the provisional embodiment of the state. When an officer commits a wrong, "he does this in his character of sheriff, *colore officii,* and not as a naked trespasser without color of authority." When, for example, Los Angeles police officers beat Rodney King, they *were* acting *as* police and not as private individuals with a personal vendetta. They were acting as police officers and, at the same time, acting in a manner neither authorized nor approved by the city, its mayor, or most of its constituents. They were acting *officially,* but not *legally.*

Thus, the problem of conduct under "color of office" is different than that addressed by the agency law doctrine of apparent authority, which protects the reliance interests of third parties who deal in good faith with an agent by binding the principal.[51] In the section 1983 context, for example, the issue is not that the injured party mistakenly thinks that the agent acts for the governmental entity.[52] If that were the issue, "a rapist who lures his victims by flashing a fake police badge would be the subject of constitutional commands, while a police officer who engages in illegal surveillance while in plainclothes would be acting beyond the reach of those commands."[53] Rather, the problem of conduct under "color of office" concerns the distinctive social meaning occasioned by abuse of official authority. This abuse arises only when the actor has a bona fide identity as a state official or when he or she acts in concert with such an official—a point confirmed by the otherwise incomprehensible state action decisions.[54]

In other words, "under color of office" connotes the sense that the evil of official misconduct is not just a matter of deception but of duplicity and betrayal as well. In this sense, the notion of "color of office" as guise of authority is different than the sense of "under color of law" as false light. The false light metaphor implies that there is some deeper truth beneath the appearance. But the fundamental difficulty addressed by the "color of office" metaphor is that there is no other reality beneath the social meaning of the state, as there is no other state separate from the officials who instantiate it. The actor *is* an officer *and* a wrongdoer.

This is why the obverse of "under color of office" is "by virtue of office" and not simply "under law" or "by authority of law." The officer who acts "under color of office" acts within his or her role as an officer, but without fidelity to that role—hence, *in malam partem* (the evil or wicked part of the office). In other words, the "color of office" metaphor signifies that the fundamental problem is not a matter of truth and falsity so much as it is a matter of integrity and corruption. Or, in the more archaic terms of Coke and *Dive*, the concern is less a matter of truth and deception than it is a matter of virtue and vice. Action "under color of law" is conduct that is understood to be that of the state and that, therefore, has all the affective power of an act of betrayal by those upon whom one relies for protection.

REDUCTIO AD ABSURDUM

Given the overlap of the metaphorical conceptions of false light and guise of authority and the overwhelming evidence from actual usage, one can say fairly that the sense of "under color of law" as false or deceptive appearance of authority is overdetermined. This is not to say, however, that the expression has a determinate or static meaning. Rather, the possible meanings are framed and constrained by the underlying metaphor. The different doctrinal manifestations of the "color of law" concept form a radial category with extensions along the two axes that correspond to the two metaphorical conceptions. The extensions reflect the different policy concerns that motivate these different doctrinal contexts. Within each of those areas, the principal disputes are less a matter of disagreement over extensions than of more fundamental differences about the nature of categorization.

The central case is defined by the shared entailment of the two metaphors. In its prototypical sense, "color" connotes an appearance that is not only false but deliberately deceptive. This is the original sense both of *colore officii* as explicated in *Dive* and of "under the color of" as Shakespeare used it. It is the central case not merely because it represents the earliest usage (though that is important evidence), but also because in our models of "action" intentional action is always the prototype.[55] This prototype is reflected in the legal presumption "that a person intends the necessary and

FIGURE 7.1   "Color" as a Radial Category

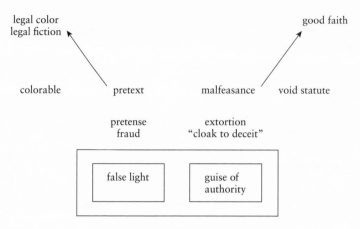

natural consequences of his acts" and in the fact that the prototypical cause of action requires intent as one of its elements.[56] Thus, the prototypical instance of action "under color of office" is action that "bears a dissembling visage of duty" where "the office is a cloak to deceit."

The uses of "color" extend from this central case in two directions, as illustrated in figure 7.1. Along one dimension, the different senses of the term vary with the nature or degree of falsity of appearance. They range from fraud and deliberate deception through the senses of "color" as pretense, pretext, mistaken appearance (as in "color of title"), and legal fiction to the sense of "colorable" as plausible argument. Related to these last two—and the greatest extension—is the late seventeenth-century English political usage of "legal color": The aspiration to "legal color" represented an effort to maintain continuity with the past by presenting a credible legal justification for action that was in an important sense extralegal. The phrase "by colour of law" connotes action that, rather than having the appearance of being governed by law, is governed by the appearance of law.

Along the "color of office" dimension, extensions from the central case connote variations in the nature of the alleged misuse of authority. Fraud, extortion, and abuse lie at the center of the category. The first-order extensions are those cases where the officer's actions were wrongful and illegal, though not necessarily dishonest or abusive. One example is provided by the surety cases where the sheriff levied on the wrong goods. Another is *Woolsey,* where a bank shareholder sued to enjoin the collection of a state tax on the ground that it was unconstitutional under the Contract Clause. There, the court reasoned that a "void law can afford no justification to any one who acts under it; and he who shall attempt to collect the tax . . . will proceed, it is true, under color of law, an act standing on the statute book, but a void act." [57]

The second-order extensions are those cases where the officer's misuse of authority was without subjective fault. In interpreting the "color of office" provisions of the nineteenth-century removal acts,* some courts construed the phrase to refer to conduct that, though ultimately proved mistaken, was at least a good faith assertion of authority. Thus, in *Woods v. Mathews*, the court allowed that "if the property sued for . . . was of such a nature as not to be liable to seizure . . . under any circumstances, it might, perhaps, be said to be apparent, that the case does not come within the act of congress." [58] A similar interpretation prevailed under the Captured and Abandoned Property Act, which provided compensation from the federal government for property taken by its officers during the Civil War, if certain conditions, including loyalty during the war, were met. The act also immunized the officer against personal liability when the seizure had been made "in virtue or under color of said act." Interpreting that provision, the Supreme Court held that "there must be good faith, or there can be no color." [59]

"Color" provides an interesting contrast case to the right-to-counsel decisions. Though both doctrinal areas represent radial categories, they differ with respect to structure, grounding, scope, and mode of extension. The right-to-counsel decisions are organized by a propositional model that, to a large degree, reflects existing legal procedures.† The "color" category, in contrast, is structured by a metaphorical model that is largely independent of legal understandings. Thus, the false light metaphor is grounded in embodied experiences that have nothing to do with law. So, too, the guise of authority metaphor is grounded in social practices and general cultural understandings only modestly influenced by legal understandings: Rules that determine who is an officer and regulations concerning uniforms and other insignia obviously play some role, since, as we have seen, an imposter cannot act "under color of his office." But they hardly go to the heart of the

---

* These statutes, first enacted during the War of 1812, provided for the removal to the federal circuit courts of all cases, both criminal and civil, brought in the state courts against federal revenue officials "for any thing done by virtue of this act or under colour thereof." The successor statute, 28 U.S.C. § 1442(a)(2), retains the phrase "under color of office."

† The relationship between the doctrine and these legal practices is not merely circular, however, because the practices are not contingent on precisely the same doctrines and decisions that they motivate. But the relationship is nevertheless reflexive, in that the practices are not independent of the legal conceptions in which they participate.

matter. Indeed, the very point of the "color of office" cases is that the legal status of official misconduct is a function of its social meaning and *not* of the legal rules governing the officer's conduct. Rather, it is social experiences of deception, duplicity, and betrayal by an authority figure that ground the metaphorical understanding and psychological impact of action "under color of law." In Brandeis's famous phrase, the "government is the potent, the omnipresent teacher." [60]

The rules governing the right to appointed counsel form a discrete doctrinal category that is implicated whenever a person faces an adversary hearing. The concept of color, in contrast, plays a role in contexts as diverse as prohibitions on extortion, medieval pleading practices, nineteenth-century property law rules, and the federal removal statutes. Moreover, the "color of office" concept plays a central role in legal contexts—such as state action doctrine and the Eleventh Amendment—for which the phrase has no apparent doctrinal relevance. What links all these cases together as a single category is an underlying problem—i.e., the difficulties that arise from the potentially deceptive appearance of authority (or, as in Shakespeare's usage, of propriety). Which is to say that "under color of" is not a *doctrinal* category but a *conceptual* one.

This difference has important consequences with respect to category extension and compositional constraint. In a doctrinal category like the right to counsel, the central model directly expresses the policies and purposes of the social practices that it reproduces: here, the value (in our system) of representation by an expert advocate when faced with a high-stakes, formal adversary proceeding. Because function is an integral dimension of the structure of the category, one can immediately recognize those situations where, in Kennedy's words, "a given general rule seems utterly obvious in its application and also utterly 'appropriate as a matter of social policy.'" As the model is extended to new contexts, disputes over the degree to which these purposes will be served are expressed as different assessments of the extent to which the new context resembles the central case.

A conceptual category like "color" is different in structure and, as a consequence, shows a different pattern of extension. Here, too, the central model is value-laden in the sense that it expresses the values and social function of the governmental practices that ground the category. But it lacks the same kind of purpose-oriented motivation: What is the "utterly obvious" central case of action "under color of" state law? A striking thing about the modern debate over the meaning of section 1983 is that each side has maintained that its interpretation better reflects the "plain meaning" of the statutory phrase.[61] But one cannot understand the meaning of this legal term just by knowing the meaning of the central case; to determine which inflection of deceptive appearance should apply to a particular legal context, one must know something about the motivations and concerns of the doctrinal context in which the concept is being deployed.

Thus, the compositional constraints on argument in the "color of law" cases are different than those in the right-to-counsel cases. In any given doctrinal area, disputes over the appropriate extension of the metaphorical conception of color will be articulated in terms of debates about the underlying purpose or function to be served. In some contexts, there will be little debate about the underlying purpose—that is, there will be strong prototype effects in which the policy behind the rule seems utterly obvious and appropriate. The Captured and Abandoned Property Act, for example, extended personal immunity to federal agents at a direct cost to the federal treasury; in this context, a narrow, "good faith" reading of the act's "under color of law" provision was an entirely predictable judicial response. But in contexts where purposes and policies are in dispute, one would expect the interpretations to vary between courts and over time—as they did, for example, in the nineteenth-century removal cases. Overall, the different judicial glosses on the "under color of" language can be understood as the different ways in which the problems arising from of the constructive nature of the state are refracted through different policy concerns.[62]

The compositional constraints in the "color of office" cases differ from those in the right-to-counsel cases in another way that is less obvious, but ultimately more profound. In *Dive* and in the surety cases, we saw that the principal alternative view is the reductive approach in which only lawful, authorized acts are treated as official. This was the position taken by Holmes and Frankfurter, dissenting in the state action cases, and subsequently adopted by Frankfurter as an interpretation of the statutory phrase "under color of law."[63]

The remarkable thing about the reductive approach is that it leads to patently absurd results. Thus, to accept Dive's reductive argument would have immunized precisely the conduct that the statute sought to prohibit. So, too, the reductive approach would have rendered meaningless the requirement that sheriffs obtain surety bonds because, by definition, illegal acts would not be "official" acts of the sheriff within the performance of his office. In the state action context, the reductive approach would mean either that "the state" could never act illegally or that the Fourteenth Amendment (which prohibits certain state actions) and the Eleventh Amendment (which immunizes the states from suit) would cancel each other out. Given the absurdity of these consequences, it is not surprising that the reductive

FIGURE 7.2   Official Action as a Graded Category

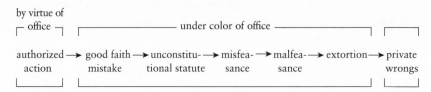

argument was usually unpersuasive. What is surprising, however, is that anyone—let alone such intellectually distinguished judges as Holmes and Frankfurter—thought it at all plausible.

It is tempting to explain the reductive approach as just another distorted product of the rationalist model, which seeks objectifiable criteria that can be specified as necessary and sufficient conditions. (Though there is something to this explanation, we shall see momentarily that it is inadequate.) On this view, the appeal of the reductive approach is its analytic rigor. It promises a clear test for determining when officers act as agents of their governmental employer—when they act pursuant to an authority expressed in positive law.[64] But advocates of the reductive approach have never applied it with any consistency or rigor for the simple reason that it does not work. Thus, courts on both sides of the issue in the surety cases agreed that the *virtute officii* concept should be extended to include cases of nonfeasance and misfeasance.[65] And even Frankfurter conceded that section 1983's prohibition of action "under color of" state law extended to "systematic and accepted custom" not sanctioned in the state's positive law.[66]

There are always instrumental reasons for pressing the reductive argument in a given case. But a purely instrumental account fails to address the problem of persuasion. To hold a position it must at least make sense; to press it on others, there must be something more to recommend it than the fact that among its many absurd results is one that favors your interests. To understand how anyone could find the reductive approach credible, one must understand how it makes sense in terms of the audience's conceptual system.

"Under color of office" is not an isolated metaphor, but—as the state action cases illustrate—part of a larger network of concepts relating to the state. One cannot have a concept of action "under color of office" without first having some concept of *office;* by the same token, the sense of "color of office" as guise of authority is necessarily contingent on a concept of *authority.* This means that the reductive approach and the metaphorical sense of "under color of office" can be understood as different parts of a single category. Indeed, that is precisely how Coke explained them: "*Colore officii* is ever taken in malam partem, as *virtute officii* is taken in bonam." As illustrated in figure 7.2, the concept "official action" forms a graded category in which action "by virtue of office" represents the prototype.

Debates over the meaning of "under color of law" are actually debates over extensions of the concept "official action." Even proponents of the reductive view support extensions from the prototype when necessary to accommodate the obvious policy concerns of the relevant legal context. Thus, the reductive approach is not an analytic definition of the state but a radical prototype effect. It survives the reductio ad absurdum of its bizarre results because it contains a kernel of truth: The paradigmatic case of official action is action that is specifically authorized by law. What renders the reductive approach absurd and self-defeating, however, is its aspiration to reduce a large and important social category to its central case.

There is an important lesson here: There is a good reason why human categorization is imaginative and flexible rather than static and definitional. The compositional structure of human rationality makes it possible to accommodate the complex and diverse concerns of social life in a way that necessary and sufficient criteria simply cannot handle. Nowhere is this more true than in law. And nowhere is this more consequential than when dealing with a powerful social construction like the state.

CHAPTER 8

How Do Rules Work?

IN THE *Rule of Law as a Law of Rules,* Justice Scalia extols the virtues of legal rules: They reduce uncertainty. They give fair notice of legal requirements. They foster a sense of justice by providing "a clear, previously enunciated rule that one can point to in explanation of the decision." And they constrain judges from "indulging" their preferences. "Only by announcing rules do we hedge ourselves in."

At the same time, Scalia concedes that "every rule of law has a few corners that do not quite fit." He recognizes, therefore, that balancing and totality-of-the-circumstances tests will always be with us. But his aversion to these modes of analysis is clear:

> At the point where an appellate judge says that the remaining issue must be decided on the basis of the totality of the circumstances, or by a balancing of all the factors involved, he begins to resemble a finder of fact more than a determiner of law. To reach such a stage is, in a way, a regrettable concession of defeat—an acknowledgment that we have passed the point where "law," properly speaking, has any further application.[1]

The concept of a rule that Scalia treats as definitional of law, "properly speaking," is a conventional one. On this view, rules are understood to be categorical—automatically applying to all instances falling within their purview. Thus, we speak of *per se* rules, *across-the-board* rules, *bright-line* rules, *clear-cut* rules, and *hard-and-fast* rules. All of the perceived advantages of rules derive from their categorical quality. The clarity, certainty, and predictability for which rules are prized are (on this view) a function of the conclusive and unconditional nature of their coverage: If the posted speed limit is fifty-five, then one may drive at fifty-five miles per hour. So, too, it is the absolute character of a rule—i.e., its status as a categorical reason for decision—that enables a decisionmaker to absolve herself of responsibility by pointing to the rule as complete justification. Rules, according to Joseph Raz, operate as second-order "exclusionary reasons" that preempt all other reasons for action.[2]

In both of these ways, the conventional notion of a rule presupposes the rationalist model of a category (as in fig. 3.1, hence, the notion of a "bright-line" or "across-the-board" rule). But, as we have seen, most categories are not categorical. It follows that most rules do not operate in the absolute or unconditional fashion supposed by the conventional view. Necessarily, rules manifest the same flexibility, variability, and sensitivity to context as the categories of which they are composed. Rules, moreover, represent legal categorizations of experience that a community (or its lawmakers) adopts for a reason. As such, they exhibit the dynamic properties characteristic of categorization as a motivated process.

Consider a simple rule prohibiting running in the halls. "Running" is a graded category that extends from a sprint to a jog, with no clear boundary to demarcate a run from a fast walk. Application of the "no running" rule necessarily involves consideration of its purposes, for it is only in light of those purposes that a decisionmaker can determine the degree of category-extension appropriate to the rule. This consideration of purpose is evident in the marginal case, as when the decisionmaker must determine whether to apply the rule to a fast walk in a crowded corridor or a slow trot in an empty one. But it is also evident in the case of a student sprinting down the hall. It might seem that the obvious applicability of the rule derives from the fact that the decisionmaker can, in a relatively mechanical manner, point to an activity that everyone would agree is clearly and properly referred to as "running." This explanation fails, however, once we consider that most people would look askance at a decision to apply the "no running" rule to stop a candidate for student counsel from campaigning in the halls. Rather, if we know immediately and automatically that the rule applies to the sprinter and not the candidate, it is only because we know what the rule is *about*. Raz is mistaken when he says: "It is only in exceptional circumstances that I must know the precise reasons for the rule in order to know what to do" (80). The easy case is easy precisely because the decision-maker has already invoked her tacit knowledge about the rule, its function, and its motivating context in order to render the rule intelligible.[3]

This simple example illustrates several more general points that shall occupy us for the balance of the chapter. Most obviously, one's view of rules is intimately related to one's understanding of language and categorization. One who holds to the position that categories can be formalized in neces-sary and sufficient conditions will conclude that rules can—at least in prin-ciple—operate in the precise, clear, and categorical manner supposed by the conventional view. By the same token, one who believes that language and meaning are indeterminate will reach the same conclusion with respect to rules. Either way, one can find evidence to bolster one's view. The conven-tional rule formalist will stress the central cases (such as sprinting in the hall) where the rule works perspicuously well. Conversely, the rule skeptic will emphasize the marginal cases (such as the fast walk) and the metaphorical extensions (such as running for office) to highlight the indeterminacy of the rule. But each view has hold of a different portion of the elephant and, thus, provides an account that is fatally incomplete in a different way.

A cognitive account, in contrast, explains what is right about both sets of intuitions. But it does so only at the cost of a dramatic change in our con-cept of a rule. Recall that according to Scalia, the whole point of a rule is to hedge-in the decisionmaker. As H. L. A. Hart explains: "There is [some-thing] in the nature of a legal rule inconsistent with all questions being open to reconsideration in light of social policy."[4] Thus, it is essential to the con-ventional view that a rule provide no occasion to advert to policy or pur-pose. If it did, it would permit the decisionmaker to make her own assess-ment of whether the application of the rule serves its purpose (or otherwise comports with the balance of interests) under the circumstances. Rules are presumed to avoid this problem because their scope is thought to be deter-mined—in a straightforward, almost mechanical manner—by the scope of their constituent categories. But, as the "no running" rule demonstrates, the conventional view has it exactly backwards: It is the reach of the rule (i.e., of its function and purpose) that determines the scope of its component cat-egories. This is how we know not to include running for office within the scope of the "no running" rule; it is how we know that a person is not an "animal" for purposes of the rule prohibiting animals on the bus.

To put the point more starkly, most rules operate like standards. A standard (e.g., "no unsafe conduct in the halls") asks the decisionmaker directly to consider the policies or values that prompt the legal directive.

A rule, in contrast, ostensibly obviates the need to consider its underlying purposes by specifying in advance the occasions for its application (e.g., "no running"). (Hence, the notion of a per se rule that is complete for *(per)* itself *(se)*.) When the operative category is a formal one or otherwise conforms to the rationalist model, rules do work in just this way. Examples might be rules such as "appoint counsel in all felony cases" or "no spitting on the subway."

Most categories, however, are flexible and functional rather than formal. To make appropriate sense of a rule, the decisionmaker necessarily begins with an understanding of its function, purpose, and motivating context. If the rule employs a graded category (e.g., "running"), a superordinate category (e.g., "animal"), or a radial category (e.g., under color of law), the decisionmaker can determine the reach of the category only by evaluating the circumstances in light of the rule's purpose. She may do so tacitly or explicitly; but she will nevertheless have to consider whether the facts of the case implicate the policies or values that prompt the rule. "In other words," Llewellyn explains, "the legal rules do not lay down any *limits within* which a judge moves. Rather, they set down *guidelines from* which a judge proceeds toward a decision."[5] Or, as Stanley Fish says, "every rule is a rule of thumb" (321).

Even the speed limit, often thought to be the epitome of a precise rule, manifests the flexibility and sensitivity to context characteristic of a standard. Despite its categorical quality, the speed limit is qualified by our understanding of its motivating context—which assumes clear weather and normal road conditions. Another section of the motor vehicle code prohibits driving at speeds that are excessive or unreasonable given road and weather conditions. Whatever the signs actually say (and there are some places on New Jersey's Garden State Parkway that are posted "55 CONDITIONS PERMITTING"), the operative legal rule is something like "Drive at a speed appropriate to road and weather conditions, but in no case more than fifty-five miles per hour."*

These examples teach a common lesson: The real world of human ac-

---

* The speed limit is further qualified by enforcement practices. Thus, the operative legal rule in most places is really "Drive at a speed appropriate to road and weather conditions, but not more than five or ten miles per hour above the posted limit (unless one is Black)." There is still a difference between the speed limit and a prototypical standard like that on Germany's Autobahns, or between the "no running" rule and a standard such as "no unsafe conduct in the halls." The point, however, is that rules are rarely as "rule-like" as normally supposed.

tion is too varied and complex to be captured by any set of categorical structures. It is not so much that every rule has a few corners that do not quite fit, as it is that life's diversity and complexity cannot be contained within square corners. Indeed, as long as we treat categories as rigid little boxes, any set of boxes we devise will be either too few to do life justice or too many to be workable.[6] Categories must be dynamic and flexible if they are to be adequate to the complexities of real-world judgments. Categorization, as I have stressed throughout these chapters, is *adaptive*. We are able to expand or adjust our categories relative to need because context, function, and purpose are built-in, constitutive dimensions of categorization by means of idealized cognitive models. Rules both compose and are composed of ICMs and, as such, are elastic to purpose. Although rules constructed of formal categories are by definition inflexible, they are almost always qualified by some more general standard to ensure that the underlying purposes of the rule are not frustrated.*

Given the inherent inadequacy of categorical structures such as formal rules, it is easy to understand the pressures that militate in favor of balancing and totality-of-the-circumstances tests. The rigid, categorical model of a rule assumed by the conventional view is deeply dysfunctional. To take such rules seriously is to conclude that rules "lie."[7] On one hand, rules claim to be appropriate directives for all cases falling within their terms— but that cannot be, because we do not really want humans excluded from the bus or candidates stopped from campaigning in the halls. On the other hand, if we temper the rule with common sense—permitting the goldfish on the bus, prohibiting fast walking in the halls—then (on the conventional model) the rule no longer means what it appears to say. One alternative is to opt for a standard, delegating to the decisionmaker the flexibility to effectuate the purpose of the directive. But this flexibility comes at the cost of the clarity and predictability for which rules are valued; it also abandons any attempt to guide subordinate decisionmakers. The other alternative, exemplified by *Mathews v. Eldridge,* is to delineate the factors to be considered in applying the standard. By using such balancing and totality-of-the-circumstances tests, one can partially mimic the dynamic quality of categorization by ICMs.

---

* Under Rule 4 of the Federal Rules of Appellate Procedure, the thirty-day time limit for filing a notice of appeal is mandatory and jurisdictional; an untimely filing requires dismissal of the appeal. Yet, Rule 4 (a) (5) provides that a district court may extend the time for filing upon a showing of "excusable neglect."

This strategy, however, represents a decidedly second-best solution. Indeed, once one recognizes the flexibility and sensitivity to context that inheres in rules organized by cognitive models, it is difficult to see exactly what is gained by substituting these tests. True, one can enumerate the factors to be considered by the decisionmaker—speed, gait, coordination, decorum, relative congestion of the hallway, and so on. But a rule prohibiting running in the halls *already* prompts the decisionmaker to consider just such factors. And it does so without sacrificing specificity, clarity, or predictability.

It may seem paradoxical to say that rules can be both flexible and clear. The incongruity arises because according to the rationalist model, adaptability to context and purpose is the antithesis of objectivity and order. How can a rule be clear, certain, and predictable if its scope is constantly being adjusted? But what seems problematic on the rationalist model is readily explicable on a cognitive one. Rules are clear and predictable when they employ basic-level categories (e.g., "running," "bus") or idealized cognitive models widely shared within the culture. There will be substantial certainty about such rules because their constitutive categories are well grounded either in embodied or social experience. Moreover, rules characterized by ICMs will produce prototype effects. For example, there will be no doubt about application of the "no running" rule to a person sprinting down a crowded hall, both because sprinting is the prototype of the category "running" and—more importantly—because running in a crowded hall is the very circumstance that motivates the rule.

Thus, rules *do* work; it is just that they do not work in the rule-like way supposed by the conventional view. We experience rules as clear, certain, and predictable because they manifest all the regularities observed in the preceding chapters: radial structure, motivation, framing and other gestalt properties, and prototype effects. For present purposes, the most significant regularities by far are those that arise as a consequence of motivation. Tacit knowledge of a rule's motivating context is both what makes a rule readable and what governs its reach. Because motivation acts as a frame for the rule's component categories, it also characterizes prototypes under the rule. These may differ subtly from the prototypes of the component category. Thus, although cows, horses, and chickens are all prototypical animals, the prototypes of the rule prohibiting animals on the bus are dogs and cats (at least in contemporary urban America).

Motivation also acts as a constraint on lawmakers. As we have observed the process thus far, motivation has two dimensions. First, and most fundamentally, motivation is a function of the existing background of sedimented cultural practice and social experience: the customs, conventions, roles, routines, institutions, objects and other artifacts that compose the repertoire of which a society is constituted. Lawmakers *begin* with the highway, the city bus, and the school hallway already in place. Each comes already encumbered with designated functions, normative social expectations (e.g., coordination, decorum), and pragmatic needs (e.g., safety, efficient travel) that cannot be redefined simply by legislative fiat. Second, these pregiven purposes and social understandings are not just "there" to be considered and (potentially) discarded; rather, they frame or otherwise characterize our categories and concepts. Some possibilities will follow from a given set of social understandings; others will be impeded by the very fact that we cognize the world in terms of a particular set of practices and categories. Thus, at the first level, motivation means that lawmakers are constrained by the material with which they must work. As Robert Cover explains: "Precepts must 'have meaning,' but they necessarily borrow it from materials created by social activity that is not subject to the strictures of provenance that characterize what we call formal lawmaking."[8]

One might think that lawmakers are nevertheless free to choose from the stock of practices produced by the culture at the "wholesale" level those practices that they will "retail" as legal rules. But, even here, lawmakers operate under constraints because their output carries a special burden of persuasion. Rules of general application must not only make sense; they must make sense *as law*. If a legal rule is to be both meaningful *and* compelling, it must use preexisting cultural knowledge in ways that will seem natural to most of those subject to its command. Otherwise, it would be impossible to sustain meaningful compliance without an unprecedented and impractical degree of enforcement. Prohibition in the 1920s may be the archetype, but the contingency of law—its dependence on preexisting practices and mores—is a more general and pervasive phenomenon: Imagine a rule requiring all citizens to genuflect whenever anyone invoked the name of Oliver Wendell Holmes. In a culture that venerates neither age nor wisdom nor leadership, who would obey it? For most people, the rule would make little sense as a valid legal requirement; most would experience it as an arbitrary and illegitimate imposition of power.

Thus, at the second level, motivation acts as a substantive constraint on lawmaking: As categories of behavior, rules too must be motivated. This is not to say that lawmakers are unable to promulgate a rule unless it is already grounded in social practice. They can do so, but only at the risk of discord, disobedience, or defiance. It is to say, rather, that rules work best *as* rules when they are derived from the practices they are intended to regulate. In other words, the ability to create cultural meanings that will be understood as *law* is contingent on the available social practices, expectations, and mores.[9] Law, then, is the unmistakable product of human interactions as they are institutionalized first in social practice and then as cultural and legal norms. Lawmakers can and do influence this development, but not in the command-and-control sense frequently supposed. Rather, the principal role of the lawmaker is to concretize preexisting social practices in a way that preserves and institutionalizes them as formal norms.

I defend these claims in the sections that follow, but the decisive point has already been made: Once we appreciate that categorization is a culturally motivated process, we can no longer hold to the conventional understanding of law as a detached, semiautonomous authority that rules "over" society—as in the inscription on the frieze of the Supreme Court building: "Equal Justice Under Law." Most of what we experience as law is merely a phenomenon of a foreground produced and shaped by larger and more basic cultural processes. Law is, in this sense, epiphenomenal: When the law grapples with the overt conflicts of social life, it can do so only against a sedimented background of concepts and categories that already bear normative orientations of real practical consequence to lawmakers and decisionmakers. The official domain of law is but the epicenter of the much larger—indeed, seismic—cultural process of law-creation that Cover calls "jurisgenesis" (11).

Thus, the argument of this chapter is both cumulative and reflexive: A more sophisticated understanding of categorization changes our notion of a rule. And a more refined understanding of rules changes our conception of law in a way that makes untenable a naïve positivism of rules.

Not So Positive about Positivism

What would it take for rules to work in the fashion supposed by the conventional view? Consider two of the more sophisticated attempts to explain decisionmaking according to rules.

In his *Playing by the Rules*,[10] Fred Schauer distinguishes two fundamentally different modes of generalization. On the first or "conversational" model, we are able to adjust for the over- and underinclusiveness of generalizations because the "give-and-take plasticity" of conversation allows us instantly to clarify, qualify, or modify our categories to suit the needs of the moment. On the "model of entrenchment," in contrast, generalization is recalcitrant to the complexity of experience: "Instead of being continuously malleable in the service of changing circumstances, generalizations become *entrenched*, and the entrenchment of past generalizations impedes the possibility of an infinitely sensitive and adaptable language" (42).

Schauer maintains that rules work on the model of entrenchment.[11] On this view, rules exist to the extent that they are treated by decisionmakers "as entrenched, having the power to provide a reason for decision even when th[e] instantiation does not serve its generating justification" (76). Thus far, Schauer's account of rules is basically the same as Raz's claim that rules act as exclusionary reasons.[12] For our purposes, the principal differences are two. First, Schauer emphasizes the fact that the real problems with rules are a consequence of the imperfections of (rationalist) categorization: "The issue of entrenchment does not arise with respect to particulars, but only in the case of under- or over-inclusive generalizations" (93). Second, Schauer's concept of entrenched generalization is not just a thesis about rules and rule-formalism; it is simultaneously and explicitly a claim about language and language-categories (42–52, 61).

As Schauer explains, the fact that a generalization (e.g., "no running in the halls") can embrace an instance that does not further its underlying justification (e.g., nondisruptive or nondangerous jogging) necessarily implies that meaning is not coextensive with purpose. Thus, he asserts "the *semantic autonomy* of language," by which he means the ability of language "to carry meaning" independent of the particular context of use or of the specific intentions of the speaker.* Schauer does not commit himself to any particular account of how this works; for his purposes, it is enough that there is something that enables him to read and understand an Australian newspaper of 1836 but not a contemporary's article on legal positivism written in Chinese. Because of this "semantic autonomy," he concludes that meaning cannot be reduced to the circumstances of use (pragmatics) or to the subjective intention of the speaker.

Having isolated the destabilizing factors of pragmatics and subjective purpose, Schauer treats what remains as "literal" and "acontextual."

> The identification of acontextual meaning involves not the denial of the necessity of context, but the recognition that a large number of contextual understandings will be assumed by all speakers of a language. These

---

* Note that Schauer presents his argument in terms of the CONDUIT metaphor-system, locating the meaning *in* the words that independently *carry* the meaning.

aspects of context might be thought of as a *universal context*, or *baseline context*, precisely because, however much these widely shared components . . . may be temporally or culturally contingent, they are largely invariant across English speakers at a given time. . . . [T]he ability of one English speaker to talk to another about whom she knows nothing is the best proof of the fact that at a particular time *some* meaning exists that can be discerned through access only to those skills and understandings that are definitional of linguistic competence. (55–58)

On Schauer's view, this "acontextual meaning" is what enables one to know that a rule comprehends a particular case even though that case does not implicate the policy or purpose behind the rule. For example, the "literal" and "acontextual" meaning of the entrenched generalization "running" enables a decisionmaker to distinguish campaigning in a crowded corridor from a slow trot in an empty one, notwithstanding the fact that neither case implicates the purpose of the rule prohibiting running in the halls.

Schauer acknowledges that what he calls "literal" meaning "incorporates substantive moral, social, and political presuppositions that could be and may yet be otherwise" (58). This admission should be fatal to Schauer's argument because it subverts the autonomy of semantics upon which Schauer's rule-formalism depends. Ordinarily, one would expect the rule's entrenched quality to be undone by the introduction of potentially controversial normative considerations. Indeed, Schauer elsewhere concedes that a positivist approach to law is not possible without the fact-value distinction.[13] But he believes he has saved the argument by establishing that meaning is sufficiently stable to allow the mechanical interpretation consonant with the conventional notion of a rule. Thus, as long as the normative dimension of a rule-term is entrenched—so that its "literal" meaning remains uniform and consistent—there should be no need for deliberation by the decisionmaker.

Schauer's argument is untenable, however, because categories do not operate in the rigidly reified manner that he supposes. We can illuminate the problem by first clarifying what Schauer gets right. He is correct that the conventional or "literal" meaning of a concept (or word) depends upon the assumption of a baseline context shared by those within a language-community. That, as we have seen, is what ICMs are all about. Schauer is also correct that concepts (or word-concepts) act as entrenched generalizations in the sense that they have ontological effects: In chapter 4, we saw that one characteristic of parallel distributive processing systems is that new knowledge about a prototype is automatically generalized to related sub-categories; in chapter 6, we saw a more extreme version of this phenomenon when we observed various assimilation-to-prototype effects. But, in point of fact, neither entrenchment nor the sharing of baseline contexts works in the totalizing way necessary to Schauer's account of rules. Ordinarily, we don't think that every category member is just like the prototype. And, as we have seen, it is precisely because the baseline context is an integral part of our processes of categorization that we are able to adjust our categories in light of the circumstances.

Schauer treats these phenomena in the all-or-nothing manner charac-teristic of the rationalist model. From the demonstration that meaning is not coextensive with purpose, he jumps to the conclusion that semantics is *autonomous* of purpose. Similarly, the baseline context becomes a *univer-sal* context "largely invariant across English speakers at a given time." Fi-nally, his concept of entrenchment is presented as if all generalizations op-erated as assimilation-to-prototype effects. Thus, his principal example is the English word "snow," which, on his account, acts as a generalization "gathering up different types of snow and suppressing differences among them." From this example he infers both that English "will ordinarily make it more difficult, albeit not impossible, to think and talk about the hetero-geneity of snow than . . . [if] the generalization 'snow' had not been so en-trenched in our language" and that the suppressed particulars "are likely in practice to be far less accessible . . . [and] less subject to recall on demand" (42–43).

As we know from chapter 4, however, this example is particularly ill-chosen. There are many English words for snow, and we can readily distin-guish sleet from slush or a blizzard from a flurry. Anyone who has ever made a snowball or shoveled a walk knows that snow can be light and powdery or wet and sticky. Nothing about our language precludes either the percep-tion or the memory of those differences. Skiers make further discriminations between kinds of snow that they express in a well-developed vocabulary.

Schauer's example actually undermines his theory of language. To make his theory of rules work, Schauer must drive a wedge between purpose and meaning. But he cannot do so without separating language from the purpose-bearing humans that speak it. Because even seemingly "objective" categories like "snow" are motivated, they can be grounded in the distinctive needs of specialized domains of experience. Thus, there is no such thing as a "universal context" even for "English speakers at a given time." (To give a different kind of example, a nineteenth-century British or Australian reader would have been quite puzzled upon encountering the distinctly American colloquialism "kangaroo court.")[14] Schauer's fundamental error is that he treats purpose and context as extrinsic factors that destabilize meaning, when, in fact, they are intrinsic factors *constitutive* of meaning. Evaluation of context and purpose, in other words, is indispensable to the "skills and understandings that are definitional of linguistic competence." Without context and purpose, one cannot ascertain when running is "running" or when an animal is an "animal."

The phenomenon of prototype effects misleads Schauer to think that there is "literal" and "acontextual" meaning. It is easy to see why he was misled. The fact of prototype effects means that there *is* some meaning available to all competent speakers of a language at a given time. The problem, however, is that the prototypical case is necessarily only a subset of the array of cases comprehended by the "literal" sense of a word-category. Thus, although the experience of prototype effects makes it seem that categories operate "acontextually" (a prototypical chair will be appropriate in *nearly* every context that calls for a chair), the relative diversity among members of a radial category (rockers, beanbag chairs) precludes any mechanical or rote application of a term. A decisionmaker cannot identify a rule's scope from its component category because she cannot know how much of that category is relevant without knowing and considering the purpose of the rule. Schauer's account fails because the more-or-less character of linguistic meaning precludes the rigid consistency required by his rule-formalism.

In contrast, H. L. A. Hart's account of rules as structured in terms of core areas of certainty and peripheral areas of indeterminacy seems a more promising alternative. Hart elaborated in a famous example:

> A legal rule forbids you to take a vehicle into the public park. Plainly this forbids an automobile, but what about bicycles, roller skates, toy automobiles? What about airplanes? Are these, as we say, to be called "vehicles" for the purpose of the rule or not? If we are to communicate with each other at all, . . . then the general words we use . . . must have some standard instance in which no doubts are felt about its application. There must be a core of settled meaning, but there will be, as well, a penumbra of debatable cases in which words are neither obviously applicable nor obviously ruled out. These cases will each have some features in common with the standard case; they will lack others or be accompanied by features not present in the standard case.

Hart recognized rules as "incurably incomplete" and maintained that "we must decide the penumbral cases rationally by reference to social aims." Nevertheless, he insisted that "the hard core of settled meaning is law in some centrally important sense." [15]

In his later treatment of this issue in *The Concept of Law,* Hart identified this "hard core of standard instances or settled meanings" in terms that we now recognize as the phenomenon of prototype effects: the "plain cases constantly recurring in similar contexts to which general expressions are clearly applicable ('If anything is a vehicle a motor-car is one') . . . , where the general terms seem to need no interpretation and where the recognition of instances seems unproblematic and 'automatic.'" [16] So, too, Hart's claim that words have a "core" meaning and "penumbral" cases describes a radial category.* Because Hart understood that natural languages are "irreducibly open textured," he appreciated that "uncertainty at the borderline is the price to be paid for the use of general classifying terms." Accordingly, he concluded that "the authoritative general language in which a rule is expressed may guide only in an uncertain way much as an authoritative example does." [17]

In these three ways, Hart's discussion foreshadowed the approach to legal rules presented at the start of this chapter: He recognized that word-categories form radial categories; that they produce prototype effects; and, consequently, that rules operate as guidelines rather than rigid directives. Even so, Hart's analysis is marred by an inadequate account of meaning. Because his description of the core relies on intuition rather than purpose, Hart's account of rules founders for much the same reason as Schauer's.

The metaphor of "open texture" captures some of the fluidity of language. But it also suggests the image of a tapestry that, though unfinished at the margins, is tightly woven at its center. In fact, Hart treated prototype effects in just this way: For him, the plain case or standard instance represented a *hard* core of *settled* meaning, rather than the contingent product of a motivated, adaptive process of categorization. Thus, both Hart and Schauer take the existence of prototype effects as evidence of meaning sufficiently stable to make the conventional model of rules work. Neither scholar appreciates the degree to which prototype effects are themselves the product of the tacit knowledge of context and purpose that is integral to categorization. Nor could they: One cannot admit a semantic role for purpose

---

* The evident congruence between Hart and recent developments in cognitive theory can be traced to the shared influence of J. L. Austin, who was Hart's colleague at Oxford.

without undermining the positivist view of law subscribed to by both Hart and Schauer.

In the traditional jurisprudential dispute, legal positivism is the rival to natural law theory. Natural law theory claims that morality is a constitutive precondition of legality and, thus, a necessary component of all (proper) acts of law identification and law application. Legal positivism, in contrast, views law as a social fact (the "is" such as the command of the sovereign or, for Hart, that which corresponds to the rule of recognition) entirely distinct from morality (the "ought"). Subsequent positivists have pointed out that this distinction is conceptual rather than empirical. Actual systems of positive law may, as a contingent matter, contain overtly moral conceptions. (The Due Process and Equal Protection Clauses of the United States Constitution are familiar examples.) Thus, the theoretical core of positivism is what Jules Coleman calls "the separability thesis"—the notion that the legal is conceptually distinguishable from the larger universe of the non-legal.[18] Schauer elaborates:

> The heart of positivism lies not in something special about the law/
> morality distinction, but in the concept of *systemic isolation*. . . . To the
> positivist, there can be systems whose norms are identified by reference
> to some identifier that can distinguish *legal* norms from other norms,
> such as those of politics, morality, economics, or etiquette. This identi-
> fier, which Hart refers to as the 'rule of recognition' and Dworkin labels
> a 'pedigree', picks out legal norms from the universe of norms. . . . If a
> norm is so selected, it is a valid legal norm, notwithstanding its moral
> repugnance, economic inconsistency, or political folly. (199–200)

The separability thesis suffers from a relatively obvious kind of category mistake. True, a lawyer will always approach an issue with the material designated "legal" firmly fixed in the foreground of her attention. But she can comprehend that material only against a larger cultural backdrop of normatively loaded understandings. The fallacy of the separability thesis is that it mistakes social distinctiveness for conceptual autonomy: There can be no purely positivist system of legal norms when categorization and comprehension already implicate the legal decisionmaker in the process of making classifications and distinctions relative to the practical commitments and normative assumptions of her culture.

The impossibility of a purely positivist system is clear on Schauer's account, which explicitly equates positivism with rule-formalism. "A positivist system," he explains, "is in many respects just the systemic analogue of a rule" (199). Given that, for Schauer, the concept of a rule is defined by the model of entrenchment, it follows that a positivist views valid legal norms as exclusionary reasons for action that preclude consideration of other decisional factors.* (Recall Hart's remark that a legal rule is, by its very nature, inconsistent with the notion that all questions are open to reconsideration in light of social aims.) In other words, the positivist considers valid legal norms as reasons for action in and of themselves—that is, without regard to their effects and without regard to whether those effects are morally repugnant or merely counterproductive. But this restriction cannot even get off the ground if the very categories in which legal rules are written require that decisionmakers take purpose and motivating context into account just to determine what a rule *means*. Consider, again, Schauer's example of a rule prohibiting animals on the bus. How can a decisionmaker distinguish dogs, goldfish, paramecia, and humans without, in Roberto Unger's words, relying "tacitly if not explicitly upon some picture of the forms of human association that are right and realistic in the areas of social life" addressed by the rule? [19]

In an important sense, the whole point of Hart's distinction between core and penumbra was to evade the force of this insight—that even the simplest cases require the decisionmaker to consider the normative underpinnings of the rule. By distinguishing a core where decision "seems unproblematic and 'automatic'" from a penumbra where "judges must necessarily legislate," [20] Hart hoped to restrict policy to the periphery and preserve the conventional concept of a rule as establishing a domain (the "is") within which decisionmakers are not free to decide in light of the considerations (the "ought") they think best. But Hart had no viable account of the core. Consequently, he had no reliable way in which to distinguish questions of the core from those of the penumbra. Moreover, once we understand how such "core" meanings actually arise, Hart's whole enterprise collapses.

This difficulty is apparent in his discussion of Holmes's 1931 opinion in *McBoyle v. United States*. The question was whether a 1919 federal statute prohibiting interstate transportation of a stolen "vehicle" applied to airplanes. Holmes concluded that it did not:

> Fair warning should be given to the world in language that the common
> world would understand. . . . When a rule of conduct is laid down in

* For Schauer, it also means that a positivist views the existing legal regime as the instantiation of its generating justification (justice, order, etc.) and treats that system in a "rule-like" fashion as providing reasons for action even when it fails to serve its goals.

words that evoke in the common mind only the picture of vehicles moving on land, the statute should not be extended to aircraft simply because
it may seem to us that a similar policy applies.[21]

Hart criticized Holmes for treating *McBoyle* as a core case to be decided by
reference to common usage instead of recognizing it as a penumbral case to
be determined by reference to policy. But one can just as plausibly say that
Holmes recognized it as a penumbral case (hence the talk of extension), but
decided it in light of the policy that criminal statutes should provide fair
notice—a point Hart grudgingly acknowledged.[22] Alternatively, one might
characterize *McBoyle* as a core case falling unequivocally within the purview of the statute but agree that it was wrongly decided. On this view,
Holmes's error lay in reducing the statutory category to its most prototypical members when he should have recognized that social and technological changes had transformed the conventional, "everyday" meaning of the
statutory term.

This view of *McBoyle* as involving a reduction-to-prototype effect has
several advantages. For one thing, it provides a better account of Holmes's
actual opinion, which explicitly rests on the policy consideration that Hart
recognized only reluctantly. For another, it is consistent with the theory of
motivation: i.e., the idea that purpose is a constitutive element of categorization suggests the correlative notion that people accommodate their purposes not arbitrarily and unpredictably but by means of regular and predictable cognitive processes. This characterization of *McBoyle* could never
have been accepted by Hart because it means that law can be made outside
the formal legal process—that is, without regard to the rule of recognition:
As Hart and Holmes implicitly agree, it is unlikely that the 1919 Congress
would have thought to include the still relatively novel airplane within the
coverage of a statute about stolen vehicles. At the same time, however, Hart
could not have defended against this characterization of *McBoyle* because
he had only a thin, intuitive account of the core. For Hart, the "plain cases
. . . are only the familiar ones, constantly recurring in similar contexts."[23]
But, by 1931, (or, if not by that time, then by the time Hart wrote), airplanes were sufficiently common and familiar to have become a "plain case"
of a vehicle.

McBoyle thus illustrates Llewellyn's observation: "All words (that is,
linguistic symbols) and all rules composed of words continuously change
meaning as new conditions emerge."[24] It also exposes the fundamental flaw
in Hart's account of rules. The relative "openness" of texture characteristic of the penumbra can extend even to the core. Meaning is not simply a

matter of regularity or familiarity; it is motivated. Change in meaning over time is, thus, but one example of the more general point that context and purpose are internal to meaning. This point, in turn, entails that meaning always remains contingent on context: Even so prototypical a chair as a dining room chair may be wrong if what is needed is a seat for the distinguished judge presiding over a moot court at the law school. By the same token, a rule prohibiting animals on the bus produces prototype effects that differ from those of the component category "animal" precisely because our comprehension of the rule is framed by our knowledge of its motivating context.

Once we recognize a semantic role for motivation, however, the distinction between a policy-free core and a penumbra of "legislative" freedom necessarily collapses. On one hand, the automatic cases are unproblematic only because the decisionmaker has already invoked her tacit knowledge of the rule's policy and purpose. On the other hand, decisions in the penumbral cases are framed and constrained by the rule's motivating context, which means that, contrary to Hart's assertion, we cannot fail "to include in the 'rule' the various aims and policies in the light of which its penumbral cases are decided." [25] Thus, it follows that the positivist claim cannot be sustained.

The fundamental flaw upon which positivism founders will, perhaps, be clearest if we revisit the famous exchange between Hart and Lon Fuller and apply the tools of cognitive theory to Hart's own example of a rule prohibiting vehicles in the park. Most of the literature commenting on this example focuses on the term "vehicle" as the locus of the rule's indeterminacy. [26] Thus, even Fuller put the point to Hart by positing a case that, if included in the rule, would yield a bizarre, counterintuitive result: Suppose, he suggested, a veteran's group mounted a working World War II truck on a pedestal in the park as a war memorial. Would it run afoul of "the 'no vehicle' rule?" [27]

Fuller criticized Hart for implying that the meaning of a rule could turn on a single word. To interpret a rule, Fuller explained, one must go beyond the formal text to read the rule in light of its purpose. Yet, he had surprisingly little to say about how one derives the purpose of the rule prohibiting vehicles:

> If the rule excluding vehicles from parks seems easy to apply in some
> cases, . . . this is because we can see clearly enough what the rule "is
> aiming at in general." . . . If in some cases we seem to be able to apply

the rule without asking what its purpose is, this is not because we can
treat a directive arrangement as if it had no purpose. It is rather because,
for example, whether the rule be intended to preserve the quiet in the
park, or to save carefree strollers from injury, we know "without thinking" that a noisy automobile must be excluded.[28]

Fuller, no less than Hart, relies on the tacit knowledge of the decisionmaker
to explain how he or she knows to apply the rule. Fuller's "what the rule 'is
aiming at in general'" is the functional equivalent of Hart's "plain case,"
where application of the rule seems unproblematic and automatic. But neither Fuller nor Hart has anything more to say about this tacit knowledge.

Tacit knowledge, however, can be specified: If we can apply the rule
"without thinking," it is because our background conception of a park in-
forms our apprehension of the rule and renders it intelligible. We know that
an automobile is to be excluded because we know that a park is for con-
templative, meditative, and recreational activities like strolling, picnicking,
exercising, and playing. And, knowing that, we also know "without thinking" that the purpose of the rule is to preserve the quiet and safety of the
park. Indeed, these conceptions are so deeply sedimented that it is hard to
conceive of any *other* reasons for prohibiting vehicles.*

In an important sense, Hart was wrong to deny that "judges are only
'drawing out' of the rule what, if it is properly understood, is 'latent' within
it." [29] Rather, the purpose of the rule *is evident* from our understanding of
its language terms. It is evident because the word "park" instantiates a cognitive process that evokes an ICM together with its motivating context: a
location, its purposes, the manner of it use, and its concomitant hazards.
The same is true of the concept "vehicle," which is structured relative to
human purpose and use. Vehicles carry us and our goods, and they do so
with greater speed and efficiency than walking. The concept "vehicle" entails mobility, transportability, and an energy source. Vehicles have varied
greatly over the course of human experience, from rickshaws, chariots,
Conestoga wagons, and cars to jet airplanes; their energy sources range
from other humans to animals to the internal combustion engine and beyond. But, in a given culture at a given moment, there are only a few con-

---

* It would be odd, indeed, for a lawyer or decisionmaker to research the question of
legislative intent behind the rule. Would she read the minutes of the meeting at which the
park department or city council adopted the rule? Would she search for some study or
commission report that examined the problem of vehicles in the park? Would she find
anything?

ventional modes of transportation that are common and recurrent. These modes will inevitably share the conditions of the vehicle ICM.

The rule against vehicles in the park presents no great difficulties—that is, it manifests a "hard core of settled meaning"—because these commonly grounded ICMs enable us to conceptualize the rule-domain with a high degree of consistency and reliability. Because the operative category ("vehicle") is framed by the concept "park," we can draw on our knowledge of its motivating context to distinguish those situations comprehended by the rule. It would be odd, for example, if an official in our culture were to apply the rule to a child's tricycle. The peculiarity of such a decision is not a function of any doubts about the proper classification of the tricycle; plainly, it is a "vehicle." Yet, because it "emits no fumes, makes no noise, and endangers no lives," [30] it does not seem to fall within the prohibition with respect to vehicles in *parks*. Indeed, unless the rule specified "no bicycles" (as some park signs do), we would be more likely to assume that tricycle riding was precisely the kind of activity the "no vehicle" rule was designed to safeguard.

This redescription of the structure of the rule changes two things. First, the gap between Hart and Fuller narrows substantially. Each emphasized a different aspect of the tacit process by which we understand the rule: Hart the standard instance of the rule's operative category; Fuller the inference of purpose that arises from our tacit knowledge of the rule's motivating context. Both views represent prototype effects. Conceptually, Fuller was more nearly correct: Ordinarily, it is the prototype of the rule rather than that of the component category that governs. But both prototype effects cohere in this case. Similarly, Fuller's counterexample of a working World War II truck mounted on a pedestal provides little problem for Hart's core/penumbra analysis. Unlike Schauer, Hart maintained that the language of the rule indicates only the prototypical example, not the entire reach of the "literal" category. Once the truck is mounted on a pedestal as a statue, it will no longer be understood to fall within the core meaning of either the category or the rule.

The second thing that changes on this redescription is that Hart's example becomes a near perfect illustration of the *anti*positivist case. Law cannot be reduced to the official domain of formal lawmaking because one cannot even *make sense* of the "no vehicles" rule without utilizing our culturally contingent, normative assumptions about the appropriate uses of a park. As Fuller explained in a later treatment:

> The proper interpretation of the ordinance will depend on the meaning
> attributed to the institution "park" by the practices and attitudes of the

society in question. In some countries . . . , a park tends to be a place of quiet and repose, where the citizen may escape the tumult of the city. In the warmer latitudes it may be a place of music and gaiety, to which the citizen will betake himself after his need for repose has been satisfied by a siesta. . . . This means that in applying the statute the judge or police sergeant must be guided not simply by its words but by some conception of what is fit and proper to come into a park; conceptions of this sort are implicit in the practices of and attitudes of the society of which he is a member.[31]

The "no vehicles" rule actually contravenes both of positivism's principal tenets. Because it cannot be applied without taking into account (whether tacitly or explicitly) the culturally approved purposes of the park, the rule cannot be isolated as a social fact divorced from an "ought." Moreover, the socially sanctioned purposes of the park do not derive from positive law but must be sought in the prevailing social practices with respect to parks. Indeed, the "no vehicles" rule is a particularly powerful example of this latter point—and, therefore, of the antipositivist case—because it depends upon cultural understandings that took shape in *direct conflict* with the official policies and rules that initially governed America's parks.

Many of the sights and activities that we now associate with the park were deemed inherently inappropriate by its mid-nineteenth-century originators—people such as William Cullen Bryan, Andrew Jackson Downing, Frederick Law Olmsted, and Horace Greeley. For them, the park was a republican institution whose pastoral scenery was expected to serve as a democratizing and civilizing reform that would "soften and humanize the rude, educate and enlighten the ignorant, and give continual enjoyment to the educated."[32] Ornaments like statuary were opposed by park advocates both because they were thought to be undemocratic (which is to say, European and aristocratic) and because they detracted from the naturalistic effect that was, in their view, the sine qua non of a park.[33] So, too, athletics were staunchly resisted—though ultimately unsuccessfully.[34] Bicycles were generally barred from the park until the 1890s, when they were accommodated with specially constructed paths.[35]

By century's end, however, the naturalistic conception of the park began to yield to the recreational demands of urban, working-class constituencies. Playgrounds were constructed in cities like New York, Chicago, Philadelphia, and San Francisco even before passage of the enabling legislation that authorized purchase of the land. By the 1920s, the typical urban park was likely to include physical facilities and organized programs for baseball, tennis, ice hockey, and swimming, as well as official programming as diverse as gardening, dancing, libraries, health clinics, and public lectures.[36] The end of the Depression saw the completion of the social transformation of the park from a special use facility to an unrestricted public resource. As aptly put in a 1940 Chicago park commission report: "The shift was not in things or properties; it was in the social meanings of those things and properties." [37]

All our current intuitions about the proper uses of the park are the contingent products of this particular cultural history. The park, in other words, is a sedimented social institution. Consequently, the concept "park" has a distinctive and inescapable normative skew. One need only compare how a "no vehicles" rule would be applied to a bicycle in Olmsted's time and in ours to see that there is no escaping the cultural and normative penetration of the ostensibly separate domain of law. As Fuller remarked: "All this adds up to the conclusion that an important part of the statute in question is not made by the legislator, but grows and develops as an implication of complex practices and attitudes which may themselves be in a state of development." [38]

LAYING DOWN THE RULES

What, then, does it mean to "follow" a rule? How is following a rule like following a story?

"Rule" is from the Latin *regula* ("straightedge") and *regere* ("to lead straight"). To comply with a rule is to act *pursuant* thereto (from the Latin *prosequerae,* "to follow," also the source of "pursue"). The concept of a rule thus reflects the same metaphorical mapping that animates the "forest of constraint" trope: ACTIONS ARE MOTIONS, PURPOSES ARE DESTINATIONS, and CONSTRAINTS ON ACTIONS ARE CONSTRAINTS ON MOTIONS. In this mapping, legal rules are paths that guide action (i.e., metaphorical motion) along an authorized course. Thus, in Deuteronomy, God admonishes the Children of Israel: "And thou shalt not turn from the words that I command you today, neither right nor left, to walk after other gods to serve them." [39] To much the same effect is the explanation of the fifteenth-century scholar, Jean Gerson, whom Richard Tuck credits with the first natural rights theory: "*Lex* is a practical and right reason *[recta ratio practica]* according to which the *movements* and workings of things are *directed toward their foreordained ends.*" [40]

This metaphorical conception—which can be represented by the mnemonic RULES ARE PATHS—is what makes sense of such familiar phrases as "following the rules laid down" and "the straight and narrow," as illustrated below in figure 8.1.[41] What differentiates the conventional concept of a rule from other kinds of legal directives is that rules are understood to provide well-defined pathways allowing little leeway. The optimal rule is "clear-cut" and "hard-and-fast." It is "clear-cut" because the trail is well-blazed and the way open for passage to the designated end.* It is "hard-and-fast" because the confines of the path are firm and unyielding (as in "to stand fast"). Thus, a clear-cut rule leaves no doubt about the proper course of action; a hard-and-fast rule admits no exceptions.

But the very fact that we have such qualifiers undermines the conventional concept of a rule. Modifiers indicate a divergence from the default assumptions that constitute the standard case—thus such idioms as "dry ice" but not "wet ice," or "working mother" but not "working father." Modifiers such as "clear-cut" and "hard-and-fast" imply that the expectations engendered by our idealized conception of rules do not fit our actual experience of them. Not surprisingly, there are several idiomatic expressions that articulate just this discrepancy. The expressions "rules are made to be broken" and "more honored in the breach" reflect that even within a rule's domain, a competent social performance often entails deviation from the rule's precise requirements. So, too, the expression "as a rule" means "usually, but not always." The familiar idiom "the exception that proves the rule" is perhaps the most revealing because it implies that the existence of outliers is necessary to determine the boundaries of appropriate behavior (i.e., to "prove the rule").

Following a rule, then, is like following a story in two related senses. First, both the rule and story ICMs employ a JOURNEY mapping as a central component of their conceptual structure. In the case of rules, the traveler maps onto the person subject to the rule (whether primary actor or legal decisionmaker); the path maps onto the constraints of the rule; and movement along the course marked out by the path maps onto compliance with— that is, the "following" of—the rule. In the case of stories, the traveler maps onto the protagonist and, by identification, the audience; the path maps onto the series of events and encounters that constitute the plot; and movement along the path maps onto the progress of the protagonist and that of the reader as he or she follows the story line. (Hence, Ricoeur's remark, "To

---

* This, too, is the import of Sir Thomas's ironic "to cut a great road through the law," which connotes a newly authorized course of action created by the abrogation or removal of existing legal constraints.

FIGURE 8.1 The "straight and narrow"

follow a story is to move forward . . . under the guidance of an expectation that finds its fulfillment in the 'conclusion' of the story.")

Compliance with a rule is not possible unless one first recognizes it as a rule and understands its requirements. Thus, the second way in which following a rule is like following a story is in the sense of the ARGUMENT IS A JOURNEY metaphor—that is, in the sense that "to follow" means "to comprehend." Both cases involve the construction of a mental space in which one recreates and then imaginatively traces the path "laid down" by the story or rule. In other words, one follows the rulemaker's lead in first reconstructing and then enacting the designated course of action.

Following a rule thus entails the same threefold mimesis that Ricoeur described with respect to narrative. Each point in the process of rule-following involves an act of culturally contingent reconstruction. The lawmaker makes use of the preexisting cultural ICMs with which she apprehends the world. She then configures them in a recognizable rule-form with an apprehensible meaning. By the time the rule is promulgated, it has already been twice rendered and shaped by cultural forms. Those governed by the rule must reconstruct it yet again, this time in relation to the cultural ICMs—e.g., "animal," "bus," "park," etc.—that *they* bring to the process. Thus, a rule risks misconstruction unless it has been fashioned from the cultural ICMs and understandings already held by those governed by the rule. If, for example, the lawmaker employs an elite or divergent conception of the park, then people are likely to understand and apply the rule prohibiting vehicles in ways that differ from the intended scope of the rule. A rule cannot work *as* a rule unless it already reflects the normatively loaded understandings of those who are expected to obey it.

Three conclusions follow. First, the clarity, certainty, and predictability associated with rules are, as Fish says, "a function of the fact that interpretive assumptions and procedures are so widely shared in a community that the rule appears to all in the same (interpreted) shape." The "ruleness" of a rule, in other words, derives not from any categorical quality but from its *conventionality:* Rules are perspicuous to the extent they reflect the categories and concepts that already define the social expectations of those whose behavior they govern. Second, rules are contingent on the very social practices they are intended to regulate: Because constraint is a function of shared understandings, and understandings are grounded in our embodied interactions with our physical and social world, rules "make sense only in reference to the very regularities they are thought to bring about" (122–23). Third, the clarity of a legal rule has nothing to do with its specificity. Even in science, as Thomas Kuhn observes, "shared examples can serve cognitive functions commonly attributed to shared rules."[42] And in law, as Judge Posner explains, "standards that capture lay intuitions about right behavior" such as the negligence standard "may produce greater legal certainty than a network of precise but technical, nonintuitive rules covering the same ground" (48).

Thus, once we understand how rules work, everything about our concept of law changes: Rules operate with the flexibility of standards; standards operate with the clarity of rules; and both forms of legal directives depend upon shared tacit understandings of their motivating contexts just to operate at all. More profoundly, one cannot give a meaningful account of legal rules (including standards) without according a fundamental, *constitutional* role to the world of social practice that the rules supposedly govern. Indeed, the concept of a formal rule is but a special case of the more general process of institutionalization by which social practice comes to be seen as normative and binding.

To see why a rule cannot be understood apart from the social practices and forms of life that give it meaning, consider an ostensibly incompatible approach such as Posner's "activity theory" of law. Posner points out that the conventional understanding of law is something of a reification: "The fact that 'the law' seems to command and empower, to channel and forbid, makes it intuitive to suppose that it is indeed a thing of some sort or perhaps a set of things, specifically rules" (221). Posner elaborates on Holmes's "prediction theory" and argues that law is not a set of concepts but a professional practice: "The law is not a thing [judges] discover; it is the name of their activity. They do not act in accordance with something called 'law'—they just act as best they can" (225).[43]

Posner is certainly correct as a philosophical matter: Whatever kind of "thing" law is, there is no "thing" separate from the mental and social activities of the people that bring "it" into existence. But activity theory is deeply problematic as a phenomenological matter. In denying the law's "thingness," Posner elides an important portion of the mental and social activity that constitutes law *as* Law. Moreover, activity theory is far too narrow and parochial in its focus on the professional activities of judges and lawyers.

Both of these problems coalesce when, with characteristic candor, Posner considers the shortcomings of his own activity theory. He notes that the very existence of a notion such as natural law shows that

> we have a concept of law that is something other than an activity. For whose activity is it to produce natural law? There are no licensed profes-

sionals to point to. The relevant concept of law in such a setting is one of law as custom or tradition rather than as professional activity, or more precisely as a professional activity bounded and shaped by custom, tradition, community feeling, and so on. (238)

Posner attempts to blunt the force of this point by folding it into his activity theory. "Positive law and natural law materials are inputs into the activity we call law" (239). True enough. Still, this solution does not suffice to save activity theory. Posner's reformulated concept of natural law admits reification in through the backdoor: "Custom" and "tradition" are no more entities, and no less activities, than positive law. In fact, custom and tradition are nothing more than labels for the social practices of real-life people. This leaves Posner with two opposed but equally fatal problems: If custom and tradition can nevertheless be reified and reduced to a set of concepts (IDEAS ARE OBJECTS) that function as mere inputs (THE MIND IS A CONTAINER) to judicial activity, then why not the law itself? If, on the other hand, custom and tradition are themselves understood as ongoing social activities of norm-creation, then it is hard to see how one can separate the strictly "legal" activity of judges (and other lawmakers) from the surrounding jurisgenerative forces.

Posner evades the second horn of this dilemma by impaling himself on the first: "The modern significance of natural law is not as a body of objective norms that underwrite positive law but as a source of the ethical and political arguments that judges use to challenge, change, or elaborate positive law—in other words to produce new positive law" (459). The reification of "custom and tradition," in other words, is integral to his positivist conception of law as an activity. By hypostatizing social practice, he maintains the conceptual distance from context and culture that enables the judge to stand aloof from it, hold it at a distance, and treat it as a resource to be self-consciously mined for the raw materials with which to produce new law.

Consider, in contrast, the position of the judge once one understands custom as an ongoing social activity with normative dimension. Even the Posnerian judge committed to a thoroughly consequentialist, empirically grounded, policy-based approach to decisionmaking cannot decide such questions as whether or which vehicles should be allowed in the park without relying on and being guided by the social practices that constitute our cultural understanding of the park and the behaviors appropriate to it. Indeed, as Fuller pointed out, the judge is likely to invoke this background knowledge automatically—"without thinking." In that event, there is no denying culture's role as a kind of dominant silent partner in the lawmaking enterprise. The judge's lawmaking activities are not only bounded but also *shaped* by the habits, practices, and understandings of his culture.

The role of social practice and understanding in shaping the law is the same whether we are talking about simple legal rules like those governing the park or the more obviously policy-laden decisionmaking in constitutional cases. Consider the controversial case of *Bowers v. Hardwick*, which upheld state sodomy laws as applied to homosexual conduct. There, the majority decided against a constitutional right to privacy because our historical and constitutional tradition had never sanctioned homosexual sodomy. The dissent, in contrast, would have upheld a right to privacy as of a piece with our society's general commitment to privacy in matters of sexuality.[44] In conventional constitutional debate, *Bowers* is understood as posing the question of the appropriate level of generality at which to frame the interpretation of constitutional guarantees.[45] But not everyone sees it quite this way. Philip Bobbitt argues that in privacy cases like *Bowers* and in the abortion case *Roe v. Wade*,[46] the level of generality is beside the point:

> If the majority in *Bowers* is persuasive, it is precisely because the actual conduct of homosexual sodomy did not, traditionally, correspond to our notions of intimacy but instead seemed (perhaps erroneously) more like licentiousness. Whether or not the argument regarding *Roe* is persuasive also depends on whether the specifics of a woman's carrying a fetus to term corresponds to our ideas of intimacy. If they don't, then the level of generality—whether or not Americans want to protect privacy, on the one hand, or fetal life on the other—is simply irrelevant.[47]

What is both striking and strikingly conventional about this debate is the degree to which it focuses on the foreground question of constitutional interpretation. "An inch from the eye is a portion of the Text; the whole living world behind is 'covered' by it."[48] Once we focus on that living world, however, we begin to notice how much of the legal and political work occurs at the epistemic level. The excerpt from Bobbitt helps us see that, in cases such as *Bowers* and *Roe*, the overt process of constitutional decisionmaking depends on preexisting, cultural processes of categorization. What ultimately decides the issue is not the legal rule but the concept of *intimacy* that the judges bring to the case. If the judges know intimacy only in the context of a traditional heterosexual marriage, if they know lesbians and gays only as Other, then *Bowers* is always and already lost. But if the society is one in which same-sex relationships can be seen and manifested in all the tender, loving capacities that human relationships can muster at their best, if the judges know of such people and can see them as people just like themselves, then the case is won (or, better yet, might never need to be brought). So, too, for *Roe.* If the judges see pregnancy as an intimate, personal matter, then it is an easy case. But if they see pregnancy and sex as fundamentally matters of procreation, then the case is already in trouble even before one gets anywhere near the Constitution.

Thus, the first lesson of activity theory is that the law cannot be understood apart from the larger social practices and forms of life—that is, how a community lives, the norms it obeys, the things it values—that give it shape and meaning. If we are to understand law as an activity, we must follow Llewellyn's lead to broaden our focus beyond the legal professionals to recognize that law involves "in one phase or another the ways of a huge number of people—well-nigh the whole population." [49] Official lawmaking is but one expression of the relentless way in which humans construct the normative world that they inhabit. "All several men need do is live together and be associated with the same task for some rudimentary rules and a beginning of law to emerge from their life in common." [50]

The second, yet more paradoxical lesson of activity theory is that, consistent with Posner's reformulation of natural law as custom and tradition, the activity of law entails a certain amount of reification. Official lawmaking is but a formalized case of the process of institutionalization that characterizes custom and tradition. We can illuminate this point by examining Peter Berger and Thomas Luckmann's account of institutionalization.[51]

Consistent with activity theory, Berger and Luckmann stress the ineradicably performative nature of social institutions. "The institution, with its assemblage of 'programmed' actions, is like the unwritten libretto of a drama" (75). The institution exists only to the extent that the actors who compose it successfully reproduce the roles, routines, and patterns of behavior that constitute it as an institution. Berger and Luckmann use habitualization as a model with which to explain this process.[52] "Any action that is repeated frequently becomes cast into a pattern, which can then be reproduced with an economy of effort and which, *ipso facto,* is apprehended by its performer *as* that pattern." Consequently, the phenomenological experience of habituation has a "There I go again" feel to it. Social institutions are constituted by the build-up of reciprocal or complementary habitualizations. "'There he goes again' becomes 'There *we* go again'" (53–54).

At this hypothetical stage, reification is only "incipient." Some measure of objectification has already occurred. But it "remains tenuous, easily changeable, almost playful" because it is still "fairly accessible to deliberate intervention" by the relevant actors.

> All this changes in the process of transmission to the new generation. The objectivity of the institutional world "thickens" and "hardens," not only for the children, but (by a mirror effect) for the parents as well. The "There we go again" now becomes "This is how these things are done." A world so regarded . . . becomes real in an ever more massive way.

Institutions "have now been crystallized" and "are experienced as existing over and beyond the individuals who 'happen to' embody them" (58–59).

Institutionalization involves both sedimentation and objectification in language.[53] Intersubjective meaning becomes "truly social only when it has been objectivated in a sign system of one kind or another, that is, when the possibility of reiterated objectification of the shared experiences arises" (67). For an institution to endure, it must be reproduced successfully in the performance of actual actors. To assure such continuity, the relevant recipe knowledge must be transmitted to those whose actions will compose the institution in the future. The necessity of reproduction creates pressure to reduce this recipe knowledge to canonical forms (70)—the "proverbial nuggets of wisdom, values and beliefs" that constitute the familiar " 'what everybody knows' about a social world" (65). In this way, "language becomes the depository of a large aggregate of collective sedimentations, which can be acquired . . . as cohesive wholes and without reconstructing their original process of formation" (65–69).[54]

The social world is, thus, "an ongoing human production" (52) that "attain[s] the character of objectivity"; it is constituted by an ongoing, three-way dialectic of externalization (i.e., continuing human activity), objectification, and internalization.[55] Berger and Luckmann explain that this "objectivity" is a social construction that, therefore, has no "ontological status apart from the human activity that produced it" (which is to say both that it is a *social* construction and that it is a social *construction*). But they emphasize that the objectivity of the social world is nevertheless real as a phenomenological matter and that this objectivity is essential to the construction of the social world. Accordingly, they insist that any "analysis of the social world that leaves out any one of these three moments will be distortive" (60–61).

Activity theory goes wrong precisely because it concentrates on the

FIGURE 8.2   Schematic of Law as Social Activity

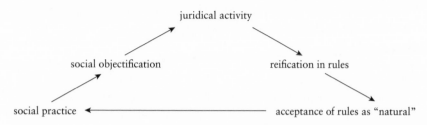

judges' externalizations, leaving out the other two moments. What it misses
is that when judges or other legal actors first approach their task they confront a sedimented field of social objectifications that they, too, have internalized.* What activity theory gets right, however, is that these objectifications have no ontological status separate from the social and mental
activities that constitute them. The value of activity theory is that it correctly identifies the reification of a naïve positivism of rules. The cost of activity theory, however, is that it overlooks the constraints that arise from the
fact that there are objectifications "out there" in the social world that are
not arbitrary.

A complete theory of law must provide an account of the reflexive process through which social practice is institutionalized as legal meaning and
accepted as appropriate because reflective of the expectations and "lay intuitions of right behavior" that arise from those very social practices (fig. 8.2).
This account is exactly what is provided by a theory of categorization as
a motivated process. Thus, one can recharacterize Berger and Luckmann's
three-way dialectic of externalization, objectification, and internalization as
a reflexive relation between experience, imagination, and meaning. Social
activity that is institutionalized as a practice already has a solidity (albeit a
socially constructed one) that makes it ripe for formalization as a legal rule.
A rule thus formulated will be perspicuous to those it supposedly governs
precisely because it is motivated by their social experience. It will, moreover, seem "natural" or "right" because people will see it as reflective of the
objective qualities of the social world in which they live. From a philosophical perspective, this putatively natural quality is a reification. Never-

---

* If they are particularly reflective, they may recognize these objectifications as such
and things may seem rather more fluid. Nevertheless, the lawmakers will be constrained by
these objectifications to the extent that they expect to persuade others of the validity of
their activity.

theless, it is a phenomenological reality, and one without which we could not have law at all. Law, in other words, is *both* something we do *and* something we have as a consequence of something we do.

LLEWELLYN

Perhaps better than any legal theorist this past century, Karl Llewellyn understood the deeply social and profoundly human dimensions of law. Today, our view of the legal realists is colored by the characterizations of their contemporaneous critics and of their more recent successors in the critical legal studies movement.[56] For entirely different reasons, both of these characterizations tend to stress the more radical rule- and fact-skepticism of Llewellyn and Jerome Frank. But Llewellyn's oeuvre represents a broader and more penetrating engagement with the social phenomenon of law.

Llewellyn, of course, has been a recurrent figure in this book. In chapter 2, we saw that he followed Holmes in appreciating the experientially based nature of reason. In chapter 4, we saw that Llewellyn long ago remarked on the phenomenon illustrated by *Bowers:* that the outcome of a case has more to do with how one categorizes the facts than with the details of the relevant legal rule. In chapter 6, I quoted his prescient (and colorful) description of the radial structure of doctrinal categories. More importantly, we have seen here how clearly he understood the phenomenon of motivation and its implications for law. This understanding is explicit in his observation that legal meaning, like all linguistic meaning, changes with the emergence of new social conditions. In a related vein, Llewellyn's approach to constitutional law reflects a sophisticated sociology and phenomenology of the sort described by Berger and Luckmann. Thus, Llewellyn explained that an institution like the Constitution "is in first instance a set of ways of living and doing. It is not, *in first instance,* a matter of words."[57]

As an admirer of Holmes, Llewellyn was also an early and embattled exponent of activity theory: "What . . . officials do about disputes is, to my mind, the law itself."[58] On the conventional view, an activity theory of law equates with an assertion of indeterminacy and judicial freedom because it defines law without reference to any external constraint. Llewellyn's statement that law is what the officials do was understood by his contemporaneous critics in just this way. And the most able of his contemporary successors in the critical legal studies movement have elaborated the activity theory in this same manner.[59]

It is the relationship between Llewellyn's appreciation of the ineradicably social dimension of law and his espousal of activity theory that I want to develop here. For Llewellyn, the idea of law as an activity implied no radical freedom for decisionmakers precisely because he understood the phenomenon of motivation. Though sometimes too exuberant to extol the values of craft, Llewellyn never lost sight of the cultural contingency of legal decisionmaking. Thus, he disparaged the lawyer's ideal of certainty:

> Far more important to me seems legal certainty for the man in the street. . . . A layman . . . fashions his norms, and consequently his expectations about the law, directly from the probabilities in real life, which change as a function of changing conditions. Legal rules provide certainty in the affairs of people . . . if, in a lawsuit, they yield a result that accord with their real-life norms. Thus, the most important legal certainty . . . depends on whether the judge can make the direction and degree of semantic change in a legal rule (or a verbal symbol used by the rule) keep up with the corresponding change in the real-life situation. If the change sanctioned by the judge keeps up more or less, but not quite, one then speaks of the law's mild conservatism. If the change on the judge's part is noticeably not keeping up, one then speaks of a crisis in decision making. And, finally, if the change on the judge's part is keeping up perfectly, neither judge nor layman realizes that any change has occurred . . . and legal certainty prevails. It *can* prevail only through change.[60]

For Llewellyn, the indeterminacy of legal rules and precedents did not amount to a general claim of indeterminacy of law understood as an activity. To the contrary, he saw the activity of dispute resolution "less as *making* order than as *maintaining* order when it has gotten out of order." [61] But he understood the maintenance of this order as anything but static. As an ongoing social institution, law

> generates *attitudes* not only of general and specific approval (in the main) of whatever happens to have become existing practice, but also attitudes less capable of definition—*sets*, or built-up predispositions in the participants, to deal with situations those participants have previously never met or thought of, *along the lines* of the ways they know.[62]

Whatever the judges' "built-up predispositions," they inevitably encounter situations that they "have previously never met or thought of." In this context, to react along the lines marked out by their sedimented knowledges is, unavoidably, to act imaginatively in a new circumstance, reasoning in terms of a known one.

How, precisely, does the judge make sure that the rule keeps up with the corresponding change in the real-life situation? Llewellyn's answer was the amalgam of intuition or tacit knowledge he called "situation-sense."[63] He offered this conception to account for and evaluate legal decisionmaking with something more than a subjectivist standard of "measurement by whether I the sparrow, with my bow and arrow, like the specific outcome for a target" (276). Thus, for Llewellyn, situation-sense was a normative ideal:

> For the standard of wisdom to which appeal is being made . . . is not any
> person's personal standard; it is rather a standard which aims to get idio-
> syncratic preferences largely hewn off until the standard becomes what
> the courts also are reaching for: something which can be hoped, on
> thought, to look reasonable to any thinking man. (277)

Even so, Llewellyn denied that situation-sense had any objective or foundational status: "It is quite independent, I repeat, of any philosophy as to the proper sources of 'Right Reason' which may be held by any 'Natural Law' philosopher. . . . It answers instead to current life, and it answers to the craft" (422–23).

Despite these qualifications, Llewellyn's concept of situation-sense was almost universally criticized. The primary ground for criticism was that the concept did not acknowledge or leave room for the inevitably subjective nature of judging.[64] This criticism is echoed today by those associated with critical legal studies, who trace their lineage to Llewellyn but reject his formulation as a mistaken objectivist bypass.[65]

Situation-sense was also criticized as internally inconsistent.[66] "This vague, subjective principle is the keystone of a system which is the antithesis of the subjective."[67] Perhaps the most telling objection to the concept of situation-sense was that no one really understood it. As one commentator put it: "Situation sense may be a Janus-faced concept."[68] Its very novelty contributed to its obscurity: "Grasp of the concept itself is made difficult by the fact that it bears no marked resemblance to any previously offered guide."[69]

Nevertheless, Llewellyn's concept of situation-sense is remarkable in its descriptive adequacy. Although it lacks the formalized coherence of Lakoff's concept of an ICM, situation-sense offers far more than the mere focus on context that it has sometimes been understood to recommend.[70] Rather, situation-sense encompasses precisely the qualities of reflexivity, cultural commonality, and experientially grounded reason that characterize an ICM.

Llewellyn's notion of situation-sense lacks only the ICM's account of internal configuration. For Llewellyn, the concept of situation-sense was identified with, if not identical to, the process of categorization. Thus, he stressed the distinction between the "facts of the individual case and the facts of the situation taken as a type" (122). He saw situation-sense as a gestalt structure: "'The' problem-situation extends only as far as you are perfectly clear, in your own mind, that you have grasped the picture fully and completely . . . and therefore know it to present a significantly single whole" (427). And he recognized situation-sense as a fundamental aspect of human rationality:

> This holds of the legal concept which is relevant just as it does of the life-situation—the sizing up of "the case" into some pattern is of the essence of getting to the case at all, and the shape it starts to take calls up familiar, more general patterns to fit it into or to piece it out or to set it against for comparison. This much, as we all know, is not a matter of method or desire, it comes close to being a matter of necessity, it is the way the normal human mind insists on working most of the time. (268)

Llewellyn also understood this process as experientially based and image-dependent: One obtains access to situation-sense by "visualizing the hands-and-feet operations in the picture, seen as a going scheme, a working setup" (261). Llewellyn saw this knowledge as widely shared in the culture, ordinarily acquired through "such experience as, like driving a car or the party system or the Christmas season, comes to most Americans in the sheer process of survival to maturity" (251). In other cases, where the knowledge is specialized, situation-sense was to come from the judge "who already knows the little area or quirk of our culture which is the crux" (ibid.). Otherwise, the advocate must educate the court by providing that knowledge in briefs and argument (211–12).

For all his perspicacity, Llewellyn nevertheless claimed too much for situation-sense as a normative ideal. (One commentator quipped that "he forsook realism for idealism.")[71] Llewellyn's classic statement of his claim provides a clue to the seeds of his misconception. In the best-known description of situation-sense in *The Common Law Tradition,* Llewellyn quoted the nineteenth-century German scholar Levin Goldschmidt:

> Every fact-pattern of common life . . . carries within itself its appropriate, natural rules, its right law. This is a natural law which . . . is not a creature of mere reason, but rests on the solid foundation of what reason can

recognize in the nature of man and of the life conditions of the time and
place; it is thus not eternal nor changeless nor everywhere the same, but
it is indwelling in the very circumstances of life. The highest task of law-
giving consists in the uncovering and implementing of this immanent
law. (122)

Critics have identified the objectivist leanings of this passage, focusing on
concepts such as "immanent law," "natural rules," and "right law." [72] And
they are correct in identifying the purely normative dimension of this passage. Yet the passage also proclaims its relativism, locating this hidden
knowledge in "the life conditions of the time and place" and maintaining
that "it is thus not eternal nor changeless nor everywhere the same."

One cannot easily harmonize these objectivist and relativist elements in
Llewellyn's description of situation-sense, though some have tried.[73] Instead,
one might acknowledge that Llewellyn was struggling to articulate an entirely novel idea. He had no paradigm with which to capture and no language
with which to express both the dynamic, particular nature of experience
and the value-laden process by which humans categorize that experience.[74]
As Twining observes:

> The central precept of Llewellyn's realism, "see it fresh," was a reminder
> of the need to stay close to the actual and the particular and thus to
> avoid the chief pitfall of formalism, that of oversimplification . . . ;
> whereas the other precept, "see it whole," emphasized the need for a
> coherent frame of reference. Cautious striving towards the establishment
> of significant patterns, as embodied in the concept "situation-sense," was
> Llewellyn's main formula for resolving the basic dilemma.[75]

But, his brilliance notwithstanding, Llewellyn could not escape this dilemma. This is manifest in the agglomeration of objectivist and relativist
elements in a single, obscure, normative formulation. Situation-sense was
Llewellyn's effort from within the distorting rationalist apparatus of the
subject-object dichotomy to express the role of idealized cognitive models in
legal analysis.

Llewellyn had no paradigm with which to describe the feel of objective
justification depicted by Goldschmidt as "a natural law" that rests on a
"solid foundation." In the absence of a formalized construct like an ICM,
Llewellyn could not capture the automatic, tacit sense of validity described
by his concept of situation-sense. "Immanent law . . . , indwelling in the
very circumstances of life," was as close to the unconscious experience of

cognitive structure as Llewellyn could come. Llewellyn was, therefore, vulnerable to the error of appearing to advocate reliance on naked social coherence as a sufficient normative ground for legal decision. And, from all appearances, he seems in fact to have succumbed to this error.

With the advantage of hindsight, it is simple to expose as a social construction the feel of objective justification provided by this model of legal reasoning. We have seen how culturally based ICMs structure both a simple rule prohibiting vehicles in the park and more complex doctrinal areas like the right-to-counsel cases. But there is nothing about this process that is objective or foundational in the philosophical sense. Both the ICMs used in ordinary interactions and the specifically legal ICMs that structure doctrine are cultural artifacts encoding particular and contingent normative conceptions. Whether described in terms of idealized cognitive models or denominated situation-sense, the process of legal reasoning remains a culturally bound phenomenon.

But, in saying this, I do not mean to criticize Llewellyn; he would plainly have agreed.[76] More importantly, his reconception of legal certainty captures a profound truth about the social and operational reality of law. Despite the heterodoxy of our society, law functions most of the time because it has a "this-is-how-these-things-are-done" quality to it. If it did not, no legal system could survive without the constant exercise of raw, repressive power. Indeed, we can go further and say that no system could *survive* the constant exercise of raw, repressive power. "That is, a society governed by a legal system may be stable either because the norms of action are truly shared to a high degree or, *momentarily,* because the norms are imposed."[77] A legal rule that is motivated—i.e., that embodies situation-sense—will seem "natural" or "right" to those governed by it because they will see the rule as a reflection of the objective qualities of the social world in which they live. The operational success of a legal system (as distinct from its *justice* or *legitimacy*) depends upon the institutionalized meaning that precedes the promulgation of the rule.

It follows that in a crucial sense legal rules are epiphenomenal. As Berger and Luckmann explain, the social control effectuated by official legal rules and their concomitant sanctions "is of a secondary or supplementary kind." The very existence of a social institution already controls

> human conduct by setting up predefined patterns of conduct, which
> channel it in one direction as against the many other directions that
> would theoretically be possible. . . . Thus, for instance, the law may provide that anyone who breaks the incest taboo will have his head chopped

off. This provision may be necessary because there have been cases where
individuals offended against the taboo. It is unlikely that this sanction
will have to be invoked continuously (unless the institution delineated by
the incest taboo is itself in the course of disintegration . . .). It makes
little sense to say, therefore, that human sexuality is socially controlled
by beheading certain individuals. (55)

And it makes as little sense to say that a system of legal rules is the only way
to have a system of law.[78]

CHAPTER 9

Reasoning by Analogy

ONE LESSON of the last chapter was that we recognize, understand, and apply rules in just the same way that we recognize, understand, and determine facts. In both cases, we depend upon the idealized cognitive models—the *same* cognitive models—by which we organize and make sense of our world. Here, I examine another of the lawyer's stock in trade, the form of legal analysis commonly referred to as "reasoning by analogy." Much valorized, often criticized, reasoning by analogy is in fact little understood. Some deny that it is any kind of reasoning at all, since it does not connect premises to conclusions.[1] This confusion over analogy is an inevitable consequence of rationalism's impoverished concept of categorization. Most of what passes for reasoning by analogy is actually the process of radial categorization by means of ICMs. Reasoning by analogy, in other words, is an ordinary mode of category extension. As such, it is governed by the same regularities of structure and motivation that we have observed throughout.

Logic's Legacy

Some clarifications to start. Most of what lawyers call reasoning by analogy is analogy in the colloquial sense of similarity or resemblance. Typically, it takes the form of an argument that case B is sufficiently like case A to warrant the same legal treatment. Thus, a lawyer might claim that flag burning is like cross burning and, therefore, a form of speech protected under the first amendment. Or, she might argue that because hate speech is like libel it, too, should be unprotected. It is not surprising, therefore, that Edward Levi characterized reasoning by analogy as an instance of what Aristotle identified as reasoning by example—that is, the process of "reasoning from part to part where both particulars are subordinate to the same term and one of them is known." [2]

Analogy can also take the form of an inductive inference, in which the known similarities between two things are taken to indicate similarities with respect to other, unknown particulars. Posner and Sunstein both give the example of a person who, having found a particular kind of car reliable in the past, concludes that other cars of the same make will also be dependable. [3] Judgments of this sort are commonly understood as weak versions of scientific induction that require empirical verification. They are weak inductions because they proceed from a meager data base. And they require verification because the existence of even extensive similarities between two entities provides no logical assurance that the inferred resemblance exists. The inferred feature (e.g., the reliability evidenced by the earlier model) may be a contingent attribute and not a necessary condition of the genus. Alternatively, the shared features that support the initial perception of similarity may themselves be contingent rather than necessary attributes of the respective entities. Thus, if I observe that a dog of a particular breed is docile, I cannot conclude that all such dogs are docile, because I do not yet know whether it is breeding or training that accounts for this trait. If the latter, then genetics would be merely a contingent condition relative to docility, and the proper inference would be to similarly trained dogs.

A third form of analogy, familiar from standardized tests such as the Scholastic Aptitude Test, consists in a comparison of the *relations* between the elements of each of a pair of items. Analogy of this kind—which, for want of a better term, I shall refer to as "classical analogy"—typically takes the form "A is to B as C is to D." An example might be the observation that "cookie is to pastry as tabby is to cat." Analogies of this sort can also be expressed as straightforward, two-term comparisons—as in the banal observation that an atom is a minisolar system. I call this form of analogy "classical" because it more nearly conforms to the original sense of the Greek *analogos* (from *ana*—"up," "back," or "again"—and *logos,* "ratio" or "reason"), which first signified proportionality and was then extended from quantity to relation. [4] This sort of analogy sometimes figures in legal argument, as we shall see below. But it is not what lawyers and legal theorists normally think of when they refer to reasoning by analogy.

Although we will question it in a moment, this initial canvas suggests that lawyer's analogy and inductive analogy are two sides of the same rationalist coin: Both kinds of analogy seem to derive their inference structure from the assumption that categorization consists in classification according to common properties. When lawyers reason by analogy, the similarities between cases are taken as an indication that they belong to the same legal category. So, too, with the more rigorous inference structure of inductive analogy: First, the observed features of case A are assumed to reflect necessary (if not sufficient) conditions for category membership. Second, the fact that case B shares some of those features is taken as evidence of membership in the same category. Finally, one infers that the second case also exhibits the unknown attribute. But note that the final inference arises if and only if (1) case B really belongs to the same category and (2) the inferred attribute really is a necessary condition of category membership.

That legal analogy is conventionally understood as a matter of rationalist categorization is readily apparent from the arguments of its defenders. It is explicit in the Aristotelian definition adopted by Levi, in which "both particulars are subordinate to the same term." The same is true of Cass Sunstein's more recent claims on behalf of analogy. He describes "the characteristic form of analogical thought in law" as consisting

> in five simple steps. (1) Some fact pattern A—the "source" case—has certain characteristics; call them x, y, and z. (2) Fact pattern B—the "target" case—has characteristics x, y, and a, or characteristics x, y, z, and a. (3) A is treated in certain way in law. (4) Some principle, created or discovered in the process of thinking through A, B, and their interrelations, explains why A is treated the way it is. (5) Because of what it shares in common with A, B should be treated in the same way. It is covered by the same principle. (65)

One could hardly ask for a more plain statement of the claim that reasoning by analogy is actually a matter of categorization by necessary and sufficient conditions—i.e., the characteristics x and y (or x, y, and z) that case B shares with A. Lest there be any doubt about the privileged normative status of the rationalist model, Sunstein makes two distinct affirmations of its hegemony. First, he confines his discussion to "analogical reasoning that is roughly propositional" (201 n.3). Second, he insists that a "requirement of principled consistency is the hallmark of analogical reasoning *(as it is of reasoning of almost all sorts)*" (67; emphasis added).

As Roberto Unger observes, it is symptomatic of the pathologies of contemporary legal thought that an "unreconstructed practice of analogical judgment turns out, in retrospect, to be the first confused steps toward reasoning from policy and principle." [5] Regardless of what Sunstein may say, his account of analogical reasoning reduces to an account of reasoning from policy or principle. This is apparent from his response to the criticism leveled against him by Judge Posner. As Sunstein reports, Posner argues that "we cannot really reason from one particular to another" without giving "an account of the policy that underlies the first particular. Once we are doing this, we are engaged in 'policy science.'" Sunstein responds by noting that policy reasoning is not the sole method of judicial decisionmaking; "we should not undervalue the process of ordering judgments about legal problems by seeing if one's judgment in the case at hand can be squared with judicial or hypothetical judgments in other cases" (97). But this response begs the question. On Sunstein's own description, it remains true that we cannot reason from one case to another without giving an account of the principle that underlies both and renders them consistent. Once we are doing that, we are engaged in reasoning according to principle.*

It may be true, as Sunstein contends, that the governing principle is not given in advance and that, therefore, it cannot be applied deductively (65). But one cannot maintain that one constructs the principle "analogically" by comparing cases, when one also insists that analogies "are no better than the principles and policies that make them work" (98). To be clear: Sunstein maintains that because "any two cases are alike and different, and both in innumerable ways," a "claim of relevant similarity *requires* a judgment of principle" (91; emphasis added). But how can the analogy be the basis of the principle when it is only our appreciation of the principle (whether tacit or explicit) that enables us to recognize the two cases as relevantly analogous in the first place? Worse yet, how do the decisionmakers know which particulars to focus on if they are not already guided by some set of policies or principles that provide the criteria of reference? Why characteristics x, y, and z rather than q, r, and s? After all, Sunstein maintains that everything is like everything else—and in innumerable ways.

---

* Sunstein maintains that his account of reasoning by analogy is superior to Dworkin's notion of law as integrity (97). But the two accounts are remarkably similar. On both accounts, decisionmaking is a matter of aligning the precedents in terms of a principle that is not dictated in advance but rather emerges in the interpretive process that best harmonizes the cases—i.e., that "squares" them with previous judgments. Sunstein's account differs, then, only in the relative ambition of his principles.

In contrast to the conventional understanding of legal analogy, classical analogy provides a mode of reasoning that does not reduce to rationalist categorization. To say "cookie is to pastry as a tabby is to cat" is not to say that a cookie, like a tabby, is a type of cat. Nor does the observation that an atom is a minisolar system mean that an atom really is a kind of solar system. To the contrary, as Mark Turner explains, one recognizes these statements as analogies precisely because they identify similarities that cut across our conventional categorizations.[6] Analogies of this kind are troubling for a rationalist like Sunstein because it seems to leave no defense against indeterminacy. If everything really is like everything else in an infinite number of ways, then there is nothing to stop legal reasoning from degenerating into a too-easy game of ad hoc analogies and distinctions. It should (at least in principle) "always be possible to find some, retrospectively, more or less convincing ways to make a set of distinctions, or failures to distinguish, look credible."[7] If someone says law is like a solar system, how can you disprove it? Why isn't law like a pastry?

We can see why Sunstein ends up where he does. A rationalist like Sunstein is like an artisan with only a single mold: He must convert everything to a problem of rationalist categorization expressed in terms of necessary and sufficient conditions because he has no other conception of reason. The rationalist, in other words, needs the discipline of a rationalizing principle because he has nothing else with which to constrain analogy and keep it from getting out of hand.[8] In this way, Sunstein's procrustean misunderstanding of analogy turns out, on reflection, to be yet another manifestation of antinomial capture.

When a House Is Not a Home

The strategy of my argument should now be clear. I have compared classical analogy with those forms of analogy that depend upon rationalist categorization because these two kinds of analogy appear maximally distinct. In drawing this contrast, I am deliberately trading on intuitions with respect to analogy and categorization that, as Turner observes, are irredeemably conventional: "The mistaken division between analogical and categorical connections as different in *kind* . . . is based on a false assumption that we categorize on the basis of shared properties, that analogies are not based on shared properties, and therefore that the two processes must be different" (6). It may seem disingenuous of me to exploit an assumption that I have striven so hard to debunk. My purpose, however, is solely to demonstrate a

kind of analogy that is neither propositional in the sense intended by Sunstein nor contingent upon rationalist categorization. We will find that even
without the discipline of rationalizing principle, analogies of this sort are
perfectly orderly and constrained. More importantly, an understanding of
the nonpropositional workings of classical analogy will enable us to see
that, in actuality, analogical reasoning in law operates—and, therefore, is
constrained—in just the same ways.

It remains true, as Posner suggests, that "a judgment of similarity or
analogy presupposes some, and possibly extensive, categorization." [9] But
the key word is "extensive." Because categorization is complex and imaginative, analogies are both more and more varied than mere judgments of
criterial similarity. A judgment that case A "is like" case B can be based on
similarities that are image-schematic, metaphorical, or relative to an ICM.
Analogy, in other words, involves the same imaginative cognitive processes
that characterize categorization as a whole.

Let us begin with an example as easy as it is familiar: the observation
that an atom is a minisolar system. The analogy consists in the similarity of
structure between a solar system and the atom, whose electrons are understood to revolve around the nucleus in much the same way that planets
revolve around the sun. Examples such as this lead Dedre Gentner to define
analogy "as a mapping of knowledge from one domain (the base) into another domain (the target), which conveys that a system of relations that holds
among the base objects also holds among the target objects." [10] In the next
section, we will question Gentner's narrow focus on relational mappings.
But notice two things in the meantime: first, that analogy involves conceptual mapping of the same sort as metaphor; and, second, that the structure-
mapping in this case is image-schematic (here involving a CENTER-PERIPHERY
and a ROTATION schema).

The term "foothill" provides a similar example. We can take it as a metaphorical projection of human body structure or as a classical analogy of the
form "hill is to mountain as foot is to body." Either way, the conception
maps the relation between foot and body onto the corresponding geologi-
cal formations of hill and mountain. And, either way, the structure-mapping
is image-schematic (here involving the UP-DOWN schema). We saw in chapter 3 that the word-category "mouth" is formed by an image-mapping of this
sort. In much the same way, the prefix "foot" forms a radial category, one
part of which consists of those extensions that map this image-schematic
relation onto various inanimate objects. Thus, *foot*notes are the citations
or parentheticals at the bottom of a page; *foot*lights are set into the floor of

the stage; and a *foot*locker is the chest that stands at the "foot" of a soldier's bed.*

At first blush, the analogy "cookie is to pastry as tabby is to cat" appears to differ from the previous examples in two ways: First, the analogy is not constitutive in the sense that we do not ordinarily understand the target domain of cookies and pastries by carrying over the structure of the source domain of tabbies and cats (nor vice versa); and, second, the analogy does not seem to involve any conceptual, metaphorical, or imagistic mapping. But closer analysis reveals that there is less to these differences than meets the eye. Because the domains of pastries and cats are independently well understood, "the effect of the analogy," as Gentner says "is not so much to import new knowledge as to focus attention on certain portions of existing knowledge" (201). When we analyze this analogy in light of the material on categorization discussed in chapters 2 and 4, we can see both that the cookie-tabby analogy involves an image-mapping and that this mapping serves to direct our attention to fresh information about each of these domains.

"Cookie" and "cat" are both basic-level categories. "Pastry" is the superordinate category immediately above "cookie" in the category-hierarchy, while "tabby" is a subordinate category subsumed under the basic-level category "cat." Thus, in each case, the second term subsumes the first within an hierarchical category-structure. And, in each case, the first term represents a prototype effect: Cookies are the most common (that is, ordinary and familiar) kind of pastry; so, too, tabbies are the most common sort of cat. In other words, the analogy "cookie is to pastry as tabby is to cat" maps across otherwise unrelated categories the very precise parallel in PART-WHOLE relations that obtains between a prototype and its overarching category.

These cases illustrate a more general point about analogy. Everything may be like everything else in an infinite number of ways, but *analogy* consists in a mapping that characterizes a *conceptual relation* between domains initially understood as separate. Typically, the "is to" relation expressed by classical analogy is image-schematic.† The prototypical classical analogy

---

* Like the case of "hand," there are also many metonymic extensions—e.g., football, footprint, footstool, and so on. Footlight and footlocker can also be understood in this way; in each case, the object's position corresponds to that of the user's feet.

† In general, prepositions (from the Latin *preaponere*, "to put in front") are image-schematic—e.g., "in," "on," "by," "to," "from," "up," "down," "over," "under."

maps the parallel PART-WHOLE (or PART-PART) relations between two sets of items—e.g., the planets of a solar system and the electrons of an atom. The mapped PART-WHOLE relation may itself be structured by other image-schemas, as in the atom-solar system and foothill examples. But it need not be. An analogy can map metaphorical relations—as in the aphorism "Ambition is but avarice on stilts and masked"*—or metonymic relations, as in the prototype effects mapped by the cookie-tabby analogy. So, too, an analogy can map within-category conceptual relations such as the causal relations between elements of an idealized cognitive model. For example, to describe a foreign policy situation as "another Munich" or "another Vietnam" is to suggest that the consequences of concession or intervention, respectively, in the current situation (the target domain) will mirror one or the other of those historical circumstances (the source domain).

Turner observes that what we "consider to be an analogy depends upon the particular details of our category structure" (3). The reason for this dependency should now be evident. Categories compose conceptual relations motivated by cognitive efficiencies, experiential regularities, and pragmatic needs. These same conceptual relations form the basis for cross-category comparisons—i.e., analogies—when a problem or occasion calls for insight or analysis not provided by our existing category structures. There is, thus, no difference in kind between categorization and analogy. Nor could there be. As the "foothill" and cookie-tabby examples illustrate, the conceptual relation mapped by a classical analogy can simultaneously instantiate a category. "Foothill" both maps a cross-category correspondence between geography and anatomy and, at the same time, is an instance of a linguistic category organized around that image-schematic relation. In much the same vein, the cookie-tabby analogy not only maps a correspondence in PART-WHOLE relations, but also instantiates the more abstract category "prototypes" of which both cookies and tabbies are members. These two cases exemplify Turner's claim that categorization and analogy differ only in degree of entrenchment: "Any analogy makes a bid to establish or influence category structures" (5).

A legal example will help illustrate this point about analogy as a conceptual operation that is of a piece with ordinary categorization. It comes from a first-hand account by William Twining of University College Lon-

---

* This analogy involves both the personification of "avarice" (as a person "on stilts and masked") and the conventional metaphor VIRTUE IS UP (as in the contrast between an *upstanding* or *upright* citizen and a person who is *underhanded* or *low-down*). Both "avarice" and "ambition," moreover, share entailments of the metaphor MORE IS UP.

don.[11] Early in his career, Twining accepted the post of reporter for the Sudanese law reports. Soon after arriving in Khartoum, he discovered that only homicide cases were reported, which meant that there could be no working system of precedent for the other offenses of the penal code. Curious about how the system worked in the absence of reported decisions, Twining investigated the application of the penal offense of "house trespass"—essentially equivalent to burglary. He found that in each of the three sections of Khartoum, the magistrates applied the offense differently. In the Moslem section, the magistrates interpreted the offense to include any penetration of the "close," including the gardens surrounding the house. In the European section, in contrast, the magistrates interpreted the offense to apply only to invasions of an actual dwelling; they did not apply it to a person arrested in the garden, for example. In the commercial part of town, where there were no actual dwellings, the magistrates interpreted the offense to apply only when the person had entered an area covered by a roof. In other words, breaking and entering a woodshed was covered by the offense, but breaking and entering a lumber yard was not.

This pattern of interpretation manifests a simple radial category of the sort encountered in chapter 6. Entry into an actual dwelling is the obvious central case—although, to be more precise, we might say that the central case concerns entry into a *prototypical* dwelling—and decisions at this level represent strong prototype effects. Differences in interpretation appear at the first level—that is, whether to extend the offense to include entry into areas peripheral to a prototypical dwelling. The disparate answers to this question reflect obvious differences in cultural practices and in assumptions that produce conspicuously different cultural prototypes.

But what accounts for the pattern of decisionmaking in the commercial section? The magistrates appear to have reasoned by analogy and concluded that an area covered by a roof "is like" a house. As a matter of policy or principle, however, this interpretation seems quite arbitrary. If, for purposes of the offense, the enclosed area of the garden "is like" a house, then why not the lumber yard? It might be true that one is more likely to surprise a person in a garden than in a lumber yard, but this fact does not provide any basis for distinguishing between the lumber yard and the woodshed. This lack of any apparent rationale, in turn, makes it hard to explain the magistrates' interpretation as just another case of an ad hoc analogy invoked to justify a decision reached on other grounds. What other grounds?

When this case of reasoning by analogy is viewed from a cognitive perspective, the magistrates' interpretation appears orderly—even ordinary. One way to understand the issue confronting the magistrates in the commercial section is that they were faced with the problem of how to extend the category "house" to a nonprototypical context. If analogy characterizes a conceptual relation between domains initially understood as separate, then the magistrates' task was to draw some *conceptual* connection between the source domain of dwellings to a target domain of commercial structures.

To trace that mapping, we must start with the conceptual structure of the underlying category. Houses vary, and so do our cultural conceptions of them. But all humans need shelter, and the basic purpose, role, and function of an igloo, Bedouin tent, or lean-to does not differ greatly from that of the single-family, suburban dwelling prototypical of our relatively affluent culture. No house works well as such without a roof, which is the minimum structure necessary to provide shelter. The roof can therefore stand for the house—a case of metonymy—as in the conventional phrase "my job is to see that we have a roof over our heads." The magistrates used this metonymy as a means of extending the category "house" to analogous cases— that is, to those cases preserving this metonymic structure.

We can get a more complete picture of this pattern of reasoning from Lakoff's description of metonymic models. Substituting "house" for "*A*" and "roof" for "*B*":

> In general, a metonymic model has the following characteristics:
> —There is a "target" concept *A* [i.e., house] to be understood for some purpose in some context.
> —There is a conceptual structure containing both *A* [house] and another concept *B* [i.e., roof].
> —[Roof] is either part of [house] or closely associated with it in that conceptual structure. Typically, a choice of [roof] will uniquely determine [house], within that conceptual structure.
> —Compared to [house], [roof] is either easier to understand . . . or more immediately useful for the given purpose in the given context.
> —A metonymic model is a model of how [house] and [roof] are related in a conceptual structure; the relationship is specified by a function from [roof] to [house].
> When such a conventional metonymic model exists as part of a conceptual system, [roof] may be used to stand, metonymically, for [house]. If [house] is a category, the result is a metonymic model of the category, and prototype effects commonly arise.[12]

The magistrates' selection of "an area covered by a roof" is a kind of prototype effect. The choice of roof as the determining characteristic reflects its

role as the prototypical feature within the conceptual structure "house"—
i.e., it is this conceptual relation that allows roof to stand metonymically for
house. To put the point somewhat differently, this metonymic model produces "roof" as a prototype effect that serves as the anchor or cognitive reference point for the analogical inference from "house" to certain commercial structures.

FEATURE PRESENTATION

What of the form of analogy that reasons from example to example?
One might concede that cases like the house trespass statute or the avarice-
ambition analogy involve conceptual reasoning of the sort I have described
and still maintain that most of what is commonly called analogy consists of
judgments of criterial similarity. We shall see, however, that even the simplest cases of feature or attribute matching are better understood as a form
of analogical processing. Even inductive analogy, whose inference structure
seems so clearly to derive from the rationalist model of categorization, is
just a subcase or variant of nonpropositional analogy. Conceptual analogy
and criterial similarity, in other words, are but different aspects of a single
cognitive process.

Dedre Gentner has done the best empirical work on analogical processes. In her early work, Gentner drew sharp distinctions between "analogy," "literal similarity," and "mere-appearance matches" (206). This taxonomy relies on a distinction between attributes and relations, where
attribute refers to a "constituent property" and relation refers to "connections between two or more objects or attributes." [13] On Gentner's account,
an analogy maps the relations between the elements of target and source; a
literal similarity maps both relations and attributes; and mere-appearance
matches map only attributes.* Implicit in this taxonomy is the conclusion
that reasoning by example is a case of criterial judgment rather than analogy. Thus, Gentner responds to pragmatic accounts that define analogy in
terms of relevance to goal-oriented behavior by invoking a case of literal

---

* As even Gentner and her colleagues recognize, the distinction between attributes
and relations is highly unstable. Accordingly, they qualified their claim to maintain only
that the distinction between attributes and relations is "psychologically salient" and "relative to a psychological representation. Logically, it is possible to define a given feature as
either an attribute or relation, and there is an indefinite number of properties and relations
that in principle apply to any entity" (65). As we shall see, however, the distinction between attributes and relations simply does not correlate with the distinction between analogy and similarity that it is offered to explain.

similarity: "'This '82 Buick is like this '83 Buick: You can use it to drive across town'. . . ; to my ear the two Buicks are literally similar whether or not a goal is involved" (220).

The appeal of Gentner's taxonomy is that it fits both with the rationalist model of categorization and with our most conventional intuitions about literal meaning. If categorization is nothing more than classification according to common properties, then the correspondence of attributes and relations would seem to entail the conclusion that target and source are "literally" similar. If, moreover, those properties are themselves understood as literal matters of fact upon which classification operates, then a judgment of criterial similarity would seem to supersede any merely analogical connection. Thus, Gentner understands the cars' mobility as a simple fact about the world that places both Buicks in the same category; they are "literally" the same in this respect, regardless of their contingent relation to the speaker's current purpose.

Gentner's taxonomy relies upon an untenable concept of literalness—one that, as we saw in chapter 4, presupposes a reductive view of meaning as reference, independent of context and purpose. The allure of the literal meaning view is that it seems to conform to our everyday experience of obvious and unproblematic meanings: A Buick is a Buick; a tabby is a cat; an atom and a solar system are different things. But, as we have seen repeatedly, the apparent clarity of these examples is misleading. The simplicity and lucidity of these cases is a product of complex processes of intelligibility involving shared, cultural ICMs, prototype effects, and basic-level categorization. So, too, with Gentner's Buick example, which presents the easy case of objects and attributes at the basic level. Thus, Gentner describes a case of objects (cars) and attributes (mobility) defined relative to human interaction and purpose.* Of course one Buick is like another with respect to the very reason that we have Buicks in the first place. Gentner's Buick example assumes the very point it is intended to rebut: The obvious similarity that she notes is a psychological datum relative to a categorization that incorporates purpose as a defining element.†

---

* Technically, "Buick" is a subordinate level category that, as a well-known make, stands as a prototype for the basic-level category "car."

† Even so, it is misleading (if not oxymoronic) to speak of "literal" similarity: The two Buicks are not "literally" alike—that is, they do not *correspond*—with respect to many other possible purposes. They are likely to differ in resale value, performance, state of repair, and color (perhaps one is a sickening green, the other a shiny red); if they represent different models, they may even differ in overall shape or mechanical design. The two cars may be "literally" the same in the desired ability to drive across town. But this simi-

Consider Gentner's distinctions from the perspective of analogy. Recall the Posner/Sunstein example of the inductive analogy that one automobile will be just as reliable as another of the same make. The inference pattern consists of an attribute mapping from case A to case B—let us say from Volvo$_1$ to Volvo$_2$. By recasting this mental operation in the form of a classical analogy—"mechanical reliability is to Volvo$_2$ as mechanical reliability was to Volvo$_1$"—we can see that the mapping consists in a projected parallel of PART-WHOLE relations: To paraphrase Gentner, the analogy maps knowledge from one domain (the source) into another domain (the target) to convey that the system of PART-WHOLE relations that holds for the source also holds for the target.

If this recharacterization seems odd, it is only because classification by common properties is conventionally understood to establish a category rather than an analogy. Nevertheless, this recharacterization reflects a perfectly ordinary and conventional aspect of our natural language competence. Expressions such as "You've seen his sleazy *side,* but he has some good *parts*" or "She presents a cheerful face, but *deep inside* she's an unhappy person" manifest an image-schematic model in which the relations between an entity and its attributes are conceptualized by means of the CONTAINER and PART-WHOLE schemas. More importantly, this seemingly dissonant recharacterization provides a more faithful description of the process of inductive inference than does the more standard conception.

On the conventional view, the inference structure of inductive analogy is understood to derive from the rationalist model of a category. But, we saw at the start of the chapter that this view of inductive analogy suffers from a logical flaw: The inference that the two Volvos will be similar in reliability is true if and only if reliability is a necessary condition of membership in the category "Volvo." Realistically, however, reliability is contingent on such practical factors as continuity in design and consistency in quality control. Accordingly, the projected reliability of Volvo$_2$ is a probabilistic judgment. In other words, the inference that the PART-WHOLE relations (in this case the *literal* part-whole relations) of Volvo$_2$ will be as good as those of Volvo$_1$ is an analogical extrapolation from past experience rather than a judgment based on a literal similarity between the two. Ex post, it will seem that the criterial similarity of the two cars was discovered in the process of experience. Ex ante, the anticipated parallel is an analogy guided by the same conceptual regularities as the atom-solar system comparison.

---

larity is an artifact of human interaction and purpose—i.e., it is relative to goal-oriented human behavior.

It remains a matter of common sense that Volvo$_1$ and Volvo$_2$ belong to the same category. But there is no inconsistency in the notion that analogical similarity and shared category membership are really the same. We have already seen that this identity often holds for linguistic categories: The word-category "mouth" includes both the human mouth and the mouth of a river; so, too, "hand" includes both human hands and the hands of a clock. We can observe the same phenomenon with respect to propositional categories. A trolley car or railroad car is a kind of "car" even though each differs from an automobile with respect to such notable features as shape, size, interior design, source of energy, and means of locomotion. Moreover, the category "mother" includes instances—such as the grandmother who carried to term her own daughter's genetic child—that resemble the central case only remotely. In any given case, therefore, the judgment that one category member will be like another—that, for example, any particular mother will bear the same relation to her child as does the prototypical mother— is actually an analogical extrapolation or probabilistic judgment premised on the expectations engendered by the standard case.*

The intuitive difference between analogy and criterial similarity has nothing to do with the distinction between attributes and relations. It is, rather, a matter of expectation and degree. One could say, for example, that cookies and tabbies are "literally" similar because both are category prototypes, or that avarice and ambition are "literally" similar because both are rapacious (and acquisitive) drives. If we perceive these as cases of analogy, it is not because the items in each pair lack common features. Rather, in each case, the entire point of the analogy is to argue that ostensibly dissimilar items should be categorized together because they are the same in some crucial but nonobvious sense. As Turner says, every analogy attempts to establish or influence category structure. In other words, the differences between analogy, similarity, and categorization are differences only in the conventional status of our connections. The more stable and conventional the connection, the more it will be perceived as a straightforward matter of categorization (or "literal" similarity): A Buick *is* a Buick; a tabby *is* a cat. A novel

---

* If you know only that Amelia is the mother of a three-year-old, you would probably be surprised to discover that Amelia is a woman in her late fifties. It is not that you have never heard of adoption; you may even be aware of the extraordinary medical advances with respect to fertility. It is, nevertheless, perfectly natural to assume that the mother of a three-year-old is of childbearing age because natural childbirth is still the default case that defines our expectations. As a statistical matter, moreover, these expectations will be borne out in the vast majority of cases.

connection, on the other hand, will be perceived as an analogy: A wood-shed is *like* a house. Turner aptly describes this difference as a reflection of the degree to which the particular connection is entrenched in our conceptual system: "When we respond to the freshness or surprise of analogy," we are reacting "to the way the analogy disrupts entrenched patterns." [14]

We can now refine our definition to say that an analogy is a conceptual mapping (whether of attributes or relations) that highlights connections that are otherwise not well established in our conceptual system. The analogical inference that one Volvo is like another in reliability can be variously characterized as an attribute mapping or as a mapping of the PART-WHOLE relations from $Volvo_1$ to $Volvo_2$. But the characterization is beside the point. The crux of the analogy is the implicit recognition that even among category members, criterial similarity is a probabilistic truth that cannot be taken for granted. It may be entirely self-evident that both cars are Volvos. But the further inference that both cars are reliable will require repeated confirmation through experience before it becomes an established category-connection.

"FLAWED" BY DESIGN

The empirical evidence on analogical processing presents an unanswerable challenge to the rationalist model of reason. As before, we will find that the rationalist model distorts and obscures what are actually quite effective and efficient cognitive processes. In contrast, a cognitive account of reason in terms of neural networks and conceptual mappings better explains the empirical data with respect to analogical reasoning.

In a series of studies, Gentner and her colleagues explored the differences between relational and attribute mappings. Initially, they observed "a developmental shift from a focus on common object attributes to a focus on common relations in analogical processing" (223). For example, a "5 year-old given the figurative comparison 'A cloud is like a sponge' produces an attributional interpretation, such as 'Both are round and fluffy.' A typical adult response is 'Both can hold water for some time and then later give it back'" (222). But Gentner also found that even after the developmental shift to relation-based analogies, attribute mappings continue as an important variable in determining the accuracy of knowledge carryover in analogical mappings (224–25). Indeed, the capacity to access the source domain (i.e., the ability, when prompted by a target domain calling for analysis, to produce an appropriate source domain for an analogy) is largely determined by resemblance among surface features. Thus, Gentner found that although "systematicity of relational structure is the dominant factor" in judging the soundness of an analogy, "surface similarity seems to be the dominant factor" in determining one's ability to draw an analogy in the first place. Moreover, she found converging evidence for the conclusion "that relational commonalities often fail to lead to access" (228–29).

Gentner initially called these findings "surprising" and "gloomy" (ibid.). One can see why. Given her restrictive definitions, these findings would imply both that we are not very good at making analogies and that our ability to draw analogies (i.e., to make relational mappings) is determined in part by the different and inferior process of mere-appearance matching. In fact, Gentner called this a "design flaw" for which she offered an unpersuasive evolutionary explanation (231).* But, as we saw with Tversky and Kahneman's cognitive fallacies, such design flaws may be nothing more than artifacts of the crude assumptions of the rationalist model. In this case, the problems arise from Gentner's foundational distinction between attributes and relations.

The most significant evidence of the attribute/relation distinction came from a study concerning judgments of similarity and difference done by Gentner and her colleagues Douglas Medin and Robert Goldstone. If judgments of similarity and difference are criterial—that is, if such judgments are based on the degree to which two items share common properties, then these judgments should be mere inverses of one another. But Gentner and her colleagues found that judgments of similarity and difference reflect processes that are not only distinct but conflicting: Judgments of similarity were governed by relational mappings; judgments of difference, in contrast, responded most to dissimilarities among attributes. As a result, a given stimulus could be judged as both more similar to a standard (because the two share relations) *and* more different than the same standard (because the two differ in their attributes). Gentner and her colleagues concluded that "the fact that the relative importance of attribute and relation matches and mismatches depends on whether similarity or dissimilarity judgments are made suggests that attributes and relations are psychologically distinct" (66). They

---

* Gentner speculated that a "conservative matching strategy . . . might be prudent for mobile biological beings, for whom a false positive might be perilous" (231). But whether false positives enhance or threaten survival depends upon the kind of match being made: When new circumstances are matched against past experiences of danger, false positives enhance survival; when new circumstances are matched against past beneficial experiences—e.g., is this attractive new berry edible?—false positives can be positively deadly. One would expect that over the course of evolution, both sorts of circumstances would be presented with roughly equal frequency.

also made the further claim that "our results support cognitive models that draw a sharp distinction between attributes and relations" (ibid.).

As we saw in the case of prototype effects, however, evidence of effects is not evidence for any particular *explanation* or *cause* of those effects. The bare fact that attributes and relations produce psychologically distinctive judgments does not tell us anything about *why* they do so. In particular, this fact does not establish that the distinction between attributes and relations is part of the ontology of our cognitive models. There may be several different explanations—not limited to different accounts of mental representations—all of which are consistent with the observed data.

As Gentner and her colleagues recognize, the "distinction between attributes and relations is relative to a psychological representation" (65). If the data seem naturally to lead to the conclusion that attributes and relations literally constitute mental representations, it is only because Gentner and her coauthors have already assumed that psychological representations are propositional—i.e., that they refer to facts and states of affairs in the world.* From that perspective, the inference that mental representations consist of object attributes (i.e., facts about those objects) and relations (i.e., states of affairs between objects) seems almost irresistible. How else could a mental model accurately reflect objects-in-the-world?

But, if this interpretation of the data seems self-evident, it also commits Gentner to a fatal contradiction in her account of analogy. The same data that provide evidence for the psychological reality of the attribute/relation distinction also support the conclusion that attribute mappings are an integral part of analogical processing. One implication of the findings about judgments of similarity and difference is that a relational mapping will more readily be seen as an analogy (i.e., the items will be *perceived* as more similar) when object attributes also map. Conversely, when object attributes do not map, the items will be perceived as more dissimilar, and the relational mapping is less likely to be seen as an analogy. In other words, an analogy that maps both attributes and relations will be judged more sound (i.e., the

---

* Some representations are propositional—the models for "bachelor" and "mother," for example. (Thus, we could say that the pope is not a prototypical bachelor because, though he has the same attributes as any other man, he lacks the key relations.) But the conceptual complexity of models that are image-schematic, metaphorical, or metonymic is not easily reduced to attributes and relations: What is the analogical mapping in the "mouth of a river" case? The attribute of being an opening? The relation between the water, on one hand, and the river's banks and the coastline, on the other? What is being mapped in the "hands of a clock" case? Models of this sort are more accurately described as imagistic.

items more similar) than an analogy that maps only relations.* "A cloud is like a sponge" is a better analogy than "A syringe is like a sponge."

This conclusion seems intuitively correct; but it is problematic for any rationalist or propositional account, in which object attributes and object relations should be separate representations corresponding to different aspects of reality with no necessary connection between them: Clouds, syringes, and sponges may all "hold" water and then release it; but it is a contingent matter that two of these are also round and fluffy. (Indeed, nowadays, most sponges seem to be flat and rectangular.) Similarly, it is not at all clear why attribute mappings should lead one to recognize a conceptual (i.e., relational) analogy, nor why attribute mappings should affect the accuracy of knowledge carryover in analogical (i.e., relational) mappings. As Gentner and her colleagues insist, attributes and relations are supposed to be "psychologically distinct." If I know that clouds and sponges are both round and fluffy, how does that help me to see that both can "hold" water and later release it?

Of course, none of this is mysterious on a cognitive account. The developmental shift from attribute matches to relational matches, the psychological salience of attribute matches, and the role of attribute mappings in knowledge carryover are all consistent with what we have learned about cognition as an embodied and experientially grounded process.

First, the phenomena of basic-level categorization, metaphor, and image-schematic reasoning tell a common story about the embodiment of human rationality. The crux of that story concerns the ways in which the sensorimotor system gives rise to and shapes more abstract processes of mind. It should not be surprising, therefore, that analogical processes have a distinctly perceptual bias. Just as basic-level categorization precedes categorization at the superordinate level, perceptual matches—what Gentner variously refers to as "surface similarities" and "mere-appearance matches" —occur earlier than more abstract analogical processes. Nor is it surpris-

---

* It might seem that Gentner has anticipated the point with her distinction between analogy and literal similarity: Cases that map relations are cases of analogy; cases that map relations *and* attributes are cases of literal similarity; and cases of literal similarity are, obviously, more "alike" than cases of analogy. In fact, however, Gentner represents analogy and literal similarity as entirely discontinuous from one another (207; fig. 7.4). Moreover, this tidy resolution is undermined by the logical instability of the attribute/relation distinction. The sponge-cloud comparison maps both attributes ("round and fluffy," "holds water") and relations ("holds, then releases water"). Yet, that does not make it a case of literal similarity, even according to Gentner.

ing that perceptual matches remain central to and dominate access to analogical processes. We have known for some time that the relative salience of visual cues has a disproportionate effect on higher-order cognitive processes.[15] Because sensorimotor processes constitute the ground or source domain for more abstract processes of mind, they continue to serve as cognitive reference points for those processes.

Second, the access and knowledge-carryover phenomena described by Gentner are merely expected qualities of neural networks. The mental processes of metaphor and analogy consist in cognitive *mappings*—i.e., in patterns of neural activation that are matched against other, preexisting patterns of neural firing. We saw in chapter 4 that the activation of one part of a neural net generally stimulates the rest of the network. This spreading activation pattern is what gives rise to a spontaneous ability to generalize across related stimuli. Recall the following example: If one learns that chimpanzees like onions, the brain incorporates this new knowledge by modifying some of the connection strengths in the relevant neural network. But this also has the effect of altering similar activity patterns. Thus, if the concept "gorilla" involves a similar activity pattern over the same set of neural units, it will be changed in similar ways.

On this model of mental processes, we can see why the ability to access an attribute mapping should enhance one's ability to draw a relational analogy. To know that $Volvo_1$ is reliable is to have made changes in various connection strengths in the "Volvo" activation pattern; when one next encounters an automobile with Volvo-like features (i.e., $Volvo_2$), the resulting sensory sheets will map with various activation patterns until they achieve the best global match. The attribute mapping (from $Volvo_1$ to $Volvo_2$) will activate the "Volvo" neural pattern, which includes the knowledge with respect to reliability. The effect will be either to import new knowledge to the target domain (as in the Volvo analogy) or, if the target is independently well understood (as in the cloud-sponge analogy), to focus attention on the relational portions of existing knowledge. Thus, knowing that clouds and sponges are both round and fluffy *can* help me see the relational analogy that both "hold" water and later release it, because the spreading activation patterns of the attribute mapping can also trigger the relational mapping.

Third, the observed role of attribute matches in prompting and enabling more abstract relational mappings is an important benefit of the experientially grounded nature of human reason. For those who cling to a strongly normative view of reason as necessarily propositional, the capacity of attribute matches to prompt relational matches may seem like a design flaw;

it remains a mere contingency that clouds and sponges are both round and fluffy. In actuality, however, this ability to prompt more abstract connections is a reflection of a rather remarkable imaginative capacity and a significant part of what makes human cognition such an effective adaptive mechanism.

Gentner considers it a design flaw that surface similarities play a determining role in the ability to draw analogies, but some of the "flaws" she found are actually artifacts of her experimental design. Consider but one example from her work of the mid-1980s. In tests of the ability to access analogies, Gentner and her colleagues employed a base story involving an eagle and a hunter. A week later, they asked subjects which of several stories reminded them of the original: Some of the comparison stories presented the original characters in a similar narrative with an essentially opposite outcome; others presented the same story using fictitious countries in the respective roles of the eagle and the hunter. When presented with the altered version of the eagle-hunter story, subjects matched the original story 78 percent of the time. In contrast, the stories presenting the purely relational but substantively more analogous mapping prompted matches in only 44 percent of the cases (226–28).*

As was true of the Tversky-Kahneman experiments discussed in chapter 4, Gentner's study finds design flaws because it misapprehends how people actually reason. Note how the study unwittingly stacks the deck in favor of the attribute mapping: The "attributes" matched are either basic-level categories (e.g., eagle) or common and familiar cultural models (e.g., hunter). The "true" analogy, on the other hand, employs unfamiliar, abstract entities (specifically, the countries "Zerdia" and "Gagrach") and, of course, abstract relations. Predictably, the more memorable attribute matches were easier to make. This particular experiment seems to reflect nothing more than the unremarkable fact that people are better at recalling and matching basic-level and other familiar sorts of items.

Gentner's more recent work supports just that conclusion.[16] In a series of studies, Gentner and her colleagues investigated the reasons for the developmental shift in which children's capacity to make analogies progresses

---

* A similar experiment with children involved stories of a chipmunk helping his friend the moose escape an evil frog. Young children were more successful at making matches when the comparison story involved a squirrel helping an elk escape a toad than when the comparison story described an elk helping a toad escape an evil squirrel. Older children, on the other hand, correctly matched even the latter group of stories containing the cross-mapped characters (223–24).

from a focus on object attributes to more relational analogies. They reviewed studies with infants that replicate Spelke's findings (discussed in chapter 2). These findings, they note, show that children are able to make some kinds of relational matches—what we would term image-schematic matches—even before the age of one. On the basis of this evidence, they hypothesized that "the shift occurs at different times for different domains because of differential knowledge: the deeper the child's domain knowledge, the earlier the relational shift" (268). This hypothesis was confirmed. Gentner and her colleagues found not only that "children can shift from object-based similarity to relational similarity in the space of a few minutes" (303), but also that this shift can be induced either by amplifying their relational knowledge or by simply increasing their exposure to relational stimuli.

One of these experiments involved sets of three identical objects of decreasing size (monotonic decrease). Having observed in a previous study that some children spontaneously applied the labels "Daddy," "Mommy," and "Baby" to describe this pattern of monotonic decrease, the experimenters taught a group of three-year-olds to use these labels with families of penguins and bears. As Gentner and her colleagues report, "The question was whether the family labels would increase children's ability to appreciate the higher-order pattern by inviting them to import a familiar relational schema. . . . The results of the labeling manipulation were dramatic" (281). Even in the cross-mapping task (i.e., where the attribute mappings *conflicted* with the relational mapping), the three-year-olds' correct relational responses improved from 54 percent to 89 percent with schematized, "sparse" objects and from 32 percent to 79 percent with more detailed, "rich" objects (ibid.).*

In another experiment, four-year-olds were asked to match sets of geometric figures presenting relations such as symmetry or monotonic increase under two sets of conditions. Under both conditions, the transparency of the mappings was varied by presenting within-dimension (e.g., symmetry as to size for triads of circles and squares) and cross-dimension (e.g., increase in size to increase in brightness) trials. In all cases, no feedback was provided. In the first version of the experiment, the trials were randomly presented. Under this condition, the four-year-olds could reliably match only the most concrete cases of same dimension and same polarity comparisons

---

* The difference between the tests involving sparse and rich objects reflects that, as Tversky had previously demonstrated, people find that rich objects are more like themselves than are sparse objects (280).

(285–86). In the second version, the children were exposed to the more concrete, within-dimension trials before the more abstract, cross-dimension trials. Even without feedback, practice on the within-dimension trials enabled the children to do better on the subsequent cross-dimension trials—showing an overall improvement on the cross-dimension trials from 49 percent correct (i.e., at the level of chance) under the random condition to 60 percent correct in the sequenced condition. More significantly, the subset of four-year-olds who had performed well on the concrete mappings (above 75 percent correct) improved their performance on the cross-dimension mappings from 48 percent in the random condition to 80 percent correct in the sequenced condition (288). Gentner and her coauthors concluded that "repeated experience on within-dimension pairs permits the child to extract deep common structures, which then form the basis for cross-dimensional alignment" (298). They suggest, therefore, that "children should be seen as domain novices rather than as underdeveloped information processors" (302).

For those who think that human reason is necessarily propositional, these findings are difficult to explain. If reason were propositional, then the initial failure to notice the relational correspondences would be just that—a failure. The children who failed initially to make the relational matches hadn't yet learned enough. (Presumably, the adults who failed to match the eagle-hunter story to the Zerdia-Gagrach story just weren't smart enough.) But this conventional view does not fit the empirical evidence: Gentner found that simply doubling the number of exposures did not produce the same results (288). Children do not learn to make cross-dimensional matches when given greater opportunities to study them; they *do* learn to make cross-dimensional matches when given the chance to first master within-dimension matches. In other words, people abstract image-schematic and other conceptual patterns from familiar experience and then use that conceptual structure to organize and understand unfamiliar new input.

This evolutionary "design" strategy is not without flaws: An ironic corollary of our reformulated definition of analogy—in which analogy is understood as a conceptual mapping that highlights connections not otherwise established in our conceptual system—is that familiar or conventional connections can easily overshadow imaginative new ones.* But this general de-

---

* This, too, is the import of the finding that there is a cognitive bias toward salient visual cues: A familiar or perceptually prominent cue is more likely to figure as the basis of a mapping than is an inconspicuous one.

sign nevertheless affords substantial overall advantages. First, it represents a remarkably adaptive capacity—already evident in Gentner's preschoolers and Spelke's infants—to make sense of a new circumstance by reasoning imaginatively from a familiar one. Second, it has the advantage of yielding significant cognitive efficiencies. In computer simulations, Gentner found that the acquisition of what she calls "higher order structure" enabled the program to make faster and more accurate matches. She concluded that "increases in domain knowledge can actually decrease the processing load associated with relational tasks in that domain" (303).

Moreover (and, for the rationalist, ironically), it is this nonpropositional, analogical form of reason that is most adequate to the real-world needs of embodied humans. Reason, it bears repeating, is an aspect and artifact of our pragmatic functioning. The perceptual bias that Gentner thought to be such a design flaw is, in many contexts, highly adaptive. As Rosch points out,[17] basic-level objects (that is, those defined relative to human sensorimotor interactions) display a strong correlation between form and function. My ability to adapt is enhanced if, knowing that this Volvo can get me across town, I am also able to recognize that this Buick can probably be used in the same way; so, too, I increase my chances of survival if the knowledge that this animal with horns can be dangerous enables me to generalize and take suitable precautions with this strange new animal with tusks. Moreover, as a pragmatic function, reason both tolerates and requires flexibility. On one hand, it is frequently enough to know that round and fluffy things are likely to have the capacity to hold water or that Volvos tend to be reliable; we can test these things by experience. On the other, the probabilistic nature of our categories and analogies better enables us to adapt in a real-world in which not all sponges are round and not all Volvos work.

House Rules

What makes a legal analogy sound or persuasive? Consider the arguments in two prominent debates—the first over the separation of power, the second over abortion.

In *Immigration and Naturalization Service v. Chadha*,[18] the Supreme Court invalidated the one-house veto as inconsistent with the constitutional provisions mandating that all legislation be approved by both the House and Senate (the bicameralism requirement) and then presented to the president for his signature or veto (the presentment requirement). At issue was an immigration statute that authorized the attorney general to suspend the deportation of otherwise deportable aliens when certain conditions of hardship were met. Suspensions were to be reported to Congress; either house could veto that decision by passing a resolution of disapproval. The attorney general had recommended that Chadha's deportation be suspended. After considering more than three hundred such recommendations, the House concluded that deportation should proceed in six of those cases including Chadha's. Chadha appealed, and the Court struck down the provision granting Congress the authority to veto the attorney general's recommendation.

Justice White, joined by Justice Rehnquist, dissented.* On White's view, the legislative veto was an "indispensable political invention" (972) designed to preserve legislative control over an administrative state in which power has increasingly been delegated to unaccountable executive agencies. White argued that the legislative veto "has not been a sword with which Congress has struck out to aggrandize itself at the expense of the other branches," but rather "a means of defense, a reservation of ultimate authority necessary if Congress is to fulfill its designated role under Article I (974)." White pointed out, moreover, that the Court's ruling leaves Congress with "a Hobson's choice: either to refrain from delegating the necessary authority, leaving itself with the hopeless task of writing laws with the requisite specificity to cover endless special circumstances across the entire policy landscape, or in the alternative, to abdicate its lawmaking function to the Executive Branch and independent agencies" (968).

White's policy arguments seem unanswerable in their own terms. Indeed, the majority did not attempt a response: "We can even concede this utilitarian argument. . . . But policy arguments supporting even useful 'political inventions' are subject to the demands of the Constitution" (945). The majority found "explicit and unambiguous" demands in the bicameralism and presentment requirements of Article 1 (ibid.). It reasoned that without the legislative veto, neither the House nor the Senate could override the attorney general's decision without passing a private bill pursuant to the ordinary procedural requirements of bicameralism and presentment. The majority pointed out, moreover, that the current procedures—that is, the delegation of decisionmaking authority to the attorney general subject to a

---

* Although Justice Powell concurred in the judgment, he saw the case differently. On his view, the one-house veto authorized Congress to act in an adjudicatory capacity: "The House did not enact a general rule; rather, it made its own determination that six specific persons did not comply with certain statutory criteria" (965).

one-house veto—had supplanted the previous "clumsy, time consuming" process by which Congress used the private bill to make the case-by-case determination whether to allow an otherwise deportable alien to remain in the country (954).

White responded with an intriguing analogy. He argued that however it is formally characterized, the one-house veto employed by this statute did not change the actual distribution of authority between Congress and the executive. Under the prior private bill procedure, a decision to allow an otherwise deportable alien to remain required the concurrence of a majority of both houses (i.e., passage of the bill in the House and Senate) and the executive (i.e., the president's signature upon presentment). But, White pointed out, just the same is true under the one-house veto provision: The executive signals its approval with the attorney general's recommendation; each house indicates its assent by its silence. Conversely, the prior private bill procedure meant that either house or the executive could insist on deportation: the House or Senate by failing to pass the private bill by majority vote; the president by vetoing the private bill. But, again, just the same is true under the one-house veto provision: A majority of either house can block the attorney general's recommendation by passing a resolution of disapproval; if the executive determines that suspension is inappropriate, it can simply fail to make a recommendation. "The President and the two Houses enjoy exactly the same say in what the law is to be as would have been true for each without the presence of the one-House veto, and nothing in the law is changed absent the concurrence of the President and a majority in each House" (995).

The majority rejected this analysis, agreeing with the lower court's assessment that the argument "would analogize the effect of the one house disapproval to the failure of one house to vote affirmatively on a private bill" (958, n.23). But that, of course, is White's point exactly: It takes a bare majority of either house to stop a private bill; so, too, it takes a bare majority of either house to disapprove the attorney general's recommendation. The majority also argued that the "legislative steps outlined in Article I are not empty formalities; they were designed to assure that both Houses of Congress and the President participate in the exercise of lawmaking authority" (ibid.). But, again, that is exactly the point of White's analogy: The bicameralism and presentment requirements *are* empty formalities in this case precisely because the one-house veto already insures that no legal action occurs unless there is agreement among both houses of Congress and the president.

In fact, the majority offered no clear reason for rejecting White's analysis. It insisted that the requirements of Article 1 "make certain that there is an opportunity for deliberation and debate" and that this responsibility cannot be evaded by "mere silence" (ibid.). But it simultaneously conceded that legislation need not be preceded by debate. Moreover, it failed to explain why the attorney general's formal submission of his or her recommendation to Congress fails to provide the requisite—indeed, the same— opportunity for deliberation and debate. True, Congress can ignore that invitation to debate the attorney general's recommendation. But, it can just as easily ignore a proposal for a private bill; even more to the point, it can go through the motions and pass a private bill without any real deliberation. So, why did the majority fail to see the cogency of White's analogy?

We know from Gentner's research that relational commonalities often fail to lead to access even for adults. We know, too, that dissimilarities among attributes can induce judgments of difference even when there is a strong relational mapping. Based in part on Gentner's subsequent work with children, I have argued that these findings reflect a more general phenomenon in which one's capacity to make conceptual connections—including imaginative, new connections—is a function of familiarity and experience. (Thus, three-year-olds could recognize abstract relations of monotonic decrease once they learned to associate that pattern with the familiar schema of "Daddy," "Mommy," and "Baby.") But, if analogy is a mapping that highlights unconventional conceptual connections, it follows that an analogy necessarily competes with more entrenched concepts and categories. (This is the flip side of Turner's point that the freshness or surprise of an analogy derives from the very fact that it disrupts our entrenched patterns of thought.) Thus, people find it more difficult to match stories containing unfamiliar or abstruse entities (e.g., the fictitious countries Zerdia and Gagrach) with their correct relational analogues when those stories must compete with other test stories containing more familiar and accessible concrete mappings.

We can, therefore, make some predictions about when analogies will work (that is, when they will be persuasive) and when they will not. For purposes of exposition, I separate these predictions into five typical situations or paradigms that I will call "maximal play," "category breakdown," "innovative recomposition," "contingent anomaly," and (borrowing from Kennedy) "the impacted field." Because these are paradigmatic cases rather than analytic distinctions, it should be understood that they are not mutually exclusive; indeed, they are probably best understood as exemplifying factors that can be present to a greater or lesser degree in any given case.

1. *Maximal play.* Analogies are most persuasive at the point where conventional concepts and categories have run out. The magistrates in the commercial section of Khartoum faced a situation of this sort, needing to adapt the offense of house trespass to a context in which there simply were no "houses." A similar situation can obtain with new social or technological developments. Sometimes, the new circumstances simply do not fit the existing categories—as in the case of the stunning developments in reproductive technologies. Other times, the new circumstances are open to multiple characterizations. Although it might seem that the first analogy has an advantage in such circumstances, the analogy or metaphor with the best chance of adoption is the one that opens up the most useful possibilities.* In the late 1970s, Mark Stefik at the Xerox Palo Alto Research Center first came up with the "windows" concept for organizing data on a computer. But the idea did not catch on until the MacIntosh was introduced; now that Microsoft has successfully commandeered the name, the idea seems almost self-evident.[19]

2. *Category breakdown.* Conventional concepts and categories frequently outlive their usefulness. In other words, there are times when the still conventional and widely applied categories have nevertheless been outstripped by changing social circumstances. In such circumstances, an analogy that accommodates the new realities by extending or otherwise changing prior conceptions is likely to succeed. Holmes's resolution notwithstanding, *McBoyle* (discussed in the last chapter) may have been such a case. We shall examine a more compelling example in the next chapter, where I discuss the 1937 sea-shift in Commerce Clause doctrine.

3. *Innovative recomposition.* Some analogies successfully compete with more conventional conceptions by drawing attention to other, equally entrenched but conventionally unrelated concepts that also fit the circumstances. Two nonlegal examples are the analogies "Ambition is but avarice on stilts and masked" and "cookie is to pastry as tabby is to cat," both of which draw attention to conceptual commonalities that nevertheless remain outside our conventional categories. We will examine a successful legal example in the next chapter, where I discuss Holmes's famous "marketplace of ideas" metaphor.

4. *Contingent anomaly.* A novel analogy may work even in the face of deeply entrenched concepts because it helps address an anomalous situa-

---

* Recall Lakoff and Johnson's pragmatist observation, quoted in chapter 3, that it is not the truth or falsity of a metaphor that matters "but the perceptions and inferences that follow from it and the actions that are sanctioned by it."

tion. For example, a conventional concept or category that works well enough in the great mass of cases may nevertheless be inadequate to or inconsistent with strongly felt social needs in a particular situation. (A conceptual first cousin of category breakdown, this case differs principally in the local or provisional nature of the anomaly.) An example is Cardozo's well-known opinion in *MacPherson v. Buick*,[20] which expanded the category of "dangerous instrumentalities" for which manufacturers were held responsible to the ultimate consumers to include ordinary goods that were negligently constructed. Another is the Supreme Court's McCarthy Era decision in *Dennis v. United States*, upholding the convictions of American Communist Party leaders for political and other nonviolent activities that merely "tended" to promote the violent overthrow of the government.[21]

5. *The impacted field.* An analogy will be least persuasive when it conflicts with highly conventional or deeply entrenched concepts or categories. The exchange between Blackmun and Burger in *Lassiter*, discussed in chapter 6, was such a case. Blackmun argued for the mandatory appointment of counsel on the ground that a parental termination proceeding resembles a criminal trial in its adversarial and stigmatizing nature. But this otherwise promising analogy was quickly skewered by Burger's matter-of-fact observation that termination proceedings are about protecting the child, not punishing the parent.

This typology of analogy's rhetorical persuasiveness parallels chapter 6's discussion of the relative indeterminacy of legal materials and chapter 8's examination of the social contingency of law. Maximal play, for example, represents the extreme case of indeterminacy of extension. Similarly, category breakdown is the extreme case—akin to Thomas Kuhn's description of a "scientific crisis"[22]—of substantive indeterminacy. Innovative recomposition is made possible by the synchronic indeterminacy that arises from multiple models. What I have called contingent anomaly reflects either an early stage of category breakdown, as in *MacPherson,* or a culturally inflected case of indeterminacy of extension, as in *Dennis*. Finally, the impacted field is a consequence of law's contingency as a social institution that reifies existing social practices, expectations, and mores. It parallels Kuhn's notion of a normal science, with its prolonged resistance to data that do not conform to its reigning paradigms.[23]

It should now be clear how the majority in *Chadha* misapprehends White's analogy in the way that it does. White sees *Chadha* as a case of contingent anomaly: The administrative state creates an anomalous condition within the traditional scheme of separation of powers; the legislative veto is the innovative political solution for this disequilibrium. White rationalizes that solution by means of an astute analogy that maps the relational schema of normal legislative action (i.e., bicameralism and presentment) onto the relatively novel procedures of the one-house veto. But this analogy fails because the majority sees the elements of the source and target domains in a more concrete and conventional fashion. For the justices who compose the majority, *Chadha* arises in an impacted field of conventional categories and concepts. They find it absurd to compare one house's affirmative vote on a resolution of disapproval with the failure by a majority of that same house to vote in favor of a private bill. Rather, the *Chadha* majority sees only what we might loosely call the familiar "attributes" of legislative action: A vote for a resolution of disapproval is the same as a vote for a private bill; both are ordinary legislative actions that must meet Article 1's bicameralism and presentment requirements. As the majority puts it: "Congress has *acted* and its action has altered Chadha's [legal] status. . . . Absent the veto provision, . . . either of them, or both of them acting together, could effectively require the Attorney General to deport an alien . . . only by legislation" (952–53; emphasis in original).

The failure of White's otherwise cogent analogy exposes the substantial gap between the *soundness* of an analogy and its *persuasiveness*. We know from Gentner's empirical studies that people judge the soundness of an analogy by the strength of its relational mappings. White's analogy does quite well on this score. But in law, as elsewhere, it is not enough to make a sound argument; one must also be persuasive. And persuasion, as I argued in chapter 6, is a function of our categories and concepts because they define our expectations and, therefore, shape what we find believable, what we judge accurate, what we perceive cogent, and what we experience as convincing. Thus, the persuasiveness of an analogy is a function not of the soundness of its relational mapping but of the degree to which it accords with our understanding (or otherwise helps to make sense) of our world. White's analogy fails not because of any lack of analytic rigor; it fails because it is too unconventional to register on the majority's conceptual radar screen. It is as if the majority had responded: "No, avarice is not at all like ambition; a cookie is absolutely nothing like a cat."

This point about the contingent nature of even a sound analogy is more forcefully illustrated (and without the *Chadha* majority's clumsy literalism) by a debate over the ethics of abortion. In a famous article, Judith Jarvis Thompson offered an analogy to undermine the seemingly self-evident logic of the right-to-life argument: Suppose you wake up one morning to find yourself in bed hooked up to an unconscious violinist. He is suffering from a potentially fatal kidney disease, and it has been determined that your blood type is a precise match for his. He has been hooked up to you for the nine months needed for his recovery. If you unplug yourself, he dies. Must you acquiesce in this arrangement? [24]

Rosalind Hursthouse suggested a different analogy in response: Suppose one is living in a house in France in 1944. The previous owners operated it as a "safe house," part of a network used to smuggle Jews out of Germany. An open window was the signal that it was safe for a refugee to enter and hide; if all the windows were shut, it meant "Danger, keep away." The first summer the new owner is in the house, she is careful to keep all the windows closed so as not to mislead any refugees. A year passes without any Jewish refugees attempting to hide anywhere in town. One hot summer day that second year, the new owner opens the window to let in some air. That night a Jewish refugee climbs in, not knowing that the house is no longer in use by the resistance as safe house. Must one risk his or her life to shelter the Jew? Or may one expel the refugee, knowing that he or she risks capture and death? [25]

Each of these analogies is sound in the sense that each of the stories forming the source domain of the analogy maps well onto the target domain of abortion. Each is composed of image-schematic (i.e., relational), metaphorical, and what we might loosely call "attribute" (or, more aptly, propositional) mappings. Thompson's violinist story uses a CONTAINER schema to map the donor's bed onto the mother's womb and a LINK schema to map the blood hookup onto the connection between mother and fetus (i.e., the placenta and the umbilical cord). The donor's bedridden condition maps metaphorically onto the potential debilities of pregnancy. Finally, the violinist's dependence on the donor for his or her life parallels the fetus's dependence, prior to viability, on the mother. So, too, Hursthouse's refugee story effectively parallels the circumstances of pregnancy by using a CONTAINER schema to map the house onto the womb, an image-metaphor of the refugee climbing through the open window to map onto the act of careless, unprotected sex, and a propositional mapping similar to the violinist story. Lastly, Hursthouse's analogy maps the Samaritan's risk of execution onto the risks to the pregnant woman's health.

The analogies differ in one respect: Thompson's was designed to parallel the case of rape, while Hursthouse's was constructed to correspond with voluntary, though careless intercourse. (With respect to the contraception issue, Hursthouse observes that the analogy still works for the case of a woman who has reason to believe that she is more than a year past the time that she is no longer capable of conception.) But we can modify Hursthouse's analogy to delete this difference: Suppose the Jewish refugee is brought to the house by an armed member of the resistance who has not heard about the change of ownership. If one's intuitions suggest that the donor is not morally bound to sustain the violinist but that the owner of the former safe house does have an ethical obligation to shelter the Jewish refugee, then how does one judge between these competing analogies? The mappings in both cases are sound. A decision on the basis of abstract principle (whether pregiven or constructed "analogically" by considering these cases) is made difficult by the fact that the analogies are now set up to conflict on all relevant points: Both present life-or-death situations in which the vulnerable party has no alternative; both present the issue of the duty owed to an "innocent" or "deserving" stranger; both involve hardship and risk to a party not responsible for creating the situation.*

Presumedly, those who support the right to choose will prefer Thompson's analogy and those who are pro-life will favor Hursthouse's. These preferences would seem to confirm the view that the persuasiveness of an analogy is ultimately subjective, depending entirely on one's preexisting values and beliefs. A pro-choice advocate might rebut this assertion by arguing that, drawing as it does on the Holocaust, Hursthouse's hypothetical presents the extraordinary case that calls for extraordinary measures. Generally, we do not require the duty to act as a Good Samaritan even in life-or-death situations. This argument has some intuitive appeal. But note that although this argument issues as an argument from principle, it draws its force from an appeal to the culture's sense that "This is how these things are done." Thus, the argument from principle actually confirms the degree to which persuasion is a function of our concepts and categories: People will find an analogy persuasive when, in Llewellyn's words, it "accord[s] with their real-life norms."

DEMOCRACY ON THE SLOPES

These last two examples might be read to suggest that there is an inherently conservative bias in analogical argument. But this cannot be if, as I have argued, reasoning by analogy is an ordinary mode of category extension. Indeed, experience—both in law and elsewhere—teaches that analogy is a common agent of change. So, too, the import of the phenomena I

---

* One can, of course, make a judgment of principle that rejects one's initial intuition about one of the source domain cases. Or, if one does not accept the implicit assumption that a fetus is a person, one can conclude that the right to an abortion follows a fortiori from Thompson's analogy. But what remains unavailable is any principle that can determine which of the two analogies better matches the abortion case.

described under the rubrics of maximal play, category breakdown, and innovative recomposition is that analogy can often be an agent of category change. Accordingly, the real lesson of these last two examples is that cultural context and social purpose operate as compositional elements of reasoning by analogy (as they do in reasoning of all sorts). In other words, context and purpose are the factors that simultaneously constrain analogical argument *and* enable it to operate as an engine of change. We can clarify this point by considering two apparently unrelated arguments, both of which misapprehend the nature of change in legal doctrine because they fail to understand how context and purpose are integral to meaning.

In an article entitled *Slippery Slopes,*[26] Fred Schauer questions the logical basis of "slippery slope" arguments. A slippery slope argument takes the following form: "The decision in the current case might not be objectionable, but it will inevitably lead to extensions whose consequences we would all agree are unacceptable." An example would be the classic First Amendment argument that permitting government to prohibit sexual material because of its offensiveness will lead to increasingly undesirable restrictions and, ultimately, to bans on such worthy literary works as *Ulysses* and *Lady Chatterley's Lover.* A slippery slope argument is inherently conservative in the sense that it is an argument for maintaining the status quo. (But it need not be *politically* conservative, as illustrated by the First Amendment example.)

Schauer argues that slippery slope arguments "are in some sense illogical" (373). "Because the slippery slope argument responds to an asserted difference between the instant case and the danger case, it presupposes a linguistic description of the instant case that distinguishes it from the danger case" (369). If the initial decisionmaker can articulate the distinction, then her successors should in principle be able to apply it to future cases to prevent the occurrence of the undesirable "danger" case. For Schauer, "a slippery slope effect is always in logical and linguistic theory eliminable" (382).

Nevertheless, Schauer acknowledges that "though not logically compelled," the slippery slope phenomenon "appears to describe a behavioral reality" (369–70). He attributes this to various human imperfections that systematically skew decisionmaking; he identifies these as "linguistic imprecision," "limited comprehension," and "distortion of risk." Linguistic imprecision, according to Schauer, arises either because we intentionally employ vague language to provide future flexibility or because even the most precise language can become vague in the face of unforeseen circumstance. "The slippery slope claimant is arguing against the move from the state of rest to the instant case because that move, the claimant fears, will increase the risk of further movement to the danger case. This argument presupposes that the linguistic boundary between the state of rest and the danger case is firmer than the linguistic boundary between the instant case and the danger case" (370).

The problem of limited comprehension arises because legal decision-making occurs over time: "The slippery slope fear arises precisely because someone other than the original formulator of the principle may be called upon to apply it. Concern about linguistic boundaries is actually a worry about the instructions we give to others in hope of constraining their decisionmaking" (373). Limited comprehension is a factor, Schauer explains, even when the potentially unfaithful future decisionmaker is oneself in different circumstances: "Just as people who are trying to stop smoking make sure that there are no cigarettes in the house, so too might formulators of principles recognize that they themselves have weaker moments" (374). Finally, distortion of risk arises because some issues present greater than normal risk of error. This risk is perspicuous in criminal and First Amendment cases where the rights-claimant—the KKK or Larry Flynt, for example—is likely to be particularly unsavory or unsympathetic.

For Schauer, in other words, slippery slope arguments address the problems that arise from "human weaknesses of bias and deficiencies of understanding" (382). He attributes the especial prevalence of slippery slope claims in legal argument to the fact that law, "perhaps more emphatically than other decisionmaking mechanisms, calls upon today's decisionmakers to consider the behavior of others who tomorrow will have to apply or interpret today's decisions" (383). In this way, he suggests, the slippery slope argument gestures toward "some larger themes about the way in which law links past, present, and future" (ibid.).

This point about time is where Schauer ends; it is, of course, precisely where he should begin. Obviously, slippery slope arguments are about the way in which the law relates to its future; the whole point of the slippery slope claim is that today's decision may have unforeseen implications. If that seems illogical to Schauer, it is only because he thinks that we already have the logical and linguistic resources with which to eliminate the slide down the slippery slope. He holds that view because, as we know, he believes that linguistic categories are characterized by entrenched "acontextual" distinctions capable of providing the requisite "linguistic boundaries." But, as we have seen, categories are flexible and dynamic and, so, cannot provide the hard-edged linguistic boundaries between the instant case and the danger case (or, even, between the state of rest and the danger case) that he supposes.

Perhaps, more to the point, Schauer's closing observation subverts his entire argument. Once we introduce the contingent future into the equation, we can no longer be certain that our logical and linguistic resources *will* be enough to staunch the slide to the "danger" case. Legal decision-making, as Schauer recognizes, occurs over time. "A perceptive decision-maker," he points out, "will therefore be attuned to the dispositional environment in which linguistically articulated rules will be evaluated by future decisionmakers" (382). But the slippery slope argument derives is force from the very fact that the environment is *dispositional*—i.e., that it has the power to arrange, manage, and control linguistic meaning.* In other words, the inexorable logic behind the slippery slope argument is, as Llewellyn observed, that all words and all rules composed of words continuously change meaning as new conditions emerge.

Edward Levi made much the same point in his classic account of legal analogy. "The words change to receive the content which the community gives to them" (104). Cass Sunstein questions Levi's "arresting claim" that legal analogy therefore "has a crucial democratic component," dismissing it as a quaint artifact of the consensus born of the postwar, post-Realist period in which Levi wrote. Sunstein complains, moreover, that Levi did not "specify the mechanism by which community wishes help settle the conflict of analogies" (74–75). Indeed, Sunstein goes further and proclaims that it would "be most surprising if we could identify *any* mechanism translating democratic wishes into analogical reasoning" (ibid.; emphasis added). After all, he points out, judges do not take polls; they "ask themselves about the principles to which they are most deeply committed" (ibid.).

In fact, however, Levi provided a cogent and coherent account of how legal analogy incorporates community values. That account seems facile to Sunstein because Sunstein is an idealist (in both senses of the term). He assumes that legal decisionmaking can be a product only of conscious investigation and deliberation: Either the judges take a public opinion poll, or they consult their innermost values and beliefs. Levi, in contrast, was a realist (in both senses of the term). He understood and assimilated John Dewey's pragmatist argument that legal decisionmaking is not driven by the logic of deracinated principles but by practical needs and purposeful reasoning.

---

* Thus, Schauer argues that "a persuasive slippery slope argument depends for its persuasiveness upon temporally and spatially contingent empirical facts rather than (or in addition to) simple logical inference" (381). But we could just as well say that meaning "depends . . . upon temporally and spatially contingent empirical facts rather than (or in addition to) simple logical inference."

As Levi described the process, judges proceed in an essentially open-ended manner, making case-by-case judgments of similarity that do not necessarily square with one another. Over time, these judgments inevitably come to reflect both the social transformations that have taken place and the resulting changes in social values and meaning. Thus, Levi described both Cardozo's reformulation of product liability law in *MacPherson* and the 1937 revolution in Commerce Clause doctrine as involving "the gradual growth of the inherently dangerous or evil category" through the "expansion of reasoning by example until previously innocuous items are included" (102). But, because meaning is social rather than subjective, this growth was

> a reflection of a period in which increasing governmental control and responsibility for the individual were thought to be proper. No one economic or social theory was responsible. . . . Rather, the growth of inventions made it hard to distinguish, when reasoning by example was used, between steam engines thought unusual and dangerous in an early day, and engines that moved and were now commonplace. A change in the method of selling and in social life made it hard to distinguish between what had once been the small known group around a seller and the vast outside world. Since the difference could no longer be felt, it fell away. And similarly in the development of a constitution, increased transactions and communication made activities previously remote and local now a matter of national concern. (102–3)

In this way, "laws come to express the ideas of the community" and remain adaptable to new circumstances "even when written in general terms, in statute or constitution" (4). Changes in social conditions, practices, routines, and behavior alter people's perception and understanding of such critical categories as "inherently dangerous," "interstate commerce," or, as in *McBoyle,* "vehicle." The prior decisions—or, at least, some of them—are then harmonized into new mediating concepts that are articulated as new doctrinal rules.

It remains true that the process, thus described, cannot settle the contest of analogies when the community is in conflict. But Sunstein asks too much of Levi, and he knows it. For, on Sunstein's own account, law's distinctive contribution is to provide imperfectly theorized agreements to resolve otherwise intractable disputes. According to Sunstein, legal reasoning proceeds by forging low-level agreements with respect to particulars because a pluralist society like ours has no supervening principles with which to resolve such conflicts. But that, precisely, is Levi's account of legal reasoning. According to Levi, legal reasoning proceeds by analogy in a case-by-case fashion until such time as a consensus emerges. Thus, Levi dismissed as naïve and self-defeating the criticism that "the result of such a method is too uncertain to compel": "The effort to find complete agreement before the institution goes to work is meaningless. It is to forget the very purpose for which the institution of legal reasoning has been fashioned" (104).

There is a critique to be made here, but it is not the conventional one that Sunstein rehearses. Mainstream legal theory is obsessed with identifying the constraints that might prevent legal decisionmakers from imposing their personal or political preferences. This concern is intensified in the case of analogical reasoning because of the rationalist misapprehension that everything is like everything else in innumerable ways. But the picture changes radically once one recognizes how deeply judges are implicated in the cultural understandings that enable meaning. Once we recognize the ways in which cultural understandings and values enable (and constrain) what counts as a meaningful and persuasive analogy, the conventional critique appears to rest on something like a category mistake. The judges' "personal" values will, in the event, be conventional or mainstream values; indeed, the judges will have little or no choice in the matter because the acceptable (i.e., persuasive) analogies are precisely those that conform to the culture's dominant understandings and expectations.

But, while this recognition of cultural constraint tends to dissolve the problem of the "rogue" judge that so bedevils mainstream theory, it does not lay to rest the concern that adjudication may be undemocratic: After all, *dominant cultural conceptions* are not the same as *majority decisions*. To be sure, both legislative and judicial decisions spring from the same social and cultural sources. As a consequence, they are likely to converge—or, at least, run in parallel—in most cases. But it remains perfectly possible to have the worst of both worlds: judicial review (or interpretation) that overturns (or undermines) democratic decisionmaking but that nevertheless fails to transcend the dominant normative assumptions implicit in our background conceptions. Social consensus, in other words, is not the same as democratic legitimacy. Thus, Levi's uncritical celebration of analogical reasoning in law—like Llewellyn's idealization of "situation-sense"—appears to commit the error of conflating naked social coherence with normatively sufficient grounds for legal decisionmaking.

Innovation

CHAPTER 1 quoted Ricoeur's statement that "innovation is a form of behavior governed by rules." This chapter tests that claim by examining three important examples of successful innovation in twentieth-century American law. Two concern the First Amendment protection of free speech. The first example is the development, in *Hague v. C.I.O.*, of modern public forum doctrine, under which public spaces like streets and parks are presumptively available for expression subject only to reasonable time, place, and manner restrictions.[1] The second example is Holmes's formulation of the "marketplace of ideas" concept, which, as we shall see, has served as the organizing metaphor for much of modern free speech law. The third example is Chief Justice Hughes's opinion for the Supreme Court in *NLRB v. Jones & Laughlin Steel Corp.*,[2] the decision that repudiated the Commerce Clause doctrine that the Old Court had used to block much of the New Deal. This is one of two contemporaneous decisions commonly referred to as the "switch in time that saved nine," because these decisions mooted President Roosevelt's controversial court-packing plan.[3]

It is easy to see these three cases as examples of self-conscious manipulation of the law to accomplish extralegal social or political goals. In fact, however, these three cases provide first-rate examples of the two central claims of this book: (1) Despite the fact that it is conventional to think of imagination as random, unpredictable, or indeterminate, it is actually orderly and systematic in operation; and (2) because legal concepts (like all concepts) depend for their coherence on the motivating contexts that ground

meaning, legal change (no less than stability) is contingent on the larger social practices and forms of life that give the law its shape and meaning.

SUNDAY IN THE PARK

Modern public forum doctrine traces its origin to the Supreme Court's
1939 decision in *Hague v. C.I.O.*, which struck down a Jersey City ordinance used to prevent labor organizers from conducting meetings or dis-
tributing handbills in town. There, Justice Roberts proclaimed:

> Wherever the title of streets and parks may rest, they have immemorially
> been held in trust for the use of the public and, time out of mind, have
> been held for purposes of assembly, communicating thoughts between
> citizens, and discussing public questions. Such use of the streets and pub-
> lic places has, from ancient times, been part of the privileges, immunities,
> rights and liberties of citizens. (515–16)

Roberts's broad proclamation is problematic in several ways. For one thing,
he wrote for only a plurality of the Court. For another, the passage is dicta—
i.e., this broad statement of principle was unnecessary to the decision in
the case. In fact, *Hague* was a straightforward application of the previous
Term's decision in *Lovell v. Griffin,* which had invalidated an ordinance
that gave local authorities unlimited discretion to grant or deny permits for
First Amendment activities.[4]

Roberts's expansive rendition of the "immemorial" tradition of free expression in the streets and parks is also problematic in a third sense: It is, as
David Kairys has pointed out, revisionist history.[5] Just forty years earlier,
in *Davis v. Massachusetts,*[6] the United States Supreme Court uncondition-
ally affirmed a state conviction for preaching on Boston Common in violation of a city ordinance. Justice Holmes had written the decision of the state
court below in *Davis;* he sustained the ordinance in part on the ground that
it was within the power of the government to regulate its property. The Supreme Court quoted this portion of Holmes's opinion with approval.[7] Not
surprisingly, Mayor Hague relied on *Davis* in his argument before the Supreme Court; Roberts's revisionist history was offered in direct response
(514–15). It appears as if Roberts simply papered over *Davis*, stretching the
history to fit the desired outcome.

Nevertheless, it would be a mistake to see the shift from *Davis* to *Hague*
as a matter of simple manipulation or self-conscious revisionism. In fact,

Roberts carefully interrogated the conceptual underpinnings of each of the *Davis* opinions. To understand how Roberts came out where he did, we need to reexamine the opinions in *Davis* and *Hague* in light of what we learned in chapter 8 about the intervening transformation of the cultural conception of the park.

On appeal to the United States Supreme Court, Reverend Davis had argued:

> Boston Common is the property of the inhabitants of the city of Boston, and dedicated to the use of the people of that city and the public in many ways, and the preaching of the gospel there has been, from time immemorial to a recent period, one of these ways. For the making of this ordinance in 1862, and its enforcement against preaching since 1885, no reason whatever has been or can be shown.[8]

The Court responded by quoting from that portion of Holmes's opinion that focused on the absolute nature of the property rights of the state. "For the legislature absolutely or conditionally to forbid public speaking in a highway or public park is no more an infringement of the rights of a member of the public than for the owner of a private house to forbid it in his house."[9] Ownership is control. Q.E.D.

It is precisely at this point—where most contemporary discussions of these cases end[10]—that Roberts began his analysis in *Hague*. Roberts first questioned the *Davis* Court's rationale: "The decision seems to be grounded on the holding of the state court that the Common 'was absolutely under the control of the legislature'" (515). But, for Roberts, the technical issue of title was beside the point: "Wherever the title of streets and parks may rest," he observed, "they have immemorially been held in trust for the use of the public" (ibid.). In effect, Roberts transformed Reverend Davis's assertion of a "time immemorial" use into "a kind of First-Amendment easement."[11] Although one can question the historical accuracy of his factual assertion, Roberts's legal characterization of the ownership issue stands on more solid ground: Contrary to the *Davis* Court's assertion, nineteenth-century law characterized parks as property held in trust for the public.[12]

To be sure, Roberts went too far in claiming that parks had always been held in trust "for purposes of assembly, communicating thoughts between citizens, and discussing public questions" (515). Even so, his rejection of *Davis* did not hinge on that assertion. Rather, Roberts turned to a ground invoked by Holmes that had been ignored by the Supreme Court on review.

The property argument relied on by the *Davis* Court and quoted by so many of the commentators was, in fact, Holmes's second argument. His first was categorical. In *Davis*, Holmes had rejected the claim that the ordinance implicated constitutional concerns. "It assumes that the ordinance is directed against free speech generally, . . . whereas in fact it is directed toward the modes in which Boston Common may be used" (511). For Holmes, the city ordinance was merely a permissible instance of the government's ordinary power to regulate parks: "There is no evidence before us to show that the power of the Legislature over the Common is less than its power over any other park dedicated to the use of the public" (ibid.). Only at that point did Holmes invoke the property rights of the state to argue that the greater power includes the lesser. Since the government could "put[] an end to the dedication to public uses," it could "take the lesser step of limiting the public use to certain purposes" (ibid.).

Roberts resurrected Holmes's characterization and made it the basis of his distinction. After summarizing the Court's reasoning in *Davis,* Roberts observed:

> The ordinance there in question apparently had a different purpose from that of the one here challenged, for it was not directed solely at the exercise of the right of speech and assembly, but was addressed as well to other activities, not in the nature of civil rights, which doubtless may be regulated or prohibited as respects their enjoyment in parks. (515)

Thus, Roberts distinguished the Jersey City ordinance because it dealt "only with the exercise of the right of assembly" and was not premised on a general authority "to promote the public convenience in the use of the streets or parks" (ibid.). Moreover, the Jersey City ordinance did "not make comfort or convenience in the use of the streets or parks the standard of official action" (516). By thus focusing on the Jersey City ordinance's "uncontrolled official suppression" of speech (ibid.), Roberts tied together his distinction of the decision in *Davis* with his reliance on the Court's then recent decision in *Lovell v. Griffin.*

Viewed from a contemporary perspective, this categorical analysis may seem disingenuous. After all, the Boston ordinance did include a clause that specifically prohibited speaking in the park; that it also regulated other activities should be irrelevant. From a contemporary perspective, therefore, it makes sense that the *Davis* Court preferred Holmes's straightforward property analysis to his abstruse categorical one. By the same token, Roberts's embrace of Holmes's peculiar characterization of the Boston ordinance seems like an unprincipled attempt to avoid an adverse precedent. Roberts reinforces this impression when he says: "We have no occasion to determine whether, on the facts disclosed, the *Davis* case was rightly decided" (515).

But, because we already know something about the history of the urban park, we know that these impressions are mistaken. To evaluate the Boston ordinance from our contemporary perspective is to understand nineteenth-century institutions through the lens of twentieth-century conceptions. Both Holmes and Roberts were born and raised in the nineteenth century, and both would have understood the Boston ordinance in light of that century's very different conception of the park.

Consider the contrast between the two city ordinances. The Jersey City ordinance stated: "No public parades or public assembly in or upon the public streets, highways, public parks or public buildings of Jersey City shall take place or be conducted until a permit shall be obtained" (502 n.1). But where the Jersey City provision was directed solely and explicitly at public speech and assembly, the Boston ordinance was directed at what to us sounds like an unusual mélange of activities. As quoted in Holmes's opinion, that ordinance provided:

> No person shall, in or upon any of the public grounds, make any public address, discharge any cannon or firearm, expose for sale any goods, wares, or merchandise, erect or maintain any booth, stand, tent, or apparatus for purposes of public amusement or show, except in accordance with a permit from the mayor. (510)

To contemporary ears, the ordinance reads less like a lucid regulation of the park than another fanciful category by Borges. But, for the drafters of the Boston ordinance in 1862,* it would have made perfect sense to include these seemingly disparate activities in a single provision governing the park: It was precisely these activities that were incompatible with the goals of the then nascent, urban park movement. In contrast to the cutthroat commercial activity of city life, "the restorative purposes of the park were

---

* Although we can only speculate, Davis's complaint that the 1862 ordinance had not been applied to prohibit speech on Boston Common until 1885 may have had something to do with the fact that Olmsted began to work with the city at just that time. It may also have had something to do with the change of municipal administrations; 1885 marked the election of the first Irish-American, a Democrat, as mayor of Boston.

[to be] accomplished through a noncompetitive, nonthreatening 'coming to-gether' and through the restful contemplation of natural scenery." [13] Thus, as Geoffrey Blodgett notes, Frederick Law Olmsted insisted

> that rural scenery could impose a calming sense of its own sacredness on the "rough element of the city." . . . Moreover, the natural simplicity of the pastoral landscape would, he hoped, inspire communal feelings among all urban classes, muting resentments over disparities of wealth and fashion. For an untrusting, watchful crowd of urban strangers, the park would restore that "communicativeness" which Olmsted prized as a central American need.[14]

In short, both aspects of the park's mission were tied to its character as a pastoral pleasure ground. Only interactions in this idyllic setting would fos-ter the sentiments of equality and community sought by nineteenth-century republican reformers like Olmsted.

These republican advocates took strong stands about what was to be permitted in their parks. They routinely opposed ornaments like statuary—though often unsuccessfully.[15] Architecture was secondary to the pastoral landscape; buildings were kept rustic and unobtrusive. Commercial activi-ties were anathema; they "smacked of the city to which the pleasure ground was an antidote" (13). So, too, most cities prohibited political and religious meetings in the parks because they were too divisive; "the pleasure ground was meant to transcend, not reflect, the evils of urban life, of which division was a prominent symptom" (23).

Thus, many of the activities that we now associate with parks were, in the nineteenth century, deemed inherently inconsistent with the fundamen-tal purposes of a park. Consider, then, how this nineteenth-century con-ception of the park changes one's understanding of the outcome in *Davis*. Understood in historical context, the Boston ordinance *is* an appropriate regulation of the park; it is no different, in principle, from a constitution-ally permissible regulation prohibiting noisy demonstrations in front of a school when classes are in session.[16] So, too, *Davis* would be correctly de-cided even under the most protective version of the modern public forum doctrine. Under that doctrine, the relevant question is "whether the man-ner of expression is basically incompatible with the normal activity of a par-ticular place at a particular time." [17] Since *any* political or religious speech was fundamentally inconsistent with the "normal" activity of the park (if viewed in its time and context), Reverend Davis's conviction under the Boston ordinance would be upheld: "The First Amendment does not forbid a viewpoint-neutral exclusion of speakers who would disrupt a non-public forum and hinder its effectiveness for its intended purpose." [18]

Considered in light of this history, Roberts's distinction between *Davis* and *Hague* looks substantially more credible. The *Davis* Court was faced with an across-the-board regulation of the park that, inter alia, included a prohibition of public speaking. In contrast, the *Hague* Court was faced with an ordinance that was not premised on a general authority "to promote the public convenience in the use of the streets or parks," but was "directed solely at the exercise of the right of speech and assembly" (515). Moreover, as was well known, the Jersey City ordinance was being invoked by Mayor Hague in a viewpoint-specific effort to thwart organized labor.*

But if the intervening changes in the uses of the park supported Roberts's distinctions in *Hague,* they also did something more important: They changed the social conception of the park in a way that thoroughly undermined the constitutional logic of Holmes's opinion in *Davis.* The republican conception was, as we have seen, already under pressure in the last quarter of the nineteenth century. "In response to a changing constituency, park administrators made provision for various forms of modern recreation. . . . The rise of active recreation marked a major shift away from the mid-century park ideal." [19] Turn-of-the-century progressives reshaped park planning to reflect their view of the needs of the urban working class.[20] "Social workers were the first professionals regularly employed by park departments" (169). Organized programming—including dancing, clinics, branch libraries, and public lectures on political topics—became a staple of the parks. Depression Era officials cynically justified park programs (and park budgets) as a solution to the problem of "the new leisure" (105). Increasingly, park officials championed programs and offered justifications that tended to support the wide-ranging use of park facilities for purposes of expression.

> Park departments . . . encouraged activities which lent themselves to festivals and pageantry—music, dramatics, dancing, art exhibits—because of their power to stimulate community interaction and integration. But

---

* Kairys reports that Hague "made it clear that labor organizers were not welcome in Jersey City. . . . Local businesses were promised that they would have no labor troubles while he was mayor; his response to the CIO was: 'I am the law'" (193). Roberts confirms this fact: "The findings are that petitioners, as officials, have adopted and enforced a deliberate policy of forbidding the respondents and their associates from communicating their views respecting the National Labor Relations Act" (505).

> it was characteristic of the era that these activities were also advocated
> by parks spokespeople who viewed them primarily as means of self-
> expression. (115)

By the time of Roberts's opinion in *Hague,* the narrow conception of the park
that stood behind the Boston ordinance would have seemed increasingly
unpersuasive. Indeed, it was no longer far-fetched for Roberts to suggest
that parks were used "for purposes of assembly, communicating thoughts
between citizens, and discussing public questions" (515).

I do not claim that by the 1930s, the park had spontaneously developed
into a First Amendment forum. Still, neither Roberts's creative rewrite of history nor his revision of legal doctrine were fashioned of whole cloth. Rather,
Roberts's interrogation of *Davis* could not help but be affected by the widespread social changes in the background assumptions that shaped the contemporary conception of the park and its proper uses. By 1939, the idea
that the urban park was an appropriate literal analogue of the metaphorical "marketplace of ideas" would have seemed increasingly apt. Consider,
again, the words of the 1940 Chicago park commission report quoted in
chapter 8: "The shift was not in things or properties; it was in the social
meanings of those things and properties."

"A Staple Commodity of Knowledge"

The public forum doctrine gives legal and institutional content to the
"marketplace of ideas." But both the doctrine and the metaphor are relatively late arrivals on the First Amendment scene. At its inception, the First
Amendment was understood more narrowly to guard only against prior restraints of speech.[21] After the fact, false or unpopular speech could be punished with a variety of coercive governmental sanctions. This was clearly
the case with the Alien and Sedition Acts, adopted not long after the
amendment itself.[22] Leonard Levy reports much the same attitude in the
pre-Revolutionary period. "Everywhere unlimited liberty existed to praise
the American cause; . . . 'liberty of speech,' as Arthur Schlesinger so aptly
said, 'belonged solely to those who spoke the speech of liberty'" (173).

It is easy to dismiss this partisan attitude toward speech as narrow and
hypocritical. But there is more here than meets the eye, for this attitude reflects a coherent view of free speech with substantial historical roots. The
Areopagitica, John Milton's famous seventeenth-century polemic against licensing of the press, framed the free speech argument as an argument for
truth. "Truth is compar'd in Scripture to a streaming fountain; if her waters

flow not in a perpetuall progression, they sick'n into a muddy pool of conformity and tradition." [23] The biblical metaphor invoked by Milton—which we can represent with the mnemonic KNOWLEDGE IS WATER—provides a systematic set of entailments: water (in its various forms) maps onto knowledge; the current (as in a river or stream) maps onto intellectual progress; the experience of torpid and, therefore, unhealthy waters maps onto the kind of conventional wisdom that amounts to nothing more than the buildup of prejudice and error; and the water's source maps onto God.* These entailments, moreover, have specific substantive implications: If truth is a "streaming fountain," the evil to be avoided is the blockage that would interrupt "the free flow of ideas" and thus impede progress toward "Truth." The objection to licensing was that it might stifle that progress by stopping or constricting the emergence of new ideas. In the words of two contemporary commentators: "What keeps knowledge from being *stagnant* is its universal vulnerability to challenge." [24]

Given its religious underpinnings, it should not surprise us that this commitment to unrestrained speech was bound to a strong concept of Truth. In another famous passage from the *Areopagitica,* Milton argued that

> though all the windes of doctrin were let loose to play upon the earth,
> Truth be in the field. . . . Let her and Falsehood grapple; who ever knew
> Truth put to the wors, in a free and open encounter. . . . For who knows
> not that Truth is strong next to the Almighty; she needs no policies no
> stratagems, nor licensings to make her victorious; Those are the shifts
> and defences that error use against her power: give her but room, and do
> not bind her. (327–28)

This passage employs the conventional conceptual metaphor RATIONAL ARGUMENT IS WAR, still a live part of our contemporary conceptual system. In this mapping, rational argument is conceptualized in terms of physical combat: "There is . . . a position to be established and defended, you can win or lose, you have an opponent whose position you attack and try to destroy and whose argument you try to shoot down. If you are completely successful, you can wipe him out." [25] On this metaphorical model, Truth is that which prevails in a "free and open" contest of ideas. Thus, Milton argued that it was important not to suppress ideas before they could compete in the

---

* For examples, see *Deuteronomy* 32:2 ("My teachings shall fall as rain; my speech shall drip as the dew."); *Proverbs* 10:11 ("The mouth of the righteous is a fountain of life."); and *Ecclesiastes* 15:3 ("waters of discernment to drink").

struggle with dogma ("the windes of doctrin"). But, ideas that had already been articulated and found not to contribute toward truth—i.e., those that had lost the battle with accepted doctrine—did not stand on the same footing and could safely be subjected to after-the-fact governmental suppression or regulation.[26]

Given these views of Truth, it is not surprising that, as Levy reports, Milton ultimately accepted a position as censor under the very licensing act he had opposed (95). So, too, the apparent hypocrisy of the founding period's partisan attitude toward speech is readily explained by this same set of understandings: Belief in the importance of free speech could go hand-in-hand with the notion of subsequent punishment because a strong belief in Truth provided the necessary theoretical assurance that after-the-fact judgments could meaningfully distinguish the true from the false and unprotected. This was the case not only for Milton (who knew Truth as strong next to the Almighty), but also for his Enlightenment successors ("We hold these truths to be self-evident"). Consistent with this view, the important innovation of the founding period was the notion that truth should operate as a defense to seditious libel—a reform carried forward in Section 3 of the Sedition Act.*

This truth-based conception of free speech, organized around the "free flow" and "open encounter" metaphors, provided only a limited model for First Amendment doctrine. This model was grounded in the historical experiences both of English pamphleteers in the seventeenth and eighteenth centuries and of the papers, protests, and committees on correspondence in the period leading to the American Revolution.[27] But the model was relatively primitive, its productivity limited by the narrow truth-based conception which left vulnerable to punishment speech that was offensive to majoritarian sensibilities. In fact, the history of First Amendment law before the twentieth century is remarkably thin.

The principal legacy of this early period is a pair of prototype effects that remain an active part of our contemporary concept of free speech: the images of a basement press cranking out seditious leaflets (the "free flow," as it were) and of an "individual mount[ed on] a soapbox on a corner in some large city . . . criticiz[ing] governmental policy."[28] The continuing importance of these prototypes can be glimpsed in the Supreme Court's 1997 decision invalidating the Communications Decency Act. In striking down

---

* English law had treated truth as an aggravating factor because truthful statements denigrating the king were considered more likely to undermine his authority than false ones.

the act's prohibitions of "indecent" material on the Internet, the Court drew a direct if somewhat awkward analogy to these free speech prototypes: "Through the use of chat rooms, any person with a phone line can become a town crier with a voice that resonates farther than it could from any soapbox. Through the use of Web pages, mail exploders, and newsgroups, the same individual can become a pamphleteer." [29]

Though these prototypes characterize a powerful set of social values and conventions, they do not provide the rich conceptual material with which one could elaborate a comprehensive notion of free speech. A truly modern First Amendment had to await a more productive conceptual model, one whose compositional structure transcended the limitations of the earlier truth-based conception. That model did not come until Holmes's World War I opinions.

The process began inauspiciously enough. Now on the United States Supreme Court, Holmes wrote three opinions for a unanimous Court affirming convictions under the Espionage Act of 1917 for urging resistance to the World War I draft. [30] The lead case was that of Charles Schenck, the general secretary of the Socialist Party, who had published leaflets counseling resistance. Holmes allowed clumsily: "It well may be that the prohibition of laws abridging the freedom of speech is not confined to previous restraints, although to prevent them may have been the main purpose." Even so, the bottom line remained much the same. As Holmes so famously put it: "The most stringent protection of free speech would not protect a man in falsely shouting fire in a crowded theatre and causing a panic." [31] More than a hundred years after the Sedition Act, little had changed: Once spoken, false or potentially injurious speech was still amenable to repressive governmental sanctions.

In just eight months, however, Holmes would dramatically change position. According to the conventional wisdom, Holmes's sudden emergence as a free speech champion was due to the influence of Zacharia Chafee. [32] But there was something more profound at work in Holmes's thought; otherwise, he would not have found Chafee's arguments persuasive, nor would he have changed position so quickly. With hindsight, moreover, we can find in Holmes's *Schenck* opinion clues to his sudden transition. Why, for example, was he so awkward in describing the scope of First Amendment protection? What, aside from prior restraints, was the First Amendment all about?

One way to approach these questions is to consider the problems posed by Holmes's analogy in *Schenck*. The analogy consists in a mapping from the source domain of a person falsely shouting fire in a crowded theater to the target domain of a political activist advocating resistance to the draft. The analogy maps the immediate and catastrophic effect of creating a panic in a crowded theater onto the harm to the war effort that might ensue if many young men took up the call to resistance. The analogy works only to the extent that the call to resistance is likely to motivate immediate and widespread action; that is the burden of Holmes's "clear and present danger" test.[33] Nevertheless, even if the exigency is real, the analogy is incomplete, for it presupposes that opposition to the war is, in some crucial sense, *false*. One need only consider our reaction to the person who, upon seeing the first lick of the flames at the theater curtains, quietly exits without alerting his or her fellow patrons. *Falsely* shouting "Fire" in a crowded theater is one thing. But crying "Fire" in a *burning* theater is quite another matter (though it might be better still to inform everyone of the fire in a calm, commanding voice).

To say that advocating resistance to the draft is like falsely shouting fire in a crowded theater, one must first be confident that the war is something like the noble cause claimed—making the world safe for democracy, the war to end all wars—and not an incendiary evil. It is one thing to obstruct the war effort in times of genuine national peril. But it is quite another matter to oppose the country's involvement in a bloody foreign conflict that will prove a tragic mistake. To equate Schenck's acts with those of the person who falsely shouts "Fire" in a crowded theater, in other words, one must be prepared to say that it is the conventional wisdom about the country's participation in the war that represents the "truth."

But that is precisely what Holmes of all people would *not* have been prepared to say. Holmes was a Social Darwinist and, on his own report, a lifelong cynic: "I used to say, when I was young, that truth was the majority vote of that nation that could lick all others."[34] It was his recognition of the contingency of truth that lay behind his famous *Lochner* dissent insisting on judicial deference to legislative action. There, Holmes had argued that a constitution, "is made for people of fundamentally differing views, and the accident of our finding certain opinions natural and familiar or novel and even shocking ought not to conclude our judgment upon the question."[35] Holmes strongly affirmed "the right of a majority to embody their opinions in law" (75) and was concomitantly skeptical of the Court's attempt "to prevent the natural outcome of a dominant opinion" (76). But, as Holmes soon came to realize, the same skepticism was in order when the attempt to forestall change came from the dominant majority itself. As he later wrote in dissent in *Gitlow:* "If, in the long run, the beliefs expressed in proletarian dictatorship are destined to be accepted by the dominant forces of the community, the only meaning of free speech is that they should be given their chance and have their way." [36]

Holmes's respect for the privilege of power to embody itself in law soon proved secondary to his Social Darwinism and skepticism. Just eight months after *Schenck,* in *Abrams v. United States,* Holmes dissented from the Court's affirmance of yet another conviction under the Espionage Act.

> Persecution for the expression of opinions seems to me perfectly logical. If you have no doubt of your premises or your power, and want a certain result with all your heart, you naturally express your wishes in law, and sweep away all opposition. . . . But when men have realized that time has upset many fighting faiths, they may come to believe even more than they believe the very foundations of their own conduct that the ultimate good desired is better reached by free trade in ideas—that the best test of truth is the power of the thought to get itself accepted in the competition of the market. [37]

This passage has provided the critical metaphor for the twentieth-century ICM of the First Amendment: "the marketplace of ideas."

Because it represents a distinct break from the immediate past, it is easy to misconceive Holmes's metaphor as a creative tour de force—in contemporary parlance, a deliberate "misreading" of what had come before. [38] But one of the fascinating things about Holmes's metaphor is that it is actually quite conventional. It is premised on the conceptual metaphors for mind and ideas that are part of the CONDUIT metaphor-system discussed in chapter 3. As we have seen, generic metaphors such as THE MIND IS A CONTAINER and IDEAS ARE OBJECTS can be used to generate additional metaphors by specifying the source domain entity with a particular example (e.g., "sieve" for CONTAINER or "plants" for OBJECTS) that provides a different set of entailments. Thus, we have the conventional conceptual metaphors:

> THE MIND IS A MACHINE—She just *grinds out* those papers; I got a lot of writing done this morning but then I *ran out of steam;* he had a nervous *breakdown.*
> IDEAS ARE PRODUCTS—That's a good hypothesis, but we need to *refine* it; she is our most *productive* writer.
> IDEAS ARE COMMODITIES—Her idea is *valuable,* but yours is *worthless;* it just won't *sell.* [39]

Holmes's "marketplace of ideas" metaphor combines these basic metaphors for mind and ideas with the economic experience of the market to provide a new view of First Amendment freedoms. The metaphor expresses a novel conception of free speech, but only by means of entirely conventional conceptual metaphors.

Holmes's metaphor carries over from the source domain of economic activity to the target domain of speech a systematic set of entailments that supersedes the limitations of the older free speech model. With respect to entities and relations, the entailments are: ideas are commodities; persuasion is selling; speakers are vendors; members of the audience are potential purchasers; acceptance is buying; intellectual value is monetary value; and the struggle for recognition in the domain of public opinion is like competition in the market. At the conceptual level, the metaphor carries over from the domain of economic activity the notion that value can be measured by demand—thus, the truth-value of speech can be measured by "the power of the thought to get itself accepted." Finally, at the normative level, the metaphor carries over from the source domain of economic activity to the target domain of speech the contingent cultural values of freedom and individual autonomy that constitute our modern notion of "free trade."

This link between freedom, autonomy, and speech is easily taken for granted today. But it became possible only because of historical and cultural contingencies having little to do with speech. Just as Roberts's doctrinal innovation in *Hague* depended upon the intervening transformation of the urban park, Holmes's "marketplace of ideas" metaphor depended upon unrelated changes in economic practices. In an earlier time, the market metaphor bore a nearly opposite meaning. Thus, in the *Areopagitica,* Milton invoked the market metaphor to *deride* the notion of licensed printing: "Truth and understanding are not such wares as to be monopoliz'd and traded in by tickets and statutes, and standards. We must not think to make a staple commodity of all knowledge in the Land, to mark and license it like our broad cloath, and wooll packs" (303–4). Milton wrote in an era of imperial mercantilism when the market was tightly regulated by the Crown and by the guilds. Holmes, in contrast, wrote in a period of laissez-faire capitalism (which, ironically, is conventionally identified with the majority opinion in *Lochner*). If Holmes was skeptical of the notion of "truth" as the inexorable outcome of the forward motion of ideas, the concept of the market provided a meaningful alternative model for the notion that "truth"—like economic well-being—could be the product of human competition. In short, the "marketplace of ideas" makes sense as a metaphor for free speech only after the advent of the economic developments of the eighteenth and nineteenth centuries.

But this is not the only cultural shift that stood between Milton and the framers, on one hand, and Holmes and the twentieth-century First Amendment, on the other. As long as Truth was understood in strong objectivist terms, a First Amendment that prohibits only censorship made some sense. After-the-fact judgments could be trusted to sort out the true from the false and unprotected. The rise of classical liberalism in the nineteenth century undermined this view because it brought with it the notion that there could be more than one "truth." [40] As Levy observes: "Neither freedom of speech nor freedom of the press could become a civil liberty until people believed that the truth of their opinions, especially their religious opinions, was relative rather than absolute" (5). Recognition of the relativity of value in turn subverts faith in the power of Truth to sustain itself against all comers. Thus, the discontinuity between the framers' First Amendment (with its focus on the prohibition of prior restraints and the introduction of truth as a defense to charges of seditious libel) and the modern First Amendment (with its more libertarian emphasis) is a function of the radically different social contexts and the distinctive concepts they each make possible. Modern free speech doctrine simply was not possible before the development of the modern practices and beliefs that give it meaning.

In both these culturally contingent ways, Holmes did not act free-form in fashioning the "marketplace of ideas" metaphor. Rather, he drew upon conventional metaphors and general cultural experience to formulate a new and innovative conception of free speech. Even so, Holmes's innovative recomposition was not immediately successful. It would be another decade before a First Amendment plaintiff actually prevailed,[41] and a full fifty years before Holmes's "clear and present danger" test would actually command a majority of the Court.[42]

SPEECH ACTS OR SEX ACTS?

Just as the metaphor of a "streaming fountain" enables some conceptions of free speech and constrains others, Holmes's market metaphor makes possible and limits the scope of First Amendment expansion. The modern First Amendment, in other words, forms a radial category that—both for good and ill—is structured by the market model and its underlying conceptual metaphors.

The heart of modern free speech law consists, in Justice Brennan's oft-quoted words, in the "profound national commitment to the principle that debate on public issues should be uninhibited, robust, and wide-open."[43] But this commitment makes little sense outside the normative cultural assumptions encompassed by the market metaphor. As Holmes observed, competition is hardly appreciated when "you have no doubt of your premises." (One might just as well invite submissions for a contest to define the proper shape of a square.) Vigorous competition becomes desirable, even indispensable, once one accepts the relativist notion that "there is no such thing as a false idea."[44] Thus, Justice Brennan's majority opinion in *New York Times v. Sullivan* affirmed that First Amendment "protection does not turn upon 'the truth, popularity, or social utility of the ideas and beliefs which are offered'" (266). Just as the economic market knows no test of product "validity" but allows demand to drive supply (relying on the market to distinguish viable and shoddy products), the constitutional regime of free speech works best when it "secure[s] 'the widest possible dissemination of information from diverse and antagonistic sources'" (271).

Yet, this otherwise expansive concept of free speech can at times be surprisingly narrow. Speech is expected to be "uninhibited, robust, and wide-open" in the freewheeling space of the public forum; but in more circumscribed contexts, there is more limited space for speech. Thus, in striking down a statute prohibiting picketing on its grounds, the Supreme Court emphasized that the "sidewalks comprising the outer boundaries of the Court grounds are indistinguishable from any other sidewalks in Washington, D.C." An earlier decision upholding restrictions on antiwar protests in the public areas of Fort Dix was different because "the streets and sidewalks at issue were located within an enclosed military reservation . . . and were thus separated from the streets and sidewalks of any municipality."[45] Under the quasi-public forum doctrine, the government may restrict the content of speech in institutional settings as long as it does not discriminate among viewpoints.[46] In practice, this doctrine means that a government employer can ban (or punish as insubordinate) communications about work-related grievances or union activities.[47] As Robert Post says, "the legally established *boundaries of public discourse* mark the point at which our commitments shift from values like autonomous self-determination to competing values like . . . managerial efficiency."[48]

The overt *spatialization* of free speech is not the only way in which our understanding of the First Amendment is shaped by the market metaphor. Equally important is the distinction between "speech" and "conduct," which continues to play a role in contemporary free speech law notwithstanding its rejection by leading constitutional law scholars such as Larry Tribe and John Hart Ely.[49]

The distinction appears in two separate doctrinal contexts. The first is the doctrine that affords less protection to "speech mixed with conduct" than to "pure speech."[50] The second is the "fighting words" doctrine of *Chaplinsky v. New Hampshire*, which recognized

> certain well-defined and narrowly limited classes of speech, the preven-
> tion and punishment of which has never been thought to raise any Con-
> stitutional problem. These include the lewd and obscene, the profane,
> the libelous, and the insulting or "fighting" words—those *words which
> by their very utterance inflict injury* or tend to incite an immediate
> breach of the peace.[51]

In his influential treatise, Tribe criticized the Court for relying on the "persistent" but "oversimplified" distinction between "speech" and "conduct." Following Ely, he argued that the speech/conduct distinction is incoherent: On one hand, all speech involves action of some sort (talking, writing, printing, etc.); on the other, many forms of conduct (wearing an armband, displaying or defacing a flag, a sit-in or other demonstration) are primarily expressive. If the distinction seems indefensible in strictly rational terms, it is even more problematic as a legal matter. Solicitation to commit a crime or the libel of a private person can be prohibited, though they are undoubtedly speech; but symbolic actions such as flag-burning are treated as speech for First Amendment purposes, notwithstanding the fact that they are unquestionably conduct. Yet, despite both the eminence and the logical force of this critique, the distinction has not been put to rest. As Cass Sunstein observes: "Free speech law has been bedeviled by the 'speech-conduct' distinction."[52]

We can observe as similar pattern with respect to *Chaplinsky*. Today its holding is largely a social and doctrinal anachronism. In 1942, the Court could say that profane and "fighting" words "are no essential part of any exposition of ideas." But that would hardly seem true after the 1960s. In *Cohen v. California*, for example, the Court treated Paul Robert Cohen's "Fuck the Draft" as a relatively obvious case of protected speech.[53] Noting that this "scurrilous epithet" (22) was "perhaps more distasteful than most others of its genre" (25), Justice Harlan nevertheless explained that words are "often chosen as much for their emotive as their cognitive force," and this "emotive function . . . may often be the more important element of the overall message sought to be communicated" (26). So, too, in *Times v. Sullivan,* the Court treated libelous statements as an inevitable part of open debate and, therefore, within the necessary "breathing space" for First Amendment freedoms (272). "Even a false statement may be deemed to make a valuable contribution to public debate, since it brings about 'the clearer perception and livelier impression of truth'" (279 n.19).[54]

About the only aspect of *Chaplinsky* that *has* survived is the idea that some forms of speech are tantamount to conduct. Today, *Chaplinsky* is regularly invoked by progressive scholars who support regulation of hate speech and pornography. Thus, the argument for prohibitions on racist speech is that it is a form of harassment—"words that wound."[55] Similarly, Sunstein initially relied on *Chaplinsky* to argue that pornography is "low value" speech that can be prohibited consistent with the First Amendment because it harms women by encouraging violence toward them.[56] In response to criticism of that argument, Sunstein specifically disclaimed any reliance on the "discredited and untenable distinction between 'speech' and 'conduct.'"[57] But, in point of fact, he employed just that notion: "Pornography does not have the special properties that single out speech for special protection; *it is more akin to a sexual aid than a communicative expression*" (606; emphasis added). Although Sunstein maintained that "pornography and obscenity are obviously 'speech'" (603 n.84), his argument at bottom was that pornography is little more than a physical stimulus: "What makes pornography different is that people 'get off on it.'"[58]

We needn't overanalyze the argument to tease out the implicit reliance on the speech/conduct distinction. Sunstein made the connection explicit. Aware of and sympathetic to the feminist argument that pornography should be banned precisely because it conveys an ideological message (i.e., devaluing women and encouraging violence toward them), Sunstein observed that "any implicit 'ideology' is communicated indirectly and noncognitively" (607). To support this position, he pointed out that even "a first amendment 'absolutist'" like Justice Black "believed that the regulation of *conduct* that also touched associated speech could, in particular circumstances, be constitutional" (607 n.109; emphasis added). Just so; Black joined Justice Blackmun's dissent in *Cohen v. California.* Blackmun argued that *Cohen* should be controlled by *Chaplinsky:* "Cohen's absurd and immature antic, in my view, was mainly conduct and little speech" (27).

How could Sunstein have lapsed into a distinction that he simultaneously insisted was thoroughly discredited? No doubt, more than one explanation is possible. But consider what we know about Sunstein: He is a died-in-the-wool rationalist. As such, he is prone to all of rationalism's paradigmatic mistakes. When Sunstein says that the speech/conduct distinction is "discredited and untenable," he means that "speech" and "conduct" lack coherence as categories because they cannot be defined consistent with the rigors of P or not-P: All forms of speech present the properties of conduct, and some forms of conduct are characterized by the same properties that identify speech as such. But, as we have seen throughout, rationalism is a peculiarly blunt instrument that tends to introduce rather than resolve indeterminacy. When rationalists look at the things-in-the-world called "speech" and "conduct," they try to identify the distinguishing features that differentiate one from the other. When they are unable to do so, they are forced to conclude that the categories "speech" and "conduct" are not useful as concepts. Thus, Tribe complains that the categories have little "determinate" content: "Any particular course of conduct may be hung almost randomly on the 'speech' peg or the 'conduct' peg as one sees fit." [59]

Nevertheless, the distinction between speech and conduct persists because the rationalist critique misses the point. The rationalist critique is literal and propositional, whereas the concepts "speech" and "conduct" are metaphorical and socially motivated. As we saw in chapter 3, the concept "speech" is structured by the conceptual mappings that compose the CON-DUIT metaphor-system. "Conduct," as we saw in chapter 1, is structured by the set of correlative metaphors represented by the mnemonic ACTIONS ARE MOTIONS. These mappings are embodied and cognitively entrenched—i.e., they are fundamental and pervasive aspects of our conceptual system upon which a host of other processes (such as semantic productivity and change) depend. The categories "speech" and "conduct," in other words, are constitutive of how we reason. Concepts like "speech" and "conduct," moreover, are not simply categories of things-as-they-exist-in-the-world; they are categorizations of social experience that reflect our speech-community's particular social understandings and purposes—the way we live, the things we value, the norms we obey. They are an essential part of "what everybody knows" about the social world. As such, they remain in place long after the rationalist critique has done its (conscious) work. Quite simply, there is no other way for us to think about such things.

To make sense of the speech/conduct distinction and the arguments and doctrines that employ it, therefore, we need carefully to examine the conceptual structure of the underlying categories. One point of the previous section was that cultural metaphors like the "marketplace of ideas" can be understood only in light of the larger cultural and conceptual structures in which they participate. Concepts, in other words, exist as parts of a *conceptual system*. This means that concepts are subject to ecological effects:

What happens in one part of the system affects what occurs in another. Competing concepts or models are not merely plastic to subjective intention—i.e., they do not simply alternate with the task at hand—but display structural and systematic linkages.[60] Thus, the doctrine that affords less protection to "speech mixed with conduct" reflects both the limits of a market model for speech and the way in which that model fits with our more general model of law: As we move from "pure speech" to action, we move from the domain of the market where IDEAS ARE PRODUCTS to be bought and sold freely to the domain of behavior where ACTIONS ARE MOTIONS subject to the control and constraint of law.[61]

This inference—that speech mixed with conduct is subject to greater regulation—is not an unmediated reflection of reality but a consequence of our conceptual models. As such, it is open to pressure from changing practices and needs. The political and social developments of the 1960s and early 1970s—sit-ins, mass demonstrations, draft card- and bra-burnings—put the conventional set of categorizations under severe strain: Forms of "conduct" once seen as peripheral to First Amendment activity have, in the space of a generation, taken center stage as major forms of political protest. Predictably, the Court responded by extending the category of protected expression to encompass these "new" forms. It did so not ad hoc but *within the conceptual system:* Conduct is "really" speech when, consistent with the CONDUIT metaphor that composes our notion of ordinary communication, it serves as a vehicle through which people convey information to others. Thus, in 1968, the Court held that conduct was to be protected as "symbolic speech" when there was "an intent to convey a particularized message . . . , and in the surrounding circumstances the likelihood was great that the message would be understood by those who viewed it." [62]

However self-evident or nonmetaphorical this definition might seem, it, too, is a product of our conceptual model and not an unmediated reflection of reality. As Post points out, there are instances of "speech," such as music and nonrepresentational art, that everyone would agree are core cases of protected expression even if no one can say exactly what the message might be.[63] We can observe the Court stumbling on just this point in its decision in *Hurley v. Irish-American Gay, Lesbian and Bisexual Group of Boston.* Struggling to explain why a St. Patrick's Day Parade with no identifiable message was nevertheless protected "speech," * the Court proclaimed:

_____

* The parade was open to most any group—except, of course, gay and lesbian Irish-Americans.

"Parades are . . . a form of expression, not just motion, and the *inherent expressiveness* of marching to make a point explains our cases involving protest marches."[64]

"Speech," in other words, is a radial category whose central case is characterized by the CONDUIT metaphor-system and its cognate, the marketplace of ideas. Speaking, writing, and publishing are the prototypical cases. First tier extensions include the protest march and the demonstration, relatively early additions that differ from the central case because they involve conduct implicating pragmatic concerns (traffic, congestion) that justify reasonable time, place, and manner restrictions. Second tier extensions include the nonprint media and symbolic and commercial speech. Thus, the broadcast media are subject to legal mandates—the fairness doctrine, the regulation of indecent but nonobscene language—that would not be tolerated for more prototypical media.[65] Symbolic speech (e.g., draft card-burning) may be restricted under a more relaxed standard that permits the government to pursue "important" interests unrelated to speech (see note 18). So, too, the protection of commercial speech allows for regulation of false and misleading advertising.[66]

As one moves farther from the core, First Amendment protections progressively weaken. Novel forms of political protest and nonprototypical instances of the traditional media receive little or no protection. When, for example, those protesting the plight of the homeless wanted to sleep overnight in a tent city set up across from the White House in Lafayette Park, the Court sustained the application of an Interior Department anticamping regulation as a reasonable "time, place, or manner" restriction.[67] By the same token, student newspapers are not treated as core cases of speech but are subject to regulation as part of the core curriculum.[68] Many of these cases are difficult to square in conventional terms of doctrine and principle. Mark Tushnet, for example, has complained that the Court's decisions appear to imply that "we are to determine the degree of protection that a category of speech gets by considering paradigmatic examples of speech in that category, not by considering unusual or merely possible examples."[69] But these outcomes are quite understandable as prototype effects—i.e., as the predictable products of radial categorization.

In an earlier piece, written during the heyday of the critical legal studies movement, Tushnet had argued that the concept of rights is a "masquerade."[70] He maintained that, while rights offer the promise of legal protection, the indeterminacy of legal doctrine in fact means that rights are easily manipulated to extend benefits to the powerful and withdraw protections from the individual.[71] But the cases that Tushnet identified as manipulations of First Amendment doctrine to favor wealth can also be explained as predictable manifestations of conceptual structure. The CONDUIT and "marketplace of ideas" metaphors both compete with and are structurally linked to the concept of property: No matter how political or important my message, I can be charged with vandalism if I write it as a graffito on your wall. Although the social and legal concept of freedom of speech has undergone many changes over the last century, the notion that private property trumps First Amendment rights has been quite stable.[72] In *Adderly v. Florida,* for example, the Court upheld the trespass convictions of civil rights protesters who had demonstrated on jail property. Justice Black's 1966 opinion in *Adderly* is an unmistakable echo of Holmes's 1895 opinion in *Davis:* "The State, no less than a private owner of property, has power to preserve the property under its control for the use to which it is lawfully dedicated."[73]

The priority of property over free speech should not be surprising. Not only is the social institution of property older, more immediate, and more thoroughly routinized,[74] but the central metaphor of the First Amendment— the "marketplace of ideas"—is itself expressed in property terms. The First Amendment protections afforded large aggregates of wealth, which Tushnet identified as products of indeterminacy and manipulation, are better understood as the expected effects of the cultural power of the social institution of private property: These protections are, one might say, part of the interest that accrues to the wealthy in a society that values wealth and power and uses them as the source domain for potent cultural metaphors. First Amendment cases privileging wealth can thus be seen as reflections of the general cultural metaphor "money talks."[75]

The phenomenon of structural linkage explains more precisely the persistence of the speech/conduct distinction. The rationalist critique is correct to the extent that there is nothing inherent or objective about the distinction between speech and conduct. The distinction persists, nevertheless, because there are fundamental structural links between the CONDUIT and ACTIONS ARE MOTIONS metaphors. Speech, too, is an activity; it, too, is conceptualized by means of the ACTIONS ARE MOTIONS metaphor. (Hence, such colloquialisms as "he talks a mile a minute" or "he talks a blue streak.") Even more importantly, several of the metaphorical mappings that constitute the CONDUIT metaphor-system are themselves premised on the ACTIONS ARE MOTIONS metaphor. The metaphors UNDERSTANDING IS GRASPING, COMMUNICATION IS SENDING, AN ARGUMENT IS A JOURNEY each represent a different aspect of the communicative process as a kind of action.

Because speech is conceptualized metaphorically in this way, there is a sense in which, *for us,* all speech *is* action. Just as any word that signifies physical acquisition can be used to signify intellectual understanding (see chapter 3), any speech act can be represented as "conduct." Thus, it is perfectly conventional to refer to an unkind word as "a cutting remark" and to say that a presentation was "powerful," "forceful," or that it "bowled me over."* In legal debate, this conventional metaphorical notion of SPEECH AS ACTION is manifested in the arguments that hate speech is a matter of *words that wound* or in the *Chaplinsky* notion that "fighting words" are *words which by their very utterance inflict injury.*

It does not follow that, as Tribe says, any particular course of behavior can arbitrarily be characterized as either speech or conduct. The metaphor of SPEECH AS ACTION merely creates the forensic space for plausible argument. Thus, Blackmun's characterization of Cohen's "Fuck the Draft" as conduct seems merely quaint rather than totally absurd. The elasticity of any category remains limited by the fact that it is socially grounded and motivated. For Blackmun's argument to succeed, it must appeal to generally accepted understandings and beliefs. And Blackmun's argument does not persuade precisely because it relies on genteel, largely old-fashioned sensibilities. Conversely, murder will readily and reliably be characterized as conduct no matter how earnest the intended message of hatred or how obvious the political motivation (e.g., Oklahoma City.) It is not that we cannot imagine a society where assassination is a mode of political expression. There have been cultures in which assassination was a regular means of determining succession. It is just that we are not (and do not particularly want to be) that kind of society. The categories "speech" and "conduct" are not infinitely manipulable because they are grounded in existing social practices and, as such, are reflections of cultural values and pragmatic social purposes. Motivation, in other words, operates as a significant if largely invisible constraint.

Kennedy's hypothetical "lie-in" by striking bus drivers, discussed in chapter 6, presents a case similar to the murder example. "Lying-in" to prevent the buses from rolling falls quite close to the core of our conventional concept of "conduct." Because the lie-in is part of a strike, it has an ideological dimension that can also be said to bear a political message. Accordingly, Kennedy's characterization of the lie-in as an arguable exercise of a First Amendment right has surface plausibility. But that description is not

---

* In the same vein, a joke or a story is said to have a "punch line." Recall, too, Rorty's wry remark (quoted in chapter 3) that "tossing a metaphor into a conversation is like suddenly . . . slapping your interlocutor's face, or kissing him."

ultimately persuasive once one focuses on the pragmatic dimensions of the lie-in—i.e., on its intended consequences and its role in the underlying labor dispute. The more traditional picket line is a statement to potential customers and strikebreakers that they should abstain from dealing with the employer because of the way it mistreats its workers (though the picket line can also be a vehicle of intimidation). The lie-in, in contrast, goes further as a practical matter; it *stops* others from dealing with the employer by preventing the buses from rolling. The difference between Kennedy's hypothetical lie-in and a flag-burning (or, for that matter, the lunch counter sit-ins of the 1960s) is that the effectiveness of the act lies not in its capacity to convey an idea in a visceral or dramatic way, but in its ability to achieve the desired concrete result—stopping the buses—even when there is no audience.[76]

Whether a speech act will be perceived as "conduct" or a course of conduct understood as "speech" depends upon its congruence with an ICM structured in terms of the CONDUIT metaphor. A speech act that uses words or "symbolic conduct" to transmit a message to an audience—i.e., one that instantiates the metaphors IDEAS ARE OBJECTS; WORDS (AND SYMBOLS) ARE CONTAINERS; COMMUNICATION IS SENDING; UNDERSTANDING IS GRASP-ING—will be understood as "speech." Conversely, a speech act that in social context and use is little more than a metaphorical OBJECT hurled at another like a brickbat* will always be open to characterization as "conduct" that should be excluded from the protections of the First Amendment. Speech acts that do not fit the ICM will be characterized based on their proximity to one or the other of these prototypical cases. Thus, an event like the St. Patrick's Day parade may not have a discrete message; but as an expression of identity or ethnic solidarity, it is more like a manifesto than a brickbat.

Because it is presently constituted as a relentlessly rationalist discourse, legal argument represents these inferences as analytic distinctions. In place of the standard doctrinal distinction between "speech" and "conduct," Sunstein offers a distinction between speech that appeals to "cognitive" and "noncognitive" capacities.† But, close attention to the actual arguments reveals the indubitable impress of the CONDUIT metaphor. When Sunstein ar-

---

* Hence the derivation of "brickbat"—literally a piece of a brick used as a missile— as an unkind or caustic criticism.

† We shall examine Sunstein's position more precisely in a moment. For now, it is enough to say that this distinction between cognitive and noncognitive corresponds roughly to the conventional distinction between reason and emotion (603 n.87).

gues that pornography is "more akin to a sexual aid than a communicative expression," he is characterizing pornography as an OBJECT employed for its physiological and autonomous psychological effects rather than as a CONTAINER for meaning. "The effect and intent of pornography are to produce sexual arousal, not in any sense to affect the course of self-government" (606). But he soon retreats from this position. Because Sunstein is sympathetic to the feminist claim that pornography conveys an ideological message (i.e., that it is a CONTAINER for misogynist meaning), he must distinguish pornography from other ideology-laden acts of communication that would ordinarily receive First Amendment protection. He does so by appealing to other aspects of the CONDUIT metaphor-system: "Whether particular speech is low-value does not turn on whether the materials *contain* an implicit ideology. . . . The question instead turns more generally on the speaker's purpose and on how the speaker communicates the message" (607; emphasis added). If COMMUNICATION IS SENDING, then it seems evident to Sunstein that what the pornographer sends is not an idea but an effect: "The pornographer's purpose in disseminating pornographic materials—to produce sexual arousal—can be determined by the nature of the material. And any implicit 'ideology' is communicated indirectly and noncognitively" (ibid.).

The plausibility of this argument depends upon the distinction between "cognitive" and "noncognitive" modes of communication, which Sunstein concedes is "thin" (604) and "difficult to defend" (606). But this concession understates the case: It is specious to argue that pornography is more like a vibrator than a tabloid simply because it can lead to arousal. After all, when spoken by the right person, the words "I love you" can have just the same effect. Pornography is no less "cognitive" than any other form of human expression; just as there can be no ideological message without a human brain to perceive it, there can be no sexual arousal without a human brain to process and experience it.* Worse yet, Sunstein's distinction is fatally self-contradictory. Sunstein cannot argue that any implicit ideology is communicated "noncognitively" when he *defines* "cognitive" as the capacity to "impart knowledge in any sense" whether it "is intended to or does in fact"

* One might try to defend Sunstein's distinction by reformulating it as a distinction between conscious and subconscious mental processes. But this defense will not wash either. Whether engaging in pillow talk or reading pornography, one is perfectly conscious of both the stimulus and the resulting arousal. Perhaps Sunstein means that First Amendment protections should extend only to speech that appeals to conscious, *deliberative* processes. But this characterization also fails, because, as we have seen, it would omit such clear cases as music, nonrepresentational art, and the St. Patrick's Day parade.

(603 n.87). On his own terms, then, the very fact that a message is communicated makes the exchange "cognitive" by definition. No matter how hard he tries, Sunstein cannot escape the inference structure of the CONDUIT metaphor: A speech act that uses words or symbols to transmit a message *is* "speech," whether the message is one of sexual libertinism or gender subordination.

In the most recent version of the argument, Sunstein concedes that the regulation of "forms of speech" like pornography "does not really stem from a distinction between speech and conduct." [77] He now views the speech/conduct distinction as a heuristic: On one hand, "'speech' refers to something that we should consider a term of art" covering "all symbols that are intended and received as messages" (833). On the other, "the treatment of some words as 'conduct' provides a shorthand, if misleading, description of a more extended argument that the speech at issue does not promote First Amendment values and creates sufficient harm to be regulable under the appropriate standards" (837). This reformulation will be appealing both to rationalists and to those familiar with the work of the legal realists. In treating "speech" and "conduct" as heuristics, Sunstein appears to reject (or, at least, temper) a misleading focus on categorical labels in favor of a rational analysis that rests solely on policy and principle.

But looks can be deceiving. In characterizing "speech" as a "term of art," Sunstein implies that the concept has a specifically *legal* meaning defined by the underlying policies and purposes of the First Amendment. Yet, as Philip Bobbitt points out, the "concepts which occur in [c]onstitutional law must also occur and have a meaning in everyday life" for it is "the use of these concepts outside law . . . that makes their use in constitutional law meaningful." [78] In fact, there is no meaning to the concept "speech" that is not governed by the social understandings composed by the CONDUIT metaphor. Once again, Sunstein's own definition—in which "speech" is a "term of art" that "covers all symbols that are intended and received as messages"—is nothing more than a restatement of the CONDUIT metaphor. And, as we have seen, it does not explain why music, nonrepresentational art, or cases like *Hurley* should count as "speech."

Of course, the question whether parades, pornography, or works of art are "speech" is difficult only in the abstract. Law, as I argued in chapter 8, is contingent on larger social practices and forms of life. This was Llewellyn's precise point when he argued that the Constitution "is in the first instance a set of ways of living and doing." Post makes much the same point with respect to the First Amendment when he says that the constitutional values it serves "inhere not in speech as such, but rather in particular social practices" (1250). If today we find "in" the First Amendment such values as liberty, democracy, autonomy, tolerance, and self-expression, it is because those are the values that we enact in diverse and pervasive contemporary practices. "The basic relation," as Charles Taylor explains, "is that ideas articulate practices. . . . That is, the ideas frequently arise from attempts to formulate and bring to some conscious expression the underlying rationale of . . . [existing] pattern[s of behavior]."[79]

Post appears to be on the right track when he suggests that we replace the search for "general principles for the constitutional protection of 'speech as such'" (1279) with "the doctrinal category of 'media for the communication of ideas'" (1255). He takes a wrong turn, however, when he tries to explain why some communicative media—navigation charts, for example—do not merit First Amendment protection:

> Social conventions, to serve the values protected by the First Amendment, must do more than merely facilitate the communication of particularized messages. They must at a minimum also presuppose and embody a certain kind of relationship between speaker and audience. We might roughly describe that relationship as dialogic and independent. . . . Navigation charts do not receive First Amendment protection . . . because we interpret them as speaking monologically to their audience, as inviting their audience to assume a position of dependence and to rely on them. (1254)

But this cannot be right. The First Amendment protects the monological and demagogic no less than the democratic and dialogic. Indeed, Post's proffered rationale fails to explain why the St. Patrick's Day parade—more Dionysian than dialogic—should receive the solicitude of the First Amendment.

If Post falters here, it is because he has betrayed his own insight and slipped from description into prescription. With the introduction of "serve" and "must," Post passes into the normative mode that insists upon a "general principle for the constitutional protection of speech." Thus, he maintains that only those social practices that enact dialogic and independent relationships between speaker and audience are deserving of First Amendment protection. But in taking this position, Post inverts the relation between practices and values; as he himself says, "all legal values are rooted in the experiences associated with local and specific kinds of social practices" (1272).

Given the constitutive relationship between social practices and legal values it should be easy enough to see why pornography is "speech." Ours is a society that uses sex to sell *everything*: not just toothpaste and tabloids, but also Charles Dickens's *Great Expectations* "in which Gwyneth Paltrow can be seen wearing—surprise—no clothes." [80] In a culture with a voracious appetite for "news" of the president's dalliances—an obsession that dominated the halls of government no less than the headlines [81]—it is little wonder that sexually explicit material is seen as a subject of constitutional protection. Here, as elsewhere, law is epiphenomenal.

METAPHOR ON THE MOVE

The legal realists were harshly critical of metaphor because they equated it with the empty conceptualisms characteristic of legal formalism. In his famous article on fundamental legal conceptions, Wesley Newcomb Hohfeld complained: "Much of the difficulty, as regards legal terminology, arises from the fact that many of our words were originally applicable only to physical things; so that their use in connection with legal relations is, strictly speaking, figurative or fictional." [82] Felix Cohen saw metaphor as one form of the "transcendental nonsense" that afflicted legal reasoning. "When the vivid fictions and metaphors of traditional jurisprudence are thought of as reasons for decisions, rather than poetical or mnemonic devices . . . , then [one] . . . is apt to forget the social forces which mold the law." [83] On the bench, judges as distinguished as Benjamin Cardozo and Charles Evan Hughes warned against the distortions caused by metaphors in law. [84]

Consistent with these views, Hughes's landmark opinion in *NLRB v. Jones & Laughlin Steel Corp.* is generally understood as a rejection of the "stream of commerce" metaphor in favor of a realistic assessment of congressional power over commerce. But here, too, appearances are deceiving. Hughes in fact held a more nuanced view of legal metaphor that recognized its usefulness in appropriate cases. [85] A closer reading of Hughes's opinion in *Jones & Laughlin* shows him reworking rather than rejecting the "stream of commerce" metaphor. Without doubt, Hughes radically reorganized the cognitive model for interstate commerce issues. But, in doing so, he did not operate free-form. Rather, he worked with the metaphorical material already in the cases to refashion the doctrine in a manner that was simultaneously constrained and enabled by the very precedents he was rejecting.

Jones & Laughlin upheld the constitutionality of the National Labor Relations Act. The case marks a watershed in Commerce Clause analysis, reflecting a major shift in the legal/social consensus on the constitutional status of the regulatory programs of the New Deal. In the proceedings before it, the National Labor Relations Board found that the Jones & Laughlin company had coerced, intimidated, and discriminated against its employees in an effort to prevent unionization. As the case came to the Supreme Court, the primary question was jurisdictional: Could the federal government exercise its Commerce Clause power to regulate labor relations in manufacturing?

The drafters of the National Labor Relations Act had addressed that question with congressional findings expressed in section 2 of the act. They found that interference with the right to organize and to bargain collectively has

> the necessary effect of burdening or obstructing commerce by (a) impairing the efficiency, safety, or operation of the instrumentalities of commerce; (b) occurring in the *current* of commerce; (c) materially affecting, restraining, or controlling the *flow* of raw materials or manufactured or processed goods from or into the channels of commerce . . . ; or (d) causing diminution of employment and wages in such volume as substantially to impair or disrupt the market for goods *flowing* from or into the *channels* of commerce. . . .
>
> It is hereby declared to be the policy of the United States to eliminate the causes of certain substantial obstructions to the *free flow* of commerce . . . by encouraging the practice and procedure of collective bargaining.[86]

Obviously, the drafters made predominant (although not exclusive) use of fluid metaphors in expressing the applicability and relevance of Congress's Commerce Clause power to labor relations.

In contrast, the steel manufacturer made a rationalist, propositional argument that treated the distinction between manufacturing and commerce according to the rigors of the essentialist categorization of P or not-P. As Hughes observed: "The argument rests upon the proposition that manufacturing is not commerce" (34). This position was, as we shall see, rooted firmly in nineteenth-century precedent. This rationalist paradigm was also mirrored in the categorical approach to the federalism question taken by Justice McReynolds in dissent:

> One who produces or manufactures a commodity, subsequently sold and shipped by him in interstate commerce, . . . has engaged in two distinct and separate activities. So far as he produces or manufactures a commodity, his business is purely local. So far as he sells and ships . . . the

commodity to customers in another state, he engages in interstate commerce. In respect of the former, he is subject only to regulation by the state; in respect of the latter, to regulation only by the federal government. (79)

The use of the CONTAINER schema for categorization fit well with the geopolitical structure of federalism: since manufacturing "is purely local," it "is subject only to regulation by the state." Thus, everything had only a single essence: either commerce or manufacture; either federal or state; either P or not-P; either in the container (manufacturing = within state borders) or across its boundaries (commerce = federal power). The *Jones & Laughlin* dissent relied, as well, on the traditional distinction between "direct" and "indirect" effects on commerce,[87] a fuzzy distinction that it defended with an ironic quote from a previous Hughes opinion: "The precise line can be drawn only as individual cases arise, but the distinction is clear in principle" (96).*

Both the board and the solicitor general, on the other hand, stayed within the metaphorical paradigm of the statute as they argued in support of congressional power. In its opinion finding an unfair labor practice, the board invoked the conventional personification metaphor for a corporation and elaborated on its fluid entailment, held in common with the statute, by using a cardiovascular analogy.[88] As quoted in Hughes's opinion, the board had argued that the steel plant

> might be likened to the *heart* of a self-contained, highly integrated *body*. They draw in the raw materials from Michigan, Minnesota, West Virginia, Pennsylvania in part through *arteries* and by means controlled by the respondent; they transform the materials and then *pump them out* to all parts of the nation through the vast *mechanism* which the respondent has elaborated. (27; emphasis added)

Similarly, the solicitor's argument in defense of the board observed that the company's "activities constitute a 'stream' or 'flow' of commerce, of which the . . . manufacturing plant is the focal point" (35). The solicitor relied on such "stream of commerce" precedents as *Stafford v. Wallace,*[89] in which the "Court found that the stockyards were a 'throat' through which the cur-

---

* The notion of a "precise line" implicates rationalist assumptions about categorization. In contrast, the characterization of the distinction as only "clear in principle" can be taken to reflect the fact that "direct" and "indirect" are structured radially with relatively clear central cases and relatively indeterminate peripheries.

rent of commerce flowed and the transactions which there occurred could not be separated from that movement" (ibid.).

These quotes from Hughes's opinion, with the metaphors "stream," "flow," and "throat" in quotation marks, suggest Hughes's self-conscious stance toward metaphor. But Hughes was neither solicitous of the company's propositional arguments nor disdainful of the government's metaphors. His classic response instead elaborated and extended those metaphors:

> We do not find it necessary to determine whether these features of defendant's business dispose of the asserted analogy to the "stream of commerce" cases. The instances in which that metaphor has been used are but particular, and not exclusive, illustrations of the protective power which the government invokes in support of the present act. The congressional authority to protect interstate commerce from burdens and obstructions is not limited to transactions which can be deemed an essential part of the "flow" of interstate or foreign commerce. Burdens and obstructions may be due to injurious action springing from other sources. The fundamental principle is that the power to regulate commerce is the power to enact "all appropriate legislation" for its "protection and advancement" . . . "and it is primarily for Congress to consider and decide the fact of the danger and to meet it." (36–37)

The most common and obvious interpretation of this passage holds that Hughes dismissed the relevance of the "stream of commerce" metaphor and adopted, instead, a broader and more pragmatic view of Congress's power over commerce. But a more careful reading suggests otherwise. What Hughes rejected was the rationalist argument that distinguishes manufacturing and commerce. Thus, Hughes first declined the company's criterial —that is, feature-based—argument, finding it unnecessary "to determine whether these features of defendant's business dispose of the asserted analogy to the 'stream of commerce' cases." He then rejected the essentialism of the prior doctrine: Congress's authority, he remarked, "is not limited to transactions which can be deemed an *essential part* of the 'flow' of . . . commerce." Manufacturing may be different than commerce, Hughes seems to be saying, but that way of thinking about the question is simply beside the point.

Rather than rejecting the conventional "stream of commerce" metaphor, Hughes sliced through to its underlying conceptualization; he treated the metaphor as "but [a] particular, and not exclusive, illustration." *What* it illustrates is an underlying image-schema: The "stream of commerce" image is merely one metaphorical elaboration of the SOURCE-PATH-GOAL schema. Returning to that level of cognitive operation, Hughes elaborated other metaphorical entailments. Suppose commerce is conceptualized not as a stream but, in the government's metaphor, as "a great movement of iron ore, coal and limestone *along well-defined paths*" (34–35; emphasis added). If commerce is a movement along a path, it can be personified as a traveler. In that case, we would not want to slow it down by undue *burdens* or allow its progress to be impeded by *obstructions*. Most important of all, we would not want it to be waylaid by attacks from ambush by the side of the road—i.e., harms "due to *injurious action springing from other sources.*" And, at the very least, we would want to see that it got off to a safe start in its journey. As Hughes asked rhetorically: "Of what avail is it to protect the facilities of transportation, if interstate commerce is *throttled* with respect to the commodities to be transported!" (42; emphasis added).

By this point in his opinion, Hughes has thoroughly reorganized the conceptual model for the commerce power from one premised on a STREAM metaphor to one premised on the much richer JOURNEY metaphor. By reconceptualizing commerce in this way, Hughes was able to change the question in a way that structured a new constitutional answer. These different metaphors entail different conceptions of the federal role. If commerce is a stream, then Congress's job is to regulate the flow and keep it free of obstructions. If, however, commerce is a traveler on a journey, then it would be absurd to exclude from consideration matters outside the "flow" of commerce; it is precisely there that danger is most likely to lurk. The concern becomes not just obstructions but harms of all sorts—"throttling," "danger," "injurious action springing from other sources." The correlative congressional power shifts from "regulation" to "protection." Congress no longer monitors the sluice gates of commerce; it becomes the interstate police protecting the always vulnerable traveler. "The fundamental principle" is now that Congress is charged with the "protection and advancement" of commerce. "And it is primarily for Congress to consider . . . the danger and to meet it" (37).

This, however, did not quite get Hughes where he needed to go. As McReynolds pointed out in dissent, it is a long way from the discharge of a single union organizer to a significant danger to the advancement of commerce (99). Hughes responded by elaborating the metaphors he had been revising so subtly. Though he started with the *obstruction* entailment common to both the STREAM and JOURNEY metaphors, he elaborated the *danger* and *protection* entailments of the latter. "The fact remains that the *stoppage* of those [manufacturing] operations by *industrial strife* would have a most serious effect on interstate commerce" (41; emphasis added). Having thus invoked the local danger to the interstate journey, Hughes rejected the previous CONTAINER schema approach to federalism by focusing on the wide scope of the company's economic operations and the concomitant breadth of the danger that Congress might be called upon to meet:

> When industries organize themselves on a national scale, making their
> relation to interstate commerce the dominant factor in their activities,
> how can it be maintained that their industrial labor relations constitute a
> forbidden field into which Congress may not enter when it is necessary
> to protect interstate commerce from the paralyzing consequences of in-
> dustrial war? (ibid.)

Silently invoking a concept of balance, Hughes was able to assert persua-sively that the scope of congressional power must be commensurate with the national scope of the company's operation and its vulnerability to violent disruption. A threat to interstate commerce cannot hide behind state bor-ders; Congress must be empowered to reach where it must. How much more so when it is "war" that must be prevented? In the end, Hughes made his point not so much by a rigorous propositional argument from policy or principle as by a cognitive and metaphorical tour de force.

Still, for the argument to have been persuasive, something more was required. Without doubt, the social and political pressure on the Court to abandon its opposition to the New Deal—which reached a high-water mark with Roosevelt's infamous court-packing plan[90]—was a crucial factor. But the crisis caused by the Court's opposition to the New Deal did not occur in a vacuum. It was, in part, a reflection of decades of industrialization and change that had fueled a more general jurisprudential crisis. In his intellec-tual history of the period, Edward Purcell observes:

> The state of American law invited and even necessitated the devas-
> tating attacks of the realists. The inconsistencies between the practices of
> a rapidly changing industrial nation and the claims of a mechanical juris-
> tic system had grown so acute by the 1920s that, in the minds of many,
> the orthodox jurisprudence could no longer justify and explain contem-
> porary practice.[91]

Perhaps nowhere was this more clear than in Commerce Clause doctrine, which was in a state of advanced category breakdown.

The "stream of commerce" metaphor dates to Holmes's 1905 opinion in *Swift & Co. v. United States,* which used the phrase "currents of commerce."[92] Before the advent of the railroads, the streams referred to in Commerce Clause cases were quite literal. Thus, in 1824, Justice Marshall wrote:

> The commerce of the United States with foreign nations is that of the whole United States. Every district has a right to participate in it. The deep streams which penetrate our country in every direction pass through the interior of almost every State in the Union, and furnish the means of exerting this right.[93]

Even so, it would be another twenty-five years before the Court asserted admiralty jurisdiction over interior waterways above the tidewaters. As the Court subsequently explained: "From the organization of the government until the era of steamboat navigation, it is not strange that no question of this kind came before this court. The commerce carried on upon the inland waters prior to that time was so small, that cases were not likely to arise requiring the aid of admiralty courts."[94]

As long as transportation remained difficult, expensive, or slow—and prior to the development of refrigeration—one could identify what seemed like more or less local markets in which goods (especially perishables) were created, sold, and consumed without actually crossing state boundaries.* But the advent of the steamboat, the railroad, and the Industrial Revolution successively transformed American commerce. By the late nineteenth century, it was increasingly difficult to distinguish interstate commerce subject to regulation by the national government from those economic transactions that were strictly intrastate. As early as 1870, Justice Field remarked:

> We are unable to draw any clear and distinct line between the authority of Congress to regulate an agency employed in commerce between the States, when that agency extends through two or more States, and when it is confined in its action entirely within the limits of a single State.[95]

The increasing blurring of these lines spawned a series of tenuous distinctions. Early on, the Court distinguished manufacturing that was local from commerce that, when interstate, could be regulated by Congress.[96]

---

* Whether such markets were truly "local," rather than connected and economically interdependent, is open to question. The point, however, is that one could *conceive* of such local markets containing only local goods.

This distinction led to the argument in *United States v. E. C. Knight* that "an attempt to monopolize, or the actual monopoly of, the manufacture" of sugar was not an attempt "to monopolize commerce, even though, in order to dispose of the product, the instrumentality of commerce was necessarily invoked" (17). In *Swift*, Holmes skirted the absurdity of this argument by distinguishing cases where the effects on commerce are "accidental, secondary, remote or merely probable" from those where the effects on commerce are the "direct object," a "necessary consequence" or "primary end." In distinguishing a monopoly over sugar production from monopoly control over stockyards, Holmes conceded that the "two cases are near to each other, as sooner or later always must happen where lines are to be drawn." But he explained that they were nevertheless distinct because

> commerce among the states is not a technical legal conception, but a practical one, drawn from the course of business. When cattle are sent from a place in one State [to] another . . . with only the interruption necessary to find a purchaser at the stock yards, . . . the current thus existing is *a current of commerce* among the States, and the purchase of the cattle is a part and incident of such commerce.[97]

As we have seen, the drafters of the National Labor Relations Act used Holmes's metaphorical conception to justify the exercise of congressional power over commerce. The same stratagem was used in other New Deal statutes; but the Old Court was not persuaded. Rather, the Court used Holmes's metaphorical conception to distinguish goods passing through "the current or flow of interstate commerce" from those same goods once they had come to rest in "a place of final destination." In *Schechter Poultry*, for example, Hughes reasoned:

> The mere fact that there may be a constant flow of commodities into a State does not mean that the flow continues after the property has arrived and has become commingled with the mass of property within the State and is there held solely for local disposition and use. So far as the poultry here in question is concerned, the flow in interstate commerce had ceased. The poultry had come to a permanent rest within the State.[98]

The increasingly fragile nature of the Court's distinctions reflected the obvious difficulty of trying to adapt a nineteenth-century concept of federalism to a robust, industrialized, twentieth-century economy. Ultimately, the enterprise could not be sustained in the face of the radical changes in the relevant social practices. Thus, as noted in chapter 9, Levi observed that changes in the method of commerce made it hard to distinguish transactions "previously remote and local" from those more extensive and intertwined dealings that compose the modern interstate economy: "Since the difference could no longer be felt, it fell away."

Jones & Laughlin articulated that shift in a new conceptual model for congressional power over commerce. No longer the sluice gate operator who assures the regular flow in the channels of commerce, Congress became the interstate police for the market. The questions that engaged the Court in cases like *E. C. Knight* and *Schechter Poultry*—i.e., where the flow of commerce begins, where it ends—were no longer pertinent. Once the Court focused on the threat to interstate traffic arising from intrastate activity, the core question became how far "the reach" of Congress's "power extends." [99] The Court concluded that federal "control is essential . . . to the security of that traffic." [100] *Wickard v. Filburn,* [101] the avatar of modern Commerce Clause analysis, was the inevitable result. Quoting this passage from Hughes's 1914 opinion in *The Shreveport Rate Cases,* Justice Jackson in *Wickard* proclaimed "the Commerce Clause exemplified by this statement has made the mechanical application of legal formulas no longer feasible" (123–24). Categorical distinctions between "production" and "commerce" (119–20) no longer addressed the appropriate model. Thus, that discourse dropped from the constitutional lexicon, and a new model gave voice to the modern Commerce Clause. [102]

CHAPTER II

Within Reason

ON SEPTEMBER 17, 1997, Intel Corporation announced a development in microchip technology that led the *New York Times* to rhapsodize: "The world is no longer flat. Earth is no longer the center of the solar system." The new technology, called "multilevel flash memory," alters "the basic physics of chip design in a way that engineers and computer scientists once thought impossible." Henceforth, computers will be able to "store not one but two bits of information on each transistor, essentially doubling the storage capacity of even the most transistor-rich chip." Intel engineers "believe they have not reached the limits of this new technology and that in the future it may be possible to build chips that can store and retrieve three, four, or even more bits on each transistor." [1]

What made this breakthrough possible? As the *Times* reports it, the new technology "is actually based on a simple idea." Conventional computer memory is stored as a series of ones and zeros. To read the code, the machine determines whether a charge is present (a "one") or absent ("zero"). The new chips can also store a graded charge that can be read as one- or two-thirds. In this way, a single transistor can register four potential states or two bits of data. Not surprisingly, Intel engineers suggest that someday it might be possible to encode further gradations to yield yet more data per chip.

The point of this vignette, of course, is that there is a steep price to be paid for the primitive mode of thought that insists on seeing everything in P-or-not-P terms. Perhaps nowhere is this more true than in law. Judges and lawyers are forever drawing lines and then struggling to defend them against

the recalcitrance of a fluid world. Most jurists, ever confident in their rationalist faith, respond to the inevitable incoherence with some solemn
demurrer: "The precise line can be drawn only as individual cases arise,
but the distinction is clear in principle." This, as we saw in the last chapter,
was the beleaguered formalist response to the progressive disintegration of
nineteenth-century Commerce Clause doctrine. But the phenomenon spans
time and methodology. In reaffirming the "central holding" of *Roe v. Wade,*
the plurality in *Planned Parenthood v. Casey* explained: "Any judicial act of
line-drawing may seem somewhat arbitrary, but *Roe* was a reasoned statement, elaborated with great care." [2] More realist judges concede the problematic nature of the line-drawing exercise but respond with a plea of necessity. Thus, Holmes insisted that "it ultimately becomes necessary to draw
a line, and the determination of the precise place of that line in nice cases
always seems somewhat technical, but still the line must be drawn." [3]

Each of these reaffirmations is a left-handed way of acknowledging that
the line-drawing exercise is, in the end, futile. Regardless of the "technical
niceness" with which one draws the line, the cases on either side will inevitably lie so near one another that the line cannot help but appear arbitrary.[4] The law is constantly dividing the world into dichotomous categories—right and wrong, law and fact, substance and procedure—only to
equivocate once confronted with the complexity of real life. May one drive
at the posted speed limit? Not when the posted rate would be unreasonable
given road and weather conditions. Is it a felony to lie under oath? Only
when the falsehood is "material." [5] Is the question whether a confession
was made voluntarily a legal issue or a matter of fact? It is *neither;* rather it
is a "mixed question of law and fact" subject to plenary appellate review.[6]
A state statute authorizes appellate courts to reduce a damage award that
deviates materially from those in comparable cases. Is the statute substantive or procedural? It is *both:* The standard for reviewing the damage award
is substantive; the assignment of that function to the appellate court is procedural.[7] And so on, and so on, down the line.[8]

A sophisticated legal realist might respond that the law works tolerably
well using this stratagem of ostensibly rule-like (that is, P or not-P) categories that nevertheless operate flexibly in light of an interpolated standard or
qualification. But, as I argued in chapter 8, such second-best solutions in-
cur significant costs. The principal cost is to the public perception of law as
stable, predictable, and detached. The law purports to offer clear delineations of right and wrong, and it expects compliance. But legal decisionmakers cannot deliver on the promise of clear, rational categories. If they

draw hard-and-fast lines, the proximity of the borderline cases will make the law seem arbitrary. If, on the other hand, they soften the ostensibly clear line with a "safety valve" of some sort, then the resulting pattern of actual decisionmaking will vary from the stated rule in ways that look suspiciously ad hoc. One regularly sees the disillusionment in the faces of first-year law students who, as they are introduced to (and, often, overwhelmed by) the sheer complexity of standard legal argumentation, quickly (all too quickly) conclude that legal analysis is so malleable that judges can just do whatever they please. What in legal theory is a problem of indeterminacy is for the public a problem of legitimacy and for the profession a problem of cynicism.

Fortunately, there is a better way. The law may remain wedded to what Tom Grey calls "the habitual and institutional rigidities of binary thought." But the human brain is not so limited. In our everyday lives, we do a superior job of expressing precisely the kind of context-sensitive discriminations with which the law seems so unable to cope. We can do so because our brains, unlike our computers, are not digital. This is the profound—and, in a theoretical sense, radical—contribution of cognitive theory and the concepts of metaphor, radial categories, and idealized cognitive models. No longer limited to the naïve notion of a rule-structure, we now have a theoretical framework that enables us to take full advantage of the remarkably complex phenomena of ordinary human comprehension.

"The Artificial Reason of the Law"

Consider the contrast between our everyday understanding of the concept "lie" and the way in which the law applies the related idea of perjury. Although people typically *define* a lie as a false statement, empirical work by Linda Coleman and Paul Kay has shown that factual falsity is the least important of the three criteria that people actually use to identify statements as lies. Rather, a "consistent pattern was found: falsity of belief is the most important element in the prototype of lie, intended deception the next most important element, and factual falsity the least important." [9] Thus, if someone insists that Babe Ruth was right-handed or reports a rumor that turns out to be false, he will have perpetuated an untruth; but he will not have lied to you. Conversely, if someone lulls you into a false sense of security by assuring you of some fact she neither knows nor believes, you may reproach her for lying to you even if—in the event—her statement turns out to be true.

In a thoughtful paper, Eve Sweetser used the tools of cognitive linguistics and the general principles of Gricean pragmatics to explain the Coleman and Kay findings.[10] The concept "lie" is understood relative to two idealized cognitive models that reflect our default expectations concerning conversation and knowledge. The first ICM assumes that conversation normally involves an intention to be helpful—i.e., an intention to share necessary information with the listener. The second ICM recognizes that most of what we "know" is a matter of having adequate reasons for belief rather than firsthand knowledge.

A "lie" is a statement that violates the social expectations and understandings reflected in these models. Ordinarily, one is helpful if one conveys truthful information. Given the assumptions of the ICM of knowledge, truth entails belief (and, conversely, lack of belief entails falsity). Accordingly, the central social criterion that identifies a statement as a "lie" is not the fact that the speaker conveyed false information but the fact that the speaker did not believe his or her own statement. This is the key factor because, given the ICM of conversation, it is falsity of belief rather than factual falsity that entails a breach of the fundamental normative assumption of intention to be helpful. Coleman and Kay's finding that intention to deceive was more important than factual falsity in identifying a statement as a "lie" follows for the same reason: It is intention to deceive, and not factual falsity, that entails a breach of the fundamental normative assumption of intention to be helpful.

The concept "lie," in other words, is socially motivated; it is understood only in relation to social conditions in which the ICM of ordinary conversation is expected to apply. As such, it is context sensitive in a way that the standard, criterial definition—in which a "lie" is simply a false statement—could never be. In fact, ordinary spoken English has an extensive and rather precise vocabulary that recognizes the differences among a broad array of false statements: "social lies," "white lies," "fibs," "fantasies," "fiction," "jokes," "tall tales," "exaggerations," "oversimplifications," and "mistakes."

Each of these expressions reflects a different social frame of reference for the evaluation of a false statement. Terms such as "joke," "tall tale," and "fiction" indicate that the informational condition of the ICM of conversation is not operative. In these cases, the speaker and listener are operating within a frame that assumes other purposes for the communication—humor or entertainment, for example. Similarly, the term "social lie"—e.g., telling the host it was a lovely party when, in fact, it was a dud—assumes a frame of communication in which politeness is more helpful than information. "White lie" and "fib" assume a frame in which the informational condition is generally applicable but the information being conveyed is of no particular importance. Terms such as "fantasy," "exaggeration," and "mistake" (as well as the hedge "for all I know") assume that the ICM of conversation is operative but the ICM of knowledge is not fully met. The speaker's belief may be deluded, overblown, or simply mistaken; in any event, the listener does not depend on it for "truth." A term like "oversimplification," or a hedge like "to the best of my knowledge," assumes that the ICM of knowledge is operative but that the acceptable "truth" conditions have been altered as specified.

Thus, the concept "lie" is the central case of the broader, radial category "false statements"—as represented in figure 11.1. A prototypical lie is defined relative to the ICMs for conversation and knowledge. When these idealized assumptions hold of the real-life situation, any false statement will *be* a lie because (within the ICM of knowledge) factual falsity entails falsity

FIGURE 11.1   "Lie" as a Radial Category

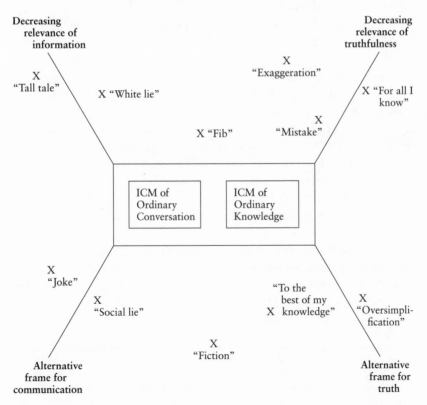

of belief and (within the ICM of conversation) falsity of belief entails intent to deceive.* The extensions represent false statements that occur in alternative motivational frameworks where all of these idealized assumptions do not hold. As indicated in the diagram, these extensions are distributed around the core along the axes that mark out the social condition that is inapplicable in a given situation.

To the skeptic, the profusion of subcategories should itself be a source of indeterminacy. Empirically, however, that is not the case. Coleman and Kay found that "subjects fairly easily and reliably assign the word *lie* to reported speech acts in a more-or-less, rather than an all-or-none fashion" and that they "agree fairly generally on the relative weights of the elements" (43). This is exactly the finding we would expect, given that "lie" and its subcases are socially motivated. These concepts, in other words, are not mere classifications subject to endless manipulation for instrumental purposes; rather, they are social categorizations grounded in the pragmatics of everyday communication in our culture.[11] Not only do these concepts embody an entire infrastructure of social experience and knowledge, but they represent a highly nuanced set of *normative* assessments of the ethics of each of these varied speech acts.[12]

Though the law of perjury starts from these same values and assumptions, it quickly goes awry. The federal perjury statute, §1621, provides: "Whoever, having taken an oath before a competent tribunal, officer, or person . . . willfully and contrary to such oath states or subscribes any material matter which he does not believe to be true, is guilty of perjury." Consistent with the ICM of knowledge, the statute focuses on falsity of belief rather than on factual falsity as the central element of the offense. Similarly, the statute's "materiality" standard recognizes (though in a rather more indefinite way than the radial category "lie") that the moral culpability of a falsehood is highly relative to context: Making a parenthetical statement one does not believe, or doing so with respect to a collateral matter, does not breach the fundamental normative expectation of helpfulness in providing information. Given the apparent congruence between the statute and our ordinary understanding of "lie," a person might be forgiven if he or she thought that the statute made it a crime intentionally to deceive the tribunal

---

* These entailments explain why people define "lie" as a false statement even though factual falsity is the least determinative criterion. When these entailments hold, a false statement is, by definition, a statement that is not believed and that is said with intent to deceive. The conventional definition is, thus, a metonym for the more complex social understandings that compose the concept "lie."

before which one was testifying—i.e., to "willfully . . . state[] any material matter which he does not believe to be true."

This, at least, was how perjury statute was read by the lower courts in *Bronston v. United States*.[13] Bronston was the sole proprietor of a business seeking relief from its creditors under Chapter 11 of the Bankruptcy Act. During that proceeding, counsel for one of those creditors asked Bronston whether he had any accounts in Swiss banks. Bronston responded that he did not. The lawyer then asked if he had ever had any such accounts, to which Bronston replied: "The company had an account there for about six months, in Zurich." In fact, Bronston also had a personal bank account in Geneva for five years during which he deposited and withdrew more than $180,000. At Bronston's subsequent perjury trial, the judge instructed the jury that the issue was whether Bronston "spoke his true belief," that he could not be convicted if he merely failed to understand the question, and that his answer should be "considered in the context in which it was given." The court of appeals affirmed the conviction, reasoning that Bronston had committed perjury because he had intentionally given "an answer containing half of the truth . . . in place of the responsive answer called for by a proper question" (354–56).

A unanimous Supreme Court reversed. It reasoned that the statute is not violated "so long as the witness speaks the literal truth" (360). The Court acknowledged that there "is, indeed, an implication in the answer to the second question that there was never a personal bank account; in casual conversation this interpretation might reasonably be drawn" (358). As ably explained at a later point in the opinion:

> Arguably, the questioner will assume there is some logical justification
> for the unresponsive answer, since competent witnesses do not usually
> answer in irrelevancies. Thus the questioner may conclude that the unre-
> sponsive answer is given only because it is intended to make a state-
> ment—a negative statement—relevant to the question asked. (362 n.5)

Indeed, the Court conceded that "only this unspoken denial would provide a logical nexus between inquiry directed to petitioner's personal account and petitioner's adverting, in response, to the company account in Zurich" (ibid.). Nevertheless, the Court concluded that Bronston had not violated the statute. "At the outset," the Court noted, there was "a serious literal problem" (357) in applying the statute because Bronston had not stated anything he did not believe to be true. The Court insisted "that the perjury statute is not to be loosely construed" (360). It explicitly rejected the jury's finding that Bronston had intended to mislead, arguing that the witness's state of mind is "relevant only to the extent that it bears on whether 'he does not believe [his answer] to be true.'" Finally, the Court put the burden on trial counsel to guard against deception by proper cross-examination: "If a witness evades, it is the lawyer's responsibility to recognize the evasion and to bring the witness back to the mark" (358–59).

Bronston is, in many ways, a curious decision. For one thing, the Court's reliance on the benefits of cross-examination proves either too much or too little. One could say just as well that it is the lawyer's responsibility to recognize a false statement and to expose it via cross-examination. After all, the Court never tires of quoting Dean Wigmore's dictum that cross-examination is "beyond any doubt the greatest legal engine ever invented for the discovery of truth." [14] As Justice Stevens observed recently in dissent: "Even if one does not completely agree with Wigmore's assertion, . . . one must admit that in the Anglo-American legal system cross-examination is the principal means of undermining the credibility of a witness whose testimony is false or inaccurate." [15] At the same time, the argument proves too little: It is true that, ex ante, counsel can always pin down an unresponsive witness by asking the next question. But this is scant comfort in a noncriminal case like *Bronston,* where the government could not have cross-examined because it was not a party. In such cases, the government can act only after-the-fact to punish a fraud on its courts that it was otherwise powerless to prevent. To say at that stage that some other lawyer should have conducted a better cross-examination is to shut the barn door only after the horse has fled.*

More peculiar still is the Court's reliance on literal meaning. The Court insisted upon the literal meaning both of the statute and of Bronston's trial

---

* Consider, too, what the Court's rule means in operation: When the witness is intent on deception, asking the next question will only elicit a further (albeit more direct) falsehood. When the question does not lead to additional falsehood, it will be in large part because the witness is not willing to commit perjury and risk prosecution. But, in that event, the lower courts' rule would produce the same result more efficiently by deterring the deception in the first instance. The Court's rule will still produce different results in two cases: (1) It protects the witness who honestly misapprehends the initial question. If there is a follow-up question, the witness will cure the error; if not, there can be no prosecution under *Bronston.* But note that under the rule applied by the lower courts, the witness could always defend by pleading honest mistake. Thus, the Court's rule makes a difference to the extent that prosecutors will proceed with weak evidence of intent to deceive and that juries will erroneously convict notwithstanding the reasonable doubt standard. (2) The Court's rule will also make a difference when the witness is not willing to utter an outright falsehood but is willing to deceive with a technical but substantively misleading truth. Exactly why one should care about such people is unclear. But the case—along with the *Dive* case discussed in chapter 7—ably illustrates how formalism serves as refuge for the scoundrel.

testimony. Yet the Court's own conclusion—that the statute does not apply "so long as the witness speaks the literal truth"—is no less a departure from the statute's literal terms: Factual falsity is not an element of the offense under §1621, which makes it a crime for a witness to "willfully . . . state[] any material matter which he does not believe to be true." A "literal" reading of the statute would mean that a witness could be prosecuted for speaking "the literal truth" so long as he harbored the subjective (though mistaken) belief that his testimony was false.[16]

These peculiarities suggest that *Bronston* cannot be taken at face value. Although the opinion is preoccupied with literal meaning, it actually stands as telling evidence against that very idea. Meaning is not a matter of words but of minds. When a court reads a statute, it can find meaning "in" it only in relation to a set of understandings and assumptions—that is, relative to an ICM. The lower courts in *Bronston* read the statute in light of the social concept of a "lie." Similarly, they understood Bronston's testimony in relation to the pragmatics of ordinary conversation—in which people do not usually answer in irrelevancies but generally respond with no more information than is necessary to be helpful.* The Supreme Court, in contrast, read the statute against the assumptions of the crude rationalism that holds sway over much of the legal system. Insisting that the perjury statute is not to be loosely construed, the Court reached for the presumed certainty and objectivity of a criterial definition: A statement is perjury if and only if it is literally untrue. Similarly, the Court understood Bronston's testimony in reductive P-or-not-P terms: The statement was either true or false, not according to how an ordinary person would understand the statement—presumedly, that would be "subjective"—but according to whether it conformed to discernible, objective criteria.

In adopting factual falsity as the sine qua non of perjury, the Court focused on the least determinative of the three criteria that people ordinarily use to identify statements as lies. Doubtless, the Court did not mean this to be the exclusive criterion. An exclusive focus on factual falsity not only would be at odds with the statutory language, but also would yield perverse results: Testimony that was merely mistaken would be subject to prosecution for perjury. A more reasonable reading of the Court's decision is that perjury involves factual falsity in addition to the statute's express requirement of falsity of belief. Understood this way, the *Bronston* ruling represents a reduction-to-prototype effect in which the Court insisted that to commit

* This is Grice's maxim of quantity. For example, consider the following exchange: "How did you two manage to get away for an entire weekend?" "My Mom's in town."

perjury a witness must tell a *prototypical* lie—i.e., one in which all three conditions (falsity of belief, intent to deceive, *and* factual falsity) are met.

In chapter 8, we saw how Hart and Schauer were misled by the phenomenon of prototype effects: The psychological salience and stability of the prototypical case led them to think that meaning is largely autonomous of purpose and, therefore, that rules could work in the relatively mechanical manner supposed by the conventional model. But this view proved illusory because prototype effects are simply products of the tacit knowledge of context and purpose that is intrinsic to categorization and meaning. The prototypical cases, moreover, are by definition only a subset of the array of cases comprehended by any radial category employed in a rule. We use tacit knowledge of the social motivation for the rule to make contextual judgments about the remaining category members—ascertaining which to include and which to exclude from the rule's purview. Prototype effects, in other words, work better as touchstones for inclusion than as rules of exclusion. Standing alone, the fact that a car is certainly a "vehicle" covered by the rule prohibiting vehicles in the park tells us little about how we should handle a bicycle, a moped, or a child's electric automobile. To make those assessments, we need both to understand the social motivation for the rule and to apply it in light of those purposes.

In a similar way, the apparent clarity of the prototypical case misled the *Bronston* majority into thinking that it had articulated a certain and stable line. But, in point of fact, the Court's reduction-to-prototype effect bleaches out the context-sensitive discriminations and nuanced normative assessments that provide the substance of our everyday concept of a "lie." The result is an incoherent line that cannot meaningfully distinguish between the cases. Consider, for example, a variation on *Bronston* in which Hedges is testifying about his assets at his bankruptcy proceeding. Hedges, who has a $100,000 in a Swiss bank account, discloses the existence of that account. The following colloquy ensues:

> Q: "How much do you have in the Swiss account?
> A: "There is $25,000 in it."

On the Court's rationale, Hedges should not be subject to a prosecution for perjury because he would have spoken "the literal truth." (After all, there *is* $25,000 in the account.) If that seems absurd (and it should), it is because we understand the response in context as a statement that there is *no more than* $25,000 in the account. As such, Hedges's reply is a deliberate misrepresentation.

It seemed that way to the Court, too. Despite its insistence on "literal" truth, the Court rejected a similar hypothetical that had been posed by the district court: "It is very doubtful that an answer which, in response to a specific quantitative inquiry, baldly understates a numerical fact can be described as even 'technically true'" (356). But it is hard to see how the Court could justify this assertion. An answer that deliberately understates an amount is still true as far as it goes. Indeed, one could just as well say that Bronston understated a numerical fact: Just as Hedges merely failed to mention that there was another $75,000, Bronston merely failed to mention that he had a second Swiss account.

Though we understand Hedges's testimony as a statement that there is no more than $25,000 in the account, this is not because of anything he actually *said*. (To make the point clear, consider a contrasting case in which the witness testified that "the *balance* is $25,000.") Our understanding of Hedges's testimony is, rather, solely a matter of *implication:* "The overt statement and the false statement are," as Sweetser explains, "linked by Gricean conversational implicature; the utterance is irrelevant or *insufficient in context,* unless the hearer also assumes the unspoken falsehood" (61; emphasis added). The understatement case may seem different, but only because the misleading statement is (as the Court inadvertently points out) made "in response to a specific quantitative inquiry." In both cases, it is the insufficiency of the answer *in context*—and not its lack of "literal" or "technical" truth—that makes the statement misleading. There is no escaping the fact that Hedges's misleading statement is structured in precisely the way the Court deemed unacceptable in *Bronston:* In both cases, the witness's statement is "untrue only by 'negative implication'" (361).

This is not to say that these cases are the same, only that their differences cannot be explained in the Court's terms of "literal" or "technical" truth. The intuition that there is a difference between the cases arises solely from the set of social understandings characterized by Grice's conversational pragmatics. Though in both cases the statement is false by implication, the perceived strength of the implication increases as the distance between the question and response diminishes: The closer one gets to the direct object of the question, the stronger the negative implication.* In Hedges's

---

* Suppose, for example, I ask you whether you have read the report I sent you. In case 1, you answer: "Don't worry, I got it." In case 2, you say: "You know, I've been reading reports all day." In case 3, you respond: "Great piece of work!" In none of these cases do you actually claim to have read the report. But, in each successive case, the implication that you did gets a little stronger. In cases 1 and 2, the response suggests that you *might* have read the report. (In case 2, contextual factors such as intonation or a rolling of the

case, the implicature arises from an answer that is both on point and sufficient on its face (if only it were accurate); in Bronston's case, the implicature arises from an answer that addresses the general issue but is nonetheless unresponsive to the precise question asked.*

The Court's reductive, line-drawing apparatus is hopelessly inadequate to such cases precisely because it eschews the social understandings that enable such context-sensitive discriminations. Worse yet, insistence on the putatively more "exact" line of technical truth produces precisely those anomalies that make the law appear arbitrary and unpredictable. On the Court's reasoning, the outcome in a case like *Bronston* will vary dramatically, depending upon the most minimal changes in the wording of the question:

Case 1:   Q: Do you have *many* Swiss accounts?
           A: My company has one. (Perjury)

Case 2:   Q: Do you have *a* Swiss bank account?
           A: My company has one. (Not perjury)

Moreover, just as the test of technical truth cannot draw any rational or coherent distinction between Bronston and Hedges, it would generate an endless set of paired cases yielding diametrically opposite results on virtually indistinguishable facts. Consider some further variations on these cases:

Case 3:   Q: Did you ever have a Swiss bank account?
           A_1: No, my company had one. (Perjury)
           A_2: My company had one. (Not perjury)

---

eyes could mark it as either an affirmative or a negative statement.) In case 3, on the other hand, one is likely to infer that you did in fact read the report.

* Hedges's answer is different in that it "contains nothing to alert the questioner that he may be sidetracked" (356). But this will be true of many "literally" true statements. Tiersma gives the example of a person who, when asked why he failed to come to work the previous day, replies "I was sick" even though he went fishing, drank to excess, and only then became sick (392). As in *Bronston*, the statement is "literally" true, but false by implication; yet it provides no indication that the questioner needs to clarify the response with a follow-up. Moreover, the point about alerting the questioner to ask a clarifying question is too easily overstated. As *Bronston* points out, the context itself will often alert the questioner to the possibility of deception: "It should come as no surprise that a participant in a bankruptcy proceeding may have something to conceal and consciously tries to do so. . . . It is the responsibility of the lawyer to probe; testimonial interrogation, and cross-examination in particular, is a probing, prying, pressing form of inquiry" (356). In the Hedges hypothetical, the careful lawyer could probe (or avoid the problem in the first place) by asking a more precise question, such as: "What is the current balance?"

Case 4:   Q: How much do you have in the Swiss account?
A_1: $25,000. (Perjury)
A_2: At least $25,000. (Not perjury)

The problem here is not simply that in social conversation all these cases would be equally misleading. Rather, it is hard to see why a legal system would want to distinguish between them.

One might abide such absurd results if the statutory language left no choice. But that is not the case. For one thing, nothing in the statute even suggests that the line be drawn at "literal" truth; for another, a sensible, more coherent reading of the statute is readily available.

The statute defines perjury as a willful statement on a material matter that the witness does not believe to be true. The Court treated the term "statement" reductively, taking it to refer to the literal words spoken. But, if meaning is in the mind rather than in the words, then a "statement" is any speech act that is understood as such. In other areas, for example, the law recognizes as statements both acts and omissions. Thus, as we saw in the last chapter, expressive conduct can be "speech" protected by the First Amendment. Similarly, the Fifth Amendment privilege not to be compelled to testify against oneself extends to the act of producing documents in response to a subpoena when that act of production has "communicative" or "testimonial aspects"—for example, when it would constitute an admission that the documents exist, that they are in the person's possession, or that he or she was aware of their contents.[17] And under federal criminal statutes governing the submission of information to the government, the failure to fill in a blank space on a form requiring disclosure of information (such as income or employment) has been held to constitute a "false statement" in violation of the act.[18]

If it still seems odd to characterize an implied falsehood as a "statement," consider the fact that the Court characterized Bronston's testimony in just this way: It specifically noted that it would be reasonable for the questioner to conclude "that the unresponsive answer is given only because it is *intended to make a statement*—a negative statement—relevant to the question asked" (362 n.5; emphasis added). Thus, a better reading of the statute would simply incorporate our everyday understanding of what it means to state something (in this case, something one does not believe to be true). In ordinary conversation, people make statements by implication and are readily understood as having done so. ("How did you two manage to get away for an entire weekend?" "My Mom's in town.") Witnesses, after all, are people too; they do not leave their ordinary communication skills behind when they take the stand.

By the same token, neither prosecutors nor jurors check their social understandings at the courtroom door. In the twenty-five years since *Bronston*, local U.S. Attorneys have continued to prosecute such cases and juries have continued to convict, only to be reversed on appeal.[19] By itself, the fact that both prosecutors and jurors persist in treating such deceptive statements as perjury despite the Court's contrary ruling is telling evidence that something is amiss. But consider what this divergence between social norm and legal rule means in practice. In *United States v. Earp*,[20] for example, the defendant Billy Carrigan stood guard with a shotgun while his fellow Klan members attempted to burn a cross on the front lawn of an interracial couple. Questioned about the incident before a grand jury, Carrigan said that he "didn't believe" in cross burnings and stated flatly: "I don't burn crosses anywhere." Carrigan subsequently told an FBI agent that he had lied to the grand jury. The agent so testified at trial, and Carrigan was convicted. The court of appeals then reversed under *Bronston* on the theory that since the Klansmen had trouble lighting the cross and fled when the victim came to the door, Carrigan's statement was literally true.*

Bronston is but a recent example of an age-old conflict that received its classic articulation in Chief Justice Edward Coke's 1612 response to King James:

> Then the King said, that he thought the law was founded upon reason, and that he and others had reason, as well as the Judges: to which it was answered by me, that true it was, that God had endowed His Majesty with excellent science, and great endowments of nature; but His Majesty was not learned in the laws of his realm of England, and causes which concern the life . . . or fortunes of his subjects are not to be decided by natural reason but by the artificial reason and judgment of law, which law is an act which requires long study and experience.[21]

Today, the claim of special legal expertise typically privileges some form of rationalism. Bruce Ackerman, for example, champions the virtues of "scientific policymaking" over the unsystematic and imprecise verities of the "ordinary observer." He advocates a form of legal policymaking that is

---

* Of course, the statement would also have been literally true if Carrigan's associates had managed to ignite the cross, since Carrigan was only the lookout, so to speak.

"scientific" in two senses: first, insofar as it implements a "comprehensive view" of the abstract ideals that the legal system is intended to serve; and, second, insofar as it does so by employing "technical concepts whose meanings are set in relation to one another by clear definitions without continuing reliance upon the way similar sounding concepts are deployed in non-legal talk." [22] In his most recent book, Roberto Unger observes that this "policy-oriented and principle-based style of legal analysis," which views the law as "a purposive social enterprise that reaches toward comprehensive schemes of welfare and right," has "achieved canonical status in professional and academic culture." Unger identifies this more general form of legal discourse, which he calls "rationalizing legal analysis," as the principal heir to Langdell's dream of a "legal science." [23]

Bronston shares with this mode of legal thought both a disdain for the insight of ordinary common sense and a conviction—actually, a naïve belief—that the law can and should impose a rationalistic "precision" upon the messy realities of social life. The irony is that rationalism repeatedly proves inadequate to the task. Faced with the complexities of social life, rationalism's crude tools are no match for the more subtle instrument of ordinary common sense. *Bronston* stands as a caution that the "artificial reason of the law" conduces to artificial lines. It is not just that, as Holmes promised, the determination of the precise line in "nice" cases will always seem abstruse in its technicality. It is rather that, given the mismatch between rationalism and life, those lines will be wholly arbitrary.

LAW AS PERSUASION

For much of the past century, legal theory has been preoccupied with the problem of meaningful constraints on judicial decisionmaking and the consequent danger of unchecked subjectivity. The fear, conventionally identified with the Supreme Court's infamous *Lochner* decision, is that without constraints judges and other powerful legal actors will be free to impose their personal values. [24] The argument of this book has been that this conventional concern is exaggerated, a consequence of the rationalist assumptions that undergird standard legal analysis. Just as objectivism (specifically, a correspondence view of meaning) introduces the problem of skepticism (How do we know that our perceptions accurately "reflect" the external world and that we are not, as Putnam playfully speculates, [25] just brains in a vat fed input by a giant computer?), rationalism (more precisely, the subject-object dichotomy) creates the problem of indeterminacy: If decisionmaking is not constrained by the objective logic of the law, then it follows that judges will be free to decide subjectively according to their personal desires, politics, or value preferences. After all, without the constraint of a rationalizing principle or some set of necessary and sufficient criteria, any two cases can be made to seem alike (or different)—and in innumerable ways.

This conventional schema defines not only the mainstream, but also the critics who contest the viability of meaningful constraints and affirm that adjudication *is* political. Yet, the entire debate rests on several related category mistakes. The fear that judges will impose their "personal" values confuses social construction with solipsism; the search for formal constraints confounds constraint with determinacy; and the effort to locate constraint *in* the law—or in some similarly rationalistic endeavor such as constitutional history (originalism), political theory, or moral philosophy—draws a false if not impossible line between the legal and the social. Ultimately, each of these errors derives from the P-or-not-P reasoning characteristic of rationalism. Once we clear away these conceptual entanglements, the way will be open for a more realistic appraisal of the constraints under which judges (and other lawmakers) operate. The resulting view, first presented in chapter 6, is the position I call "law as persuasion."

In his book *Critique of Adjudication*,[26] Duncan Kennedy argues that lawmaking by adjudication is characterized by the denial of the ideological nature of judging. This denial, he claims, has distinctive political consequences, which he identifies as the moderation, empowerment, and legitimation effects. This denial arises, Kennedy explains, as a defense against judicial anxiety: Judges (at least many of them) are caught in a genuine role conflict. They are expected to decide cases according to law—to the exclusion of ideology or their own policy preferences; in the familiar formula, judges should apply the law and not make it. At the same time, however, judges (at least many of them) realize that both legal reasoning and the materials with which they work are actually quite plastic:

> First, they are very much aware that their task is to decide "questions of law," meaning questions of rule definition, and that these are questions of interpretation, rather than of application of rules to disputed facts. Second, they are very much aware that "the law" as it appears at the end of the decision process is a function of the work they do on the legal materials, and that different work strategies are likely to produce different law—that is, different legal rules—with no intralegal criteria available to indicate which work strategy is correct. (203)

The inability to resolve this conflict provokes the psychological defense of denial. The rest of us (the audience) are complicit in this denial. We, too, are invested in the conventional picture of the judge as standing above politics, though we fear that this may be impossible.

Kennedy's argument presupposes that the law is indeterminate—at least to some degree. Yet, he has moderated his position on this score. He does not maintain that legal doctrine is always indeterminate. Rather, he affirms that judges committed to the ideal of interpretive fidelity will often experience themselves as constrained by the text and by the reactions they expect from others: "What a given judge will do in a case depends on what she thinks will 'fly' as 'good legal argument' in the minds of others, as well as on what she herself thinks about the matter" (161). Kennedy also affirms that judges sometimes reach a point of "closure" at which they are reasonably certain both that they have reached the right result and that no additional analysis would change the outcome. But this closure, Kennedy says, does not prove that the law in that case was determinate: "That everyone unselfconsciously adopted a view, or no one objected, isn't evidence that the outcome was determinate in any sense we are interested in" (170).

The reason this experience of closure does not prove that the law was determinate, Kennedy explains, is

> that there are gaps, conflicts, and ambiguities, that these are a function of legal work as well as of the materials the judge works with, that the experience of "freedom" to shape the legal field is common, and that one cannot say with certainty that when closure occurs it is a product or property of the field rather than of the work strategy adopted under particular circumstances. (396 n.2)

Indeed, Kennedy goes further: He says that the very question whether a particular legal issue has a determinate answer is

> meaningless if it is a question about *the question of law,* rather than a question about the interaction between a particular, situated historical actor and this particular question of law situated in this particular field. Because determinacy is a complex function of work as well as of facts and materials, a function of an interaction, it makes no sense to predicate determinacy or indeterminacy of the question as it exists independently of the particular actor who is trying to answer it. (170; emphasis added)

From even this brief summary, it should be apparent that Kennedy's argument is structured according to the conventional, polarized schema. The giveaway is his remark that even complete agreement on a legal issue would provide no evidence that the outcome was determinate *in any sense we are interested in.* What sense would that be? Presumedly, it would have to be a sense in which *the law itself*—that is, independent of any particular actor—determined the answer (though he has already pronounced that inquiry meaningless). In fact, that is precisely what Kennedy means.* When he describes the judge's anxiety over the fact that different work strategies may produce different legal rules, Kennedy says that the problem arises because there are no *intralegal criteria* that govern the choice between rules. When Kennedy discusses legal education, he observes that "the student learns no *metadiscourse* that permits necessitarian choice between necessitarian discourses" (366; emphasis added). When he acknowledges that the expected reactions of others act as a constraint on the judge, he pronounces it "a peculiar kind of constraint, because the judge is a participant and can affect the community's reaction to the interpretation in question, rather than having simply to register it *as an immovable, external fact*" (161; emphasis added). Finally, when Kennedy acknowledges but then discounts the judges' experience of closure as evidence of determinacy, he maintains that those experiences provide no warrant to think that they "are 'reflections' of an external reality, or truth of the matter, that exist independently of their own efforts" (170).

In other words, constraint only counts as constraint if it is an independent, objective property of the materials themselves, like the physical obstruction of the trees that impede my movement through the forest of law. As soon as one introduces the subjectivity of a human actor, it becomes a "peculiar" constraint because the judge is now a participant who may affect the outcome in untold ways. Once one introduces subjectivity, "it makes no sense to predicate determinacy or indeterminacy of the question as it exists independently of *the particular actor who is trying to answer it.*"

---

* He describes deduction as "the paradigm case of constraint or determinacy or legal necessity" (164). One might have thought this was just internal critique. But Kennedy devotes an earlier passage to the rehabilitation of deductive reasoning in law; he maintains both that a "good part of legal reasoning is deductive" (101) and that the legal realist critique of formalism was not a critique of deduction per se, but of a systematic tendency to overestimate the power of deduction (103–7). (But read Dewey, Holmes, or Llewellyn *op. cit.*) According to Kennedy, the realists merely criticized specific deductions as unwarranted.

Kennedy not only reifies the subject-object dichotomy in this thoroughly conventional way, but also explicitly eschews any analysis of the social factors that might stabilize meaning. "My approach," he explains, "neither answers nor rejects, but rather defers or brackets, the question of what, if anything, lies behind ('in' the legal materials) the experiences of openness and closure. . . . We can explore the 'surface,' rather than trying to penetrate the depths" (171). But what if we did not confine ourselves to the surface? What if we were to ask what lies beneath those experiences of openness and closure? What if we were to take seriously the notion that the relative determinacy of law is, to paraphrase Kennedy, a question about the interaction between particular, situated historical actors and particular questions of law situated in particular social fields? The answer is that, if we did, we would get something like the argument of this book.

Kennedy's earlier work conceptualizing judicial decisionmaking as work-in-a-field represented a significant advance over previous accounts—both formalist accounts of decision-according-to-rule and critical legal studies accounts of law-as-politics. In that article, he provided a typology of six typical field configurations to describe the different ways in which judges experience their work with the legal materials relevant to a given case.[27] But, despite its insight, that effort came up short in two ways. First, the lessons it drew were overly simplistic. The mere fact that decisions are not determinate as suggested by the model of deduction tells us nothing important about whether the decisions are sufficiently regular and predictable to do the work we expect of law. Second, Kennedy concluded (as he does, again, in the subsequent book) that there is no way to predict when a body of precedent will yield one particular field structure as opposed to another. Consistent with his argument about the effects of different work strategies, Kennedy maintained that there is no way to know that one didn't miss "the catch that releases the secret panel" that would have led to a different outcome (561). Yet, these skeptical conclusions are not supported by argument—neither in his earlier article nor in his subsequent book. Moreover, as this book has shown, these skeptical conclusions are inconsistent with much of what we know about human reasoning.

Although I have taken issue with Kennedy's account, I have also been building on it. At the outset, I observed that law is a product of human minds and suggested that our understanding of law could be improved through an analysis informed by recent developments in the study of the mind. This book can therefore be read as addressing the question of how our understanding of law changes once we take seriously the insight (common to

Holmes, Llewellyn, Posner, and Kennedy) that law is something that judges do. We have looked at how human reasoning works and then traced precisely those cognitive processes via case studies of actual judges' minds (including, in chapter 10, some of our greatest judges' minds) at work. What we have found is that because law is a product of human minds, it displays all the regularities both of structure and of context-dependence predicted by cognitive theory. We have found, moreover, that the indeterminacy of the standard legal materials (upon which Kennedy's account trades so heavily) *is* very much a surface phenomenon. It is the product of a deracinated rationality that, as we saw in *Bronston,* brackets precisely those social understandings that constitute meaning and make communication work. Most importantly, we have seen that judges (and other lawmakers) nevertheless operate under significant constraints for three, closely intertwined reasons. By way of summary, I discuss them in ascending order of importance under the rubrics of *cognition, categorization,* and *persuasion.*

1. *Cognition.* The one thing judges cannot bracket is the vital elements of their own thought processes. No matter how distorting the surface rhetoric of the law, judges' brains work just like yours and mine. Consequently, their thought processes will reproduce all the regularities of radial categories, prototype effects, compositional structure, motivation, framing and other gestalt processes. Thus, the *Bronston* Court articulates a rule of literal truth or falsity but instead produces a series of judgments—such as its insistence on a prototypical lie and its claim that a response like Hedges's is not even "technically true"—more consistent with our ordinary social understandings than with the Court's rationalist rule. So, too, the justices in the right-to-counsel cases (discussed in chapter 6) insist on abstracting a principle to govern decision in the case before them, but the actual pattern of their decisionmaking produces a radial category structured in terms of a more complex, culturally grounded model. This model is, as the dissenters found, recalcitrant to pure political manipulation. At the same time, however, it also creates opportunities or "forensic space" for strategically motivated judicial action.

2. *Categorization.* Judges are, as Kennedy suggests, situated historical actors grappling with legal questions in a particular historical field. Kennedy implies that because legal decisions are a function of this complex interaction, they are somehow unreliable or subjective. But just the opposite is true: To paraphrase Merleau-Ponty (quoted in chapter 5), it is because of our historical inherence that we have whatever degree of determinacy we do. The fact that determinacy is a function of a complex interaction means only that determinacy is a complicated phenomenon. One can shrug one's

shoulders in the face of complexity. Or one can take up the challenge and try to map the complex patterns of constraint and indeterminacy in a way that proves useful. As indicated above, I think that Kennedy's earlier work is best understood as an effort of that sort. That, in any event, is the project I have taken up here.

One way to approach that task is to ask what it means to be a situated historical actor. At the simplest level, being situated means being "in" a historical context that must be taken into account as an external precondition for action. But this understanding of what it means to be situated is ultimately self-defeating because it recapitulates the conventional subject-object dichotomy by reinscribing a distinction between the internal (the subject) and the external (the object). To locate the subject *within* a social, cultural, and historical situation is to reestablish that actor as an entity somehow separate from that situation.

To get beyond this naïve view, we must first relinquish the conventional schema of subject and object. "The mistake," Merleau-Ponty explains, "lies in treating the social as an object" rather than as "a permanent field or dimension of existence."[28] To be a situated actor, we might say, is to be the function of a complex, social interaction. Indeed, no human infant could survive without the nurturance and instruction of other people. Yet these earliest interactions already provide the person with an entire repertoire of psychological mechanisms, defenses, complexes, and personality traits.[29] Even more important for our purposes, these earliest interactions provide an entire world of sedimented constructions—theories, presuppositions, and concepts—that form the very ground or field of one's existence. Thus, to be a situated actor is to be a person who, in Merleau-Ponty's words, "thinks in terms of his situation, forms his categories in contact with his experience, and modifies this situation and this experience by the meaning he discovers in them."[30]

It follows that to talk about a *particular* actor trying to answer a legal question is to confuse social construction with solipsism: "If we could . . . cut the *solus ipse* [the self alone] off from others and from Nature . . . , there would be fully preserved, in this fragment of the whole which alone was left, the references to the whole it is composed of. In short, we still would not have the *solus ipse*."[31] When judges first approach any task, they confront a sedimented field of concepts and categories that they, too, have internalized. Meaning is a shared social phenomenon that constrains how we as embodied and culturally situated humans understand our world. Chapter 8 quoted Unger's observation "that every branch of doctrine must rely tacitly if not explicitly upon some picture of the forms of human associa-

tion that are right and realistic in the areas of social life with which it deals."
But this is true of every category. Even "simple" concepts such as "park,"
"mother," and "lie" incorporate normative assumptions about the conventional roles, proper social functions, and appropriate behaviors governing
that particular corner of social life. Because these modes of being constitute
how judges *think,* they cannot be dispensed with by any simple act of will
or mere political desire. And, as we have seen repeatedly, those assumptions
actively shape legal decisionmaking.

One could object that, even so, the categories will nevertheless under-
determine the decision in any given case. After all, I have stressed throughout that categorization is an imaginative, adaptive process. Necessarily, this
means that no system of categorization, however extensive, could provide
the answers to all legal questions. It does not follow, however, that judges
are therefore free to operate in the interstices in any way they please. The
existing categories may be modified or extended; the judge may innovate.
But innovation remains a form of behavior governed by rules. Even the most
groundbreaking legal changes take place only within the constraints defined by the compositional structure of the conceptual material and by the
motivating context of judicial action. What was true of Holmes's formulation of "the marketplace of ideas" and Hughes's reconceptualization of
Commerce Clause doctrine is true a fortiori of the mine-run case where the
judge wishes to push the law in one direction or another. Indeed, as we saw
in chapter 9, even the most cogent analogy works only when the social circumstances and understandings permit.

Legal decisionmaking, as I have described it thus far, could be characterized as relatively constrained or (if one prefers) as moderately indeterminate. But it would be more accurate still to say that the law is indeterminate
in more-or-less predictable ways: Rarely do the legal materials provide a
single "right" answer to a legal question; but, despite the ineluctable flexibility of legal materials, legal decisionmaking is nevertheless regular, systematic, and largely predictable.

I will say more about why this is so in a moment. But note, first, that
this position is quite different from the center/periphery model advanced by
H. L. A. Hart. For Hart, the law consists in a core of settled meaning and a
periphery in which the judge is free to "legislate." But, as the case studies
in this book have shown, extension or innovation in the peripheral cases is
highly constrained both by the conceptual materials and by the social contexts that are constitutive of meaning. Conversely, Hart's settled meanings
are but prototype effects themselves dependent on context and purpose.
Consequently, the core meanings that Hart claims are "law in some centrally

important sense" are frequently unsettled by adventitious changes in social practices and conditions; as a historical matter, moreover, these changes have often taken place in the very teeth of the law. The center and periphery, in other words, are both constrained by the social contexts and processes that constrain and enable meaning. In both cases, moreover, the law that can effectively be made is, in a centrally important sense, a socially contingent artifact or epiphenomenon.

3. *Persuasion.* Kennedy is exactly right when he says that the question of whether a particular legal issue has a determinate answer is simply unintelligible if it is a question about the law *in the abstract.* But, instead of pursuing that insight, Kennedy brackets everything but the "surface" question of the legal materials themselves. This strategy is not just a blind alley; it is *irrelevant:* Legal materials cannot decide cases, only people can. To paraphrase Kennedy, it makes no sense to predicate the determinacy or indeterminacy of a legal question as it exists independently of the particular *community* that is trying to answer it. Constraint, as explained in chapter 6, is a social phenomenon that can exist only within the collective decisionmaking processes of some actual group of people.

A lawyer with actual, hands-on experience would never make such a mistake. If there is one thing that practicing lawyers certainly know, it is that the life of the law is not logic but *persuasion.*** At each and every turn in the process, the participants are trying to persuade one another to take a particular action on the basis of both a particular interpretation of the relevant events and a particular normative/legal understanding. The law that emerges from this process is a social product—that is, the product of an interaction between particular, situated historical actors. It is not—and, as Robert Cover points out, can never be—the work of a single "heroic" judge trying to advance some particular political or social agenda.[32] It follows that any theory of law that takes seriously the insight that law is not a "thing" but an activity that judges do, must take into account the role of persuasion in the decisionmaking process.

Rationalists have an account of persuasion: For them, it is a distorting factor that introduces capricious elements that make the law less predictable. A lawyer may sway judge or jury with eloquence; the decisionmaker may be swept along by an advocate's appeal to sympathy or some other emotion. Rationalists view these events as unfortunate realities for which the

---

* In the fall of 1984, I argued a case before the United States Supreme Court. My wife (we were then dating) was finishing her masters in social work at the time. Her first words to me after the argument were: "I didn't realize it was such a *psychological* process."

proper antidote is a more dispassionate exercise of reason. But, then, rationalists *must* think this way because they have no concept of constraint outside the discipline of rationalizing principle and criterial logic. Everything
else is *subjective*.

As Stanley Fish points out, however, this conventional view faces a conceptual conundrum because the

> success that rhetoric may have in turning the mind away from purely ra-
> tional considerations is a function as much of tendencies in the mind as
> it is of pressuring forces external to the mind; an illegitimate appeal can
> hardly have an effect if there is nothing to appeal to.[33]

It makes no sense, Fish observes, to talk about reason free from the appeal
of interest and emotion unless there are minds free of interest and emotion.
But, "were every preconception, acquired belief, assumed point of view,
opinion, bias, and prejudice removed from the mind, there would be nothing left with which to calculate, determine, and decide" (518). Reason, in
other words, is a faculty of situated historical actors. Consequently, it cannot be abstracted from the contexts, perspectives, and understandings that
constitute those actors as such.

The conventional view is self-contradictory in another, more profound
way. Recall that the central concern of the conventional view is to avoid subjectivity in legal decisionmaking. It requires reason to do so because it does
not recognize any other kind of constraint. On this model, persuasion represents the antithesis of reason—and, thus, is understood to exacerbate the
danger of subjectivity—because it appeals to extrarational considerations.
Fish's provocative and perceptive rejoinder is that these considerations are
not outside reason but constitutive of it. We can press the point further still:
If persuasion works only to the extent that the decisionmaker already shares
the values being appealed to, then it is hard to see in what sense the resulting process could be said to be "subjective." Quite the contrary. Persuasion
is, by definition, an *intersubjective* process—not only in the trivial sense
that it takes at least two people to occasion persuasion, but also in the more
important sense that persuasion can proceed only on the basis of shared
values and perspectives. And decisionmaking constrained by shared, social
values, as will be recalled, is precisely what the conventional view was trying to secure in the first place.

There is an obvious rejoinder. Before addressing it, however, it will be
helpful to consider the problem from the opposite perspective—i.e., from

the perspective of the advocate who wants to lead a decisionmaker in a particular direction. If he heeds the rationalist, he will rely solely on reason to constrain the decisionmaker in the desired direction. If he is hell-bent on winning, he may succumb to the temptation to use rhetoric and other persuasive devices to trump reason. Or so the conventional view would have it.

But the practicing lawyer knows, and a moment's reflection will confirm, that eloquence and the emotional appeal are no more reliable than the logic so prized by the rationalist. Neither logic nor eloquence work in the abstract; both depend for their efficacy on the values, beliefs, and understandings of the decisionmakers to whom one must appeal. To take a particularly strong example, consider the situation faced by Thurgood Marshall in 1952 as he stood to make the closing argument in Walter Lee Irvin's capital rape case.[34] The trial was the concluding chapter of an incendiary racial episode that began in 1949 when Irvin, Samuel Shepherd, Charles Greenlee, and Ernest Thomas—all African Americans—were accused of raping a seventeen-year-old white woman near Groveland, Florida. Thomas was shot to death during the course of his arrest. The remaining defendants had to be transferred to the state prison to save them from a lynch mob—though, as the reported opinions reflect, they were first savagely beaten by the sheriff (and illegal confessions probably obtained). In the ensuing mob violence, the homes of Shepherd's parents and other Black residents were burned. Most of the Black residents fled or were evacuated for their own safety. The National Guard was called in to restore order; two days later the 116th Field Artillery had to be mobilized as well. All this (including alleged confessions that were never introduced at trial) was meticulously reported by the local papers under such headlines as "Night Riders Burn Lake Negro Homes" and "Flames From Negro Homes Light Night Sky in Lake County."

The U.S. Supreme Court reversed Irvin's and Shepherd's capital rape convictions and remanded the cases for a new trial. (Greenlee, who as the youngest received a life sentence, decided not to appeal.) Shepherd was shot to death by the local sheriff as he was allegedly trying to escape. At that point, Marshall (then director-counsel of the NAACP Legal Defense Fund) personally undertook Irvin's defense on retrial. The capstone of the defense, which according to the *New York Times* "brought gasps from several hundred white and Negro persons in the Marion County courtroom," was the testimony of a Miami forensic expert who concluded that the plaster casts of the defendant's footprints taken at the scene had been fabricated by the sheriff: The casts were convex (toes and heels curving downward), as if the impressions had been made by shoes with shoe trees in them, whereas an actual footprint would have been concave (the toes curling upward).* Summing up the next day, Marshall acknowledged that an acquittal would be a "pretty tough proposition" given the sensational nature of the case; but he eloquently appealed to the jury to remember that federal, state, and local laws were all designed to assure fairness before the courts without regard to race. The all-white jury emerged from their deliberations only a short time later. As they entered the jury box, the foreman turned to the man next to him and said in a voice loud enough to be heard throughout the hushed courtroom: "That Nigger was good!" Moments later he pronounced the verdict: Guilty, without recommendation of mercy.

The rationalist would no doubt be quick to point out that if ever there was a case that needed the dispassionate exercise of reason as a safeguard against prejudice and injustice, this surely was it. But while this conclusion fits well with the rationalist's presuppositions, it does not quite jibe with the facts. If the story shows anything at all, it shows that reason cannot guarantee anything like the constraint that rationalism claims to offer—and for a simple reason: Even a *legitimate* appeal can hardly have an effect if there is nothing to appeal to.

Others might object that the overt racism of the jury makes this an unrepresentative case. But, precisely because it is an extreme case, the story helps us see the dynamic at work in every case. What is true for reason is true for eloquence; both must find receptive ground if they are to do any work at all. To be effective, the advocate must not only know the audience but also be able to speak to it. Persuasion, in other words, is constrained by what the audience already believes.† Let us call this (with all intended irony) "the iron law of persuasion."

We can now return to the point deferred above. The obvious objection

---

* The plaster casts, which had been used at the first trial, were not actually introduced at the second trial because they had been shattered mysteriously. Rather, the prosecution put on the stand a deputy sheriff who testified that he placed the defendant's shoes in the tracks at the scene and that the shoes fitted the tracks exactly.

† To be clear, I am not arguing that people can never be persuaded to change their beliefs, only that one must be able to refer to some other aspects of their beliefs, values, and understandings in order to effect that change. Thus, one cannot persuade a bigot to embrace racial equality as long as he persists in seeing Blacks as inferior or does not regard equality as an important social or moral value. Persuasion is nevertheless possible if one can bring the bigot to see Blacks as humans just like himself (or those he loves) or if one can convince him of the instrumental benefits of equality (or the concomitant costs of inequality).

to my argument is that nothing about the process of persuasion as I have so far described it protects us from the idiosyncratic decisionmaker. The fact that a lawyer (in this case, the prosecutor) has succeeded in convincing a particular decisionmaker (here, a white southern jury) is no guarantee that the decision accords with any values that the rest of us share; as a logical matter, it means only that those particular actors happen to share the same values.

Though the logic is impeccable, the conclusion is wrong. The flaw lies with its faulty premise, which presupposes an atomized picture of adjudication. But legal decisionmaking *never* occurs in a social vacuum. (Irvin's death sentence, for example, was later commuted by Governor Collins.) Judgments are subject to appeal; every decision depends for its efficacy on the compliance either of an unhappy losing party or of an enforcement official who must be willing to take coercive, sometimes violent action; and all cases stand as potential precedents for future decisions. A truly idiosyncratic decision, in other words, risks reversal, recalcitrance, or irrelevance. It remains true that nothing stops the rogue judge from deciding any way he or she wants. Judges are nevertheless constrained to the extent that they expect to be effective. And make no mistake about it; judges *do* expect to be effective. Its follows, as Cover observes, that

> legal interpretation . . . can never be "free"; it can never be the function of an understanding of the text or word alone. . . . Legal interpretation must be capable of transforming itself into action; it must be capable of overcoming inhibitions against violence in order to generate its requisite deeds. (1617)

Judges know that a purely political decision will not succeed unless it can appeal beyond the judges' "personal" preferences to some larger set of values shared by the wider audience. Kennedy concedes as much when he acknowledges that "what a given judge will do in a case depends on what she thinks will 'fly' as 'good legal argument' in the minds of others." But the point is broader: What a given judge will do in a case depends on what she thinks will fly with the much larger constituency to which she must appeal both for her legitimacy and efficacy. Kennedy's response is that when judges deny the ideological in adjudication they are practicing bad faith in a conscious or half-conscious attempt to maintain their legitimacy by cloaking political decisions behind a facade of legal necessity. My own experience of judges is rather different. Those judges that I have observed close-up were all too aware—sometimes to the point of painful self-consciousness—that what they did was constrained by the public's perception of it. But you needn't take my word for it. The point is confirmed both by logic and by direct evidence.

The particular focus of the conventional concern has always been on appellate courts and, in particular, the Supreme Court. Likewise, Kennedy's critique of adjudication is a critique of appellate lawmaking; he explicitly defends this narrow focus against the criticisms of more sophisticated sociological analyses that emphasize the hands-and-feet practices of judges, lawyers, sheriffs, clerks, and other low-level officials (65–68, 266–80). Common sense has it that the higher the court, the greater its freedom to act—hence Justice Jackson's famous quip that the Supreme Court is "not final because we are infallible, but we are infallible only because we are final." [35]

But the conventional wisdom has it exactly backwards: The higher the court, the greater the constraints on its actions, for it should be apparent that the higher the court, the larger the audience that must be persuaded. The trial judge decides alone (though he or she can *act* only in concert with others). The appellate judge, in contrast, must first convince one or more colleagues to join together to form a majority.* The opinion that ensues must speak to an audience that becomes larger as the court's authority increases. The wider that audience, the more the court's decisions are con-

---

* It is this intuition that underpins the institution of the three-judge district court that, over the course of the twentieth century, Congress has used as a brake on judicial action in controversial areas. The three-judge court was employed at the beginning of the century in antitrust cases and in suits challenging orders of the Interstate Commerce Commission. During the *Lochner* Era, the three-judge court requirement was extended to injunctive actions challenging state statutes on constitutional grounds; during the New Deal, this requirement was extended again to include cases challenging federal statutes on constitutional grounds. The three-judge court was largely abandoned in 1976, except for reapportionment and voting rights cases. In 1997, Representative Bill Paxon (R–NY) proposed legislation to revive the three-judge court requirement in injunctive actions challenging state or federal statutes or state administrative orders on constitutional grounds (H.R. 1027 IH).

A similar idea can be discerned in the Judiciary Act of 1789, which established the federal court system. The act set up a two-tiered system of trial courts consisting of a district court staffed by a single district judge and a circuit court made up of one district court judge and one or two justices riding circuit. The circuit courts were authorized to hear civil cases where the matter in dispute exceeded $500, all criminal cases under federal law, and appeals from certain decisions of the district courts. The district courts were authorized to hear all admiralty cases, suits for forfeitures under federal law, tort suits brought by aliens, suits brought by the United States, and criminal cases where the punishment was confined to "whipping, not exceeding 30 stripes, a fine not exceeding one hundred dollars, or a term of imprisonment not exceeding six months." 1 Stat. 70, 73–79 (1789).

strained by the need to appeal to common values and understandings in order to persuade those affected that its decisions are indeed correct. In a society where "law" is synonymous with objective delineations of right and wrong (which, as far as I can tell, includes all Western societies), a court can produce that automatic, tacit sense of validity only if its judgments conform with the most conventional values of the culture. Like the "lowest common denominator" factor at work in popular culture, the court's need to appeal to the masses forces it to act within the most mainstream values and understandings.

There is nothing particularly new in this observation. It was implicit in Llewellyn's notion of situation-sense (discussed in chapter 8). It is, also, the ultimate lesson of a brilliant but much neglected article that Jan Deutsch published thirty years ago. In a dazzling deconstruction of Herbert Wechsler's concept of neutral principles, Deutsch demonstrated that it makes no sense to talk about consistency, generality, or principle in judicial decisionmaking *except* as a function or artifact of the cultural and historical understandings that reign at any given moment.[36] Deutsch first observed that a principle will be understood as "neutral" only if it is sufficiently general. He then demonstrated that there is no logical or objective way in which to specify the correct level of generality for a given principle. Famously, Wechsler had argued "that the main constituent of the judicial process is precisely that it must be genuinely principled, resting with respect to every step that is involved in reaching judgment on analysis and reasons quite transcending the immediate result that is achieved" (15). Wechsler's examples of unprincipled, "ad hoc" decisions were hypothetical cases in which claims are approved or disapproved solely because they were "put forward by a labor union or a taxpayer, a Negro or a segregationist, a corporation or a Communist" (12). Deutsch pointed out, however, that it is logically possible to have a consistently applied general rule that, for example, all claims brought by labor unions or those exercising the right of free speech should win. Such rules would still be "neutral" in the sense defined by Wechsler because they would not, in Wechsler's words, "turn on the immediate results" (ibid.) but rather on "standards that transcend the case at hand" (17).

If, nevertheless, it seems self-evident that a decisionmaking "principle" always to prefer the claims of African Americans would be an illegitimate one, it is not because such a principle lacks support in positive law. After all, Deutsch observed, the express purpose of the Thirteenth, Fourteenth, and Fifteenth amendments was to protect the then newly freed slaves (193–94). Rather, the intuition of illegitimacy "rests on our society's deep-seated aversion to attaching legal consequences to the fact of group membership vel non," an aversion that Deutsch attributed to the need of a heterogeneous society to avoid the divisive consequences of distrust (194–95). In other words, the perception that a particular rule is not sufficiently general really expresses a value judgment about the content of the proposed principle. And this value judgment is itself a historically contingent artifact: in this case, the product of our "melting pot" heritage. But, if "the historical context may well determine the proper classification of a given principle," then

> a neutral principle becomes one that is perceived as adequately general in terms of the historical context in which it is applied. The question that such a reformulation raises, however, is this: perceived as adequately general by whom? The answer can be derived from the fact that the legitimacy of the principle approving all Negro claims was ultimately traced to a deeply held social aversion to the attaching of legal consequences to memberships in groups. . . . Adequate generality in a judicial decision— neutrality, if you will—is, therefore, that degree of generality perceived as adequate by the very society that imposes the requirement of adequate generality to begin with—that same public whose agreement that the principle approving all Negro claims is illegitimate serves to make Wechsler's illustrations persuasive. (195)

Today, the point about the circularity of neutral principles—like the argument that there is no logical or objective way to determine the right level of generality for a legal principle—would most likely be taken as an argument that the law is indeterminate; indeed, that is exactly how Deutsch's students (of whom, incidentally, Kennedy was one) have since presented it.[37] But the precise point of Deutsch's argument is that social values and understandings constitute what counts as "neutral" and "principled" (that is the import of his reference to "adequate generality in a judicial decision" as "neutrality, if you will"). Thus, a more sophisticated reading would recognize in Deutsch's circularity a Hegelian reflexivity of the sort described by Charles Taylor, and articulated with great clarity in the quote from Merleau-Ponty above (at note 30).[38] Deutsch made the point again at the close of the article when he argued that "the phenomenon of the internalized community agenda" best explains the constraints experienced by all political actors:

> If we inquire into the source of the particular set of existing checks and balances or ask why the actors accept the constraints represented by those checks and balances, we are led directly to the community agenda

of alternatives: the consensus that defines the existing set of checks and
balances and whose internalization by the actors results in the acceptance of the constraints that it imposes. (257)

Deutsch concluded the article with the observation that constraints on the
Court could be disclosed "only by examining the extent to which individ-
ual Justices have internalized the community consensus that defines the
Court's sphere of competence" (259).

The point about the "circularity" of values is a profound one that we
shall return to in the final chapter. For present purposes, I want to highlight
a different but related aspect of the argument. Deutsch observed that Wechsler's illustrations of illegitimate deviations from "neutrality" are persuasive
because they appeal to deep-seated social values against group preferences
(values that, if anything, are more deeply entrenched now than when Wechsler and Deutsch wrote). What this observation means, however, is that the
cogency of Wechsler's argument for neutral principles—like the cogency of
the geocentric view of the universe prior to Copernicus and Galileo, New-
tonian physics prior to Einstein and Böhr, or rationalism today—stems
from the automatic sense of validity that arises when someone insists on a
truism: What is perceived as detached and objective is just the familiar "what
everybody knows" or, in Wallace Stevens's words, the "stiff and stubborn,
man-locked set" of conceptions that constitute our reality. If the iron law of
persuasion is that an appeal can hardly have an effect if there is nothing to
appeal to, then its first corollary is that one can always persuade people to
the truth of what they already believe. Deutsch's point, prefigured in Llewellyn's account of the layman's notion of legal certainty discussed in chapter 8, is that one of the names we give to this experience of validity is "neutrality." Or, as Deutsch elsewhere observes, lawmaking by an astute judge
such as Holmes works "as all good stories work, not by retailing the murky
and confusing truth of how things are, but by confirming our felt certain-
ties about how we know they should be." [39]

Deutsch's observation about the perception of neutrality that arises from
conformity to the community's expectations points the way to a broader,
more profound conclusion: In a society where the judiciary is expected to
be neutral rather than political and to apply the law rather than make it,
judges will be constrained to replicate the conventional understandings and
values that characterize the culture. True, judges can always pretend that
"the law" is clear and that they are just conforming to its dictates. But this
pretense will not suffice if no one *believes* them. Perhaps everyone will sim-

ply accede to their authority (and, in societies more deferential to authority than our own, that might indeed be enough). Perhaps, as Kennedy suggests, everyone will play along in one giant act of collective denial. But maybe they won't—in which case, the judge has an overwhelming incentive to find in the law just those things that the society at large will accept as neutral, principled, and right.

We have direct evidence of this very proposition in the plurality opinion of Justices O'Connor, Kennedy, and Souter in *Planned Parenthood v. Casey*. Despite some of their personal misgivings, the plurality reaffirmed what it characterized as the "central holding" of *Roe v. Wade*. (Three other justices continued to adhere to *Roe* in its entirety.) The plurality justified adherence to precedent on the ground that "overruling *Roe*'s central holding would not only reach an unjustifiable result under principles of *stare decisis*, but would seriously weaken the Court's capacity to exercise the judicial power and to function as the Supreme Court of a Nation dedicated to the rule of law" (865).

As the plurality explained: "The Court's power lies . . . in its legitimacy, a product of substance and perception that shows itself in the people's acceptance of the Judiciary as fit to determine what the Nation's law means and to declare what it demands." The plurality insisted that the "underlying substance of this legitimacy is of course the warrant for the Court's decisions in the Constitution and the lesser sources of legal principle on which the Court draws." But, consistent with Kennedy's point that the law is a product of the work that judges do, the plurality conceded that "that substance is expressed in the Court's opinions." Even so, the plurality identified an important constraint on its work:

> Our contemporary understanding is such that a decision without principled justification would be no judicial act at all. But even when justification is furnished by apposite legal principle, something more is required. Because not every conscientious claim of principled justification will be accepted as such, the justification claimed must be beyond dispute. The Court must take care to speak and act in ways that allow people to accept its decisions on the terms the Court claims for them, as grounded truly in principle, not as compromises with social and political pressures having, as such, no bearing on the principled choices that the Court is obliged to make. Thus, the Court's legitimacy depends on making legally principled decisions under circumstances in which their principled character is sufficiently *plausible* to be accepted by the Nation. (865–66; emphasis added)

At first blush, this passage seems to confirm the strongest version of Kennedy's thesis that judges are acting in bad faith.* After all, in place of decisions that are "beyond dispute" because "grounded truly in principle," the plurality offers a confidence game in which judicial decisions (or, what is much the same, their principled character) need only be "sufficiently plausible to be accepted by the Nation." From a solemn declaration that judicial decisions must find their warrant in the Constitution and the law, the opinion moves quickly (all too quickly) to the concealment of doubt in self-conscious illusion: "The Court," we are told, "must take care to speak and act in ways that allow people to accept its decisions on the terms the Court claims for them."

But, even the cynical reading of this passage confirms my argument: The plurality is self-conscious of its need to be persuasive. It knows that if it is to retain its effectiveness as "the Supreme Court of a Nation dedicated to the rule of law," it must speak and act in ways that permit people to accept its opinions as principled. It can do so, as Deutsch's argument makes clear, only if its opinions accord with the expectations engendered by people's real-life norms. Consider, for example, Judge Posner's observation with respect to the recent cases claiming a constitutional right to die.

> The Justices did not explain why they ducked the philosophical issue, but they had compelling practical reasons for doing so. The first is that given the balance between the opposing philosophical arguments as they would appear to most people . . . , the Court could not have written a convincing endorsement of either position; it would have been seen as taking sides on a disagreement not susceptible of anything normally resembling an objective resolution.[40]

Thus, it would not matter even if Kennedy is correct and judges are acting in bad faith when they claim that their decisions are required by legal principle. The need to make such claims credible will nevertheless operate as a constraint on what those positions can reasonably be. This constraint, moreover, will be operative regardless of the conscious bad faith or explicit political motivation of the judge.

* Kennedy finesses the question whether bad faith is a self-conscious phenomenon. Of judges, Kennedy says, "It seems enough to say that the desire is half-conscious, or conscious and unconscious at the same time, or that the ego wills its own unconsciousness of something that it must therefore in some sense know" (200). Of liberalism, generally, Kennedy says: "I mean to attribute a disreputable motive, albeit a half-conscious one, for this distortion" (294).

But it is unclear whether Kennedy *is* correct. While the cynical reading fits well with the text of the plurality opinion in *Casey,* it nevertheless presents a problem. Judges acting in self-conscious bad faith would never acknowledge so explicitly the conceptual sleight of hand inherent in "principled" decisionmaking: When one is trying to pull the wool over people's eyes, it is usually advisable not to tell them so to their face. It is possible that the plurality's surprising candor is really a parapraxis or Freudian slip, which would tend to confirm Kennedy's claim that judges are in denial. But this reading would suggest a strong sense of denial, one bordering on repression. The plurality, after all, seems utterly unself-consciousness in disclosing that its decision is "grounded truly in principle" not because it is logically rigorous but because the justices have taken "care to speak and act in ways that allow people to accept its decisions on the terms the Court claims for them" and have done so "under circumstances in which their principled character is sufficiently plausible to be accepted" as such.

What this disclosure suggests is not bad faith so much as cognitive dissonance. Ordinarily, the Court speaks and acts in ways that allow the justices *themselves* to accept their reasoning as grounded truly in principle. But they can do that only when their conclusions are in accord with the prevailing understandings that they themselves have been socialized to. If, in *Casey,* the plurality struggles so painfully and self-consciously with the idea of principle in constitutional adjudication, it is because the plurality on some level grasps (though perhaps only dimly) that it is unable in this case to do what it ordinarily does: The controversy over abortion means that there is no consensus, either of practice or values, that could support a perception of neutrality for any legal principle the Court would adopt.

Precisely because *Casey* is a controversial case, it forces open a window on the dynamic at work in every case. The plurality opinion unwittingly exposes the way in which the social constraint of persuasion operates even at the highest levels of lawmaking. Still, the lessons of *Casey* are decidedly mixed. On one hand, it reassures us that the social processes of constraint are at work even in the most controversial cases. On the other hand, *Casey* demonstrates the epistemic limits of law and of legal reasoning. The insight that law is a socially contingent artifact or epiphenomenon implies that legal meaning is possible only to the extent that the society enjoys a relative stability of context: When there is a consensus in practices and consequent values—that is, when the social and legal categories are firmly motivated—then the courts will be able to articulate "principled" decisions that people will recognize as valid. By the same token, the judges will experience the legal materials as "determinate" and their own legal reasoning as "principled." But, when social practices and values are controversial or in disarray, the legal rules and principles will be too. It follows that we cannot expect the law to resolve difficult, controversial cases in a way that is different or removed from the realm of politics.*

It is important, however, not to misunderstand the import of the term "stability." Stability is not stasis; it is a dynamic balance or equilibrium like that of a market or homeostatic system. Since we are speaking of a social system, stability is actually a dynamic pattern of interaction, reformulation, and adaptation. One might think that I have undermined my own argument—that is, that time and social change are destabilizing factors that vitiate the constraints I have described. In fact, however, precisely because the constraint of persuasion is itself a dynamic social phenomenon, it is responsive to rather than vitiated by social change.

In times of social change, the judges may modify or extend the existing categories. But they nevertheless remain constrained by the need to articulate innovations that others will find persuasive as logical extensions of existing law. At a minimum, these extensions must comport with the compositional structure of the conceptual material with which the judges work; otherwise, the innovations they propose will not even seem reasonable. More importantly, the legal changes must track the changes in people's real-life norms or they will not elicit the perception of validity and neutrality that sustains the law as such. Again, as Llewellyn explained:

> If the change sanctioned by the judge keeps up more or less, but not
> quite, one then speaks of the law's mild conservatism. If the change on
> the judge's part is noticeably not keeping up, one then speaks of a crisis
> in decision making. And, finally, if the change on the judge's part is keeping up perfectly, neither judge nor layman realizes that any change has
> occurred.[41]

In other words, it is controversy and heterogeneity rather than change that undermine the social phenomenon of constraint. A dynamic cultural context, in contrast, enables legal change. But this dynamic quality does not

---

* What, then, does law contribute in controversial cases? A legal decision may effect an uneasy compromise between strongly felt but incompatible positions; this is one way to characterize the plurality opinion in *Casey* (and, perhaps, the original line-drawing exercise in *Roe v. Wade*). Or, as Levi suggests, reasoning case-by-case by analogy may keep the larger issue open until such time as a meaningful consensus forms. Finally, as Sunstein suggests, law may contribute by brokering low-level agreements on particular disputes when there is no consensus capable of supporting a perception of "principle."

make the law unstable or indeterminate because this enablement is simultaneously a constraint. As we saw in chapter 10, innovation is not a release from constraint but a function of it.

That constraint in law is a dynamic social phenomenon means that it is partial, rather than total. This dynamic often leaves the forensic space for the strategic, ideological behavior that Kennedy is concerned to demonstrate. It is, in other words, a "peculiar" constraint because it does not provide determinate answers on the model of deduction. But the fact that constraint in law is a dynamic social phenomenon rather than an immovable, external fact should be a scandal only to those still operating within the two-dimensional framework of objectivity versus subjectivity. Constraint in law is the same as constraint in life; the problem with law is that it pretends to clothe itself in objectivity and then invites us to expect more than human rationality can deliver. Disillusioned, some people overreact and proclaim loudly that the emperor has no clothes.* But to think that we should replace legal decisionmaking with a more direct politics is to labor under a self-defeating misconception. Turning from law to politics will not change who we are.

Once we recognize that constraint is not an all-or-nothing phenomenon, it becomes easier to see that different areas of law exhibit different degrees of constraint and, thus, of stability. The degree of constraint in any given case—and, conversely, the forensic space for judicial improvisation—is not a matter of a priori theory. Rather, as skilled practitioners already know, constraint is something that can be mapped only after careful, context-sensitive investigation. Not all issues are as controversial as abortion; in many cases, social practices (and their concomitant values) will be sufficiently stable to enable reasoning that feels deductive in its certainty. In other cases, social practices may be as unsettled as the abortion question but without its notoriety. More obscure questions may claim the attention of only a small, specialized audience; the technical issues of federalism, for example, speak to little in people's real-life norms and, therefore, provide judges with greater leeway for strategic action. In chapters 6 and 9, I suggested typologies for predicting the contexts that will support determinacy or create indeterminacy. But the relative (in)determinacy of law is not a unitary or universal matter. It is, rather, a function of where and when.

---

* Consider in this regard Deutsch's quip (in correspondence) that Wittgenstein was just a disappointed Platonist. Kennedy's account of his own conversion experiences (312–14) resonates well with this description.

Still, it would be a significant mistake to think that judges act ideologically only in cases of instability or obscurity. Kennedy is concerned to show the overtly political motivations of judges as they apply their work strategies to the legal materials at hand. This focus is surprisingly shortsighted for a radical; the earlier Duncan Kennedy would never have set his sights so low. The truly radical insight is that judges are ideological precisely when they are *not* acting in an overtly political way. The insight that categorization is socially motivated means that categorization—including even the most straightforward, uncontroversial case of legal decisionmaking—is always a normatively loaded process. Every category and every legal doctrine relies tacitly if not explicitly upon some picture of the forms of human association that are right and realistic in the areas of social life with which it deals. Two (only slightly) paradoxical conclusions follow. First, law works as "law" because the social processes of persuasion mean that judges will be constrained to replicate the most mainstream values and understandings.* Second, and as a direct consequence, law is always ideological in the sense that it enforces (and reinforces) the dominant normative views of the culture. Indeed, the ideological dimension of law is most pronounced precisely when judges are acting in good faith, unaware of the normative entailments of the conceptual materials with which they work. And *that*, precisely, is what makes adjudication a profoundly political activity.

* Kennedy claims that the denial of the ideological nature of adjudication leads to a "moderation effect" in which the strategic efforts of liberal and conservative judges cancel each other out (217–24). But, this moderation effect can be explained more simply as the predictable consequence of the constraints on decisionmaking we have examined under the rubrics of cognition, categorization, and persuasion.

CHAPTER 12

Meaning and Making

UPON SEEING a shooting star or some other wonder of nature, the observant Jew is enjoined to make a *Brachah* or blessing: "Blessed art thou, Lord our God, King of the Universe, who makes the work of creation." Similarly, every Sabbath and holiday meal begins with the *Kiddush* or sanctification over a cup of wine that marks the day's special quality. These rituals work *as* rituals because they call upon the adherent to enact the meaning that the words express. The very act of making the blessing, in other words, is an act of dedication that constitutes the special significance of the moment.

Legal meaning is, ultimately, of the same *performative* order as the *Brachah* or *Kiddush*. This, then, is the paradox of law: We conceive of law as an exogenous, impersonal constraint—in Frank Michelman's apt description, law is "an autonomous force" that provides "an external untouchable rule of the game." [1] But, as it turns out, the "truth" or viability of a law depends upon its realization in our ongoing social practices. Thus, in chapter 8, we saw how the intelligibility of a legal rule is a function of the very cultural practices that it purports to regulate. And, in the last chapter, we saw that the objectivity and neutrality of law is but an artifact of the de facto consensus in social practices and consequent values that may prevail in society at a given time. Here, I press the point to its radical conclusion: The social processes that make law meaningful and those by which we make law are, necessarily, one and the same. Law is constituted and sustained not by edict or statute but in the forms of life that give meaning to our categories, concepts, and values. And, as we shall see, it is precisely there that freedom lies. [2]

The Body of Law

In *Nomos and Narrative,* Robert Cover draws on his religious experience to explain the profoundly human nature of law. He writes movingly of the "jurisgenerative" or lawmaking quality of communal life and the "jurispathic" or law-killing role of the state and its courts.[3] "The creation of legal meaning," Cover explains, "takes place always through an essentially cultural medium" (11).[4] The resulting *nomos* is "not merely a system of rules to be observed, but a world in which we live" (5). The legal world thus conceived "requires no state" (11), for it is "held together by the force of interpretive commitments" (7). Cover explains:

> Creation of legal meaning . . . requires not only the movement of dedication and commitment, but also the objectification of that to which one is committed. The community posits a law, external to itself, that it is committed to obeying and that it does obey in dedication to its understanding of that law. Objectification is crucial to the language games that can be played with the law and to the meanings that can be created out of it. If the Amish lived as they do because it was fun to do so, they might still fight for their insularity. They would not, however, be disobedient to any articulable principle were they to capitulate. And they could not hold someone blameworthy—lawless—were he to give in.
>
> Creation of legal meaning entails, then, subjective commitment to an objectified understanding of a demand. It entails the disengagement of the self from the "object" of law, and at the same time requires an engagement to that object as a faithful "other." The metaphor of separation permits the allegory of dedication. (45)

Cover emphasizes, however, that interpretation, commitment, and dedication are not mere matters of belief. In law, he points out, "interpretation always takes place in the shadow of coercion" (40). It follows that law "is never just a mental or spiritual act. A legal world is built only to the extent that there are commitments that place bodies on the line."[5] Cover gives the powerful example of the civil rights demonstrators of the 1960s (of whom he was one) who affirmed their interpretation of the Equal Protection Clause with their bodies and their lives: "In acting out their own, 'free' interpretation of the Constitution, protesters say, 'We do mean this in the medium of blood' (or in the medium of time in jail)" (47).

Cover's radical account strips lawmaking down to its roots in human thought and action. In doing so, he seeks to rip away the veil of objectivity and rationality that attends most conventional judicial and academic expositions of law—whether positivist paeans to "The Rule of Law" or Dworkinian celebrations of "Law's Empire." In stressing the psychological and material underpinnings of law over the more prosaic processes of formal lawmaking, Cover aims to expose a "radical dichotomy between the social organization of law as power and the organization of law as meaning" (18). The ineradicable social dimensions of meaning, Cover elsewhere explains, "doom the positivist enterprise to failure, or, at best, to only imperfect success." [6]

Cover makes a distinctive cognitive and linguistic claim about how we as humans constitute law through metaphorical reasoning. "Objectification," Cover tells us, "is crucial to the language games that can be played with the law and to the meanings that can be created out of it." As we saw in chapter 1, one cannot even talk about law without the metaphor of "object": To know that someone has "broken" the law, we must first conceptualize it as a "thing" that can be broken; it must be an "object" that the outlaw or vigilante can "take into his own hands." So, too, to ascertain what the law "is," we must first give it metaphorical form as an object that can be "found," "discovered," or "made." And, as we learned from Berger and Luckmann's account of institutionalization (discussed in chapter 8), this objectification is both a feature and consequence of the process by which a social world becomes real to its participants. There is no law without reification.

But Cover is also telling us that this objectification must take a specific form if it is to work as law. It must be the kind of "object" that can be obeyed or disobeyed. Law, in other words, is a *person*—Michelman's "autonomous force." It is the "other" from whom we "disengage" but whom we continue to perceive as "faithful" to us and thus deserving of obedience.[7] The metaphor of separation that Cover invokes is not just a generalized metaphor of personification, but an invocation of the childhood experience of separation from parent. The process of law-creation is a projection of developmental experience.[8] Law is the projected parent, the internalized superego.[9] In Brandeis's famous and quite Freudian metaphor, the "Government is the potent, the omnipresent teacher." When it is no longer faithful, when "Government becomes a lawbreaker" and not the embodiment of law, "it breeds contempt for law; it invites everyman to become a law unto himself; it invites anarchy." [10]

Consider Nietzsche's very different conception of law in *The Genealogy of Morals*. Describing his view of the origin and meaning of law, Nietzsche says:

> Wherever Justice is practiced and maintained, we see a stronger power
> intent on finding means to regulate the senseless raging of rancor *[ressen-*
> *timent]* among its weaker subordinates. This is accomplished by wresting
> the object of rancor from vengeful hands. . . . But above all, by the estab-
> lishment of a code of laws *[Gesetz]* which the superior power imposes
> upon the forces of hostility and resentment whenever it is strong enough
> to do so; by a categorical declaration of what it considers to be legiti-
> mate and right *[Recht]*, or else forbidden and wrong *[Unrecht]*. Once
> such a body of law has been established, all acts of highhandedness on
> the part of individuals or groups are seen as infractions *[Frevel]* of the
> law, as rebellion against the supreme power. . . . It follows that only after
> a corpus of laws has been established can there be any talk of "right"
> and "wrong" (and not, as Dühring maintains, after the act of injury).[11]

Nietzsche, too, employs the metaphors of objectification and personification. He has the strong "wresting the object of rancor from vengeful hands"
and transmuting it into a thing called "Justice." Once this code or body of
law *(Gesetz)* is established, all infractions (from the Latin *fractus,* "broken")
or offenses *(Frevel)* are treated as a "rebellion." Nietzsche's law is also a
very particular kind of object, for it must be the kind of object—a "supreme
power"—against which one can rebel. It is (here, in the translator's rendition) "a *body* of law." As the passage concludes, it is "only after a *corpus*
of laws has been established" that there can "be any talk of 'right' and
'wrong.'"

The use of the personification metaphor to constitute such different concepts of law is hardly fortuitous. To paraphrase Cover, personification is crucial to the conventional language games we play with law. We speak of the
corpus juris. Fundamental legal principles are described as "embodied" in
the Constitution or statutes.[12] So, too, we employ our knowledge of human
physiology to elaborate other conventional legal expressions. Criminals are
warned of the "long arm of the law," and "long arm" statutes are what we
use in civil cases to exercise jurisdiction over out-of-state defendants. When
we want to know what the law requires, we ask what the statute (or case or
constitutional provision) "says." A statute may be held unconstitutional
"on its face," in which case the court "strikes it down."[13] Personified entities can reproduce; it is thus common to refer to important cases as "seminal" cases and to the cases that follow as their "progeny." In the same vein,
Nietzsche entitled his treatise "The *Genealogy* of Morals." Like people, legal concepts have determinate life spans. Consider Grant Gilmore's famous
account of the "brief, happy life of the general theory of contract."[14] More-

over, like our real-life forebears, "dead" legal concepts may yet retain surprising power to influence their offspring: thus Maitland's famous dictum that "the forms of action we have buried, but they still rule us from their graves." [15]

Some may object that these expressions are nothing more than clichés. But, as we know from chapter 3, reality is a cliché that we make and remake by metaphor. These expressions, in other words, reflect a highly conventional metaphorical mapping that is constitutive of our very concept "Law." This conclusion is confirmed by the facts that the mapping is systematic and productive, which shows that it is a live part of our conceptual system, and that it remains consistent even across antithetical jurisprudential theories, which shows that it is deeply entrenched. All of which is precisely what one would expect of a conceptual mapping that, as Cover suggests, uses as its source domain the childhood experience of internalization and separation from parent.

Much the same conclusion is reflected in the observation that "only after a corpus of laws has been established can there be any talk of 'right' and 'wrong.'" On the surface, Nietzsche is making a positivistic observation about law: It is the creation of the strong and imposed upon the weak by superior power. Armed with this understanding, we can see through the false legitimation often entailed by the assertion of legality. As Cover observes:

> Legal positivism may be seen, in one sense, as a massive effort that has gone on in a self-conscious way to strip the word "law" of these resonances. . . . Positivism breaks down psychological barriers to outright conscription of the word "law" to nefarious purposes which natural law thinking might create.[16]

Nietzsche's description of law as a human construct is iconoclastic and liberating; it is intended to free us from the tyranny of false, imposed delineations of "right" and "wrong."

The translation of Nietzsche I have used above makes his point in a more robustly conventional way. The medium motivates the message: Nietzsche's positivistic point is made more powerful precisely because the metaphor employed by the translator bears an intimate cognitive relationship to our underlying conception of law. The statement that it is "only after a corpus of laws has been established" that there can "be any talk about right" reveals the deep psychological connection between the personification metaphor and the meaning of "right."

It is not accidental that we use the same word in these ostensibly distinct ways—i.e., to mean both "correct" and "the opposite of left." More analytic approaches to linguistic theory treat such instances as cases of homonymy: ostensibly different words that, quite fortuitously, happen to be spelled or pronounced the same. But, as was true of the cases discussed in previous chapters (i.e., "mouth," "hand," and "foot"), most homonyms are actually cases of polysemy—that is, metaphorically related meanings of the same word. Here, both senses of "right" are related to each other by the conventional personification metaphor that forms a central part of our concept "Law." If the Law has a body, it must also have a right arm with which to enforce its commands. The "long arm of the law" has been identified: It is the right arm that enforces that which is acceptable and that which is not.[17] It is the law's sanction—i.e., its potentially violent sanction—that determines what is right. Or, as Nietzsche might say: Might makes right.

This underlying image and metaphorical conceptualization of law is widely shared and cognitively real; it is, therefore, constitutive of our social reality. It is reflected not only in cultural imagery and common language but also in conventional legal materials. Consider, first, the predominant Western iconography of justice: the Goddess Justicia (fig. 12.1), the familiar image of the blindfolded woman who holds aloft the scales of justice, in her left hand, also carries a sword in her right.[18] So, too, the principal word for "law" in so many European languages is the same word that connotes the opposite of left: in French, *droit* and *Droit*; in Spanish, *derecho* and *Derecho*; in German, *recht* and *Recht*; and, in English, "right" and "legal rights."* *Black's Law Dictionary*, perhaps the most conventional of legal sources, defines the Roman legal concept *jus* as a "*quasi* personified factor in human history or conduct or social development" and as "'a right'; that is, a power . . . or a capacity residing in one person of controlling, with the assent and assistance of the state, the actions of another." Indeed, *Black's* concludes: "It is thus seen to possess the same ambiguities as the words '*droit*,' '*recht*,' and '*right*.'"[19]

The English word "right" derives most immediately from the German *recht*, which derives in turn from the Latin *rectus* or "straight." Thus, the notion of a legal right is a conceptual counterpart to the idea of a rule: Both are understood in terms of the legally defined behaviors or metaphorical paths marked out by the law. This metaphorical conception, moreover, is closely related to the personification metaphor for law. It is "the Law" per-

---

* Italian is the exception: There the terms are, respectively, *destra* and *Direto*. The latter, however, shares with the English "right" the same root in the Latin—*rectus*, for "straight."

FIGURE 12.1   Statue of Justicia atop Borough Hall, Brooklyn, N.Y.

(Photo by Les Morsillo)

sonified that lays down the rules (from the Latin *regula,* meaning "straight-edge"; and *regere,* meaning "to lead straight") or paths that we are to follow, as in *the rule of law.*[20] Thus, our very concept of rights is intimately bound up with our notions of power: "Meaningful" rights are those backed up by a sanction administered by some authority.[21] To put it another way, the concepts "right" and "legal rights" both have a specific entailment of violence.*

---

* This notion of rights is also an entailment of the conventional metaphor RATIONAL ARGUMENT IS WAR (discussed in chapter 10). The entailment of violence is systematic in the way we talk about rights, whether one advocates for or against the concept (the references are given in n.21). Thus, Tushnet writes: "The language of rights attempts to describe how people can *defend* the interests they have by virtue of their humanity." Minow maintains that rights are "the language we use to try to persuade others to let us *win this round.*" Commenting on the work of Roberto Unger, Hutchinson and Monahan explain: "The vocabulary of rights is enlisted as a *rhetorical weapon* in a larger ideological and po-

To understand the underlying cognitive structure of the concept "Law" is, in an important sense, to understand what law "really is." As Peter Gabel explains, "when we realize that we routinely speak these ideas and images to each other . . . , we can begin to form an understanding of how the law is actually constitutive of our social experience."[22] To understand this conceptual structure is, thus, to understand something fundamentally important about law's *social* meaning: How we think about and understand law affects how we behave towards it; and this is true whether—and whenever—we defer to it, challenge it, or actively seek to change it.

Consider the conceptual model implicit in our language and thought. On that model, law is an authority figure who rules through the threat or imposition of force. (Let us call this "the command model.") We may think—or hope—that law rules wisely, fairly, and well. But, as Schauer remarks, obedience is expected in any event: "law does not just stand there to be watched. We expect people to obey its mandates, even when they disagree."[23] Respectful noncompliance is simply not an option when every failure to comply is seen as an act of defiance—that is, a "rebellion against the supreme power." This, too, is the understanding reflected in legal doctrine: Disobedience of a court's order is punishable as a "contempt," and that is true even when the order or the statute under which it was issued is subsequently held unconstitutional.[24] The same incipient authoritarianism is evident in Owen Fiss's controversial remark that "in legal interpretation there is only one school and attendance is mandatory."[25]

Representation or Artifact?

We are now ready to unpack the argument implicit in the previous section. The argument has two parts. We can summarize the first part as follows: Like the ritual of the *Brachah,* the law is at bottom a belief, concept, or mental artifact; but, it is a mental artifact that emerges as meaningful only as it is externalized and realized in social practice. To put it more sharply, we understand law in a certain way and *make* it real whenever we (or Owen Fiss or the Supreme Court) act on that understanding. By juxtaposing Cover's and Nietzsche's substantively distinct but metaphorically similar accounts of law, we were able to tease out the metaphors of objectification and personification that form the core of that understanding.

---

litical *conflict.*" And Unger himself expresses the point in the darkest, but most colorful metaphor: "The right," he says, "is a loaded gun that the rightholder may shoot at will in his corner of town. Outside that corner the other licensed gunmen may shoot him down."

Within traditional jurisprudence, Cover's and Nietzsche's views represent overtly antagonistic approaches to law. Viewed from a cognitive perspective, however, these disparate accounts reflect two complementary moments or truths about our social understanding of law. Indeed, when viewed in terms of the personification metaphor, these putatively disparate accounts manifest a surprising psychological and conceptual coherence: We understand law as an authority worthy of our commitment and deserving of our obedience; we understand law as a coercive authority whose unflinching long arm brings to justice those who would ignore her commands. Law, in other words, is a complex cognitive and social artifact. The traditional jurisprudential accounts such as natural law theory (including its contemporary successors) and legal positivism (including its contemporary variants) simply do not do justice to the deeper psychological resonance of our core conception of law. We might say that each is a pale, deracinated reflection of a richer, more vibrant cognitive reality.

The second part of the argument concerns the implications of that core conception of law. In our idealized cognitive model, it is the Law personified that lays down the rules or paths we are to follow and that enforces these constraints by threat of force.* One consequence of this model is that legal positivism—at least in its crude, command-model form—seems merely constitutive of common sense. In technical terms, legal positivism is a prototype effect arising from our cognitive model of law, which explains the stubborn persistence of the positivist understanding of law notwithstanding the blistering critiques to which it has been subject. As we shall see in a moment, legal positivism (in both its crude *and* sophisticated versions) is simply untenable as a theory of law.

Of course, to argue against common sense is to fight an uphill battle. Thus, many people will find it more sensible to conclude that the command model is the representation of reality and that Nietzsche's metaphors are just tropes. So, too, many people will view Cover's explanation of the law as nothing more than a perhaps astute account of our internal psychology; they will find more congenial the contemporary legal positivist account that, as we have seen, identifies law with a set of authoritative sources and authorized social institutions. After all, the command model has an obvious real-world referent in the criminal justice system, where it is enacted and

---

* We can represent this conception in terms of the conventional metaphors: LAW IS A PERSON, ACTIONS ARE MOTIONS, CONSTRAINTS ON ACTIONS ARE CONSTRAINTS ON MOTIONS, CONTROL IS UP, and RULES (AND LEGAL RIGHTS) ARE PATHS.

confirmed every time an offender is arrested and punished. And it is simple common sense that what legislatures and judges write is *law,* while what I write isn't.

Why do these disparate accounts of law matter? Here is one reason one might think that it does: In chapter 1, we saw that the conventional understanding of law presents a paradox. As epitomized by the "forest of constraint" trope, the crux of our concept of law is that it operates as an external constraint. The conventional personification of law is but an instantiation of this more general concept; as Cover says, it is the community that "posits a law, external to itself." But when the external constraint of the law turns out to be a mental artifact—i.e., the product of a metaphorical projection—it becomes hard to see how the conventional view can defend itself against the disenchantment (or cynical disillusion) occasioned by self-reflection. This is the situation of sophisticated legal actors, whether critics or participants. We saw this disenchantment and disillusion with respect to Duncan Kennedy in the last chapter. Much the same is true of Judge Posner, whose activity theory (discussed in chapter 8) reduces precedent to "only one source of information on which to base judgment." [26] Let us call this reification, in which we treat our own projection as an external reality, "the ontological fallacy." And, for reasons that should be apparent from the last chapter, I will use the term "empowerment fantasy" to describe the false sense of freedom that seems to arise from the recognition of this fallacy.

There are those who, like Nietzsche, pursue the positivist project for its capacity to reveal the ontological fallacy and thereby demystify law. But many mainstream legal positivists are engaged in the very different project of (to paraphrase Hart) vindicating law in some centrally important sense. Indeed, if one attraction of the positivist view is that it seems to conform best with common sense, another must be the fear that there could be no rule of law without an authoritative body of determinate legal rules and a hierarchical set of legal institutions with which to enforce them.

Both motivations rest on misapprehensions. As we have seen repeatedly, common sense is but a surface effect of more complex cognitive processes. And the fear of lawlessness is obviously unfounded. After all, the *nomoi* that Cover describes are permeated by law of the strongest sort—i.e., law capable of inspiring not just obedience but commitments spelled out "in the medium of blood." Rather, the common sense view and the fear associated with it are distortions born of the subject-object dualism that frames conventional thinking about law: Specifically, they are manifestations of the standard view that understands constraint as necessarily external and, therefore, defines freedom as the absence of constraint. And it is this mistaken understanding that leads to the misplaced fear that an artifactual law—i.e., one that we construct for ourselves "of whole cloth," so to speak—cannot be a meaningful constraint.

Legal positivism, whether the crude positivism of the command model or the more sophisticated version espoused by contemporary legal positivists, is a project doomed to failure for the reason identified by Cover: Positivist law (i.e., state law) is an attempt to organize and direct social power, but law cannot organize or cabin the social meaning upon which that exercise of power depends.* We can further characterize positivism's shortcomings as: (1) the epistemic objection; (2) its corollary, the circularity problem; (3) the existential objection; and (4) the problem of conceptual collapse.

1. *The epistemic objection.* The first problem can be rehearsed quickly, for we have developed it at length. Recall that the heart of legal positivism lies in the notion that one can differentiate conceptually and analytically between that which is law and that which is not, between the legal and the larger social world of the nonlegal. Thus, Schauer explains that "positivism is about normative systems smaller than and distinguishable from the entire normative universe" (199). But, as we have seen, this separation is impossible because every legal prescription is necessarily situated in and, therefore, inextricable from its larger, meaning-conferring context. As Cover observes: "No set of legal institutions or prescriptions exists apart from the narratives that locate it and give it meaning" (4), nor could they. "Precepts must 'have meaning,' but they necessarily borrow it from materials created by social activity that is not subject to the strictures of provenance that characterize what we call formal lawmaking" (18).

2. *The circularity problem.* The second problem both follows from and deepens the epistemic objection. It is not just that the law is constructed out of and, therefore, permeated by the larger culture. It is, rather, that (as elaborated in chapter 8) rules cannot work *as* rules unless they already reflect the normatively loaded understandings of those who are expected to obey them. Rules thus formulated will be perceived as natural, right, and deserving of obedience because they will be experienced as confirmed by the ob-

---

* As Cover points out, the same is true of Dworkin: "Dworkin's critique of the 'positivism' articulated by Hart does not deny the social control over precept articulation that I am positing here. Though Dworkin disagrees with Hart about how the judge, in particular, as one source of privileged precept articulation, goes about his or her judicial task, Dworkin does not deny the special social control exercised by virtue of the office" (17 n.44).

jective qualities of the social world (just as the command model seems to be confirmed by the criminal justice system). The positivist may respond that a legal rule that departs from existing social practices, expectations, and mores is nonetheless law. But it is a weaker, degraded form of law precisely because it will be experienced as less compelling by those it supposedly governs. (Recall the examples of Prohibition in the 1920s and the hypothetical law requiring citizens to genuflect with each mention of Holmes.) What makes law *Law* is not the simple matter of its provenance or pedigree. The "lawfulness" of law is a function of cultural significance and social motivation. Contrary to the suppositions of both the command model and the separation thesis, the most powerful determinants of law are embodied in the social interactions and practices that give rise to one's senses of order and cultural truth. The ultimate "rule of recognition" is that dictated by social experience.

3. *The existential objection.* Where the first two objections go to the conceptual plausibility of positivist law, the existential objection challenges its psychological viability. Legal meaning can neither be restricted nor reduced to the manifestations of positive law because, as Cover points out, every legal prescription is a call to human action. "If there existed two legal orders with identical legal precepts and identical, predictable patterns of public force, they would nonetheless differ essentially in meaning if, in one of the orders, the precepts were universally venerated while in the other they were regarded by many as fundamentally unjust" (7).

Cover gives as an example the contrast between positivist judges like Chief Justice Taney and Garrisonian abolitionists like Wendell Phillips. Both Taney and Phillips agreed on the dictates of positive law—i.e., both agreed that, as written, the Constitution countenanced and protected slavery. Taney authored the infamous *Dred Scott* decision that upheld the property rights of the slaveholder, voided the Missouri Compromise, and helped precipitate the Civil War.[27] Phillips and the Garrisonians, in contrast, "opted for a radically different course. . . . They eschewed participation in and renounced obligation to government under such a Constitution" (36). In one sense, Cover explains, Phillips and Taney "agreed" on the meaning of Article 4, Section 2, Clause 3 of the Constitution: Both thought that it provided for the compulsory return of fugitives from slavery. But, in a more important sense, they did not agree.* Taney's reading "assumed a principle

---

* We can highlight that disagreement by saying that where Taney read the Constitution to require the return of escaped slaves, the abolitionists read it to force the return to slavery of people who had escaped.

justifying obedience to the Constitution" (37), while Phillips and the Garrisonians read the Constitution as a corrupt national bargain—in William Lloyd Garrison's famous words, "A Covenant with Death and an Agreement with Hell"—that could not state a valid norm. "The two groups," Cover elaborates,

> could only be said to agree on the meaning of the document abstracted from any need or desire to act upon it. But by its own terms the text is a ground for action. And no two people can be said to agree on what the text requires if they disagree on the circumstances in which it will warrant their actions. (37 n.104)

The fundamental problem is that neither the crude nor the sophisticated version of positivism grasps the psychological rigors of interpretation. Positivism understands interpretation as nothing more than a problem of communication: It can be done poorly or well; for the positivist, however, interpretation is nothing more than a mental act that requires the appropriate level of fidelity to a text (or the framers' intent, etc.). Cover's response is that this can never be true of law, first, because legal interpretation always occurs "in the shadow of coercion" and, second, because legal materials "present not only bodies of rules or doctrine to be understood, but also worlds to be inhabited" (6).

This latter point states a profound truth not limited to law: Commitment is a phenomenological condition of all interpretation. As we saw in chapter 5, every narrative invites the reader to enter its world and to view that world in a particular way; indeed, every narrative requires the reader to *construct* that world in order just to enter into it. We might say that empathy of this sort is the sine qua non of interpretation. It follows that interpretation always entails a degree of ethical commitment because, in Ricoeur's words, "what is interpreted in a text is the proposing of a world that I might inhabit and into which I might project my ownmost powers." The positivist model of interpretation is abstracted from—and, therefore, oblivious to—the social contexts and situations that make human action meaningful. Deliberately applied, positivism represents an ethic of psychological denial hiding behind a mask of judicial obligation. But every interpretation implicates the commitments of the interpreter, and every legal interpretation implicates the commitments both of the interpreter and of those subject to her judgments—each of whom must decide whether to follow, ignore, or enforce the law's demand.

4. *Conceptual Collapse.* Though the final objection applies to both versions of positivism, the details differ. For crude positivism, it is intrinsic. Recall Nietzsche's characterization of law as something the superior power *imposes* upon its weaker subordinates. As Bernard Williams observes, this is a view already discredited in Plato's *Republic:*

> Thrasymachus says that the conventions that enjoin respect for others' interests—"justice," as it may be called—are an instrument of the strong to exploit the weak. This immediately raises the question, what makes these people strong? Thrasymachus speaks as if political or social power were not itself a matter of convention, and that is a view barely adequate to the school playground. His position is rapidly followed in the *Republic* by another, which takes this point. According to this, justice is the product of a convention adopted by a group of people to protect themselves. It is a contractual device of the weak to make themselves strong.[28]

We can see the same problem in Posner's Nietzschean assertion (though, in fact, he is paraphrasing Holmes) that "truth" in law is based on force:

> To be blunt, the *ultima ratio* of law is indeed force. . . . If you ask how we know that Venus exerts a gravitational pull on Mars, the answer is that the people who study these things agree it does. If you ask how we know that the Fourteenth Amendment forbids the states to prohibit certain abortions, the answer is that the people who have political power to decide the issue—namely, the Justices of the Supreme Court—have so determined by majority vote. (83)

What this argument actually demonstrates is that law is necessarily based on convention—both the convention that the Supreme Court decides by majority vote (and not, say, by the relative physical strength of the justices) and the convention that prompts litigants, states, and the other branches of the federal government to treat the Court's decisions as authoritative despite the fact that it wields neither the power of the sword nor of the purse. For just this reason, Hamilton, in *The Federalist* No. 78, referred to the Court as the "least dangerous" branch of government.

It is, thus, meaningless to explain law (or identify its provenance) as based on power or force. "Power" cannot work as a foundational account of justice, morality, law, or anything else because at each and every step of the way, the capacity to exercise power is itself contingent on some complex set of social conventions and understandings.[29]

Because contemporary legal positivism takes as its point of departure the rejection of John Austin's command theory of law, it does not face the same problem of conceptual collapse. Still, it has a comparable problem of origins. Contemporary legal positivists identify law by reference to a norm or set of norms that picks out legal norms from the universe of all other norms (such as those of morality, politics, or culture). H. L. A. Hart calls this norm the "rule of recognition"; Hans Këlsen refers to it as the "gründ-norm"; and Dworkin (in critiquing positivism) dubs it a "pedigree." The problem the positivists face, however, is that the rule of recognition cannot itself be a legal rule, for what could identify it as such? Accordingly, Schauer notes that contemporary legal positivists acknowledge that "the validity of a system [of law] is not a question of validity at all, but of the social fact that a certain system is treated as the law of some community by that community" (120). In other words, as he says elsewhere: "The ultimate rule of recognition is a matter of social fact, and so determining it is for empiri-cal investigation rather than legal analysis. . . . It may be less distracting to think of the ultimate source of recognition, following Brian Simpson, as a *practice*." [30] What this statement means, of course, is that it is only a matter of social practice or convention that certain norms are identified as legal norms and accorded the force of law. To paraphrase Cover, it is the community that posits the law as something above itself that it is commit-ted to obey.

But the game is up once it is conceded that the social determines the le-gal. Once it is acknowledged that social practices and understandings are what identify the legal as such, it becomes difficult to see why that is not true in every case. If it is a social fact that our community treats the Consti-tution as the rule of recognition, then the question whether it continues to do so is a question that—to paraphrase Schauer—calls for empirical in-vestigation rather than philosophical analysis. Perhaps the community has simply ignored the process of formal amendment prescribed by Article 5 and changed the Constitution *tout court*. (This is one way to read Acker-man's theory of "constitutional moments.") [31] Perhaps it has, for whatever social and political reasons, lost or withdrawn the sense of validity previ-ously accorded a constitutional right—liberty of contract, for example. Perhaps it has come to expect legal protection for the sexual autonomy that large numbers of citizens have come to enjoy. [32] There is simply no practi-cal, logical, or philosophical reason why law should be socially contingent at the wholesale level but not at the retail level. The problem of conceptual collapse thus leads us back to the circularity problem.

Ultimately, each of these arguments derive their force from legal positivism's failure to take social contingency seriously. Recall that in chapter 9, Schauer's analysis of slippery slope arguments was undone by the introduction of time and contingency into the equation. In effect, positivism takes a thin, synchronic slice of social life and spins an entire theory of law upon it. But law has both past and future: The antecedent reality that positivism fails to address—law's situated social meaning—is reflected in the epistemic objection, the circularity problem, and the problem of conceptual collapse. The problem of the subsequent social reality of law—law's implications—is reflected in the existential objection.

What positivism gets right is the notion that law is the product of human beings and human institutions rather than of some transcendent set of fundamental moral principles. But on this score, even Cover is a "positivist." He is not, however, a *legal* positivist because he understands law as an ongoing cultural production of human communities rather than as the result of formal lawmaking. The problem with legal positivism is not that it sees law as a social fact—that is certainly correct. The problem with legal positivism is that it commits the worst version of the ontological fallacy: It offers an alienated, elitist vision of law as an external phenomenon that emanates only from approved sources. In doing so, it obscures a more profound, productive, and humane understanding of law and, thus, estranges us from ourselves.

THE MEANING AND POSSIBILITY OF RIGHTS

We can now answer the question, posed earlier, why it matters that law is an artifact rather than a representation. What is at stake is nothing less than the content and substance of law: The question about the nature of law is, necessarily, a question of what makes law meaningful as *Law*. And the question of what makes law meaningful is also a question of how one makes law.

We know how the positivist answers that question: If it is to be law, it must be made by the authorized institutions acting in a manner consistent with the authorized sources. This view accords, as we have seen, both with common sense and with the command model implicit in our language and thought. But this understanding has the psychological consequence of orienting us to the law as its passive and alienated subjects. As Peter Gabel explains:

> First, to the extent that individuals are represented as "having" rights, . . .
> we represent each individual ontologically as being a passive locus of pos-

sible action, rather than as in action with others already. Second, these rights are conceived as being granted to the individual from an outside source, from "the State" which either creates them (in the positivist version of the constitutional thought-schema) or recognizes them (in the natural-law version) through the passage of "laws." Thus, insofar as the individual emerges from his passive station to act and interact with others on the basis of his rights, he does so because he has been "allowed" to do so in advance. (1576–77)

Gabel's Sartrean phenomenology of rights consciousness—and his argument against the utility of rights—goes much deeper, however. In his view, the state is a hallucinatory projection that takes the place of real community, and legal rights are the media of alienation that, in ordering our relationships, take the place of real relatedness. "How can a group haunted by an absence of community reassure itself that it is characterized by the presence of connection?" he asks. "By conspiring to represent itself to itself as politically constituted" (1573). Gabel sees legal rights as reifications "intended to solve the problem of contingency by pretending that the next moment can be colonized in advance" (1569). Thus understood, rights are "drained of existential quality, which is to say of all vitality" (1575), because they displace "the immediacy and contingency of truly lived encounters" (1576).

Gabel argues, therefore, that empowering social movements (such as those of labor, civil rights, and feminism) are doomed to co-optation and failure the minute they turn to the state to seek the security of legal rights. Gabel acknowledges that the rights won by such movements never lose their resonance entirely: "Once this meaning has been realized in social experience even a little bit, we retain it like an ethical memory enveloped by its alienated meaning but not wholly erased by it" (1597).* But he rejects the possibility of the objectification and retention of this meaning in legal form. It is wrong, he explains, to think that

we could produce a quantity of movement and freeze it in stone, and then another and freeze that in stone, until we had the right to everything we wanted. To think any of these things is to participate in the illusion that the right to an experience can create the experience itself, and

* In a footnote at this point, Gabel notes that his article "could be rewritten from this point of view, focusing on the ways that rights exert a positive force on social relationships in the form of such ethical memories" (1547 n.41).

to reverse the true relationship between the meaning of verbal concepts
and the qualitative or lived milieu out of which they arise. (1598)

In the end, Gabel's argument is unpersuasive because he falsely polar-
izes the alternatives. The choice between an unequivocal objective meaning
"fixed in stone" and a romanticized, holistic meaning that can be lived only
in its unalienated fullness is a spurious choice. Neither absolute is available
to us. All meaning is grounded in experience, and all experience is shaped
by our preexisting concepts and understandings. To assess the meaning and
possibility of rights, we must attend to the middle ground that lies between
Gabel's false extremes.

Still, the main thrust of Gabel's critique of rights is very much on point.
Law's project is, as he says, "to solve the problem of contingency by pretending that the next moment can be colonized in advance." But contingency cannot be cabined in this way; as we saw in chapter 8, the complexity and flux of life cannot be contained within the square corners of a legal
rule (even if one could be written in stone). And, though Gabel romanticizes
the relationship between the meaning of verbal concepts and "the qualitative or lived milieu out of which they arise," he is certainly correct that
there is a loss of meaning when concepts are detached from their grounding practices. To paraphrase Llewellyn, rights are in the first instance a set
of ways of living and doing that include accompanying patterns of thought
and emotion.

The ontological fallacy, in other words, has consequences. Its necessary
effect is to separate meaning from the social practices and understandings
that make things meaningful. This effect finds its corollary in the standard
methodology of legal reasoning that abstracts meaning from context and
reduces it to a set of legal principles or rules. The reification of "Law"—i.e.,
its metaphorical projection as OBJECT—is paralleled by a reification in legal reasoning in which the content of the law is also projected as an OBJECT
detached from the social practices and experiences that would make it
meaningful. This parallelism is natural in the sense that both reifications are
metaphorical entailments or subcases of the IDEAS ARE OBJECTS mapping
that is part of the CONDUIT metaphor-system—that is, both reifications instantiate similar sets of neural activation patterns. But these reifications are
a parallelism and not an equivalence, which means that it is not a logical or
necessary entailment of the metaphorical projection of law as OBJECT. Self-
reflection is possible; we can be conscious of "Law" as a metaphorical projection and still appreciate that law (no less than language) must draw its
meaning from life.

Gabel points to studies by critical legal scholars documenting specific historical instances in which courts and legislatures have manipulated rights gains through a series of interpretive strategies that denature the movements' rights-victories.[33] But the success of these strategies has less to do with the statist identity of these interpreters than with the deracinated methodology that dominates legal reasoning. Alan Freeman's classic analysis of anti-discrimination law, for example, shows how rights won by racial minorities were systematically eviscerated by refocusing the law away from the victim's perspective to that of the perpetrator: Central to the former perspective "is an insistence on concrete historical experience rather than timeless abstract norms." The latter view, in contrast, is concerned "with eradicating the behaviors of individuals" and centers, accordingly, on "the principle of individual (or sometimes institutional) fault."[34]

The emptiness of legal rights in this form—i.e., their loss of meaning—is the inevitable consequence of cutting rationality loose from its grounding in human experience. To say that *Brown v. Board of Education* is a case about "freedom of association" or a constitutional requirement of state "color-blindness" is to falsify meaning precisely because it fails to see that the meaning of *Brown* is written in the lived experience of slavery and segregation, of civil war and social struggle.[35] Pat Williams puts the point with characteristic eloquence:

> Blacks believed in [rights] so much and so hard that we gave them life where there was none before. We held onto them, put the hope of them into our wombs, and mothered them—not just the notion of them. We nurtured rights and gave rights life. And this was not the dry process of reification, from which life is drained and reality fades as the cement of conceptual determinism hardens round—but its opposite. This was the resurrection of life from 400-year-old ashes; the parthenogenesis of un-fertilized hope.[36]

We are the context, the larger frame, that gives legal interpretation its meaning and resonance. As Cover says: "Law connects 'reality' to alternity constituting a new reality with a bridge built out of committed social behavior."[37]

It does not follow, of course, that we can fix the meaning of such rights in stone. As Gabel observes, the meaning of such rights will always remain

> *contingent* in the sense that it is rooted in the particularity of a concrete, lived experience, and *determinate* in the sense that it is expressive only of

the existential quality of this experience, as this quality might be realized in its universality through an infinite number of particular, historical instances. (1590)

Gabel thinks this true only of the rights consciousness that arises from empowering social movements. But the ethical memory that Gabel acknowledges does not simply evaporate when a movement wanes. Once something has been realized in social experience, it remains as motivation for the imaginative abstraction and encoding of legal concepts. The idealized cognitive models that work in every other aspect of our cognitive and communicative life are no less available to law. Rights and other legal concepts continue to be meaningful because we can recall and reflect on the lived experience that gave them birth. That is what it means to be human and rational. And that is the way in which law contributes to social structure and the institutionalization of social meaning.

But reality must always be remade, lest the committed actions of yesterday dissolve into tomorrow's clichés. A law can be promulgated, but *legal meaning* must be lived if it is to continue to be recognized as such. Many people will find this claim disquieting; after all, the whole purpose of law is, in the words of the Preamble to the U.S. Constitution, to "secure the Blessings of Liberty to ourselves and our Posterity." The point, however, is that there is no constitutional or other legal stone in which to engrave our liberties: That reification *is* the ontological fallacy. Rights are real only to the extent that they are realized in lived human experience and sustained by committed social action. And, whatever its shortcomings, a precarious reality is still preferable to a complacent but unreliable illusion.

To *make* meaning, one must *do* meaning. Legal meaning must first germinate in action and then take root in our forms of life. The possibility of rights, in other words, lies in learning to rediscover their locus in our practices and commitments. Without that ground, there can be no rights and no law worth speaking of.

And it's a good thing, besides. As Merleau-Ponty observes: "The idea of a fortuitous humanity which has no cause already won is what gives absolute value to our *virtue*." [38]

Roots Thrust into the World

In his magisterial *Doing What Comes Naturally*, [39] Stanley Fish challenges the belief, cherished by many in the literary and legal academies, that the insights of antifoundationalist theory can be harnessed to politically progressive ends. Fish calls this belief "anti-foundationalist theory hope." The central antifoundationalist claim is that all human knowledge is situated knowledge, "that human history is the context in which we know" (324). The implicit minor premise is that there can never be an Archimedean point outside of some situated, historical practice or perspective. Fish agrees with this insight, of course. What he objects to is the assumption that it can free "us from the hold of unwarranted absolutes so that we may more flexibly pursue the goals of human flourishing or liberal conversation." He does not believe that once we "know that our convictions about truth and factuality have not been imposed on us by the world," we will then be able to "set them aside in favor of convictions that we choose freely" (323). That is impossible, Fish argues, because the insight that everything is socially constructed cannot open a way to a better, more free, or unconstructed context. If the antifoundationalist insight is correct, there is no place to go but to some other historically situated, socially constructed context. Critique, no matter how rigorously deconstructive, merely "delivers us from the grip of one system only to deposit us in the (equally frozen) grip of another" (457).

One may recognize in this argument the model for my skepticism of the empowerment fantasy. For Fish, however, the argument against mutability is but one consequence of a more general argument that theory and critical self-consciousness are impossible. Thus, he maintains that the mind is an extension of the system of beliefs in which it is situated. Beliefs, he explains, "are not what you think about but what you think with, and it is within the space provided by their articulations that mental activity—including the activity of theorizing—goes on" (326). Reflection is not possible because it "requires a space in which it can occur, and . . . that space of reflection cannot already be occupied by what are to be its objects." He continues:

> If reflection must occur in a place or moment apart from the "prevailing realm of purposes," and if the first thesis of critical thought is that the "prevailing realm of purposes" covers the field, then reflection can never get off the ground because it is always tethered to the ground from which it claims to set us free. (455)

He concludes that the antifoundationalist insight teaches us that we can believe only what we believe: "Being situated not only means that one cannot achieve a distance on one's beliefs, but that one's beliefs do not relax their hold because one 'knows' that they are local and not universal" (467).

This argument has the profoundly disturbing implication that there is no such thing as freedom; with characteristic bravado, Fish does not flinch from drawing precisely this conclusion. He denies that "there are degrees of constraint, or, more precisely, that there is a continuum on which forms of thought and social organization can be ranked" because

> the degree of constraint—at least in relation to an ideal condition of freedom—is always the same and always total. By this I do not mean that we are never free to act, but that our freedom is a function of—in the sense of being dependent on—some other structure of constraint without which action of any kind would be impossible. This may seem counterintuitive to those who are accustomed to identify freedom with the *absence* of constraints but, in fact, such a state, if it could be achieved, would produce not free actions, but *no* actions. An action is only conceivable against a background of alternative paths, a background that is already a constraint in that by marking out some actions as possible it renders unavailable others that might emerge as possibilities against a different background. . . . It follows, then, that it makes no sense to imagine conditions of *no* constraint, and it follows, too, that there can be no continuum which differentiates institutions or structures as being more or less constrained, more or less free, because freedom, in whatever shape it appears, is another name for constraint. (459)

The problem is that this argument loses all persuasive force once we expose its all-or-nothing structure: Why must all liberation and constraint be measured against an "ideal condition of freedom"? This all-or-nothing way of framing the argument is, as Merleau-Ponty says, but the "rationalist's dilemma: either the free act is possible, or it is not—either the event originates in me or is imposed on me from outside." [40] Fish, moreover, fashions his argument by means of the conventional metaphors of freedom and constraint with which we began this book.* We "are accustomed," he says, "to identify freedom with the *absence* of constraints." Fish writes as if he were rejecting this notion, when, in fact, he is exploiting it. He knows that we *all* identify freedom with the absence of constraints. He uses that understanding as the fulcrum of his argument: Once he has shown that we are never without constraints, it will follow that we are never really free.

---

* Fish invokes the conventional metaphorical conception ACTIONS ARE MOTIONS and CONSTRAINTS ON ACTION ARE CONSTRAINTS ON MOTION: "An action," he observes, "is only conceivable against a background of alternative paths." But, he points out, without such paths "marking out some actions as possible" and "render[ing] unavailable others," there could be no action at all. Where there can be no action, there can of course be no freedom.

How else could we conceptualize freedom? Fish himself suggests an alternative when he says that "our freedom is a function of—in the sense of being dependent on—some other structure of constraint." Of course, he immediately invokes the rationalist logic of P or not-P to assert that "that there can be no continuum which differentiates institutions or structures as being more or less constrained, more or less free, because freedom, in whatever shape it appears, is another name for constraint." But this is a false logic. To say that freedom is dependent on constraint is not the same as saying that freedom is a synonym for constraint. Dependence is a relation, not an identity. I depend on my wife for emotional and physical nurturance, on my job for economic security, on my computer to get my work done. Each of these dependencies constrains my freedom of action in significant ways; each also enables me to do things—like write this book—that I could not otherwise accomplish. The fact that "I am a psychological and historical structure," Merleau-Ponty points out, "does not limit my access to the world, but on the contrary is my means of entering into communication with it" (455).

What if we were to take seriously the notion that our constraints provide the enabling conditions of possibility? Two things would follow. First, the focus would shift to the different concrete possibilities that are enabled. There is, for example, an obvious difference between the degree of constraint experienced by the adherent of a strict religious faith and that experienced by the typical member of secular culture. Both ways of being in the world are socially constructed; and, in Fish's absolute sense, they are thus equally constraining. But in a more significant sense—and in the only sense that can matter for us as situated humans—they are not. Both the artist and the professional house painter are constituted in part by their social roles, each the function of what Fish would call a "structure of constraint." But the artist and the house painter experience neither the same constraints nor the same possibilities of creativity and expression.

Second, to reconceptualize freedom as a function of constraint rather than its absence is profoundly to change our sense of self and place in the world. It is quintessentially modern to understand constraint as something to be overcome. It is theoretically radical (and characteristically postmodern) to understand that constraints cannot be avoided because they provide the enabling conditions of possibility. Fish's argument would have it that we are not, then, free; but this is just another manifestation of antinomial capture. In an antifoundationalist world, one does not ask for absolutes. All one has are possibilities; either they are taken up and maximized, or they are not.

Merleau-Ponty understood that "without the roots which it thrusts into the world, it would not be freedom at all" (456). Our freedom is exercised not *in* a situation, but *through* it. Freedom is not a capacity to transcend one's context but to transform it by retracing or reworking the grounds of one's social situation to create possibilities that would not otherwise exist.[41]

To make this point concrete, consider the question of freedom in the extreme case of compulsion under torture. Sartre and Merleau-Ponty took up this issue in a famous exchange written in the shadow of Nazi occupation. In *Being and Nothingness,* Sartre argued that "even the red-hot pincers of the torturer do not exempt us from being free."[42] He did not mean by this that the victim had an unlimited physical capacity to resist. What he meant was that, as an existential matter, "the *very impossibility* of continuing in a certain direction must be freely constituted" (506). One might think that the victim's surrender is induced by the inability to withstand more pain; but, for Sartre, it is the impossibility of continuing that is induced "by means of the free renunciation" (ibid.). In the most controversial passage, he elaborated this claim:

> In fact no matter what pressure is exerted on the victim, abjuration remains *free;* it is a spontaneous production, in response to a situation; it manifests human-reality. No matter what resistance the victim has offered, no matter how long he has waited before begging for mercy, he would have been able despite all to wait ten minutes, one minute, one second longer. He has *determined* the moment at which the pain becomes unbearable. The proof of this is the fact that he will later live out his abjuration in remorse and shame. Thus he is entirely responsible for it. (403)

Merleau-Ponty rejected Sartre's claim of complete existential freedom. "True reflection," he argued, leads me to recognize my subjectivity "not despite my body and historical situation, but, on the contrary, by being this body and this situation." But, once I take this point of view: "I can no longer pretend to be a nihilation *(néant),* and to choose myself continually out of nothing at all" (452).

> Let us suppose that a man is tortured to make him talk. If he refuses to give the names and addresses which it is desired to extract from him, this does not arise from a solitary and unsupported decision: the man still feels himself to be with his comrades, and, being still involved in the common struggle, he is as it were incapable of talking. Or else, for months or years, he has, in his mind, faced this test and staked his whole life upon

it. . . . These motives do not cancel out freedom, but at least ensure that
it does not go unbuttressed in being. What withstands pain is not, in
short, a bare consciousness, but the prisoner with his comrades or with
those he loves and under whose gaze he lives. (453–54)

If the prisoner is sustained by his connection with those outside the torture
chamber, it is a connection that he has actively cultivated: "And probably
the individual in his prison daily reawakens these phantoms, which give back
to him the strength he gave to them" (454).

Merleau-Ponty's astuteness is remarkable, as made clear by contemporaneous events in Poland. On August 2, 1943, approximately sixty Jewish
prisoners staged a successful revolt at the Treblinka death camp—where a
million people (including the entire Warsaw Ghetto) were exterminated in
little over a year. The prisoners killed the guards and burned the camp. About
700 prisoners escaped, though most did not survive the war. (The Nazis soon
demolished what was left of the camp, planting it over with trees and lu-
pines.) As documented by Jean-François Steiner in his masterful and moving account, the organized resistance began with a group that formed to
dissuade the nightly suicides in the barracks. The argument that succeeded
with their fellow prisoners, and that sustained the underground through the
revolt, was that the prisoners had an obligation to those on the outside to survive the camp in order to bear witness.[43]

Thankfully few of us are tested in this way. But freedom, even in our quo-
tidian lives, consists in the fact that we are situated beings who mutually construct and reconstruct the world in which we live. Consider the constraints
of the many social roles that each of us play. These roles do not originate
from us, but neither do they exist without us. Every role must be enacted,
and every enactment is also a potential reconstruction. The world, in other
words, is not simply a context in which we find ourselves; it is a dimension
of our existence. It is not a constraint to be overcome, but a product of our
interactions. As Merleau-Ponty says: "We can see, beneath these noisy debates and the fruitless efforts to 'construct' ourselves, the tacit decisions
whereby we have marked round ourselves the field of possibility" (438).

As long as we accept the view that the only reflective position is an im-
possibly transcendent position, we will have to accept Fish's conclusion that
critical self-consciousness is inconceivable and freedom impossible. But once
we recognize that meaning is constituted in our imaginative interactions with
the environment, we can begin to understand ourselves as human—that is,
as beings who think in terms of our situation, form our categories in contact
with our experience, and modify that situation and that experience by the

meaning we discover in them. "Reflection," Merleau-Ponty explains, "does not withdraw from the world . . . ; it steps back to watch the forms of transcendence fly up like sparks from a fire; it slackens the intentional threads which attach us to the world and thus brings them to our notice" (xiii). Once we have noticed the tacit decisions that mark out the social field, we are in a position to rework them from the very place we stand: situated not just in our cultural and historical tradition, but in a real physical and social world that we construct and reconstruct through acts of imagination and commitment.

Which is not to say that we are free to remake the world in any way we please. There are always constraints, and they are difficult to escape precisely because they are embodied in and constantly reinforced by the sedimented social field of public interactions, cultural objects, and common experiences—"the meaning-saturated milieu" in which we are always implicated as participants.[44] If we are to get beyond these sedimentations, it will only be because we have acted to transform that social field directly. Until that time, we will remain prisoners of the social field—the very clearing in the forest—that we ourselves have made.

EPIGRAPH

1. THE WRITINGS OF WILLIAM JAMES: A COMPREHENSIVE EDITION 629, 630–31 (John J. McDermott ed. 1968).

PREFACE

1. RICHARD RORTY, PHILOSOPHY AND THE MIRROR OF NATURE 246 (1979).

2. HILARY PUTNAM, REASON, TRUTH, AND HISTORY 54 (1981) (emphasis deleted).

3. Culombe v. Connecticut, 367 U.S. 568, 604-5 (1961) (Frankfurter, J., concurring); see also Miller v. Fenton, 474 U.S. 104 (1985).

4. I discuss some of these experiences in Steven L. Winter, Cursing the Darkness, 48 U. MIAMI L. REV. 1115 (1994).

5. MARTHA C. NUSSBAUM, LOVE'S KNOWLEDGE: ESSAYS ON PHILOSOPHY AND LITERATURE 229 (1990); see also Steven L. Winter, Human Values in a Postmodern World, 6 YALE J.L. & HUMAN. 233 (1994).

6. As Merleau-Ponty observes:
Superficially considered, our inherence destroys all truth; considered radically, it founds a new idea of truth. As long as I cling to the ideal of an absolute spectator, of knowledge with no point of view, I can see my situation as nothing but a source of error. But if I have once recognized that . . . [history] contains everything which can exist for me, then my contact with the social in the finitude of my situation is revealed to me as the point of origin of all truth, including scientific truth.
MAURICE MERLEAU-PONTY, SIGNS 109 (Richard C. McCleary trans., 1964).

7. See Steven L. Winter, The Cognitive Dimension of the Agon Between Legal Power and Narrative Meaning, 87 MICH. L. REV. 2225 (1989); Steven L. Winter,

Indeterminacy and Incommensurability in Constitutional Law, 78 CAL. L. REV. 1441 (1990); and Steven L. Winter, *Contingency and Community in Normative Practice,* 139 U. PA. L. REV. 963 (1991).

8. WALLACE STEVENS, *Chocorua to Its Neighbors, in* THE COLLECTED POEMS OF WALLACE STEVENS 300 (1954).

CHAPTER ONE

1. Robert Bolt, *A Man for All Seasons* 66 (1960).

2. Sir Howard Beale, *A Man for All Seasons, in* FELIX FRANKFURTER: A TRIBUTE 18–19 (Wallace Mendelson ed., 1964).

3. Duncan Kennedy, *Freedom and Constraint in Adjudication: A Critical Phenomenology of Judging,* 36 J. LEGAL EDUC. 518 (1986). Subsequent page numbers are given in the text.

4. Berkey v. Third Ave. Ry. Co., 244 N.Y. 84, 94, 155 N.E.2d 58, 61 (1930). Typically, this suspicion of metaphor has been shared both by those within the mainstream and by those critical of mainstream jurisprudence. *Compare* David A. Anderson, *Metaphorical Scholarship,* 79 CAL. L. REV. 1205, 1214–15 (1991), *with* Felix Cohen, *Transcendental Nonsense and the Functional Approach,* 35 COLUM. L. REV. 809, 812 (1935).

5. DONALD DAVIDSON, INQUIRIES INTO TRUTH AND INTERPRETATION 245–64 (1984); RICHARD RORTY, CONTINGENCY, IRONY, AND SOLIDARITY 16–20 (1989).

6. John Dewey, *Logic and Legal Method,* 12 CORNELL L.Q. 1 (1924).

7. Even a legal positivist such as Steve Burton, for example, concedes the force of the indeterminacy of legal doctrine and seeks to sidestep it with his "good faith thesis." On this view, a judge is deciding in good faith as long as she considers and applies only "legal" reasons. *See* STEVEN J. BURTON, JUDGING IN GOOD FAITH (1993).

8. DUNCAN KENNEDY, A CRITIQUE OF ADJUDICATION {fin de siècle} 191–212 (1997).

9. 1 PAUL RICOEUR, TIME AND NARRATIVE 69 (Kathleen McLaughlin & David Pellauer trans., 1984).

10. *See* HUBERT L. DREYFUS, WHAT COMPUTERS *STILL* CAN'T DO: A CRITIQUE OF ARTIFICIAL REASON 53 (2d ed. 1979) (observing that "our sense of our situation" is formed, inter alia, "by our sensory-motor skills for coping with objects and people—skills we develop by practice without ever having to represent to ourselves our body as an object, our culture as a set of beliefs, and our propensities as situation → action rules.") For a poststructuralist critique, arguing that the computational approach to the mind is rooted in overly technocratic forms of rationality, see FRED J. EVANS, PSYCHOLOGY AND NIHILISM: A GENEALOGICAL CRITIQUE OF THE COMPUTATIONAL MODEL OF MIND (1993).

11. The principal books by Lakoff and Johnson are (in chronological order): GEORGE LAKOFF & MARK JOHNSON, METAPHORS WE LIVE BY (1980); GEORGE LAKOFF, WOMEN, FIRE, AND DANGEROUS THINGS: WHAT CATEGORIES REVEAL ABOUT THE MIND (1987); MARK JOHNSON, THE BODY IN THE MIND: THE BODILY BASIS OF MEANING, IMAGINATION, AND REASON (1987); GEORGE LAKOFF & MARK JOHNSON, PHILOSOPHY IN THE FLESH: THE EMBODIED MIND AND ITS CHALLENGE TO WESTERN THOUGHT (1999); and GEORGE LAKOFF & RAFAEL F. NÚÑEZ, WHERE MATHEMATICS COMES FROM: HOW THE EMBODIED MIND BRINGS MATHEMATICS

INTO BEING (2000). Edelman's books on the brain include: GERALD M. EDELMAN, NEURAL DARWINISM: THE THEORY OF NEURONAL GROUP SELECTION (1988); THE REMEMBERED PRESENT: A BIOLOGICAL THEORY OF CONSCIOUSNESS (1989); BRIGHT AIR, BRILLIANT FIRE: ON THE MATTER OF THE MIND (1992); and GERALD M. EDELMAN & GIULIO TONONI, A UNIVERSE OF CONSCIOUSNESS: HOW MATTER BECOMES IMAGINATION (2000). See also STEPHEN M. KOSSYLN, IMAGE AND MIND (1980). Subsequent page references in the text are to *The Remembered Present*.

12. LAKOFF, *supra* note 11, at 445.

13. On the indispensability of imagination to morality, see MARK JOHNSON, MORAL IMAGINATION: IMPLICATIONS OF COGNITIVE SCIENCE FOR ETHICS (1993).

14. The landmark study, which we shall discuss at length, is George Lakoff's *Women, Fire, and Dangerous Things, supra* note 11. See also JOHN R. TAYLOR, LINGUISTIC CATEGORIZATION: PROTOTYPES IN LINGUISTIC THEORY (2d ed. 1996).

15. *See* ROBERT BORK, THE TEMPTING OF AMERICA: THE POLITICAL SEDUCTION OF THE LAW 265 (1989) ("[L]egal reasoning must begin with a body of rules or principles or major premises that are independent of the judge's preferences"). Most of the modern debate has taken place within constitutional law driven by the anxiety that the Supreme Court's protection of minority rights and individual liberties, epitomized by Brown v. Board of Education, 347 U.S. 483 (1954), and Roe v. Wade, 410 U.S. 113 (1973), may be indistinguishable in theory from an earlier Court's imposition of laissez-faire in cases like Lochner v. New York, 198 U.S. 45 (1905). But the issue of constraint is more general: In the early part of this century, most of the sophisticated debate about the determinacy of legal rules took place in the context of private law. *See* Steven L. Winter, *Indeterminacy and Incommensurability in Constitutional Law*, 78 CAL. L. REV. 1441 (1990).

16. For examples among sophisticated mainstream legal theorists, see RONALD DWORKIN, LAW'S EMPIRE 70–72 (1987) (distinguishing between an idea or principle, a "concept," and its particular expression, a "conception"); Owen M. Fiss, *Why the State?*, 100 HARV. L. REV. 781, 783 (1987) ("Adjudication is one process by which these abstract ideals are given concrete meaning and expression and are thereby translated into rights."). This view of the reasoning process is so ingrained that even its staunchest critics are wont to fall back upon it. Thus, Mark Tushnet assumes that to the extent that "[w]e can gain an interpretive understanding of the past" we do so "by working from commonalities in the use of large abstractions to reach the unfamiliar particulars of what those abstractions really meant in the past." MARK TUSHNET, RED, WHITE, AND BLUE: A CRITICAL ANALYSIS OF CONSTITUTIONAL LAW 44 (1988).

17. *See, e.g.*, Joseph William Singer, *The Player and the Cards: Nihilism and Legal Theory*, 94 YALE L.J. 1 (1984); Mark Tushnet, *Following the Rules Laid Down: A Critique of Interpretivism and Neutral Principles*, 96 HARV. L. REV. 781 (1983); Mark Kelman, *Interpretive Construction in the Substantive Criminal Law*, 33 STAN. L. REV. 591 (1981); Duncan Kennedy, *The Structure of Blackstone's Commentaries*, 28 BUFF. L. REV. 205, 211–19, 354–60 (1979).

18. The term "relativist" connotes a wide variety of positions, including my own. I will not try to sort them out beyond the brief discussion offered in the text. For helpful discussions of the degrees and dimensions of different relativisms, see LAKOFF, *supra* note 11, at 304–37, and PAUL FEYERABEND, FAREWELL TO REASON 19–89 (1987).

19. *See, e.g.*, Paul Brest, *Interpretation and Interest*, 34 Stan. L. Rev. 765 (1982); Duncan Kennedy, *Legal Education as Training for Hierarchy, in* The Politics of Law: A Progressive Critique 54, 60–64 (David Kairys ed., 3d ed. 1998); Kennedy, *supra* note 17, at 217–18; Tushnet, *supra* note 17, at 144.

20. "'Reason,' as the term is used in the Platonic and Kantian traditions, is interlocked with the notion of truth as correspondence, of knowledge as discovery of essence, of morality as obedience to principle." Richard Rorty, Consequences of Pragmatism 172 (1982).

21. Thomas Kuhn, The Structure of Scientific Revolutions 64 (2d ed. 1970) ("[N]ovelty emerges only with difficulty, manifested by resistance, against a background provided by expectation.").

22. This view is frequently referred to as "metaphysical realism." Within the legal academy, Michael Moore is one of the few who explicitly endorse this view. *See* Michael S. Moore, *The Interpretive Turn in Modern Theory: A Turn for the Worse?*, 41 Stan. L. Rev. 871, 879 (1989).

23. Stanley Fish, Doing What Comes Naturally: Change, Rhetoric, and the Practice of Theory in Literary and Legal Studies 2 (1989).

24. Friedrich Nietzsche, *On Truth and Falsity in Their Ultramoral Sense, in* The Complete Works of Friedrich Nietzsche 80 (O. Levy ed., M. Magge trans., 1974).

25. Fish, *supra* note 23, at 323, 440, 518–19 ("[R]eason cannot operate independently of some content—of some proposition or propositions made up of definitions, distinctions, and criteria already assumed."); Rorty, *supra* note 20, at xli (describing rationality within a normal discourse as "made possible by agreement on criteria" that, in turn, enables "[r]igorous argumentation issu[ing] in agreement in propositions.").

26. Singer, *supra* note 17, at 16 (emphasis added).

27. Duncan Kennedy, *Form and Substance in Private Law Adjudication*, 89 Harv. L. Rev. 1685, 1723–24 (1976) (emphasis changed from original); *see also* Kennedy, *supra* note 3, at 534 ("I assert my policy as 'valid' and as 'requiring' an outcome, and then blithely reject it and in the next case, endorse its exactly matching opposite without giving any *meta-level explanation* of what keys me into one side or the other.") (emphasis added).

28. *Cf.* Singer, *supra* note 17, at 4–5 n.8 ("The nihilist . . . would argue that a rational foundation is necessary to sustain values but that no such foundation exists or can be identified. . . . My position rejects *both* assumptions. We do not have a rational foundation and method for legal or moral reasoning . . . ; we do not, however, need such a foundation or method to develop passionate commitments and to make our lives meaningful.")

29. *See, e.g.*, Philip Bobbitt, Constitutional Interpretation (1992); John Stick, *Can Nihilism Be Pragmatic?*, 100 Harv. L. Rev. 332 (1986); Joan Williams, *Critical Legal Studies: The Death of Transcendence and the Rise of the New Langdells*, 62 N.Y.U. L. Rev. 429 (1987); *see also* Brian Langille, *Revolution Without Foundation: The Grammar of Scepticism and Law*, 33 McGill L.J. 451 (1988).

30. The hidden complicity between objectivism and subjectivism was identified by Merleau-Ponty nearly fifty years ago: "We pass from absolute objectivity to absolute subjectivity, but this second idea is no better than the first and is upheld only

against it, which means by it. The affinity between intellectualism [i.e., idealism] and empiricism [i.e., objectivism] is thus much less obvious and much more deeply rooted than is commonly thought." MAURICE MERLEAU-PONTY, THE PHENOMENOLOGY OF PERCEPTION 39 (Colin Smith trans., 1962). Recently, this insight and its implications have begun to take on something of the status of conventional wisdom. *See, e.g.,* Cass R. Sunstein, *Incommensurability and Valuation in Law*, 92 MICH. L. REV. 779, 854 n.280 (1994); Allan C. Hutchinson, *Inessentially Speaking (Is There Politics After Postmodernism?)*, 89 MICH. L. REV. 1549, 1562–63 (1991).

31. *See* George Lakoff, *The Contemporary Theory of Metaphor, in* METAPHOR AND THOUGHT 202, 209 (Andrew Ortony ed., 2d ed. 1992):

This view of metaphor is thoroughly at odds with the view that metaphors are just linguistic expressions. If metaphors were merely linguistic expressions, we would expect different linguistic expressions to be different metaphors. Thus, "We've hit a dead end street" would constitute one metaphor. "We can't turn back now" would constitute another, entirely different metaphor. "Their marriage is on the rocks" would involve still a different metaphor. And so on for dozens of examples. Yet we don't seem to have dozens of different metaphors here. We have one metaphor, in which love is conceptualized as a journey. . . . And this unified way of *conceptualizing* love metaphorically is realized in many different *linguistic* expressions.

32. The source of this term is the Anglo-Saxon practice of outlawry as punishment. "The effect was that [the outlaw] was put outside the kings peace and protection, and could probably till 1329, be slain by anyone." 2 SIR WILLIAM HOLDSWORTH, A HISTORY OF ENGLISH LAW 605 (4th ed. 1936) (footnotes omitted).

33. JOHNSON, *supra* note 11, at 29.

34. LAKOFF, *supra* note 11, at 445; EDELMAN, REMEMBERED PRESENT, *supra* note 11, at 195.

35. EVE SWEETSER, FROM ETYMOLOGY TO PRAGMATICS: METAPHORICAL AND CULTURAL ASPECTS OF SEMANTIC STRUCTURE 49–75 (1990).

36. JOHNSON, *supra* note 11, at 48–57. Similarly, Turner has shown how the concepts and categories of classical rhetoric are instantiations of these schemas and related metaphors. MARK TURNER, READING MINDS: THE STUDY OF ENGLISH IN THE AGE OF COGNITIVE SCIENCE 99–120 (1991).

37. JOHN RAWLS, A THEORY OF JUSTICE 19–22, 46–51 (1971).

38. *See* LAKOFF & JOHNSON, METAPHORS WE LIVE BY, *supra* note 11 at 41–44; GEORGE LAKOFF & MARK TURNER, MORE THAN COOL REASON: A FIELD GUIDE TO POETIC METAPHOR 4–7, 11–12 (1989).

39. Adamson v. California, 332 U.S. 46, 68 (1947) (Frankfurter, J., concurring) (emphasis added).

40. Goldberg v. Kelly, 397 U.S. 254, 276–77 (1970) (Black J., dissenting) (emphasis added).

41. *Id.* at 272–73 (emphasis added). Even those who criticize Justice Black's textualism employ the same images. Sanford Kadish, for example, has argued that the Court's opinions "belie the notion that the literal language of these provisions *directs* and *confines* judicial inquiry *along specific lines.*" Kadish, *Methodology and Criteria in Due Process Adjudication—A Survey and Criticism*, 66 YALE L.J. 319, 338 (1957) (emphasis added).

42. Planned Parenthood of Southeastern Pennsylvania v. Casey, 505 U.S. 833, 847 (1992) (Opinion of O'Connor, Kennedy, & Souter, J.J.) (emphasis added).

43. *Id.* at 965 (Rehnquist, C.J., concurring & dissenting) (quoting Griswold v. Connecticut, 381 U.S. 479, 502 (1965) (Harlan, J., concurring)) (emphasis added).

44. *Id.* at 988 (Scalia, J., concurring & dissenting) (emphasis added).

45. It should be noted, however, that Holmes never actually used that particular metaphorical expression. *See* Abrams v. United States, 250 U.S. 616, 630 (1919) (Holmes, J., dissenting) ("The ultimate good desired is better reached by free trade in ideas—that the best test of truth is the power of the thought to get itself accepted in the competition of the market."). But, for reasons already discussed, we readily recognize these different expressions as instances of the same metaphor.

46. LAKOFF & JOHNSON, METAPHORS WE LIVE BY, *supra* note 11, at 47.

47. The claim that poetic metaphor is an extension of conventional conceptual metaphor is developed more fully in LAKOFF & TURNER, *supra* note 38, and TURNER, *supra* note 36.

48. Peter Gabel & Duncan Kennedy, *Roll Over Beethoven,* 36 STAN. L. REV. 1, 40 (1984).

49. ALASDAIR MACINTYRE, WHOSE JUSTICE? WHICH RATIONALITY? 382 (1988).

CHAPTER TWO

1. Sandra Blakeslee, *Theory on Human Brain Hints How Its Unique Traits Arose,* N.Y. TIMES, November 8, 1994, at C1.

2. Henrietta C. Leiner et al., *Cognitive and Language Functions of the Human Cerebellum,* 16 TRENDS IN NEUROSCI. 444 (1993).

3. S. E. Petersen & J. A. Fiez, *The Processing of Single Words Studied with Positron Emission Tomography,* 16 ANN. REV. OF NEUROSCI. 509 (1993); J. A. Fiez et al., *Impaired Nonmotor Learning and Error Detection Associated with Cerebellar Damage: A Single Case Study,* 115 BRAIN 155 (1992).

4. Frank Middleton & Peter Strick, *Anatomical Evidence for Cerebellar and Basal Ganglia Involvement in Higher Cognitive Function,* 266 SCIENCE 458 (1994).

5. Leiner, *supra* note 2, at 445.

6. GERALD M. EDELMAN, BRIGHT AIR, BRILLIANT FIRE: ON THE MATTER OF THE MIND 7 (1992). Subsequent page references are provided in the text.

7. ROGER BROWN, SOCIAL PSYCHOLOGY 321 (1965). Subsequent page references appear in text.

8. *See* BRENT BERLIN ET AL., PRINCIPLES OF TZELTAL PLANT CLASSIFICATION (1974); EUGENE S. HUNN, TZELTAL FOLK ZOOLOGY: THE CLASSIFICATION OF DISCONTINUITIES IN NATURE (1977); Eleanor Rosch, *Principles of Categorization, in* COGNITION AND CATEGORIZATION 27 (Eleanor Rosch & Barbara B. Lloyd eds., 1978). Subsequent references to Rosch's summary are given in the text.

9. GEORGE LAKOFF, WOMEN, FIRE, AND DANGEROUS THINGS: WHAT CATEGORIES REVEAL ABOUT THE MIND 50 (1987).

10. *See, e.g.,* Roger A. Nicoll & Robert C. Malenka, *Contrasting Properties of Two Forms of Long-term Potentiation in the Hippocampus,* 377 NATURE 115 (Sept. 14, 1995).

11. *See* GERALD M. EDELMAN, THE REMEMBERED PRESENT: A BIOLOGICAL THEORY OF CONSCIOUSNESS 43–46 (1989). As Edelman explains:

Neurons in a group tend to be more highly interconnected anatomically and to have changes in their synaptic strengths that differentially enhance responses of other neurons in that group. While the various structures of neuronal groups in different parts of the brain are based on local anatomical patterns, such groups are dynamic entities whose characteristics are affected by their developmental and functional history and by the nature of the signals they receive at any time. (44)

12. Antonio R. Damasio & Hanna Damasio, *Brain and Language,* SCI. AM. 89, 91 (Sept. 1992).

13. LAKOFF, *supra* note 9, at 445.

14. This is the problem with Steven Pinker's discussion of imagistic thought. STEVEN PINKER, HOW THE MIND WORKS 284–98 (1998). After recounting some of the extensive evidence supporting the role of "images" in thought, he dismisses imagistic thought as no more than an adjunct to computational thought. Images, he asserts, "cannot serve as our concepts, nor can they serve as the meaning of words in the mental dictionary." But, in defending the latter claim, he considers only highly concrete images such as "Fred MacMurray" and the "Statue of Liberty." *Id.* at 296–98. This is, of course, a straw man: No one claims that people carry in their heads a picture of Fred MacMurray that they use to represent "all men."

15. MARK JOHNSON, THE BODY IN THE MIND: THE BODILY BASIS OF MEANING, IMAGINATION, AND REASON 29 (1987); *cf.* IMMANUEL KANT, CRITIQUE OF PURE REASON A 141, B 180 (N. K. Smith trans., 1963) ("No image could ever be adequate to the concept of a triangle in general. It would never attain that universality of the concept which renders it valid of all triangles. . . . The schema of the triangle can exist nowhere but in thought. . . . [It] is a rule of synthesis of the imagination.").

16. GEORGE LAKOFF & MARK JOHNSON, PHILOSOPHY IN THE FLESH: THE EMBODIED MIND AND ITS CHALLENGE TO WESTERN THOUGHT 54–58 (1999).

17. EDELMAN, *supra* note 11, at 195 (footnote deleted) (discussing JOHNSON, *supra* note 15, and Elizabeth S. Spelke, *The Origins of Physical Knowledge, in* THOUGHT WITHOUT LANGUAGE 168 (Lawrence Weiskrantz ed., 1988)).

18. Edelman's Darwin III—a computer simulation using reentrant mappings—is programmed only with the knowledge that striped, bumpy objects are harmful. Without additional training, it is capable of learning to discriminate between striped objects, bumpy objects, and striped-and-bumpy objects and then to activate its mechanical arm to swat away only the latter. EDELMAN, *supra* note 11, at 57–63.

19. MICHAEL S. GAZZANIGA, NATURE'S MIND: THE BIOLOGICAL ROOTS OF THINKING, EMOTIONS, SEXUALITY, LANGUAGE, AND INTELLIGENCE 37 (1992). William Wimsatt's concept of generative entrenchment provides a powerful model that captures both the experience-dependent and sequence-dependent nature of genetically driven development. William C. Wimsatt, *Developmental Constraints, Generative Entrenchment, and the Innate-Acquired Distinction, in* INTEGRATING SCIENTIFIC DISCIPLINES 185 (William Bechtel ed., 1986). As Wimsatt explains his nuanced account, "it does not follow . . . either that if something is coded in a genetic program, it is 'genetically determined' or that the information which determines it is entirely in the genome." *Id.* at 186.

20. Sandra Blakeslee, *Recipe for a Brain: Cup of Genes and Dash of Experience*, N.Y. TIMES, November 4, 1997, at F4.

21. The evidence comes from a computer simulation performed by Bradley Seebach and his colleagues. Adults English speakers perceive the stop consonants [b], [p], [d], [t], [g], and [k] as different categories. When it was shown that infants, too, make these category distinctions, some took this as proof that there were neural mechanisms innately attuned to the acoustics of human speech. *See* PHIL LIEBERMAN, UNIQUELY HUMAN: THE EVOLUTION OF SPEECH, THOUGHT, AND SELFLESS BEHAVIOR (1991). Seebach and his colleagues tested this claim using a neural net that had been successfully deployed to model experience-dependent synaptic modification in the kitten's visual cortex. Bradley S. Seebach, Nathan Intrator, Phil Lieberman, and Leon N. Cooper, *A Model of Prenatal Acquisition of Speech Patterns*, 91 PROC. NAT'L ACAD. SCI. 7473, 7473 (1994). They hypothesized that the same process of spontaneous learning might occur during the last trimester of fetal development—i.e., after the onset of hearing in the fetus—in response to the "acoustically rich environment" that is dominated by, but not limited to, the mother's voice. To test this claim, Seebach and his colleagues used an unsupervised net that was trained without back-propagation or feedback on a set of 74 examples of the unvoiced stop syllables [ka], [pa], and [ta]—the unvoiced stop consonants plus the vowel [a]—as pronounced by a single speaker. The network was trained with random presentations of the set until there were only minimal changes in neuronal selectivity.

Once trained, the net was tested by exposing it to unvoiced stop consonants as articulated by two additional speakers, one male and the other female. The network correctly classified their enunciations at a 98 percent rate of accuracy. When exposed to *voiced* stop consonants as pronounced by each of the three speakers, the net was able to recognize these new sounds as related to the previously learned unvoiced stop consonants and make correct classifications at a 96 percent rate of accuracy. As the researchers noted, this "generality of solutions is atypical for speech recognition systems and indicates that the . . . net is discovering features that yield categorical place-of-articulation distinctions" (7475).

The network's stunning success in learning to distinguish these sounds even when presented in novel contexts provides strong support for the experiential model of cognition. The researchers concluded that "the high degree of generalization across states of voicing, loudness, and speakers of both sexes gives reason to believe that neuronal selectivities such as those that develop in this model might provide a basis for perceptual abilities seen in early infancy" (7475).

22. THOMAS KUHN, THE STRUCTURE OF SCIENTIFIC REVOLUTIONS 62–65, 112–13 (2d ed. 1970) (discussing Jerome S. Bruner & Leo Postman, *On the Perception of Incongruity: A Paradigm*, 18 J. PERSONALITY 206–23 (1949)).

23. EDELMAN, *supra* note 11, at 78–90; GAETANO KANIZSA, ORGANIZATION IN VISION: ESSAYS ON GESTALT PERCEPTION (1979).

24. LAKOFF & JOHNSON, *supra* note 16, at 255–56. *See also* LAKOFF, *supra* note 9, at 338–52.

25. MAURICE MERLEAU-PONTY, SENSE AND NON-SENSE 133–34 (Hubert L. Dreyfus & Patricia A. Dreyfus trans., 1964). *See also* HILARY PUTNAM, REASON, TRUTH, AND HISTORY xi (1981) ("[T]he mind and the world jointly make up the mind and the world.").

26. STEPHEN M. KOSSLYN & OLIVIER KOENIG, WET MIND: THE NEW COGNI-

TIVE NEUROSCIENCE 145–47 (1992); PINKER, *supra* note 14, at 285; Steven Pinker, *His Brain Measured Up,* N.Y. TIMES, June 24, 1999, at A27.

27. Oliver Wendell Holmes, Jr., *Law in Science and Science in Law,* 12 HARV. L. REV. 443, 460 (1899). The full quote is: "[W]e must think things not words, or at least we must constantly translate our words into the facts for which they stand, if we are to keep to the real and the true." One can see from the context why Judge Posner would read this as indicating Holmes's adherence to a correspondence view of meaning. RICHARD A. POSNER, THE PROBLEMS OF JURISPRUDENCE 13 n.20 (1990). For the reasons discussed in the text, I think that Posner's reading is nevertheless mistaken.

28. In private, Holmes confided to Brandeis the joy at mastering "the trick of working out what he calls 'a form of words' to express desired result." Melvin I. Urofsky, *The Brandeis-Frankfurter Conversations,* 1985 SUP. CT. REV. 299, 334.

29. Donald Schön, *Generative Metaphor: A Perspective on Problem-Setting in Social Policy, in* METAPHOR AND THOUGHT, 132 (Andrew Ortony ed., 2d ed. 1992).

30. Oliver Wendell Holmes, Jr., *Law and the Court, in* THE ESSENTIAL HOLMES, 145–46 (Richard A. Posner ed., 1992).

31. 283 U.S. 25, 26 (1931).

32. LAKOFF, *supra* note 9, at 445–46; STEVEN KOSSYLN, IMAGE AND MIND (1980).

33. *See* JEAN PIAGET, THE ORIGINS OF INTELLIGENCE AND CHILDHOOD (1952); JEAN PIAGET, THE CONSTRUCTION OF REALITY IN THE CHILD (1954).

34. These experiments are described and discussed in Spelke, *supra* note 17, and in Elizabeth S. Spelke et al., *Origins of Knowledge,* 99 PSYCHOL. REV. 605 (No. 4, 1992). Specific page references are given in the text as Spelke 1988 and Spelke 1992.

35. *See* Dedre Gentner et al., *Two Forces in the Development of Relational Similarity, in* DEVELOPING COGNITIVE COMPETENCE: NEW APPROACHES TO PROCESS MODELING 263, 267 (T. Simon & G. Halford eds., 1995).

36. *See* Alan M. Leslie, *The Necessity of Illusion: Perception and Thought in Infancy, in* THOUGHT WITHOUT LANGUAGE, *supra* note 17, at 185, 195–99 (showing that Spelke's results cannot be explained as resulting from built-in limitations of the perceptual system).

37. Thomas C. Grey, *Langdell's Orthodoxy,* 45 U. PITT. L. REV. 1, 3–4 (1983) (Langdell's "classical orthodoxy is the thesis to which modern legal thought has been the antithesis."). *See also* EDWARD PURCELL, JR., THE CRISIS OF DEMOCRATIC THEORY: SCIENTIFIC NATURALISM & THE PROBLEM OF VALUE 74–77 (1973); WILLIAM TWINING, KARL LLEWELLYN, AND THE REALIST MOVEMENT 10–14 (1973); GRANT GILMORE, THE DEATH OF CONTRACT 59 (1974). For a partially dissenting view, see NEIL DUXBURY, PATTERNS OF AMERICAN JURISPRUDENCE (1995).

38. Robert W. Gordon, *American Law Through English Eyes: A Century of Nightmares and Noble Dreams,* 84 GEO. L.J. 2215, 2224 (1996) (reviewing Duxbury). The latter maxim is from Holmes's famous dissent in Lochner v. New York, 198 U.S. 45, 76 (1905).

39. OLIVER WENDELL HOLMES, JR., THE COMMON LAW 5 (Mark Howe ed., 1963) (1881).

40. Richard Michael Fischl, *Some Realism About Critical Legal Studies,* 41 U.

Miami L. Rev. 505, 522 (1987); *see also* Joseph William Singer, *Legal Realism Now,* 76 Cal. L. Rev. 465, 504 (1988).

41. Thomas C. Grey, *Holmes and Legal Pragmatism,* 41 Stan. L. Rev. 787, 816 (1989).

42. Clark A. Remington, *Llewellyn, Antiformalism, and the Fear of Transcendental Nonsense: Codifying the Variability Rule in the Law of Sales,* 44 Wayne L. Rev. 29 (1998).

43. Twining, *supra* note 37, at 369.

44. Karl N. Llewellyn, The Common Law Tradition: Deciding Appeals 122, 268, 427 (1961); Karl N. Llewellyn, *The Constitution as an Institution,* 34 Colum. L. Rev. 1, 8 (1934). *See also* Karl N. Llewellyn, The Bramble Bush: On Our Law and Its Study 138 (1930).

45. *Id.* at 12.

Chapter Three

1. Thomas C. Grey, The Wallace Stevens Case: Law and the Practice of Poetry 7 (1991). Subsequent page numbers are given in the text.

2. *See* Thomas C. Grey, *Holmes and Legal Pragmatism,* 41 Stan. L. Rev. 787, 798 (1989) (The pragmatists "treated thinking as contextual and situated; it came always embodied in *practices*—habits and patterns of perceiving and conceiving that had developed out of and served to guide activity."). Elsewhere, I have identified and explained this tendency of pragmatist thought as the "particularist fallacy." *See* Steven L. Winter, *The Constitution of Conscience,* 72 Tex. L. Rev. 1805, 1813–16 (1994).

3. The classical sources are Herbert Wechsler, *Toward Neutral Principles of Constitutional Law,* 73 Harv. L. Rev. 1, 15 (1959) ("[T]he main constituent of the judicial process is precisely that it must be genuinely principled, resting with respect to every step that is involved in reaching judgment on analysis and reasons quite transcending the immediate result that is achieved."), and Lon Fuller, *The Forms and Limits of Adjudication,* 92 Harv. L. Rev. 353, 369 (1978) ("[A]djudication is a form of decision that defines the affected party's participation as that of offering proofs and reasoned arguments."). *Cf.* Thomas C. Grey, *Langdell's Orthodoxy,* 45 U. Pitt. L. Rev. 1 (1983).

4. Milner Ball argues that the "and" in Law and Literature "gives too much away as though law is discrete . . . as though we are exploring an equivocal, analogical relation (similarities between two admittedly different things, law and literature) rather than a univocal, metaphorical relation." Milner S. Ball, *Confessions,* 1 Cardozo Stud. L. & Literature 185, 188 (1989).

5. John Locke, An Essay Concerning Human Understanding bk. 3, ch. 10, at 508 (Peter H. Nidditch ed., 1975).

6. Audre Lorde, *The Master's Tools Will Never Dismantle the Master's House, in* Sister Outsider: Essays and Speeches 110 (1984).

7. Friedrich Nietzsche, *On Truth and Falsity in Their Ultramoral Sense, in* Early Greek Philosophy and other Essays 180 (Maximillian A. Mugge trans., Dr. Oscar Levy ed., 1964).

8. Richard Rorty, Contingency, irony, and solidarity 16 (1989). Subsequent pages numbers are indicated in the text.

9. Percy Bysshe Shelley, A Defense of Poetry 80 (John E. Jordan ed., 1965).

10. Donald Davidson, Inquiries into Truth and Interpretation 262 (1984). Subsequent citations to this essay are provided in the text.

11. *See also* Richard Rorty, *Unfamiliar Noises: Hesse and Davidson on Metaphor, in* 1 Objectivity, Relativism, and Truth: Philosophical Papers 162 (1991).

12. This reference is to Donald Davidson, *A Nice Derangement of Epitaphs, in* Philosophical Grounds of Rationality 157 (R. Grandys & R. Warner eds., 1986).

13. Paul Ricoeur, *The Metaphorical Process as Cognition, Imagination, and Feeling, in* On Metaphor 141, 141 (Sheldon Sacks ed., 1979). Ricoeur is explicitly responding to Davidson but also to those on the other side of the metaphor question such as I. A. Richards and Max Black.

14. *Id.* at 148.

15. On the role of image-mappings in poetry, see George Lakoff & Mark Turner, More than Cool Reason: A Field Guide to Poetic Metaphor 89–96 (1989).

16. As Lakoff and Turner explain, proverbs like these

are both concrete and information-rich: they have rich imagery associated with them, they are memorable, they are connected to our everyday experiences, and they contain a relatively large amount of information about those concrete everyday experiences. Proverbs use both kinds of power: they lead to general characterizations, which nevertheless are grounded in the richness of the special case.

Such specific-level schemas tend to be evoked by short, common words, like "blind," "blame," and "ditch." As a result short proverbs tend to be packed with information and imagery. Consequently, the knowledge they call up includes a great deal of generic-level information as well as specific level-information.

Id. at 165.

17. Eve Sweetser, From Etymology to Pragmatics: Metaphorical and Cultural Aspects of Semantic Structure 32 (1990). Subsequent pages numbers are given in the text.

18. Michael J. Reddy, *The Conduit Metaphor—A Case of Frame Conflict in Our Language About Language, in* Metaphor and Thought 164 (Andrew Ortony ed., 2d ed. 1993). Reddy provides a "partial listing" of 141 examples. *Id.* at 189–97.

19. Wallace Stevens, *Description Without Place, in* The Collected Poems of Wallace Stevens 345–46 (1954).

20. Wallace Stevens, *An Ordinary Evening in New Haven, in id.* at 465, 473. On the claim that poetic metaphor is an extension of conventional conceptual metaphor, see Lakoff & Turner, *supra* note 15, and Mark Turner, Reading Minds: The Study of English in the Age of Cognitive Science (1991).

21. Anyone who has watched an infant grasp an unfamiliar object and test it with his or her mouth should understand why a metaphor like ideas are objects would have as a corollary the metaphor ideas are food. *See* George Lakoff & Mark Johnson, Metaphors We Live By 46–47 (1980) ("Now there's a theory

you can really *sink your teeth into*. . . . That's *food for thought*. He's a *voracious* reader. We don't need to *spoon-feed* our students.").

22. Richard Rorty, Philosophy and the Mirror of Nature 12 (1979); *see also* Rorty, *supra* note 11, at 3–4 (describing his view as "anti-representationalist").

23. Richard A. Posner, The Problems of Jurisprudence 38–39 (1990). Subsequent page references are provided in the text.

24. *See* Richard A. Posner, Law and Literature: A Misunderstood Relation (2d ed. 1998) (concluding that, in spite of what each has to offer the other, law and literature are best preserved as separate disciplines).

25. George Lakoff, Women, Fire, and Dangerous Things: What Categories Reveal About the Mind 380–415 (1987); George Lakoff and Zoltán Kövecses, *The Cognitive Models of Anger Inherent in American English, in* Cultural Models in Language and Thought 195–221 (Dorothy Holland & Naomi Quinn eds., 1987).

26. Lakoff, *supra* note 25, at 412–15; Mark Johnson, The Body in the Mind: The Bodily Basis of Meaning, Imagination, and Reason 5–11 (1987).

27. William James, *Pragmatism, in* The Writings of William James: A Comprehensive Edition 364–65, 369–71 (John J. McDermott ed., 1968).

28. Richard Rorty, Consequences of Pragmatism xviii (1982).

29. Ricoeur, *supra* note 13, at 142.

30. Wallace Stevens, *Connoisseur of Chaos, in* The Collected Poems, *supra* note 21, at 215.

31. Ricoeur, *supra* note 13, at 141.

32. Lakoff & Johnson, *supra* note 21, at 157.

33. Wallace Stevens, *Adagia, in* Opus Posthumous 195 (1957). Subsequent citations to the *Adagia* are given in the text.

34. Wallace Stevens, *Angel Surrounded by Paysans, in* The Collected Poems, *supra* note 19, at 496, 497.

35. Thomas S. Kuhn, The Structure of Scientific Revolutions 115 (2d ed. 1970).

36. I do not claim that Stevens would have put it this way. Although he questioned it, Stevens never quite escaped the dichotomization of mind and world, of realism and idealism, of truth and fiction. In an essay on the integration of the poetic and the philosophic, Stevens maintained: "If the philosopher's world is this present world plus thought, then the poet's world is this present world plus imagination." Stevens, *A Collect of Philosophy, in* Opus Posthumous, *supra* note 33, at 267, 278. Here, Stevens not only separates the "present world" from what is added by the mind, but also divides the workings of the mind into the philosopher's "thought" and the poet's "imagination."

37. Letters of Wallace Stevens 413–14 (Holly Stevens ed., 1966).

Chapter Four

1. *See, e.g.,* Cass R. Sunstein, *Analogical Reasoning in Law,* 106 Harv. L. Rev. 741, 755–57 (1993). In chapter 9, I discuss Sunstein's more recent version of the argument made in this article.

2. GEORGE LAKOFF, WOMEN, FIRE, AND DANGEROUS THINGS: WHAT CATEGO-RIES REVEAL ABOUT THE MIND 92–104 (1987). All subsequent page numbers are given in the text.

3. LUDWIG WITTGENSTEIN, PHILOSOPHICAL INVESTIGATIONS 31e–32e (G. E. M. Anscombe trans., 1953).

4. BENJAMIN LEE WHORF, LANGUAGE, THOUGHT, AND REALITY: SELECTED WRITINGS OF BENJAMIN LEE WHORF 260 (John Carroll ed., 1956).

5. JORGE LUIS BORGES, OTHER INQUISITIONS 108 (1966).

6. Thus, Jacques Derrida was asked by Gerald Graff whether he didn't run the risk "of keeping certain linguistic superstitions alive in order to legitimate the project of calling them into question?" Derrida responded: "Every concept that lays claim to any rigor whatsoever implies the alternative of 'all or nothing.'" *Afterword,* *in* JACQUES DERRIDA, LIMITED INC. 115–16 (Samuel Weber & Jeffrey Mehlmann trans., 1988).

7. GEORGE LAKOFF & MARK JOHNSON, METAPHORS WE LIVE BY 15 (1980).

8. "Metonymic concepts allow us to conceptualize one thing by means of its re-lation to something else." *Id.* at 39. *See also* LAKOFF, *supra* note 2, at 77–79; GILLES FAUCONNIER, MENTAL SPACES 3–5 (1985). As used here, the notion of conceptual metonymy includes what rhetoricians call synecdoche.

9. Eleanor Rosch, *Cognitive Reference Points,* 7 COGNITIVE PSYCHOL. 532 (1975).

10. Lance J. Rips, *Inductive Judgments About Natural Categories,* 14 J. VERBAL LEARNING & VERBAL BEHAV. 665 (1975).

11. Amos Tversky & Daniel Kahneman, *Probability, Representativeness, and the Conjunction Fallacy,* 90 PSYCHOL. REV. 293 (1983). Similar evidence of reason-ing from prototypes can be found in Amos Tversky & Daniel Kahneman, *Causal Schemas in Judgments under Uncertainty, in* JUDGMENTS UNDER UNCERTAINTY: HEURISTICS AND BIASES 117 (Daniel Kahneman et al. eds., 1982). The former article is discussed below; subsequent page numbers are provided in the text.

12. RICHARD A. POSNER, THE PROBLEMS OF JURISPRUDENCE 38–39 (1990).

13. *See* Sharon Lee Armstrong et al., *What Some Concepts Might Not Be,* 13 COGNITION 263 (1983); Daniel Osherson & Edward Smith, *On the Adequacy of Prototype Theory as a Theory of Concepts,* 9 COGNITION 35 (1981). *See* discussion *infra* notes 20–21.

14. Eleanor Rosch, *Principles of Categorization, in* COGNITION AND CATEGO-RIZATION 27, 35–37 (Eleanor Rosch & Barbara B. Lloyd eds., 1978).

15. *Id.* at 38–39; Eleanor Rosch, *Prototype Classification and Logical Classifi-cation: The Two Systems, in* NEW TRENDS IN COGNITIVE REPRESENTATION: CHAL-LENGES TO PIAGET'S THEORY 73 (E. Scholnick ed., 1981).

16. Rosch found that when three-to-four-year-olds were asked to "show a color to the experimenter," "focal" colors were more frequently selected than were "nonfocal" colors; "focal" colors were also more accurately matched and more fre-quently chosen to represent the color name. Eleanor Rosch Heider, *"Focal" Color Areas and the Development of Color Names,* 4 DEVELOPMENTAL PSYCHOL. 447 (1971). In a later experiment, she found that the reaction-time disparities in verifying good and poor examples of a category were more extreme for ten-year-olds than for

adults, "indicating that the children had learned the category membership of the pro-totypical members earlier than that of other members." Rosch, *supra* note 14, at 38.

17. Eleanor Rosch Heider, *Universals in Color Naming and Memory,* 93 J. Ex-PERIMENTAL PSYCHOL. 10, 19 (1972); Eleanor Rosch Heider & Donald C. Olivier, *The Structure of the Color Space in Naming and Memory for Two Languages,* 3 COGNITIVE PSYCHOL. 337 (1972); Eleanor H. Rosch, *Natural Categories,* 4 COGNI-TIVE PSYCHOL. 328, 331 (1973).

18. Rosch, *supra* note 14, at 38.

19. Lawrence W. Barsalou, *Ad-hoc Categories,* 11 MEMORY & COGNITION 211, 224 (1983) ("The ad hoc categories observed here had typicality gradients as salient as those in common categories . . . , and subjects showed equal agreement when judging typicality for both category types.").

20. Armstrong, *supra* note 13, at 277. Armstrong and her colleagues offer this evidence in support of the "core-plus-identification" theory. However, their argu-ment rests on the premise that prototype effects occur only when a category has a graded structure—that is, one that yields *degrees* of membership. They reason that the natural numbers are not a graded category but rather a classical category defined by necessary and sufficient criteria. They conclude, therefore, that these prototype ef-fects must be the result of a psychological identification procedure that is merely sup-plemental to a definitional core expressed in analytic terms. The problem with the argument, of course, is its premise. As we shall see shortly, graded structure is not the only nor even the chief cause of prototype effects. And, as discussed in the next note, Armstrong, Gleitman, and Gleitman's results can be explained easily in terms of a models-based theory of reasoning.

21. Lakoff explains (*supra* note 2, at 149–51) that although numbers are de-fined in formal mathematics by necessary and sufficient criteria, it does not follow that people actually *think* about numbers in formal terms. Rather, people compre-hend and reason about numbers by means of a series of submodels—the base-ten model, the multiples of five model, and so on. Most of these submodels produce pro-totype effects; the notable exceptions are the prime numbers and odd-even subcate-gories. When the submodels with their various prototype effects are taken together with the odd-even subcategories, the net result is a subcategory that is not graded—i.e., all odd numbers are equally members of the subcategory—but that nevertheless displays prototype effects. That is exactly what Armstrong, Gleitman, and Gleitman found. *Id.* at 151.

22. BRENT BERLIN & PAUL KAY, BASIC COLOR TERMS: THEIR UNIVERSALITY AND EVOLUTION 7–12 (1969).

23. Paul Kay & Willett Kempton, *What Is the Sapir-Whorf Hypothesis?* 86 AM. ANTHROPOLOGIST 65, 71 (1984). Earlier, Rosch found the same results with the Dani who, as noted previously, have only two colors categories, *mili* and *mola.* When asked to select the best examples of these two categories, different speakers of Dani chose different colors. But even though they differed in their choice of which color within a particular category was the "best example," the colors they did choose were "focal" white or "focal" red, for example, and not pinkish-white or purple. *See* sources cited *supra* note 17.

24. PAUL M. CHURCHLAND, THE ENGINE OF REASON, THE SEAT OF THE SOUL: A PHILOSOPHICAL JOURNEY INTO THE BRAIN 24–25 (1995).

25. Paul Kay & Chad K. McDaniel, *The Linguistic Significance of the Meanings of Basic Color Terms,* 54 LANGUAGE 610, 617–26 (1978).

26. *See* CHURCHLAND, *supra* note 24, at 25–26.

27. *Id.* at 82–83 (discussing R. P. Gorman & T. J. Sejnowski, *Analysis of Hidden Units in a Layered Network Trained to Classify Sonar Targets,* 1 NEURAL NETWORKS (1988)).

28. "If we view concepts as stable patterns, they are much less discrete in character. It is possible, for example, to differentiate one stable pattern into two closely related but different variants by modifying some of the weights slightly." DAVID E. RUMELHART, JAMES L. MCCLELLAND, ET AL., 1 PARALLEL DISTRIBUTED PROCESSING: EXPLORATIONS IN THE MICROSTRUCTURE OF COGNITION 87 (1986).

29. *See id.* at 85 ("It is hard to make a clean distinction between systems that use local representations plus spreading activation patterns and systems that use distributed representations. In both cases the result of activating a concept is that many different hardware units are active.").

30. *Id.* at 82 (emphasis added).

31. Bradley S. Seebach, Nathan Intrator, Phil Lieberman, and Leon N. Cooper, *A Model of Prenatal Acquisition of Speech Patterns,* 91 PROC. NAT'L ACAD. SCI. 7473 (1994). Subsequent citations are given in the text.

32. GERALD M. EDELMAN, THE REMEMBERED PRESENT: A BIOLOGICAL THEORY OF CONSCIOUSNESS 89 (1989).

33. Eleanor Rosch, *Cognitive Representations of Semantic Categories,* 104 J. EXPERIMENTAL PSYCHOL. (GENERAL) 192 (1975).

34. Developed by Lotfi Zadeh, fuzzy set logic basically allows membership values other than 1 (i.e., in the set) or 0 (i.e., not a member of the set) so that degrees of membership can be characterized (e.g., .5). Increasingly, fuzzy logic is finding broad technological applications. For example, the braking systems for the Tokyo subway and on some Japanese automobiles are controlled by computer programs using fuzzy logic that actually provide safer and smoother stops. On fuzzy logic and its many ramifications, *see generally,* BART KOSKO, FUZZY THINKING: THE NEW SCIENCE OF FUZZY LOGIC (1993); DANIEL MCNEIL & PAUL FREIBERGER, FUZZY LOGIC: THE REVOLUTIONARY COMPUTER TECHNOLOGY THAT IS CHANGING OUR WORLD (1993).

35. Rosch, *supra* note 14, at 40–41.

36. *See* Stephen Dopkins & Theresa Gleason, *Comparing Exemplar and Prototype Models of Categorization,* 51 CANADIAN J. EXPERIMENTAL PSYCHOL. 212, 213 (1997) (stating that "the mental representation of a category is its prototype" and defining a prototype as "the exemplar with average values on all of the dimensions along which the category's exemplars vary"); J. David Smith & John Paul Minda, *Prototypes in the Mist: The Early Epochs of Category Learning,* 24 J. EXPERIMENTAL PSYCHOL. 1411 (1998); J. David Smith et al., *Straight Talk About Linear Separability,* 23 J. EXPERIMENTAL PSYCHOL. 659 (1997).

37. Dopkins & Gleason, *supra* note 36, at 214.

38. Smith & Minda, *supra* note 36, at 1412.

39. *Id.* Again, given the limitations noted in the text, it is difficult to tell whether these findings of a shift from so-called prototype models to exemplar models reflect a change in cognitive processing or the well-established fact that experts in

any domain work with a more finely grained set of models and categories. See discussion *infra* chapter 9.

40. Lawrence W. Barsalou, *Intraconcept Similarity and Its Implications for Interconcept Similarity, in* SIMILARITY AND ANALOGICAL REASONING 76 (Stella Vosniadou & Andrew Ortony eds., 1989).

41. RONALD DWORKIN, LAW's EMPIRE 72 (1986).

42. Charles J. Fillmore, *Frame Semantics, in* LINGUISTICS IN THE MORNING CALM 111, 112 (The Linguistic Society of Korea ed., 1982).

43. Charles J. Fillmore, *Toward a Descriptive Framework for Spatial Deixis, in* SPEECH, PLACE, AND ACTION 31, 34 (R. J. Jarvella & W. Klein eds., 1982).

44. Other hedges include: "strictly speaking," "loosely speaking," and "regular" (as in "He's not just a bachelor, he's a *regular* Casanova!"). For a more detailed account of these hedges and how each works, see LAKOFF, *supra* note 2, at 122–24, 138–39. *See also* George Lakoff, *Hedges: A Study in Meaning Criteria and the Logic of Fuzzy Concepts,* 2 J. PHIL. LOGIC 458 (1973).

45. *See* Fillmore, *supra* note 42, at 111; ROGER C. SCHANK & ROBERT P. ABELSON, SCRIPTS, PLANS, GOALS, AND UNDERSTANDING: AN INQUIRY INTO HUMAN KNOWLEDGE STRUCTURES (1977); David E. Rumelhart & Andrew Ortony, *The Representation of Knowledge in Memory, in* SCHOOLING AND THE ACQUISITION OF KNOWLEDGE 99 (R. Anderson et al. eds., 1977); David Rumelhart, *Notes on a Schema for Stories, in* REPRESENTATION AND UNDERSTANDING: STUDIES IN COGNITIVE SCIENCE (D. G. Bobrow & A. M. Collins eds., 1975); Gerald P. López, *Lay Lawyering,* 32 UCLA L. REV. 1 (1984); LAKOFF, *supra* note 2, at 45, 56–57.

46. López, *supra* note 45, at 6.

47. SCHANK & ABELSON, *supra* note 45, at 37–38, 42–46.

48. For a discussion of the image-schematic model that structures the legal conception of a cause of action and its distorting consequences for the law of standing, see Steven L. Winter, *The Metaphor of Standing and the Problem of Self-Governance,* 40 STAN. L. REV. 1371 (1988).

49. PATRICIA J. WILLIAMS, THE ALCHEMY OF RACE AND RIGHTS: DIARY OF A LAW PROFESSOR (1991).

50. WALLACE STEVENS, *Sunday Morning, in* THE COLLECTED POEMS OF WALLACE STEVENS 46, 69 (1954) ("Death is the mother of beauty, mystical, / Within whose burning bosom we devise / Our earthly mothers waiting, sleeplessly."). On the cognitive source and systematic poetic usage of such kinship metaphors for causation, see MARK TURNER, DEATH IS THE MOTHER OF BEAUTY: MIND, METAPHOR, CRITICISM (1987).

51. Some, though not all, of the questions used in Tversky and Kahneman's study of the asymmetry of causal inferences reflect this same problem. For example, they asked subjects to rate which of the following two events is more probable: "(a) that an athlete won the decathlon, if he won the first event in the decathlon"; or "(b) that an athlete won the first event in the decathlon, if he won the decathlon." Tversky and Kahneman found a marked asymmetric preference for probability (b), notwithstanding the fact that, prospectively, both are equally probable. Tversky & Kahneman, *Causal Schemas, supra* note 11, at 120–21. Unfortunately, however, the question does not indicate that it calls for a prospective assessment; to the contrary, the use of the past tense might very well have been taken to indicate that the

decathlon had already occurred. On that understanding, people might well have inferred that (b) was more likely, not because they thought it statistically more probable but because they thought that winning the entire event was more indicative of athletic ability than merely winning the first event. Similar problems of abstraction or indefiniteness trouble Tversky and Kahneman's mercury, fuel rationing, and burglary examples. No doubt, the subjects understood these examples (as Tversky and Kahneman conclude) as statements of causal relations rather than as the statements of statistical covariance intended by the researchers and against which the responses were measured (122–25).

52. López, *supra* note 45, at 6.

53. The term "sedimentation" comes from Husserl by way of Merleau-Ponty. The metaphor connotes the alluvial build-up of categories and conceptions deposited by the flow of our interactions and experiences in the physical and social world. For a more extended discussion, see Steven L. Winter, *Indeterminacy and Incommensurability in Constitutional Law,* 78 CAL. L. REV. 1441, 1485–93 (1990).

54. PETER BERGER & THOMAS LUCKMANN, THE SOCIAL CONSTRUCTION OF REALITY: A TREATISE ON THE SOCIOLOGY OF KNOWLEDGE 67–70 (1966) ("The experiences that are so retained [in consciousness] become sedimented, that is, they congeal in recollection as recognizable and memorable entities.").

55. Fillmore, *supra* note 42, at 131.

56. *See* BERGER & LUCKMANN, *supra* note 54, at 39 ("[T]he sum of linguistic objectifications . . . constitutes [a] semantic field, which meaningfully orders . . . the routine events I encounter. . . . Within the semantic fields thus built up it is possible for . . . historical experience to be objectified, retained, and accumulated."); *see also id.* at 41 (discussing "linguistic objectification").

57. GEOFFREY K. PULLUM, THE GREAT ESKIMO VOCABULARY HOAX 170 (1991); *see also* LAKOFF, *supra* note 2, at 308 ("English-speaking skiers have reported to me that there are at least a dozen words for snow.").

58. *See id.* ("Anyone with an expert knowledge of some domain of experience is bound to have a large vocabulary about things in that domain—sailors, carpenters, seamstresses, even linguists."); *see also* PULLUM, *supra* note 57, at 165–66. We will return to these issues in chapters 8 and 9.

59. LAKOFF & JOHNSON, *supra* note 7, at 164.

60. Karl N. Llewellyn, *A Realistic Jurisprudence—The Next Step,* 30 COLUM. L. REV. 431, 431 (1930).

61. Karl N. Llewellyn, *The Constitution as an Institution,* 34 COLUM. L. REV. 1, 8 (1934); KARL N. LLEWELLYN, THE BRAMBLE BUSH: ON OUR LAW AND ITS STUDY 65 (2d ed. 1951) ("Your application of a rule of law bears then on what you have already decided to be the meaning of the facts. It does not touch the raw evidence at all."); *see also* ALEXANDER E. SILVERMAN, MIND, MACHINE, AND METAPHOR: AN ESSAY ON ARTIFICIAL INTELLIGENCE AND LEGAL REASONING 54 (1993).

62. Frederick Schauer, *Formalism,* 98 YALE L.J. 509, 533 n.70 (1988).

63. *Id.* at 532.

64. Unfortunately, Schauer illustrates his singular notion with the singularly inapt example that English has only a single word to "gather up different types of snow and suppress differences among them." FREDERICK F. SCHAUER, PLAYING BY

THE RULES: A PHILOSOPHICAL EXAMINATION OF RULE-BASED DECISION-MAKING IN LAW AND LIFE 42 (1991).

65. This is the first definition given in THE RANDOM HOUSE DICTIONARY OF THE ENGLISH LANGUAGE 82 (2d ed. unabridged 1987) (further noting that "some classification schemes include protozoa . . . that have motility and animal-like nutritional modes").

66. *Id.* (definition 3).

CHAPTER FIVE

1. *Cf.* NATHAN AUSUBEL, A TREASURY OF JEWISH FOLKLORE 4 (1948) (recounting a different version in which the marksman uses a gun and in which the magid explains that he merely collects good stories to be prepared for any occasion).

2. Robert M. Cover, *The Supreme Court 1982 Term—Foreword:* Nomos *and Narrative,* 97 HARV. L. REV. 4, 4 (1983).

3. MAURICE MERLEAU-PONTY, THE PHENOMENOLOGY OF PERCEPTION 442 (Colin Smith trans., 1962); *cf.* RICHARD J. BERNSTEIN, BEYOND OBJECTIVISM AND RELATIVISM: SCIENCE, HERMENEUTICS, AND PRAXIS 16–19 (1983) (discussing the "Cartesian Anxiety.").

4. Cover, *supra* note 2, at 4–5 ("No set of legal institutions or prescriptions exists apart from the narratives that locate it and give it meaning . . . , nor can prescription, even when embodied in a legal text, escape its origin and end in experience, in the narratives that are the trajectories plotted upon material reality by our imaginations.").

5. *Cf.* MERLEAU-PONTY, *supra* note 3, at 455 ("I am a psychological and historical structure. . . . All my actions and thoughts stand in a relationship to this structure. . . . The fact remains that I am free, not in spite of, or on the hither side of, these motivations, but by means of them.")

6. The model of basic story structure and the account of narrative that follows first appeared in 1989 as part of the Michigan Law Review's widely noted Symposium on Legal Storytelling. Steven L. Winter, *The Cognitive Dimension of the* Agon *Between Legal Power and Narrative Meaning,* 87 Mich L. Rev. 2225 (1989). Restatements of this model have recently surfaced in books published by those associated with Tony Amsterdam's Lawyering Program at NYU. *See* ANTHONY G. AMSTERDAM & JEROME BRUNER, MINDING THE LAW 113–14 (2000); RICHARD K. SHERWIN, WHEN LAW GOES POP: THE VANISHING LINE BETWEEN LAW AND POPULAR CULTURE 43 (2000). For a comparison of the two models and an evaluation of the remaining differences between the two accounts of narrative, *see* Steven L. Winter, *Making the Familiar Conventional Again,* 98 MICH. L. REV. (2001).

7. RONALD DWORKIN, LAW'S EMPIRE 228–38 (1986); Owen M. Fiss, *Objectivity and Interpretation,* 34 STAN. L. REV. 739 (1982). Subsequent references to Dworkin's *Law's Empire* are given in the text.

8. *See, e.g.,* RICHARD A. POSNER, LAW AND LITERATURE: A MISUNDERSTOOD RELATION (2d ed. 1992); Anne M. Coughlin, *Regulating the Self: Autobiographical Performances in Outsider Scholarship,* 81 VA. L. REV. 1229 (1995); Daniel A. Farber and Suzanna Sherry, *Telling Stories out of School: An Essay on Legal Narratives,* 45 STAN. L. REV. 807 (1994); Mark Tushnet, *The Degradation of Constitutional Dis-*

course, 81 GEO. L.J. 251 (1993); *see also* Kathyrn Abrams, *Hearing the Call of Stories,* 79 CAL. L. REV. 971 (1991).

9. OXFORD LATIN DICTIONARY 768, 1155 (P. G. W. Glare ed., 1985). Both Latin terms derive from the Indo-European *gna* ("to know"), which is the root of the Greek *gnoscere* and the Latin *cognoscere;* these yield the English words "know," "cognition," and "noun," among others. Victor Turner, *Social Dramas and Stories About Them, in* ON NARRATIVE 163 (W. J. T. Mitchell ed., 1980).

10. Cover, *supra* note 2, at 5.

11. 1 D. H. FREEDMAN & MAURICE SIMON, THE MIDRASH RABAH 310–12 (1977) (commenting on *Genesis* 11:28—"And Haran died 'on the face of' his father Terach, in the land of his birth, in Ur of the Chaldees."). The midrash is the collection of rabbinic parables that was part of the development of the Oral Law starting in the fifth century B.C. and extending well into the third and fourth centuries A.D. Epstein, *Foreword, in id.* at x–xvii.

12. David E. Rumelhart & Andrew Ortony, *The Representation of Knowledge in Memory, in* SCHOOLING AND THE ACQUISITION OF KNOWLEDGE 99, 131 (R. Anderson et al. eds., 1977).

13. 1 PAUL RICOEUR, TIME AND NARRATIVE 65 (Kathleen McLaughlin & David Pellauer trans., 1984). Subsequent page references are given in the text.

14. ARISTOTLE, POETICS 50b.

15. *Cf.* GEORGE LAKOFF, WOMEN, FIRE, AND DANGEROUS THINGS: WHAT CATEGORIES REVEAL ABOUT THE MIND 285–86 (1987) (describing a "scenario" as structured by the SOURCE-PATH-GOAL schema in the time domain).

16. *See also* WILLIAM STRUNK, JR. & E. B. WHITE, THE ELEMENTS OF STYLE 67 (1959) ("[T]he one truly reliable shortcut in writing is to choose words that are strong and sure-footed, to carry the reader on his way."); VLADÍMIR PROPP, MORPHOLOGY OF THE FOLKTALE 92 (2d ed. 1968) ("Morphologically, a tale . . . may be termed any development *proceeding from* villainy . . . or a lack . . . , *through* intermediary functions *to* marriage . . . or *to* other . . . [*t*]*erminal functions.*") (emphasis added); Cover, *supra* note 2, at 5 ("[N]arratives . . . are the *trajectories* plotted upon material reality by our imaginations.") (emphasis added).

17. *See* Cover, *supra* note 2, at 5 ("[E]very narrative is insistent in its demand for its prescriptive point, its moral").

18. *See* Paul Grice, *Logic and Conversation, in* 3 SYNTAX AND SEMANTICS: SPEECH ACTS 41 (P. Cole & J. Morgan eds., 1975).

19. Conflict is already central to storytelling in childhood. At this early stage, however, children's stories have little recognizable structure. Rather, they tend to be about conflicts and crises beyond the child's control. *See* Brian Sutton-Smith, *The Origins of Fiction and the Fictions of Origin, in* TEXT, PLAY, AND STORY: THE CONSTRUCTION AND RECONSTRUCTION OF SELF AND SOCIETY 117–23 (Edward Bruner ed., 1984).

20. *Genesis* 32:22–32. For contrasting structuralist and deconstructionist readings of this story, see ROLAND BARTHES, IMAGE-MUSIC-TEXT 125 (S. Heath ed., 1977).

21. HOMER, THE ODYSSEY (A. Pope trans., 1942).

22. *See* PROPP, *supra* note 16, at 36–39.

23. JACK KEROUAC, ON THE ROAD (1955).

24. *See* LAKOFF, *supra* note 15, at 285–86. Stories have an internal time structure, or "story-time," that can be different from the temporal order of the storytelling itself, the "discourse-time." Seymour Chatman, *What Novels Can Do that
Films Can't (and Vice Versa), in* ON NARRATIVE, *supra* note 9, at 118.

25. KEROUAC, *supra* note 23, at 5, 250–253.

26. PROPP, *supra* note 16, at 39–50. Propp identified the recursive structure of
many folkstories, although he characterized the basic units somewhat differently. *Id.*
at 92 ("Each new act of villainy, each new lack creates a move. One tale may have
several moves."). My account of story structure is influenced by Propp and his structuralist successors, particularly Barthes, and owes a great deal to conversations with
George Lakoff and Mark Turner.

27. FREEDMAN & SIMON, *supra* note 11, at 311 (quoting *Genesis* 11:28; brack-
eted material in original). The rabbis of the midrash interpreted *'al pene* as if the
verse read *'al yideh.* The latter phrase translates literally as "on the hands of" or,
more properly, "by means of." The intimation is that Terach's trade in idols led to
Haran's death. *Id.* at 311 n.2. In the traditional Jewish account, Abraham's father left
Ur of the Chaldees to go to Canaan because of this incident. Commentary of Rashi
on *Genesis* 11:31. On the name change from Abram to Abraham, see *Genesis* 17:5.

28. GEORGE LAKOFF & MARK JOHNSON, METAPHORS WE LIVE BY 61–65
(1980).

29. *See Genesis* 4:1–15. Cover traces the systematicness of the sibling rivalry
theme in the context of the ascendancy of the younger to the birthright of the elder.
Cover, *supra* note 2, at 19–24. *Cf.* FREEDMAN & SIMON, *supra* note 11, at 311–12
& n.1 (The rabbis of the midrash assumed that Abraham must have excelled Haran
at everything).

30. *See* CLAUDE LÉVI-STRAUSS, THE SAVAGE MIND 16–22 (1969).

31. MAURICE MERLEAU-PONTY, SENSE AND NON-SENSE 131 (Hubert L. Dreyfus & Patricia A. Dreyfus trans., 1964); KERRY WHITESIDE, MERLEAU-PONTY AND
THE FOUNDATION OF AN EXISTENTIAL POLITICS 75 (1988) ("What *constitutes* a community is the meaning-saturated milieu that it creates for itself and that it transmits
to its members.").

32. *See* MICHEL FOUCAULT, POWER/KNOWLEDGE: SELECTED INTERVIEWS AND
OTHER WRITINGS 1972–77, 131 (Colin Gordon ed., 1980) ("Truth is a thing of this
world; it is produced only by virtue of multiple forms of constraint. And it induces
regular effects of power.").

33. From a postmodern perspective, indeterminacy arises from the surfeit
rather than the lack of foundations. *See* Steven L. Winter, *Human Values in a Postmodern World,* 6 YALE J. L. & HUMAN. 233, 242 (1994); *cf.* Cover, *supra* note 2, at
16 ("It is the problem of the multiplicity of meaning—the fact that never only one
but always many worlds are created by the too fertile forces of jurisgenesis—that
leads at once to the imperial virtues and the imperial mode of world maintenance.").

34. MARTHA C. NUSSBAUM, LOVE'S KNOWLEDGE: ESSAYS ON PHILOSOPHY AND
LITERATURE 391 (1990).

35. *See* Steven L. Winter, *Contingency and Community in Normative Practice,*
139 U. PA. L. REV. 963, 989–94 (1991); *see also* Cover, *supra* note 2, at 5 ("[O]ur

apprehension of the structure of the normative world is no less fundamental than our appreciation of the structure of the physical world.").

36. MAURICE MERLEAU-PONTY, SIGNS 109 (Richard C. McCleary trans., 1964).

37. *See* MARK JOHNSON, THE BODY IN THE MIND: THE BODILY BASIS OF MEANING, IMAGINATION AND REASON, 89–95 (1987); *see also* GEORGE LAKOFF, MORAL POLITICS: WHAT CONSERVATIVES KNOW THAT LIBERALS DON'T (1996).

38. *Compare Exodus* 21:24, tractate *Baba Kamah* 84a, and *Matthew* 5:38–39 ("You have heard the saying, *An eye for an eye and a tooth for a tooth.* But I tell you, you are not to resist an injury: whoever strikes you on the right cheek, turn the other to him as well.").

39. LAKOFF, *supra* note 15, at 310.

40. *See* CLAUDE LÉVI-STRAUSS, A VIEW FROM AFAR 105–8 (Joachim Neugroschel & Phoebe Hoss trans., 1985). Lévi-Strauss uses these stories to make different structuralist claims.

41. *See* PROPP, *supra* note 16, at 107.

42. Nelson Goodman, *Twisted Tales; or, Story, Study, and Symphony, in* ON NARRATIVE, *supra* note 9, at 104–6.

43. BARTHES, *supra* note 20, at 92–103. Subsequent page references are given in the text.

44. TOM STOPPARD, ROSENCRANTZ AND GUILDENSTERN ARE DEAD (1967).

45. Samuel Beckett, *Waiting for Godot, in* SEVEN PLAYS OF THE MODERN THEATER (1962) (subsequent page references given in the text). *Godot* has been called "the play that was to alter the course of theater in the 20th century." Mel Gussow, *The Tramps Who Remade the Theater,* N.Y. TIMES, November 6, 1988, § 2, at 1. "After 'Godot' plots could be minimal; exposition, expendable; characters, contradictory; settings, unlocalized; and dialogue, unpredictable. Blatant farce could jostle tragedy." *Id.* at 20 (quoting the critic Ruby Cohn).

46. The play begins with the stage direction: "A country road. A tree." Beckett *supra* note 45, at 3. For Beckett, stage directions were integral to the play. Mel Gussow, *Critic's Notebook: Enter Fearless Director, Pursued by Playwright,* N.Y. TIMES, Jan. 3, 1985, at 14. (discussing Beckett's threatened suit over a change of scenery in a production of *Endgame*). The characterization of the two protagonists as fellow travelers is made explicitly at the close of act 1, when Estragon says: "I sometimes wonder if we wouldn't have been better off alone, each one for himself. We weren't made for the same road." Beckett *supra* note 45, at 44 (stage direction omitted).

47. On the systematicity of these metaphors, see GEORGE LAKOFF & MARK TURNER, MORE THAN COOL REASON: A FIELD GUIDE TO POETIC METAPHOR 6, 13–14, 31–37 (1989).

48. On reader-response theory, see STANLEY FISH, IS THERE A TEXT IN THIS CLASS? (1980); NORMAN HOLLAND, 5 READERS READING (1975).

49. NELSON GOODMAN, WAYS OF WORLDMAKING (1978).

50. Chatman, *supra* note 24, at 126–36 & n.4.

51. Nelson Goodman, *Metaphor as Moonlighting, in* ON METAPHOR 180 (Sheldon Sacks ed., 1979).

52. LIVIA POLANYI, TELLING THE AMERICAN STORY: A STRUCTURAL AND CULTURAL ANALYSIS OF CONVERSATIONAL STORYTELLING 4–5 (1985).

53. Gerald P. López, *Lay Lawyering,* 32 UCLA L. REV. 1, 6 (1984).

54. *Cf.* Charles R. Lawrence, III, *The Id, the Ego, and Equal Protection: Reckoning with Unconscious Racism,* 39 STAN. L. REV. 317, 338 (1987) ("In ambiguous social situations, it will always be easier to find evidence supporting an individual's presumed group characteristics than to find contradictory evidence.").

55. The cases include Riggs v. Palmer, 115 N.Y. 906, 22 N.E. 188 (1889) (the case of the murdering heir); Tennessee Valley Authority v. Hill, 437 U.S. 153 (1978) (the snail darter case); and Brown v. Board of Education, 347 U.S. 483 (1954) (the school desegregation case).

56. STANLEY FISH, DOING WHAT COMES NATURALLY: CHANGE, RHETORIC, AND THE PRACTICE OF THEORY IN LITERARY AND LEGAL STUDIES 87–119, 356–71 (1989).

57. Ronald Dworkin, *My Reply to Stanley Fish (and Walter Benn Michaels): Please Don't Talk About Objectivity Any More, in* THE POLITICS OF INTERPRETATION 287 (W. J. T. Mitchell ed., 1980).

58. FISH, *supra* note 56, at 364–65.

59. PATRICIA J. WILLIAMS, THE ALCHEMY OF RACE AND RIGHTS: DIARY OF A LAW PROFESSOR 44–46 (1991). Subsequent page references are given in the text. The story first appeared as *Spirit-Murdering the Messenger: The Discourse of Fingerpointing as the Law's Response to Racism,* 42 U. MIAMI L. REV. 127 (1987).

60. RICHARD A. POSNER, OVERCOMING LAW 372, 369 (1995). Subsequent page references appear in the text.

61. Coughlin, *supra* note 8, at 1268–75.

62. *Id.* at 1271 (quoting HAYDEN WHITE, TROPICS OF DISCOURSE 121 (1978)). *See also id.* at 1253–54 (affirming that "actual lived experiences and narratives of those experiences occupy different orders of existence") (citing HAYDEN WHITE, THE CONTENT OF THE FORM 2–5 (1987)).

63. *See* GOODMAN, *supra* note 49, at 2–3 ("If I ask about the world, you can offer to tell me how it is under one or more frames of reference; but if I insist that you tell me how it is apart from all frames, what can you say?"); HILARY PUTNAM, REASON, TRUTH, AND HISTORY 54 (1981) (quoted in the *Preface* at note 3).

64. *Cf.* DONALD DAVIDSON, *On the Very Idea of a Conceptual Scheme, in* INQUIRIES INTO TRUTH AND INTERPRETATION 183 (1984).

65. The locus classicus is Kuhn's *Structure of Scientific Revolutions.* Significantly, Posner subjectivizes Kuhn's insight, attributing to him the claim "that scientific theories are a function of human need and desire rather than the way things are in nature." Posner, *supra* note 60, at 391.

66. *See* Clark Freshman, *Were Patricia Williams and Ronald Dworkin Separated at Birth?,* 95 COLUM. L. REV. 1568 (1995) (reviewing POSNER, *supra* note 60).

67. Note that there is hoary jurisprudential precedent for using practices of courtesy as a proxy for legal rules. H. L. A. HART, THE CONCEPT OF LAW 121–22 (1961).

68. Dworkin's point has roots in Hart's distinction between the internal and external perspective. *See* HART, *supra* note 67, at 10–11, 55–56, 197.

69. Lena Williams, *When Blacks Shop, Bias Often Accompanies Sale,* N.Y.

TIMES, April 30, 1991, at A1. *See also* Ian Ayres, *Fair Driving: Gender and Race Discrimination in Retail Car Negotiations,* 104 HARV. L. REV. 817 (1991).

70. Judi Dash, *Black Travelers Talk About Bias,* CONDÉ NAST TRAVELER, November 1992, at 45. When Oprah later spoke to the president of the company that owned the store, he explained that the store had recently been robbed by Black people and the manager was afraid to let her in.

71. Farber & Sherry, *supra* note 8, at 850–51. Much the same argument appears in their more recent treatment of the same material. DANIEL A. FARBER & SUZANNA SHERRY, BEYOND ALL REASON: THE RADICAL ASSAULT ON TRUTH IN AMERICAN LAW 84–94 (1997).

72. Farber & Sherry, *supra* note 8, at 819, 849.

CHAPTER SIX

1. 452 U.S. 18, 25–27 (1980). Subsequent page numbers are given in the text.

2. KARL N. LLEWELLYN, THE BRAMBLE BUSH: ON OUR LAW AND ITS STUDY 74 (2d ed. 1951) (emphasis deleted).

3. Johnson v. Zerbst, 304 U.S. 458 (1938) (federal cases); Betts v. Brady, 316 U.S. 455 (1942) (state cases).

4. Gideon v. Wainwright, 372 U.S. 335 (1963) (overruling *Betts v. Brady*); *In re* Gault, 387 U.S. 1 (1968); Argersinger v. Hamlin, 407 U.S. 25 (1972); Scott v. Illinois, 440 U.S. 367, 373 (1979).

5. 455 U.S. 480, 493 (1979).

6. 411 U.S. 778, 782 (1973); Morrissey v. Brewer, 408 U.S. 471 (1972) (parole revocation).

7. 442 U.S. 584 (1979).

8. *Vitek,* 445 U.S. at 495–97, 498–99.

9. *Gagnon,* 411 U.S. at 783, 788.

10. *See Argersinger,* 407 U.S. at 49–50 (Powell, J., dissenting) (discussed *infra* in text accompanying note 35); *Gault,* 387 U.S. at 15–20 (rejecting the benign characterizations and aspirations of the early juvenile justice reformers); *see also id.* at 39 n.65 (quoting the observation of the National Crime Commission Report: "Fears have been expressed that lawyers would make juvenile court proceedings more adversary. No doubt this is partly true, but it is partly desirable. Informality is often abused.").

11. *Argersinger,* 407 U.S. at 32.

12. *Gault,* 387 U.S. at 35.

13. *Scott,* 440 U.S. at 373.

14. *See* Karl N. Llewellyn, *Some Realism About Realism—Responding to Dean Pound,* 44 HARV. L. REV. 1222, 1239 (1931); Duncan Kennedy, *Form and Substance in Private Law Adjudication,* 89 HARV. L. REV. 1685, 1712–13 (1976); Richard Michael Fischl, *Some Realism About Critical Legal Studies,* 41 U. MIAMI L. REV. 505, 513–522 (1987).

15. KARL N. LLEWELLYN, THE COMMON LAW TRADITION: DECIDING APPEALS 263 (1961).

16. *Compare* Goldberg v. Kelly, 397 U.S. 254 (1970) (requiring a hearing prior

to termination of welfare benefits in part because recipients often depend on continued benefits for survival), *with* Mathews v. Eldridge, 424 U.S. 319 (1976) (finding a
post-termination hearing sufficient in disability cases because survival is rarely at
stake for this class of recipients). In Addington v. Texas, 441 U.S. 418 (1979), for
example, the Court explained that the standard of proof "reflects the value society
places on individual liberty." The "typical civil case involving a monetary dispute" is
determined by "a preponderance of the evidence." Proof in criminal cases must be
"beyond a reasonable doubt." The intermediate "clear and convincing evidence"
standard, in contrast, is typically used "in civil cases involving allegations of fraud
or some other quasi-criminal wrongdoing." *Id.* at 423–25.

17. Powell v. Alabama, 287 U.S. 45, 69 (1932).

18. *Gault,* 387 U.S. at 24–29.

19. *Argersinger,* 407 U.S. at 32–37.   21. *Gagnon,* 411 U.S. at 785.

20. *Vitek,* 445 U.S. at 491–94.   22. *Id.* at 786–87.

23. *Id.* at 789; *see also id.* at 781 ("Revocation deprives an individual, not of
the absolute liberty to which every citizen is entitled, but only of the conditional liberty properly dependent on observance of special parole restrictions.") (quoting
Morrisey v. Brewer, 408 U.S. 471, 480 (1972)). *Gagnon's* reliance on the "more limited due process right of one who . . . has been convicted of a crime," *id.* at 781, suggests that what governs the Court's assessment of the right to counsel is the legal interest in liberty (i.e., formal liberty) rather than practical freedom from confinement.
This conclusion is corroborated by the line of cases declining to extend the right to
counsel to convicted prisoners challenging the legality of their confinement via dis-
cretionary Supreme Court review on direct appeal, Ross v. Moffit, 417 U.S. 600
(1974); via state post-conviction relief, Pennsylvania v. Finley, 481 U.S. 551 (1987);
or via federal habeas corpus, Murray v. Giarratano, 492 U.S. 1 (1989).

24. *Parham,* 442 U.S. at 620.

25. *Id.* at 610.

26. *Id.* at 600 (arguing that the "adverse social consequences" of commitment
"need not be equated with the community response resulting from being labeled by
the state as delinquent, criminal, or mentally ill and possibly dangerous.").

27. *Cf.* Duncan v. Louisiana, 391 U.S. 145, 149–50 n.14 (1968) ("The recent
cases . . . have proceeded on the valid assumption that state criminal processes are
not imaginary and theoretical schemes but actual systems bearing every characteristic of the common-law system that has been developing contemporaneously in England and in this country.").

28. *Eldridge,* 424 U.S. at 335.

29. *Cf.* Richard A. Posner, Economic Analysis of Law 550 (4th ed. 1992)
(noting that, "as with the Hand Formula *[B<PL]* . . . , it is rarely possible (or at least
efforts are not made) to quantify the terms" of the *Eldridge* three-factor test). Posner
finds the *Eldridge* test valuable, nevertheless. In support of this conclusion, he offers
contrasting cases involving simple deprivations of property. But these examples are
misleading because the variables are few, discrete, and easily quantified; the "weighing" of the interests is, then, just a matter of simple arithmetic. Posner's examples
are, thus, atypical of such constitutional due process cases as *Lassiter* or *Goldberg v.
Kelly* (*supra* note 16).

30. *See, e.g., Goldberg,* 397 U.S. at 263–64.

31. Steven L. Winter, *The Metaphor of Standing and the Problem of Self-Governance*, 40 STAN. L. REV. 1371, 1385–86 (1988).

32. *See* GORDON W. ALLPORT, THE NATURE OF PREJUDICE 17–27 (3d ed. 1979); GEORGE LAKOFF, WOMEN, FIRE, AND DANGEROUS THINGS: WHAT CATEGORIES REVEAL ABOUT THE MIND 85–86 (1987).

33. *Gault*, 387 U.S. at 17.

34. *Gagnon*, 411 U.S. at 789.

35. *Argersinger*, 407 U.S. at 49–50.

36. Joseph William Singer, *The Reliance Interest in Property*, 40 STAN. L. REV. 611, 624 n.40 (1988); Mark Tushnet, *Following the Rules Laid Down: A Critique of Interpretivism and Neutral Principles*, 96 HARV. L. REV. 781, 819 & n.119 (1983).

37. *Cf.* Joseph William Singer, *The Player and the Cards: Nihilism and Legal Theory*, 94 YALE L.J. 1, 21–22 (1984) (suggesting that "[c]onvention, rather than logic, tells us that judges will not interpret the Constitution to require socialism.").

38. *Cf.* Thomas Kuhn, *Second Thoughts on Paradigms, in* THE STRUCTURE OF SCIENTIFIC THEORIES 459, 460 (Frederick Suppe ed., 1972) ("A paradigm is what the members of a scientific community, and they alone, share. Conversely, it is their possession of a common paradigm that constitutes a scientific community of a group of otherwise disparate men.").

39. LLEWELLYN, *supra* note 2, at 48.

40. *Parham*, 442 U.S. at 602–3 (commitment by parents); *id.* at 617–19 (commitment by the state's Department of Family and Children Services).

41. MAURICE MERLEAU-PONTY, SENSE AND NON-SENSE 39 (Hubert L. Dreyfus & Patricia Allen Dreyfus trans., 1964).

42. "Social systems are constructed out of, as well as constrained by, what human beings are; and how human beings cognize their worlds constrains and shapes how humans-in-societies reproduce them." Roger M. Keesing, *Models, "Folk" and "Cultural": Paradigms Regained? in* CULTURAL MODELS IN LANGUAGE AND THOUGHT 369, 388–89 (Dorothy Holland & Naomi Quinn eds., 1989).

43. Joseph C. Hutcheson, Jr., *The Judgment Intuitive: The Function of the "Hunch" in Judicial Decisions*, 14 CORNELL L.Q. 274, 278 (1929).

44. Duncan Kennedy, *Freedom and Constraint in Adjudication: A Critical Phenomenology of Judging*, 36 J. LEGAL EDUC. 518, 535 (1986).

45. HILARY PUTNAM, REASON, TRUTH, AND HISTORY 54 (1981) (emphasis deleted).

CHAPTER SEVEN

1. Snowden v. Hughes, 321 U.S. 1, 16 (1944) (Frankfurter, J., concurring); *cf.* Tennessee v. Davis, 100 U.S. 257, 263 (1880).

2. In Peter Gabel's colorful phrase, the state is a "hallucinatory projection." Peter Gabel, *The Phenomenology of Rights Consciousness and the Pact of the Withdrawn Selves*, 62 TEX. L. REV. 1563, 1573–74 (1984). But, as Benedict Anderson points out, "this formulation . . . implies that 'true' communities exist which can be advantageously juxtaposed to nations. In fact, all communities larger than primordial villages of face-to-face contact (and perhaps even these) are imagined." BENEDICT

ANDERSON, IMAGINED COMMUNITIES: REFLECTIONS ON THE ORIGIN AND SPREAD OF NATIONALISM 6 (rev. ed. 1991).

3. GEORGE LAKOFF, WOMEN, FIRE, AND DANGEROUS THINGS: WHAT CATE-GORIES REVEAL ABOUT THE MIND 208 (1987); *see also* Karl N. Llewellyn, *The Constitution as an Institution*, 34 COLUM. L. REV. 1, 17–18 (1934) ("An institution is in the first instance a set of ways of living and doing. . . . The existence of an institution lies first of all and last of all in the fact that people do behave in certain patterns, . . . and it involves not patterns of doing (or of inhibition) merely, but also accompanying patterns of thinking and of emotion.").

4. For example, the Nazi occupation of France during World War II and the formation of a collaborationist government at Vichy "meant that suddenly each citizen was thrust into a situation where he had to . . . 'reconstitute a state by choice.' . . . Where before there had been habitual allegiance, now there was necessarily a deliberate decision for or against the Vichy regime." KERRY H. WHITESIDE, MERLEAU-PONTY AND THE FOUNDATION OF AN EXISTENTIAL POLITICS 185–86 (1988) (quoting MAURICE MERLEAU-PONTY, HUMANISM AND TERROR: AN ESSAY ON THE COMMU-NIST PROBLEM 36–37 (John O'Neill trans., 1969)).

5. Luther v. Borden, 48 U.S. (7 How.) 1, 2, 46–47 (1849).

6. *Compare* Home Telephone & Telegraph Co. v. City of Los Angeles, 227 U.S. 278, 288 (1913), *with* Barney v. City of New York, 193 U.S. 430, 437 (1904).

7. *Compare Ex parte* Young, 209 U.S. 123, 159 (1908), *with* Pennhurst State School & Hospital v. Halderman, 465 U.S. 89, 107 (1984).

8. MASS. CONST., pt. 1, art. XXX ("A Declaration of the Rights of the Inhabi-tants of the Commonwealth of Massachusetts"); *see also* Marbury v. Madison, 5 U.S. (1 Cranch) 137, 163 (1803). On the origins of the phrase, see Frank I. Michel-man, *The Supreme Court 1985 Term—Foreword: Traces of Self-Government*, 100 HARV. L. REV. 4, 4 n.2 (1986).

9. *See Young*, 209 U.S. at 159–60 ("[T]he officer . . . is in that case stripped of his official or representative character and is subjected in his person to the conse-quences of his individual conduct.").

10. *See Home Telephone*, 227 U.S. at 284 (rejecting the reductive argument be-cause "the enforcement of the doctrine would hence render impossible the perfor-mance of the duty with which the Federal courts are charged under the Constitution. Such paralysis would inevitably ensue.").

11. *See* Robert Hale, *Coercion and Distribution in a Supposedly Non-Coercive state*, 38 POL. SCI. Q. 470 (1923). *See also* Duncan Kennedy, *Form and Substance in Private Law Adjudication*, 89 HARV. L. REV. 1685, 1748–51 (1976).

12. *Home Telephone*, 227 U.S. at 283 ("Under this hypothesis . . . , it could not be assumed that the state had authorized its officers to do acts in violation of the state constitution until the court of last resort of the state had determined that such acts were authorized."). This, in effect, is the position taken by the Court in many of its recent decisions. Henry Paul Monaghan, *State Law Wrongs, State Law Remedies, and the Fourteenth Amendment*, 86 COLUM. L. REV. 979, 982 (1986).

13. 42 U.S.C. § 1983 (1986).

14. The statute provided: "That no Escheator, Sheriff, nor other Bailiff of the King, by Colour of his Office, without special Warrant, or Commandment, or Au-thority certain pertaining to his Office, disseise any Man of his Freehold, nor of any

Thing belonging to his Freehold." Statute of 3 Edw. 1, ch. 24 (1275), *reprinted in* 1 STATUTES AT LARGE 92–93 (Danby Pickering ed., 1762). The appearance of the phrase in this statute is almost a hundred years earlier than any of the entries in *The Oxford English Dictionary* for legal uses of the term "colour" and fifteen years earlier than the earliest example given for a nonlegal use. 3 THE OXFORD ENGLISH DICTIONARY 499–500 (2d ed. 1989) (definitions 2.a., 11.c. & d.) [hereinafter OED].

15. SIR EDWARD COKE, THE SECOND PART OF THE INSTITUTES OF THE LAWES OF ENGLAND 206 (facsimile ed. 1979) (1642).

16. *See* Dive v. Maningham, 1 Plowden's Reports 60, 67, 75 Eng. Rep. 96, 107 (Common Bench 1551) (first reported in 1578).

17. Statute of 23 Hen. 6, c. 10 (1444), *reprinted in* 3 STATUTES AT LARGE 269, 271–72 (Danby Pickering ed., 1762).

18. *Dive,* 1 Plowden at 63, 75 Eng. Rep. at 100–01.

19. *Id.* at 67, 75 Eng. Rep. at 107–8.

20. *Id.* at 67–68, 75 Eng. Rep. at 108 (emphasis in original).

21. STATUTES AT LARGE, *supra* note 17, at 269–70.

22. *Dive,* 1 Plowden at 64, 75 Eng. Rep. at 102.

23. *Ex parte* Reed, 4 Hill 572, 574 (N.Y. Sup. Ct. 1843), *overruled by* The People *ex rel.* Kellog v. Schuyler, 4 N.Y. 173 (1850); *see also* United States v. Cranston, 25 F. Cas. 692 (C.C.D.C. 1828) (No. 14,889) (sureties not liable for action without legal process); Governor *ex rel.* Simmons v. Hancock, 2 Ala. 728 (1841) (sureties not liable for fraud).

24. *Schuyler,* 4 N.Y. at 180.

25. *Reed,* 4 Hill at 572–75.

26. Ohio *ex rel.* Story v. Jennings, 4 Ohio St. 419, 423 (1854); *accord* City of Lowell v. Parker, 51 Mass. (10 Met.) 309, 313–14 (1845) (Shaw, C.J.).

27. Sangster v. Commonwealth, 58 Va. (17 Gratt.) 124, 130 (1866).

28. Lammon v. Feusier, 111 U.S. 17, 20–22 (1884) (canvassing cases); *see also* Van Pelt v. Littler, 14 Cal. 194 (1859); Commonwealth for Davy v. Stockton, 21 Ky. (5 T.B. Mon.) 192 (1827); Carmack v. Commonwealth *ex rel.* Boggs, 5 Binn. 184 (Pa. 1812).

29. 18 U.S.C. § 242 (1988). This statute was the model for section 1983. Cong. Globe, 42d Cong., 1st Sess. App. 68 (statement of Rep. Shellabarger).

30. 365 U.S. 167, 184 (1961); United States v. Classic, 313 U.S. 299, 326 (1941).

31. *See* GEORGE LAKOFF & MARK JOHNSON, METAPHORS WE LIVE BY 14–17 (1980).

32. *Id.* at 15, 48.

33. 3 OED, *supra* note 14, at 499 (definition 1).

34. William Shakespeare, *The Two Gentlemen of Verona,* act 1, scene 2, lines 1–4: "Already I have been false to Valentine, / And now I must be as unjust to Thurio. / Under the color of commending him, / I have access my own love to prefer."

35. Virginia v. De Hart, 119 Fed. 626, 628 (C.C.W.D. Va. 1902).

36. *See, e.g.,* Cong. Globe, 42d Cong., 1st Sess. 364 (1871) (statement of Rep. Archer opposing the bill) ("[U]nder color of maintaining the manhood of man in the

political equality of the colored man, the manhood of man is denied in the political degradation of the white man."). Archer also quoted a similar usage from Justice Story on the Guarantee Clause. *Id.* at 366 ("Every pretext for intermeddling with the domestic concerns of any state, under color of protecting it against domestic violence, is taken away by that part of the provision."). The OED gives a related nonlegal usage of "colour" as "[a] show of reason, a specious or plausible reason or ground; fair pretense, pretext, cloak." 3 OED, *supra* note 14, at 500 (definition 12.a.).

37. *See* HOMERSHAM COX, THE INSTITUTIONS OF THE ENGLISH GOVERNMENT 218 (1863).

38. 30 Fed. Cas. 606, 608 (C.C.D. Ohio 1854) (No. 18,032), *aff'd,* 59 U.S. 331 (1855). The reference to "jurisdiction" is to the court's equity jurisdiction.

39. EDWARD JENKS, A SHORT HISTORY OF ENGLISH LAW 163–64 (6th ed. 1949); 9 SIR WILLIAM HOLDSWORTH, A HISTORY OF ENGLISH LAW 299–302 (1925) ("The doctrine of colour was founded on a fiction."). Already extant by 1400, this practice continued in use in England until the beginning of the nineteenth century.

40. Pillow v. Roberts, 54 U.S. 472, 477 (1851); *see also* Beaver v. Taylor, 68 U.S. 637, 641 n.2 (1863); Wright v. Mattison, 59 U.S. 50, 56 (1855).

41. HOWARD NENNER, BY COLOUR OF LAW: LEGAL CULTURE & CONSTITUTIONAL POLITICS IN ENGLAND, 1660–1689, at 83 (1977); *see also id.* at 130 ("Legal process, or at least its appearance 'by colour of law,' would serve as the constant guide to political action from 1660 on.").

42. 3 OED, *supra* note 14, at 499 (definitions 2.b. & 6.a.).

43. *Monroe,* 365 U.S. at 171–72 (emphasis added). Similarly, Frankfurter recognized: "Certainly the night-time intrusion of the man with a star and a police revolver is a different phenomenon than the night-time intrusion of a burglar." *Id.* at 238.

44. 8 OED, *supra* note 14, at 46 (definition 4).

45. *Ex parte* Virginia, 100 U.S. 339, 347 (1880) (emphasis added); *accord Home Telephone,* 227 U.S. at 287 ("[T]he theory of the Amendment is that where an officer or other representative of a state in the exercise of *the authority with which he is clothed* misuses the power possessed to do a wrong forbidden by the Amendment, inquiry concerning whether the state has authorized the wrong is irrelevant.") (emphasis added). *See also* Screws v. United States, 325 U.S. 91, 110 (1945) (plurality opinion) (noting that the statute at issue in *Ex parte Virginia* did not contain the "under color of law" language).

46. *Monroe,* 365 U.S. at 238 (emphasis added); *see also* Terry v. Adams, 345 U.S. 461, 475 (1953) (Frankfurter, J., concurring).

47. *Young,* 209 U.S. at 159–60 (emphasis added).

48. HOWARD P. FINK & MARK V. TUSHNET, FEDERAL JURISDICTION: POLICY AND PRACTICE 127 (2d ed. 1987) ("[T]he *Young-Home Telephone* pair retains the air of mysticism that surrounds most legal fictions."); Akhil Reed Amar, *Of Sovereignty and Federalism,* 96 YALE L.J. 1425, 1490 n.257 (1987); Pennhurst State School & Hospital v. Halderman, 465 U.S. 89, 106–7 (1984) (describing the reductive approach of *Ex parte Young* as a necessary "fiction" and characterizing the dissent's ultra vires theory of *Young* as "out of touch with reality").

49. *Ex parte* Virginia, 100 U.S. at 347.

50. Hafer v. Mello, 502 U.S. 21, 27 (1991).

51. To the contrary, the common-law rule was that a municipal corporation was not liable for the action of its agents committed "under color of office." Thayer v. City of Boston, 36 Mass. (19 Pick.) 511, 516–17 (1837) (Shaw, C. J.). Similarly, under section 1983, a municipality is not responsible for the constitutional violations committed by its officers "under color of law" unless they act pursuant to an official policy or custom; the officers are personally responsible to the victim for the damages. Monell v. Department of Social Services, 436 U.S. 658 (1978); Hafer, 502 U.S. at 27–28.

52. In some other legal contexts, the "color of office" concept has been used to address the problem of apparent authority. See Cocke v. Halsey, 41 U.S. 71, 86–87 (1842) (The irregular appointment of a clerk would still confer "color of title" to office and subsequent acts would be colore officii and binding on third parties).

53. LARRY ALEXANDER & PAUL HORTON, WHOM DOES THE CONSTITUTION COMMAND?: A CONCEPTUAL ANALYSIS WITH PRACTICAL IMPLICATIONS 33 (1988).

54. One need only compare Lugar v. Edmundson Oil Co., 457 U.S. 922 (1982), where the participation of the clerk of the court in issuing the ex parte writ of attachment and of the sheriff in executing that writ was sufficient to establish state action "under color of law," with Flagg Bros., Inc. v. Brooks, 436 U.S. 149 (1978), where the unaided action of a private storage company was not considered state action even though it acted pursuant to the authorization of positive state law establishing a warehouseman's lien. One can make sense of these cases only in light of the social understanding in which the officer embodies the abstraction called "the state." Under the reductive analysis, these cases cannot be rationalized at all.

55. LAKOFF & JOHNSON, supra note 31, at 54–55 (Intentional action is part of our basic model of causation.); Eve E. Sweetser, The Definition of Lie: An Examination of the Folk Models Underlying a Semantic Prototype, in CULTURAL MODELS IN LANGUAGE AND THOUGHT 43, 50–51 (D. Holland & N. Quinn eds., 1987); and Linda Coleman & Paul Kay, Prototype Semantics: The English Verb 'Lie,' 57 LANGUAGE 26, 43 (1981) (Falsity of belief and intended deception are more important elements of what people judge to be a "lie" than factual falsity.).

56. On the presumption, see United States v. U.S. Gypsum Co., 438 U.S. 422, 430 (1978); Sandstrom v. Montana, 492 U.S. 510 (1979); Morrisette v. United States, 342 U.S. 248, 250–51 (1952) ("A relation between some mental element and punishment for a harmful act is almost as instinctive as the child's familiar exculpatory 'But I didn't mean to.'"). On causes of actions, see Steven L. Winter, The Metaphor of Standing and the Problem of Self-Governance, 40 STAN. L. REV. 1371, 1389–90 & n.90 (1988) (collecting sources). See also Asahi Metal Indus. Co. v. Superior Court, 107 S. Ct. 1026, 1033 (1987) (Jurisdiction based on minimum contacts requires "an action of the defendant purposefully directed toward the forum state.") (plurality opinion; emphasis deleted).

57. Woolsey, 30 Fed. Cas. at 607.

58. 30 Fed. Cas. 465 (C.C.D. Vt. 1852) (No. 17,955); Findley v. Satterfield, 9 Fed. Cas. 67, 68 (C.C.N.D. Ga. 1877) (No. 4,792) (Congress's authority to prescribe removal extends to "acts done, or in good faith alleged to have been done, in the course of their duty."). See also Tennessee v. Davis, 100 U.S. at 261–62.

59. Lamar v. McCulloch, 115 U.S. 164, 186 (1885); McLeod v. Callicott, 16

Fed. Cas. 295, 297 (C.C.D.S.C. 1869) (No. 8,897). The statute is the Act of July 27, 1868, ch. 276, § 3, 15 stat. 243–44.

60. Olmstead v. United States, 277 U.S. 438, 485 (1928) (Brandeis, J., dissenting); *see also* Owen v. City of Independence, 445 U.S. 622, 651 (1980) (identifying the harm as worse because committed by "the government itself—'the social organ to which all in our society look to for the promotion of liberty, justice, fair and equal treatment, and the setting of worthy norms and goals of social conduct'") (quoting Adickes v. S. H. Kress & Co., 398 U.S. 144, 190 (1970) (Brennan, J., concurring and dissenting)).

61. *Compare Monroe,* 365 U.S. at 222 (Frankfurter, J., dissenting) ("[T]he prior decisions . . . have given 'under color of [law]' a content that ignores the meaning fairly comported by the words of the text."), *with Screws,* 325 U.S. at 111 (plurality opinion) ("If, as suggested, the statute was designed to embrace only actions which the state in fact authorized, the words 'under color of state law' were hardly apt words to express the idea.").

62. For a more extended discussion, see Steven L. Winter, *The Meaning of "Under Color of" State Law,* 91 MICH. L. REV. 323, 348–52, 360–61, & 405–7 (1992).

63. Raymond v. Chicago Union Traction Co., 207 U.S. 20, 41 (1907) (Holmes, J., dissenting) ("I am unable to grasp the principle on which the state is said to deprive the appellee of his property without due process of law because a subordinate board, subject to the control of the Supreme Court of the state, is said to have . . . disobeyed the authentic command of the state."); *Snowden,* 321 U.S. at 17 (Frankfurter, J., concurring) (paraphrasing Holmes in *Raymond*); *Screws,* 325 U.S. at 147–48 (Roberts, Frankfurter, & Jackson, JJ., dissenting). Frankfurter claimed that "'under color of' law meant by authority of law in the nineteenth century." *Monroe,* 365 U.S. at 244. This is obviously false, and Frankfurter probably knew it. *See* Winter, *supra* note 62, at 362–84.

64. *See, e.g.,* City of St. Louis v. Praprotnik, 485 U.S. 112, 125 (1988) (plurality opinion) ("[W]e can be confident that state law . . . will always direct a court to some official or body that has the responsibility for making law or setting policy in any given area of a local government's business.").

65. *Schuyler,* 4 N.Y. at 181 ("The English statutes and our own refer to acts done 'virtute officii,' and yet they have uniformly been held to extend to acts of misfeasance."); *Reed,* 4 Hill at 572–73 ("The words cannot be extended beyond nonfeasance or misfeasance in respect to acts which by law [the sheriff] is required to perform.").

66. *Monroe,* 365 U.S. at 246, 254–55.

CHAPTER EIGHT

1. Antonin Scalia, *The Rule of Law as a Law of Rules,* 56 U. CHI. L. REV. 1175, 1178–80 (1989).

2. JOSEPH RAZ, PRACTICAL REASON AND NORMS 61 (2d ed. 1990) ("Following a rule entails its acceptance as an exclusionary reason for not acting on conflicting reasons even though they may tip the balance of reasons."). Subsequent page references are provided in the text. *See also* RONALD DWORKIN, TAKING RIGHTS SERIOUSLY 22–28, 72–80 (1977) (treating rules as, by definition, dispositive when applicable).

3. *Cf.* Stanley Fish, Doing What Comes Naturally: Change, Rhetoric, and the Practice of Theory in Literary and Legal Studies 320–21 (1989) ("[T]here are sentences which . . . seem to be intelligible in isolation, independently of any contextual setting. This simply means, however, that the context is so established, so deeply assumed, that it is invisible to the observer."). Subsequent page references are given in the text.

4. H. L. A. Hart, *Positivism and the Separation of Law and Morals,* 71 Harv. L. Rev. 593, 615 (1958) (emphasis deleted).

5. Karl N. Llewellyn, The Case Law System in America 80 (Paul Gewirtz ed., Michael Ansaldi trans., 1989) (emphasis in original). *See also* Richard A. Posner, The Problems of Jurisprudence 51 (1990) ("The rules [of skiing] are really guides, and maybe this is what rules of law are to judges."). Subsequent references are given in the text.

6. Anthony G. Amsterdam, *Perspectives on the Fourth Amendment,* 58 Minn. L. Rev. 349, 376–77 (1974).

7. Larry Alexander & Emily Sherwin, *The Deceptive Nature of Rules,* 142 U. Pa. L. Rev. 1191, 1192 (1994) (defining "a serious rule" as "one that dictates the course of action to be taken in all cases that fall within its terms" and arguing that, since rules are overgeneralizations, "rule-makers 'lie' to rule followers.").

8. Robert M. Cover, *The Supreme Court 1982 Term—Foreword:* Nomos *and* Narrative, 97 Harv. L. Rev. 4, 18 (1983). Subsequent page references are provided in the text.

9. For the more detailed argument that power cannot be reduced to the capacity to use force but must be understood as a social construction, see Steven L. Winter, *The "Power" Thing,* 82 Va. L. Rev. 721 (1996).

10. Frederick F. Schauer, Playing by the Rules: A Philosophical Examination of Rule-Based Decision-Making in Law and Life 38–52 (1991). Subsequent page numbers appear in the text.

11. One of the sophisticated aspects of Schauer's discussion is that he treats the entrenched generalization, and not the canonical formulation, as *the* rule. This allows his theory to comprehend those cases in which the justification is itself treated as the "rule," acting as an entrenched generalization with respect to higher-order justifications. *Id.* at 62–76, 207–15.

12. *See id.* at 92 ("Although all rules are exclusionary (or inclusionary) second-order reasons, not all exclusionary or inclusionary second-order reasons are rules."). Schauer argues (correctly in my view) that exclusionary reasons operate in a presumptive rather than preemptive fashion. *Id.* at 90–91.

13. Frederick Schauer, *Constitutional Positivism,* 25 Conn. L. Rev. 797, 826–27 (1993).

14. This phrase, which originated in America in the 1850s, does not even appear in the first edition of the *Oxford English Dictionary. Compare* 5 The Oxford English Dictionary 651–52 (1933) (definition 4.b.), *with* 8 The Oxford English Dictionary 348 (2d ed. 1989) (definition 4.b.).

15. Hart, *supra* note 4, at 606–15.

16. H. L. A. Hart, The Concept of Law 123–25 (1961).

17. *Id.* at 123–25.

18. Jules L. Coleman, *Negative and Positive Positivism,* 11 J. LEGAL STUD. 139, 140–43, 148–49 (1982); SCHAUER, *supra* note 10, at 197–99.

19. ROBERTO MANGABEIRA UNGER, THE CRITICAL LEGAL STUDIES MOVEMENT 8 (1986).

20. Hart, *supra* note 4, at 609.

21. 283 U.S. 25, 26 (1931).

22. Hart, *supra* note 4, at 610–11 (noting that "this itself is a social policy (though possibly a bad one)").

23. HART, *supra* note 16, at 123.

24. LLEWELLYN, *supra* note 5, at 83.

25. Hart, *supra* note 4, at 614. Hart backed off this claim in his later treatment in *The Concept of Law,* though he continued to treat purpose as an *attribution* rather than as an integral part of *meaning.* HART, *supra* note 16, at 124 ("In the case of legal rules, the criteria of relevance and closeness of resemblance depend on . . . the aims or purposes which may be attributed to the rule.").

26. *See, e.g.,* James D. A. Boyle, *The Politics of Reason: Critical Legal Theory and Local Social Thought,* 133 U. PA. L. REV. 685, 711–13 (1985); Anthony D'Amato, *Can Legislatures Constrain Judicial Interpretations of Statutes?,* 75 VA. L. REV. 561, 595–602 (1989); Frederick Schauer, *Formalism,* 97 YALE L.J. 509, 524–26, 532–34, 540–41 (1988); Steven L. Winter, *Transcendental Nonsense, Metaphoric Reasoning, and the Cognitive Stakes for Law,* 137 U. PA. L. REV. 1105, 1172–80 (1989); *see also* MARK KELMAN, A GUIDE TO CRITICAL LEGAL STUDIES 12 (1987) (using "vehicle" to illustrate the linguistic indeterminacy thesis).

27. Lon Fuller, *Positivism and Fidelity to Law—A Reply to Professor Hart,* 71 HARV. L. REV. 630, 662–63 (1958).

28. *Id.* at 662–63.

29. Hart, *supra* note 4, at 612; *see also id.* at 614.

30. Schauer, *supra* note 26, at 540.

31. LON FULLER, ANATOMY OF THE LAW 58–59 (1968).

32. DAVID SCHUYLER, THE NEW URBAN LANDSCAPE: THE REDEFINITION OF CITY FORM IN NINETEENTH-CENTURY AMERICA 62–66 (1986) (quoting Downing); MELVIN KALFUS, FREDERICK LAW OLMSTED: THE PASSION OF A PUBLIC ARTIST 278–81 (1991); IRVING FISHER, FREDERICK LAW OLMSTED AND THE CITY PLANNING MOVEMENT IN THE UNITED STATES 5, 102–3 (1986) ("In Olmsted's view, the park was an aesthetic instrument to achieve a social and psychological change in a business oriented, urban society."); Geoffrey Blodgett, *Frederick Law Olmsted: Landscape Architecture as Conservative Reform,* 62 J. AM. HIST. 869, 877–78 (1976) ("[Olmsted's] parks may be understood to reflect as accurately as civil service reform or tariff reform or Mugwump journalism a common group desire to counter the headlong popular impulses of the Gilded Age.").

33. GALEN CRANZ, THE POLITICS OF PARK DESIGN: A HISTORY OF URBAN PARKS IN AMERICA 55–56 (1982). *See also* SCHUYLER, *supra* note 32, at 186–87 (Park advocates opposed the Soldiers and Sailors Monument in Grand Army Plaza at the entrance to Brooklyn's Prospect Park.).

34. *See* Blodgett, *supra* note 32, at 881. Olmsted thought that Central Park had been ruined by the introduction of baseball diamonds; when he left New York in the

1880s to work in Boston, he made sure to place alongside the main park a smaller, antepark designed separately to accommodate more active recreation. SCHUYLER, *supra* note 32, at 141; KALFUS, *supra* note 32, at 299–300.

35. CRANZ, *supra* note 33, at 13–19.

36. *Id.* at 61–77.

37. *Id.* at 122 (quoting Chicago South Park Commission, Report 1940).

38. FULLER, *supra* note 31, at 59.

39. *Deuteronomy* 28:14 (translation from original Hebrew); *see also Leviticus* 26:3 (Soncino ed.) ("If you walk in my statutes. . . ."). In the latter quote, the Hebrew word that is usually translated as *statute* actually has a connotation closer to *fiat*.

40. RICHARD TUCK, NATURAL RIGHTS THEORIES 25–27 (1979) (translation by Tuck) (emphasis and excerpt from original Latin added). *Cf.* Oliver Wendell Holmes, Jr., *The Path of the Law,* 10 HARV. L. REV. 457 (1897).

41. The illustration, by David Gothard, appeared with an article concerning controversies over the ethics of various government officials. John Herbers, *Pentagon Bribery Inquiry; Demand for Ethics in Government Has Outstripped Supply,* N.Y. TIMES, June 19, 1988, § 4, at 4.

42. Thomas Kuhn, *Second Thoughts on Paradigms, in* THE STRUCTURE OF SCIENTIFIC THEORIES 459, 482 (F. Suppe ed., 1972).

43. Discussing Holmes, *supra* note 40, at 460–61 ("The prophecies of what the courts will do in fact, and nothing more pretentious, are what I mean by the law.").

44. 478 U.S. 186, 190–94 (1986) (majority opinion); *id.* at 199 (Blackmun, J., dissenting).

45. *See* MARK TUSHNET, RED, WHITE, AND BLUE: A CRITICAL ANALYSIS OF CONSTITUTIONAL LAW 135 (1988) (discussing *Bowers*); RONALD DWORKIN, LAW'S EMPIRE 70–72 (1986) (arguing that courts should attend to the concept or principle incorporated in a constitutional provision rather than to the particular conception of that provision held by its framers); LAURENCE TRIBE & MICHAEL DORF, ON READING THE CONSTITUTION 98 (1991). *See also* Michael H. v. Gerald D., 491 U.S. 110, 127 n.6 (1989) (opinion by Scalia, J., joined by Rehnquist, C.J.).

46. 410 U.S. 113 (1973).

47. Philip Bobbitt, *Is Law Politics?,* 41 STAN. L. REV. 1233, 1294–96 (1989) (reviewing TUSHNET, *supra* note 45).

48. Karl N. Llewellyn, *The Constitution as an Institution,* 34 COLUM. L. REV. 1, 17 (1934).

49. *Id.* at 18.

50. MAURICE MERLEAU-PONTY, SENSE AND NON-SENSE 118 (Hubert L. Dreyfus & Patricia Allen Dreyfus trans., 1964).

51. PETER L. BERGER & THOMAS LUCKMANN, THE SOCIAL CONSTRUCTION OF REALITY: A TREATISE ON THE SOCIOLOGY OF KNOWLEDGE 47–92 (1966). Subsequent page numbers appear in the text.

52. This is only a model and not a claim of methodological individualism. *See id.* at 54 ("[E]ven . . . a solitary individual . . . will habitualize his activity in accordance with biographical experience of a world of social institutions preceding his solitude.").

53. *Id.* at 67–70 ("The experiences that are so retained [in consciousness] become sedimented, that is, they congeal in recollection as recognizable and memorable entities.").

54. *See also id.* at 41 ("Within the semantic fields thus built up it is possible for both biographical and historical experience to be objectified, retained, and accumulated. . . . By virtue of this accumulation a social stock of knowledge is constituted, which is transmitted from generation to generation and which is available to the individual in everyday life.").

55. Following Hegel and Marx, they use the term "objectivation." *See id.* at 60–61 ("The process by which the externalized products of human activity attain the character of objectivity is objectivation.") (footnote omitted).

56. For an example of the contemporaneous criticisms, see 1 ROSCOE POUND, JURISPRUDENCE 271 (1959). For examples of CLS characterizations of realism, see MORTON HORWITZ, THE TRANSFORMATION OF AMERICAN LAW, 1870–1960: THE CRISIS OF LEGAL ORTHODOXY (1992); Joseph William Singer, *Legal Realism Now,* 76 CAL. L. REV. 465 (1988) (review essay); Gary Peller, *The Metaphysics of American Law,* 73 CAL. L. REV. 1151 (1985); Boyle, *supra* note 26, at 691–705.

57. Llewellyn, *supra* note 48, at 17–18 (emphasis in original; footnotes omitted). For my attempt to apply these insights to contemporary constitutional law, see Steven L. Winter, *Indeterminacy and Incommensurability in Constitutional Law,* 78 CAL. L. REV. 1441 (1990).

58. KARL N. LLEWELLYN, THE BRAMBLE BUSH: ON OUR LAW AND ITS STUDY 3 (2d ed. 1951). For Llewellyn's discussion of the "teapot tempest" caused by these words, see *id.* at ix–x. On Llewellyn's admiration for Holmes, see Karl N. Llewellyn, *Holmes,* 35 COLUM. L. REV. 485 (1935).

59. *See* Duncan Kennedy, *Freedom and Constraint in Adjudication: A Critical Phenomenology of Judging,* 36 J. LEGAL EDUC. 518, 539, 546–47, 551, 560–62 (1986). I discuss Kennedy's most recent iteration of this position in chapter 11.

60. LLEWELLYN, *supra* note 5, at 82–83.

61. LLEWELLYN, *supra* note 58, at 14.

62. Llewellyn, *supra* note 48, at 27 (emphasis in original).

63. KARL N. LLEWELLYN, THE COMMON LAW TRADITION: DECIDING APPEALS 60–61, 122–23 (1961). Subsequent page numbers are given in the text.

64. Charles E. Clark & David M. Trubek, *The Creative Role of the Judge: Restraint and Freedom in the Common Law Tradition,* 71 YALE L.J. 255 (1961).

65. *See, e.g.,* Richard Michael Fischl, *Some Realism About Critical Legal Studies,* 41 U. MIAMI L. REV. 505, 520–21 (1987) ("To overstate the matter somewhat, . . . Realists [like Llewellyn] sought to substitute one form of science for another."); Jay Feinman, *Promissory Estoppel and Judicial Method,* 97 HARV. L. REV. 678, 704 (1984) (referring to the "quasi-empirical—and therefore determinate—activity prescribed by the method of situation-sense"); Peller, *supra* note 56, at 1240–45, 1247–50.

66. Patrick J. Rohan, *The Common Law Tradition: Situation Sense, Subjectivism or "Just-Result Jurisprudence"?,* 32 FORDHAM L. REV. 51, 63–64 (1963). *See also* Feinman, *supra* note 65, at 704–5 (arguing that in determining the "type-situation," the level of categorization can always be varied to yield any desired result).

67. Clark & Trubek, *supra* note 64, at 261.

68. Rohan, *supra* note 66, at 56. *See also* Note, *Commercial Law and the American Volk: A Note on Llewellyn's German Sources for the Uniform Commercial Code*, 97 YALE L.J. 156, 158 (1987) ("[N]o scholar has been able to explain what Llewellyn thought 'immanent law' to be.").

69. Rohan, *supra* note 66, at 71.

70. *See, e.g.,* Feinman, *supra* note 65, at 704–5. Situation-sense still may not offer quite as much as Llewellyn hoped. Because of synchronic substantive indeterminacy, a decisionmaker may find that there is more than one ICM that fits and, therefore, has situation-sense.

71. Rohan, *supra* note 66, at 72.

72. This is the passage focused on by Feinman and Fischl, *supra* note 65, and referred to by the Note, *supra* note 68. The student note reports that Llewellyn actually misidentified the source of the quote and locates the quote in a later work by Goldschmidt. *Id.* at 158 n.16.

73. The most sophisticated and most nearly successful attempt is Kenneth M. Casebeer, *Escape from Liberalism: Fact and Value in Karl Llewellyn*, 1977 DUKE L.J. 671, 697 (recognizing that "there are passages seemingly impossible to reconcile").

74. *Id.* at 697 ("[O]ne should expect such difficulty given a very different dominant tradition subverting the language in another direction.").

75. WILLIAM TWINING, KARL LLEWELLYN AND THE REALIST MOVEMENT 369 (1973).

76. LLEWELLYN, *supra* note 58, at 117:
As to tools, law has borrowed copiously from the rest of culture: language, logic, writing; and for the subject matter of its thinking it borrows the whole stock of practices, standards, ethics that make up the social, economic and religious phases of society. What is dominant in society, then, is dominant in law.

77. Casebeer, *supra* note 73, at 693 (emphasis in original).

78. *See generally* KARL N. LLEWELLYN & E. ADAMSON HOEBEL, THE CHEYENNE WAY: CONFLICT AND CASE LAW IN PRIMITIVE JURISPRUDENCE (1941).

CHAPTER NINE

1. *See* RICHARD A. POSNER, THE PROBLEMS OF JURISPRUDENCE 93 (1990); RICHARD A. POSNER, OVERCOMING LAW 521 (1995) ("Analogy brings candidates for legal governance forward for our consideration, and this is a valuable function, akin to that of emotions like fear and desire in directing our thoughts along one channel rather than another."). *See also* Larry Alexander, *Bad Beginnings*, 145 U. PA. L. REV. 57, 86 n.96 (1996) (arguing that analogical reasoning in law that is based solely on the similarities and differences between the cases "lacks any rational force").

2. EDWARD H. LEVI, AN INTRODUCTION TO LEGAL REASONING 1, 1–2 n.2 (1949) (quoting ARISTOTLE, ANALYTICA PRIORA 69a).

3. POSNER, JURISPRUDENCE, *supra* note 1, at 91–92 (Volvo); CASS R. SUNSTEIN, LEGAL REASONING AND POLITICAL CONFLICT 64 (1996) (Honda). Subsequent page numbers are given in the text.

4. 1 THE OXFORD ENGLISH DICTIONARY 425, 432 (2d ed. 1989).

5. Roberto Mangabeira Unger, What Should Legal Analysis Become? 59 (1996).

6. Mark Turner, *Categories and Analogies, in* Analogical Reasoning: Perspectives of Artificial Intelligence, Cognitive Theory, and Philosophy 3, 9–11 (David H. Hellman ed., 1988). Subsequent citations to this article are given in the text. The argument is further developed in Mark Turner, Reading Minds: The Study of English in the Age of Cognitive Science 118–50 (1991).

7. *See* Roberto Mangabeira Unger, The Critical Legal Studies Movement 8 (1986).

8. This is no less true of Scott Brewer's "modestly rationalistic" account of legal analogy as an instance of reasoning by "abduction." Scott Brewer, *Exemplary Reasoning: Semantics, Pragmatics, and the Rational Force of Legal Argument by Analogy,* 109 Harv. L. Rev. 923 (1996). Brewer has captured something of the tenor of analogy with the Peircian notion of abductive reasoning, particularly with respect to a propositional analogy like the Volvo case. But, as we shall see, this hardly does justice to the full range of analogical thinking—which cannot be reduced to rule-governed "theories" of the sort suggested by Brewer.

9. Posner, Jurisprudence, *supra* note 1, at 90.

10. Dedre Gentner, *The Mechanisms of Analogical Learning, in* Similarity and Analogical Reasoning 199, 201 (Stella Vosniadou & Andrew Ortony eds., 1989). Subsequent page references are given in the text.

11. This report was made by Professor Twining at a faculty seminar at the University of Miami School of Law on September 29, 1989.

12. George Lakoff, Women, Fire, and Dangerous Things: What Categories Reveal about the Mind 84–85 (1987).

13. Douglas L. Medin, Robert L. Goldstone, & Dedre Gentner, *Similarity Involving Attributes and Relation: Judgments of Similarity and Difference Are Not Inverses,* 1 Psychol. Sci. 64, 65 (1990). Subsequent citations appear in the text.

14. Turner, *supra* note 6, at 123, 140–42.

15. *See, e.g.,* Amos Tversky, *Features of Similarity,* 84 Psychol. Rev. 327, 342 (1977); *see also id.* at 344 ("The intensity of a feature is determined by perceptual and cognitive factors that are relatively stable across contexts.").

16. Dedre Gentner et al., *Two Forces in the Development of Relational Similarity, in* Developing Cognitive Competence: New Approaches to Process Modeling 263, 271 (Tony J. Simon & Graeme S. Halford eds., 1995). Subsequent references are provided in the text. In this more recent work, Gentner both confirms and embraces the fact that "even for adults, the process of interpreting a comparison involves both object matches and relational matches" (302).

17. Eleanor Rosch, *Principles of Categorization, in* Cognition and Categorization 27, 40–41 (Eleanor Rosch & Barbara B. Lloyd eds., 1978).

18. 462 U.S. 919 (1983). Subsequent page numbers are given in the text.

19. Edward Rothstein, *The Internet Needs Technological Innovation and Social Transformation,* N.Y. Times, October 28, 1996, at D4.

20. 217 N.Y.382, 111 N.E. 1050 (1916).

21. 341 U.S. 494 (1951). In *Dennis,* the Court adopted Learned Hand's revision of the "clear and present danger" test—"'whether the gravity of the "evil" dis-

counted by its improbability, justifies such invasions of free speech as is necessary to avoid the danger.'" *Id.* at 510 (quoting lower court).

22. Crisis occurs when anomalous data (that is, data that do not conform to the paradigms that constitute a "normal science") accrue to such an extent that they can no longer be ignored. THOMAS KUHN, THE STRUCTURE OF SCIENTIFIC REVOLUTIONS 67–68 (2d ed. 1970). This process is itself the product of normal science, which "ultimately leads only to the recognition of anomalies and to crises." *Id.* at 122.

23. *Id.* at 64 ("[N]ovelty emerges only with difficulty, manifested by resistance, against a background provided by expectation.").

24. Judith Jarvis Thompson, *A Defense of Abortion*, 1 PHIL. & PUB. AFF. 47, 48–49 (1971).

25. ROSALIND HURSTHOUSE, BEGINNING LIVES 189–91 (1987).

26. Frederick Schauer, *Slippery Slopes*, 99 HARV. L. REV. 361 (1985). Additional page references are provided in the text.

CHAPTER TEN

1. 307 U.S. 496 (1939). *See also*, United States v. Grace, 461 U.S. 171 (1983). Subsequent references to *Hague* are provided in the text.

2. 301 U.S. 1 (1937). Subsequent page numbers are provided in the text.

3. The other is West Coast Hotel v. Parrish, 300 U.S. 379 (1937). For a discussion of the communitarian underpinnings of *West Coast Hotel,* see my *Indeterminacy and Incommensurability in Constitutional Law*, 78 CAL. L. REV. 1441, 1523–27 (1990).

4. Lovell v. Griffin, 303 U.S. 444, 451–52 (1938). *See* GERALD GUNTHER & KATHLEEN M. SULLIVAN, CONSTITUTIONAL LAW 1237 (13th ed. 1997); Geoffrey Stone, *Fora Americana: Speech in Public Places,* 1974 SUP. CT. REV. 233, 238. For the ordinance at issue in *Hague,* see *infra* p. 263.

5. David Kairys, *Freedom of Speech in* THE POLITICS OF LAW: A PROGRESSIVE CRITIQUE 190, 192–97 (David Kairys ed., 3rd ed. 1998). Subsequent page references appear in the text.

6. 167 U.S. 43 (1897).

7. *Id.* at 45 (quoting Commonwealth v. Davis, 162 Mass. 510, 511 (1895)). Subsequent references to Holmes's opinion for the state court are given in the text.

8. *Davis*, 167 U.S. at 46.

9. *Id.* at 45 (quoting *Commonwealth v. Davis*, 162 Mass. at 511).

10. *See, e.g.,* GUNTHER & SULLIVAN, *supra* note 4, at 1237; GEOFFREY STONE ET AL., CONSTITUTIONAL LAW 1335–36 (3d ed. 1996). Though Kairys observes that "Holmes, like almost all state and lower federal court judges, viewed such an ordinance as simply a city regulation of the use of its park" (192), he does explain why judges might have understood the ordinance in that way.

11. Harry Kalven, *The Concept of the Public Forum: Cox v. Louisiana,* 1965 SUP. CT. REV. 1, 13.

12. *See* Brooklyn Park Comm'rs v. Armstrong, 45 N.Y. 234, 244 (1871) ("[T]he city took the title to the lands . . . for the public use as a park, and held it in trust for that purpose.") (cited in *Commonwealth v. Davis,* 162 Mass. at 511).

13. MELVIN KALFUS, FREDERICK LAW OLMSTED: THE PASSION OF A PUBLIC ARTIST 281 (1991); IRVING FISHER, FREDERICK LAW OLMSTED AND THE CITY PLANNING MOVEMENT IN THE UNITED STATES 5, 103 (1986).

14. Geoffrey Blodgett, *Frederick Law Olmsted: Landscape Architecture as Conservative Reform,* 62 J. AMER. HIST. 869, 878 (1976).

15. GALEN CRANZ, THE POLITICS OF PARK DESIGN: A HISTORY OF URBAN PARKS IN AMERICA 55–56 (1982); DAVID SCHUYLER, THE NEW URBAN LANDSCAPE: THE REDEFINITION OF CITY FORM IN NINETEENTH-CENTURY AMERICA 186–87 (1986). Subsequent page references to Cranz are given in the text.

16. Grayned v. Rockford, 408 U.S. 104, 121 (1972).

17. *Id.* at 116. Some commentators have suggested that the nature of the forum is no longer the primary concern in public forum doctrine. *See* LAURENCE TRIBE, AMERICAN CONSTITUTIONAL LAW § 12–24, at 989–93 (2d ed. 1988). Rather, the Court has increasingly collapsed the doctrine permitting reasonable "time, place, or manner" restrictions into the more lenient standard under United States v. O'Brien, 391 U.S. 367 (1968), which allows content-neutral regulation that furthers an important or substantial governmental interest unrelated to speech even though it results in incidental restriction of speech. *See* Susan Williams, *Content Discrimination and the First Amendment,* 139 U. PA. L. REV. 615 (1991).

18. Cornelius v. NAACP Legal Defense & Educational Fund, 473 U.S. 788, 811 (1985). To put the matter somewhat anachronistically, the dominant nineteenth-century conception of the park was that of a place that functioned as a special use forum. *Cf.* Kalven, *supra* note 11, at 12 ("Clearly it is easy to think of public places, swimming pools, for example, so clearly dedicated to recreational use that talk of their use as a public forum would in general be totally unpersuasive.").

19. SCHUYLER, *supra* note 15, at 186 (discussing Brooklyn's Prospect Park in the late 1880s).

20. Cranz refers to this as the Reform Era, which he dates from 1900 to 1930 (63–80). On his account, the Reform Era was succeeded by the Recreation Era, which he dates from 1930–65, and the Open Space System, which he dates from 1965 and thereafter (101–17, 135–42). Cranz's formalistic periodization has been criticized. KALFUS, *supra* note 13, at 299, 394 n.6; SCHUYLER, *supra* note 15, at 239. I draw on Cranz's extensive reports of data and trends without relying on his specific periodization.

21. LEONARD W. LEVY, EMERGENCE OF A FREE PRESS 65 (1985). Subsequent page numbers are given in the text.

22. An Act Concerning Aliens, 1 Stat. 570 (June 25, 1798); An Act in Addition to the Act, Entitled "An Act for the Punishment of Certain Crimes Against the United States," 1 Stat. 596 (July 14, 1798). More than a century later, Holmes argued: "I wholly disagree . . . that the First Amendment left the common law as to seditious libel in force. History seems to me against the notion. I had conceived that the United States, through many years, had shown its repentance for the Sedition Act of 1798, by repaying fines that it imposed." Abrams v. United States, 250 U.S. 616, 630 (1920) (Holmes, J. dissenting). The full Court later adopted this view in New York Times Co. v. Sullivan, 376 U.S. 254, 273 (1964), where it cited Levy's earlier work and concluded: "Although the Sedition Act was never tested in this Court, the attack upon its validity has carried the day in the court of history" (276). *See* LEONARD W. LEVY, LEGACY OF SUPPRESSION (1960).

23. John Milton, *Areopagitica: A Speech for the Liberty of Unlicensed Printing, To the Parliament of England* (1644), *in* THE PROSE OF JOHN MILTON 265, 310 (J. M. Patrick ed., 1967) (all spellings as in original). Subsequent page references are provided in the text.

24. DANIEL A. FARBER AND SUZANNA SHERRY, BEYOND ALL REASON: THE RADICAL ASSAULT ON TRUTH IN AMERICAN LAW 27 (1997) (emphasis added).

25. GEORGE LAKOFF & MARK JOHNSON, METAPHORS WE LIVE BY 63 (1980).

26. *Cf.* Chaplinsky v. New York, 315 U.S. 568, 572 (1942) (permitting regulation of certain categories of speech because, in part, "such utterances are no essential part of any expression of ideas and are of such slight social value as a step to truth").

27. For the story of these political pamphleteers, also central to the development of the Fourth Amendment, see Vincent Blasi, *The Checking Value in First Amendment Theory*, 1977 AM. B. FOUND. RES. J. 521, and Eric Schnapper, *Unreasonable Searches and Seizures of Papers*, 71 VA. L. REV. 869 (1985). With respect to the pre-Revolutionary period, Levy reports: "The press along with pulpit, platform, and parliamentary forum, became an enormously effective vehicle for advertising the Whig position, and so long as England maintained control of the situation, the revolutionary journalists, whose newspapers doubled in number between 1763 and 1775, unceasingly urged the value of open debate" (62). In addition to these founding experiences, the modern First Amendment is also grounded in the more recent social experiences of the labor and civil rights movements. This part of the history is recounted in David Kairys, *Freedom of Speech, in* THE POLITICS OF LAW: A PROGRESSIVE CRITIQUE 149–53, 156–59 (David Kairys ed., 1982).

28. Owen Fiss, *Free Speech and Social Structure*, 71 IOWA L. REV. 1405, 1408 (1986).

29. Reno v. ACLU, 521 U.S. 844, 870 (1997).

30. Schenck v. United States, 249 U.S. 47 (1919); Frohwerk v. United States, 249 U.S. 204 (1919); Debs v. United States, 249 U.S. 211 (1919).

31. *Schenck*, 249 U.S. at 52.

32. *See, e.g.*, G. EDWARD WHITE, JUSTICE OLIVER WENDELL HOLMES: LAW AND THE INNER SELF 42–30 (1993) (noting, too, the influence of Frankfurter, Laski, and Hand).

33. *Schenck*, 249 U.S. at 52 ("The question in every case is whether the words used are used in such circumstances and are of such a nature as to create a clear and present danger that they will bring about the substantive evils that Congress has a right to prevent.").

34. Oliver Wendell Holmes, Jr., *Natural Law*, 32 HARV. L. REV. 40, 40 (1918).

35. Lochner v. New York, 198 U.S. 45, 75–76 (1905) (Holmes, J., dissenting). Subsequent page numbers are given in the text.

36. Gitlow v. New York, 268 U.S. 652, 673 (1925) (Holmes, J., dissenting).

37. Abrams v. United States, 250 U.S. 616, 630 (1919) (Holmes, J., dissenting). Subsequent page numbers are given in the text.

38. David Cole, *Agon at the Agora: Creative Misreadings in the First Amendment Tradition*, 95 YALE L.J. 857 (1986).

39. LAKOFF & JOHNSON, *supra* note 25, at 27–28, 47–48.

40. A first step along this road was the realization of human fallibility. *See, e.g.*,

JOHN STUART MILL, ON LIBERTY 21–22 (C. V. Shields ed., 1956) ("To refuse a hearing to an opinion because they are sure that it is false is to assume that their certainty is the same thing as absolute certainty. All silencing of discussion is an assumption of infallibility.") (emphasis in original).

41. Stromberg v. California, 283 U.S. 359 (1931) (voiding state statute prohibiting display of red flag); Near v. Minnesota, 283 U.S. 697 (1931) (striking down state infringement on freedom of the press). The expansion of First Amendment freedoms picked up steam in the late New Deal and postwar periods. *See* Grosjean v. American Press Co., 297 U.S. 233 (1936); De Jonge v. Oregon, 299 U.S. 353 (1937); Herndon v. Lowry, 301 U.S. 242 (1937); *Lovell v. Griffin, supra* note 4; *Hague v. CIO, supra* note 1; Schneider v. State, 308 U.S. 147 (1939); Thornhill v. Alabama, 310 U.S. 88 (1940); Cantwell v. Connecticut, 310 U.S. 296 (1940); Martin v. City of Struthers, 319 U.S. 141 (1943); West Virginia State Bd. of Educ. v. Barnette, 319 U.S. 624 (1943); Schneiderman v. United States, 320 U.S. 118 (1943); Marsh v. Alabama, 326 U.S. 501 (1946); Saia v. New York, 334 U.S. 558 (1948); Terminiello v. Chicago, 337 U.S. 1 (1949).

42. *Compare* Brandenburg v. Ohio, 395 U.S. 444 (1969), *with* Dennis v. United States, 341 U.S. 494 (1951) (upholding Smith Act prosecutions of Communist Party leaders).

43. *Times v. Sullivan,* 376 U.S. at 271. Subsequent page numbers are given in the text.

44. Gertz v. Welsh, 418 U.S. 323, 339 (1974).

45. *Grace,* 461 U.S. at 179.

46. *See, e.g.,* Perry Educ. Ass'n v. Perry Local Educators' Ass'n, 460 U.S. 37, 52–53 (1983) ("The Court of Appeals would have been correct if a public forum were involved here. But the internal mail system is not a public forum."); FCC v. Pacifica Foundation, 438 U.S. 726, 750–51 (1978) ("[W]hen . . . a pig has entered the parlor, the exercise of . . . regulatory power does not depend on proof that the pig is obscene."); Greer v. Spock, 424 U.S. 828, 838 (1976) ("The notion that federal military reservations, like municipal streets and parks, have traditionally served as a place for free public assembly and communication of thoughts by private citizens is thus historically and constitutionally false."); *see also* Consolidated Edison Co. v. Public Service Comm'n, 447 U.S. 530, 544–45 (1980) ("Any student of history who has been reprimanded for talking about the World Series during a class discussion of the First Amendment knows that it is incorrect to state that a 'time, place, or manner restriction may not be based upon either the content or subject matter of speech.'") (Stevens, J., concurring; quoting majority opinion).

47. Connick v. Myers, 461 U.S. 574 (1983); *Perry, supra* note 46.

48. Robert Post, *Recuperating First Amendment Doctrine,* 47 STAN. L. REV. 1249, 1278 (1995) (emphasis added; internal quotes omitted). Specific page numbers are given in the text.

49. TRIBE, *supra* note 17, at § 12-7, p. 827; John Hart Ely, *Flag Desecration: A Case Study in the Roles of Categorization and Balancing in First Amendment Analysis,* 88 HARV. L. REV. 1482, 1495–96 (1975). For an earlier articulation of this point, see Louis Henkin, *The 1967 Supreme Court Term—Foreword: On Drawing Lines,* 82 HARV. L. REV. 63, 79–80 (1968) ("A constitutional distinction between speech and conduct is specious. . . . [The] meaningful constitutional distinction is between conduct that speaks, communicates, and other kinds of conduct.").

50. *See, e.g.,* Texas v. Johnson, 491 U.S. 397, 406 (1989) ("[T]he Government generally has a freer hand in restricting expressive conduct than it has in restricting the written or spoken word."); Broadrick v. Oklahoma, 413 U.S. 601, 615 (1973) (The doctrine of facial overbreadth "attenuates as the otherwise unprotected behavior that it forbids the State to sanction moves from 'pure speech' toward conduct."); Teamsters Union v. Vogt, Inc., 354 U.S. 284 (1957); Giboney v. Empire Storage & Ice Co., 336 U.S. 490 (1949).

51. *Chaplinsky,* 315 U.S. at 571–72 (emphasis added; footnotes omitted).

52. Cass R. Sunstein, *Words, Conduct, Caste,* 60 U. Chi. L. Rev. 795, 833 (1993).

53. 403 U.S. 15 (1971). Specific page references are provided in the text.

54. *See also* Hustler Magazine v. Falwell, 485 U.S. 46 (1988).

55. Richard Delgado, *Words That Wound: A Tort Action for Racial Insults, Epithets, and Name-Calling,* 17 Harv. C.R.-C.L. L. Rev. 133 (1982).

56. Cass R. Sunstein, *Pornography and the First Amendment,* 1986 Duke L.J. 589, 606–7. Subsequent page references are given in the text. Sunstein's most recent treatment of this issue, which I discuss below, abandons the argument that pornography is more like conduct than speech. *See* Sunstein, *supra* note 52, at 808.

57. Cass R. Sunstein, *The First Amendment and Cognition: A Response,* 1989 Duke L.J. 433, 436.

58. *Id.* at 434.

59. Tribe, *supra* note 17, at 827.

60. *See* Dorothy Holland & Naomi Quinn, *Culture and Cognition, in* Cultural Models in Language and Thought 10–11, 34–35 (D. Holland & N. Quinn eds., 1987).

61. *Cf.* Hurley v. Irish-American Gay, Lesbian, and Bisexual Group of Boston, 515 U.S. 557, 571 (1995) ("While the law is free to promote all sorts of conduct in place of harmful behavior, it is not free to interfere with speech.").

62. Spence v. Washington, 418 U.S. 405, 410–11 (1968); *see also* Texas v. Johnson, 491 U.S. at 403–4 (the first flag burning case).

63. Post, *supra* note 48, at 1252–53 (quoting *Hurley,* 515 U.S. at 569) ("A narrow, succinctly articulable message is not a condition of constitutional protection, which if confined to expressions conveying a 'particularized message,' . . . would never reach the unquestionably shielded painting of Jackson Pollock, music of Arnold Schönberg, or Jabberwocky verse of Lewis Carroll.").

64. *Hurley,* 515 U.S. at 568.

65. *Compare* Red Lion Broadcasting Co. v. FCC, 395 U.S. 367 (1969), *with* Miami Herald Pub. Co. v. Tornillo, 418 U.S. 241 (1974) (newspaper cannot be required to publish retraction of erroneous story). *Red Lion* is particularly problematic when one considers the now conventional point that cable has rendered irrelevant the standard justification about the scarcity of the airwaves. For the Court's recent treatment of the cable system, see Turner Broadcasting System, Inc. v. FCC, 512 U.S. 622, 653 (1994) ("Cable programmers and cable operators engage in and transmit speech, and they are entitled to the protection of the speech and press provisions of the First Amendment."). On indecency, see FCC v. Pacifica Foundation, 438 U.S. 726 (1978) (the "seven dirty words" case).

66. *See* Virginia State Board of Pharmacy v. Virginia Citizens Consumer Council, 425 U.S. 728 (1976); Bates v. State Bar of Arizona, 433 U.S. 350 (1977).

67. Clark v. Community for Creative Non-Violence, 468 U.S. 288 (1984). For another explanation that relates the Court's reasoning to our historical conceptions of the park, see Steven L. Winter, *An Upside/Down View of the Countermajoritarian Difficulty,* 69 Tex. L. Rev. 1881 (1991).

68. Hazelwood Sch. Dist. v. Kuhlmeier, 484 U.S. 260 (1988). Of course, one can question the Court's characterization of the school paper as part of the core curriculum. But, in relating the student paper to an alternative ICM, the Court's characterization seems a rather clear example of what, in chapter 6, I identified as an assimilation-to-prototype effect.

69. Mark Tushnet, Red, White, and Blue: A Critical Analysis of American Constitutional Law 307 (1987). Characteristically, he proclaims this approach "analytically unsatisfying" and "likely to be manipulated" (309).

70. Mark Tushnet, *An Essay on Rights,* 62 Tex. L. Rev. 1363, 1364 (1984).

71. The cases extending First Amendment protections to powerful interests are Central Hudson Gas & Elec. Corp. v. Public Service Comm'n, 447 U.S. 557 (1980), First National Bank v. Bellotti, 435 U.S. 765 (1978), and Buckley v. Valeo, 424 U.S. 1 (1976). For a discussion of the quasi- and nonpublic forum cases, see *supra* notes 46–47.

72. *Compare* Lloyd Corp. v. Tanner, 407 U.S. 551 (1972) (holding that the First Amendment does not prevent a private shopping center from prohibiting handbill distribution on its premises), *with Marsh v. Alabama, supra* note 41 (company owned town treated as public forum like ordinary streets and parks), and Pruneyard Shopping Center v. Robins, 447 U.S. 74 (1980) (upholding state's power to enforce state constitutional right to pursue First Amendment activities in private shopping center open to general public).

73. 385 U.S. 39, 47 (1966).

74. *See* David Van Zandt, *Commonsense Reasoning, Social Change, and the Law,* 81 Nw. U.L. Rev. 894, 924 (1987) (footnotes omitted):

People routinely think of and treat material goods, whether personal articles, real estate, or capital, as owned by them. This conclusion is not merely abstract theory, but is bolstered and evidenced in everyday activities. Individuals in routine activity treat things as subject to the absolute control of particular persons, and such treatment is consistently validated by the reactions of others and the pragmatic usefulness of the treatment.

75. In a 1982 article, Tushnet had characterized First Amendment protection of corporate speech as the natural product of three metaphors: "(1) the corporation is a person; (2) the free marketplace of ideas; and (3) money talks." Mark Tushnet, *Corporations and Free Speech,* in Kairys, *supra* note 5, at 253–55. Tushnet concluded, moreover: "A simple instrumental explanation—the Court, behaving as it often does, gave corporations what they really needed—is inadequate. That kind of explanation must be augmented by emphasizing the sense of naturalness that the significant metaphors have" (260).

76. To much the same effect is the Second Circuit's decision in Young v. New York City Transit Authority, 903 F.2d 146, 153–54 (2d Cir. 1990), upholding a regulation prohibiting panhandling in the subways. The court reasoned that "begging is

much more 'conduct' than it is 'speech,'" because its object "is the transfer of money." As the court explained: "Speech . . . is not of the essence of the conduct. Although our holding today does not ultimately rest on an ontological distinction between speech and conduct, we think this case presents a particularly poignant example of how the distinction subsists in right reason and coincides with common sense."

77. Sunstein, *supra* note 52, at 837. Subsequent references are to this article and are given in the text.

78. PHILIP BOBBITT, CONSTITUTIONAL FATE 237 (1982).

79. CHARLES TAYLOR, SOURCES OF THE SELF: THE MAKING OF THE MODERN IDENTITY 204 (1989).

80. Terry Teachout, *Classics That Sizzle,* N.Y. TIMES, December 20, 1997, at A13 (op-ed) (noting that "the film industry's latest fling with the classics is being driven by [the] equation: Famous Title + Naked Babes − Author's Original Dialogue = Box Office Smash").

81. James Bennet, *In Washington, There's Still Only One Topic of Conversation,* N.Y. TIMES, March 19, 1998, at A1 ("It is the sexual content of the accusations now that is sustaining press and public attention at fever pitch, in the view of White House advisers and other political experts here.").

82. Wesley Newcomb Hohfeld, *Some Fundamental Legal Conceptions as Applied in Judicial Reasoning,* 23 YALE L.J. 16, 24 (1913) (footnote omitted).

83. Felix Cohen, *Transcendental Nonsense and the Functional Approach,* 35 COLUM. L. REV. 809, 812 (1935)

84. Berkey v. Third Ave. Ry. Co., 244 N.Y. 84, 94, 155 N.E.2d 58, 61 (1930) (Cardozo, J.) ("Metaphors in law are to be narrowly watched, for though starting as devices to liberate thought, they end often by enslaving it."); BENJAMIN CARDOZO, *What Medicine Can Do for Law,* in LAW AND LITERATURE 100 (1930) ("A metaphor, however, is, to say the least, a shifting test whereby to measure degrees of guilt that mean the difference between life and death."); Liverpool & London & Globe Ins. Co. v. Board of Assessors, 221 U.S. 346, 354 (1911) (Hughes, C.J.) ("When it is said that intangible property, such as credits on open account, have their situs at the creditor's domicile, the metaphor does not aid. Being incorporeal, they can have no actual situs."); New York *ex rel.* Whitney v. Graves, 299 U.S. 366, 372 (1937) (Hughes, C.J.) ("When we speak of a 'business situs' of intangible property in the taxing state we are indulging in metaphor.").

85. *See* Graves v. Elliot, 307 U.S. 383, 390 (1939) (Hughes, C.J., dissenting) ("This general rule proceeds in the view that intangibles, as such, are incapable of an actual physical location and that to attribute to them a 'situs' is to indulge in metaphor. Still, in certain circumstances the use of the metaphor is appropriate.").

86. 29 U.S.C. § 151 (emphasis added).

87. Quoting Schechter Poultry Corp. v. United States, 295 U.S. 495, 546 (1935). *See also* Carter v. Carter Coal Co., 298 U.S. 238, 307–8 (1936); Swift & Co. v. United States, 196 U.S. 375, 397 (1905) (*see infra* text accompanying notes 92 & 97–98).

88. On the conventional use of the personification metaphor to structure our understanding of a "corporation," see Steven L. Winter, *Transcendental Nonsense, Metaphoric Reasoning, and the Cognitive Stakes for Law,* 137 U. PA. L. REV. 1105, 1163–65 (1989).

89. 258 U.S. 495 (1922).

90. Although the origins of the court-packing plan are unknown, the idea had been suggested by Llewellyn as early as 1934. Karl N. Llewellyn, *The Constitution as an Institution,* 34 COLUM. L. REV. 1, 23 n.33, 39 n.45 (1934).

91. EDWARD PURCELL, JR., THE CRISIS OF DEMOCRATIC THEORY: SCIENTIFIC NATURALISM & THE PROBLEM OF VALUE 79 (1973).

92. 196 U.S. at 399.

93. Gibbons v. Ogden, 22 U.S. (9 Wheat.) 1, 195 (1824). The "stream of commerce" metaphor thus had a grounding in historical experience.

94. The Hine v. Trevor, 71 U.S. 555, 562 (1866) (discussing The Genesee Chief, 53 U.S. (12 How.) 443 (1851), *overruling* The Thomas Jefferson, 21 U.S. (10 Wheat.) 428 (1825)).

95. The Daniel Ball, 77 U.S. 557, 566 (1870).

96. Kidd v. Pearson, 128 U.S. 1 (1888); United States v. E. C. Knight Co., 156 U.S. 1 (1895); *Carter Coal,* 298 U.S. at 299–303.

97. *Swift,* 196 U.S. at 397, 398–99 (emphasis added).

98. *Schechter Poultry,* 295 U.S. at 543; *accord Carter Coal,* 298 U.S. at 305–6.

99. United States v. Wrightwood Dairy Co., 315 U.S. 110, 119 (1942).

100. The Shreveport Rate Cases, 234 U.S. 342, 351 (1914) (Hughes, C.J.). This early use of the "traffic" and "security" metaphors illustrates yet another way in which Hughes's innovation in *Jones & Laughlin* was prefigured and constrained by existing, conventional metaphors.

101. 317 U.S. 111 (1942). In *Wickard,* the Court upheld regulation of wheat grown only for home consumption on the theory that it affected the interstate market for wheat by reducing demand. With respect to the resulting unfairness to the local farmers, the Court simply observed: "It is the essence of regulation that it lays a restraining hand on the self-interest of the regulated" (129).

102. In recent decisions, however, the Court has drawn a mechanical decision between "economic" matters that may continue to be regulated by Congress and "noneconomic" matters left to local control unless they have a "substantial effect" on interstate commerce. United States v. Lopez, 514 U.S. 549 (1995); United States v. Morrison, 529 U.S. 598 (2000). While this leaves intact much of the midcentury regime of *Jones & Laughlin* and *Wickard,* it does have the effect of reinstating the direct/indirect distinction of the older Commerce Clause cases.

CHAPTER ELEVEN

1. John Markoff, *Innovation to Double Chip Power May Cut Life Span of Computers,* N.Y. TIMES, September 17, 1997, at A1.

2. Planned Parenthood of Southeastern Pennsylvania v. Casey, 505 U.S. 833, 870 (1992) (opinion of O'Connor, Kennedy, & Souter, JJ.). Subsequent page references are given in the text.

3. Ellis v. United States, 206 U.S. 246, 260 (1907) (Holmes, J.). To much the same effect is Cardozo's observation in Burnet v. Wells, 289 U.S. 670, 681 (1933):

The line of division between the rational and the arbitrary in legislation is not to be drawn with an eye to remote possibilities. What the law looks for in establishing its standards is a probability or tendency of general validity.

If this is attained, the formula will serve, though there are imperfections here and there. The exceptional, if it arises, may have its special rule.

4. Swift & Co. v. United States, 196 U.S. 375, 397 (1905) (Holmes, J.) (conceding that the "two cases are near to each other, as sooner or later always happens when lines are to be drawn").

5. 18 U.S.C. § 1621 (1996). The text of the statute is quoted below at p. 300.

6. Miller v. Fenton, 474 U.S. 104 (1985).

7. Gasperini v. Center for Humanities, Inc., 518 U.S. 415 (1996).

8. Pierre Schlag, *Cannibal Moves: An Essay on the Metamorphoses of the Legal Distinction,* 40 STAN. L. REV. 929, 942–44 (1988).

9. Linda Coleman & Paul Kay, *Prototype Semantics: The English Verb* Lie, 57 LANGUAGE 26, 43 (1981). Sissela Bok's philosophical discussion of lying starts from the premise that to settle the "moral question of whether you are lying . . . we must know whether you *intend your statement to mislead.*" SISSELA BOK, LYING: MORAL CHOICE IN PUBLIC AND PRIVATE LIFE 6 (2d ed. 1999) (emphasis in original).

10. Eve Sweetser, *The Definition of* lie: *An Examination of the Folk Models Underlying a Semantic Prototype, in* CULTURAL MODELS IN LANGUAGE AND THOUGHT 43 (D. Holland & N. Quinn eds., 1987). The account that follows is greatly simplified. Sweetser's paper, written in 1984, is further developed in subsequent discussions by GEORGE LAKOFF, WOMEN, FIRE, AND DANGEROUS THINGS: WHAT CATEGORIES REVEAL ABOUT THE MIND 71–74 (1987), and Steven L. Winter, *Transcendental Nonsense, Metaphoric Reasoning, and the Cognitive Stakes for Law,* 137 U. PA. L. REV. 1105, 1151–56 (1989). The reference to "Gricean pragmatics" is to Paul Grice's seminal *Logic and Conversation,* which appears in 3 SYNTAX AND SEMANTICS: SPEECH ACTS 41 (P. Cole & J. Morgan eds., 1975).

11. For cross-cultural comparisons, see Sweetser, *supra* note 10, at 59–62.

12. For a more detailed account that considers the moral ambiguity of such familiar cases as the altruistic person who lies to the Nazis to protect the Jews hiding in the attic and the doctor who, believing it to be in the patient's best interest, lies to that patient about his or her condition, see *id.* at 59, and Winter, *supra* note 10, at 1237 n.152.

13. The court of appeals' decision is reported at 453 F.2d 555 (2d Cir. 1972). The Supreme Court's decision reversing the conviction is reported at 409 U.S. 352 (1973). Subsequent page references are to the Supreme Court's opinion and are provided in the text.

14. 5 J. WIGMORE, EVIDENCE § 1367, p. 32 (J. Chadbourn ed., rev. ed. 1974), *quoted in* Maryland v. Craig, 497 U.S. 836, 846 (1990); California v. Green, 399 U.S. 149, 158 (1970).

15. United States v. Salerno, 505 U.S. 317, 328–29 (1992) (Stevens, J., dissenting).

16. Up to this point, my argument has been consistent with Peter Tiersma's earlier analysis applying the principles of Gricean pragmatics to critique *Bronston.* Peter Tiersma, *The Language of Perjury, "Literal Truth" Ambiguity, and the False Statement Requirement,* 63 S. CAL. L. REV. 373 (1990) (subsequent references provided in the text). But Tiersma seems to have been misled—whether by the Court's focus on the truth or falsity of Bronston's statement or by the Gricean principles themselves seems unclear—to focus on the conversational *meaning* of the witness's testimony.

The statute, however, defines the crime of perjury in terms of the witness's state of mind—i.e., falsity of *belief* in his or her own statement. Consequently, it is hard to know exactly what Tiersma means when he advocates a "communicative approach to false statements in perjury law" that would concentrate "on how the speaker intends the hearer to understand the utterance" without imposing any "further requirement that the speaker intend to mislead" (376, 408). If one focuses on the statutory language, then how the speaker intends the hearer to understand the statement is entirely irrelevant: It matters only whether the speaker understood her own statement to be (in some sense) false. If one understands the statute in terms of the social concept of a "lie," then the speaker's intention to mislead is the expected entailment of the focus on falsity of belief. Indeed, it is crux of the matter.

17. United States v. Doe, 465 U.S. 605, 612 (1984). And, as Peter Tiersma points out, Rule 801 of the Federal Rules of Evidence defines a "statement" to include "nonverbal conduct" (p. 410 n.84).

18. *See, e.g.,* United States v. Ryan, 828 F.2d 1010, 1017 (3d Cir. 1987); United States v. Mattox, 689 F.2d 531 (5th Cir. 1982). The statute is 18 U.S.C. §§ 1001 *et seq.* (1990) (discussed by Tiersma at 409–12).

19. *See, e.g.,* United States v. Shotts, 145 F. 3d 1289 (11th Cir. 1998); United States v. Boone, 951 F.2d 1526 (9th Cir. 1991); United States v. Martinez, 836 F.2d 684 (1st Cir. 1987); United States v. Lighte, 782 F.2d 367 (2d Cir. 1985); United States v. Eddy, 737 F.2d 564 (6th Cir. 1984); United States v. Tonelli, 575 F.2d 194 (3d Cir. 1978).

20. 812 F.2d 917 (4th Cir. 1987). The defendants—Earp, Childers, and Carrigan—were each convicted under 18 U.S.C. § 241 of conspiracy to deprive persons of their civil rights and under 18 U.S.C. § 1623(a) of making false declarations to the grand jury. Only Carrigan's conviction under § 1623 was reversed.

21. Prohibitions del Roy, 12 Co. 63, 64–65, 77 Eng. Rep. 1342, 1343 (K.B. 1655).

22. Bruce A. Ackerman, Private Property and the Constitution 10–22 (1977). For a clear statement of this preference, see Bruce A. Ackerman, Reconstructing American Law (1983). There, Ackerman criticizes "undue reliance upon the situation sense in which the Realists took so much pride" because "it is not enough to react intuitively to particular features of individual cases." Rather, he maintains that "to fill the vacuum left by the disintegration of Realistic situation sense, . . . [o]nly a theory that locates market freedom within [a] larger legitimating framework could possibly provide a general interpretive schema for an understanding of existing American law." *Id.* at 93–94.

23. Roberto Mangabeira Unger, What Should Legal Analysis Become? 36, 46 (1996).

24. Lochner v. New York, 198 U.S. 45, 57 (1905). As Tribe points out, however, the conventional reading of *Lochner* as an imposition of values is vastly overstated. Laurence Tribe, American Constitutional Law viii (2d ed. 1988).

25. Hilary Putnam, Reason, Truth, and History 5–8 (1981).

26. Duncan Kennedy, A Critique of Adjudication *{fin de siècle}* (1997). Specific page references are provided in the text.

27. The six typical field configurations are: (1) the impacted field "with long straight boundaries, reenforced at regular intervals with precedents" that will prove

difficult to manipulate; (2) the case of first impression, traditionally viewed as a "kind of clearing of freedom in the endless forest of constraint"; (3) the unrationalized field, in which the existing precedents are scattered in chaotic fashion, yielding maximum freedom to the decisionmaker; (4) the contradictory field, in which there are "rapid fluctuations along a contorted boundary line" and, therefore, "[e]very point not occupied by a recent precedent is contestable"; (5) the collapsed field, like state action doctrine after Shelly v. Kraemer, 334 U.S. 1 (1948), in which there is "no coherent argument for a line that would hold against the collapsing argument"; and (6) the loopified field, like the law governing the family which is both constitutionally protected as private and extensively regulated by the states, where the core areas of opposing precedents are more alike than their peripheries. Duncan Kennedy, *Freedom and Constraint in Adjudication: A Critical Phenomenology of Judging*, 36 J. LEGAL EDUC. 518, 538–42 (1986). Portions of this discussion (but without the typology) appear in chapters 6 and 7 of Kennedy's *Critique of Adjudication*.

28. MAURICE MERLEAU-PONTY, PHENOMENOLOGY OF PERCEPTION 362 (Colin Smith trans., 1962).

29. *See id.* at 455 ("I am a psychological and historical structure, and have received, with existence, a manner of existing, a style. All my actions and thoughts stand in a relationship to this structure.").

30. MAURICE MERLEAU-PONTY, SENSE AND NON-SENSE 133–34 (Hubert L. Dreyfus & Patricia A. Dreyfus trans., 1964).

31. MAURICE MERLEAU-PONTY, SIGNS 173–74 (Richard C. McCleary trans., 1964) (discussing Husserl) (footnotes omitted).

32. *See* Robert M. Cover, *Violence and the Word*, 96 YALE L.J. 1604, 1612 (1986) (subsequent references given in the text):

> The legal philosopher may hold up to us a model of a hypothetical judge who is able to achieve a Herculean understanding of the full body of legal and social texts relevant to a particular case, and from this understanding to arrive at the single legally correct decision. But that mental interpretive act cannot give itself effect. The practice of interpretation requires an understanding of what others will do with such a judicial utterance.

33. STANLEY FISH, DOING WHAT COMES NATURALLY: CHANGE, RHETORIC, AND THE PRACTICE OF THEORY IN LITERARY AND LEGAL STUDIES 517 (1989).

34. The reported decisions in the case are Shepherd v. State, 46 So. 2d 880 (1950), *rev'd*, 341 U.S. 50, *remanded for new trial*, 52 So. 2d 903 (1951); *on appeal after retrial*, Irvin v. State, 66 So. 2d 288 (1953), *cert. denied*, 346 U.S. 927 (1954); and, *on habeas*, Irvin v. Chapman, 75 So. 2d 591 (1954), *cert. denied*, 348 U.S. 915 (1955). The account that follows comes in part from these opinions, from contemporaneous stories in the *New York Times*, and from the report of Jack Greenberg, who was present and participated in the trial. *See Florida Killer Reprieved: Told of Overhearing Escape Plot by Two in Groveland Case*, N.Y. TIMES, Jan. 5, 1952, at 28; Richard H. Parke, *2d Race-Case Jury All White*, N.Y. Times, Feb. 13, 1952, at 33; Richard H. Parke, *Irvin Says Florida Planted Evidence*, N.Y. TIMES, Feb. 14, 1952, at 28; Richard H. Parke, *Irvin Is Convicted, Sentenced to Die*, N.Y. TIMES, Feb. 15, 1952, at 42; *Groveland, Fla.*, N.Y. Times, Feb. 17, 1952, § 4, at 2.

Marshall's work in these cases was continued by the Legal Defense Fund after he left for the bench. It reached a culmination of sorts in the Supreme Court's decision in Coker v. Georgia, 433 U.S. 584 (1977), which held that death was a constitutionally disproportionate penalty for the crime of rape. My very first project for LDF as a law student was to provide research assistance (amounting to two footnotes in the brief) to David Kendall, who argued *Coker*.

35. Brown v. Allen, 344 U.S. 443, 540 (1954) (Jackson, J., concurring).

36. Jan G. Deutsch, *Neutrality, Legitimacy, and the Supreme Court: Some Intersections Between Law and Political Science*, 20 STAN. L. REV. 169 (1968). The focus of Deutsch's analysis is Herbert Wechsler, *Toward Neutral Principles of Constitutional Law*, 73 HARV. L. REV. 1 (1959). Subsequent references to both of these articles are given in the text.

37. *See* Mark V. Tushnet, *Following the Rules Laid Down: A Critique of Interpretivism and Neutral Principles*, 96 HARV. L. REV. 781 (1983). Portions of this article appear as chapter 5 of Tushnet's subsequent book. MARK TUSHNET, RED, WHITE, AND BLUE: A CRITICAL ANALYSIS OF CONSTITUTIONAL LAW (1988).

38. CHARLES TAYLOR, SOURCES OF THE SELF: THE MAKING OF THE MODERN IDENTITY 306–8 (1989) (describing the relation between ideas and practices as "plainly circular").

39. Jan G. Deutsch, The Reality of Law in America: An Invitation to Dialogue 103 (1988) (unpublished manuscript).

40. Richard A. Posner, *The Problematic of Moral and Legal Theory*, 111 HARV. L. REV. 1637, 1700 (1998). The cases, which rejected the claim, are Vacco v. Quill, 521 U.S. 793 (1997), and Washington v. Glucksberg, 521 U.S. 702 (1997).

41. KARL N. LLEWELLYN, THE CASE LAW SYSTEM IN AMERICA 82–83 (Paul Gewirtz ed., Michael Ansaldi trans., 1989).

CHAPTER TWELVE

1. Frank Michelman, *Political Truth and the Rule of Law*, 8 TEL AVIV STUDIES IN LAW 287 (1988).

2. *Cf.* MAURICE MERLEAU-PONTY, THE PHENOMENOLOGY OF PERCEPTION 455 (Colin Smith trans., 1962) ("My freedom can draw life away from its spontaneous course, but only by a series of unobtrusive deflections which necessitate first of all following its course—not by any absolute creation.").

3. Robert M. Cover, *The Supreme Court 1982 Term—Foreword: Nomos and Narrative*, 97 HARV. L. REV. 4, 4 (1983) Subsequent page references are given in the text. Cover writes: "It is remarkable that in myth and history the origin of and justification for a court is rarely understood to be the need for law. Rather, it is understood to be the need to suppress law, to choose between two or more laws, to impose upon laws a hierarchy. It is the multiplicity of laws, the fecundity of the jurisgenerative principle, that creates the problem to which the court and the state are the solution" (40).

4. *See also* Robert M. Cover, *Violence and the Word*, 95 YALE L.J. 1601, 1602 n.2 (1986) ("[T]he thrust of *Nomos* was that the creation of legal meaning is an essentially cultural activity which takes place (or *best* takes place) among smallish groups.").

5. *Id.* at 1605. "Legal interpretation," Cover explains, "is either played out on the field of pain and death or it is something less (or more) than law." *Id.* at 1606–7. The legal academy, Cover observes sardonically in Nomos *and Narrative,* is engaged in something decidedly less: "The community that writes law review articles has cre-

ated a law—a law under which officialdom may maintain its interpretation merely by suffering the protest of the articles" (47).

6. Robert M. Cover, *The Folktales of Justice: Tales of Jurisdiction,* 14 CAP. U.L. REV. 179, 180 (1985).

7. *See* NANCY CHODOROW, THE REPRODUCTION OF MOTHERING: PSYCHO-ANALYSIS AND THE SOCIOLOGY OF GENDER 42 n.** (1978) ("In psychoanalytic parlance 'objects' are people, parts of people, or symbols of people.").

8. See IVAN BOSZORMENYI-NAGY & J. SPARK, INVISIBLE LOYALTIES 54 (1984) ("We believe that the concept of justice of the human order is a common denominator for individual, familial, and societal dynamics. . . . Individuals who have not learned a sense of justice within their family relationships are likely to have a distorted judgment of social justice."); *cf.* JEROME FRANK, LAW AND THE MODERN MIND 21(1930) ("Why do men seek unrealizable certainty in law? Because . . . they have not yet relinquished the childish need for an authoritative father and unconsciously have tried to find in the law a substitute for the those attributes of firmness, sureness, certainty and infallibility ascribed in childhood to the father.").

9. *Cf.* CHODOROW, *supra* note 7, at 50 ("[S]ociety constitutes itself psychologically in the individual not only in the moral strictures of the superego. All aspects of psychic structure, character, and emotional and erotic life are social, constituted through a 'history of object-choices.'"); EDITH JACOBSON, THE SELF AND THE OB-JECT WORLD 50 (1964) ("The child's desires to remain part of his love objects, or to make them part of his own self, will slowly recede and give way to wishes for realistic likeness within. This goal can be achieved by virtue of selective identification, based on mechanisms of partial introjection.").

10. Olmstead v. United States, 277 U.S. 438, 485 (1928) (Brandeis, J., dissenting). Note that Brandeis uses a kinship metaphor to express the way in which lawless government causes anarchy. Thus, the government is the *potent* teacher who *breeds* contempt.

11. FRIEDRICH NIETZSCHE, THE GENEALOGY OF MORALS, essay 2, aphorism 11, at 208 (F. Golffing trans., 1956). Kaufmann's translation is different in several of the relevant particulars. FRIEDRICH NIETZSCHE, ON THE GENEALOGY OF MORALS AND ECCE HOMO 75–76 (Walter Kaufmann ed., 1969) (subsequent references are to the Kaufmann translation). Accordingly, I have interpolated the original German words (as well as Nietzsche's use of the French term *ressentiment*), and, in the text that follows, tried to indicate the relevant differences.

12. *See* United States v. Bailey, 444 U.S. 394, 414 (1980) (invoking "[t]he Anglo-Saxon tradition of criminal justice, embodied in the United States Constitution and federal statutes"); Fay v. Noia, 372 U.S. 391, 433 (1963) (referring to "the ancient principles of the writ of habeas corpus, embodied both in the Federal Constitution and in the habeas corpus provisions of the Judicial Code"); Weeks v. United States, 232 U.S. 383, 393 (1914) (describing "those great principles established by years of endeavor and suffering which have resulted in their embodiment in the fundamental law of the land.").

13. *See* Coates v. City of Cincinnati, 402 U.S. 611, 619–20 (1971) ("The statute, in effect, is stricken down on its face."); Gooding v. Wilson, 405 U.S. 518 (1972).

14. GRANT GILMORE, THE DEATH OF CONTRACT 85 (1974). For another famous example, see Louis Brandeis and Charles Warren, *The Right to Privacy,* 4 HARV. L.

Rev. 193 (1890) ("[T]he common law, in its eternal youth, grows to meet the demands of society.").

15. Fredrick Maitland, Equity and the Forms of Action at Common Law 296 (1909).

16. Cover, *supra* note 6, at 180 & n.6.

17. John Finnis uses the metaphor in just this way, though it may seem incongruous with his philosophical argument for natural law. "The modern language of rights," he observes, "provides . . . a supple and potentially precise instrument for sorting out and expressing the demands of justice." John Finnis, Natural Law and Natural Rights 210 (1980). Here, Finnis has personified Justice, which issues demands and expresses them by the (moral) force of the "supple and precise instrument" of "rights." The metaphor of rights as physical appendages (that is, "literal" rights) appears as well in Grotius's seventeenth-century work, *De Iure Bellis:* "Right is a moral Quality *annexed to the person,* enabling him to *have,* or *do,* something justly." Richard Tuck, Natural Rights Theories 74 (1979) (translation by Tuck) (emphasis added).

18. Occasionally, the sword is in Justicia's left hand, as in the painting by Sir Joshua Reynolds that appears in the overleaf of Robert M. Cover et al., Procedure (1988). This painting, however, contains other variations of the conventional image; for example, Justicia's eyes are not blindfolded but shaded by the scale she holds aloft in her right hand.

19. Black's Law Dictionary 994 (4th ed. 1968).

20. Or, as Nietzsche says: "Where right *rules,* a state and degree of power is preserved." Friedrich Nietzsche, *The Dawn,* § 112, *supra* note 11, at 189–90 (emphasis in original).

21. Since the 1920s, the legal realists have stressed the connection between private law and state power. *See, e.g.,* Robert Hale, *Law Making by Unofficial Minorities,* 20 Colum. L. Rev. 451, 452–53 (1920); Felix S. Cohen, *Dialogue on Private Property,* 9 Rutgers L. Rev. 357, 374 (1954) ("Any definition of property, to be useful, must reflect the fact that property merges by imperceptible degrees into government, contract, force, and value.").

The examples given in the footnote in the text are taken from: Mark Tushnet, *An Essay on Rights,* 62 Tex. L. Rev. 1363, 1382 (1984) (emphasis added); Martha Minow, *Interpreting Rights: An Essay for Robert Cover,* 96 Yale L.J. 1860, 1876 (1987) (emphasis added); Allan C. Hutchinson & Patrick J. Monahan, *The "Rights" Stuff: Roberto Unger and Beyond,* 62 Tex. L. Rev. 1477, 1482 (1984) (emphasis added); and Roberto Mangabeira Unger, The Critical Legal Studies Movement 36 (1983). Minow (in correspondence) maintains that her line intended not boxing, but a round of cards. Even so, a potentially competitive agon like a card game is structured metaphorically in terms of combat.

22. Peter Gabel, *The Phenomenology of Rights Consciousness and the Pact of the Withdrawn Selves,* 62 Tex. L. Rev. 1563, 1564 (1984). Subsequent page references given in the text.

23. Frederick Schauer, Playing by the Rules: a Philosophical Examination of Rule-based Decision-making in Law and in Life 202 (1991) Subsequent page references are given in the text. Note the personification implicit in "stand" and "watched."

24. Walker v. City of Birmingham, 388 U.S. 307 (1967); United States v. United Mine Workers, 330 U.S. 258, 293 (1947); Howat v. Kansas, 258 U.S. 181, 189–90 (1922). Concurring in *United Mine Workers,* Frankfurter wrote: "If one man can be allowed to determine for himself what is law, every man can. That means first chaos, then tyranny. . . . The greater the power that defies law the less tolerant can this Court be of defiance" (312).

25. Owen M. Fiss, *Objectivity and Interpretation,* 34 STAN. L. REV. 739, 747 (1982).

26. RICHARD A. POSNER, THE PROBLEMS OF JURISPRUDENCE 94 (1990). But, as argued in chapters 8 and 11, even disenchanted judges will nevertheless be constrained to the extent that they expect to persuade others of the validity of their activity. For example, Posner at a later point remarks that "strictly legal materials are used only for help in setting an initial orientation and in providing specific data, and later as sources of possible constraints" (133).

27. Scott v. Sandford, 60 U.S. (19 How.) 393 (1857). Cover's earlier and longer treatment of these issues appears in ROBERT M. COVER, JUSTICE ACCUSED (1975).

28. BERNARD WILLIAMS, ETHICS AND THE LIMITS OF PHILOSOPHY 30–31 (1985) (footnote omitted). *See also* HANNAH ARENDT, ON VIOLENCE 44 (1970) ("The strength of even the strongest individual can always be overpowered by the many, who will often combine for no other purpose than to ruin strength precisely because of its peculiar independence.").

29. For the complete argument, see Steven L. Winter, *The "Power" Thing,* 82 VA. L. REV. 721 (1996); *see also id.* at 733 ("One need only contrast the events of Tiananmen Square in June 1989 with those in Moscow in August 1991 to [see that, i]n an organized society where force is deployed through a social organization like an army or police force, the effective use of violence as an instrument of policy is dependent upon the set of social conventions that constitute a chain of command: If soldiers refuse to fire on people, it's a safe bet that the generals will soon be headed for the airport.")

30. Frederick Schauer, *Amending the Presuppositions of a Constitution, in* RESPONDING TO IMPERFECTION: THE THEORY AND PRACTICE OF CONSTITUTIONAL AMENDMENT 145, 150 (Sanford Levinson ed., 1995) (emphasis in original).

31. BRUCE ACKERMAN, 1 WE THE PEOPLE (1995).

32. *See* Griswold v. Connecticut, 381 U.S. 479 (1965); Eisenstadt v. Baird, 405 U.S. 438 (1972); and Roe v. Wade, 410 U.S. 113 (1973).

33. Alan Freeman, *Legitimizing Racism Through Antidiscrimination Law,* 62 MINN. L. REV. 1049 (1978); Karl Klare, *Judicial Deradicalization of the Wagner Act and the Origins of Modern Legal Consciousness, 1937–1941,* 62 MINN. L. REV. 265 (1978); Katherine van Wetzel Stone, *The Post-War Paradigm in American Labor Law,* 90 YALE L.J. 1509 (1981).

34. Alan Freeman, *Antidiscrimination Law: The View from 1989,* 64 TUL. L. REV. 1407, 1411–12 (1990).

35. Brown v. Board of Education, 347 U.S. 383 (1954). The "freedom of association" characterization is from Herbert Wechsler, *Toward Neutral Principles of Constitutional Law,* 73 HARV. L. REV. 1, 31–34 (1959). For two of the better statements of the historical dimensions of the point that the meaning of *Brown* is written in lived experience, see Charles Black, *The Lawfulness of the Segregation Decisions,*

69 YALE L.J. 421 (1960); H. Jefferson Powell, *Parchment Matters: A Meditation on the Constitution as Text,* 71 IOWA L. REV. 1427, 1430 (1986).

36. Patricia J. Williams, *Alchemical Notes: Reconstructing Ideals from Deconstructed Rights,* 22 HARV. CIV. RTS.-CIV. LIB. L. REV. 401, 430 (1987) (footnote omitted); *cf.* PATRICIA J. WILLIAMS, THE ALCHEMY OF RACE AND RIGHTS: DIARY OF A LAW PROFESSOR 163 (1991).

37. Cover, *supra* note 6, at 181.

38. MAURICE MERLEAU-PONTY, SIGNS 219 (Richard C. McCleary trans., 1964).

39. STANLEY FISH, DOING WHAT COMES NATURALLY: CHANGE, RHETORIC, AND THE PRACTICE OF THEORY IN LITERARY AND LEGAL STUDIES (1989). Subsequent page references are provided in the text.

40. MERLEAU-PONTY, *supra* note 2, at 442. Subsequent page references are provided in the text.

41. KERRY H. WHITESIDE, MERLEAU-PONTY AND THE FOUNDATION OF AN EXISTENTIAL POLITICS 68–69 (1988) ("Freedom consists not in an unrestricted capacity to define meaning, but in an ability to modulate meanings by transforming elements of the sedimented field of perception. Our freedom comes from our ability to focus our attention on those background decisions, to bring them to the foreground, and to see previously unperceived possibilities for change"). *Cf.* Margaret Jane Radin, *Market-Inalienability,* 100 HARV. L. REV. 1849, 1905 (1987) ("The relationship between personhood and context requires a positive commitment to act so as to create and maintain particular contexts of environment and community.").

42. JEAN-PAUL SARTRE, BEING AND NOTHINGNESS: A PHENOMENOLOGICAL ESSAY ON ONTOLOGY 506 (Hazel E. Barnes trans., 1956). Further page references are given in the text.

43. JEAN-FRANÇOIS STEINER, TREBLINKA (Helen Weaver trans., 1994).

44. WHITESIDE, *supra* note 41, at 75.